Readings in Dual Diagnosis

International
Association of
Psychosocial
Rehabilitation
Services

D1444531

edited by

Robert E. Drake, M.D., Ph.D.

Carolyn Mercer-McFadden, Ph.D.

Gregory J. McHugo, Ph.D.

Kim T. Mueser, Ph.D.

Stanley D. Rosenberg, Ph.D.

Robin E. Clark, Ph.D.

Mary F. Brunette, M.D.

Middlesex County College
Library
2600 Woodbridge Avenue
Edison, NJ 08818

Library of Congress Cataloging-in-Publication Data

Readings in dual diagnosis / edited by Robert E. Drake ... [et al.].
        p.   cm.
      Includes bibliographical references.
      ISBN 0-9655843-2-1
      1. Dual diagnosis.   I. Drake, Robert E., M.D., Ph.D.
    II. International Association of Psychosocial Rehabilitation
    Services.
      [DNLM: 1. Substance Use Disorders--diagnosis--collected works.
    2. Substance Use Disorders--therapy--collected works. 3. Mental
    Disorders--diagnosis--collected works. 4. Mental Disorders-
    -therapy--collected works. 5. Mental Disorders--complications-
    -collected works. 6. Diagnosis, Dual (Psychiatry)--collected works.
    WM 270 R287 1997]
    RC564.68.R42   1997
    616.89--dc21
    DNLM/DLC
    for Library of Congress   97-37262
                                                                   CIP

The International Association of Psychosocial Rehabilitation Services has worked to ensure that all information in this book is accurate as of the publication date and consistent with good industry practices. It is recommended, however, that readers evaluate the applicability of this information in light of particular situations and changing standards. It is sold with the understanding that the publisher is not engaged in rendering legal, accounting, or other professional service. If professional advice is required, the services of a competent professional should be sought.

Copyright © 1998 by International Association of Psychosocial
                    Rehabilitation Services

ISBN 0-9655843-2-1

Design and production management by ColburnHouse Publishing & Marketing

International Association of Psychosocial Rehabilitation Services
10025 Governor Warfield Parkway, #301
Columbia, MD 21044-3357

Printed in the United States of America

CONTENTS

Section Three: Assessment

Section Four: Clinical Issues

Section Five: Treatment

Section Six: Special Issues

ABOUT THE EDITORS

Robert E. Drake, M.D., Ph.D., is Professor of Psychiatry and Community and Family Medicine at Dartmouth Medical School and Director of the New Hampshire-Dartmouth Psychiatric Research Center in Concord and Lebanon, NH.

Carolyn Mercer-McFadden, Ph.D., is a senior researcher and public policy specialist at the New Hampshire-Dartmouth Psychiatric Research Center.

Gregory J. McHugo, Ph.D., is Research Assistant Professor in the Department of Community and Family Medicine at Dartmouth Medical School and a senior researcher at the New Hampshire-Dartmouth Psychiatric Research Center.

Kim T. Mueser, Ph.D., is Professor of Psychiatry and Community and Family Medicine at Dartmouth Medical School and a senior researcher at the New Hampshire-Dartmouth Psychiatric Research Center.

Stanley D. Rosenberg, Ph.D., is Professor of Psychiatry and Director of the Psychology Internship Program at the Dartmouth Medical School and a senior researcher at the New Hampshire-Dartmouth Psychiatric Research Center.

Robin E. Clark, Ph.D., is Associate Professor of Community and Family Medicine and Psychiatry at the Dartmouth Medical School, a senior researcher at the New Hampshire-Dartmouth Psychiatric Research Center, and Director of the Cost-Effectiveness Laboratory at Dartmouth Medical School.

Mary F. Brunette, M.D., is Assistant Professor of Psychiatry and a clinical psychiatrist at Dartmouth Medical School and is a junior research associate at the New Hampshire-Dartmouth Psychiatric Research Center.

PREFACE

In the early 1980s, substance abuse began to be recognized as a common co-occurring condition among young people with severe mental illnesses such as schizophrenia and bipolar disorder. In the intervening years clinicians and researchers have clarified many aspects of what has come to be called the dual-diagnosis problem. We now know, for example, that half of all persons who suffer with severe mental illness also experience the complications of adjustment, course, and treatment that are related to comorbid substance use disorder. Fortunately, we are also learning many lessons about treatment and recovery. In many parts of the U.S., clinicians are combining mental health and substance abuse interventions in what are called integrated treatment programs, and the research on these integrated treatments is thus far promising.

Because substance abuse is so common and so devastating in its effects on severe mental illness, all administrators and clinicians in mental health, substance abuse, and rehabilitation programs need to know about dual diagnosis. Those who suffer from dual disorders and their families also need access to the latest developments in the field so that they can understand the issues and advocate for high quality services. The purpose of this book of readings is to provide a selection of the best articles in the field to all of these interested stakeholders.

The articles reprinted here were recommended by a national panel of experts in the dual-diagnosis field. The readings represent overviews, seminal contributions, and recent updates from the literature. Because the literature on dual disorders has grown vastly in the past ten years, we have selected only a representative group of readings. To supplement the readings and to place them in the larger context of the literature, they are grouped into six sections (overview, etiology, assessment, clinical issues, treatment, and special issues), and each section begins with an introduction. The introductions are intended not only to create context but also to provide information to help the reader understand the more technical articles.

A few terms should be defined at the beginning. *Severe mental illness* refers to the group of major mental illnesses that are associated with long-term impairments and extensive service needs. These illnesses include schizophrenia, schizoaffective disorder, bipolar disorder, recurrent major depression, and some of the severe personality disorders such as borderline personality disorder. *Substance use disorder* denotes abuse of or dependence on alcohol or other drugs according to criteria in the American Psychiatric Association's Diagnostic and Statistical Manuals (DSM). Although the specific diagnostic details change with each new edition of the DSM, the core of the definition is recurrent use of a psychoactive substance (alcohol or other drugs) despite adverse social, psychological, or physical consequences. The term *substance abuse* is often used as shorthand for substance use disorder. The co-occurrence of severe mental illness and substance use disorder is referred to variously as *dual diagnosis, dual disorders, comorbidity, mental illness/chemical abuse (MICA), mental illness/substance abuse (MISA),* or *co-occurring addiction and mental disorder (COAMD)*.

A final and most important point on language relates to the terminology used for referring to the people who have dual diagnoses. The different terms used—*patients, clients,* or *consumers,* for example—have different literal meanings, and they also imply different connotations or values. Literally, individuals who suffer from co-occurring disorders would correctly be referred to as *patients* when they were in hospitals, as *clients* when they were receiving treatment in mental health clinics or programs, and as *consumers* when the focus was on their perspective as people seeking services. The terms are sometimes used interchangeably, though, either because speakers or writers are not using the language precisely, or more often, because they wish to emphasize particular values in relation to the people being referred to. Since the articles are reprinted in their original copyrighted form, the uses of these terms and other terminology of the original articles have been retained. Terminology and usages that seem old and inappropriate after only five or ten years signal the rapid changes in a field.

Robert E. Drake
Carolyn Mercer-McFadden
Gregory J. McHugo
Kim T. Mueser
Stanley D. Rosenberg
Robin E. Clark
Mary F. Brunette

ACKNOWLEDGMENTS

A number of individuals deserve thanks for their efforts in putting this volume together. Karen Dunn labored tirelessly to obtain permissions to reprint from publishers, and to collect, scan, and proofread all articles. A national group of researchers, including Kate Carey, Brian Cuffel, Lisa Dixon, Tony Lehman, Ken Minkoff, Fred Osher, and Susan Ridgely, helped us to choose readings for the book.

The New Hampshire-Dartmouth Psychiatric Research Center is one of several centers that are conducting services research studies related to people with dual disorders. As the editors of this volume, we have had the difficult task of choosing not to reprint many articles that were suggested. We have also had the pleasure of including those works of our colleagues and collaborating centers that have been particularly influential in our work.

A large group of investigators and staff at the New Hampshire-Dartmouth Psychiatric Research Center has participated in our efforts to study and review dual disorders over the years. We would especially like to thank Tim Ackerson, Marianne Alverson, Stephanie Acquilano, Krista Anderson, Linda Antosca, Bill Baber, Steve Bartels, Jeremy Biesanz, Karen Carrieri, Mary Dionne, Lindy Fox, Tom Fox, Dan Freeman, Sara Koury, Kathy Luger, Pat McKenna, Keith Miles, Doug Noordsy, Joan Packard, Tom Paskus, Susan Ricketts, Don Shumway, Greg Teague, Will Torrey, Marion Wheeler, Rosemarie Wolf, Haiyi Xie, and Nancy Yovetich. We also greatfully acknowledge several grants and contracts from the National Institute of Mental Health, the National Institutes on Alcohol Abuse and Alcoholism, the Substance Abuse and Mental Health Services Administration, the Robert Wood Johnson Foundation, the New Hampshire Division of Behavioral Health, and West Central Services, Inc. Finally, we thank our publisher LeRoy Spaniol for his wise guidance at each step in the process of producing this book.

The Editors

INTRODUCTION TO SECTION ONE

The Overview section includes three articles that look broadly at the problem of dual disorders — as a personal problem and as a social problem. Consumers, family members, and clinicians have for decades recognized that substance use causes many personal problems for individuals who have serious and persistent mental illnesses. A problem does not become a social problem, though, until it is perceived as affecting the well-being of many individuals and thus as requiring society's organized attention. Dual disorders did not receive much attention as a social problem until the early 1980s. According to the histories (e.g., Osher & Drake, 1996), public and professional attention grew at this time due to the combined effects of deinstitutionalization, the growing population of young people, and the official recognition by psychiatry that two disorders could co-occur. As a personal problem and as a social problem, the problem of dual disorders poses many challenges for consumers, clinicians, and systems of care.

The articles in this section provide current perspectives on "the problem of dual disorders." They offer complementary views on three questions: What is the problem? Why does the problem require public attention? What should be done about the problem? The perspectives move from the viewpoint of an individual who has experienced the problem, to some observations on one group of individuals, and finally to the broadest societal outlook, the observations of numerous researchers on many groups of individuals.

In the first article, Virginia Green describes and analyzes the problem of dual disorders from the perspective of one who has experienced the problem. In "The resurrection and the life," she tells of the hopelessness and frustration that plagued her. The dual disorders and their tenacious symptoms are exacerbated by unorganized and unresponsive services. Like many other consumers, Ms. Green has personally endured the well-known link between substance use and increased use of hospitals and jails. In her experience, substance use and its attendant difficulties seemed preferable to other pains, and the substances thus seemed to be a kind of medicine. Real help came slowly — from friends and family members and from a precious few professional people. With her personal account, Ms. Green provides compelling advocacy for the integration of treatment services and for a full partnership with consumers in the governance of systems of care. Many consumers with serious and persistent mental illness and many of their family members have felt the dire emotional and financial consequences of a consumer's substance use. Yet even one who has suffered so many of these problems need not abandon the hope that greater understanding and help will come. As Ms. Green's poem suggests, many mysteries remain hidden.

The second article looks at manifestations of the dual disorders problem in a group of individuals with major mental illnesses. Kim Mueser and his colleagues conducted their study at a time when clinical treatments for dual disorders were proliferating rapidly, but when the problems of dual disorders were not well understood clinically. These authors aimed to understand how the substance abuse of their study participants was associated with other attributes of the participants. Conceivably, such an understanding would help to identify more specific treatments. The results of their study highlight the societal links of the dual-disorders problem. Commonplace attributes like gender, age, race, and education were more predictive of the types of substances that the clients used than were their types of mental illnesses. In addition, the patterns of substance use mirrored patterns in the general population. For example, substance abuse among individuals with schizophrenic disorders increased dramatically since the 1960s, and this has also occurred in the general population. These observations have been valuable in designing additional research that is sensitive to demographic differences and in conceiving of psychosocial treatments.

The third article brings the overview to its broadest perspective. From the perspective of society as a whole, Robert Drake and Kim Mueser provide an overview of what is now known about the dual-disorders problem following a decade of research. Discussing drug use disorder as well as alcohol use disorder, they report on what we know today about the size of the dual-disorders problem (prevalence), its possible causes (etiology), the factors associated with it (correlates), the course and outcome of dual disorders, and the prospects for effective assessment and treatment. Substance abuse is more common among people with severe mental disorders than among other people in the general population. About half of people with severe mental illnesses develop substance use disorders at some point during their lives. Why people with severe mental illnesses use substances more than others will most likely be explained by a combination of factors, including biological, psychological, and social factors. Whatever the causes, the problem of dual disorders is known to be associated with many serious consequences. For example, substance use among individuals with severe mental illness is associated with worsening of psychiatric symptoms, with disruptive behaviors, with HIV risk and infection, with family problems, and with homelessness. Despite the complexity and complications of the dual-disorders problem, particularly among people who are homeless, there is cause for optimism. Better assessment and treatment interventions are becoming available. In providing a glimpse of some of these innovations, this article also provides a bird's-eye view of material covered in detail in the other sections of this book.

REFERENCE

Osher, F.C., & Drake, R.E. (1996). Reversing a history of unmet needs: Approaches to care for persons with co-occurring addictive and mental disorders. *American Journal of Orthopsychiatry, 66*, 4-11.

THE RESURRECTION AND THE LIFE

Virginia L. Green

Reprinted from *American Journal of Orthopsychiatry*, 66(1):12-16, 1996

This first-person account of a woman undergoing manic-depression concurrent with alcohol and drug problems highlights the difficulties of attaining help from a system geared toward treating one or the other but not both, and hints at the positive outcomes possible when an integrated approach to co-occurring addictive and mental disorders— one that incorporates the knowledge and perspectives of the client and the family as well as the professional—is available.

My name is Virgina and I am an alcoholic. My name is Virginia and I am a drug addict. My name is Virginia and I am manic-depressive. If it were possible to divide Virginia into three, each illness could be treated according to the traditional yet differing approaches and philosophies of the substance abuse and mental health fields. But alas, or hooray, Virginia is one person. My name is Virginia and I am an alcoholic, drug-addicted person with a major mental illness.

For me these disorders are inextricably interconnected. Until I was able to overcome my own denial regarding my substance abuse, I was not able to seek the help I needed. When I had overcome my denial, the help I needed was difficult to find.

Before that day came, I had spent a dozen years in the mental health system, garnering more than a dozen diagnoses and nearly as many hospitalizations. The quality of my life and my ability to function deteriorated year by year. My alcohol and drug abuse continued unabated and unaddressed, my drugs of choice changing with the times. I reached the nadir in my thirty-third year. I entered the local psych ward, psychotically depressed.

Six months previously, I had abruptly discontinued the use of benzodiazepines and barbiturates, upon which I had been dependent for six years. I was not linked with a physician at that point and I stopped the drugs "cold-turkey." While hospitalized, my depression worsened. For the first time, I was extremely paranoid. I made an ineffectual, if dramatic, suicide attempt and was committed to the state hospital where I languished for months in a nearly catatonic state. My sister has written about my illness:

> Virginia's mental illness has always been hard for me. Whenever she got sick and had to be hospitalized I have felt frustrated and cut off from the process of her recovery. I've often thought

there must be a way that the medical profession, counselors, and concerned persons in her life could collaborate and intervene in a supportive and safe way. The lack of communication and means to understand her treatment program have always fallen short.

I'll always remember driving into the state hospital. The grounds were so huge and buildings looked so bleak and I felt fear about where I was going and what I would see. Going past locked doors and seeing sedated people shuffling in the halls was as hard as I expected. There was something final about that place; I wondered how anyone could ever return to the outside world. The feeling of hopelessness is what struck me the most.

Virginia's doctor seemed to hear me about the substance abuse and was willing to take that into consideration, although there still wasn't a clear plan. At the same time, I had been attending Alanon and was trying to sort out what was enabling and what was support for Virginia. I'll always remember the picnic that I brought her to have on the grounds of the state hospital. Virginia and I sat on the lawn and I told her that I believed her behavior and attitude had contributed to where we now sat. I told her that I felt the only hope was to stop drinking and drugging herself on the outside.

As I write about the details, what comes back are my feelings of frustration, hopelessness, helplessness, and inadequacy concerning my part in the process. I hope that today there is a better way for families and other concerned people to contribute and not simply to care-take in the process of recovery.

I had lost all hope. There were those, however, who carried hope for me: my family, some friends, and, luckily for me, one of the first clinicians in our state to specialize in working with people who were dually diagnosed. Mary Jean McKelvy, who piloted the Augusta Mental Health Institute program for co-occurring addictive and mental disorders, would come and literally get me out of bed and take me to AA meetings and to groups with other patients identified as having alcohol or drug dependencies, or both. When I told her my fear of being moved to a back ward to spend the rest of my potentially long life, she responded that it was a definite possibility and that the only person who could alter my course was me. My sister, who visited often, echoed that truth. Deep within me, my spirit took the challenge.

Upon discharge, I entered a psychiatric halfway house. Within days I was back in bars, drinking and reconnecting with old drinking and drugging friends. While there was a policy forbidding alcohol or drug use in the house itself, a blind eye was turned upon one's behavior beyond its four walls.

Within weeks, I was heavily abusing a variety of substances. It occurred to me that I was on a fast track back to the hell from which I had so recently emerged. One night I passed out in bed with a lit cigarette. When I awoke, there was a hole the size of a small plate burned in the blanket. I felt deeply ashamed that I had put the lives of the other people in the house in such jeopardy. That morning I walked to the only alcohol rehab facility of which I was aware, a place used primarily by the city's indigent. They took me in, and I spent four days in detox before being transferred to a woman's alcohol and drug rehab in the country.

Philosophically, it was an AA-oriented program. The staff was neither prepared for nor familiar with treating mental illness. A compromise was struck: I could remain on lithium but not on Mellaril. I was sent to the hospital's psych unit for several days to be taken off Mellaril. The rehab program combined education, AA, and confrontational groups. The discontinuation of the phenothiazines, the stress of groups and difficult relationships with other clients, combined to create in me a state of hypomania. I could not sleep. The family practitioner who was a physician for the program told me that because of my former dependence on benzodiazepines I would probably not sleep for one to two years. Added stress. After two weeks the staff was ready to see me go and I was eager to oblige. But where? The mental health providers were unable to treat my addictions; the substance abuse providers had made no provisions for mental illness. My mother recalls:

> I shall always remember a lovely fall afternoon. Virginia and I were pacing back and forth in the parking lot of an alcohol and drug rehab for women. I hoped there would be someone on the staff to give me advice. But, it soon became clear that they had agreed that this was not the place for Virginia. Furthermore, the staff did not have any suggestions of where Virginia could go from there to find some meaningful help. Virginia was feeling upset because she did not want to stay either. Virginia was beginning to feel manic and this made her unable to sleep and too nervous to join in the discussion groups. I was very upset because her father and I were hoping so much that our daughter would receive some help.
>
> Virginia and I were each feeling miserable in our own ways when the name of a doctor whom we both respected came into our conversation. We went into the building and called her and, as a result of our conversation, we learned of one of the few places in the northeast that treated people with the problems of both alcohol addiction and mental illness. Virginia agreed to try once again. And I might add that it is not an easy thing to do—to commit oneself to a strange place and an unknown treatment. Thank goodness she did.

I viewed the dual diagnosis program as my last chance, literally the alternative to death, as I was unwilling to spend my life in a hospital. The integrated approach is what I needed. I learned that I could be on medication for my mental illness and still be sober. Though it was tempting to believe people in AA who told me I was a "garden variety drunk," I knew better. I finally had a complete set of tools.

I didn't move back to my adopted home town for two years. I felt I needed to avoid old friends and old haunts until I was secure in my recovery. Shortly after moving back home, I became hypomanic. With the help of my trusted physician, I came to terms with the fact that I did indeed have a bipolar disorder.

Although it is by no means easy to remain abstinent from alcohol and drugs, nor to learn to manage an affective disorder, it is possible. While it was not helpful to be labeled with many misdiagnoses, ultimately I have come to believe that it is not possible to recover from any mental illness if one is abusing chemicals. Nor, in many cases, is it possible to diagnose mental illness accurately in a person who is self-medicating or using substances addictively. While I have heard many interesting chicken-or-egg discussions concerning which came first, mental illness or substance abuse, I hear too little emphasis, even amongst those specializing in treating people with co-existing disorders, on achieving and maintaining sobriety as the necessary first steps on the path to recovery from mental illness, to integrated healing and personal growth.

Relapse prevention is an essential element in maintaining wellness. Like it or not, even in recovery, one is likely to continue to experience the symptoms of one's mental illness. I had been sober for six years when I had my first relapse. I was experiencing a longer than usual period of depression; the antidepressants did not seem to be helping; I was feeling desperate. I thought I would feel better if I smoked some marijuana. I felt much better, for about two weeks. Then I stopped sleeping and, within another week, was fully manic. I was hospitalized for the first time since I had begun recovery. In the following three years I experienced two more psychotic breaks, both precipitated by marijuana and alcohol use.

I have learned that although the pain and feelings of hopelessness that accompany depression can be temporarily alleviated by self-medication, the consequences probably will include loss of sanity and loss of freedom, and almost certainly will exacerbate the depth of the depression to follow. I have learned to be vigilant and to be honest with my caregivers. I have become willing to put one foot in front of the other even when I have lost the desire to move forward.

I have been lucky. I have loving and supportive family and friends. My mother and father, sisters and brothers, and good friends never ceased to love and believe in me in the bleakest of times. My father, who died in 1986, and my mother stuck by me through hell and high water. My mother continues to contribute to my financial support so that I do not have to be dependent on a program like SSI. I have been able gradually to increase the hours that I work; I have had the flexibility to take time off, in order to maintain my wellness, or to regain my balance when I have become ill.

In learning to manage my disorders I have had a marvelous teacher in Jane P. Pringle, M.D., who is both my physician and my friend. Although she is a specialist in internal medicine, she was willing to manage my psychiatric needs. We became partners in my care. I learned the importance of personal responsibility in maintaining my own good health. She listened carefully and was willing to make adjustments in dosages or to try different medicines when I was experiencing side effects or doubted the effectiveness of the medicine. She encouraged me to take risks, when I was able, in both my personal and work lives. When I was sick, she was my advocate when I needed hospitalization, and she often kept in such close touch that I was able to avoid hospitalization entirely.

In my work as a consultant on dual diagnosis issues, I have had a kind and intelligent mentor in Marlene McMullen-Pelsor, currently director of Maine's Office of Substance Abuse. She has been the state's foremost leader in the development of dual diagnosis education and treatment opportunities. As a result of the work of the Reimbursement Task Force, which she headed and upon which I served, grants were obtained from foundations and from the state of Maine to develop regional dual diagnosis collaboratives. I have served as a consultant to the Cumberland County Dual Diagnosis Collaborative since it began in 1992.

The Collaborative is made up of more than 20 mental health and substance abuse agencies in the greater Portland area. Consumers and family members are encouraged to participate in all aspects of the work, and are remunerated for their time. The Collaborative sponsors training in the community. It has developed an interdisciplinary team called ACCESS to provide outreach and treatment to those dually diagnosed persons who have been inadequately served by the existing system, especially those who are homeless. There is also an Enhanced Community Care Coordinator whose job it is to encourage communication between agencies and providers and to expedite appropriate care for clients within the traditional system.

Through the work with which I have been involved, I have become knowledgeable regarding barriers to care for people with co-existing disorders that were outside of my personal experience. One of these is the need for change in both the public and private reimbursement systems. The division of the reimbursement structure into mental health and substance abuse benefits affects consumers in a variety of ways.

The person who is aware of having more than one disorder may choose services based on the type of care and degree of reimbursement available through his or her insurance coverage. Reimbursement can range from 0% to 100%. Frequently, policies offer 80% toward substance abuse services and 50% toward the mental health counterparts. If a choice based on immediate savings to the consumer results in inappropriate or incomplete treatment, there is a long-term loss to the consumer and to the insurer. People with inadequate or no coverage often avoid treatment until a crisis precipitates an inpatient stay. Upon discharge, aftercare remains unaffordable and the costly cycle continues.

Reimbursement policies perpetuate and reinforce the separations of skills, methods, and philosophies between substance abuse and mental health providers. It discourages integration of treatment and a holistic approach to the needs of people with coexisting disorders.

The current system emphasizes diagnosis over functionality. Often a person acquires a diagnosis based on behavior and symptoms observed during a crisis. Because of this, people who are abusing substances often receive misdiagnoses. Diagnoses can become labels of stigma. They can dictate the type of treatment, sometimes inappropriate and incomplete, which an individual receives for years, even a lifetime.

Integration of reimbursement delivery will encourage care for the whole person. The results will include less recidivism, fewer inpatient stays, and, consequently, greater cost-effectiveness.

While progress has been made in unifying treatment for people with co-existing disorders, the knowledge remains scattered. For the most part, innovative dual diagnosis theories and practice are not taught in medical schools, social work schools, and addiction programs. In most communities there are no widely known agencies or providers with dual diagnosis expertise. Consequently, primary care physicians and others who may recognize the complexity of a person's needs have no identified outpatient center to which to refer.

Consumers have invaluable experience and perspectives to bring to system change, policy development, and the overall improvement of treatment, yet their inclusion in those processes has not been widely achieved. This will not happen naturally or easily. Effort must be made on all sides to bridge the valleys of mistrust and stigma. There are divisions and resentments separating family organizations and consumer groups which diminish both groups' abilities to achieve the changes they seek. There is internal conflict within and between consumer advocacy coalitions. Some will not proceed beyond the adversarial stance that was necessary at their inception. Policy makers and providers sometimes invite consumers to participate in meetings and efforts for change without offering to pay for a consumer-contributor's time. Often, consumers are overwhelmed by unfamiliar jargon and acronyms, and feel left out of the discussion.

The collaboration of providers, consumers, and family members can have enormous power and produce creative solutions and directions. The journey can be fraught with discord and frustrations, and leavened with humor and mutual respect. A shared vision and investment will ultimately reward us with a system in which we can take pride.

As a young adult, the promises of my early years seem squandered and gone forever. But I have been fortunate. Through the loving help of family, physician, friends, and caregivers in the truest sense, and through the determination of my own spirit, I have been given a second chance to live. I feel compelled to give back the best of myself.

My name is Virginia and I am a poet.

THE IDES OF OCTOBER

We are fooled by history, lulled to security
*   by salient events we half understand.*
The threats we watch for, the errors we seek
*   to avoid are the least of it.*
We examine the past as if the future held
*   no answers.*

It is the future that will take us unawares;
*   unprepared, the seeds we planted*
*   in the spring are hybrids, like*
*   we, ourselves.*
We count on outcomes.
We count our incomes.
We count the costs.
We discount early frosts.

For centuries the harvest moon has risen
*   orange and full.*
Toil and celebration our age-old response.
Who will note the orange seep to blood red?
Who will hear the hoofbeats beyond
*   the tractor tread?*

Our history is barely written.
We younger than the newest star; the universe
*   expanding, we have no sense of where we are,*
The universe contracting and still we can-
*   not see that far.*

Who looks in the mirror and sees beyond
*   the surface?*
We contemplate a future both opaque and foretold;
*   are we the quick and the dead also infinitely old?*

Are there answers to our questions?
Would we want to know the truth?
We are secure in limitations.
We enjoy the protection of our straw,
*   wooden, asbestos roofs.*
We cry out to the Lord, praying
*   that God remain aloof.*

ABOUT THE AUTHOR

Virginia L. Green is affiliated with the State of Maine Office of Substance Abuse, Augusta, and Cumberland County Dual Diagnosis Collaborative, Portland, ME.

Copyright 1996 by the American Orthopsychiatric Association, Inc. Reproduced by permission.

Diagnostic and Demographic Correlates of Substance Abuse in Schizophrenia and Major Affective Disorder

Kim T. Mueser, Paul R. Yarnold, and Alan S. Bellack

Reprinted from *Acta Psychiatrica Scandinavica*, 85:48-55, 1992

The relationship between history of specific types of substance abuse (alcohol, stimulants, cannabis, hallucinogens, narcotics) and demographic and diagnostic variables was evaluated in a large (n = 263) sample of schizophrenic, schizoaffective, major depression and bipolar disorder patients. Prevalence rates were also compared with rates observed in a previous study (1983-1986) conducted using the same methods. Demographic characteristics (gender, age, race, educational level) were strong predictors of type of substance abuse. Patients with a history of cocaine abuse had fewer prior hospitalizations, suggesting that less impaired psychiatric patients may be more prone to illicit substance abuse. Diagnoses were not related to most types of substance abuse, although there was a trend for bipolar patients to have a history of alcohol abuse. The results demonstrate the importance of matching groups on demographic characteristics when exploring diagnostic differences in preference to abuse specific types of substances.

Estimates of the prevalence of substance abuse in schizophrenia and major affective disorder vary widely as a function of setting (for example, inpatient *vs* outpatient), demographic characteristics of the sample and assessment methods, with most prevalence rates ranging between 15% and 65% (1-6). In recent years, as knowledge about the pathophysiological bases of major mental disorders and mechanisms underlying effective pharmacological intervention has accumulated, increased attention has been given to examining the influence of substance abuse on the onset and course of the illness (7, 8), as well as drug-type preference as a function of diagnosis (9-11). Recognition of the importance of substance abuse to the psychiatric population, even in the absence of a convergence of findings about the nature of its effects, has led to a proliferation of new treatments for the dual-diagnosed patient (12-14).

Despite recent attention to this area, relatively little is known about the diagnostic and demographic characteristics of psychiatric patients who abuse psychoactive substances. The hypothesis that patients abuse specific classes of drugs or alcohol as a function of their diagnosis in an attempt to self-medicate their symptoms (for example, the increased rate of stimulant abuse for schizophrenics) has received limited support (5, 15-18). Many studies of substance abuse in psychiatric patients have failed to examine different classes of drugs, focusing on alcohol alone (19-21), a single class of illicit substances (18, 22) or polysubstance abuse (3, 6, 22-25). The studies that have investigated the relationship between substance abuse class and diagnosis typically suffer from other methodological limitations, such as small sample sizes (5, 17, 26) or the inclusion of only men (15).

A final lacuna in this area concerns the influence of demographic characteristics on the propensity to abuse drugs among psychiatric patients. It is widely recognized that demographics are important predictors of substance abuse patterns in the general population (27, 28). Because most schizophrenics in study samples are young men, the same group most prone to substance abuse in the general population, the relationship between demographic characteristics and substance abuse needs to be determined in studies of psychiatric patients. However, many studies give the demographic characteristics of the patient sample scant attention. Little research has investigated the relationship between specific classes of substance abuse and both diagnostic and demographic variables in a large sample of patients. In a previous study conducted on a large sample of schizophrenic and schizoaffective patients ($n = 149$), we found that demographic variables were strong predictors of specific classes of substance abuse, whereas diagnosis was a comparatively weak predictor (29). The present study was conducted as a replication and extension of our previous findings by examining diagnostic and demographic variables as predictors of substance abuse in a large sample of schizophrenic, schizoaffective, and major affective disorder patients.

MATERIALS AND METHODS

The study sample included 263 patients between 18 and 76 years old with diagnoses of schizophrenia, schizoaffective disorder, major depression or bipolar disorder. Patients were admitted to the Medical College of Pennsylvania at Eastern Pennsylvania Psychiatric Institute between 1986 and 1990 for treatment of an acute exacerbation. Diagnoses were established using DSM-III-R criteria (30) by patients' resident and attending psychiatrists. Patients with drug-induced psychoses, organic brain disease or unspecified psychoses were excluded from the study. The demographic and clinical characteristics of the patients are summarized in Table 1.

Table 1. Characteristics of study sample

	Diagnosis			
	Schizophrenia	Schizoaffective disorder	Major depression	Bipolar disorder
Categorical variables: number (percentage)				
Gender[1]				
Male	54 (62)	20 (24)	31 (40)	14 (32)
Female	33 (38)	62 (76)	19 (60)	30 (68)
Race[2]				
White	49 (56)	50 (61)	29 (59)	32 (70)
Non-white	38 (44)	32 (39)	20 (41)	12 (30)
Marital status[3]				
Never married	66 (76)	54 (66)	24 (48)	16 (37)
Married/divorced/widowed	21 (24)	28 (34)	26 (52)	28 (63)
Legal admission Status[4]				
Voluntary	43 (49)	61 (74)	40 (80)	25 (67)
Involuntary	44 (51)	21 (26)	10 (20)	19 (33)
Continuous variables: mean (standard deviation)				
Age[5]	32.3 (8.5)	35.6 (10.0)	40.8 (13.4)	37.1 (10.6)
Educational level[6]	11.2 (2.2)	11.3 (2.1)	11.3 (2.6)	11.3 (2.6)
Number of prior hospitalizations[7]	4.7 (4.3)	6.5 (5.7)	2.8 (3.9)	4.9 (5.0)
Length of current hospitalization (days)[8]	36.0 (17.7)	39.9 (19.3)	28.2 (15.6)	29.8 (15.8)

[1]χ^2 (3) = 15.5, $P < 0.001$; a higher percentage of schizophrenics were male. [2]Information on race missing for 1 major depression patient and 2 bipolar disorder patients. χ^2 (3) = 2.8, NS. A total of 94.1% (96/102) of the non-white patients were black. [3]χ^2 (3) = 23.6, $P < 0.0001$; a higher percentage of schizophrenics and schizoaffective disorder patients had never married than major depression and bipolar disorder patients. [4]χ^2 (3) = 18.5, $P < 0.0001$; a higher percentage of schizophrenics and bipolar disorder patients were involuntarily hospitalized than schizoaffective disorder and major depression patients. [5]F(3,259) = 7.3, $P < 0.0001$; Duncan's multiple range test indicated that patients with major depression were older than schizophrenics and schizoaffectives, and bipolar patients were older than schizophrenics. [6]F(3,244) = 0.01, NS. [7]F(3,253) = 6.2, $P < 0.0005$; Duncan's multiple range test indicated that patients with major depression had fewer hospitalizations than other patients. [8]F(3,259) = 2.56, NS.

The lifetime history of substance abuse or dependence, based on DSM-III-R criteria, was evaluated by interviews with patients and (when available) relatives, and examination of all previous medical records. Reports from significant others (usually parents) on patients' substance abuse history were available for approximately 25% of the sample. In most cases, the relatives' reports of patient substance abuse were obtained from social history interviews conducted by the inpatient social worker. A history of substance abuse or dependence was recorded as definitely absent, unknown or definitely present for each of 6 classes of substances: alcohol, stimulants (cocaine, amphetamines and related compounds), sedatives (anxiolytics, barbiturates, hypnotics and tranquilizers), cannabis (hashish and marijuana), hallucinogens (LSD, MDA, mescaline, PCP and psilocybin) and narcotics (codeine, heroin, morphine and opium). Patients with a history of stimulant abuse were also rated separately for history of cocaine and amphetamine abuse. Use of nicotine and caffeine was not evaluated. Interrater reliability for the assessment of specific classes of substance abuse, conducted on 10% of the total patient sample, was high, with percentage of agreement ranging from 73% (cocaine) to 100% (sedatives and hallucinogens). The substance abuse history of 16 patients could not be ascertained reliably, either because of unresolved discrepancies between the patients and significant others or poor quality of the patient's report and lack of sufficient information in the medical records. Hence, these patients were dropped from subsequent statistical analysis.

RESULTS

To correct for alpha inflation because of the number of statistical tests conducted, Bonferroni bounds were calculated for an overall alpha significance level of $P < 0.05$ (31). To facilitate comparison of these results with results reported by others who do not correct for multiple statistical tests, we also note the tests that were significant at the $P < 0.05$ and $P < 0.10$ unadjusted significance levels. We refer here to significant effects as those that are statistically significant at the Bonferroni bounds criterion, trends as effects significant at the unadjusted $P < 0.05$ level, and weak trends as effects significant at the unadjusted $P < 0.10$ level.

The percentage of patients in each diagnostic group (schizophrenia, schizoaffective disorder, major depression and bipolar disorder) with a history of abuse for any of the different classes of substances is displayed in Table 2. To determine whether substance abuse was related to diagnostic group, gender, race, marital status or legal status upon admission to the hospital, separate chi-square tests were performed between each class of substance abuse and each of the categorical variables. The statistics for these tests are contained in Table 3 and the results are summarized below.

Table 2. Percentage of patients in each diagnostic group with a positive history of substance abuse

	Schizophrenic (n=85)	Schizo-affective (n=74)	Major depression (n=47)	Bipolar (n=41)
Alcohol	45	42	47	66
Stimulants	31	34	38	34
Cocaine	29	17	36	29
Amphetamines	14	10	20	21
Sedatives	7	8	11	20
Cannabis	22	8	11	22
Hallucinogens	8	15	2	10
Narcotics	9	15	11	10

Only patients with complete data on substance abuse history are included, resulting in a slightly smaller sample size than listed in Table 1.

Diagnosis

In general, diagnosis was not related to the abuse of different classes of substance. There was a weak trend for bipolar patients to abuse alcohol more than the other diagnostic groups. Stimulant abuse, however, did not differ as a function of diagnosis.

Gender

Men were significantly more likely than women to have a history of alcohol and narcotic abuse, and there were trends for men to also be more likely to abuse cannabis and hallucinogens than women. Surprisingly, women were more likely to have a history of stimulant abuse than men. Within the group of patients with a history of stimulant abuse, there were not gender differences between cocaine or amphetamine abuse. Similarly, men and women did not differ in history of sedative abuse. To explore the relationship between gender and stimulant abuse further, chi-square tests were computed within each of the 4 diagnostic groups. The chi-square was significant only for the schizoaffective group ($\chi^2 (1) = 10.2$, $P < 0.001$), but not the schizophrenia, major depression or bipolar disorder groups, indicating that female schizoaffective patients were more likely to have a history of stimulant abuse.

Table 3. Summary of chi-square tests of independence between substance abuse history and categorical clinical and demographic variables

| | Categorical clinical and demographic variables | | | | | | | | | |
| | Gender | | Race | | Marital status | | Legal status | | Diagnosis | |
Substance	χ^2	n	χ^2	n	χ^2	n	χ^2	n	χ^2	n
Alcohol	16.7**	247	3.5	244	0.1	247	1.8	247	6.7+	247
Stimulants	7.9*	247	0.3	244	4.4*	247	1.0	247	0.8	247
Cocaine	0.1	64	4.7*	63	1.6	64	0.2	64	1.0	64
Amphetamines	0.1	62	7.6*	61	2.7	62	0.1	62	0.2	62
Sedatives	2.8	247	5.3*	244	0.9	247	0.2	247	5.2	247
Cannabis	8.1*	247	0.4	244	6.7*	247	1.1	247	5.3	247
Hallucinogens	9.1*	247	7.6*	244	0.8	247	0.3	247	5.7	247
Narcotics	12.2**	247	2.4	244	4.2*	247	0.2	247	1.4	247

Substance abuse history = absent/present; diagnosis = schizophrenia/schizoaffective/major depression/bipolar; race = white/non-white; marital status = never married/currently or previously married; legal status = voluntary/involuntary. For discharge diagnosis, df=3; for all other variables, df=1. + $P < 0.10$, unadjusted. * $P < 0.05$, unadjusted. ** $P < 0.05$, Bonferroni-adjusted.

Race

There were trends for more white patients to have a history of amphetamine, sedative, and hallucinogen abuse than non-white (mainly black) patients. Black patients, on the other hand, tended to be more likely to have abused cocaine than white patients, whereas there were no differences in alcohol, cannabis or narcotic abuse.

Marital status

Trends were present for patients who had never married to be more likely to have abused stimulants, cannabis and narcotics than patients who were currently or previously married. Within the group of stimulant abusers, marital status was not related to cocaine or amphetamine abuse, nor was it related to a history of alcohol, sedative or hallucinogen abuse in the overall sample.

Legal status

There were no differences in history of substance abuse between patients who were voluntarily admitted to the hospital and those who were involuntarily admitted.

To evaluate whether substance abuse history was related to any of the continuous demographic (age, or educational level) or chronicity (prior hospitalization or length of current hospitalization) variables, t-tests were performed for each type of substance comparing patients who had a history of abuse with patients with no abuse history. The results of this analysis are contained in Table 4 and are summarized below.

Age

Younger patients were significantly more likely to have a history of stimulant and cannabis abuse and there were trends for them to have abused more hallucinogens and narcotics than older patients. Age was not related to either a history of alcohol or sedative abuse, nor was it significantly related to cocaine or amphetamine abuse within the group of stimulant abusers.

Educational level

There was a trend for patients with fewer years of education to have a history of alcohol and stimulant abuse, but there were no differences in the other substances. Additionally, among the stimulant abusers, level of education was not related to cocaine or amphetamine abuse.

Number of prior hospitalizations

Patients with a history of cocaine abuse had significantly fewer prior hospitalizations than other patients, whereas number of hospitalizations was unrelated to any other types of substance abuse.

Table 4. Summary of *t*-tests for independent groups between substance abuse history and continuous demographic and chronicity variables

	Continuous demographic and chronicity variables							
	Age		Educational level		Number of prior hospitalizations		Length of current hospitalizations (days)	
Drug	*t*	df	*t*	df	*t*	df	*t*	df
Alcohol	0.53	245	2.66*	232	-1.36	239	-0.13	245
Stimulants	3.96**	245	2.71*	232	-0.53	239	0.75	245
Cocaine	1.14	62	-1.48	58	3.62**	62	1.40	62
Amphetamines	0.67	60	1.34	56	-1.50	60	0.39	60
Sedatives	1.55	245	0.87	232	1.04	239	1.17	245
Cannabis	4.08**	245	0.59	232	-1.24	239	-0.27	245
Hallucinogens	2.58*	245	-0.42	232	-0.01	239	-0.46	245
Narcotics	1.97*	245	0.24	232	1.03	239	0.63	245

A positive value for *t* indicates that patients with a history of substance abuse had a lower mean value than did patients with no history of abuse on the demographic or chronicity variable. Sample sizes vary because of missing data. * *P* < 0.05, unadjusted. ** *P* < 0.05, Bonferroni-adjusted.

Length of current hospitalization

There was no relationship between the number of days patients were hospitalized for the current admission and history of any type of substance abuse.

Changes in substance abuse from
1983-1986 to 1986-1990

This investigation examined substance abuse patterns of patients hospitalized between 1986 and 1990, whereas our previous study (29) examined patients hospitalized between 1983 and 1986. Because the prevalence of different types of substance abuse can vary over time in the general population (32), we compared the prevalence rates of substance abuse for schizophrenic and schizoaffective patients across the 2 studies (data on patients with major depression and bipolar disorder were not obtained in the earlier study). The differences in prevalence rates are illustrated in Fig. 1. Comparison of the substance abuse patterns between the earlier and later studies revealed similar rates of abuse across the 2 time periods for alcohol and sedatives. For stimulant abuse, schizoaffectives had comparable rates to schizophrenics in the 1986-1990 study, whereas in previous years schizoaffectives had a lower rate of stimulant abuse than schizophrenics. There were similar patterns of changes for 4 drugs for schizophrenic and schizoaffective patients: rates of abuse increased from 1983-1986 to 1986-1990 for cocaine and narcotics, and decreased for amphetamine and cannabis. Finally, there was a slight reduction in the rate of hallucinogen abuse for the schizophrenic, but not the schizoaffective patients over the 2 study periods.

DISCUSSION

The comparison of substance abuse patterns between patients assessed in 1983-1986 and 1986-1990 has important implications for the interpretation of differences obtained between substance abuse and the demographic and clinical variables. The most apparent change in pattern of abuse was in the rates of cannabis abuse and specific types of stimulant abuse. In 1983-1986, cannabis was the most commonly abused illicit drug. In 1986-1990, rates of cocaine abuse had increased so that it became the most popular illicit drug, while rates of both cannabis and amphetamine abuse had declined. These trends are consistent with patterns of abuse in the general population, particularly with respect to changes in cocaine and cannabis abuse in the United States (32).

The influence of the recent cocaine epidemic and the corresponding reduction in cannabis abuse can account for several of the differences in results between the 2 studies. In 1983-1986, race (black), educational level (low) and number of prior hospitalizations (few) were all related to a history

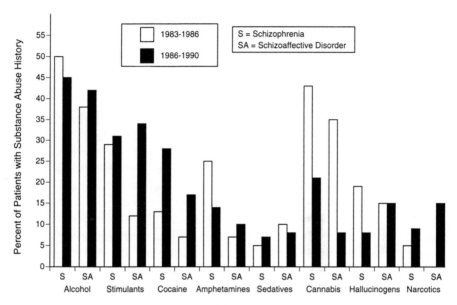

Figure 1. **Percentage of schizophrenic and schizoaffective disorder patients with a history of substance abuse or dependence admitted to the hospital in 1983–1986 and 1986–1990**

of cannabis abuse (29). In 1986-1990, the same relationship was found between each of these variables and history of cocaine abuse, with cannabis abuse no longer related to any of these variables. This suggests that the availability of illicit drugs is an important determinant of who abuses which substance, irrespective of its psychoactive effects.

A particularly intriguing result was that patients with a history of cocaine abuse had fewer prior hospitalizations than patients who had not abused cocaine, similar to our previous findings on cannabis abuse. Since most patients in the current study had been ill for a relatively long period of time and patients with drug-induced psychoses were deliberately excluded from the study, the relationship between cocaine abuse and number of prior hospitalizations does not seem to be caused by the effect of cocaine on provoking mental disorders in patients who would otherwise not have become ill. A more likely explanation, first suggested by Cohen & Klein (33), is that severely symptomatic patients may lack the social skills and personal contacts to sustain heavy illicit drug use, and these patients may be more prone to relapses and rehospitalization because of a stronger biological diathesis to the disorder. This possibility is also in line with a recent study by Dixon et al. (34) on substance abuse in schizophrenia, in which patients with a history of drug abuse had better premorbid sexual adjustment and were less symptomatic at discharge than patients with no history of substance abuse. In a similar vein, it has been found that psychiatric patients who avoid the use of alcohol tend to be more severely ill than patients who drink either socially or abusively (19, 35). Thus, although stimulant use has been reported to worsen the symptoms of mental disorders (36-38), patients currently prone to cocaine abuse may be a slightly less ill subgroup.

The relationships between substance abuse and demographic characteristics observed in the overall sample were robust and similar to our previous study on schizophrenic and schizoaffective patients (29). Men tended to be more likely to have a history of alcohol, cannabis, hallucinogen and narcotic abuse, in line with our previous study, as well as other studies with psychiatric patients (2) and prevalence rates in the general population (39). The finding that female schizoaffectives were more likely than men to have a history of stimulant abuse was unexpected and is difficult to account for.

As previously found (29), there were trends for the pattern of substance abuse to be related to patients' race. White patients tended to abuse sedatives, amphetamines and hallucinogens more than black patients, who in turn were more prone to a history of cocaine abuse. It is interesting that blacks tended to abuse cannabis more than whites in 1983-1986, whereas in 1986-1990, when the rate of cocaine abuse surpassed that of cannabis, black patients abused more cocaine than white patients. The consistent trend for whites to be more likely to abuse sedatives than blacks and for blacks to abuse the most commonly used illicit drug suggests that socioeconomic factors may play a role in determining drug type selection. White patients, who tend to have a higher socioeconomic status than black patients in Philadelphia, may have greater access to prescription sedatives, whereas black patients probably have more exposure and access to street drugs, such as cannabis (1983-1986) or cocaine (1986-1990). Few studies have examined the relationship between specific types of substance abuse and race. In a recent study by Sevy et al. (40), there was a trend for nonwhite schizophrenics to have a history of cocaine abuse and, more than 20 years ago, Hensela (41) reported that white patients were more likely to abuse hallucinogens than blacks; both findings are consistent with those reported here. Several studies examining race differences in psychiatric patients' history of alcohol abuse have produced contradictory results (4, 21, 23, 42-43). These findings show the importance of examining specific drug types when exploring race differences in substance abuse among patients with major mental disorder.

Similar to our patients assessed in 1983-1986 and numerous other reports (5, 17-18, 21, 42, 44), younger patients were more likely to abuse most types of drugs, particularly stimulants and cannabis, but also narcotics and hallucinogens. It is interesting that age was not related to a history of abusing central nervous system depressants (alcohol and sedatives), similar to many other reports. Younger patients appear to have a preference to abuse more activating or euphoric drugs, although the high availability of these substances in the past several decades may also account for this effect.

There were trends for patients with fewer years of formal education to be more likely to have a history of alcohol or stimulant abuse. Comparatively few studies have examined the relationship between substance abuse and educational level. Dixon et al. (34) reported that their sample of schizophrenic patients with a history of drug abuse had worse school performance during adolescence, despite better overall clinical functioning. The present findings suggest that drug abuse during adolescence may interfere with and eventually disrupt schooling, leading to fewer years of education for heavy substance abusers.

A prominent theory to account for the propensity of psychiatric patients to abuse drugs and alcohol is that substance abuse is an attempt to self-medicate distressing symptoms (9, 10, 45). In our previous study, schizophrenics were more likely to have a history of stimulant abuse (29), particularly amphetamines, than schizoaffective patients, a finding similar to that reported by several others (15, 17, 18). However, there were no differences in stimulant abuse between any of the 4 diagnostic groups in this study. The lack of agreement between the 2 studies suggests that differences in stimulant abuse between schizophrenics and other diagnostic groups may not be stable over time and could, in part, be influenced by varying base rates of stimulant abuse across different study populations.

A weak trend was present for patients with bipolar disorder to have a higher rate of alcohol abuse (66%) than patients with other diagnoses (range: 42-47%). This finding is consistent with extensive other research on alcohol abuse in bipolar disorder (1, 20, 46-48), and some genetic research showing a higher rate of alcoholism in the relatives of bipolar patients (49, 50). Previous research on other types of substance abuse in bipolar disorder has produced mixed results, although fewer studies have examined this issue (46, 51, 52). The weak statistical significance of this result and the absence of comparable data from other studies precludes speculation as to the inflated rate of alcohol abuse in the bipolar group.

Several caveats regarding the assessment procedures used need to be stated. First, DSM-III-R diagnoses were established in the context of standard inpatient psychiatric treatment and not by use of a structured clinical interview administered by a trained research psychiatrist or psychologist, resulting in some additional variation in the diagnostic groups. Second, history of substance abuse was not determined with a standardized research instrument. Future research in this area needs to be conducted using standardized instruments to assess diagnosis and substance abuse history.

The study provides strong confirmation for the importance of demographic variables such as gender, age, race and education as predictors of substance abuse in persons with major mental disorders. To the extent that demographic characteristics reflect the availability and prevalence of specific types of psychoactive substance use in the environments in which patients were raised and currently reside, these results suggest that social learning factors are primarily responsible for determining which patients abuse which types of drugs. Self-medication hypotheses pertaining to the predilection of specific diagnostic groups to abuse specific types of illicit substances are difficult to demonstrate consistently because of changing abuse patterns in the dominant culture. Additional research needs to be conducted on demographically matched groups of patients with different diagnoses to determine whether diagnosis predisposes persons to abuse specific types of substances.

REFERENCES

1. Parker JB, Meiller RM, Andrews GW. Major psychiatric disorders masquerading as alcoholism. *Southern Medical Journal* 1960: 53: 560-564.
2. Bowers MB, Swigar ME. Vulnerability to psychosis associated with hallucinogen use. *Psychiatry Research* 1983: 9: 91-97.
3. Safer DJ. Substance abuse by young adult chronic patients. *Hospital and Community Psychiatry* 1987: 38: 511-514.
4. Westermeyer J, Walzer V. Sociopathy and drug use in a young psychiatric population. *Diseases of the Nervous System* 1975: 36: 673-677.
5. Siris SG, Kane JM, Frechen K, Sellow AP, Mandeli J, Fasanodube B. Histories of substance abuse in patients with post-psychotic depressions. *Comprehensive Psychiatry* 1988: 29: 550-557.
6. Atkinson RM. Importance of alcohol and drug abuse in psychiatric emergencies. *California Medicine* 1973: 118: 1-4.
7. Alterman AI, Ayres ER, Williford WO. Diagnostic validation of conjoint schizophrenia and alcoholism. *Journal of Clinical Psychiatry* 1984: 45: 300-303.
8. Tsuang MT, Simpson JC, Kronfol Z. Subtypes of drug abuse with psychosis. *Archives of General Psychiatry* 1982: 39: 141-147.
9. Pope HG. Drug abuse and psychopathology. *New England Journal of Medicine* 1979: 301: 1341-1343.
10. Khantzian EJ. The self-medication hypothesis of addictive disorders: focus on heroin and cocaine dependence. *American Journal of Psychiatry* 1985: 142: 1259-1264.
11. Schneier FR, Siris SG. A review of psychoactive substance use and abuse in schizophrenia: patterns of drug choice. *Journal of Nervous & Mental Disease* 1987: 175: 641-650.
12. Minkoff K. An integrated treatment model for dual diagnosis of psychosis and addiction. *Hospital and Community Psychiatry* 1989: 40: 1031-1036.
13. Carey KB, Carey MP. Social problem-solving in dual diagnosis patients. *Journal of Psychopathology and Behavioral Assessment* 1990: 12: 247-254.

14. Evans K, Sullivan JM. *Dual diagnosis: counseling the mentally ill substance abuser.* New York: Guilford Press, 1990.

15. McLellan AT, Druley KA. Non-random relation between drugs of abuse and psychiatric diagnosis. *Journal of Psychiatric Research* 1977: 13: 179-184.

16. McLellan AT, Woody GE, O'Brien CP. Development of psychiatric illness in drug abusers: possible role of drug preference. *New England Journal of Medicine* 1979: 301: 1310-1314.

17. Breakey WR, Goodell H, Lorenz PC, McHugh PR. Hallucinogenic drugs as precipitants of schizophrenia. *Psychological Medicine* 1974: 4: 255-261.

18. Richard ML, Liskow BI, Perry PC. Recent psychostimulant use in hospitalized schizophrenics. *Journal of Clinical Psychiatry* 1985: 46: 79-83.

19. O'Farrell TJ, Connors GJ, Upper D. Addictive behaviors among hospitalized psychiatric patients. *Addictive Behaviors* 1983: 8: 329-333.

20. Bernadt MW, Murray RM. Psychiatric disorder, drinking and alcoholism: what are the links? *British Journal of Psychiatry* 1986: 148: 393-400.

21. Alterman AI, Erdlen FR, Murphy E. Alcohol abuse in the psychiatric hospital population. *Addictive Behaviors* 1981: 6: 69-73.

22. Rockwell DA, Ostwald P. Amphetamine use and abuse in psychiatric patients. *Archives of General Psychiatry* 1968: 18: 612-616.

23. Hall RCW, Popkin MK, Devaul R. The effect of unrecognized drug abuse on diagnosis and therapeutic outcome. *American Journal of Drug & Alcohol Abuse* 1977: 4: 455-465.

24. Ananth J, Vandewater S, Kamal M, Brodsky A, Gamal R, Miller M. Mixed diagnosis of substance abuse in psychiatric patients. *Hospital and Community Psychiatry* 1989: 40: 297-299.

25. Whitlock FA, Lowrey JM. Drug dependence in psychiatric patients. *Medical Journal of Australia* 1967: 1: 1157-1166.

26. Barbee JG, Clark PD, Crapanzano MS, Heintz GC, Kehoe CE. Alcohol and substance abuse among schizophrenic patients presenting to an emergency psychiatric service. *Journal of Nervous & Mental Disease* 1989: 177: 400-407.

27. Tien AY, Anthony JC. Epidemiological analysis of alcohol and drug use as risk factors for psychotic experiences. *Journal of Nervous & Mental Disease* 1990: 178: 473-480.

28. Regier DA, Boyd JH, Burke JD et al. One-month prevalence of mental disorders in the United States: based on five Epidemiological Catchment Area sites. *Archives of General Psychiatry* 1988: 45: 977-986.

29. Mueser KT, Yarnold PR, Levinson DF et al. Prevalence of substance abuse in schizophrenia: demographic and clinical correlates. *Schizophrenia Bulletin* 1990: 16: 31-56.

30. American Psychiatric Association. *Diagnostic and statistical manual of mental disorders.* 3rd edn., revised. Washington, DC: APA, 1987.

31. Kleinbaum DG, Kupper LL, Muller K. *Applied regression analysis and other multivariable methods.* Boston: PWS-Kent Publishing, 1988.

32. Pope HG, Ionescu-Pioggia M, Aizley HG, Varma DK. Drug use and life style among college undergraduates in 1989: a comparison with 1969 and 1978. *American Journal of Psychiatry* 1990: 147: 998-1001.

33. Cohen M, Klein DF. Drug abuse in a young psychiatric population. *American Journal of Orthopsychiatry* 1970: 40: 448-455.

34. Dixon L, Haas G, Weiden PJ, Sweeney J, Frances AJ. Drug abuse in schizophrenic patients: clinical correlates and reasons for use. *American Journal of Psychiatry* 1991:148: 224-230.

35. Ritzler BA, Strauss JS, Vanord A, Kokes RF. Prognostic implications of various drinking patterns in psychiatric patients. *American Journal of Psychiatry* 1977: 134: 546-549.

36. Janowsky DS, Davis JM. Methylphenidate, dextroamphetamine, and levamphetamine. *Archives of General Psychiatry* 1976: 33: 304-308.

37. Brady K, Anton R, Ballenger JC, Lydiard RB, Adinoff B, Selander J. Cocaine abuse among schizophrenic patients. *American Journal of Psychiatry* 1990: 147: 1164-1167.

38. West AP. Interaction of low-dose amphetamine use with schizophrenia in outpatients: three case reports. *American Journal of Psychiatry* 1974: 131: 321-323.

39. Myers JK, Weissman MM, Tischler GL et al. Six-month prevalence of psychiatric disorders in three communities. *Archives of General Psychiatry* 1984: 41: 959-967.

40. Sevy S, Kay SR, Opler LA, Vanpraag HM. Significance of cocaine history in schizophrenia. *Journal of Nervous & Mental Disease* 1990: 178: 642-648.

41. Hensala JD, Epstein LJ, Blackel KH. LSD and psychiatric inpatients. *Archives of General Psychiatry* 1967: 16: 554-559.

42. Fischer DE, Halikas JA, Baker JW, Smith JB. Frequency and patterns of drug abuse in psychiatric patients. *Diseases of the Nervous System* 1975: 36: 550-553.

43. Pokorny AD. The multiple readmission psychiatric patient. *Psychiatric Quarterly* 1965: 39: 70-78.

44. Hekimian LJ, Gershon S. Characteristics of drug abusers admitted to a psychiatric hospital. *Journal of the American Medical Association* 1968: 205: 125-130.

45. Kushner MG, Sher KJ, Beitman BD. The relation between alcohol problems and the anxiety disorders. *American Journal of Psychiatry* 1990: 147: 685-695.

46. Estroff TW, Dackis CA, Gold MS, Pottash ALC. Drug abuse and bipolar disorders. *International Journal of Psychiatry in Medicine* 1985: 15: 37-40.

47. Freed EX. Alcohol abuse by manic patients. *Psychological Reports* 1969: 25: 280.

48. Miller FT, Busch F, Tanenbaum JH. Drug abuse in schizophrenia and bipolar disorder. *American Journal of Drug & Alcohol Abuse* 1989: 15: 291-295.

49. Dunner DL, Patrick V, Fieve RR. Rapid cycling manic depressive patients. *Comprehensive Psychiatry* 1977: 18: 561-566.

50. Winokur G, Reich T, Rimmer J, Pitts FN. Alcoholism. III. Diagnosis and familial psychiatric illness in 259 alcoholic probands. *Archives of General Psychiatry* 1970: 23: 104-111.

51. Weiss RD, Mirin SM, Michael JL, Sollogub AC. Psychopathology in chronic cocaine abusers. *American Journal of Drug & Alcohol Abuse* 1986: 12: 17-29.

52. Liskow B, Mayfield D, Thiele J. Alcohol and affective disorder: assessment and treatment. *Journal of Clinical Psychiatry* 1982: 43: 144-147.

ABOUT THE AUTHORS

Kim T. Mueser, Ph.D., is affiliated with the New Hampshire-Dartmouth Psychiatric Research Center, Concord, NH. Alan S. Bellack, Ph.D., is affiliated with the University of Maryland Medical School in Baltimore, MD. Paul R. Yarnold, Ph.D., is affiliated with Northwestern University Medical School and University of Illinois at Chicago, Chicago, IL.

ACKNOWLEDGMENTS

This research was supported by NIMH grants 38636, 39998, 41577, and by a grant from the National Alliance for Research in Schizophrenia and Depression (NARSAD).

Copyright 1992. Munksgaard International Publishers, Ltd., Copenhagen, Denmark. Reprinted with permission.

Alcohol-Use Disorder and Severe Mental Illness

Robert E. Drake and Kim T. Mueser

Reprinted from *Alcohol Health & Research World*, 20(2):87-93, 1996

Alcohol-use disorders (AUD's) commonly occur in people with other severe mental illnesses, such as schizophrenia or bipolar disorder, and can exacerbate their psychiatric, medical, and family problems. Therefore, to improve detection of alcohol-related problems, establish correct AUD diagnoses, and develop appropriate treatment plans, it is important to thoroughly assess severely mentally ill patients for alcohol and other drug abuse. Several recent studies have indicated that integrated treatment approaches that combine AUD and mental health interventions in comprehensive, long-term, and stagewise programs may be most effective for these clients.

Alcohol-use disorder[1] (AUD) is the most common co-occurring disorder in people with severe mental illnesses, such as schizophrenia and bipolar disorder. This article reviews several aspects of AUD among mentally ill patients—prevalence and etiology, clinical correlates, course and outcome, assessment, and treatment—emphasizing practical clinical implications within each of these categories. Because people with AUD also frequently suffer from other drug-use disorders with similar clinical correlates, similar impacts on the course of mental illnesses, and similar principles of treatment as AUD, the information summarized in this article pertains to the broader problem area of alcohol and other drug (AOD)-use disorders among people with severe psychiatric disorders.

Prevalence and Etiology

Severe mental disorders frequently are complicated by comorbid disorders, such as medical illnesses, mental retardation, and AOD abuse. Co-occurring AOD-use disorders represent the most frequent and clinically most significant comorbidity among mentally ill patients, and alcohol is the most

---

[1]The term "alcohol-use disorder" used in this article encompasses alcohol abuse and dependence as defined in the American Psychiatric Association's *Diagnostic and Statistical Manual of Mental Disorders, Fourth Edition* (DSM-IV). The terms "alcohol-use disorder" and "alcohol abuse" are used interchangeably in this article. The definitions for these terms vary among the studies reviewed and frequently are based on earlier editions of the DSM.

commonly abused drug (Cuffel 1996). Undoubtedly, the fact that alcohol is readily available and that its purchase and consumption are legal for anyone age 21 and older contributes to its widespread abuse. For example, in community samples evaluated for the Epidemiologic Catchment Area (ECA) study, 33.7 percent of people diagnosed with schizophrenia or schizophreniform disorder and 42.6 percent of people with bipolar disorder also met the lifetime criteria for an AUD diagnosis, compared with 16.7 percent of people in the general population (Regier et al. 1990). Furthermore, according to the National Comorbidity Study, people with mania are 9.7 times as likely as the general population to meet the lifetime criteria for alcohol dependence (Kessler et al. 1996).

Because of the ways in which AOD-use disorders complicate severe mental illness, comorbidity rates tend to be particularly high among young males and clients in high-risk settings, such as hospitals, emergency rooms, and homeless shelters. The high rates of AOD-use disorders, especially among young adults, may be due partly to changes in the United States' mental health care system during the past few decades. An entire generation of people with severe mental illnesses developed their disorders during the era of deinstitutionalization. These people resided predominantly in their communities rather than in hospitals; they received few vocational, recreational, and social opportunities but experienced regular exposure and ready access to AOD's. As a result, the rates of diagnosed AOD-use disorders in mental health settings have continued to rise. In addition, clinicians have become more aware of the high prevalence of AOD-use disorders and more skilled at identifying them (Cuffel 1996).

Although people with severe mental illnesses probably experiment with AOD's for the same reasons as other members of the general population, several additional factors may contribute to the elevated rates of AOD-use disorders among severely mentally ill people. These factors include a downward social drift into poor, urban living settings, resulting in increased exposure and access to AOD's; attempts to alleviate, or self-medicate, the symptoms of mental illness, the side effects of psychotropic medications, and the dysphoria associated with mental illness; and attempts to avoid being labeled a "mental patient" (Minkoff and Drake 1991). Other factors involved in the underlying mechanisms (i.e., the etiology) of AOD-use disorders for this population may include early experimentation due to social pressure; desire to experience alcohol's short-term effects, such as relief of anxiety; and clinical correlates, such as antisocial behavior.

Although more research must be conducted on the etiology of AOD-use disorders in mentally ill people, most likely these disorders are determined, as in other people, by a complex set of biological, psychological, and social (i.e., biopsychosocial) factors. However, distinguishing the causes of AOD-use disorders from factors that sustain AOD use or that are correlates or consequences of AOD use often is difficult. For example, the following items appear to be related to sustained AUD, regardless of the reasons for initial alcohol use: positive reinforcement in the brain's reward system; association with internal or external cues through classical conditioning; poor cognitive, social, and vocational functioning; and lack of significant social and material resources (Donovan 1988).

SOCIAL AND PSYCHOLOGICAL CORRELATES OF AUD

Several studies have indicated that AUD among people with severe mental illnesses is associated with various manifestations of poor psychological and social adjustment (Dixon et al. 1990; Drake et al. 1989; Kozaric-Kovacic et al. 1995). These manifestations include relapses of psychiatric symptoms; psychosocial instability; other drug-use disorders; disruptive behavior; medical problems, such as HIV infection; family problems (e.g., in managing finances or maintaining positive relationships with family members); and institutionalization in hospitals and jails. Moreover, patients with dual diagnoses of severe mental illness and AUD are particularly prone to unstable housing arrangements and homelessness (see Appendix). Finally, dually diagnosed patients tend to be noncompliant with outpatient treatment and frequently receive health services in emergency rooms, hospitals, and jails (Bartels et al. 1993). Not all these correlates, however, have been observed consistently (e.g., the exacerbation of schizophrenic symptoms), and some correlates (e.g., violence or HIV infection) may be linked more closely with the abuse of drugs other than alcohol.

Although one is tempted to regard AUD as the cause of the above-mentioned social and psychological problems, many additional factors may contribute to poor adjustment. For example, alcohol-abusing patients with mental disorders also are prone to abuse other potentially more toxic drugs, to be noncompliant with medications, and to live in stressful circumstances without strong support networks (Drake et al. 1989). Moreover, these patients may differ premorbidly from patients with the same mental disorders who do not abuse drugs. Laboratory experiments may help clarify some of the relationships between AUD and poor adjustment, but the circumstances, quality, and quantity of alcohol use in a laboratory may differ significantly from the typical alcohol-use patterns of people in the community (Dixon et al. 1990). Support for the role of AUD in causing poor adjustment, however, comes from findings indicating that severely mentally ill patients who become abstinent show many signs of improved well-being. These patients either resemble severely mentally ill people who have never experienced AUD (Drake et al. 1996a) or rate between non-AOD users and current users on many clinical and functional measures (Kovasznay 1991; Ries et al. 1994).

COURSE AND OUTCOME

Data regarding the course and outcome of co-occurring mental illness and AUD are accumulating rapidly. Short-term studies (i.e., those lasting 1 year or less) of patients in traditional treatment systems indicate that these dually diagnosed people are prone to negative outcomes, such as continuing AUD, as well as to high rates of homelessness, disruptive behavior, psychiatric hospitalization, and incarceration. For example, outpatients with schizophrenia and co-occurring AUD had twice the rate of hospitalization during 1-year followup compared with patients with only schizophrenia (Drake et al. 1989). Fewer studies have been conducted on the long-term outcomes (i.e., results more than 1 year later), but findings tend to show persistent AUD and poor adjustment (Drake et al. 1996a; Kozaric-Kovacic et al. 1995).

Conversely, dually diagnosed patients who achieve abstinence appear to experience better prognoses and more positive adjustment, including improved psychiatric symptoms and decreased rates of hospitalization. For example, ECA study participants with schizophrenia and AUD who attained abstinence had decreased rates of depression and hospitalization at 1-year followup (Cuffel 1996). These optimistic findings have fueled attempts to develop more effective AUD interventions among psychiatric patients (see the section "Treatment").

ASSESSMENT

Thorough AOD-use assessment includes three overlapping but conceptually separable tasks: detection, diagnosis, and treatment planning (Drake et al. 1996b). Detection refers to the identification of harmful or dangerous substance-use patterns, whether or not they fulfill the criteria of abuse or dependence. Conversely, diagnosis denotes the assignment of a label of AOD-use disorder, based on the criteria of the American Psychiatric Association's *Diagnostic and Statistical Manual of Mental Disorders* (DSM). Treatment planning entails a more thorough analysis of the biopsychosocial factors sustaining AOD abuse and a specific plan to address them.

Detection

Numerous studies have shown that AOD-use disorders typically are underdiagnosed in acute-care psychiatric settings (Drake et al. 1993a). Several factors account for the high rates of nondetection, including mental health clinicians' inattention to AOD abuse; patients' denial, minimization, or inability to perceive the relationships between AOD use and their medical and social problems; and the lack of reliable and valid detection methods for this population. Failure to detect AOD abuse in psychiatric settings can result in misdiagnosis; overtreatment of psychiatric syndromes with medications;

neglect of appropriate interventions, such as detoxification, AOD education, and AOD abuse counseling; and inappropriate treatment planning.

Several procedures could improve the detection of AOD-use disorders and of potentially harmful AOD use among psychiatric patients. For example, mental health clinicians should be educated about AOD's and, subsequently, should maintain both a high index of suspicion for AOD-use disorders and an awareness of their clinical correlates. Little evidence exists indicating that psychiatric patients can sustain moderate AOD use over long periods of time without incurring problems (Drake et al. 1996a), although AOD use without abuse may occur at any time (Lehman et al. 1996). Consequently, clinicians should pay attention to any current AOD use, even if there appear to be no harmful consequences. Furthermore, clinicians should pay attention to reports of clients' past AOD-related problems, because the clients are more likely to report past use than current use (Barry et al. 1995).

Multiple tools are available that detect the majority of mentally ill people who abuse alcohol. These tools include brief screening tests, such as the CAGE and the Michigan Alcoholism Screening Test (MAST). Other standard detection approaches include assessment using more than one type of information (e.g., patient self-reports combined with laboratory tests) and information from multiple sources (e.g., family members or friends) (Drake et al. 1993a). In addition, Rosenberg and colleagues (1996) recently developed a screening instrument, the Dartmouth Assessment of Lifestyle Instrument, that detects AOD-use disorders in psychiatric patients with greater accuracy than other instruments.

Diagnosis

According to the DSM criteria, persistent alcohol use resulting in social, vocational, psychological, or physical problems should be considered abuse or dependence. This definition has several implications for diagnosing AOD-use disorders in severely mentally ill patients. For example, in psychiatric patients, who are more vulnerable to the effects of psychoactive drugs, use of relatively small amounts of AOD's may result in psychological problems or relapse of the symptoms of mental illness or may evolve into an obvious use disorder (Dixon et al. 1990; Drake et al. 1989). Moreover, clinicians must be aware that in many patients with apparent dual diagnoses, AOD use may have induced the second psychiatric disorder (Lehman et al. 1994).

Treatment Planning

During treatment planning, the clinician, together with the patient, reviews all data and specifies a strategy for further exploration or change of AOD-use behavior. Treatment planning includes a thorough biopsychosocial evaluation encompassing the following areas (Donovan 1988):

- Historical information and family history
- Current frequency and patterns of use
- Physiological factors
- Cognitive-behavioral expectancies related to the use of different drugs
- Environmental cues, social networks, and other social and behavioral patterns that sustain abuse
- Interrelationships between AOD use, medications, and psychiatric illnesses
- Previous attempts to control or treat AOD use.

Thus, treatment planning is a continuous, dynamic, and long-term process based on the clinician's and patient's collaboration.

TREATMENT

For historical reasons, the mental health and AOD-abuse treatment systems in the United States are quite separate. Despite attempts to link the two treatment systems in traditional approaches to the care of patients with dual diagnoses, poor coordination between the systems may act as a treatment barrier for these patients (Osher and Drake 1996; Ridgely et al. 1987).

Over the past 15 years, however, mental health programs serving people with severe mental illnesses have moved toward integrating AOD-abuse treatment into a comprehensive treatment approach in which the same clinicians or teams of clinicians combine both mental health and AOD-abuse philosophies and treatment components (Carey 1996; Drake et al. 1993b; Drake and Mueser 1996; Lehman and Dixon 1995; Minkoff and Drake 1991). In addition to integrating mental health and AOD-abuse treatments, many of these programs also incorporate intensive case management approaches and outreach to facilitate engagement in treatment; comprehensive services and a team orientation; various types of group interventions; and a longitudinal, stagewise approach (Mueser and Noordsy 1996). A longitudinal, stagewise approach is based on the findings that the recovery process typically occurs over years rather than weeks and often proceeds in several steps (e.g., the clients require motivational interventions before they are ready to participate in abstinence-oriented interventions).

Osher and Kofoed (1989) conceptualized four overlapping stages of AOD treatment for patients with severe mental illnesses: engagement, persuasion, active treatment, and relapse prevention. Engagement includes developing a trusting relationship, or working alliance, with the patient, whereas persuasion entails helping the patient to perceive and acknowledge the adverse consequences of AOD use in his or her life and develop motivation for recovery. During active treatment, the clinician helps the patient achieve stable recovery in the form of either controlled use or, preferably, abstinence. Relapse prevention focuses on helping the patient maintain stable recovery. During each stage, a range of treatment options are available, and the specific treatment plan should reflect the patient's preferences. For example, some patients may benefit from participating in self-help programs (e.g., Alcoholics Anonymous) during active treatment or relapse prevention, whereas other patients may not. Clinicians employing a stagewise treatment approach may find it useful to consult a growing number of clinical guides describing various strategies for integrating mental health and AOD treatments for patients with dual diagnoses (e.g., Daley and Thase 1994; Evans and Sullivan 1990; Gold and Slaby 1991; Miller 1994; as well as the articles cited in the preceding paragraph).

Most programs integrating mental health and AOD treatment provide services on a long-term, outpatient basis in the community and attempt to minimize the time spent in inpatient, detoxification, or residential settings. Community-based treatment is emphasized because skills acquired by severely mentally ill patients in one setting (e.g., in a clinic) often fail to generalize to other settings (e.g., everyday life in the community). Thus, a premium is placed on working with patients in their natural environments. Nevertheless, brief treatment components in inpatient and detoxification settings can provide valuable opportunities for clinicians to establish or reestablish therapeutic relationships with patients during the engagement stage and to motivate patients to examine their AOD use and its possible consequences during the persuasion stage. Inpatient and outpatient services must be coordinated, however, in order to maximize long-term treatment gains.

Several recent studies indicate that integrated treatment programs combining AOD-abuse and mental health interventions within the same setting result in more positive outcomes than traditional, nonintegrated treatment systems (Drake et al. 1996a; Godley et al. 1994; Mueser et al. 1997). These studies show a steady reduction in AOD use, with the number of stably abstinent patients increasing with each year of consistent treatment. Other findings support the concept of treatment stages in the recovery process (McHugo et al. 1995). For example, in a recent study in New Hampshire, clients moved steadily through the stages of engagement, persuasion, active treatment, and relapse prevention, and approximately 50 percent of them achieved abstinence after 3 years of treatment (Mueser et al. 1996).

Not all investigators, however, have reported positive results of integrated treatment for dual-diagnosis patients. For example, Lehman and colleagues (1993) failed to find a beneficial effect of integrated treatment, possibly because the AOD-abuse measure they employed (i.e., the Addiction Severity Index) was not sufficiently sensitive to changes in AOD use in the severely mentally ill population studied (Corse et al. 1995). Also, not all integrated treatment approaches may be equally effective. Jerrell and Ridgely (1995) reported that an integrated treatment program with a focus on behavioral skills training reduced AOD abuse more effectively than a more traditional 12-step approach or a case management approach. The accumulated evidence suggests that providing integrated mental health and AOD treatment to dually diagnosed patients improves outcome compared with traditional, nonintegrated approaches. More research is needed, however, before definitive conclusions about the effectiveness of integrated treatment can be reached.

Summary

Approximately 50 percent of clients with severe mental illnesses, such as schizophrenia and bipolar disorder, who are in community mental health settings develop AOD-use disorders during their lifetime. The rate probably is even greater among high-risk groups, such as young men with histories of violence or homelessness, and among patients in acute-care settings. AOD-use disorders among severely mentally ill patients are correlated with poor concurrent adjustment in several domains and with adverse short-term outcomes, including high rates of homelessness, hospitalization, and incarceration.

Clinicians often overlook AOD abuse among psychiatric patients. The use of standard screening and evaluation procedures could, however, greatly improve detection and diagnosis of AOD-related problems as well as treatment planning for this patient population. AOD-abuse treatment should be provided in stages over the long term by dual-diagnosis experts. Current research suggests that for patients with dual diagnoses, treatment approaches that integrate mental health and AOD treatment are particularly effective.

References

Barry, K.L.; Fleming, M.F.; Greenley, J.; Widlak, P.; Kropp, S.; and McKee, D. Assessment of alcohol and other drug disorders in the seriously mentally ill. *Schizophrenia Bulletin* 21:313-321, 1995.

Bartels, S.J.; Teague, G.B.; Drake, R.E.; Clark, R.E.; Bush. P.; and Noordsy, D.L. Service utilization and costs associated with substance abuse among rural schizophrenic patients. *Journal of Nervous and Mental Disease* 181:227-232, 1993.

Carey, K.B. Substance use reduction in the context of outpatient psychiatric treatment: A collaborative, motivational, harm reduction approach. *Community Mental Health Journal* 32:291-306, 1996.

Corse, S.J.; Hirschinger, N.B.; and Zanis, D. The use of the Addiction Severity Index with people with severe mental illness. *Psychiatric Rehabilitation Journal* 19:9-18, 1995.

Cuffel, B.J. Comorbid substance use disorder: Prevalence, patterns of use, and course. In: Drake, R.E., and Mueser, K.T., eds. *Dual Diagnosis of Major Mental Illness and Substance Abuse: Recent Research and Clinical Implications.* San Francisco: Jossey-Bass, 1996. pp. 93-105.

Daley, D., and Thase, M. *Dual Disorders Recovery Counseling.* Independence, MO: Herald House/Independence Press, 1994.

Dixon, L.; Haas, G.; Weiden, P.; Sweeney, J.; and Frances, A. Acute effects of drug abuse in schizophrenic patients: Clinical observations and patients' self-reports. *Schizophrenia Bulletin* 16: 69-79, 1990.

Donovan, D.M. Assessment of addictive behaviors: Implications of an emerging biopsychosocial model. In: Donovan, D.M., and Marlatt, G.A., eds. *Assessment of Addictive Behaviors.* New York: Guilford Press, 1988. pp. 3-8.

Drake, R.E.; and Mueser, K.T., eds. *Dual Diagnosis of Major Mental Illness and Substance Abuse: Recent Research and Clinical Implications.* San Francisco: Jossey-Bass, 1996.

Drake, R.E.; Osher, F.C.; and Wallach, M.A. Alcohol use and abuse in schizophrenia: A prospective community study. *Journal of Nervous and Mental Disease* 177:408-414, 1989.

Drake, R.E.; Alterman, A.I.; and Rosenberg, S.R. Detection of substance use disorders in severely mentally ill patients. *Community Mental Health Journal* 29:175-192, 1993a.

Drake, R.E.; Bartels, S.J.; Teague, G.B.; Noordsy, D.L.; and Clark, R.E. Treatment of substance abuse in severely mentally ill patients. *Journal of Nervous and Mental Disease* 181:601-611, 1993b.

Drake, R.E.; Mueser, K.T.; Clark, R.E.; and Wallach, M.A. The course, treatment, and outcome of substance disorder in persons with severe mental illness. *American Journal of Orthopsychiatry* 66:42-51, 1996a.

Drake, R.E.; Rosenberg, S.D.; and Mueser, K.T. Assessing substance use disorder in persons with severe mental illness. In: Drake, R.E., and Mueser, K.T., eds. *Dual Diagnosis of Major Mental Illness and Substance Abuse: Recent Research and Clinical Implications.* San Francisco: Jossey-Bass, 1996b. pp. 3-17.

Evans, K., and Sullivan, J.M. *Dual Diagnosis: Counseling the Mentally Ill Substance Abuser.* New York: Guilford Press, 1990.

Godley, S.H.; Hoewing-Roberon, R.; and Godley, M.D. *Final MISA Report.* Bloomington. IL: Lighthouse Institute, 1994.

Gold, M., and Slaby, A., eds. *Dual Diagnosis in Substance Abuse.* New York: Marcel Dekker, Inc., 1991.

Jerrell, J., and Ridgely, M.S. Comparative effectiveness of three approaches to serving people with severe mental illness and substance abuse disorders. *Journal of Nervous and Mental Disease* 183:566-576, 1995.

Kessler, R.C.; Nelson, C.B.; McGonagle, K.A.; Edlund, M.J.; Frank, R.G.; and Leaf, P.J. The epidemiology of co-occurring addictive and mental disorders: Implications for prevention and service utilization. *American Journal of Orthopsychiatry* 66:17-31, 1996.

Kovasznay, B. Substance abuse among veterans with a diagnosis of schizophrenia. *Hospital and Community Psychiatry* 42:948-949, 1991.

Kozaric-Kovacic, D.; Folnegovic-Smalc, V.; Folnegovic, Z.; and Marusic, A. Influence of alcoholism on the prognosis of schizophrenic patients. *Journal of Studies on Alcohol* 56:622-627, 1995.

Lehman, A.F.; and Dixon, L.B.. *Double Jeopardy: Chronic Mental Illness and Substance Abuse.* New York: Harwood Academic Publishers, 1995.

Lehman, A.F.; Herron, J.D.; Schwartz, R.P.; and Myers, C.P. Rehabilitation for young adults with severe mental illness and substance use disorders: A clinical trial. *Journal of Nervous and Mental Disease* 181:86-90, 1993.

Lehman, A.F.; Myers, C.P.; Corty, E.; and Thompson, J.W. Prevalence and patterns of "dual diagnosis" among psychiatric inpatients. *Comprehensive Psychiatry* 35:1-5, 1994.

Lehman, A.F.; Myers, C.P.; Dixon, L.B.; and Johnson, J.L. Detection of substance use disorders among psychiatric inpatients. *Journal of Nervous and Mental Disease* 184:228-233, 1996.

McHugo, G.J.: Drake, R.E.; Burton, H.L.; and Ackerson, T.M. A scale for assessing the stage of substance abuse treatment in persons with severe mental illness. *Journal of Nervous and Mental Disease* 183:672-677, 1995.

Miller, N.S., ed. *Treating Coexisting Psychiatric and Addictive Disorders.* Center City, MN: Hazelden, 1994.

Minkoff, K., and Drake, R.E., eds. *Dual Diagnosis of Major Mental Illness and Substance Disorder.* San Francisco: Jossey-Bass, 1991.

Mueser, K.T., and Noordsy, D.L. Group treatment for dually diagnosed clients. In: Drake, R.E.; and Mueser, K.T., eds. *Dual Diagnosis of Major Mental Illness and Substance Abuse: Recent Research and Clinical Implications.* San Francisco: Jossey-Bass, 1996. pp. 33-51.

Mueser, K.T.; Drake, R.E.; and Miles, K.M. *The Course and Treatment of Substance Use Disorder in Patients with Severe Mental Illness.* National Institute on Drug Abuse Research Monograph. Rockville, MD: U.S. Department of Health and Human Services, 1997.

Osher, F.C., and Drake, R.E. Reversing a history of unmet needs: Approaches to care for persons with co-occurring addictive and mental disorders. *American Journal of Orthopsychiatry* 66:4-11, 1996.

Osher, F.C., and Kofoed, L.L. Treatment of patients with psychiatric and psychoactive substance abuse disorders. *Hospital and Community Psychiatry* 40: 1025-1030, 1989.

Regier, D.A.; Farmer, M.E.; Rae, D.S.; Locke, B.Z.; Keith, S.J.; Judd, L.J.; and Goodwin, F.K. Comorbidity of mental disorders with alcohol and other drug abuse: Results from the Epidemiologic Catchment Area (ECA) study. *Journal of the American Medical Association* 264:2511-2518,1990.

Ridgely, M.S.; Osher, F.C.; and Talbott, J.A. *Chronic Mentally Ill Young Adults with Substance Abuse Problems: Treatment and Training Issues.* Baltimore, MD: University of Maryland Mental Health Policy Studies Center, 1987.

Ries, R.; Mullen, M.; and Cox, G. Symptom severity and utilization of treatment resources among dually diagnosed inpatients. *Hospital and Community Psychiatry* 45:562-568, 1994.

Rosenberg, S.D.; Drake, R.E.; Wolford, G.L.; Mueser, K.T.; Oxman, T.E.; and Vidaver, R.M. "Development of a Brief Screen for Substance Use Disorder in the Severely

Mentally Ill." Paper presented at the annual meeting of the American Association of Behavior Therapy, New York, November 1996.

ABOUT THE AUTHORS

Robert E. Drake, M.D., Ph.D., is Professor in both the Department of Psychiatry and the Department of Community and Family Medicine at Dartmouth Medical School and Director of the New Hampshire-Dartmouth Psychiatric Research Center, Concord, NH. Kim T. Mueser, Ph.D., is Professor in both the Department of Psychiatry and the Department of Community and Family Medicine at Dartmouth Medical School and a senior researcher at the New Hampshire-Dartmouth Psychiatric Research Center, Concord, NH.

ACKNOWLEDGMENTS

The writing of this article was supported by U.S. Public Health Service grant MH-46072 from the National Institute of Mental Health (NIMH) and the Substance Abuse and Mental Health Services Administration; National Institute on Alcohol Abuse and Alcoholism grants AA-08341, AA-08840, and AA-10265; and NIMH grants MH-00839 and MH-52822.

Appendix: Homelessness and Dual Diagnosis

Homeless people with co-occurring severe mental illnesses and alcohol use disorder (AUD) represent a particularly vulnerable subgroup of the homeless with complex service needs (Drake et al. 1991). Although often referred to as dually diagnosed, these people typically are impaired by several additional problems, including abuse of drugs other than alcohol, general medical illnesses, and legal problems. This group also has histories of trauma and behavioral disorders, deficient social and vocational skills, and support networks that include people involved in alcohol and other drug (AOD) abuse or other illegal behavior. Compared with other homeless subgroups, those with co-occurring severe mental illnesses and AUD are more likely to experience harsh living conditions, such as living on the streets rather than in shelters; suffer from psychological distress and demoralization; grant sexual favors for food and money; be picked up by police; become incarcerated; be isolated from their families; and be victimized (Fischer 1990).

Much of our current knowledge of homeless adults with dual disorders comes from National Institute on Alcohol Abuse and Alcoholism initiatives funded by the Stewart B. McKinney Act (Huebner et al. 1993). These initiatives include a 3-year, 14-project demonstration to develop, implement, and evaluate interventions for homeless adults with AOD-related problems. Two of the projects specifically have targeted homeless people with co-occurring severe mental illnesses and AOD-use disorders.

Prevalence and etiology

In a comprehensive review, Fischer (1990) found that between 3.6 and 26 percent of homeless adults suffered from both a mental disorder and AUD. The rates of co-occurring mental and AOD-use disorders ranged from 8 to 31 percent. Other recent reviews also have determined that the rates of dual diagnoses among the homeless range from 10 to 20 percent (Drake et al. 1991).

Many studies investigating the causes (i.e., etiology) of homelessness and dual diagnoses have suggested that people with co-occurring mental and AOD-use disorders are particularly prone to losing family supports and stable housing and becoming homeless (Drake et al. 1991). One reason for this increased risk appears to be that dually diagnosed clients often are excluded from housing and treatment programs designated specifically for people with single disorders (Drake et al. 1991).

Management of Homeless People With Dual Diagnoses

Several consistent themes have emerged in the literature on interventions for homeless people with dual disorders. Most important, interventions should focus primarily on meeting the clients' basic needs related to subsistence and safety. Moreover, appropriate interventions should provide needed structure, support, and protection. Specific treatment recommendations include the following (Drake et al. 1991):

- Integration of mental health and substance abuse interventions—for example, through intensive case management and group interventions
- Provision of services to families as well as to individual clients
- Development of culturally relevant services
- Development of long-term, stagewise interventions.

Recent studies have examined the integration of mental health, AOD abuse, and housing interventions in various configurations. These studies show that both engaging and retaining dually diagnosed homeless people in treatment programs are extremely difficult, especially in short-term or residential programs (Blankertz and Cnaan 1994; Burnam et al. 1995; Rahav et al. 1995). Furthermore, any gains that the clients make during short-term or residential treatment tend to erode rapidly following discharge. Several observations may help explain these findings. For example, behaviors that may represent common adaptations to homeless living, such as intimidating or threatening other people, often are incompatible with participation in treatment and recovery programs (Weinberg and Koegel 1995). Homeless people also often have difficulty participating in treatment or rehabilitation before they have attained some measure of stable subsistence (Baxter and Hopper 1981). Finally, rehabilitation and recovery are long-term endeavors that take years for most dually diagnosed people. Consequently, programs that first address the clients' subsistence needs and then provide long-term treatment in progressive stages are best suited for dually diagnosed homeless people (Drake et al. 1994).

Summary

Among the homeless, those with severe mental illnesses and co-occurring AUD constitute a complex subgroup. Meeting their needs requires an intensive effort over months or years, with multidisciplinary teams providing outreach; addressing subsistence needs; integrating mental health, substance abuse, and housing interventions; and allowing for a longitudinal, stagewise recovery process. Because researchers have identified some of the pathways by which dually diagnosed individuals frequently become homeless, interventions to prevent homelessness also may be possible. Such preventive interventions could focus on unstable housing situations and evictions, more careful discharge planning from institutional settings, greater support for families, more efficient use of resources, and help with money management (Substance Abuse and Mental Health Services Administration 1996).

–Robert E. Drake and Kim T. Mueser

References

Baxter, E., and Hopper, K. *Private Lives/Public Spaces: Homeless Adults on the Streets of New York City.* New York: Community Service Society, 1981.

Blankertz, L.E., and Cnaan, R.A. Assessing the impact of two residential programs for dually diagnosed homeless persons. *Social Service Review* 68:536-560, 1994.

Burnam, M.A.; Morton, S.C.; McGlynn, E.A.; Petersen, L.P.; Stecher, B.M.; Hayes, C.; and Vaccaro, J.V. An experimental evaluation of residential and nonresidential treatment for dually diagnosed homeless adults. *Journal of Addictive Diseases* 14(4):111-134, 1995.

Drake, R.E.; Osher, F.C.; and Wallach, M.A. Homelessness and dual diagnosis. *American Psychologist* 46:1149-1158,1991.

Drake, R.E.; Yovetich, N.A.; Bebout, R.R.; Harris, M.; and McHugo, G.J. "Integrated Treatment for Dually Diagnosed Homeless Adults." Paper presented at the NIAAA Cooperative Agreement Program for Homeless Persons with Alcohol and Other Drug Problems meeting, Rockville, MD, September 1994.

Fischer, P.J. *Alcohol and Drug Abuse and Mental Health Problems Among Homeless Persons: A Review of the Literature, 1980-1990.* Rockville, MD: National Institute on Alcohol Abuse and Alcoholism and National Institute of Mental Health, 1990.

Huebner, R.B.; Perl, H.I.; Murray, P.M.; Scott, J.E.; and Tutunjian, B.A. The NIAAA Cooperative Agreement Program for Homeless Persons with Alcohol and Other Drug Problems: An overview. *Alcoholism Treatment Quarterly* 10(3/4):5-20, 1993.

Rahav, M.; Rivera, J.J.; Nuttbrock, L.; Ng-Mak, D.; Sturz, E.L.; Link, B.G.; Struening, E.L.; Pepper, B.; and Gross, B. Characteristics and treatment of homeless, mentally ill, chemical-abusing men. *Journal of Psychoactive Drugs* 27:93-103,1995.

Substance Abuse and Mental Health Services Administration. *Cooperative Agreements for DMHS/CSAT Collaboration Program to Prevent Homelessness.* GFA No. SM 96-01. Rockville, MD: U.S. Department of Health and Human Services, 1996.

Weinberg, D., and Koegel, P. Impediments to recovery in treatment programs for dually diagnosed homeless adults: An ethnographic analysis. *Contemporary Drug Problems* 22:193-236, 1995.

INTRODUCTION TO SECTION TWO

The focus of the six articles in the Etiology section is on the causes of substance abuse in the psychiatric population. Two articles in the Overview section documented the high rate of substance use disorders in persons with a severe mental illness (Drake & Mueser, 1996; Mueser, Yarnold, & Bellack, 1992). Upwards of one-half of all persons with a psychiatric disability experience problems related to substance abuse sometime during their lives, compared with fewer than one fifth of all people in the general population. These observations lead quite naturally to a frequently asked question: Why are people with a psychiatric disorder at such high risk of developing substance use disorders?

There are many different theories that have been proposed to explain widespread substance abuse in psychiatric clients, and probably no single theory can completely explain the high rates of substance abuse in this population. Rather, different explanations may apply to different clients, with more than one explanation possible for any given individual. Identifying factors that may have contributed to, or are currently maintaining, substance abuse in psychiatric clients is important for treatment planning. Those factors that play a critical role in substance abuse may need to be addressed if treatment is to be successful. For example, a client who uses substances to facilitate social interactions may need help developing skills for establishing satisfying social relationships that are not based on the mutual use of substances.

The articles in this section address some of the most prominent theories of etiology of dual disorders. Lisa Dixon and her colleagues review several different models of the relationship between substance abuse and schizophrenia. The authors point out that although there is strong evidence that substance use can worsen psychiatric symptoms and lead to relapses, some clients report immediate positive effects of substances, such as less depression and more energy, that may be related to their continued use. Research has not provided strong support for the hypothesis that clients use substances to regulate, or self-medicate, their symptoms as an explanation for the high rates of comorbidity (cf., Brunette, Mueser, Xie, & Drake, 1997), but this hypothesis may nevertheless be important because many clients perceive substance use as having beneficial effects on at least some symptoms (Noordsy et al., 1991; Test, Wallisch, Allness, & Ripp, 1989). Dixon and colleagues also review several other models of comorbidity, including the etiological model (substance use leads to psychopathology), the dopamine dysfunction model (dopamine imbalance increases vulnerability to substance abuse), the socialization model (substance use facilitates social interactions), and the independence model (psychiatric illness and substance use problems may be unrelated in some clients). Although this article (and several others in this section) focus on schizophrenia, the findings apply to other diagnostic groups with severe mental illness.

The article by Helen Bergman and Maxine Harris reviews one of the first studies to examine client's self-reports regarding their reasons for using substances and their knowledge of the effects of substance abuse. A number of different reasons for using substances were identified, with the most common reasons including socialization (e.g., membership in a peer group, reduction of social anxiety) and self-medication. Of equal importance, few clients understood the debilitating consequences of substances on their psychiatric illness.

Although clients with dual diagnoses commonly identify a variety of different motives for their substance use, the reliability and validity of these self-reports is unknown. Kim Mueser and his colleagues evaluated the internal consistency of standardized scales for assessing motives and expectancies for substance use, and examined their relationships to substance use disorders. *Internal consistency* is a type of scale reliability. Measures of internal consistency such as coefficient alpha reflect the extent to which the constituent items of a scale cohere in assessing the target construct. *Motives* refer to the reasons clients give for using substances. *Expectancies* refer to clients' beliefs about the effects of substances. Mueser and colleagues found that scales developed for measuring motives and expectancies for substance use in the general population showed good reliability when used in psychiatric populations. In addition, clients with substance use disorders endorsed stronger motives and more positive expectancies for use than those clients without substance use disorders.

Clinicians who work with clients who have dual diagnoses have observed that many clients are sensitive to the effects of even small quantities of substances. For example, a few alcoholic drinks or uses of marijuana or cocaine can have potent negative consequences for people with a major psychiatric disorder. The article by Robert Drake and Michael Wallach shows that few clients with a severe mental illness are able to sustain asymptomatic drinking over time. Clients from two studies, who were drinking moderate amounts of alcohol and experiencing no negative consequences at the initial evaluation, either tended to develop alcohol use disorders or to became abstinent during the follow-up periods. Fewer than five percent of clients sustained asymptomatic drinking over two successive six-month assessments. This article suggests that the supersensitivity of persons with a major mental illness to psychoactive substances may account partly for the high rate of co-occurring substance use disorder.

Persons with severe mental illnesses may experience high rates of substance abuse because of an accumulation of known risk factors such as poverty, joblessness, poor social skills, and dysphoria. For example, people in the general population with a family history of substance abuse have an increased vulnerability to developing a substance use disorder. That is, persons with close relatives who are alcoholic are more likely to develop an alcohol use disorder than persons with no alcohol abuse in their immediate family. A logical extension of this is to evaluate the relationship between family history and substance abuse in clients who have dual diagnoses. The article by Douglas Noordsy and his colleagues describes such a study with a focus on alcoholism, the most commonly abused substance. The authors found that clients with a family history of alcoholism were more likely to have alcohol and drug use disorders. Of equal importance, among clients with alcoholism, family history was associated with more severe alcoholism and a poorer response to treatment. One implication of these findings is that clinicians need to explore family history of substance abuse with their clients, because those with relatives who have had substance use problems may require more intensive or specialized interventions.

Kushner and Mueser (1993) described the *common factor model* of comorbidity as suggesting that the high rate of substance abuse in psychiatric clients could be caused by a third factor that increases vulnerability to both disorders. The article by Carol Caton and her colleagues examines the potential importance of one such common factor, antisocial personality disorder (APD). Rates of APD are higher among substance abusers (Regier et al., 1990) and those with psychiatric disorders (Jackson, Whiteside, Bates, Rudd, & Edwards, 1991) than in the general population. In their study, Caton and colleagues compared homeless persons with schizophrenia to similar persons who had never been homeless on a variety of measures, including APD. One of the most important factors that distinguished the two groups was APD. Among the never-homeless group, only 9% had APD, compared with 25% of the group who had been homeless. The significance of these findings is underscored by a recent study by Mueser and colleagues (in press) in which APD in clients with schizophrenia and co-occurring substance use disorder was found to be related to more severe substance abuse, as well as worse legal problems, more severe psychiatric symptoms, and a stronger family history of substance use disorders.

REFERENCES

Brunette, M.F., Mueser, K.T., Xie, H., & Drake, R.E. (1997). Relationships between symptoms of schizophrenia and substance abuse. *Journal of Nervous and Mental Disease*, 185, 13-20.

Drake, R.E., & Mueser, K.T. (1996) Alcohol-use disorder and severe mental illness. *Alcohol Health and Research World*, 20, 87-93.

Jackson, H.J., Whiteside, H.L., Bates, G.W., Rudd, R.P., & Edwards, J. (1991). Diagnosing personality disorders in psychiatric inpatients. *Acta Psychiatrica Scandinavica*, 83, 206-213.

Kushner, M.G., & Mueser, K.T. (1993). Psychiatric co-morbidity with alcohol disorders. In *Eighth special report to the U.S. Congress on alcohol and health* (NIH Publication No. 94-3699, pp. 37-59). Rockville, MD: U.S. Department of Health and Human Services.

Mueser, K.T., Drake, R.E., Ackerson, T.H., Alterman, A.I., Miles, K.M., & Noordsy, D.L. (in press). Antisocial personality disorder, conduct disorder, and substance abuse in schizophrenia. *Journal of Abnormal Psychology.*

Mueser, K.T., Yarnold, P.R., & Bellack, A.S. (1992). Diagnostic and demographic correlates of substance abuse in schizophrenia and major affective disorder. *Acta Psychiatrica Scandinavica, 85,* 48-55.

Noordsy, D.L., Drake, R.E., Teague, G.B., Osher, F.C., Hurlbut, S.C., Beaudett, M.S., & Paskus, T.S. (1991). Subjective experiences related to alcohol use among schizophrenics. *Journal of Nervous and Mental Disease,* 179, 410-414.

Regier, D.A., Farmer, M.E., Rae, D.S., Locke, B.Z., Keith, S.J., Judd, L.L., & Goodwin, F.K. (1990). Comorbidity of mental disorders with alcohol and other drug abuse. *Journal of the American Medical Association,* 264, 2511-2518.

Test, M.A., Wallisch, L., Allness, D., & Ripp, K. (1989). Substance use in young adults with schizophrenic disorders. *Schizophrenia Bulletin,* 15, 465-476.

ACUTE EFFECTS OF DRUG ABUSE IN SCHIZOPHRENIC PATIENTS: CLINICAL OBSERVATIONS AND PATIENTS' SELF-REPORTS

Lisa Dixon, Gretchen Haas, Peter Weiden, John Sweeney, and Allen Frances

Reprinted from *Schizophrenia Bulletin*, 16(1):69-79, 1990

Substance abuse among schizophrenic patients is an increasingly recognized clinical phenomenon. The authors review experimental and observed clinical effects of drug abuse and patients' subjective experiences of acute intoxication. Though drug abuse may exacerbate psychotic symptoms, abused drugs may also lead to transient symptom reduction in subgroups of schizophrenic patients. Some patients report feeling less dysphoric, less anxious, and more energetic while intoxicated. Models of the relationship of drug abuse and schizophrenia, particularly the self-medication hypothesis, are discussed in reference to these data.

The comorbidity of schizophrenia and substance abuse is well documented, with up to 60 percent of schizophrenic patients being reported to use or abuse illicit drugs (Alterman et al. 1980; Richard et al. 1985; Negrete et al. 1986; Dixon et al. 1989a; Miller and Tanenbaum 1989; and Dixon et al., submitted for publication). The lack of outpatient treatment programs which treat dual-diagnosis patients has compounded this problem (Gottheil and Weinstein 1980; Solomon 1986). If rational treatment strategies are to be designed, it is necessary to develop empirical and theoretical foundations to understand why schizophrenic patients abuse psychoactive drugs.

To date, experimental studies have examined the acute effects of psychoactive drugs on the psychopathology of schizophrenic patients. Clinical observations of drug-abusing patients have focused on the impact of drugs on psychotic symptoms. Very few data describe the schizophrenic patients' self-reported reasons for drug use and their subjective experience of the intoxicated state. The focus on how drug use affects psychotic symptoms may have resulted in neglect of other significant drug effects—for example, on depression, anxiety, and negative symptoms. Attention to the heterogeneity of drug effects across different patient groups, different drugs, and different symptoms may offer insight into the reasons underlying the abuse of drugs by schizophrenic patients. While a number of models previously offered to explain the interaction of drug abuse and schizophrenia have merit, the application of these data to the self-medication hypothesis offers an important perspective, especially when considering schizophrenic patients' apparent drug preferences.

ACUTE DRUG EFFECTS

The majority of reports in the literature indicate that abused drugs generally cause an acute worsening of psychotic symptoms in schizophrenia. However, a significant heterogeneity of response has been observed in the empirical investigations of acute drug effects, and careful examination of the data suggests that abused drugs may produce possible benefits as well as adverse effects. Data on drug effects come from the following three general sources: (1) experimental observation, (2) clinical reports, and (3) retrospective studies of patient groups (primarily inpatient).

Experimental studies

Experimental observations of schizophrenic patients under the influence of drugs have been reported primarily for hallucinogens, phencyclidine (PCP), amphetamines, benzodiazepines, and opiates. Experimental studies from the 1950's and 1960's in which schizophrenic patients were given hallucinogenic drugs showed that most subjects in these studies exhibited exacerbation of anxiety and psychosis, but a minority of subjects experienced euphoria and relaxation or were not affected (Hoch 1951; Hoch et al. 1952; Pennes 1954). Ellinwood and Petrie (1979) commented that these drug effects were similar to the acute disorganizing effects of schizophrenia, and they noted that the chronic patient may be less vulnerable to the psychotomimetic drug effects of hallucinogens. Fink et al. (1966) administered varying doses of lysergic acid diethylamide (LSD) to 65 psychotic subjects and found only a 2 percent incidence of prolonged psychotic exacerbations characterized by an initial irritable period followed by thought disorder, visual hallucinations, and elevated mood. PCP increased psychotic symptoms and agitation in most schizophrenic patients in whom it was tested, similar to an acute exacerbation of their underlying illness (Luby et al. 1959; Levy et al. 1960).

While even small doses of stimulant drugs like the amphetamines are known to induce psychosis and to worsen symptoms (Janowsky et al. 1973; West 1974; Janowsky and Davis 1976; Angrist et al. 1980), this effect is not uniform, and some authors have found that amphetamine caused no effects or even improvements in negative symptoms (Kornetsky 1977; Angrist et al. 1982; van Kammen et al. 1982; Cesarec and Nyman 1985). Opiates and opiatelike peptides, endorphins, have been reported to have antipsychotic properties (Comfort 1977; Gold et al. 1977), although clinical trials of opiates have, as with amphetamines, yielded inconsistent results with moderate overall improvements (Berger et al. 1980), reduction of psychotic symptoms (Brizer et al. 1985), and worsening of negative symptoms (Judd et al. 1981). Opioid antagonists have also been reported to reduce psychotic symptoms (Gunne et al. 1977), but this finding is again inconsistent (Davis et al. 1977). Benzodiazepines have been found to worsen psychotic symptoms and produce intolerable side effects in some patients (Dixon et al. 1989b), but also appear to reduce anxiety, positive symptoms, and negative symptoms (Jimerson et al. 1982; Csernansky et al. 1984; Kahn et al. 1988; Wolkowitz et al. 1988; Douyon et al. 1989) in subgroups of schizophrenic patients. Moreover, benzodiazepines are now commonly used in the treatment of neuroleptic-induced akathisia. Thus, almost all drugs tested have the potential to exacerbate psychosis—psychostimulants and hallucinogens more so than benzodiazepines. Opiates alone have not consistently been demonstrated to worsen psychosis. However, reductions of depression, anxiety, and negative symptoms also have been observed in subgroups of schizophrenic patients experimentally medicated with classically abused drugs.

Clinical reports and epidemiologic surveys

Clinical studies of drug-abusing schizophrenic patients have generally focused on the co-occurrence of psychotic symptoms and relapse with substance abuse. Unfortunately, these reports have very rarely used systematic assessment procedures and standardized scales. Treffert (1978) and Knudsen and Vilmar (1984) reported exacerbation of psychosis in small samples of schizophrenic patients who use cannabis. Negrete et al. (1986) evaluated 137 schizophrenic outpatients and found that cannabis users had significantly more delusional and hallucinatory activity than nonusers. Heavy cannabis users showed the most symptomatology. Bernhardson and Gunne (1972) found that in 7 of the 14 patients whose psychosis predated cannabis use, cannabis abuse produced a further psychotic deterioration; cannabis did not appear to exert any effect on the remaining 7 patients. Hekimian and Gershon (1968) evaluated 112 patients who had abused drugs within 48 hours of their admission to Bellevue Hospital (of whom 39 percent had a predrug diagnosis of schizophrenia). Although the findings were given by drug rather than by psychiatric diagnosis, Hekimian and Gershon reported that all drugs increased psychosis or psychopathology for the large majority of users. Alterman et al. (1980) reported that schizophrenic inpatients who abused alcohol while in the hospital had unspecified changes in sleeping patterns, mood, and behavior. Alterman et al. (1982) also reported that a cohort of drug-abusing hospitalized inpatients, 80 percent of whom were schizophrenic, had more mood changes than nondrug abusers but demonstrated the same degree of depression, paranoia, delusions, and hallucinations. Several reports have found increased hospitalizations among schizophrenic drug abusers (Craig et al. 1985; Richard et al. 1985; Rader et al. 1988).

Critique/summary

Interpretation of the above sources of data on drug effects in schizophrenia must take into account certain specific limitations. Data from laboratory studies should be interpreted with caution because experimental paradigms to test drug effects may not duplicate the environment, or the type, dose, and purity of drugs schizophrenic patients encounter when abusing drugs outside of the laboratory. Furthermore, clinical observations of drug-abusing schizophrenic inpatients are likely to overrepresent exacerbations and underrepresent benefits, since the study population is a relapsing one, and adverse effects are more likely to come to clinicians' attention.

Despite these difficulties, the evidence is compelling that a wide range of drugs are associated with exacerbation of psychotic symptoms in many patients. However, there are two important qualifications to this observation: (1) drug response is heterogeneous among schizophrenic patients (e.g., across acute vs. chronic, anxious vs. nonanxious, and other subgroups); (2) not all drugs have a pathological effect on specific symptoms (e.g., amphetamines, opiates, and benzodiazepines). Patients' self-reports also reflect this heterogeneity.

Drug Effects Reported by Schizophrenic Patients

Clinical reports

Reports of schizophrenic patients' subjective responses to drugs have been largely anecdotal and often vague. Alpert and Silvers (1970) found that some schizophrenic patients reported that alcohol reduced discomfort caused by hallucinations. Hansell and Willis (1977) also found that patients reported symptom reduction with alcohol. In contrast, Kesselman et al. (1982) reported that 75 percent of patients who commented had felt that alcohol worsened their "schizophrenic" symptoms.

Cannabis has also generated a varied response. Weil (1970) reviewed adverse reactions to cannabis and reported that many schizophrenic patients found marijuana unpleasant with frequent feelings of "derealization." Negrete et al. (1986) found that schizophrenic subjects who reported previous cannabis experience tended to stop this practice more readily than nonschizophrenic users. They speculated that this tendency might be due to a high frequency of untoward reactions; all except 7 of the 76 subjects in their sample reported adverse psychic effects, although these effects are not defined specifically. In contrast, Hekimian and Gershon (1968) reported that in their sample of eight cannabis users, of whom six had a predrug and postdrug diagnosis of schizophrenia, five reported a "favorable subjective response" to cannabis. Knudsen and Vilmar (1984) presented descriptions of 10 schizophrenic patients medicated with neuroleptics of whom 7, they contended, used cannabis to reverse neuroleptic effects. For example, one patient reported that cannabis allowed her to "regain experiences blotted out by medication." Knudsen and Vilmar described patients' experiences with cannabis in detail; responses were characterized by an initial feeling of being "inspired," "relaxed," "energized," or "active," followed by an exacerbation of symptoms and feeling "bad," "aggressive," or "splitting of thoughts."

Subjective effects of other drugs in groups of schizophrenic patients have been less commonly reported. Judd et al. (1981) administered the Profile of Mood States (McNair et al. 1971) to six schizophrenic patients undergoing drug challenge with methadone. Self-ratings by patients indicated significant increases of depression-dejection and fatigue with methadone. The majority of Hekimian and Gershon's (1968) groups of amphetamine users and hallucinogen users had schizophrenia, and they reported favorable and unfavorable subjective experiences for each drug, respectively.

In a study of 83 consecutively admitted *DSM-III-R* (American Psychiatric Association 1987) schizophrenic (*n* = 65), schizoaffective (*n* = 12), and schizophreniform (*n* = 3) inpatients, Dixon and colleagues asked 40 patients who also met criteria for a lifetime diagnosis of *DSM-III-R* drug or alcohol abuse or dependence (Dixon et al. 1988, 1989) to indicate the direction in which selected symptoms and affects changed during acute drug intoxication (i.e., drug-abusing patients were asked to say whether cannabis acutely increased, decreased, or produced no effect on anxiety). Alcohol, cannabis, and cocaine were the drugs abused commonly enough for meaningful results to be obtained. The large majority of substance-abusing patients felt that all three drugs decreased depression (table 1). In contrast, reported effects on anxiety, energy, and psychotic symptoms differed for the three drugs. For example, drug-abusing patients reported that cannabis and alcohol decreased anxiety but that cocaine made them more anxious.

Table 1. Schizophrenic patients' subjective report of acute drug effects

	Alcohol	Cannabis	Cocaine
Anxiety	▼	▼	▲
Depression	▼	▼	▼
Calm	▲	▲	▲▼
Suspiciousness	◆	▲	▲◆▼
Trust	▲◆	◆▼	▼
Hallucinations	◆	▲◆	▲◆▼
Energy	▼	▲▼	▲

Note.
▲ Indicates increase.
▼ Indicates decrease.
◆ Indicates no change.
Different symbols within same category indicate mixed response.

Critique/summary

The method of obtaining posthoc reports of subjective drug effects has many limitations. It relies on patients' memories of feelings and experiences while intoxicated (state-dependent recall). It is subject to reporting biases of recall and more general problems of unreliability. Moreover, a self-report assessment of motivation for drug use and drug effects may be largely based on posthoc rationalizations of impulsive acts or acts driven by other factors. Nevertheless, the individuals' perceptions of drug effects may be integral to the development or maintenance of drug-seeking behavior. While the data are limited, subgroups of patients clearly report feeling less depressed, less anxious, and, in some cases, more energized while intoxicated, in spite of frequent awareness of the psychotogenic potential of drugs they abuse.

SELF-REPORTED REASONS FOR DRUG USE

There is a remarkable paucity of studies describing the self-perceived reasons that schizophrenic patients abuse drugs. In Hekimian and Gershon's (1968) study of 112 patients who had used drugs within 48 hours of hospital admission, the desire for euphoria (which included the desire to "get high" or "relieve depression") was most important for heroin, amphetamines, and hallucinogens, while the influence of friends or environment was most important for marijuana. The majority of amphetamine, hallucinogen, and marijuana users had schizophrenia. Three of the 10 patients described by Knudsen and Vilmar (1984) stated that they used cannabis for the social contacts and "Bohemian lifestyle" surrounding cannabis use. Two patients described by Treffert (1978) smoked cannabis to decrease depression and to improve social relationships.

In our study (Dixon et al. 1989a; Dixon et al., 1991), patients were read a series of statements, such as "I use [drug] to relieve anxiety" or "I use [drug] to increase my number of thoughts," and were asked to respond, "yes," "no," or "uncertain," depending on whether the statement was true for them. The patients' particular drug(s) of choice had already been identified in the interview and were substituted into the statement. In contrast to data on subjective effects, no drug differences appeared in patients' responses to reasons for drug use.

Almost 75 percent of patients acknowledged that they used drugs "to get high" and "to relax." In about half of the cases, patients also endorsed the responses that were probing for the desire for negative symptom relief—"to increase pleasure," "to increase energy," "to increase emotions," and "to talk more." These statements, of course, might not necessarily apply exclusively to negative symptoms and could represent efforts to reduce symptoms of depression. Approximately half of the patients also endorsed the statement, "I use [drug] to go along with the group," suggesting that social pressures play an important role for certain patients across all drugs. Patients infrequently acknowledged the use of drugs to increase concentration, to help them work better, and to relieve neuroleptic-induced side effects, and psychotic symptoms.

Critique/summary

These data are limited as are the data on reported subjective effects above; self-reported reasons for drug use are biased, without proven reliability, and could be posthoc rationalizations rather than accurate representations of subjects' intent and motivations. Nevertheless, they do suggest that dysphoria, anxiety, desire for socialization, and possibly the anergia associated with negative symptoms may impel schizophrenic patients to abuse drugs.

SITUATIONAL FACTORS

With the exception of Hekimian and Gershon's (1968) observations on the social and environmental factors associated with the use of marijuana, there is a dearth of information about the specific circumstances or external stimulus/reinforcement conditions associated with drug use among schizophrenic patients. In our study, we asked patients where and with whom they used their preferred drugs. Over half of the patients reported using drugs alone at least some of the time. Patients seemed as likely to use drugs on the street or in a public place as at home (table 2).

Table 2. Where and with whom schizophrenic patients used drugs

	Alcohol (%)	Cannabis (%)	Cocaine (%)	Total (%)
With whom do you use [drug]?				
Always alone	28	32	7	25
Usually alone	17	8	7	11
As likely to be alone as not	33	12	27	28
Usually with other people	22	32	27	28
Always with other people	0	12	33	14
Where do you usually use [drug]?				
On the street or a public place	42	37	43	40
At home	47	42	29	40
At a friend's home	0	4	14	5
At school or work	0	8	0	4
Other	11	8	14	11

DISCUSSION

These data illustrate a core clinical problem of drug abuse in schizophrenia: schizophrenic patients abuse drugs which can increase psychosis, but from which some patients apparently derive beneficial effects. These data are discussed in the context of models that have been advanced to understand the interaction of drug abuse and schizophrenia. It is important to note that the discussion focuses only on how the psychological and subjective data presented can be informative in generating hypotheses to understand the interaction of drug abuse and schizophrenia. Other approaches to the problem of comorbidity (e.g., biological or behavioral) may be equally valid and informative.

Etiological model

Drug abuse has been hypothesized to be an etiological factor in a subgroup of patients with schizophrenia (e.g., Bowers 1987). This model derived from early experimental observations of the psychotogenic properties of many drugs, and it has received support from the finding of McLellan et al. (1979) that amphetamine users were significantly more likely to develop psychotic disorders than were barbiturate abusers. Andreasson et al. (1987) reviewed the records of 45,570 Swedish conscripts and found that the relative risk of schizophrenia among high consumers of cannabis was 6.0 times that of nonusers. They concluded that cannabis use is an independent risk factor in the development of schizophrenia, although documentation of subjects' early functioning has been questioned. Studies reporting that drug-abusing schizophrenic patients have an earlier age of onset of illness (Breakey et al. 1974; Tsuang et al. 1982; Alterman et al. 1984; Weller et al. 1988) and better premorbid functioning (Breakey et al. 1974; Tsuang et al. 1982) than schizophrenic patients who do not abuse drugs have been used to support the hypothesis that drug abuse played a role in the onset of schizophrenia. Finally, the observation that schizophrenic patients may preferentially abuse substances that induce psychosis (Schneier and Siris 1987; Weller et al. 1988) may support this model.

Cross-sectional data on observed or subjective response to drug abuse are subject to systematic biases and do not allow critical assessment of the etiological model. Without prospective controlled studies, conclusions about drug abuse as an etiological factor in schizophrenia are largely inferential.

Dopamine dysfunction model

Evidence of the involvement of the dopamine system in reinforcement and reward function (Prosser and Pickens 1979; Ritz et al. 1987), combined with the large body of indirect evidence implicating dopamine in schizophrenia (Snyder 1976), has led to suggestions that dopamine disturbances may heighten vulnerability to both schizophrenia and drug abuse in some patients (Prosser and Pickens 1979). This model is largely theoretical without direct clinical or experimental evidence to support it at this point.

Socializing effects model

Drug use by schizophrenic patients may be a socializing phenomenon, providing isolated, socially handicapped individuals with an identity and a social group (Treffert 1978; Hall et al. 1979; Millman and Sbriglio 1986). Schizophrenic patients in the samples of Hekimian and Gershon (1968) and Knudsen and Vilmar (1984) used marijuana and hallucinogens for social contacts and because of the "influence of friends." In our sample, approximately half of the patients reported using drugs to "go along with the group," suggesting that social factors are operative, for at least some patients, across all drugs. However, this explanation does not hold for all drug use. A large number of patients did not endorse the socialization item in our sample, and a substantial portion of patients used drugs unaccompanied by others. The abundance of solitary drug use argues against drug abuse as a purely socializing phenomenon. More research on the setting and circumstances of drug use by schizophrenic patients is necessary to evaluate this model.

Self-medication model

Drug-abusing schizophrenic patients may self-medicate depression (Freed 1975; Siris et al. 1988), negative symptoms (Schneier and Siris 1987), or neuroleptic-induced extrapyramidal side effects (Treffert 1978; Knudsen and Vilmar 1984) with drugs. The self-medication model has been advanced to explain drug use not only in schizophrenia, but also in the general population (Khantzian 1985).

The self-medication model has a biochemical logic in that schizophrenic patients may prefer drugs with dopaminergic action (Schneier and Siris 1987) which have the potential to reverse neuroleptic-induced extrapyramidal side effects. Moreover, if negative symptoms are due to dopamine hypoactivity as suggested by Weinberger (1987) and Friedhoff (1983), then the self-medication hypothesis is even more compelling from a neurochemical point of view, since abused drugs with dopaminergic function may reverse this purported dopamine deficit in the same way, perhaps, that the decreased brain dopamine levels associated with chronic cocaine use may help to maintain cocaine addiction (Wyatt et al. 1988). Thus, although the remainder of the discussion focuses on psychological factors, there may also be parallel or complementary biological determinants driving the "self-medication."

The actions of drugs may allow inferences about motivations for drug-seeking behavior. To that end, the most striking aspect of the literature review on drug effects is how commonly the abuse of drugs induced psychotic exacerbations in schizophrenic patients. Is psychosis just an unwanted side effect of illicit drug use, or an *intended* effect? We have no data to answer that question adequately. However, data are available to support the notions that (1) the drugs abused by schizophrenic patients may diminish other symptoms such as dysphoria, anxiety, and anergia; and (2) that patients believe that drugs diminish such symptoms.

Experimental studies indicated that some stimulant drugs produced improved functioning and reduced symptoms in some patients, and interestingly, schizophrenic patients may preferentially abuse stimulants (Schneier and Siris 1987). Opiates and benzodiazepines have also been found to exhibit antipsychotic as well as anxiolytic and antidepressant qualities in patients with schizophrenia. The suggestion that schizophrenic patients may use opiates and benzodiazepines less than other populations (Schneier and Siris 1987) warrants discussion. Drugs with antipsychotic properties might mask psychotic symptoms so that patients would receive relatively less clinical attention. Such patients might also receive treatment in methadone clinics with a primary focus on drug abuse rather than schizophrenia. These factors would make schizophrenic opiate and benzodiazepine abusers relatively less visible in the traditional hospital and community settings where schizophrenic patients receive care. Alternatively, schizophrenic patients may in fact use opiate drugs less frequently than other populations for various reasons—for example, if opiates are too difficult for schizophrenic patients to obtain, if the depressant effects reported by Judd et al. (1981) generalize to other patients, or if schizophrenic patients intend to increase, not to reduce, psychosis with drug abuse.

The subjective response of schizophrenic patients to drug abuse suggests that they may perceive themselves as self-medicating symptoms. In our sample, schizophrenic drug abusers reported an overall subjective antidepressant effect common to the three most popularly abused drugs—cannabis, cocaine, and alcohol—and attributed differential anxiolytic, activating and psychotogenic effects to each, perhaps using the drugs in patterns specific to their symptomatology. Thus, a way of understanding the popularity of cannabis abuse is that cannabis, in addition to its reported acute antidepressant effects (common to cocaine and alcohol), was perceived to have desirable anxiolytic and activating effects.

Patients' reasons for drug use apply directly to the self-medication model. Almost all reports in the literature indicated that patients reported using drugs to relieve dysphoria and to feel more relaxed. In our study, many of the responses were consistent with a desire for relief of negative symptoms. Fewer patients reported "medicating" themselves to affect extrapyramidal side effects, but it is often difficult for patients (and clinicians) to determine the etiology of symptoms; for example, a patient might not recognize that neuroleptics cause the "depression" or listlessness that they acknowledge self-medicating.

The application of the self-medication model to substance abuse in schizophrenia must be examined in light of the severity and nature of the impairments in schizophrenia. For example, although evidence may suggest that schizophrenic patients self-medicate negative symptoms, negative symptoms presumably diminish the patients' capacities to seek and obtain drugs. Thus, patients with the most severe negative symptoms would be unlikely to abuse drugs (e.g., a profoundly apathetic, withdrawn schizophrenic patient). Significant motivation and activity are required to sustain drug-seeking/drug-using behavior. Indeed, Andreasen (1982) found that schizophrenic patients with negative symptoms as measured by the Scale for the Assessment of Negative Symptoms were less likely to have histories of drug abuse than were patients with positive symptoms. Perhaps there is a "critical window" for the propensity to self-medicate; patients with too few, or too many, negative symptoms may not effectively seek or maintain a drug-use habit.

An alternative explanation is that dysphoria may be the final common pathway to drug abuse. Perhaps only those patients whose symptoms (positive, negative, or extrapyramidal) lead to distress or depression are the ones who abuse drugs. Siris et al. (1988) reported that in a sample of patients with postpsychotic depression (from which active drug users were excluded), patients with a history of drug abuse had more features of endogenous depression, suggesting that previous drug abusers had been self-medicating depression. Dysphoria secondary to neuroleptics or negative symptoms might escape measurement by standard instruments designed for endogenous depression. Investigation of this hypothesis would thus benefit from increased sophistication in methodologies designed to evaluate schizophrenic patients' subjective experience of their illness, symptoms, and treatments.

Despite all the questions raised, the self-medication model appears to have heuristic value for further research on drug abuse among schizophrenic patients. Subgroups of schizophrenic patients improve with experimental administration of classically abused drugs. Moreover, many patients report feeling less depressed, less anxious, and more energized with their drug of choice, and they report using drugs for that reason. Treatments with anxiolytic agents or antidepressants, as well as reductions in neuroleptic dosage, might be logical corollaries to these data.

Independence model

Finally, it has been postulated that determinants of drug abuse in schizophrenia may not differ from those in the general population. Historically, explanations of drug abuse have included, among others, the desire for euphoria and escape (Khantzian 1985); sociodemographic factors such as poverty, age, and sex (Falk and Feingold 1987); familial and genetic factors (Cadoret et al. 1986); and self-medication (Kolb 1962; Khantzian 1985).

The schizophrenic patients' stated reasons for drug use and descriptions of drug effects are similar to those reported in nonschizophrenic subjects (Fischman et al. 1976). The self-medication and socialization models may apply to schizophrenic patients no differently than to other populations. Even if that is so, it seems inescapable that the targets of self-medication are at least partially determined by schizophrenic symptomatology (or effects of neuroleptic treatment). In addition, the apparent preference of schizophrenic patients for psychotomimetic agents (Schneier and Siris 1987), consistent with our data (Dixon et al. 1989a; Dixon et al. submitted for publication), suggests some selective matching of psychotomimetic agents with schizophrenia.

Factors independent of schizophrenia undoubtedly play an important role in determining which schizophrenic patients become drug abusers. At a very basic level, drug exposure is required. The question may not be whether independent factors are involved but, rather, to what extent factors specific to schizophrenia determine drug abuse. To answer this question will require controlled studies that compare schizophrenic patients to other groups of psychiatric patients and drug abusers.

CONCLUSION

The answer to the question of which schizophrenic patients abuse drugs and why may lie in a combination of models. A schizophrenic patient who has a family history of drug abuse, is exposed to drugs, and has little impairment of affect and only mild negative symptoms may be at highest risk for substance abuse. While the role of substance abuse in the pathogenesis of schizophrenia is not well understood, the available evidence linking substance abuse with the onset of the disorder should be taken as an important public health warning for individuals at high risk for schizophrenia to avoid psychotomimetic agents. Application of the self-medication hypothesis to the subjective responses of schizophrenic patients to drug abuse suggests the need for increased clinical sensitivity to experiences of anxiety and depression, whether they are primary, neuroleptic-induced, or a consequence of coping with a disabling, stigmatizing, and isolating illness. Treatment implications derived from the self-medication model include the need to develop cognitive and rehabilitative strategies to help schizophrenic patients find alternative ways to cope with dysphoria as well as the consideration of pharmacological treatments.

REFERENCES

Alpert, M., and Silvers, K.N. Perceptual characteristics distinguishing auditory hallucinations in schizophrenia and acute alcoholic psychoses. *American Journal of Psychiatry,* 127:298-302, 1970.

Alterman, A.J.; Ayre, R.R.; and Williford, WO. Diagnostic validation of conjoint schizophrenia and alcoholism. *Journal of Clinical Psychiatry,* 45:300-303, 1984.

Alterman, A.J.; Erdlen, D.L.; Laporte, D.J.; and Erdlen, F.R. Problem drinking in hospitalized schizophrenic patients. *Addictive Behavior,* 5:273-276, 1980.

Alterman, A.J.; Erdlen, D.L.; Laporte, D.J.; and Erdlen, F.R. Effects of illicit drug use in an inpatient psychiatric population. *Addictive Behavior,* 7:231-242, 1982.

American Psychiatric Association. *DSM-III-R: Diagnostic and Statistical Manual of Mental Disorders.* 3rd ed., revised. Washington, DC: The Association, 1987.

Andreasen, N.C. Negative symptoms in schizophrenia: Definition and reliability. *Archives of General Psychiatry,* 39:784-788, 1982.

Andreasson, S.; Engstrom, A.; Allebeck, P.; and Rydeberg, U. Cannabis and schizophrenia: A longitudinal study of Swedish conscripts. *Lancet,* II:1483-1486, 1987.

Angrist, B.; Rotrosen, J.; and Gershon, S. Differential effects of amphetamine and neuroleptics on negative and positive symptoms in schizophrenia. *Psychopharmacology,* 72:17-19, 1980.

Angrist, B.; Peselow, E.; Rubinstein, M.; Corwin, J.; and Rotrosen, J. Partial improvement in negative schizophrenic symptoms after amphetamine. *Psychopharmacology,* 78:128-130, 1982.

Berger, P.A.; Watson, S.J.; and Akil, H. Beta-endorphin and schizophrenia. *Archives of General Psychiatry,* 37:642-647, 1980.

Bernhardson, G.; and Gunne, L.E. Forty-six cases of psychosis in cannabis users. *International Journal of Addiction,* 7:9-16, 1972.

Bowers, M.B., Jr. The role of drugs in the production of schizophreniform psychoses and related disorders. In: Meltzer, H.Y., ed. *Psychopharmacology: The Third Generation of Progress.* New York: Raven Press, 1987. pp. 819-823.

Breakey, W.R.; Goodell, H.; Lorenz, P.C.; and McHugh, P.R. Hallucinogenic drugs as precipitants of schizophrenia. *Psychological Medicine* 4:255-261, 1974.

Brizer, D.A.; Hartmen, N.; Sweeney J.; and Millman, R.B. Effect of methadone plus neuroleptics on treatment-resistant chronic paranoid schizophrenics. *American Journal of Psychiatry,* 142:1106-1107, 1985.

Cadoret, R.J.; Troughton, E.; O'Gorman, T.W.; and Heywood, E. An adoption study of genetic and environmental factors in drug abuse. *Archives of General Psychiatry,* 43:1131-1136, 1986.

Cesarec, Z., and Nyman, A.K. Differential response to amphetamine in schizophrenia. *Acta Psychiatrica Scandinavica,* 71:523-528, 1985.

Comfort, A. Morphine as an antipsychotic. *Clinical Toxicology,* 11:383-386, 1977.

Craig, T.J.; Lin, S.P.; El-Defrawi, M.H.; and Goodman, A.B. Clinical correlates of readmission in a schizophrenic cohort. *Psychiatric Quarterly,* 57:5-10, 1985.

Csernansky, J.G.; Lombrozo, L.; Gulevich, G.; and Hollister, L. Treatment of negative schizophrenic symptoms with alprazolam: A preliminary open-label study. *Journal of Clinical Psychopharmacology,* 4:349-352, 1984.

Davis, G.C.; Bunney, W.E., Jr.; DeFraites, E.G.; Kleinman, J.E.; van Kammen, D.P.; Post, R.M.; and Wyatt, R.J. Intravenous naloxone administration in schizophrenia and affective illness. *Science,* 197:74-77 1977.

Dixon, L.; Haas, G.H.; Dulit, R.A.; Weiden, P.J.; Sweeney, J.; and Hien, D. Substance abuse in schizophrenia: Preferences, predictors and psychopathology. *Schizophrenia Research,* 2:6, 1989a.

Dixon, L.; Haas, G.H.; Weiden, P.J.; Sweeney, J.; and Frances, A.J. "Schizophrenia and Drug Abuse: Who, What, and Why?" Presented at the Annual Meeting of the American Psychiatric Association, San Francisco, CA, May 1988.

Dixon, L.; Haas, G.H.; Weiden, P.J.; Sweeney, J.; and Frances, A.J. "Drug Abuse in Schizophrenic Patients: Clinical Correlates and Reasons for Use." *American Journal of Psychiatry,* 148:224-230, 1991.

Dixon, L.; Weiden, P.J.; Frances, A.J.; and Sweeney, J. Alprazolam intolerance in stable schizophrenic outpatients. *Psychopharmacology Bulletin,* 25:213-214, 1989b.

Douyon, R.; Angrist, B.; Peselow, E.; Cooper, T.; and Rotrosen, J. Neuroleptic augmentation with alprazolam: Clinical effects and pharmacokinetic correlates. *American Journal of Psychiatry,* 146:231-234, 1989.

Ellinwood, E.H.; and Petrie, W.M. Drug-induced psychoses. In: Pickens, R.W., and Heston, L.L., eds. *Psychiatric Factors in Drug Abuse.* New York: Grune and Stratton, 1979. pp. 301-336.

Falk, J.L., and Feingold, D.A. Environmental and cultural factors in the behavioral actions of drugs. In: Meltzer, H.Y., ed. *Psychopharmacology: The Third Generation of Progress.* New York: Raven Press, 1987. pp. 1503-1510.

Fink, M.; Simeon, J.; Haque, W.; and Itil, T. Prolonged adverse reactions to LSD in psychotic subjects. *Archives of General Psychiatry,* 15:450-454, 1966.

Fischman, M.W.; Resnekov, L.; Schick, J.F.E.; Krasnegor, N.A.; Fennel, W.; and Freedman, D.X. Cardiovascular and subjective effects of intravenous cocaine administration in humans. *Archives of General Psychiatry,* 33:983-989, 1976.

Freed, E.X. Alcoholism and schizophrenia: The search for perspectives—A review. *Journal of Studies on Alcohol,* 36:853-881, 1975.

Friedhoff, A.J. A strategy for developing novel drugs for the treatment of schizophrenia. *Schizophrenia Bulletin,* 9:555-562, 1983.

Gold, M.S.; Donabedian, R.K.; Dillard, M.; Slobetz, F.W.; Riordan, C.E.; and Kleber, H.D. Antipsychotic effect of opiate agonists. *Lancet,* II:398-399, 1977.

Gottheil, E., and Weinstein, S.P. Staffing patterns, treatment setting, and perceived psychiatric problems in alcoholism services. In: Gottheil, E.; McLellan, A.T.; and Druley, K.A., eds. *Substance Abuse and Psychiatric Illness.* Elmsford, NY: Pergamon Press, 1980.

Gunne, L.M.; Lindstrom, L.; and Terenius, L. Naloxone-induced reversal of schizophrenic hallucinations. *Journal of Neural Transmission,* 40:13-19, 1977.

Hall, R.; Stickney, S.K.; Gardner E.R.; Perl, M.; and LeCann, A.F. Relationship of psychiatric illness to drug abuse. *Journal of Psychedelic Drugs,* 11:337-342, 1979.

Hansell, N.; and Willis, G.L. Outpatient treatment of schizophrenia. *American Journal of Psychiatry,* 134:1082-1086, 1977.

Hekimian, L.J., and Gershon, S. Characteristics of drug abusers admitted to a psychiatric hospital. *Journal of the American Medical Association,* 205:125-130, 1968.

Hoch, D.H. Experimentally produced psychoses. *American Journal of Psychiatry,* 107:607-611, 1951.

Hoch, P.H.; Cattell, J.P.; and Pennes, H.H. Effects of mescaline and lysergic acid (D-LSD-25). *American Journal of Psychiatry,* 108:579-584, 1952.

Janowsky, D.S., and Davis, J.M. Methylphenidate, dextroamphetamine, and levamfetamine: Effects of schizophrenic symptoms. *Archives of General Psychiatry,* 33:304-308, 1976.

Janowsky, D.S.; El-Yousef, M.K.; Davis, J.M.; and Sekerke, H.J. Provocation of schizophrenic symptoms by IV administration of methylphenidate. *Archives of General Psychiatry,* 28:185-191, 1973.

Jimerson, D.C.; van Kammen, D.P.; Post, R.M.; Docherty, J.P.; and Bunney, W.E., Jr. Diazepam in schizophrenia: A preliminary double-blind trial. *American Journal of Psychiatry,* 139:489-491, 1982.

Judd, L.L.; Janowsky, D.S.; Segal, D.S.; Parker, D.C.; and Huey, L.Y. Behavioral effects of methadone on schizophrenic patients. *American Journal of Psychiatry,* 138:243-245, 1981.

Kahn, J.P.; Puertollano, M.A.; Schane, M.D.; and Klein, D.F. Adjunctive alprazolam for schizophrenics with panic anxiety: Clinical observations and pathogenic implications. *American Journal of Psychiatry,* 145:742-744, 1988.

Kesselman, M.S.; Solomon, J.; Beaudett, M.; and Thornton, B. Alcoholism and schizophrenia. In: Solomon, J., ed. *Alcoholism and Clinical Psychiatry.* New York: Plenum Press, 1982. pp. 69-80.

Khantzian, E.J. The self-medication hypothesis of addictive disorders: Focus on heroin and cocaine dependence. *American Journal of Psychiatry,* 142:1259-1264, 1985.

Knudsen, P., and Vilmar, T. Cannabis and neuroleptic agents in schizophrenia. *Acta Psychiatrica Scandinavica,* 69:162-174, 1984.

Kolb, L. *Drug Addiction: A Medical Problem.* Springfield, IL: Charles C Thomas, Publisher, 1962.

Kornetsky, C. Hyporesponsivity of chronic schizophrenic patients to dextroamphetamine. *Archives of General Psychiatry,* 33:1425-1428, 1977.

Levy, L.; Cameron, D.E.; and Aitken, R.C.G. Observation of two psychomimetic drugs of piperidine derivation-CLI 395 (Sernyl) and Cl 400. *American Journal of Psychiatry,* 116:843-844, 1960.

Luby, E.D.; Cohen, B.D.; Rosenbaum, G.; Gottlieb, J.S.; and Kelly, R. Study of a new schizophrenomimetic drug Sernyl. *Archives of Neurology and Psychiatry,* 81:363-369, 1959:

McLellan, A.T.; Woody, G.E.; and O'Brien, C.P. Development of psychiatric illness in drug abusers: Possible role of drug preference. *New England Journal of Medicine,* 301:1310-1314, 1979.

McNair, D.M.; Lorr, M.; and Droppelman, L.F. *Profile of Mood States Manual.* San Diego, CA: EDITS, 1971.

Miller, E, and Tanenbaum, J.H. Drug abuse in schizophrenia. *Hospital and Community Psychiatry,* 40:847-849, 1989.

Millman, R.B., and Sbriglio, R. Patterns of use and psychopathology in chronic marijuana users. *Psychiatric Clinics of North America,* 9:533-545, 1986.

Negrete, J.C.; Knapp, W.P.; Douglas, D.E.; and Smith, W.B. Cannabis affects the severity of schizophrenic symptoms: Results of a clinical survey. *Psychological Medicine,* 16:515-520, 1986.

Pennes, H.H. Clinical reactions of schizophrenics to sodium amytal, pervitin hydrochloride, mescaline sulfate, and D-lysergic acid diethylamide (LSD$_{25}$). *Journal of Nervous and Mental Disease,* 119:95-112, 1954.

Prosser, R.A., and Pickens, R. Catecholamines, drug abuse and schizophrenia. In: Pickens, R.W., and Heston, L.L., eds. *Psychiatric Factors in Drug Abuse.* New York: Grune and Stratton, 1979. pp. 285-300.

Rader, L.E.; Rodell, D.E.; Beck, C.M.; Kashner, T.M.; Buchanon, S.; and Westerdorp, F. Hospital utilization in schizophrenia. *New Research Programs and Abstracts, American Psychiatric Association, 141st Annual Meeting,* Montreal, Canada, 1988. p.55.

Richard, M.L.; Liskow, B.I.; and Perry, P.J. Recent psychostimulant use in hospitalized schizophrenics. *Journal of Clinical Psychiatry,* 135:79-83, 1985.

Ritz, M.C.; Lamb, R.J.; Goldberg, S.R.; and Kuhar, M.J. Cocaine receptors on dopamine transporters are related to self-administration of cocaine. *Science,* 237:1219-1223, 1987.

Schneier, F.R., and Siris, S.G. A review of psychoactive substance use and abuse in schizophrenia: Patterns of drug choice. *Journal of Nervous and Mental Disease,* 175:641-642, 1987.

Siris, S.G.; Kane, J.M.; Frechen, K.; Sellew, A.P.; Mandeli, J.; and Fasano-Dube, B. Histories of substance abuse in patients with post-psychotic depressions. *Comprehensive Psychiatry,* 29:550-557, 1988.

Snyder, S.H. The dopamine hypothesis of schizophrenia: Focus on the dopamine receptor. *American Journal of Psychiatry,* 133:197-202, 1976.

Solomon, P. Receipt of aftercare services by problem types: Psychiatric, psychiatric/substance abuse and substance abuse. *Psychiatric Quarterly,* 87:180-188, 1986.

Treffert, D.A. Marijuana use in schizophrenia: A clear hazard. *American Journal of Psychiatry,* 135:1213-1215, 1978.

Tsuang, M.T.; Simpson, J.C.; and Kronfol, Z. Subtypes of drug abuse with psychosis. *Archives of General Psychiatry,* 39:141-147, 1982.

van Kammen, D.P.; Bunney, W.E., Jr.; Docherty, J.P.; Marder, S.R.; Ebert, M.H.; Rosenblatt, J.E.; and Rayner, J.N. *d*-Amphetamine induced heterogeneous changes in psychotic behavior in schizophrenia. *American Journal of Psychiatry,* 139:997-999, 1982.

Weil, A.T. Adverse reactions to marijuana. *New England Journal of Medicine,* 282:997-1000, 1970.

Weinberger, D.R. Implications of normal brain development for the pathogenesis of schizophrenia. *Archives of General Psychiatry,* 44:660-669, 1987.

Weller, M.P.; Ang, P.C.; Latimer-Sayer, D.T.; Weller, M.P.; Ang, P.C.; Zachary, A.; and Latimer-Sayer, D.T. Drug abuse in mental illness. *Lancet,* I:997, 1988.

West, P. Interaction of low-dose amphetamine use with schizophrenic outpatients: Three case reports. *American Journal of Psychiatry,* 131:321-323, 1974.

Wolkowitz, O.M.; Breier, A.; Doran, A.R.; Kelsoe, J.; Lucas, P.; Paul, S.M.; and Pickar, D. Alprazolam augmentation of the antipsychotic effects of fluphenazine in schizophrenic patients. *Archives of General Psychiatry,* 45:664-670, 1988.

Wyatt, R.J.; Karoum, F; Suddath, R.; and Fawcett, R. Persistently decreased brain dopamine levels and cocaine. *Journal of the American Medical Association,* 259:2996, 1988.

ABOUT THE AUTHORS

Lisa Dixon, M.D., M.P.H., is Associate Professor of Psychiatry at the University of Maryland, Baltimore. Gretchen Haas, Ph.D., is Director of Family and PSR Studies Programs, Department of Psychology at the University of Pittsburgh School of Medicine and the Western Psychiatric Institute and Clinic. Peter Weiden, M.D., is Director of the Neurobiologic Disorders Service of St. Luke's-Roosevelt Hospital Center and is Associate Professor of Clinical Psychiatry at Columbia University. John Sweeney, Ph.D., is Associate Professor of Psychiatry at the University of Pittsburgh. Allen Frances, M.D., is Professor and Chair, Department of Psychiatry, at Duke University.

Reprinted with permission from *Schizophrenia Bulletin.*

SUBSTANCE ABUSE AMONG YOUNG ADULT CHRONIC PATIENTS

Helen C. Bergman and Maxine Harris

Reprinted from *Psychosocial Rehabilitation Journal*, IX(1):49-54, 1985

Drugs and alcohol used by young adult chronic patients are often part of their social life in the community. Few patients understand the psychiatrically debilitating consequences of such usage. The Community Connections program offered its young adult patients education and led groups to help patients recognize the adverse effects of drugs on themselves and their friends. Preliminary findings of a survey on the reasons for drug use are presented.

Recent literature (Schwartz & Goldfinger, 1981; Pepper, Kirshner, & Ryglewicz, 1981; Bachrach, 1982; Pepper & Ryglewicz, 1984; Goldfinger, Hopkin, & Surber, 1984; Crabtree, 1984), in describing the characteristics of the subgroup now known as the young adult chronic patient, has noted that substance abuse is a growing problem for a substantial portion of the population. Although there is an increased awareness among clinicians of the difficulties encountered by the patients who abuse alcohol and/or various drugs, detailed studies describing the reasons for drug use and its correlation with decompensation and readmissions have not appeared, to our knowledge. This report describes the preliminary findings of one such study, which was undertaken to ascertain the extent of substance use and abuse and to discover why young adult chronic patients engage in such activity. This article also includes treatment approaches we have implemented to address the misuse of drugs and to avert severe decompensation.

Community Connections is an intensive inpatient and outpatient program geared toward treating the young adult chronic patient. The treatment philosophy is predicated on both psychodynamic and psychosocial theory and continuity of care principles for this population (Harris, Bergman, & Greenwood, 1982; Harris & Bergman, 1984). More recently, Community Connections has become an independent nonprofit agency serving chronic patients in the community. At the time of this study, the program operated out of Saint Elizabeth's Hospital in Washington, D.C. Located in an urban, lower income area, the study population is over 70% Black and originates from a lower socioeconomic class. The age range is 31 years. All patients have psychiatric histories of at least 2 years duration, and the average number of hospitalizations at the time of entry to the Community Connections inpatient unit is nine.

The program emphasizes continuity of care through aggressive outreach and case management. After an initial inpatient stay, Community Connections patients remain connected to the same treatment team as they move into the community. The locus of treatment changes to the community where the treatment team sees the patient at home or at work. Treatment goals include the development and maintenance of a support network in order to prevent relapse. We have been successful in reducing the relapse rate by 50 percent over a period of five years.

Intensive community outreach work has allowed us to watch more carefully the stresses our patients experience in readjusting to community life. We have observed that while some patients relapse when stress among social relationships becomes too great, others do not fit this pattern and seem to become psychotic rather suddenly. This unpredicted decompensation occurs despite at least weekly contact with a clinician who has been trained to be sensitive to the individual's particular early warning signals. In our clinical work we have noted that these groups demonstrate different patterns of alcohol and substance abuse prior to relapse.

In order to examine the effects of alcohol and substance use on readmissions, baseline data from the clinical records of 65 patients were gathered. Histories dating back to 1976 revealed that 34 patients (52%) had histories of drug and/or alcohol use that were associated with a hospitalization. Of these 34 patients, investigators found that 14 (41%) used marijuana only, and 10 (29%) used alcohol only. In addition, 7 (21%) used marijuana and PCP, and 3 (9%) used alcohol and marijuana. We also determined that an additional 6 patients had recorded histories of excessive use of alcohol or drugs although the use was not cited in the record as a direct precipitant of a hospitalization. In total, 39 patients (60%) had recorded histories of substance abuse prior to entry into Community Connections.

METHODOLOGY AND RESULTS

In view of the high use of addictive substances and its effect on relapse and readmission, we wanted to explore further the reasons why patients engaged in such activity as well as whether or not they had knowledge of the consequences of alcohol or drug usage. Toward that end we conducted structured interviews with each patient who was either readmitted to Community Connections or who displayed signs of relapse that required crisis management by our treatment teams. Subjects were asked if they used drugs, why they engaged in drug taking, and whether they were aware of the personal consequences of abusing marijuana or alcohol. In addition to assessing the reasons for taking the drugs, the interviewers evaluated the effects of the substance use on the individuals' psychiatric condition through clinical assessment and the impact on the social support system as reported by network members. During the course of the 1-year study, there were a total of 16 readmissions. Eleven readmissions (60%) were found to be drug-related. Twelve additional drug episodes that required crisis management but not a rehospitalization were recorded.

Different reasons for taking drugs were expressed. Two-thirds of the patients who smoked marijuana and/or PCP did so to be part of a peer group. Drugs were an integral part of their social life and peer pressure encouraged these patients to smoke. Those who simply smoked marijuana did not tend to require readmission, although chronic use did cause disruption on the job and a relapse of the clinical condition. For others, smoking "reefer" allowed them to tolerate social contact that they otherwise avoided. Those who smoked marijuana laced with PCP (7) seemed to do so inadvertently. The marijuana available on the streets near the hospital (which is where most patients congregated to socialize) was often laced with PCP at no extra expense. Patients who thought they were smoking "reefer" were surprised to learn that the drug screens found PCP in their systems. Most had little knowledge of this more potent drug. The marijuana/PCP users who reported smoking together socially relapsed in rapid succession to one another after the ingestion. These users relapsed and required hospitalization with no early warning signs of other stresses.

Forty percent of the patients reported using both marijuana and alcohol to self-medicate. Those patients in this group who were diagnosed as schizophrenic stated that marijuana kept voices away and "makes me feel different." This altered state of being seems preferable to the unmedicated feeling of emptiness.

An unexpected finding revealed in the clinical interviews was the extent of Cogentin abuse (6 patients, 38%). Cogentin, a popular drug prescribed to counter the side effects of phenothiazines, offered users a high similar to amphetamines. After ingesting extra Cogentins, marijuana is commonly used to come down from the high induced by the Cogentin. Marijuana then acts as a sedative drug for the patients. Several patients tried to obtain extra Cogentin by either reporting increased side effects or by seeking different physicians to prescribe the drug.

In contrast to the social smokers, the alcohol users tended to drink to relieve anxiety. Anxiety was attributed directly to stresses in social relationships. Interestingly, the alcohol abusers who were readmitted did show other early warning signs and clinicians predicted the crises, whereas the social marijuana/PCP users who were readmitted did so without other precipitating stresses. In sum, patients tend to use alcohol to relieve stress while the smokers do so, in part, to be social.

DISCUSSION

Drugs used by young adult chronic patients are often a part of their social life and secondary to their diagnoses of schizophrenia and character disorders. Most patients in our study had only minimal understanding of the effects of these drugs and the correlation to relapse. Few patients were aware that drug use potentiated an already debilitating psychiatric condition. Because the patients studied do not carry primary diagnoses of addictive disorders, the usual treatment of alcohol and drug abuse is not applicable to this group.

Young adult chronic patients are also young adults. They find themselves struggling with the common social problems encountered in the late 20's and early 30's. Though they have typical reasons to use drugs (to be sociable or to relieve anxiety), they unfortunately have atypical responses to such use. The patients' peer group has a significant effect in encouraging continued usage of drugs.

The patients' environment also influences their patterns of drug use. The urban subculture where these patients live condones substance use and, to some extent, substance abuse. Patients reported that drug running was a common means of earning extra cash. Drug involvement made patients feel a part of the neighborhood mainstream. For many patients, neighbors and friends were themselves drug traffickers and users.

Community Connections has adopted a two-pronged approach consisting of education and peer pressure in combating these problems. We have introduced an education component, the results of which will be the subject of a future study.

In the educative component, patients are informed of the consequences, both physical and mental, of drug and alcohol abuse. We describe patients' inability to use drugs as similar to having an allergic reaction. Some people are allergic to drugs and become sick while others are able to use drugs in moderation without repercussions. We stress that the reaction to drugs is not the fault of the individual but is merely an unfortunate clinical condition beyond one's control. Such a descriptive explanation avoids individual blame and parental reproach and gives young adults an acceptable excuse to refuse drugs or to monitor ingestion. The education also includes movies depicting the hazards of PCP and alcohol use, and pamphlets to enlighten patients about the dangers of drug and alcohol use with prescribed medication.

The education sessions reinforce the need for patients to be aware of and streetwise to the adverse effects of drugs. Following these sessions, patients are asked to take responsibility for each other openly. In this way the secretiveness and adolescent-like fear of reprisal are minimized. Patients learn that they must be intelligent users if they choose to smoke or drink and that they must be watchful of their friends.

Patients appear to be responsive to this educative approach. They have begun to take care of one another at home and have also voluntarily enlisted the aid of staff when a particular friend is in trouble. In one instance, residents in a group home took turns sitting up all night with a woman who became psychotic while smoking an excessive amount of marijuana. By staying at her side, offering her food, and supporting her through her crisis, they enabled her to avoid a rehospitalization.

SUMMARY

Our preliminary findings indicate a serious lack of knowledge regarding drug and alcohol use among young adult chronic patients. In the environment where these patients reside, particularly within their young adult peer group, substance use and abuse represent a common part of daily life. Young adult patients want to feel a part of the "normal" world and thus may use these substances, at least in part, in order to be accepted and liked by others. However, drug use potentiates already serious impairments for these patients, and subsequent rehospitalization or reinstitutionalization further decreases their capacity to live productive lives. There is a high price to pay for each psychotic episode; rarely does the chronic patient return to a premorbid level of functioning (Docherty, Van Kammen, Siris, & Marder, 1978).

Widespread cultural acceptance of drug use and abuse, coupled with the lack of knowledge of the negative effects of such usage, contribute to the problem of drug use among young adult chronic patients. Patients tend to make a better adjustment to community life when they return to their natural neighborhoods than when they are placed in new, unfamiliar neighborhoods. We have found that our patients, as they blend into the culture of their lower socioeconomic neighborhoods of origin, cannot avoid the drug use existent in these areas. While clinicians have little control over the environment, we do have some control over the lack of education regarding drug use. In preparing patients to return to the community, drug education must be emphasized.

We do not expect that drug use will be eradicated among these patients. The perceived benefits of drug use—social acceptance, an altered state of being, and relief from anxiety—and the widespread availability of drugs may outweigh concerns about relapse and readmission. However, through education sessions and through the encouragement of peer support, we may anticipate more cautious and moderate use of these drugs and heightened awareness by the patients of the early warning signs of relapse for themselves and for their friends. In this way, patients may seek help sooner and may avoid a more serious decompensation or rehospitalization.

REFERENCES

Bachrach, L. (1982). The young adult chronic patient: An analytical review of the literature. *Hospital and Community Psychiatry,* 33(3), 189-197.

Crabtree, L. (1984). Disability in young adult chronic patients at discharge from a private psychiatric hospital. *New Directions for Mental Health Services,* 21, 39.

Docherty, J., Van Kammen, D., Siris, S., & Marder, S. (1978). Stages of onset of schizophrenia psychosis. *American Journal of Psychiatry,* 135(4), 420-428.

Goldfinger, S., Hopkin, J., & Surber, R. (1984). Treatment resisters or system resisters?: Toward a better service system for acute care recidivists. *New Directions for Mental Health Services,* 21, 18.

Harris, M., & Bergman, H. (1984). Reassessing the revolving door: A developmental perspective on the young adult chronic patient. *Journal of Orthopsychiatry,* 54(2), 281-289.

Harris, M., Bergman, H., & Greenwood, V. (1982). Integrating hospital and community systems for treating revolving door patients. *Hospital and Community Psychiatry,* 33, 225-227.

Pepper, B., & Ryglewicz, H. (1984). Advances in treating the young adult chronic patient. *New Directions for Mental Health Services,* 21, 9.

Pepper, B., Kirshner, M., & Ryglewicz, H. (1981). The young adult chronic patient: Overview of a population. *Hospital and Community Psychiatry,* 32(7), 463-469.

Schwartz, S., & Goldfinger, S. (1981). The new chronic patient: Clinical characteristics of an emerging subgroup. *Hospital and Community Psychiatry,* 32(7), 470-474.

ABOUT THE AUTHORS

Helen C. Bergman, A.C.S.W., is Co-Director of Community Connections, a community-based program of aggressive outreach and case management in Washington, D.C. Maxine Harris, Ph.D., is a clinical psychologist and Co-Director of Community Connections.

Reprinted with permission from *Psychosocial Rehabilitation Journal.*

EXPECTATIONS AND MOTIVES FOR SUBSTANCE USE IN SCHIZOPHRENIA

Kim T. Mueser, Pallavi Nishith, Joseph I. Tracy,
Joanne DeGirolamo, and Max Molinaro

Reprinted from *Schizophrenia Bulletin, 21(3):367-378, 1995*

This study examined the internal reliability of standardized measures of substance use expectancies and motives in a schizophrenia population (n = 70) and the relationship of these expectancies and motives to alcohol and drug use disorders. Internal reliabilities were uniformly high for the subscales of the expectancy and motive measures. Analyses of the relationship between substance use disorders and expectancies revealed strong substance-specific expectations. Alcohol expectancies were related to alcohol disorders but not to drug disorders; cocaine expectancies were related to drug but not to alcohol disorders; and marijuana expectancies were more strongly related to drug than to alcohol use disorders. In contrast, motives were related to substance use disorders, and self-reported substance use problems were related to expectancies and motives in a nonspecific manner. These results suggest that expectancy and motive questionnaires developed for the primary substance abuse population may be valid for psychiatric populations. Research on motives and expectancies may help to clarify the functions of substance abuse in persons with schizophrenia.

Over the past decade, there has been a growing awareness of the problem of comorbid substance use disorders in schizophrenia. Estimates of the prevalence of comorbidity among persons with schizophrenia are high, usually ranging between 20 and 60 percent (Mueser et al. 1990; Regier et al. 1990). This is of particular concern considering the negative impact of substance use disorders on the course of the illness (Drake et al. 1989), as well as the increased service utilization and costs associated with comorbidity (Bartels et al. 1993). Yet, very little is known about why schizophrenia patients use substances, what they expect from that use, and how either of these factors relates to the etiology or maintenance of the substance abuse.

With increased research being directed toward the development of more effective interventions for schizophrenia patients with substance use disorders, some investigators have been exploring the reasons patients give for their substance use and the perceived effects of such use. Current treatment modalities for patients with schizophrenia who abuse substances often assume that these individuals have the same expectancies and reasons for use as primary substance abusers; however, such an assumption has yet to be tested. The ability to obtain valid assessments of motives or perceived effects from patients with schizophrenia might facilitate the tailoring of interventions for substance use disorders to address the specific needs of individual patients.

Surveys of schizophrenia patients with a substance use disorder conducted by Test et al. (1989), Dixon et al. (1991), and Noordsy et al. (1991) have reported a range of different motives for patients' substance use, the most common among them being to reduce anxiety or depression, improve sleep, facilitate socialization, and enhance pleasure (or reduce anhedonia). These studies suggest that patients with schizophrenia are capable of articulating their reasons for using substances. However, the validity of these reports is unknown. Moreover, the conclusions that can be drawn from these studies are limited. First, standardized instruments were not used to assess motives for substance use or its perceived effects. Second, self-reports were obtained from patients with a history of substance use disorder but not from patients with no such history; therefore, it is unclear whether there was a relationship between the reasons given for substance use and the presence of a substance use disorder.

The present study was conducted to examine the relationship between expectancies and motives for substance use, and a history of substance use disorder in patients with schizophrenia. It goes beyond previous research on reasons for substance abuse in schizophrenia by using instruments that have been standardized in the general population and by assessing patients both with and without a substance abuse history. We elected to examine substance use expectancies in addition to motives because prior studies have shown that expectancies for the effects of substances are related to a history of substance abuse in the general and alcoholic population (Brown et al. 1987; Schafer and Brown 1991; Goldman 1994). Expectancies and motives for substance use theoretically are distinct, with the latter thought to be more proximate to actual substance abuse behavior (Cooper 1994). Although both have been posited as etiological factors in the development of alcohol and drug use disorders (e.g., Cox and Klinger 1988; Cooper et al. 1992a), research has not examined these constructs together in the population of patients with schizophrenia. Thus, one goal of this study was to examine whether a similar pattern of associations was found in substance use disorders and in expectancies or motives.

We examined two general hypotheses: (1) that patients with a history of alcohol or drug use disorder would endorse stronger expectancies and motives for substance use than patients with no substance use disorder; and (2) that the associations between substance use disorder and the motives for and expectancies of use would be stronger within a given substance than across different substances. In other words, we expected that patients with a history of alcohol use disorder would endorse stronger expectancies and motives for alcohol use than for drug use and, conversely, that patients with a history of drug use disorder would endorse stronger expectancies and motives for drug use than for alcohol use.

METHOD

Subjects

The subjects were 70 patients with diagnoses of either schizophrenia ($n = 51$, 73%) or schizoaffective disorder ($n = 19$, 27%). Patients were selected if they had a chart diagnosis of schizophrenia or schizoaffective disorder based on *DSM-III-R* (American Psychiatric Association 1987) criteria or were diagnosed based on the Structured Clinical Interview for *DSM-III-R* (SCID; Spitzer et al. 1990). SCID interviews for a primary diagnosis of schizophrenia or schizoaffective disorder were available for 37 subjects (53%).[1] Patients with neurologic conditions having a clear central nervous system impact, based on chart review, were excluded.

Subjects were assessed in three different psychiatric settings: an acute inpatient setting (Medical College of Pennsylvania at Eastern Pennsylvania Psychiatric Institute [MCP/EPPI]), where patients were admitted for brief (2-4 week) treatment of a symptom exacerbation ($n = 22$, 31%); an outpatient clinic at MCP/EPPI ($n = 29$, 41%), where the average patient had been treated for 4 years; and a chronic inpatient setting (Norristown State Hospital; $n = 19$, 27%).

A total of 45 patients (64%) were male, and 20 (29%) were African-American. The mean age was 36.7 years (standard deviation [SD] = 8.68; range: 21-59), with a mean of 7.1 prior hospitalizations (SD = 5.70; range: 0-30). The mean age at onset of schizophrenia symptoms was 22.2 years (SD = 6.82; range: 7-41); for onset of alcohol abuse symptoms, 16.2 years (SD = 4.39; range: 0-24); and for onset of drug abuse symptoms, 16.7 years (SD = 6.73; range: 0-34).

Measures

Measures were used to assess two broad areas: (1) motives for and expectancies from substance use; and (2) substance use disorders and problems.

---

[1]To determine whether a history of substance use disorder was related to how a diagnosis of schizophrenia or schizoaffective disorder was made, two chi-square analyses were performed, one for alcohol use disorder (never, past, recent) and diagnostic method (SCID, chart) and one for drug use disorder and diagnostic method. The chi-square for alcohol use disorder was significant ($\chi^2 = 9.01$, $df = 2$, $p = 0.01$), but that for drug use disorder was not ($\chi^2 = 4.66$, $df = 2$, not significant). Patients with a current or past history of alcohol use disorder were more likely to have been diagnosed with schizophrenia or schizoaffective disorder by chart (70% and 56%, respectively) than were patients with no history of alcohol abuse (29%).

Motives and expectancies

Motives for alcohol use were assessed with the Drinking Motives Measure (DMM; Cooper et al. 1992b). This instrument measures three different motives for drinking: social motives, coping motives, and enhancement of positive affect. It includes 15 items, each rated on a 4-point Likert scale (1 = almost never/never, 4 = almost always). Following the procedure of Cooper et al. (1992b), the scale was administered orally to patients who drank at least once during their lifetime. The DMM was developed and validated in the general population, and it has good internal reliability and predictive validity (e.g., it discriminates people with a history of alcohol abuse from alcohol use).

To our knowledge, there is no available scale comparable to the DMM for assessing motives for using drugs. However, schizophrenia patients frequently cite similar motives for using drugs as for using alcohol, such as socialization, pleasure enhancement, and coping with symptoms (Test et al. 1989; Dixon et al. 1991). Therefore, to obtain a measure of drug use motives, we adapted the DMM by substituting the words "drug use" for "drinking"—hence, the Drug Use Motives Measure (DUMM). The DUMM was administered in the same fashion as the DMM to those patients who used an illicit drug (e.g., cannabis, cocaine) at least once in their lifetime.

Surveys of substance use disorders and patterns of abuse in psychiatric patients have found that alcohol is the most frequently abused substance, followed by marijuana and cocaine (Mueser et al. 1990, 1992; Regier et al. 1990; Cuffel et al. 1993). Therefore, substance use expectancies were assessed for the effects of these three classes of substances using three scales: the Alcohol Effect Expectancy Questionnaire (AEEQ; Brown et al. 1987), the Marijuana Effect Expectancy Questionnaire (MEEQ; Schafer and Brown 1991), and the Cocaine Effect Expectancy Questionnaire (CEEQ; Schafer and Brown 1991). These scales contain items describing the common effects of each substance (e.g., "When I smoke marijuana it helps me escape reality"). Subjects are asked to agree or disagree with each item according to their own current thoughts, feelings, and beliefs about the effects of the substance. The AEEQ and MEEQ each contain six subscales whereas the CEEQ contains five. The expectancy scales have high test-retest reliabilities and have been found to distinguish between patterns of nonuse and varying degrees of use in the general population. Patients with adequate reading skills completed the expectancy questionnaires themselves; others had the questions read to them. In contrast to the DMM and the DUMM, the expectancy measures were administered to all patients, regardless of whether they had ever tried the substance, in line with procedures recommended by the developers of these scales.

Substance use disorders and problems

Alcohol use disorders (using *DSM-III-R* criteria) were assessed with the Case Manager Rating Scale (CMRS-Alcohol; Drake et al. 1990), which was based on both a semistructured interview and a chart review. A parallel form of this instrument was used to assess drug use disorders (CMRS-Drug; Drake et al. 1990). These scales were used to assess both lifetime and recent (past year) alcohol and drug use disorders separately. Previous research on the CMRS indicates that it has good reliability and validity in patients with schizophrenia when compared with structured clinical interviews for substance use disorders, such as the SCID (Drake et al. 1990). Ratings are made on 5-point, behaviorally anchored rating scales. The low end of the scales corresponds to either no alcohol/drug use (1) or alcohol/drug use without any problems (2), whereas higher scores (3-5) indicate increasing degrees of problem severity, corresponding to the symptoms required to diagnose *DSM-III-R* alcohol/drug use disorders.

To check on the reliability of the CMRS ratings, 43 percent of all patients were also evaluated by an independent rater. Intraclass correlation coefficients, computed using the case 2 formula from Shrout and Fleiss (1979), indicated satisfactory reliability for all CMRS ratings (range: 0.58 for CMRS—Alcohol Lifetime, to 0.82 for CMRS—Drug Recent). CMRS—Alcohol ratings were collapsed to form three mutually exclusive groups: no history of alcohol use disorder (n = 34, 49%), past history of alcohol use disorder but not recent (past year) history (n = 16, 23%), and recent (past year) alcohol use disorder (n = 20, 28%). Similar categories were formed for the CMRS—Drug ratings: no history of drug use disorder (n = 35, 50%), past history of drug use disorder but not recent (past year) history (n = 17, 24%), and recent (past year) drug use disorder (n = 18, 26%). Chi-square analyses indicated that history of alcohol or drug use disorder (no history, past but not recent disorder, recent disorder) was not related to hospital (χ^2 = 5.48, 2.24, df = 2, p > 0.05).

Self-reported problems related to alcohol were assessed with the Michigan Alcoholism Screening Test (MAST; Selzer 1971). The MAST contains 24 yes/no questions pertaining to alcohol use and problems related to alcohol. Used extensively as a screening instrument in the general population, it has been found to discriminate schizophrenia patients with and without an alcohol use disorder (McHugo et al. 1993). To obtain a parallel measure of drug use, items from the MAST were adapted for the context of drug use. Two items referring specifically to alcohol-related problems were dropped (liver cirrhosis, delirium tremens), and three items related to drug use were added (arrest for sale of drugs, arrest for possession, physical problems related to drug use). The resultant instrument, the Michigan Drug Screening Test (MDST), is similar to Skinner's (1982) Drug Abuse Screening Test. The MAST and the MDST were given only to patients who had at least one drink or one incident of illicit drug use in their lifetime.

Procedure

Sequential admissions to MCP/EPPI were screened for project eligibility. Potentially eligible outpatients at MCP/EPPI and inpatients at Norristown were identified through hospital staff referral. Approximately 80 percent of the patients approached for the project agreed to participate. Unfortunately, information regarding the characteristics of patients who declined to participate was not obtained. Patients who provided informed consent were administered the instruments in the following order: MAST, MDST, DMM, DUMM, AEEQ, MEEQ, CEEQ, CMRS—Alcohol, and CMRS—Drug. The assessment was usually broken down into two or three meetings to avoid fatiguing the patient. Before completing all assessments, patients were assured that all information would be held strictly confidential and would not influence their treatment or discharge planning.

RESULTS

The analyses were organized as follows. First, we examined the overlap between alcohol and drug use disorders. Second, we evaluated the correspondence between interview-based measures of substance use disorders and self-reported substance-related problems. Third, we calculated the internal reliabilities of the substance use expectancy and motives measures. Fourth, we determined the relationship between motives, expectancies, and history of substance use disorder. Last, we explored the relationship between motives, expectancies, and self-reported problems related to substance use.

Overlap of alcohol and drug use disorders

Based on the CMRS, a history of alcohol use disorder was present in 51 percent of the sample, and a history of drug use disorder was present in 50 percent. The overlap between lifetime history of drug use disorder and alcohol use disorder was very high, with only 11 subjects (16%) having a history of one type of substance use disorder but not of the other ($\chi^2 = 32.94$, $df = 1$, $p < 0.001$). Recent alcohol and drug use disorders were present in 29 and 26 percent of the sample, respectively. Similar to lifetime history of substance use disorder, recent alcohol use disorder was strongly related to recent drug use disorder ($\chi^2 = 17.23$, $df = 1$, $p < 0.001$). In short, these data indicate a high comorbidity between alcohol and drug use disorders in this sample.

Interview-based and self-reported substance use problems

To evaluate the relationship between history of substance use disorders and self-reported problems, we first collapsed the history data obtained from the CMRS to form two categorical variables (three levels for alcohol = no alcohol use disorder / past alcohol use disorder / recent alcohol use disorder; and three levels for drugs = no drug use disorder/past drug use disorder/recent drug use disorder). For each variable, past substance use disorder referred to a history of disorder but not recent (past year) substance use disorder.

To evaluate whether past or recent alcohol use disorders were related to self-reported problems on the MAST and the MDST, two one-way analyses of variance (ANOVAs) were performed. Alcohol use disorder served as a between-subject factor, and the MAST and the MDST were the dependent variables. Both of these ANOVAs were statistically significant ($F = 28.78$, $df = 2,55$, $p < 0.001$; $F = 12.99$, $df = 2,41$, $p < 0.001$, respectively). Similar ANOVAs were performed to examine whether past or recent drug use disorders were related to the MAST and MDST. Both of these ANOVAs were also statistically significant ($F = 9.42$, $df = 2,55$, $p < 0.001$; $F = 44.41$, $df = 2,41$, $p < 0.001$, respectively). In all cases, Tukey's honestly significant difference (HSD) tests ($p < 0.05$) indicated that the patients with no history of the relevant substance had lower self-reported problems than patients with a past or recent history, who did not differ. The descriptive statistics for the self-report ratings on the MAST and the MDST are shown in table 1.

Internal reliabilities of expectancy and motives scales

To evaluate whether the subscales of the expectancy and motives measures were internally reliable in a schizophrenia population, coefficient alphas were computed for each of the subscales. For the 17 subscales of the AEEQ, MEEQ, and CEEQ, coefficient alphas ranged from 0.55 (relaxation and tension reduction on the CEEQ) to 0.92 (global positive effects on both the CEEQ and the AEEQ), with a median coefficient alpha of 0.84.

For the six subscales of the DMM and DUMM, coefficient alphas ranged from 0.74 (socialization motives on the DMM) to 0.91 (pleasure enhancement motives on the DUMM), with a median coefficient alpha of 0.77. The internal reliabilities of the expectancy and motive subscales in this sample are comparable to those reported for these measures in the general population, suggesting acceptable internal consistency (except for the DUMM, which has not been previously used).

Relationship of substance use disorder to expectancies and motives

To evaluate whether past or recent alcohol use disorder (CMRS—Alcohol) was related to expectancies, three multivariate analyses of variance (MANOVAs) were performed, one for each expectancy scale (AEEQ, MEEQ, CEEQ). For each MANOVA, the independent variable was a history of alcohol use disorder (no history, past history, recent history) and the dependent variables were the subscales on each of the respective expectancy questionnaires (six for the AEEQ, six for the MEEQ, five for the CEEQ). The MANOVAs for the AEEQ and the MEEQ were statistically significant ($F = 2.05$, $df = 12,110$, $p < 0.05$; $F = 2.16$, $df = 12,112$, $p = 0.05$, respectively), but the MANOVA for the CEEQ was not. The descriptive statistics for the AEEQ and MEEQ subscales and for Tukey's HSD tests are provided in table 2. Inspection of this table shows that higher scores on all of the AEEQ subscales were related to history of alcohol use disorder, whereas only one MEEQ subscale was related to a history of alcohol use disorder.

Table 1. MAST and MDST scores for schizophrenia patients with different histories of substance abuse

	Alcohol				Drugs			
	No alcohol abuse (N)	Past alcohol abuse (P)	Recent alcohol abuse (R)	Tukey	No drug abuse (N)	Past drug abuse (P)	Recent drug abuse (R)	Tukey
MAST	4.87 (n = 23; SD = 2.38)	12.93 (n = 15; SD = 4.54)	12.95 (n = 20; SD = 4.87)	P, R > N[1]	6.65 (n = 26; SD = 4.72)	12.00 (n = 15; SD = 4.91)	12.53 (n = 17; SD = 5.14)	P, R > N[1]
MDST	5.59 (n = 17; SD = 5.48)	12.50 (n = 14; SD = 4.55)	14.69 (n = 13; SD = 5.38)	P, R > N[1]	3.20 (n = 15; SD = 2.48)	13.25 (n = 12; SD = 4.00)	14.94 (n = 17; SD = 4.35)	P, R > N[1]

Note.–MAST = Michigan Alcoholism Screening Test (Selzer 1971); MDST = Michigan Drug Screening Test; SD = standard deviation.
[1] $p < 0.001$

Table 2. Means (standard deviations) on the AEEQ and MEEQ for patients with different histories of alcohol abuse

	No alcohol abuse (N)	Past alcohol abuse (P)	Recent alcohol abuse (R)	Tukey
AEEQ subscales[1]	(n = 30)	(n = 14)	(n = 18)	
Global positive effects	7.20 (7.17)	12.71 (5.82)	13.33 (5.50)	P, R > N[2]
Sexual enhancement	1.70 (2.09)	3.79 (2.45)	3.56 (2.43)	P, R > N[3]
Physical and social pleasure	3.87 (2.84)	6.43 (1.74)	6.89 (2.30)	P, R > N[2]
Social assertiveness	3.27 (3.12)	6.00 (2.75)	7.17 (3.24)	P, R > N[2]
Relaxation and tension reduction	4.03 (3.48)	6.21 (2.52)	7.00 (2.25)	P, R > N[2]
Arousal and power	3.23 (2.47)	4.79 (1.80)	5.50 (2.12)	R > N[3]
MEEQ subscales[4]	(n = 31)	(n = 15)	(n = 17)	
Cognitive and behavioral impairment	6.23 (4.33)	7.53 (3.36)	8.65 (3.67)	NS
Relaxation and tension reduction	4.00 (3.14)	5.07 (2.91)	4.59 (2.76)	NS
Social and sexual facilitation	4.03 (3.06)	5.67 (2.38)	4.65 (1.93)	NS
Perceptual and cognitive enhancement	3.55 (2.73)	5.00 (2.51)	5.18 (2.16)	NS
Global negative effects	3.94 (3.39)	4.13 (1.81)	4.65 (2.70)	NS
Craving and physical effects	2.71 (2.08)	4.47 (1.46)	4.71 (1.79)	P, R > N[2]

Note.—AEEQ = Alcohol Effect Expectancy Questionnaire (Brown et al. 1987); MEEQ = Marijuana Effect Expectancy Questionnaire (Schafer and Brown 1991); NS = not significant

[1] Multivariate $F = 2.05$, $df = 12,110$, $p < 0.05$.
[2] $p < 0.001$.
[3] $p < 0.01$.
[4] Multivariate $F = 2.16$, $df = 12,112$, $p < 0.05$.

The relationship between a history of drug use disorder and expectancies was examined by performing a similar set of MANOVAs with drug use history (CMRS—Drug) as the independent variable. The multivariate group effect was significant for the MEEQ and the CEEQ ($F = 1.81$, $df = 12,112$, $p = 0.05$; $F = 2.05$, $df = 10,110$, $p < 0.05$, respectively), but not for the AEEQ. Tukey's HSD tests indicated that three of the six MEEQ subscales were significantly different, and four of the five CEEQ subscales were different. Patients with a history of drug use disorder tended to have higher expectancies than did patients with no history. The descriptive statistics for the MEEQ and the CEEQ by drug use disorder group are presented in table 3.

The relationship between a history of alcohol or drug use disorders and motives (the DMM and the DUMM) was explored in a series of MANOVAs similar to those described above. Both of the MANOVAs on history of alcohol use disorder were statistically significant (DMM, $F = 6.82$, $df = 6,110$, $p < 0.001$; DUMM, $F = 2.16$, $df = 6,82$, $p = 0.05$), as were both of the MANOVAs on history of drug use disorder (DMM, $F = 3.06$, $df = 6,110$, $p < 0.01$; DUMM, $F = 2.98$, $df = 6,82$, $p = 0.01$). The descriptive statistics for these measures and for Tukey's HSD tests are summarized in tables 4 and 5. As with the expectancies, patients with a history of alcohol or drug use disorder tended to endorse motives more strongly than did patients with no substance use disorder history.[2]

Relationship of self-reported substance use problems with expectancies and motives

To evaluate whether patients who reported more problems related to alcohol (MAST) or drugs (MDST) also reported stronger expectancies (AEEQ, MEEQ, CEEQ) and motives (DMM, DUMM) for alcohol or drug use, Pearson

---

[2]Additional analyses were conducted to evaluate whether the same pattern of results would be obtained if the patients with chronic schizophrenia (assessed at Norristown State Hospital) were excluded. To address this question, the 14 MANOVAs (previously described) evaluating the relationships between alcohol- or drug-related problems (MAST, MDST), expectancy (AEEQ, MEEQ, CEEQ), motives (DMM, DUMM), and history of alcohol or drug use disorder (never, past, recent) were repeated, dropping the chronic patients. The pattern of results obtained was similar but not identical to that found with the entire sample. Similar to the findings with the entire sample, a history of alcohol use disorder was related to MAST, MDST, AEEQ, and DMM, and a history of drug use disorder was related to MAST, MDST, and marginally ($p < 0.1$) to CEEQ. Also similar to findings with the entire sample, a history of alcohol use disorder was not related to CEEQ, and a history of drug use disorder was not related to AEEQ. However, in contrast to the previous findings, a history of alcohol abuse was not related to MEEQ or DUMM, and a history of drug abuse was not related to MEEQ, DMM, or DUMM. Thus, 10 out of the 14 MANOVAs (including CEEQ and drug abuse) in the restricted sample produced the same findings as in the complete sample. The failure of some MANOVAs to achieve significance appears to be at least partly owing to the reduced power in the subsample analyses, in which the sample size was reduced from 70 to 51 patients.

Table 3. Means (standard deviations) on the MEEQ and CEEQ for patients with different histories of drug abuse

	No drug abuse (N)	Past drug abuse (P)	Recent drug abuse (R)	Tukey
MEEQ subscales[1]	(*n* = 31)	(*n* = 15)	(*n* = 17)	
Cognitive and behavioral impairment	6.48 (4.19)	8.20 (3.78)	7.59 (3.87)	NS
Relaxation and tension reduction	3.74 (3.13)	5.93 (2.40)	4.29 (2.80)	NS
Social and sexual facilitation	3.71 (2.66)	5.93 (2.63)	5.00 (2.29)	P > N[2]
Perceptual and cognitive enhancement	3.45 (2.59)	5.67 (1.95)	4.76 (2.68)	P > N[2]
Global negative effects	4.03 (3.17)	4.67 (2.16)	4.00 (2.96)	NS
Craving and physical effects	2.74 (2.05)	4.80 (1.37)	4.35 (1.97)	P, R > N[3]
CEEQ subscales[4]	(*n* = 29)	(*n* = 16)	(*n* = 16)	
Global positive effects	5.41 (4.86)	10.56 (4.18)	6.69 (4.94)	P > N[2]
Global negative effects	8.07 (5.48)	12.06 (2.69)	8.25 (4.49)	P > N[5]
General arousal	3.79 (2.99)	6.56 (1.67)	5.31 (2.63)	P > N[2]
Anxiety	3.41 (2.64)	5.25 (1.44)	4.56 (2.22)	P > N[5]
Relaxation and tension reduction	1.24 (1.24)	1.81 (1.22)	1.44 (1.26)	NS

Note.—MEEQ = Marijuana Effect Expectancy Questionnaire (Schafer and Brown 1991); CEEQ = Cocaine Effect Expectancy Questionnaire (Schafer and Brown 1991); NS = not significant

[1] Multivariate $F = 1.81$, $df = 12,112$, $p < 0.05$.
[2] $p < 0.01$.
[3] $p < 0.001$.
[4] Multivariate $F = 2.05$, $df = 10,110$, $p < 0.05$.
[5] $p < 0.05$.

Table 4. Means (standard deviations) on the DMM and DUMM for patients with different histories of alcohol abuse

	No alcohol abuse (N)	Past alcohol abuse (P)	Recent alcohol abuse (R)	Tukey
DMM subscales[1]	(*n* = 24)	(*n* = 16)	(*n* = 19)	
Socialization	9.42 (3.20)	13.62 (3.48)	13.16 (3.76)	P, R > N[2]
Coping	8.04 (3.25)	11.19 (4.00)	13.84 (3.67)	P, R > N[2]
Pleasure enhancement	8.12 (3.40)	14.19 (4.71)	13.79 (3.60)	P, R > N[2]
DUMM subscales[3]	(*n* = 10)	(*n* = 16)	(*n* = 19)	
Socialization	9.58 (4.25)	12.25 (3.70)	10.76 (4.16)	NS
Coping	8.08 (2.87)	10.44 (3.52)	12.06 (4.23)	R > N[4]
Pleasure enhancement	10.17 (5.46)	14.69 (4.45)	13.47 (4.62)	P > N[4]

Note.—DMM = Drinking Motives Measure (Cooper et al. 1992b); DUMM = Drug Use Motives Measure; NS = not significant.

[1] Multivariate F = 6.82, df = 6,110, $p < 0.001$.
[2] $p < 0.001$.
[3] Multivariate F = 2.16, df = 6,82, $p < 0.05$.
[4] $p < 0.05$.

Table 5. Means (standard deviations) on the DMM and DUMM for patients with different histories of drug abuse

	No drug abuse (N)	Past drug abuse (P)	Recent drug abuse (R)	Tukey
DMM subscales[1]	**(n = 27)**	**(n = 16)**	**(n = 16)**	
Socialization	10.33 (4.05)	12.50 (3.72)	13.44 (3.20)	R > N[2]
Coping	9.26 (4.32)	11.31 (3.50)	12.75 (4.39)	R > N[2]
Pleasure enhancement	9.07 (4.00)	13.75 (4.20)	13.69 (4.67)	P, R > N[3]
DUMM subscales[4]	**(n = 13)**	**(n = 16)**	**(n = 16)**	
Socialization	9.23 (4.60)	11.81 (4.00)	11.56 (3.46)	NS
Coping	7.00 (1.96)	11.25 (3.15)	12.37 (4.13)	P, R > N[3]
Pleasure enhancement	10.31 (6.14)	13.56 (4.72)	14.69 (3.48)	P > N[2]

Note.—DMM = Drinking Motives Measure (Cooper et al. 1992b); DUMM = Drug Use Motives Measure; NS = not significant.

[1]Multivariate F = 3.06, df = 6,110, $p < 0.01$.
[2]$p < 0.05$.
[3]$p < 0.001$.
[4]Multivariate F = 2.98, df = 6,82, $p < 0.05$.

correlations were computed between the two sets of measures. There are a total of 17 subscales for the expectancy measures and 6 subscales for the motives measures, yielding a total of 23 subscales. Each subscale was correlated with the MAST and the MDST. Of the 46 computed correlations, 2—the MAST and the relaxation and tension reduction subscale of the CEEQ ($r = 0.12$) and the MDST and the relaxation and tension reduction subscale of the CEEQ ($r = 0.21$)—were nonsignificant ($p > 0.05$). The remaining 44 correlations ranged between 0.26 and 0.65, with a median of 0.51. Thus, problems that patients perceived to be due to the use of alcohol or drugs were strongly related to patients' expectations and motives for substance use.

Demographic and chronicity correlates of substance use disorders

A series of analyses was conducted to evaluate whether any of the following demographic or clinical variables—sex, race, age, number of prior hospitalizations, and age at onset of schizophrenia symptoms—were related to substance use disorders. (Age at onset of alcohol or drug abuse symptoms was not examined because this variable was available for only a subset of patients—those with alcohol or drug use disorders.) For sex and race, separate chi-square analyses were conducted to determine whether each variable was related to a history (never, past, recent) of alcohol or drug use disorder. None of these four analyses was significant ($p > 0.1$), suggesting that these demographic characteristics were not related to a history of substance use disorder.

To evaluate whether age, number of hospitalizations, or age at onset of schizophrenia symptoms was related to substance use disorder, one-way ANOVAs were conducted on each variable, separately, for alcohol and drug abuse history. For each ANOVA, age, age at onset, or number of prior hospitalizations was the dependent variable, and a history of alcohol (or drug) use disorder (never, past, recent) was the independent variable. One of these six ANOVAs was significant: age at onset of schizophrenia symptoms and history of alcohol use disorder ($F = 3.21$, $df = 2,60$, $p < 0.05$). A post hoc Tukey HSD test indicated that patients with a past history of alcohol abuse had an earlier age at onset of schizophrenia symptoms than patients with no history (means = 19.37 and 24.39 years, respectively), whereas patients with a recent history of alcohol abuse (mean = 21.26 years) did not differ significantly from either group.

Subsequent exploratory MANOVAs included age at onset of schizophrenia symptoms as a covariate in analyses examining the relationship between history of alcohol use disorder and expectancies (AEEQ, MEEQ, CEEQ) or motives for use (DMM, DUMM). The results were significantly different for only one of these five MANOVAs: the multivariate effect for history of alcohol use and the AEEQ was no longer statistically significant ($p < 0.2$). A minor difference was that the multivariate effect for the MEEQ was only marginally significant ($p = 0.07$), whereas when age at onset of schizophrenia symptoms was not included as a covariate, the effect was significant at the $p < 0.05$ level. These findings suggest that differences in age at onset of schizophrenia symptoms did not mediate the observed relationships between history of alcohol abuse, and expectancies and motives for use.

DISCUSSION

The internal reliabilities of the expectancy and motives were satisfactory for all subscales. These findings are consistent with other reports of the internal reliability or item coherence within a scale (based on factor analysis) in the general population and among primary substance abusers (Brown et al. 1987; Schafer and Brown 1991; Cooper et al. 1992b). These data are, to our knowledge, the first reliability reports for these measures in a schizophrenia population or, for that matter, a primary psychiatric population. Future research on these instruments needs to examine their test-retest reliability to determine whether they measure stable, trait-like dimensions, as hypothesized by expectancy and motive theories of substance use.

Analyses examining the relationship between alcohol or drug use disorder and expectancies and motives for substance use provide some support for the validity of the expectancies and motives measures. Patients with a history of alcohol use disorders reported higher expectancies for the effects of substances and more motives for using substances than did patients with no such history. These effects were consistent across the subscales of the AEEQ, but were present for only one of six MEEQ subscales and for none of the CEEQ subscales. Regarding a history of drug use disorders, an opposite pattern emerged, with effects present across four of the five CEEQ subscales, less consistent across the MEEQ subscales (three of the six), and present for none of the AEEQ subscales. The differential association between substance abuse and the expectancies for effects of different substances is particularly noteworthy considering the overlap of patients with alcohol and drug use disorders. Thus, there was an association between a history of alcohol or drug use disorder and an elevation in expectancies for those same substances.

The finding that schizophrenia patients with a history of alcohol or drug use disorder endorsed stronger expectations for the effects of those substances is consistent with prior studies on persons with a primary substance use disorder (Brown et al. 1985, 1987; Schafer and Brown 1991). Previous studies, however, have not measured multiple substance use histories or multiple expectancies; therefore, they have not provided evidence for true substance-specific effects (i.e., expectancies for one type of substance related to a history of use of that substance but not of another substance). For example, the finding that alcohol expectancies in this sample were related to a history of alcohol use disorder but not of drug use disorder is evidence in support of a substance-specific association. Additional research on the expectancies of groups of patients who do not overlap in their alcohol or drug use histories (e.g., comparisons of patients with a history of alcohol abuse but not of drug abuse with patients with a history of drug abuse but not of alcohol abuse) would provide further support for the specificity of expectations for different types of substances. Such an analysis could not be conducted in the present study because of the limited sample size.

Higher motives for using alcohol (DMM) were related to a history of both alcohol and drug use disorders. The parallel version we employed to assess drug use motives (DUMM) was also related to both alcohol and drug use disorders in the expected direction. Thus, in contrast to the pattern for expectancies, substance-specific effects for motives were not observed. Cooper et al. (1992a) reported that the DMM was related to a history of alcohol use symptoms in the general population. Our data raise the possibility that motives for using drugs are related to symptoms of alcohol abuse. However, these data must be interpreted with caution because the validity of the measure of motives for drug use employed here (DUMM) has not yet been established. Furthermore, the overlap between the alcohol and drug use disorder groups may have made it less likely to detect substance-specific motives on these measures. Nevertheless, the differential pattern of associations between the expectancies and motives scales and a history of substance use disorder supports the distinctiveness of these two constructs. In addition, it raises the question of whether the assessment of expectancies for the effects of alcohol and drugs might mediate the use of specific substances.

These findings raise questions about the relationship between motives, expectancies, and substance use behavior in patients with schizophrenia. One hypothesis is that motives are the driving or proximate explanation underlying substance use, whereas expectations are correlated with the specific types of substances used. It is interesting that socialization, coping, and pleasure-enhancement motives were all strongly related to a history of alcohol use disorders, whereas only coping motives were strongly related to a history of drug abuse. Cooper et al. (1992a) reported in a large community sample that drinking to cope with negative emotions was more strongly associated with alcohol-related problems than was drinking for socialization or pleasure enhancement. The present data suggest that in schizophrenia, a similar relationship is found between drug use motivated by coping with negative emotions and drug-related problems. At the same time, while problematic drug use may be primarily motivated by efforts to cope, patients are aware of (and develop expectancies for) a range of other positive (as well as negative) effects of drug use. The results reported here are consistent with the hypothesis that motives are the more proximate determinant of substance use behavior, although the data are not well suited to evaluate this possibility.

Examination of demographic and clinical correlates of substance use disorders revealed few significant associations, perhaps partly because of the modest sample size. The one significant finding, out of 10 statistical analyses indicating that age at onset of schizophrenia symptoms was earlier in patients with a history of alcohol use disorders, could simply be a chance finding. Other data on age at onset of schizophrenia and alcoholism are mixed, with some studies finding an earlier onset in patients with alcohol use disorders (Alterman et al. 1982, 1984) but most reporting no differences (Bernadt and Murray 1986; Hays and Aidroos 1986; Barbee et al. 1989; Mueser et al. 1990). Regardless of the replicability of this result, inclusion of age at onset as a covariate in analyses examining the relationship between a history of alcohol use disorder and expectations and motives resulted in few changes, suggesting that age at onset was not a critical mediating variable.

Patients with a history of recent or past alcohol use disorders reported more problems related to the use of drugs or alcohol on the MAST and MDST than did patients with no such history. Similarly, patients with past or recent drug use disorders also had elevations on the MAST and MDST. Previous research on the MAST with a schizophrenia sample has also shown that self-reported problems related to alcohol are associated with a history of alcohol use disorders (McHugo et al. 1993). Evidence that a history of alcohol or drug use disorders is associated with problems for both the same and a different substance type reflects the high rate of comorbidity for alcohol and drug use disorders in this sample. This is in line with findings from other surveys of substance use disorders in schizophrenia (Mueser et al. 1990; Regier et al. 1990). Since the same pattern of results was observed for both the MAST and the MDST, these data suggest that the MDST, developed for the purpose of this study, may have the same properties (i.e., validity) as the MAST. The MDST results reported here, however, are in need of replication.

Our data suggest that in schizophrenia and schizoaffective disorder, where there is a high rate of both alcohol and drug use disorders, strong substance-specific expectations may be present. That is, experience with the distinct effects of different substances may cause divergent expectancies to develop, which may play a role in subsequent use (and abuse) of those substances. In contrast, motives appear associated with either an alcohol or a drug use disorder, suggesting that they do not play a role in substance choice. Similarly, self-reported problems were related nonspecifically to both expectancies and motives. These data suggest that expectancy and motive questionnaires, although developed for the primary substance abuse population, may be valid for psychiatric populations. Research on motives and expectancies may help to clarify the functions of substance use in persons with schizophrenia, leading to better treatments. For example, patients whose primary substance abuse is motivated by attempts to cope with negative affect may benefit from learning alternative strategies for coping with these negative feelings, whereas patients whose substance abuse is primarily motivated by social facilitation may require help establishing different social networks or social skills for resisting overtures to use drugs or alcohol. In this sense, identifying individual differences in expectancies and motives may lead to the development of more targeted interventions for substance use disorders in this population.

REFERENCES

Alterman, A.I.; Ayres, F.R.; and Williford, W.O. Diagnostic validation of conjoint schizophrenia and alcoholism. *Journal of Clinical Psychiatry,* 45:300-303, 1984.

Alterman, A.I.; Erdlen, D.L.; LaPorte, DJ.; and Erdlen, F.R. Effects of illicit drug use in an inpatient psychiatric population. *Addictive Behaviors,* 7:231-242, 1982.

American Psychiatric Association. *DSM-III-R: Diagnostic and Statistical Manual of Mental Disorders.* 3rd ed., revised. Washington, DC: The Association, 1987.

Barbee, J.G.; Clark, P.D.; Crapanzano, M.S.; Heintz, G.C.; and Kehoe, C.E. Alcohol and substance abuse among schizophrenic patients presenting to an emergency psychiatric service. *Journal of Nervous and Mental Disease,* 177:400-407, 1989.

Bartels, S.J.; Teague, G.B.; Drake, R.E.; Clark, R.E.; Bush, P.W.; and Noordsy, D.L. Substance abuse in schizophrenia: Service utilization and costs. *Journal of Nervous and Mental Disease,* 181:227-232, 1993.

Bernadt, M.W., and Murray, R.M. Psychiatric disorder, drinking, and alcoholism: What are the links? *British Journal of Psychiatry,* 148:393-400, 1986.

Brown, S.A.; Christiansen, B.A.; and Goldman, M.S. The Alcohol Expectancy Questionnaire: An instrument for the assessment of adolescent and adult expectancies. *Journal of Studies on Alcohol,* 48:483-491, 1987.

Brown, S.A.; Goldman, M.S.; and Christiansen, B.A. Do alcohol expectancies mediate drinking patterns of adults? *Journal of Consulting and Clinical Psychology,* 53:512-519, 1985.

Cooper, M.L. Motivations for alcohol use among adolescents: Development and validation of a four-factor model. *Psychological Assessment,* 6:117-128, 1994.

Cooper, M.L.; Russell, M.; Skinner, J.B.; Frone, M.R.; and Mudar, P. Stress and alcohol use: Moderating effects of gender, coping, and alcohol expectancies. *Journal of Abnormal Psychology,* 101:139-152, 1992a.

Cooper, M.L.; Russell, M.; Skinner, J.B.; and Windle, M. Development and validation of a three-dimensional measure of drinking motives. *Psychological Assessment,* 4:123-132, 1992b.

Cox, M., and Klinger, E. A motivational model of alcohol use. *Journal of Abnormal Psychology,* 97:168-180, 1988.

Cuffel, B.J.; Heithoff, K.A.; and Lawson, W. Correlates of patterns of substance abuse among patients with schizophrenia. *Hospital and Community Psychiatry,* 44:247-251, 1993.

Dixon, L.; Haas, G.; Weiden, P.J.; Sweeney, J.; and Frances, A.J. Drug abuse in schizophrenic patients: Clinical correlates and reasons for use. *American Journal of Psychiatry,* 148:224-230, 1991.

Drake, R.E.; Osher, F.C.; Noordsy, D.L.; Hurlbut, S.C.; Teague, G.B.; and Beaudett, M.S. Diagnosis of alcohol use disorders in schizophrenia. *Schizophrenia Bulletin,* 16(1):57-67, 1990.

Drake, R.E.; Osher, F.C.; and Wallach, M.A. Alcohol use and abuse in schizophrenia: A prospective community study. *Journal of Nervous and Mental Disease,* 177:408-414, 1989.

Goldman, M.S. The alcohol expectancy concept: Applications to assessment, prevention, and treatment of alcohol abuse. *Applied and Preventive Psychology,* 3:131-144, 1994.

Hays, P., and Aidroos, N. Alcoholism followed by schizophrenia. *Acta Psychiatrica Scandinavica,* 74:187-189, 1986.

McHugo, G.J.; Paskus, T.S.; and Drake, R.E. Detection of alcoholism in schizophrenia using the MAST. *Alcoholism, Clinical and Experimental Research,* 17:187-191, 1993.

Mueser, K.T.; Yarnold, P.R.; and Bellack, A.S. Diagnostic and demographic correlates of substance abuse in schizophrenia and major affective disorder. *Acta Psychiatrica Scandinavica,* 85:48-55, 1992.

Mueser, K.T.; Yarnold, P.R.; Levinson, D.F.; Singh, H.; Bellack, A.S.; Kee, K.; Morrison, R.L.; and Yadalam, K.G. Prevalence of substance abuse in schizophrenia: Demographic and clinical correlates. *Schizophrenia Bulletin,* 16(1):31-55, 1990.

Noordsy, D.L.; Drake, R.E.; Teague, G.B.; Osher, F.C.; Hurlbut, S.C.; Beaudett, M.S.; and Paskus, T.S. Subjective experiences related to alcohol use among schizophrenics. *Journal of Nervous and Mental Disease,* 179:410-414, 1991.

Regier, D.A.; Farmer, M.E.; Rae, D.S.; Locke, B.Z.; Keith, S.J.; Judd, L.L.; and Goodwin, F.K. Comorbidity of mental disorders with alcohol and other drug abuse: Results from the Epidemiologic Catchment Area (ECA) study. *Journal of the American Medical Association,* 264:2511-2518, 1990.

Schafer, J., and Brown, S.A. Marijuana and cocaine effect expectancies and drug use patterns. *Journal of Consulting and Clinical Psychology,* 59:558-565, 1991.

Selzer, M.L. The Michigan Alcoholism Screening Test: The quest for a new diagnostic instrument. *American Journal of Psychiatry,* 127:1653-1658, 1971.

Shrout, P.E., and Fleiss, J.L. Intraclass correlations: Uses in assessing rater reliability. *Psychological Bulletin,* 86:420-428, 1979.

Skinner, H.A. The Drug Abuse Screening Test. *Addictive Behaviors,* 7:363-371, 1982.

Spitzer, R.L.; Williams, J.B.W.; Gibbon, M.; and First, M.B. *Structured Clinical Interview for DSM-III-R—Patient Edition.* Washington, DC: American Psychiatric Press, 1990.

Test, M.A.; Wallisch, L.S.; Allness, D.J.; and Ripp, K. Substance use in young adults with schizophrenic disorders. *Schizophrenia Bulletin,* 15(3):465-476, 1989.

About the Authors

Kim T. Mueser, Ph.D., is Professor, Departments of Psychiatry and Community and Family Medicine, Dartmouth Medical School, Concord, NH. Pallavi Nishith, Ph.D., is Assistant Research Professor of Psychology, University of Missouri, St. Louis, MO. Joseph I. Tracy, Ph.D., is Associate Professor of Psychiatry. Joanne DeGirolamo, B.A., is Research Assistant, Allegheny University of the Health Sciences, Philadelphia, PA. Max Molinaro, M.Ed., is Staff Psychologist, Catch, Inc., Philadelphia, PA.

Acknowledgments

Portions of this research were presented at the 27th Annual Convention of the Association for the Advancement of Behavior Therapy in Atlanta, GA, in 1994 and at the Conference on Comorbidity Between Psychiatric Disorders and Addictive Behavior in Hamburg, Germany, in 1993.

The authors thank Jack J. Blanchard for valuable discussions about this topic; Richard C. Josiassen for providing access to patients and staff at the MCP Research Unit at Norristown State Hospital; Sandra K. Brown for the expectancy scales; Lynne Cooper for information concerning administration of the Drinking Motives Measures; and Janet Holec, Sylvia Gratz, Linda Roth, and Ruthanne Vendy for their help in other aspects of the study.

Reprinted with permission from *Schizophrenia Bulletin*.

MODERATE DRINKING AMONG PEOPLE WITH SEVERE MENTAL ILLNESS

Robert E. Drake and Michael A. Wallach

Reprinted from *Hospital and Community Psychiatry*, 44(8):780-782, 1993

Along with the increased recognition of substance abuse in the community mental health field, a clinical controversy about the advisability of moderate drinking for persons who have severe mental illnesses has developed. Many clinicians argue that mentally ill individuals should be able to drink moderately, as do the majority of Americans (1). Other clinicians argue that severely mentally ill persons should be encouraged to pursue abstinence because they are extremely sensitive to the negative effects of alcohol and highly prone to develop an alcohol use disorder.

The dearth of research data about the effects of moderate drinking for this population undoubtedly contributes to the controversy. Longitudinal data about the maintenance of moderate drinking would be particularly helpful in psychoeducational work with clients and their families. Mentally ill clients have the same legal right to drink as other citizens, but they and their families deserve to have accurate information on the consequences of moderate drinking.

The purpose of this report is to evaluate the long-term stability and consequences of moderate drinking among severely mentally ill persons by examining longitudinal ratings of alcohol use from two independent clinical groups. The clinical controversy about moderate drinking was conceptualized in terms of competing hypotheses. On one hand, if moderate drinking is a realistic lifestyle choice for severely mentally ill persons, a large proportion of moderate drinkers should be able to sustain regular drinking without adverse consequences over time. On the other hand, if moderate alcohol consumption is an unrealistic choice for severely mentally ill persons, only a small proportion should stay at that level of drinking over time, while many who appeared to be moderate drinkers should show evidence of abuse over longitudinal follow-up.

METHODS

Study groups

The study groups were drawn from clients with severe and persistent mental disorders at two separate mental health centers, one urban and the other rural. The urban group, studied originally in 1983 and described in detail elsewhere (2,3), consisted of 187 severely mentally ill clients who had been discharged from an urban state hospital to a comprehensive case management team. At the time of the initial evaluation, the mean±SD age of the subjects was 40.1±12.1 years. More than half (55 percent) were male. Their major primary diagnoses were schizophrenia (61 percent) and bipolar disorder (20 percent).

At follow-up seven years later, in 1990-91, a total of 170 clients (91 percent) were traced. Fifteen of the 170 clients (9 percent) were deceased, seven of the clients or their clinicians (4 percent) declined to participate, and 148 clients (87 percent) cooperated fully. Thus we obtained complete follow-up information on 86 percent (148 of 172) of the clients not known to be deceased (4).

The rural group, originally studied in 1987 and also described in detail elsewhere (5,6), consisted of 75 schizophrenic outpatients in a community mental health center. Their mean±SD age was 43.6±14.3 years. Slightly more than half (52 percent) were female.

At follow-up four years later, in 1991, 73 of the clients (97 percent) were traced. Seven of the 73 (10 percent) were deceased, three of the clients or their clinicians (4 percent) refused to participate, and 63 (86 percent) cooperated fully. Thus complete follow-up information was obtained for 93 percent of the rural clients not known to be deceased (7).

Procedures

Clients in the two study groups were assessed by their case managers for alcohol use at two points in time, the original evaluation and the follow-up evaluation four or seven years later. Alcohol use was assessed by the Case Manager Rating Scale (CMRS), developed as a research instrument for use by clinicians to rate the extent of alcohol-related problems over at least the previous six months among severely ill clients in the community (5). The scale includes five categories with descriptive anchors: abstinence, nonproblematic (or moderate) drinking, alcohol abuse, alcohol dependence, and severe alcohol dependence. Moderate drinking is defined as the use of alcohol without persistent or recurring social, vocational, medical, or psychological consequences. Abuse and dependence are defined in terms of *DSM-III-R* criteria. The CMRS has high reliability and validity (5).

All case managers were individually trained to use the CMRS. Follow-up ratings of recent alcohol use were based on use in the previous six months. To further check on longitudinal course of drinking and because some clients may become abstinent for reasons other than loss of control, we interviewed the clients from the rural setting who had been moderate drinkers at the initial evaluation and their case managers about the clients' lifetime drinking histories.

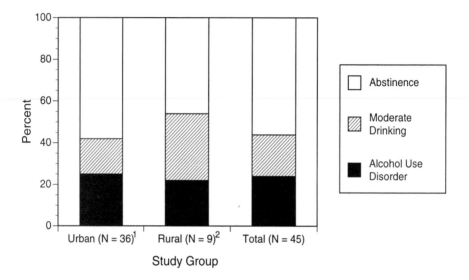

[1]Assessed seven years after initial evaluation
[2]Assessed four years after initial evaluation

Figure 1. Alcohol-use status at follow-up of severely mentally ill persons who were moderate drinkers at initial evaluation

RESULTS

At the time of the original evaluation, 36 of the 148 available severely mentally ill clients in the urban group (24 percent) were rated as moderate drinkers, and nine of the 63 available schizophrenic clients in the rural sample (14 percent) were so rated. Figure 1 shows the status of these 45 clients at follow-up. More than half of these originally moderate drinkers (55.6 percent) were abstinent at follow-up. Approximately one in four (24.4 percent) manifested an alcohol use disorder, and only one in five (20 percent) was still drinking moderately. Overall, less than 5 percent of the clients in both study groups (six of 148 and three of 63, respectively) appeared to sustain moderate drinking during the two evaluation intervals.

Follow-up interviews with the nine rural subjects who had been moderate drinkers at initial evaluation and with their case managers confirmed that two clients had developed alcohol use disorders between the two evaluations and were actively abusing alcohol during the six-month follow-up interval. Three additional clients were classified as abstinent at follow-up but had evidence of alcohol abuse occurring outside the two assessment intervals. The four who persisted as moderate drinkers all drank infrequently and in ritualized fashion—for example, one glass of wine with dinner on Saturday nights. Thus, none of the nine clients in this study group actually maintained regular drinking over time without evidence of alcohol-related problems.

DISCUSSION

A large proportion of Americans in the general population drink alcohol regularly without developing abuse or dependence (1,8). In contrast, less than 5 percent of the severely mentally ill persons in each of the two study groups sustained nonproblematic drinking over two separate six-month assessment intervals. Follow-up interviews with one study group indicated that the actual proportion who sustained moderate drinking over time may have been considerably less than 5 percent.

Large proportions of moderate drinkers in these two groups became nondrinkers over time, perhaps because they experienced alcohol-related problems outside of the two assessment intervals. Moreover, clients who drank moderately at the initial evaluation but did not choose abstinence were highly likely to develop an alcohol use disorder.

Alcohol has many short-term and long-term effects that may interact with severe mental illness, which may account for its potency in this population. For example, alcohol use rapidly produces disinhibition, aggression, and poor judgment (9)—difficulties that often accompany severe mental illness—and may be worsened in clients who drink. In animals, alcohol use has direct neurotoxic effects in the hippocampus, mammillary bodies, cerebral cortex, and cerebellar cortex, and chronic alcohol use produces cortical atrophy in humans (10). Many of these effects overlap with areas of brain dysfunction found in severe mental illness.

Mental health programs typically focus on the disorder of alcoholism rather than on moderate drinking. Because many clients attempt to drink moderately, further research should focus on the consequences of this lifestyle choice. Our data indicate that moderate drinking is only rarely a stable long-term strategy and that what in a cross-sectional study appears to be nonproblematic drinking often becomes an alcohol use disorder when viewed over the long term. Clients seem to become aware of this risk over time, and many adopt abstinence.

Little research has been available on this controversial issue, but it is hoped that these and other empirical data will begin to replace ideological positions. Research evidence may be particularly helpful in psychoeducational activities with severely mentally ill clients and their families.

REFERENCES

1. Hilton ME: Drinking patterns and drinking problems in 1984: results from a general population survey. *Alcoholism: Clinical and Experimental Research* 11:167-175, 1987
2. Drake RE, Wallach MA: Mental patients' attitudes toward hospitalization: a neglected aspect of hospital tenure. *American Journal of Psychiatry* 145:29-34, 1988
3. Drake RE, Wallach MA: Substance abuse among the chronic mentally ill. *Hospital and Community Psychiatry* 40:1041-1046, 1989
4. Bartels SJ, Drake RE, Noordsy DL: A seven-year follow-up of mentally ill substance abusers. Presented at the annual meeting of the American Psychiatric Association, Washington, DC, May 2-7, 1992
5. Drake RE, Osher FC, Noordsy DL, et al: Diagnosis of alcohol use disorders in schizophrenia. *Schizophrenia Bulletin* 16:57-67, 1990
6. Drake RE, Wallach MA, Teague GB, et al: Housing instability and homelessness among rural schizophrenic patients. *American Journal of Psychiatry* 148:330-336, 1991
7. Noordsy DL, Bartels SJ, Drake RE: Treatment of dual disorders: four-year outcomes. Presented at the annual meeting of the American Psychiatric Association, Washington, DC, May 2-7, 1992
8. Vaillant GE: *The Natural History of Alcoholism.* Cambridge, Mass, Harvard University Press, 1983
9. Ciraulo, DA, Renner JA: Alcoholism, in *Clinical Manual of Chemical Dependence.* Edited by Ciraulo DA, Shader RI. Washington, DC, American Psychiatric Press, 1991
10. *Alcohol and Health: Sixth Special Report to the US Congress.* DHHS pub ADM 87-1515. Rockville, MD, National Institute on Alcohol Abuse and Alcoholism, 1987

ABOUT THE AUTHORS

Robert E. Drake, M.D., is Professor of Psychiatry at Dartmouth Medical School, and Michael A. Wallach, Ph.D., is Professor of Psychology at Duke University.

ACKNOWLEDGMENTS

This research was supported by contract 89M007842601D from the National Institute on Alcohol Abuse and Alcoholism and by U.S. Public Health Service grant K02-MH-00839 from the National Institute of Mental Health.

Copyright 1993. The American Psychiatric Association. Reprinted by permission.

FAMILY HISTORY OF ALCOHOLISM IN SCHIZOPHRENIA

Douglas L. Noordsy, Robert E. Drake,
Jeremy C. Biesanz, and Gregory J. McHugo

Reprinted from *Journal of Nervous and Mental Disease,* 182:651-655, 1994

Previous research has shown that family history of alcoholism (FHA) is associated with several aspects of the development and expression of alcohol use disorder in people who are not mentally ill. This study examined FHA in a group of 66 schizophrenic outpatients who were well characterized in terms of their alcohol use and were followed prospectively in treatment for 4 years. The FHA-positive probands (42.4% of the group) were more likely to have alcohol use disorder. Contrary to our prediction, the relationship between FHA and alcoholism in the probands was significant for women but not for men. Among schizophrenic probands with alcoholism, positive FHA was associated with more severe alcoholism and with the use of other drugs. Probands with positive FHA also responded less well to alcoholism treatment than did probands with negative FHA. These exploratory findings have significant implications for understanding risk, for conducting assessment, and for studying treatment, but should be confirmed in larger and more representative samples of people with schizophrenia.

Previous research has established that the presence of a family history of alcoholism (FHA) is associated with the development and expression of alcoholism in people who are not mentally ill. Positive FHA has been correlated with dependence rather than abuse (Goodwin et al., 1973, 1992; Vaillant, 1983). The relationship between FHA and probands' alcohol dependence has sometimes been stronger in men than in women (Kosten et al., 1991; McGue et al., 1992; Pickens et al., 1991). FHA has been related to several other aspects of alcoholism: earlier onset (Penick et al., 1987; Svanum and McAdoo, 1991; Volicer et al., 1985), greater severity (Latcham, 1985; McKenna and Pickens, 1981; Schuckit, 1984), more severe course (Penick et al., 1987), poor response to alcoholism treatment (Frances et al., 1984), and co-occurring abuse of other drugs (Alterman, 1988; Schuckit, 1984; Svanum and McAdoo, 1991).

Although people with schizophrenia have a threefold increased risk of developing alcohol use disorder relative to people who are not mentally ill (Regier et al., 1990), little is known about the relationships between FHA and alcoholism in schizophrenia. Kendler and Tsuang (1988) found an association between FHA and schizophrenic probands' divorced marital status, but did not examine their alcohol status. Caton et al. (1989) found a significant correlation between probands' substance abuse and parental substance abuse among young mentally ill patients, but only 21% had diagnoses of schizophrenia.

The purpose of this study was to examine several hypotheses, derived from previous research on nonschizophrenic samples, regarding FHA in a group of schizophrenic outpatients who were well characterized for alcohol use. The specific hypotheses were:

1. FHA is positively associated with alcohol use disorder among schizophrenic probands.
2. The association between FHA and alcoholism is stronger among schizophrenic men than among schizophrenic women.
3. Among alcoholic, schizophrenic probands, FHA is associated with: a) earlier age of onset of alcoholism; b) greater severity of alcoholism; c) more severe psychiatric symptoms; d) poorer psychosocial functioning; e) greater use of other drugs of abuse; and f) poorer response to alcoholism treatment.

METHODS

Study group

The potential subjects for this study were 75 outpatients who participated in a previous study of alcohol use in schizophrenia (Drake et al., 1990; Noordsy et al., 1991; Osher et al., 1994). Schizophrenia diagnoses were determined according to DSM-III-R criteria (American Psychiatric Association, 1987), based on direct interviews and a review of records by research psychiatrists. Patients for whom psychotic symptoms appeared only in association with substance use were excluded. Diagnoses of alcohol use disorder were also established according to DSM-III-R criteria. As described in our previous report (Drake et al., 1990), current and lifetime (current plus past disorder in remission) diagnoses were established by combining interview data using the Alcohol Dependence Scale (ADS; Horn et al., 1984), the CAGE (Mayfield et al., 1974), and the Michigan Alcoholism Screening Test (MAST; Selzer, 1971) with clinicians' ratings using the Case Manager Rating Scales (Drake et al., 1990). In addition, subjects were rated by clinicians for other drug use, psychiatric symptoms, and psychosocial adjustment at the time of the original evaluation (Osher et al., 1994).

At 4-year follow-up in 1991, we assessed family history of alcoholism in 66 of the 75 subjects. We were unable to obtain family history data on two deceased subjects who had no known relatives, one subject who was lost to follow-up, and six subjects who did not have information on both biological parents.

The study group of 66 schizophrenic patients had a mean ± SD age of 42.4 ± 14.2 years at original evaluation in 1987; of the group, 53.0% were men and 47.0% were women. All were non-Hispanic white. Only 15.2% were currently married, 63.6% were single, and 21.2% were separated, divorced, or widowed. Of the 66 patients, 89.4% (N = 59) had a diagnosis of schizophrenia, and 10.6% (N = 7) had a diagnosis of schizoaffective disorder. At baseline in 1987, 54.5% (N = 36) had a lifetime (i.e., current plus past) diagnosis of alcohol use disorder, and 25.8% (N = 17) had a current diagnosis of alcohol use disorder. At 4-year follow-up, 10.6% (N = 7) had current alcohol use disorder.

Procedures and measures

All subjects were followed up in 1991, 4 years after their initial evaluation, using similar methods of structured interview and clinician ratings. Most of the subjects (86.4%) were interviewed directly to assess family history; family interviews were used to assess family history on five deceased subjects and on four subjects who were too disorganized to be reliably interviewed. Family history of alcoholism was assessed using the family history section of the Addiction Severity Index (McLellan et al., 1992). McLellan and colleagues (personal communication, 1992) have reported good test-retest reliability and a high correlation between subjects' reports and those of a close relative with this instrument. The instrument assesses family history of alcoholism, drug abuse, and other psychiatric disorders in first- and second-degree biological relatives of the proband. Subjects are asked whether each relative had "a significant drinking... problem, one that did, or should have, led to treatment," and a positive FHA is coded only if the response is "clearly yes" (McLellan et al., 1990). We used the parental method of classifying FHA, in which subjects with at least one alcoholic parent are classified as FHA-positive (Alterman, 1988). The parental method is generally the most reliable classification of FHA (Mann et al., 1985) and, in this study, maximized size of the group, since several subjects were unable to provide complete data on second-degree relatives.

RESULTS

Twenty-eight (42.4%) of the schizophrenic probands reported at least one parent with alcoholism and were therefore classified as FHA-positive. Positive FHA was associated with alcoholism in probands, both current ($\chi^2 =$

Table 1. Rates of alcohol use disorder among schizophrenic outpatients with and without parental history of alcoholism

Assessment Interval	Proband Alcohol Use Disorder						χ^2 (df)
	None		Abuse		Dependence		
	N	%	N	%	N	%	
Lifetime							
Parental FHA negative	22	73.3	8	61.5	8	34.8	8.03 (2)*
Parental FHA positive	8	26.7	5	38.5	15	65.2	
Current							
Parental FHA negative	32	65.3	5	62.5	1	11.1	9.23 (2)**
Parental FHA positive	17	34.7	3	37.5	8	88.9	

*p < .05; **p < .01

4.65, 1 *df, p* <.05) and lifetime (χ^2 = 5.59, 1 *df, p* <.05). The influence of maternal alcoholism could not be separated from paternal alcoholism because there were so few cases in which the mother was alcoholic and the father was not. When both parents were alcoholic, eight of nine probands (88.9%) had alcohol use disorders.

As shown in Table 1, positive FHA was associated with alcohol dependence rather than alcohol abuse. Table 2 indicates that alcoholism was significantly associated with positive FHA among women but not among men.

Family history of alcoholism was not associated with age of onset in the 36 probands who developed alcoholism. The probands with positive FHA reported an average ± SD age of onset of 21.7 ± 8.1 years, as opposed to 23.0 ± 7.6 years for those without a parental history (t[34] = .49, NS). The association was nonsignificant for each gender.

Table 3 shows the relationship between FHA and measures of the severity of probands' alcoholism among those 36 probands who had a lifetime alcohol use disorder. Alcoholic probands with a positive FHA had significantly higher mean scores on the ADS and the MAST, and nonsignificantly higher scores on the CAGE and Case Manager Rating Scales. An

Table 2. Parental alcoholism history and proband lifetime alcoholism diagnosis by gender

| | Parental FHA | | | | | |
| | Negative (N = 38) | | Positive (N = 28) | | | |
Probands	N	%	N	%	χ^2 (1 df)	Phi
Males (N = 35)						
Alcoholic	10	55.6	12	70.6	0.85	.16
Not alcoholic	8	44.4	5	29.4		
Females (N = 31)						
Alcoholic	6	30.0	8	72.7	5.23*	.41*
Not alcoholic	14	70.0	3	27.3		

* $p < .05$

Table 3. Relationships between parental history and alcoholism severity measures among schizophrenics with alcoholism (N = 36)

| | Parental FHA | | | | |
| | Negative | | Positive | | |
Variable	Mean	SD	Mean	SD	t (df)
ADS	2.00	2.85	7.55	10.64	-2.23 (22.3)[a]*
MAST	14.00	11.30	25.75	12.05	-2.99 (34)**
CAGE	2.13	1.36	2.50	1.36	- .82 (34)
Case Manager Rating Scale					
Lifetime	3.38	1.31	4.00	1.12	-1.54 (34)
Current	2.00	1.03	2.60	1.39	-1.44 (34)

[a]Degrees of freedom reduced by separate variance estimate for each group.
* $p < .05$; ** $p < .01$

analysis of variance was used to test for any influence of gender on this relationship. Although there was a weak association between male gender and higher mean scores on the ADS and MAST, no interaction between gender and family history was found. Family history of alcoholism was also associated with the lifetime use of other drugs of abuse, both for the entire study group ($t[64] = 2.69$, $p < .01$) and for probands with alcoholism ($t[30] = 2.05$, $p = .02$). On the other hand, FHA was not significantly related to clinicians' ratings of psychiatric symptoms (multivariate analysis of variance: $F[10,25] = 1.40$, NS) or psychosocial problems (multivariate analysis of variance: $F[8,27] = 1.43$, NS) among alcoholic patients.

At the time of initial evaluation in 1987, 17 subjects in this sample had a current alcohol use disorder (following DSM-III-R, defined as active abuse within the previous 6 months). After 4 years of active dual diagnosis treatment, many of these patients were stably in remission (Drake et al., 1993). However, only 5 of the 11 FHA-positive probands (45.5%) achieved remission, while 5 of the 6 FHA-negative probands (83.3%) did so. These numbers are too small for statistical analysis, but certainly suggest a possible effect of FHA on treatment success.

DISCUSSION

This exploratory study suggests that FHA is a significant contributing factor in the development of alcohol use disorder among schizophrenic outpatients. Since the rate of alcoholism was high, even among FHA-negative probands, our data suggest that schizophrenia and FHA may represent additive factors that contribute to the risk of alcoholism. Our findings are consistent with the model of additive, independent risk factors for alcoholism proposed by Stabenau (1990). The exact nature of transmission represented by FHA remains uncertain (Schuckit, 1994).

One surprising finding in this study was the interaction between FHA and gender. Schizophrenic men in our study group had a high rate of alcoholism that was increased, but not significantly, in relation to FHA, whereas schizophrenic women had a much lower rate of alcoholism when they were FHA-negative but a high rate when they were FHA-positive. This gender-specific finding is contrary to research in nonschizophrenic samples, and may be an artifact due to the small study group size. The relative contributions of schizophrenia, FHA, and gender to probands' alcoholism should be investigated in larger samples.

There may be two groups of alcoholic, schizophrenic patients—one characterized by extreme psychiatric vulnerability on exposure to small amounts of alcohol and the other, more typical group characterized by heavier drinking and the dependence syndrome (Bartels et al., in press). In our data, positive FHA was related to dependence rather than abuse, to measures of severity of alcoholism, and to the use of other drugs. The FHA-negative group had an extremely low average score on the ADS, both in relation to the FHA-positive patients and in relation to established norms on this instrument, indicating that they had few signs of the alcohol dependence syndrome. These findings suggest that use patterns and the dependence syndrome may be different in FHA-positive and FHA-negative patients with co-occurring schizophrenia and alcohol use disorder. However, even the FHA-positive alcoholic patients in this study scored in the low range on the ADS while scoring moderately high on the MAST, CAGE, and Case Manager Rating Scales, consistent with the view that many schizophrenic patients develop alcohol-related adverse consequences with relatively small amounts of use before they develop the full alcohol dependence syndrome. The hypothetical dichotomy (or perhaps continuum) between two groups of alcoholic, schizophrenic patients should be investigated further to clarify possible differences in FHA, expression, and treatment response.

The possible relationship between FHA and treatment response is particularly intriguing. It raises the possibility that different treatment strategies might be appropriate for FHA-positive and FHA-negative patients in this population. The influence of FHA on treatment is, however, confounded with severity of alcoholism and other factors in this small study group. The relationship between FHA and treatment response should be investigated in larger samples in which other prognostic factors can be controlled for statistically.

This report represents an exploratory study on a small group of schizophrenic outpatients. The failure to find significance in several relationships could be due to the small size of the study group, and the positive findings could be due to selection biases related to clinical, rural, or other factors. Another methodological caveat is the use of self-report to establish FHA. Kendler et al. (1991) found that probands are able to recall FHA validly, and Thompson et al. (1982) found that probands identified alcoholism in their relatives more reliably than other psychiatric disorders. These findings have not been verified for schizophrenic patients, but people with schizophrenia have generally been found to give highly reliable responses to personal history questions in structured interviews (Lehman, 1988).

Future research should include larger and nonclinical samples, other diagnostic groups, as well as non-mentally ill comparison groups, and multiple methods of collecting family data. Since our study points toward several hypotheses that have implications for risk, assessment, and treatment, all of these issues should be studied in greater depth. For example, if FHA proves to be a strong risk factor in schizophrenic women, it should be helpful in the difficult process of detection. Similarly, if FHA predicts treatment response in this population, FHA-positive patients should be studied separately to determine effective interventions.

Summary and Conclusions

In this pilot study, self-reported FHA was associated with an increased prevalence of alcoholism among schizophrenic outpatients. The association was significant for females, but not males. Family history of alcoholism was also associated with greater severity of alcoholism, with greater use of other drugs, and possibly with poorer treatment response. These findings should be considered hypotheses for future research; if confirmed, they would have significant implications for understanding risk, for clinical assessment, and for treatment.

References

Alterman AI (1988) Patterns of familial alcoholism, alcoholism severity, and psychopathology. *Journal of Nervous & Mental Disease* 176:167-175.

American Psychiatric Association (1987) *Diagnostic and statistical manual of mental disorders* (3rd ed, revd). Washington, DC: Author.

Bartels SJ, Drake RE, Wallach MA (in press) Long-term course of substance use disorders in severe mental illness. *Hospital and Community Psychiatry.*

Caton CLM, Gralnick A, Bender S, Simon R (1989) Young chronic patients and substance abuse. *Hospital and Community Psychiatry* 40:1037-1040.

Drake RE, McHugo GM, Noordsy DL (1993) A pilot study of outpatient treatment of alcoholism in schizophrenia: Four-year outcomes. *American Journal of Psychiatry* 150:328-329.

Drake RE, Osher FC, Noordsy DL, Hurlbut SC, Teague GB, Beaudett MS (1990) Diagnosis of alcohol use disorders in schizophrenia. *Schizophrenia Bulletin* 16:57-67.

Frances RJ, Bucky S, Alexopoulos GS (1984) Outcome study of familial and nonfamilial alcoholism. *American Journal of Psychiatry* 141:1469-1471.

Goodwin DW, Penick E, Gabrielli W, Jensen P, Knop J, Schulsinger F (1992, May 7) *Thirty-year follow-up of sons of alcoholics.* Presented at the American Psychiatric Association annual meeting, Washington, DC.

Goodwin DW, Schulsinger F, Hermansen L, Guze SB, Winokur G (1973) Alcohol problems in adoptees raised apart from alcoholic biological parents. *Archives of General Psychiatry* 28:238-243.

Horn JL, Skinner HA, Wanberg KW, Foster FM (1984) *Alcohol Dependence Scale* (ADS). Toronto: Addiction Research Foundation of Ontario.

Kendler KS, Silberg JL, Neale MC, Kessler RC, Health AC, Eaves LJ (1991) The family history method: Whose psychiatric history is measured? *American Journal of Psychiatry* 148:1501-1504.

Kendler KS, Tsuang MT (1988) Outcome and familial psychopathology in schizophrenia. *Archives of General Psychiatry* 45:338-346.

Kosten TR, Rounsaville BJ, Kosten TA, Merikangas K (1991) Gender differences in the specificity of alcoholism transmission among the relatives of opioid addicts. *Journal of Nervous & Mental Disease* 179:392-400.

Latcham RW (1985) Familial alcoholism: Evidence from 237 alcoholics. *British Journal of Psychiatry* 147:54-57.

Lehman AF (1988) A quality of life interview for the chronically mentally ill. *Evaluation & Program Planning* 11:51-62.

Mann RE, Sobell LC, Sobell MB, Pavan D (1985) Reliability of a family tree questionnaire for assessing family history of alcohol problems. *Drug & Alcohol Dependence* 15:61-67.

Mayfield D, McCleod G, Hall P (1974) The CAGE questionnaire: Validation of a new alcoholism screening questionnaire. *American Journal of Psychiatry* 131:1121-1123.

McGue M, Pickens RW, Svikis DS (1992) Sex and age effects on the inheritance of alcohol problems: A twin study. *Journal of Abnormal Psychology* 101:3-17.

McKenna T, Pickens R (1981) Alcoholic children of alcoholics. *Journal of Studies on Alcohol* 42:1021-1029.

McLellan AT, Kushner H, Metzger D, Peters R, Smith I, Grissom G, Pettinati H, Argeriou M (1992) The fifth edition of the Addiction Severity Index. *Journal of Substance Abuse Treatment* 9:199-213.

McLellan AT, Luborsky L, O'Brien CP, Woody GE (1990) The *Addiction Severity Index* (5th ed). Philadelphia: Penn-VA Center for Studies of Addiction.

Noordsy DL, Drake RE, Osher FC, Teague GB, Hurlbut SC, Beaudett MS (1991) Subjective experiences related to alcohol use among schizophrenics. *Journal of Nervous & Mental Disease* 179:410-414.

Osher FC, Drake RE, Noordsy DL, Teague GB, Hurlbut SC, Biesanz J, Beaudett MS (1994) Correlates and outcomes of alcohol use disorder among rural schizophrenic outpatients. *Journal of Clinical Psychiatry* 55:109-113.

Penick EC, Powell BJ, Bingham SF, Liskow BI, Miller NS, Read MR (1987) A comparative study of familial alcoholism. *Journal of Studies on Alcohol* 48:136-145.

Pickens RW, Svikis DS, McGue M, Lykken DT, Heston LL, Clayton PJ (1991) Heterogeneity in the inheritance of alcoholism: A study of male and female twins. *Archives of General Psychiatry* 48:19-28.

Regier DA, Farmer ME, Rae DS, Locke BZ, Keith SJ, Judd LL, Goodwin FK (1990) Comorbidity of mental disorders with alcohol and other drug abuse. *Journal of the American Medical Association* 264:2511-2518.

Schuckit MA (1984) Relationship between the course of primary alcoholism in men and family history. *Journal of Studies on Alcohol* 45(4):334-338.

Schuckit MA (1994) A clinical model of genetic influences in alcohol dependence. *Journal of Studies on Alcohol* 55:5-17.

Selzer ML (1971) The Michigan Alcoholism Screening Test. The quest for a new diagnostic instrument. *American Journal of Psychiatry* 127:89-94.

Stabenau JR (1990) Additive independent factors that predict risk for alcoholism. *Journal of Studies on Alcohol* 51:164-174.

Svanum S, McAdoo WG (1991) Parental alcoholism: An examination of male and female alcoholics in treatment. *Journal of Studies on Alcohol* 52:127-132.

Thompson WD, Orvaschel H, Prusoff BA, Kidd KK (1982) An evaluation of the family history method for ascertaining psychiatric disorders. *Archives of General Psychiatry* 39:53-58.

Vaillant GE (1983) *The natural history of alcoholism.* Cambridge, MA: Harvard University Press.

Volicer L, Volicer B, D'Angelo N (1985) Assessment of genetic predisposition to alcoholism in male alcoholics. *Alcohol and Alcoholism* 29:63-68.

ABOUT THE AUTHORS

Douglas L. Noordsy, M.D., is Medical Director of The Mental Health Center of Greater Manchester, Manchester, NH, and is also Assistant Professor of Psychiatry at Dartmouth Medical School and Research Associate at the New Hampshire-Dartmouth Psychiatric Research Center, Concord, NH. Robert E. Drake, M.D., Ph.D., and Gregory J. McHugo, Ph.D., are affiliated with the New Hampshire-Dartmouth Psychiatric Research Center, Concord, NH. Jeremy Biesanz, B.A., is a graduate student in psychology at the University of Arizona.

ACKNOWLEDGMENTS

This work was supported by U.S. Public Health Service grants R18-MH-46072 from SAMSHA, K02-MH-00839 from NIMH, and R01-AA-08341 from NIAAA.

Reprinted with permission from *Journal of Nervous and Mental Disease.*

RISK FACTORS FOR HOMELESSNESS AMONG SCHIZOPHRENIC MEN: A CASE-CONTROL STUDY

Carol L. M. Caton, Patrick E. Shrout, Paula F. Eagle, Lewis A. Opler, Alan Felix, and Boanerges Dominguez

Reprinted from *American Journal of Public Health.* 84:265-270, 1994

Objectives. To identify risk factors for homelessness among the severely mentally ill, we conducted a case-control study of 100 indigent schizophrenic men meeting criteria for literal homelessness and 100 such men with no homeless history.

Methods. Subjects were recruited from shelter, clinic, and inpatient psychiatric programs in Upper Manhattan. Clinical interviewers employed standardized research instruments to probe three domains of risk factors: severity of mental illness, family background, and prior mental health service use.

Results. Homeless subjects showed significantly higher levels of positive symptoms, higher rates of a concurrent diagnosis of drug abuse, and higher rates of antisocial personality disorder. Homeless subjects experienced greater disorganization in family settings from birth to 18 years and less adequate current family support. Fewer homeless subjects than subjects in the never-homeless comparison group had a long-term therapist. These differences remained when demographic variables were adjusted statistically.

Conclusions. Homeless schizophrenic men differed from their domiciled counterparts in all three domains we investigated: family background, nature of illness, and service use history. Findings are discussed in relation to policy and programs for the severely mentally ill.

INTRODUCTION

A recent governmental report estimates that 1 in 20 of the severely mentally ill experience homelessness.[1] Using different definitions of homelessness or housing instability, empirical studies of state mental hospital constituents have found that from 9% to 28% have been homeless.[2-4] The crisis nature of homelessness, both for the individual and for society, demands a clearer understanding of why some of the severely mentally ill become homeless while others do not.

Previous studies in which differences between the homeless and the residentially stable have been explored suggest that the homeless have more psychiatric disorders meeting standard diagnostic criteria[5,6] and higher rates of hospitalization and arrest.[5,7] Studies focused on defined psychiatric populations have found that the homeless are more likely to abuse alcohol[3,8] and/or drugs,[3,4,6] have higher symptom levels,[3,7,8] and are less likely to comply with prescribed treatments.[3,8] The use of different definitions of homelessness, the employment of varied approaches to the assessment of psychiatric disorder, and the selection of different subgroups of the homeless population in these investigations limit their generalizability.

Attempts to identify areas of differences between the homeless and the never homeless outside of the illness domain are more limited. Studies of childhood antecedents of adult homelessness have revealed that homelessness (or its duration) is associated with placement in foster care[9,10] or group homes,[10] physical abuse,[9] and runaway episodes.[10] Although the breakdown of family ties has been thought to play a role in the genesis of homelessness, perceptions of the kinship bond in adulthood have not been found to be as important as patient characteristics in distinguishing the homeless from the nonhomeless.

In spite of the discourse on deinstitutionalization of mental health services as a possible factor in homelessness among the severely mentally ill,[11,12] the service use histories of homeless and never-homeless persons have not been compared with regard to access to and utilization of community-based treatment and support services. Although the literature suggests that multiple factors may separate the homeless from the never homeless, there has been no prior attempt to incorporate multiple risk factors into a single study.

We recently completed a case-control study of indigent schizophrenic men in New York City designed to test hypotheses about differences between the homeless and never-homeless mentally ill. To facilitate an adequate test of hypotheses about differences between the homeless and never homeless, we elected to focus our study on a homogeneous group of indigent adults suffering from schizophrenia. Schizophrenia is the most common diagnosis leading to chronic mental illness[13] and is widely prevalent among those living in shelters.[1,14,15] Because four of five homeless adults are male,[16] it is possible that pathways to homelessness are gender-specific. Therefore, our sample was stratified by gender. Findings from our study of women will be reported later.

We probed three domains of influence on homelessness: severity of illness, family background, and prior mental health service use. We hypothesized that schizophrenic men who became homeless would have poorer pre-illness social functioning, higher levels of the positive and negative symptoms of schizophrenia, greater abuse of drugs and alcohol, and more antisocial personality disorder. In addition, we hypothesized that the homeless would have experienced greater family disorganization in childhood, would have imposed a greater caretaker burden after becoming mentally ill, and would have less current family support. Finally, we hypothesized that the homeless would be less adherent to prescribed treatment and would have less help from the mental health system in finding adequate housing and procuring long-term follow-up care.

METHODS

We employed a case-control design with 100 men in the (sheltered) homeless group and 100 men in the never-homeless group. All 200 subjects had experienced at least one psychiatric hospitalization and were between the ages of 18 and 44 years. To be eligible for inclusion, the men were required to meet DSM-III-R criteria for schizophrenia or schizoaffective disorder, determined through a research diagnostic interview, the Structured Clinical Interview for DSM-III-R (SCID).[17] Voluntary informed consent was elicited from each subject after a treating clinician attested to the subject's ability to fully comprehend the implications of participation in our research.

Case subjects met criteria for literal homelessness, meaning that they had no fixed abode and were forced to sleep in the street or in shelters.[18] They were recruited by a mental health day treatment program located on-site at a municipal shelter for homeless men in Upper Manhattan.

Control subjects had no lifetime history of literal homelessness, as determined by a screening instrument.[4] They were discharge-ready inpatients or outpatients recruited from Columbia University–affiliated psychiatric services in Upper Manhattan. More than four of five control subjects resided in a family setting, usually with a parent or sibling.

Because Blacks have been found to be overrepresented among the sheltered homeless in New York City,[19] we made every effort to match case and control subjects on ethnicity (Black, White, Hispanic). When we encountered difficulty in finding an adequate number of Black subjects who had never been homeless, we abandoned our matching strategy. Reasons for the paucity of Black never-homeless subjects constitute a topic in need of further study.

A total of 248 men were asked to participate in the study. Eleven (4.4%) refused, and 22 (8.9%) dropped out before completing the interview battery. Four of five dropouts were homeless men who precipitously left the shelter without letting the mental health staff know how to reach them. Fifteen (6.1%) of the homeless subjects with completed interviews were eliminated from the study because of inconsistent or poor-quality data that could not be improved with a reinterview. In such cases the subject was either too delusional or too disorganized to function as a reliable informant. It is possible that the more disturbed subjects were not included in the final sample.

Subjects were interviewed by mental health clinicians specially trained to administer the assessment battery. Clinical and anamnestic data were verified with information contained in the clinical case record. A family member was also interviewed for 57% of the homeless and 68% of the never homeless. The most common reason for the lack of a family interview was the subject's estrangement from kin.

Instruments

The following research instruments were used to assess key study variables:

Pre-illness social functioning was rated with the Los Angeles Social Attainment Scale, a seven-item instrument focused on peer relationships and social participation in late adolescence.[20] The alpha reliability coefficient for this scale is .80.

The positive (active psychotic symptoms such as delusions, hallucinatory behavior, and conceptual disorganization) and negative (deficit symptoms such as blunted affect, emotional withdrawal, and difficulty with abstract thinking) dimensions of schizophrenia were assessed with the Positive and Negative Syndrome Scale, a 30-item rating scale evaluating symptoms present during the 7-day period prior to the interview.[21] The alpha reliability coefficient was .79 for the positive scale, .84 for the negative scale, and .83 for the general psychopathology scale.

Current and lifetime alcohol and drug abuse or dependence were evaluated with the SCID, which yields information on the extent to which heavy use of alcohol or seven classes of drugs meets criteria for a diagnosis based on standards commonly applied in psychiatry.[17]

Antisocial personality disorder was evaluated with the SCID-II, the segment of the SCID dealing with personality disorders.[17] This instrument probes the presence of conduct problems—such as running away from home, being truant from school, initiating physical fights, or belonging to a gang—occurring before the age of 15, as well as patterns of irresponsible, destructive, or illegal activity carrying over into adulthood. For a subject to meet criteria for a diagnosis of antisocial personality disorder, a conduct disorder must have been present in early adolescence.

Family disorganization in childhood was evaluated with 4-point rating scales contained in the Community Care Schedule.[22] These ratings are based on carefully defined anchor points for the assessment of nurturing constancy, residential stability, adequacy of income, dependence on public assistance, family violence, parental criminality, parental mental illness, and parental substance abuse—the components of an index of family disorganization.

Information for this instrument was elicited from both the subject and a family member (whenever possible) to obtain the most complete picture of family life during the subject's childhood. The alpha reliability coefficient for the seven-item index of family disorganization is .69.

Current family support was rated on a scale of adequacy, based on the degree of support and assistance available from family members regarding money, shelter, food, clothing, advice, and companionship.[22] Information for this rating was obtained from the subject and corroborated by a relative when possible.

Caretaker burden was assessed with a semistructured interview that yielded a 3-point rating of overall burden.[23] Unlike other family variables, family burden required an assessment from a family member with firsthand knowledge of the family experience of living with the patient. Family burden data were missing for one third of never-homeless and nearly one half of homeless case subjects.

Prior service use was explored with items contained in the Community Care Schedule[22] that were designed to elicit detailed information on medication adherence patterns, long-term follow-up care, and housing placement at hospital discharge. Medication adherence was rated on a 4-point scale on the basis of the subject's self-report. Long-term follow-up care was defined in terms of the number of months in outpatient treatment with the same therapist.

Statistical methods of analysis

The case subjects (homeless) were compared with the control subjects (never homeless) with respect to three classes of key variables. In the illness domain, there were six variables: premorbid social attainment scale, positive symptom score, negative symptom score, and binary indicators of alcohol abuse, drug abuse and antisocial personality disorder. In the family domain, there were three variables: family disorganization index, adequacy of family support, and assessment of burden. In the service use domain, there were two variables: medication adherence and existence of a long-term therapist.

First we compared the case and control subjects without taking into account sampling characteristics of the groups, and then we compared them after making statistical adjustments for demographic variables that could possibly account for observed differences. Statistical adjustments were made by means of logistic regression, with the binary case/control variable treated as the outcome and the risk variables and possible confounders treated as explanatory variables. Possible confounders were chosen from those demographic variables shown in Table 1 that were at all related to the case/control variable (at the $P < .15$ level). These included place of birth, New York City residence history, ethnicity, and veteran status. We did not adjust for current income variables, because they can be expected to be related to homelessness structurally rather than incidentally.

To facilitate the comparison of adjusted and unadjusted associations between the risk variables and the case/control distinction, we presented both using results from logistic regression analyses. The test statistic we present is the likelihood ratio chi-square from the logistic analyses.[24] For the unadjusted case/control comparisons the pattern of significance results from the likelihood ratio chi-square is the same as would be obtained by means of t tests or Pearson chi-square statistics.

RESULTS

Demographic profile

The homeless (case) group and never-homeless (control) group had many traits in common, including median age (32 years); marital status (four fifths had never married or were currently single); median level of education (11 years); and employment status (more than four fifths were unemployed). Moreover, most (89% of the homeless and 76% of the never homeless) were members of ethnic minorities. However, there were more Blacks among the homeless (66% vs 22%) and more Hispanics among the never homeless (54% vs 23%). Ethnic differences were reflected in differences in religious background (Catholics predominated among the never homeless, whereas Catholics and Protestants were nearly equally represented among the homeless) and place of birth. Nearly twice as many never homeless as homeless (39% vs 21%) were foreign-born.

Table 1. Background characteristics of never-homeless and homeless schizophrenic men

	Never Homeless (n=100)	Homeless (n=100)
Current age, yrs		
Mean	33.86	32.95
Median	32.00	32.00
Mode	32.00	30.00
SD	9.15	6.39
Education, yrs		
Mean	11.01	11.02
Median	11.00	11.00
Mode	12.00	11.00
SD	2.99	2.25
Place of birth, %		
United States	61	79
Foreign	39	21
Residence history, % (residence for the greatest % of time from birth to 18 years)		
New York City area	67	66
Other	33	34
Race/ethnicity, %		
Black	22	66
Hispanic	54	23
White	24	11
Religion, %		
Protestant	20	43
Catholic	61	40
Other	11	11
None	8	6
Marital status, %		
Single	78	79
Married/conjugal	7	3
Separated/divorced	14	16
Widowed	1	1
Veteran status, %		
Yes	7	22
No	93	78
Employment status, %		
Employed	10	11
Unemployed	90	89
Income from entitlements, %		
Yes	78	59
No	22	41
Earned income, %		
Yes	13	19
No	87	81
Income from family, %		
Yes	33	8
No	67	92

Both groups were heavily dependent on public assistance. Nearly four fifths of the never homeless and three fifths of the homeless were receiving income from entitlements, averaging about $430 per month. Thirteen percent of the never homeless and 19% of the homeless earned an average of $100 per month at unskilled jobs. Thirty-three percent of the never homeless and 8% of the homeless also received some financial support from their families. For subjects who had ever worked, the longest duration of steady employment was an average of 12 months. Unemployed subjects had been out of work for an average of 4 to 5 years. Nine percent of the never homeless and 22% of the homeless had served in the armed forces.

Family history and illness onset

Thirty-five percent of the never homeless and 23% of the homeless had lived with both biological parents from birth to 18 years of age. The majority in both groups experienced one or more changes in the primary nurturing adult in childhood and adolescence. One fourth of the never homeless and more than one third of the homeless had experienced two or more such changes. One never-homeless subject and six homeless subjects experienced foster care placement; four homeless subjects had been placed in a group home. Four never-homeless subjects and 20 homeless subjects had a father, mother, or sibling with a history of homelessness.

The median age of onset of psychiatric disorder was 21 years for the never homeless and 20 years for the homeless. Never-homeless subjects experienced their first psychiatric hospitalization at a median age of 22 years; for homeless subjects it was 21 years. Most subjects had extensive hospitalization histories. Fifty-eight percent of the never homeless and 56% of the homeless had been hospitalized in the 12-month period preceding the interview. The median number of hospital days in this time period was 60 for the never homeless and 43 for the homeless subjects. At the termination of the most recent hospitalization episode, 11 homeless subjects and 1 never-homeless subject had been discharged against medical advice. Ninety-six percent of the never homeless and 83% of the homeless had been given a recent prescription for neuroleptic medication (the class of psychotropic drugs often used to treat schizophrenia).

Subjects with substance abuse problems had initiated alcohol and drug use in midadolescence. The median age of onset of drug abuse (any drugs) was 18 years for never-homeless subjects (44%) and 16 years for homeless subjects (77%). The median age of onset for alcohol abuse was 18 years for both groups (44% of the never homeless and 49% of the homeless). Fifteen percent of the never homeless and 34% of the homeless had received some form of substance abuse treatment in the 12-month period preceding the interview.

Thirteen percent of the never homeless and 46% of the homeless had had severe conduct problems before the age of 15 years. Six percent of the never homeless and 28% of the homeless reported that they had run away from home at least once during early adolescence. Nine percent of the never homeless and 42% of the homeless were given a research diagnosis of adult antisocial personality disorder, and 25% of the never homeless and 72% of the homeless had jail or prison histories.

Distinctions between the homeless and the never homeless

Table 2 summarizes tests of study hypotheses about the differences between never-homeless and homeless schizophrenic men. The tests are presented in two forms, one that is unadjusted for possible case-control differences that may confound the group comparisons and one that adjusts for demographic factors that may be related to selection into the study.

Within the illness domain, there were no significant differences between the homeless and the never homeless on the Los Angeles Social Attainment Scale scores in either unadjusted or adjusted tests. Average ratings on peer socialization and social participation in late adolescence were at the "poor premorbid" level in both groups. Homeless subjects did show significantly higher levels of positive symptoms than did the never-homeless subjects ($P < .01$, unadjusted; $P < .05$ adjusted). However, there were no major differences in negative symptom levels. There were no meaningful differences in the proportion of subjects in each group with a concurrent diagnosis of alcohol abuse, but a significantly larger number of homeless subjects had a concurrent diagnosis of drug abuse ($P < .01$ for both unadjusted and adjusted tests). Similarly, a significantly larger number of homeless subjects had a concurrent diagnosis of antisocial personality disorder ($P < .01$ for both unadjusted and adjusted tests).

Within the family domain, the mean score on the index of family disorganization was higher, indicating greater impairment, for homeless subjects ($P < .01$, unadjusted; $P < .05$, adjusted). Family support was less adequate for the homeless ($P < .01$ for both tests). However, there were no significant differences in the overall levels of caretaker burden.

In terms of service use issues, the homeless initially appeared to adhere less to prescribed medication regimens ($P < .01$, unadjusted), but that difference did not withstand adjustment for potential confounders ($P < .10$). Fewer homeless subjects had a long-term therapist, an indicator of continuity of care ($P < .01$, both adjusted and unadjusted).

At discharge from the most recent psychiatric hospitalization, 50% of the homeless (undomiciled before hospitalization) were discharged to a shelter or the streets. The 95% confidence interval for the proportion P is between 40% and 60%.

Table 2. Test of key hypotheses about differences between homeless and never-homeless urban schizophrenic men

	Never Homeless (n = 100)		Homeless (n = 100)		Unadjusted[a]		Adjusted[b]	
	Mean	SD	Mean	SD	LRT	P	LRT	P
Illness domain								
Social attainment score	19.24	6.93	19.92	5.97	0.54	.46	0.03	.87
Postive symptoms score	13.00	5.82	15.73	6.72	9.28	<.01	4.57	<.05
Negative symptoms score	15.53	6.04	15.99	6.29	0.28	.60	0.56	.45
Alcohol abuse (0 = no, 1 = yes)	0.44	0.50	0.49	0.50	.50	.48	0.16	.69
Drug abuse (0 = no, 1 = yes)	0.44	0.50	0.77	0.42	23.33	<.001	17.55	.001
Antisocial personality disorder (0 = no, 1 = yes)	0.09	0.29	0.42	0.50	30.54	<.001	17.99	<.001
Family domain								
Index of family disorganization	11.88	3.29	13.98	4.65	12.18	<.001	4.64	<.05
Adequacy of family support	1.42	0.88	2.28	1.20	65.81	<.001	36.6	.001
Overall assessment of burden	2.03	0.63	1.95	0.65	0.54	.46	0.25	.62
		(67 cases)		(55 cases)				
Service use domain								
Medication adherence	1.52	0.83	1.96	1.09	10.24	<.01	3.13	<.10
Long-term therapist	36.78	36.97	19.36	23.08	14.77	<.01	7.86	<.01

[a]Likelihood ratio test (LRT) and P value from logistic regression models with no other variables held constant.
[b]LRT and P value from logistic regression models holding constant immigration status, New York City residence history, ethnicity, and veteran status.

Table 2 shows how each of the individual risk variables relates to homelessness after demographic factors that might be related to selection are controlled. We carried out additional analyses to determine the extent to which these variables accounted for the same variation in the homelessness distinction. When all the risk variables in Table 2 were entered simultaneously in a logistic model fitting log odds of homelessness (along with the demographic control variables), one variable in each domain remained either significant or a trend. Still significant by the Wald statistic were drug abuse (from the illness domain) (Wald = 5.28, $df = 1$, $P < .05$) and adequacy of family support (from the family domain) (Wald = 14.41, $df = 1$, $P < .001$), whereas having a long-term therapist (from the service use domain) was reduced to a trend (Wald = 3.07, $df = 1$, $P < .10$). These three variables seem to reflect different aspects of the differences between the homeless and never-homeless groups.

Two variables under the illness domain that are significant in Table 2 are not significant when adjusted for the other risk variables. Positive symptoms is no longer a discriminating variable when other illness domain variables are controlled, but antisocial personality disorder loses significance only when adequacy of current family support is adjusted.

Adequacy of family support also appears to be the variable that accounts for the effects of family disorganization index and having a long-term therapist. These variables are significant in Table 2, but they do not appear to differentiate the homeless from the never homeless when adequacy of family support is adjusted.

DISCUSSION

In this study we have attempted to identify factors that differentiate economically disadvantaged schizophrenics who live in private homes from those who are homeless and who live in public shelters. Although not definitive in terms of causal pathways, a case-control design such as ours is an efficient way to spot potential risk factors for homelessness. Some variables we explored preceded the first homeless experience and may play a causal role. In addition to childhood antecedents, our data indicate that drug abuse and antisocial personality disorder had their onset prior to homelessness. The cross-sectional nature of our study prevents us from determining whether other variables are a cause or a consequence of homelessness. Our data show an association between family disorganization in childhood and poor family support in adulthood in assessing the risk of homelessness. However, a longitudinal approach is needed to establish that breakdown of family relationships plays a causal role in homelessness.[7] Higher current levels of positive symptoms and the lack of a long-term therapist could be either a cause or a consequence of homelessness. Higher symptom levels can precipitate behaviors that undermine housing stability, but the vicissitudes of street or shelter living can increase distress and disrupt usual patterns of mental health care. Our data on hospital discharge practices for homeless subjects suggest that the pattern of discharging patients to shelters or streets functions to perpetuate homelessness.

The sampling design of our study formally limits us to generalizing our findings only to persons who have the same demographic and clinical characteristics as our study subjects and who are enrolled in mental health treatment programs similar to those from which we drew our sample. However, the pattern of findings suggests that they may be more general, particularly among the severely mentally ill. We found that the homeless schizophrenic men differed from their domiciled counterparts in all three domains we investigated: family background, nature of illness, and service use history.

Schizophrenic men who came from families with high levels of family disorganization, characterized by lack of nurturing constancy, residential instability, economic inadequacy, dependence on public assistance, family violence, mental illness, substance abuse, or criminality in a parent, were more likely to be in the homeless group than in the never-homeless group, even when demographic variables such as place of birth and ethnicity were controlled. Our findings broaden the scope of childhood antecedents of adult homelessness to include family economic problems and parental pathology, the latter being strongly associated with out-of-home placement.[25] However, the logistic regression analysis revealed that poor family support is a more important risk factor for homelessness than childhood antecedents. We thought it reasonable to ask whether the overall burden experienced by the family in taking care of the schizophrenic relative might differentiate the homeless from the never homeless. Our negative findings should be interpreted cautiously because our ability to measure family burden was limited.

The men who ended up in our homeless group do appear to have a strikingly different profile of psychopathology. They were more likely to have positive symptoms of psychosis and to have concurrent drug abuse and antisocial personality disorder. The logistic regression analysis revealed that drug abuse was the most important risk factor in the illness domain. There were no significant differences between the homeless and the never homeless in premorbid social adjustment, negative symptoms, or alcohol abuse. Thus, the homeless in our study were not more severely ill in all dimensions of psychopathology.

The finding that 50% of the homeless (undomiciled before hospitalization) were discharged to a shelter or the streets indicates that the homeless in our study had less access to adequate care. Although this finding may reflect local mental health practices, similar findings have emerged from studies carried out in Chicago[26] and rural Ohio.[27] The logistic regression analysis revealed that the most important risk factor in the service use domain was not having a long-term therapist. Future work will have to determine whether lack of a long-term therapist is an access problem or a consequence of resistance to treatment.

Clearer identification of risk factors for homelessness can lead to the development of preventive intervention strategies. For example, thorough assessment of patterns of substance use, family support, and prior outpatient service use in concert with routine discharge planning can identify those who require additional services and supportive housing. Patients with co-disorders can be singled out for intensive case management to improve the successful coordination of mental health and substance abuse treatment services.[28-31] Finally, although risk factors aid in identifying those individuals most vulnerable to homelessness, they do not obviate the need for policymakers at all levels of government to address the chronic shortage of affordable housing for indigent Americans.

REFERENCES

1. Federal Task Force on Homelessness and Severe Mental Illness. *Outcasts on Main Street.* Washington, DC: Interagency Council on the Homeless; 1992:18.
2. Mowbray CT, Johnson US, Solar A. Homelessness in a state hospital population. *Hospital and Community Psychiatry.* 1987; 38:880-882.
3. Drake RE, Wallach MA, Hoffman JS. Housing instability and homelessness among aftercare patients of an urban state hospital. *Hospital and Community Psychiatry.* 1989;40:46-51.
4. Susser ES, Lin SF, Conover SA. Risk factors for homelessness among patients admitted to a state mental hospital. *American Journal of Psychiatry.* 1991;148:1659-1664.
5. Fischer PJ, Shapiro S, Breakey WR, Anthony JC, Kramer M. Mental health and social characteristics of the homeless: a survey of mission users. *American Journal of Public Health.* 1986;76:519-524.
6. Koegel P, Burnam A, Farr RK. The prevalence of specific psychiatric disorders among homeless individuals in the inner city of Los Angeles. *Archives of General Psychiatry.* 1988;45:1085-1092.
7. Tessler RC, Gamache GM, Rossi PR, Lehman AF, Goldman HH. The kindred bonds of mentally ill homeless persons. *New England Journal of Public Policy.* 1992;8:265-280.
8. Drake RE, Wallach MA, Teague GB, Freeman DH, Paskus TS, Clark TA. Housing instability and homelessness among rural schizophrenic patients. *American Journal of Psychiatry.* 1991;148:330-336.
9. Winkleby MA, Rockhill B, Jatulis D, Fortmann SP. The medical origins of homelessness. *American Journal of Public Health.* 1992;82:1394-1398.
10. Susser ES, Lin SP, Conover SA, Struening EL. Childhood antecedents of homelessness in psychiatric patients. *American Journal of Psychiatry.* 1991;148:1026-1030.

11. Lamb HR. Deinstitutionalization and the homeless mentally ill. *Hospital and Community Psychiatry.* 1984;35:899-907.
12. Lamb HR. Will we save the homeless mentally ill? *American Journal of Psychiatry.* 1990;147:649-651.
13. Goldman HH, Manderscheid RW. Chronic mental disorder in the United States. In: Manderscheid RW, Barrett SA, eds. *Mental Health, United States, 1987.* Rockville, MD: US Dept of Health and Human Services, National Institute of Mental Health; 1987:1-11.
14. Arce AA, Tadlock M, Vergare MJ, Shapiro SH. A psychiatric profile of street people admitted to an emergency shelter. *Hospital and Community Psychiatry.* 1983;34:812.
15. Bassuk EL, Rubin L, Lauriat A. Is homelessness a mental health problem? *American Journal of Psychiatry.* 1984;141:1546-1549.
16. Burt MR, Cohen BE. *America's Homeless: Numbers, Characteristics, and Programs That Serve Them.* Washington, DC: Urban Institute Press; 1989:36.
17. Spitzer RL, Williams JBW, Gibbon M, First MB. *Structured Clinical Interview for DSM-III-R.* Washington, DC: American Psychiatric Press; 1990.
18. Rossi PH, Wright JD, Fisher GA, Willis G. The urban homeless: estimating composition and size. *Science.* 1987;235:1336-1341.
19. Susser E, Struening EL, Conover S. Psychiatric problems in homeless men. *Archives of General Psychiatry.* 1989;46:845-859.
20. Goldstein MJ. Further data concerning the relation between premorbid adjustment and paranoid symptomatology. *Schizophrenia Bulletin.* 1978;4:236.
21. Kay SR, Fiszbein A, Opler LA. The Positive and Negative Syndrome Scale (PANSS) for schizophrenia. *Schizophrenia Bulletin.* 1987;13:261-275.
22. Caton CLM. *The Community Care Schedule.* New York, NY: New York State Psychiatric Institute; January 1989.
23. Pai S, Kapur RL. The burden on the family of a psychiatric patient: development of an interview schedule. *British Journal of Psychiatry.* 1981;138:332-335.
24. Hosmer DW, Lemeshow S. *Applied Logistic Regression.* New York, NY: John Wiley & Sons Inc; 1989.
25. Caton CLM, Eagle P, Felix A, Shrout P. Family factors in the genesis of homelessness. Presented at the 120th Annual Meeting of the American Public Health Association; November 11, 1992; Washington, DC.
26. Sosin MR, Grossman S. The mental health system and the etiology of homelessness: a comparison study. *Journal of Community Psychology.* 1991;19:337-351.
27. Belcher JR. On becoming homeless: a study of chronically mentally ill persons. *Journal of Community Psychology.* 1989;17:173-185.
28. Osher FC, Kofoed LL. Treatment of patients with psychiatric and psychoactive substance abuse disorders. *Hospital and Community Psychiatry.* 1989;40:1025-1030.
29. Caton CLM, Wyatt RJ, Felix A, Grunberg J. Follow-up of chronically homeless mentally ill men. *American Journal of Psychiatry.* 1993;150:1639-1642.

30. Abram KM, Teplin LA. Co-occurring disorders among mentally ill jail detainees. *American Psychologist.* 1991;46:1036-1045.

31. Steadman HJ, McCarty DW, Morrissey JP. *The Mentally Ill in Jail: Planning For Essential Services.* New York, NY: Guilford Press; 1989.

ABOUT THE AUTHORS

Carol L. M. Caton, Ph.D., Paula F. Eagle, M.D., Lewis A. Opler, M.D., Ph.D., Alan Felix, M.D., and Boanerges Dominguez, M.S., are affiliated with the Department of Psychiatry and School of Public Health, College of Physicians and Surgeons, Columbia University, New York, NY. Patrick E. Shrout, Ph.D., is affiliated with the Department of Psychology, New York University.

ACKNOWLEDGMENTS

The research on which this report is based was supported by the National Institute of Mental Health, grant MH44705.

Our thanks to our dedicated and talented research support staff, including Luz Romero, B.S. (who also assisted in the preparation of the manuscript); Andrea Cassells, M.P.H.; Louis Caraballo, B.A.; Diane Engel, C.S.W.; Lee Futrovsky, Ph.D.; Barbara Holton, C.S.W.; Elizabeth Margoshes, Ph.D.; and Mary Ellen Russell, M.S. We are also grateful to Richard Jed Wyatt, M.D., and Jerome K. Myers, Ph.D., for their critical reading of an earlier draft.

Copyright 1994. American Public Health Association. Reprinted with permission.

INTRODUCTION TO SECTION THREE

The Assessment section contains five articles that deal with the importance of, and strategies for, assessing substance use disorders in persons with severe mental illness. The problem of co-occurring substance use disorders in people with severe mental illnesses is extremely common and yet is frequently overlooked. Approximately half of all persons with severe mental illnesses will have a diagnosis of substance use disorder at some time in their lives, which is considerably higher than rates in the general U.S. population. Many studies show that the three primary substances of abuse in this population are alcohol, cannabis, and cocaine. Without systematic efforts at screening and diagnosis, substance use disorder is not likely to be detected. Numerous studies show that substance use disorder is significantly underdiagnosed in acute care psychiatric settings. For example, Ananth and colleagues (1989) found that only 2% of substance use disorder diagnoses among patients with severe mental illnesses were detected in a university emergency room and only 15% in a state hospital.

The assessment of substance use is complicated by many factors. For example, substance abuse engenders shame and guilt, and the use of many drugs is illegal. Many people who abuse alcohol and drugs minimize or deny their use and the associated problems. Standard alcohol and drug screening tests often rely on obvious items. For example, they ask the respondent if he or she has tried to cut down on alcohol or drug use, which implies that the individual recognizes a problem. When people have reason to hide their substance-using behavior, or when they do not recognize the consequences of their substance use, these tests may fail to detect abuse and dependence. Another problem is that most of the popular tests have been developed with groups of white, male alcoholics in substance abuse treatment. The tests often do not function as well in special populations, such as women or people with a psychiatric illness. For example, people with schizophrenia do not often report that alcohol use has caused problems with work, driving a car, or spouses, because usually they are not employed, do not drive, and are not married. For an excellent review of the performance of standard self-report alcohol abuse measures in psychiatric populations, see Teitelbaum and Carey (1996).

The research reported in this section highlights a number of specific and practical findings about assessment of substance use in people with severe mental illnesses, including the need to tailor the assessment approach to the particular setting, resources, and clients, to the primary substance(s) of abuse, and to the differing stages of treatment. The order of the articles follows the assessment sequence of screening, diagnostic procedures, and specialized assessment procedures, as outlined in the first reading by Robert Drake and his colleagues. They describe a number of assessment methods, including self-report, structured interviews, laboratory testing, and collateral ratings, and they review the applicability of each to different treatment situations.

Currently available substance abuse screening instruments probably all have poor detection accuracy in the population of individuals who have severe mental illnesses. Because of this difficulty, we recently developed a screen for alcohol, cannabis, and cocaine abuse in people with severe mental illnesses: the DALI (Rosenberg et al., in press). The DALI is brief, easily administered by a nonclinician interviewer, and appears to have superior diagnostic properties when compared with other available tests. The DALI is available from the authors.

Various procedures are used to enhance validity when interviewing clients about their substance use. These include establishing rapport with the client before asking about substance use; asking clients about substance use in the context of other lifestyle issues such as smoking, diet, and exercise; assuring them about the confidentiality of the interview; and asking questions in a nonjudgmental, matter-of-fact way. Yet even the better designed self-report methods appear to underestimate the rate of substance use disorders in people with severe mental illnesses. One common way to get around the problem of self-report is to use urine drug screens. As Andrew Stone and his colleagues demonstrate in their article, laboratory tests such as urine drug screening may be very helpful in detecting frequent drug use in an inner-city, outpatient setting where cocaine abuse is common.

Another way around the problems of self-report is to use clinician ratings of substance use. The Clinician Rating Scale (CRS) (Drake et al., 1990) is a method by which a trained clinician establishes a current (most recent six months) substance abuse or dependence diagnosis, by DSM criteria, through the collation of self-report data, observers' reports, consultation with families, laboratory findings, medical history, psychiatric evaluation, and personal longitudinal contact with the client. Because of these multiple modes of observation, signs and symptoms of use disorder are more likely to be detected. As the article by Kate Carey and her colleagues reports, the CRS is reliable and valid when used by case managers who follow their clients with severe mental illnesses over time in the community.

Individualized assessment that enables treatment planning involves much more than detection and diagnosis. Clinicians must identify critical components of the disorder and the conditions that sustain it in order to develop a detailed treatment plan. The last two articles in this section address some of the complexities of specialized assessment. Anthony Lehman points out that clients with dual diagnoses may differ from one another in their primary diagnoses, their substances of abuse, and their other medical and psychosocial problems. In addition, a client's substance use disorder profile may also change over time. Assessment procedures must be chosen with this heterogeneity and evolution in mind.

In the final article Gregory McHugo and his colleagues describe the concept and measurement of stages of substance abuse treatment in persons with severe mental illnesses. This approach to recovery addresses the client's motivation for, and involvement in, treatment of substance abuse and follows the four-stage process described by Osher and Kofoed (1989): engagement, persuasion, active treatment, and relapse prevention. The Substance Abuse Treatment Scale (SATS) is introduced in this article and is evaluated as a research and clinical tool for obtaining clinician ratings of the stage of treatment. Knowing a client's stage of substance abuse treatment is critically important in treatment planning, as it determines the types of interventions that are appropriate at a particular point in time (Drake & Noordsy, 1994).

To understand better the articles in the Assessment section, familiarity with a few basic terms will be helpful. *Reliability* refers to how consistently a test measures what it is supposed to measure. For example, does a test produce the same score over time (test-retest reliability) or when it is administered by different people (interrater reliability)? If these two types of reliability are not high, then the test is unlikely to be very useful. *Validity* refers to the degree that a test score reflects the person's true score on that attribute. A perfectly valid diagnostic test would yield no false negatives (i.e., everyone with the disorder would be so classified) and no false positives (i.e., everyone without the disorder would be so classified). False negatives and positives are also described in terms of sensitivity and specificity. *Sensitivity* refers to the rate of detecting true positives; a test with high sensitivity correctly classifies most persons with the disorder. *Specificity* refers to the rate of detecting true negatives; a test with high specificity correctly classifies most persons without the disorder.

REFERENCES

Ananth, J., Vandewater, S., Kamal, M., Brodsky, A., Gamal, R., & Miller, M. (1989). Missed diagnosis of substance abuse in psychiatric patients. *Hospital and Community Psychiatry, 40,* 297-299.

Drake, R.E., & Noordsy, D.L. (1994). Case management for people with co-existing severe mental disorder and substance use disorder. *Psychiatric Annals, 24,* 427-431.

Drake, R.E., Osher, F.C., Noordsy, D.L., Hurlbut, S.C., Teague, G.B., & Beaudett, M.S. (1990). Diagnosis of alcohol use disorders in schizophrenia. *Schizophrenia Bulletin, 16,* 57-67.

Osher, F.C., & Kofoed, L.L. (1989). Treatment of patients with psychiatric and psychoactive substance abuse disorders. *Hospital and Community Psychiatry, 40,* 1025-1030.

Rosenberg, S.D., Drake, R.E., Wolford, G.L., Mueser, K.T., Oxman, T.E., Vidaver, R.M., & Carrieri, K. (in press). The Dartmouth Assessment of Lifestyle Instrument (DALI): A substance use disorder screen for people with severe mental illness. *American Journal of Psychiatry*.

Teitelbaum, L.M., & Carey, K.B. (1996). Alcohol assessment in psychiatric patients. *Clinicial Psychology Science and Practice*, 3, 323-338.

Assessing Substance Use Disorder in Persons with Severe Mental Illness

Robert E. Drake, Stanley D. Rosenberg, and Kim T. Mueser

Reprinted from *Dual Diagnosis of Major Mental Illness and Substance Abuse. Volume 2: Recent Research and Clinical Implications.* New Directions for Mental Health Services, No. 70, R.E. Drake & K.T. Mueser (Eds.). San Francisco: Jossey-Bass, Inc. (pp. 3-17), 1996

Assessment of dually diagnosed patients consists of three steps: detection, diagnosis, and specialized assessment for treatment planning. Each of these is informed by recent research.

Case Study: John D

A lawyer called the mental health center about a twenty-seven-year-old homeless man, John D, who had been arrested several times after threatening women in public. John, who was disheveled, paranoid, and verbally abusive, explained to an outreach case manager that the FBI was following him and directing women on the streets to control his thoughts. This problem had been worsening for three or four years. John had been hospitalized and given medications involuntarily on several occasions. He denied using alcohol or other drugs. Hospital records, obtained subsequently, corroborated this history, including the lack of alcohol and drug problems.

The outreach case manager began to meet John each morning for coffee and helped him to secure entitlements and housing. After several weeks of building a relationship, John agreed to take a small dose of medicine to alleviate his problems with sleep, anxiety, and fears. Nevertheless, his psychosis and public invective flared up periodically and he continued to have difficulties with the police. During another hospitalization precipitated by further threats, a urine drug test revealed high levels of cannabis. John then admitted to his case manager a pattern of heavy cannabis use over several years. The treatment plan changed as John and his case manager began to explore the role of marijuana in his life and in his course of illness. He suffered from delusions, hallucinations, and paranoia even when he was not using cannabis, and his symptoms became much worse and led to threatening behavior when he was using cannabis heavily. He was given two diagnoses—schizophrenia and cannabis use disorder.

After several months of exploring the nature of his substance abuse, John and his case manager had identified six risk factors that led to cannabis use: feeling anxious around people, eating at the soup kitchen where cannabis was sold and traded, hanging around with other homeless persons who used cannabis daily, boredom, not having a safe place to sleep, and getting angry with his parents. Next, they developed a treatment plan that both addressed each of these problems with specific behavioral strategies and provided further drug education and treatment. John's cannabis use gradually decreased and stopped over the course of ten months.

SUBSTANCE ABUSE ASSESSMENT

Over the past decade awareness of substance abuse and dependence in persons with severe mental illness has grown steadily (Lehman and Dixon, 1995; Minkoff and Drake, 1991; Ridgely, Osher, and Talbott, 1987). Despite this awareness and the costly consequences of nondetection (Kofoed, 1991; Lehman, Myers, and Corty, 1989), substance disorders are still underdiagnosed in this population (Ananth and others, 1989; Drake and others, 1990). Nondetection is attributable to a variety of factors, some generic to the problem of asking people to disclose their own socially proscribed behavior, and some specific to the complications of substance abuse diagnoses in persons with psychiatric illness. Concealing substance use patterns is very common in our culture; additional problems related to communication, memory, attitudes, and perception arise when assessing persons with severe mental illness. More valid, practical procedures have been developed, but assessment is still complicated by the technical limitations of available procedures and by the complex overlaps and interactions between severe mental illness and psychoactive substance use. In this chapter we review issues related to assessing substance use disorders in severely mentally ill patients, provide information from recent research, and discuss current procedures and new research directions.

SCOPE OF PROBLEM

In this review, we will discuss three primary functions of assessment: detection, diagnosis, and specialized assessment for treatment planning. *Detection* refers to procedures for identifying substance dependence, substance abuse, or harmful or dangerous use that does not qualify for a diagnosis (Babor, Kranzler, and Lauerman, 1989). The *diagnostic* term "substance use disorder" refers to a habitual pattern of alcohol use or other drug use that results in significant impairments in areas of adjustment (American Psychiatric Association, 1987; 1994). Use disorders are divided into two mutually exclusive classifications—*substance abuse* and *substance dependence*—with the latter characterized by greater severity, physiological dependence, and compulsive use. *Specialized assessment* involves measuring the severity of the substance-related problems, the client's motivation and participation in treatment, and the conditions associated with the occurrence of problematic use that become targets for treatment interventions (Drake and Mercer-McFadden, 1995). Before discussing these three aspects of assessment, we briefly review research on prevalence and the problem of nondetection.

Prevalence

Substance use disorder is the most common comorbid complication among severely mentally ill persons (Minkoff and Drake, 1991). The Epidemiological Catchment Area (ECA) study (Regier and others, 1990) found that all persons with psychiatric disorders were more prone to substance disorder than the general population, but those with severe mental illness were especially vulnerable, with lifetime prevalence of approximately 50 percent. For example, persons with schizophrenia were more than four times as likely to have had a substance use disorder during their lifetimes and those with bipolar disorder were more than five times as likely to have such a diagnosis than persons in the general population. The evidence that persons with severe mental disorders are at increased risk for substance use disorders is reviewed in this volume by Cuffel.[1]

Nondetection

Many studies show that substance disorders are underdetected and underdiagnosed in acute-care psychiatric settings, with rates of nondetection as high as 98 percent (Ananth and others, 1989). Failure to detect substance use disorder results in misdiagnosis of the psychiatric disorder, suboptimal pharmacological treatment of psychiatric syndromes, neglect of appropriate interventions for substance abuse (such as detoxification, education, and counseling) and inappropriate treatment planning and referral (Crowley, Chesluk, Dilts, and Hart, 1974; Kofoed, 1991; Lehman, Myers, and Corty, 1989).

The underdetection of comorbid substance disorders in psychiatric settings is caused by a combination of factors (Drake and others, 1990; Magliozzi, Kanter, Csernansky, and Hollister, 1983; Safer, 1987; Test, Wallisch, Allness, and Ripp, 1989), including clinicians' lack of awareness of the high rates of substance disorders in psychiatric populations; clinicians' inattention to substance abuse as a problem; the inadequacy of standard assessment instruments in this population; psychiatric patients' denial, minimization, and failure to see the relation between their substance use and problems of adjustment; and patients' cognitive, psychotic, and other impairments related to their psychiatric illness.

---

[1]Editors' Note: The authors refer to a chapter that appears in the book where this reading was originally published. The full reference for that chapter is Cuffel, B.J. (1996). Comorbid substance use disorder: Prevalence, patterns of use, and course. In R.E. Drake & K.T. Mueser (Eds.), *Dual diagnosis of mental illness and substance abuse: Vol. 2. Recent research and clinical implications* (pp. 93-105). San Francisco: Jossey-Bass.

DETECTION PROCEDURES

To overcome the problem of invalid assessment of substance disorder in psychiatric patients, clinicians and researchers have recommended using multiple instruments, multiple perspectives, or multiple modes of assessment (Blankertz and Cnaan, 1994; Corse, Hirschinger, and Zanis, 1995; Drake, Alterman, and Rosenberg, 1993; Drake and Mercer-McFadden, 1995; Goldfinger and others, in press; Kofoed, 1991; Safer, 1987). Studies that have included these procedures have demonstrated greater sensitivity to detection (Drake and others, 1990; Galletly, Field, and Prior, 1993; Goldfinger and others, in press; Shaner and others, 1993; Stone, Greenstein, Gamble, and McLellan, 1993; Test, Wallisch, Allness, and Ripp, 1989). Ideally, substance abuse screening should incorporate an awareness of base rates and clinical and behavioral correlates, a self-report instrument designed specifically for persons with severe mental illness, and concurrent procedures to circumvent the problem of unreliable and invalid self-reports. Additional procedures that have proved useful in detecting substance abuse in other settings are laboratory evaluations, collateral reports, and physical signs and symptoms. Many of these procedures have not been carefully studied in psychiatric patients.

Index of suspicion

Because co-occurring substance disorder is the most common complicating feature of severe psychiatric illness, mental health clinicians need to develop and maintain assessment skills and a high index of suspicion, especially when demographic features or other aspects of the patient's presentation suggest substance disorder. For example, although substance disorder affects approximately half of all patients with severe mental illness, it is even more common among young males (Cuffel, this volume;[1] Drake, Osher, and Wallach, 1989; Mueser, Yarnold, and Bellack, 1992). The correlates of alcohol and drug abuse that increase risk status in this population include younger age, male gender, family history of substance abuse, homelessness, disruptive behavior, poor relationships with family, repeated hospitalizations, legal difficulties, and incarceration (Alterman and Erdlen, 1983; Alterman, Erdlen, McLellan, and Mann, 1980; Drake, Osher, and Wallach, 1989; Haywood and others, 1995; Mueser, Yarnold, and Bellack, 1992; Negrete and Knapp, 1986; Noordsy, Drake, Biesanz, and McHugo, 1994; Richard, Liskow, and Perry, 1985; Yesavage and Zarcone, 1983).

Self-report

Assessment usually begins with direct interview, and a number of studies have shown that structured interviews yield valuable information that is reliable and specific but not necessarily sensitive (Drake and others, 1990;

Goldfinger and others, in press). Self-report is less sensitive for detecting illicit drugs (Galletly, Field, and Prior, 1993; Shaner and others, 1993; Stone, Greenstein, Gamble, and McLellan, 1993) and should therefore be supplemented by collateral information or laboratory assessments (Drake, Alterman, and Rosenberg, 1993).

Standard interview instruments have several limitations with this population. For example, lengthy interviews are not practical in many treatment settings (Barbee and others, 1989), and standard instruments often assess consequences that are inappropriate or irrelevant for psychiatric patients (Corse, Hirschinger, and Zanis, 1995). If interview is the only means of assessment available, combining more than one instrument has been found useful (Drake and others, 1990; Goldfinger and others, in press).

We currently use the following procedures for direct interview: First, screen for lifetime difficulties by using, for example, the screening portion of the Structured Clinical Interview DSM-IV-R (Spitzer, Williams, Gibbon, and First, 1988). Second, use a calendar method to document use patterns in recent months (Sobell and others, 1980). Third, if there is any evidence of use of alcohol or other drugs, use a brief checklist such as the MAST (Selzer, 1971) or DAST (Skinner, 1982) to assess consequences. Supplement the MAST or DAST by asking about problems that are more common in psychiatric illness, such as homelessness, legal problems, and exacerbation of psychiatric disorder. Fourth, assess moderate alcohol use, which may have adverse consequences or portend future problems for this population (Drake, Osher, and Wallach, 1989; Drake and Wallach, 1993); recent, regular use, which may offer a better indicator of need for treatment than abuse (Dixon and others, 1993); and past history, which often provides a sensitive indicator of current problems (Barry and others, 1995). Finally, when conducting interviews, employ several general procedures that increase the validity of self-reported information: If possible, use self-report instruments when the client is stabilized; in the context of a careful, nonjudgmental, clinical interview that enables the client to relax and assures confidentiality; and in conjunction with laboratory assessment. Repeat self-report assessments on a regular basis (Babor, Stephen, and Marlatt, 1987).

Collateral sources

People who know the client well can often provide accurate information about substance use and adverse consequences. Several studies have shown that clinicians are able to monitor substance use among psychiatric patients (Drake and others, 1990; Drake, Osher, and Wallach, 1989; Goldfinger and others, in press; Barry and others, 1995; Mueser and others, 1995; Test, Wallisch, Allness, and Ripp, 1989). Case managers, for example, can easily be trained to assess substance use and consequences according to standard criteria, and we have developed scales and rating forms—the Alcohol

Use Scale and the Drug Use Scale—for this purpose (Drake, Mueser, and McHugo, 1996). When available, close personal contacts such as family members, friends, and housemates can help the clinical case manager with screening and monitoring (Osher and Kofoed, 1989; Ryglewicz, 1991). Patients with severe mental illness, however, often have constricted social networks and live in isolated settings so that collaterals are unavailable. In addition, because illicit drug use is often secretive, collateral informants may be more aware of alcohol use than of illicit drug use.

Laboratory tests

Clinical investigators often recommend routine urine drug screening for all incoming psychiatric patients (Safer, 1987). Several studies have used urine drug tests to detect high rates of unreported illicit substance use in this population (Blumberg, Cohen, Heaton, and Klein, 1971; Galletly, Field, and Prior, 1993; Shaner and others, 1993; Stone, Greenstein, Gamble, and McLellan, 1993). Moreover, using laboratory tests is likely to increase the accuracy of clients' self-reports (Stone, Greenstein, Gamble, and McLellan, 1993).

The obvious shortcoming of urine drug tests is that they provide a limited indication of the frequency and amount of use and yield no information about the consequences of use. Some indirect information on frequency and amount can be obtained through repeated tests, and even one positive test serves to include substance abuse in the differential diagnosis. Clinicians should also be aware of issues related to sensitivity, quality control, and detection interval after use with specific tests, laboratories, and drugs (Gold and Dackis, 1986).

Blood chemistries and Breathalyzers are not as satisfactory for the detection of alcohol use as urine drug testing is for illicit drug use. Blood tests such as liver enzymes and red blood cell morphology are primarily sensitive to heavy alcohol use in the past three to six weeks (Babor, Kranzler, and Lauerman, 1989) and have only moderate sensitivity for detecting heavy drinking in psychiatric patients (Toland and Moss, 1989). Breathalyzer assessments are limited by the short time window (several hours or less), the high initial investment for equipment, the need for frequent recalibration, and a high need for technician support. We instead use a simple, inexpensive saliva test to detect the presence of alcohol (Cox and Crifasi, 1990).

Other procedures

Other procedures for detecting substance use have not been tested in psychiatric patients. Procedures that deserve study include medical history and examination (Skinner, Holt, Sheu, and Israel, 1986), questions regarding traumatic injuries and clinical signs (Babor, DeLaFuente, Saunders, and Grant, 1989), and historical indicators such as childhood conduct disorder (Babor, DeLaFuente, Saunders, and Grant, 1989).

Table 1 lists currently used procedures for detection and diagnosis.

Table 1. Techniques for identifying alcohol and illicit drug use

Technique	Advantages	Disadvantages
Lab tests	-Increases accuracy of self-report. -Adds sensitivity when patients are defensive or cognitively impaired.	-Limited indication of frequency and amount of use. -Temporal range very limited.
Self-report	-Data on both current and lifetime use. Patients may be more willing to admit to alcohol use than drug use.	-Poor validity when there are reasons to deny or minimize substance use. -Interviews not always feasible in acute treatment settings. Patients may be defensive or cognitively impaired.
Physical signs and symptoms	-Case managers are capable of making longitudinal observations that are quite sensitive to alcohol use, and are sensitive to the changes that accompany drug abuse.	-Sensitivity of physical exam and medical history not tested in this population. -Several signs and symptoms overlap with psychotic and agitated states.
Collateral sources	-Collaterals may be more aware of alcohol use than illicit drug use. -When available, close personal contacts can help with screening and monitoring.	-Many severely mentally ill persons do not have collaterals. -Collaterals typically have incomplete information.
Sociodemographic and other correlates	-Age, gender, and clinical correlates can be used to identify high-risk patients.	-Relatively little data on this specific population.
Indirect measures	-May increase sensitivity when patients are defensive or cognitively impaired.	-Not yet fully developed.

DIAGNOSIS

Making the diagnosis of substance use disorder in persons with severe mental illness is complicated in several ways. The specific criteria and thresholds for diagnosis have not been validated in patients with severe psychiatric illness and may need clarification. Evidence for a reconsideration of criteria and thresholds includes the following: These patients may be especially vulnerable to small amounts of substances (Knudsen and Vilmar, 1984; Drake, Osher, and Wallach, 1989; Lieberman, Kinon, and Loebel, 1990). They appear to have less severe substance disorders than primary substance abusers according to traditional criteria (Lehman, Myers, Corty, and Thompson, 1994), but they often experience adverse effects that are different from those experienced by primary substance abusers (Corse, Hirschinger, and Zanis, 1995). Finally, the physiological dependence syndrome may be less significant in patients with severe mental illness than in other substance abusers (Drake and others, 1990).

Although considered a residual category in DSM-III-R, substance abuse (as opposed to dependence) is actually quite common in persons with severe mental illness (Drake and others, 1990). Furthermore, the abuse versus dependence distinction may be etiologically important and prognostically useful in the population of severely ill psychiatric patients. Those with abuse rather than dependence are less likely to have family histories of substance disorder (Noordsy, Drake, Biesanz, and McHugo, 1994) and appear to have a better long-term prognosis, which suggests the possibility of different treatment needs (Bartels, Drake, and Wallach, 1995).

The current DSM-IV definition of abuse (American Psychiatric Association, 1994) involves a maladaptive pattern of use leading to adverse consequences in the absence of dependence. Recurrent exacerbation of psychological problems, however, which was a sufficient criterion for an abuse diagnosis in DSM-III-R, has been omitted from DSM-IV—a change that may be particularly significant for dually diagnosed persons, because the maladaptive nature of their use often involves interaction with mental illness. How these and other changes from DSM-III-R to DSM-IV will affect classification of persons with severe mental illness remains to be studied. National survey data suggest that in the general population the DSM-IV diagnosis of substance abuse without dependence will be far less prevalent (.06 percent) than was the DSM-III-R diagnosis (2.38 percent) (Grant, 1992).

The issue of diagnostic heterogeneity and its possible role in matching patients with treatments is poorly understood. Using latent class analysis, Cuffel, Heithoff, and Lawson (1993) identified two groups of dually diagnosed schizophrenic patients: alcohol or marijuana abusers and multiple-drug abusers. This diagnostic difference may have implications for treatment; it was later found to be important in predicting community violence, with multiple-drug abusers exhibiting higher level of violence (Cuffel, Shumway, Chouljian, and MacDonald, 1994).

Although this chapter focuses on assessing substance use, the co-occurring psychiatric diagnosis is equally important in determining heterogeneity. Substance disorder comorbidity clearly affects diagnostic validity and makes differential diagnosis very difficult in some cases (Lehman, Myers, and Corty, 1989). Patients with psychiatric syndromes that are induced by substance disorder probably have different treatment needs from those who have two independent, co-occurring disorders (Lehman, Myers, Thompson, and Corty, 1993). Diagnostic heterogeneity within the dual-disorder population undoubtedly has further implications for treatment. For example, research indicates that patients with severe and persistent affective disorders, as opposed to psychotic disorders, are more socially competent and more able to participate in groups that require higher functioning, including self-help groups (Noordsy, Schwab, Fox, and Drake, 1996).

SPECIALIZED ASSESSMENT

Once substance use disorders have been detected and diagnosed, the transition to treatment planning requires more detailed, individual information. Specialized assessment yields specific information for planning treatment by exploring three areas: the nature and severity of the problematic substance-using behaviors, the stage of treatment, and the factors associated with the maintenance of the problematic substance-using behaviors.

Nature and severity of substance-using behaviors

Substance-using behaviors should first be thoroughly described, including time, duration, frequency, level of intensity, and quantity of use; severity; developmental use history; physiological, cognitive, behavioral, and environmental systems involved in the behaviors; and the immediate and delayed consequences of use (Donovan, 1988). Physiological factors include tolerance, dependence, and withdrawal, as well as the medical sequelae of substance use. Cognitive factors include positive and negative expectancies related to use, such as enhanced mood, improved social ease, or enhanced feelings of arousal. Behavioral factors include interpersonal coping strategies and communication skills. Environmental factors include the social context of use, such as peer pressure. Although a number of instruments are available, no standardized measures for assessing the nature and severity of substance disorder have been validated in dual-disorder patients.

Assessment should investigate all relevant domains but should be individualized and should correspond to the duration of the substance-using behavior. For example, extensive neuropsychological testing may not be important for the young, moderate drinker, but is often critical for an older person with a long drinking history (Donovan, Kivlahan, Walker, and Umlauf, 1985).

Severity of psychiatric symptoms and response to antipsychotic medications may also be important dimensions. Our clinical experience suggests that persistent psychosis often renders substance abuse treatment ineffective, and case studies indicate that a positive response to clozapine is associated with reduced substance use (Marcus and Snyder, 1995).

Stage of treatment

One central aspect of assessment is the individual's stage of change and stage of treatment. Prochaska, DiClemente, and Norcross (1992) have found that individuals with substance use disorder change in a predictable sequence, whether they do so on their own or in relation to a treatment program. Although assessing this process might have implications for treatment, there are currently no studies of this scheme in psychiatric patients.

Osher and Kofoed (1989) independently derived a similar model for the stage of treatment, which focuses less on internal motivational states and more on the client's level of behavioral involvement in substance abuse treatment. A client in the *engagement* stage develops a trusting relationship with treatment staff. During *persuasion,* clients learn more about the role that alcohol and drugs have played in their lives and develop motivation for change. They use specific strategies and interventions during *active treatment* to reduce their substance use. When these gains are stable, other specific strategies are employed as part of *relapse prevention.* Our group operationalized these stages of recovery in order to create a psychometrically sound scale to determine stage of treatment: the Substance Abuse Treatment Scale (SATS), which can be used reliably by clinicians or researchers (McHugo, Drake, Burton, and Ackerson, 1995).

The SATS helps clinicians determine the range of interventions that might be effective in relation to the client's current level of motivation and behavioral change (Drake and Noordsy, 1994). Thus the most immediate goal when working with a client in the engagement phase is to establish a helping relationship, or treatment alliance. Efforts to convince clients to address their substance abuse before such a relationship is established are usually premature and may drive clients away from treatment. In the persuasion phase, several strategies may enable the client to perceive the relationship between substance use and problems in living (see Carey's chapter in this volume).[2] During active treatment, clients may make use of different interventions to modify risk factors such as lack of employment, a substance-abusing peer network, and craving. It should be noted that the efficacy of specific interventions and of the stagewise concept of treatment needs to be studied in depth.

---

[2]Editors' Note: The authors refer to a chapter that appears in the book where this reading was originally published. The full reference for that chapter is Carey, K. B. (1996). Treatment of co-occurring substance abuse and major mental illness. In R.E. Drake & K.T. Mueser (Eds.), *Dual diagnosis of mental illness and substance abuse: Vol. 2. Recent research and clinical implications* (pp. 19-31). San Francisco: Jossey-Bass. See also Dr. Carey's article in the Treatment section of this volume.

Conditions associated with abuse

Substance abuse is currently viewed as a complex biopsychosocial disorder in which genetic, biological, psychological, cognitive, social, and environmental factors combine to predispose an individual to disorder; another combination of potentially overlapping factors sustains the disorder (Donovan, 1988). Thus, for example, for a particular individual with schizophrenia, factors such as family history of alcoholism, social anxiety, expectancies of decreased anxiety and increased social friendships, boredom, hopelessness, lack of activities, and living with substance-abusing peers may all contribute to a drug disorder. The essence of treatment planning is to identify these specific factors as targets of intervention. This approach underlies cognitive (Beck, Wright, Newman, and Liese, 1993) and behavioral (Monti, Abrams, Kadden, and Cooney, 1989) approaches to substance abuse treatment. As an example, for the patient described above the treatment team might consider some combination of the following interventions: a multiple-family group to address family issues, social skills training to overcome social anxiety without alcohol, cognitive therapy to modify expectancies, participation in a supported employment program to combat boredom and inactivity, and modification of the subject's living situation. Typically, not all of these can be changed at once, which is why recovery tends to take place over months and years rather than weeks (Drake, Mueser, Clark, and Wallach, 1996).

Recent evidence indicates that one important risk factor for substance abuse—trauma history—has often been ignored in treatment. Research shows that a high proportion of patients with severe mental illness have evidence of recent and past sexual and physical trauma, and that trauma history is associated with substance disorder (Goodman, Dutton, and Harris, 1995; Rosenberg, Drake, and Mueser, in press). Anecdotally, trauma history is identified as critical by clinicians in almost every dual-diagnosis program that we have visited. Clinicians are beginning to develop interventions that focus specifically on the poor self-care and self-destructive behaviors associated with trauma history in dually diagnosed persons (Harris, in press). Although no outcome data are yet available, we expect that this will be an important line of research in coming years.

Only limited evidence supports the efficacy of the type of individualized assessment and treatment planning discussed in this section. Two recent quasi-experimental studies show that the specific types of cognitive-behavioral and social networking interventions that are implied by this approach are effective with dually diagnosed individuals (Drake and others, 1996; Jerrell and Ridgely 1995). In each study specific, individualized interventions with a focus on cognitive, behavioral, and social network factors produced better outcomes than other treatments.

FUTURE RESEARCH

There is a great need to develop substance use assessment instruments that are specifically tailored for persons with severe mental illness. Ideally such instruments should address the utility of multimodal procedures and should also address the three phases of screening, diagnostic assessment, and specialized assessment. Our group is now engaged in developing optimal screening and diagnostic instruments based on available interviews, questionnaires, laboratory procedures, collateral interviews, and indirect measures. By administering these assessment procedures to a large sample of severely mentally ill patients, we are working to develop a brief screening instrument for identifying substance-abusing patients in acute-care psychiatric settings. We are also working to develop a multimodal, diagnostic procedure for alcohol, cannabis, and cocaine abuse and dependence in persons with severe mental illness. This latter procedure is being designed for acute situations in which time, patient cooperation, and other resources allow a more extensive assessment. In addition to these studies, the field needs comprehensive instruments specific to persons with severe mental illness that assess the nature and severity of substance disorder and the specific factors that are associated with the substance-using behaviors.

CONCLUSION

Severely ill psychiatric patients constitute an extremely vulnerable, high-risk group for substance abuse and dependence. They should therefore receive routine screening in all treatment programs. Currently, substance abuse is frequently underdetected in acute-care psychiatric settings. A few simple procedures could improve current rates of detection dramatically. Mental health professionals assessing patients in acute-care settings need to be educated about the high rates of substance abuse among severely mentally ill persons, the common correlates of substance abuse, basic detection techniques, and the importance of accurate diagnosis for appropriate treatment.

Some progress has been made in terms of understanding the limits of instruments currently used for primary substance abusers. More work is needed to develop and refine screening instruments and procedures to detect and diagnose alcohol- and drug-related problems in severely mentally ill persons. In addition, the development of instruments that enable clinicians to go from diagnosis to treatment planning should be a priority for researchers.

REFERENCES

Alterman, A. I., and Erdlen, D. L. "Illicit Substance Use in Hospitalized Psychiatric Patients: Clinical Observations." *Journal of Psychiatric Research and Evaluation,* 1983, 5, 377-380.

Alterman, A. I., Erdlen, F. R., McLellan, A. T., and Mann, S. C. "Problem Drinking in Hospitalized Schizophrenic Patients." *Addictive Behaviors,* 1980, 5, 273-276.

American Psychiatric Association. *Diagnostic and Statistical Manual of Mental Disorders* (3rd ed., revised). Washington, D.C.: American Psychiatric Press, 1987.

American Psychiatric Association. *Diagnostic and Statistical Manual of Mental Disorders* (4th ed.). Washington, D.C.: American Psychiatric Press, 1994.

Ananth, J., Vandewater, S., Kamal, M., Broksky, A., Gamal, R., and Miller, M. "Missed Diagnosis of Substance Abuse in Psychiatric Patients." *Hospital and Community Psychiatry,* 1989, 4, 297-299.

Babor, T. F., DeLaFuente, J. R., Saunders, J., and Grant, M. *AUDIT: The Alcohol Use Disorders Identification Test, Guidelines for Use in Primary Health Care.* Geneva, Switzerland: World Health Organization. 1989.

Babor, T. F., Kranzler, H. R., and Lauerman, R. J. "Early Detection of Harmful Alcohol Consumption: Comparison of Clinical, Laboratory, and Self-Report Screening Procedures." *Addictive Behaviors,* 1989, 14, 139-157.

Babor, T. F., Stephen, R. S., and Marlatt, G. A. "Verbal Report Methods in Clinical Research on Alcoholism: Response Bias and its Minimization." *Journal of Studies on Alcohol,* 1987, 48, 410-424.

Barbee, J. G., Clark, P. D., Crapanzano, M. S., Heintz, G. C., and Kehoe, C. E. "Alcohol and Substance Abuse Among Schizophrenic Patients Presenting to an Emergency Psychiatric Service." *Journal of Nervous and Mental Disease,* 1989, 177, 400-407

Barry, K. L., Fleming, M. F., Greenley, J., Widlak, P., Kropp, S., and McKee, D. "Assessment of Alcohol and Other Drug Disorders in the Seriously Mentally Ill." *Schizophrenia Bulletin,* 1995, 21, 315-321.

Bartels, S. J., Drake, R. E., and Wallach, M. A. "Long-Term Course of Substance Use Disorders in Severe Mental Illness." *Psychiatric Services,* 1995, 46, 248-251.

Beck, A. T., Wright, P. D., Newman, C. F., and Liese, B. S. *Cognitive Therapy of Substance Abuse.* New York: Guilford Press, 1993.

Blankertz, L. E., and Cnaan, R. A. "Assessing the Impact of Two Residential Programs for Dually Diagnosed Homeless Individuals." *Social Services Review,* 1994, 68, 536-560.

Blumberg, A. G., Cohen, M., Heaton, A. M., and Klein, D. F. "Covert Drug Abuse Among Voluntary Hospitalized Psychiatric Patients." *Journal of the American Medical Association,* 1971, 217, 1659-1661.

Corse, S. J., Hirschinger, N. B., and Zanis, D. "The Use of the Addiction Severity Index with People with Severe Mental Illness." *Psychiatric Rehabilitation Journal,* 1995, 19 (1), 9-18.

Cox, R. A., and Crifasi, J. A. "A Comparison of a Commercial Microdiffusion Method and Gas Chromatography for Ethanol Analysis." *Journal of Analytic Toxicology,* 1990, 14, 211-212.

Crowley, T. J., Chesluk, D., Dilts, S., and Hart, R. "Drug and Alcohol Abuse Among Psychiatric Admissions." *Archives of General Psychiatry,* 1974, *30,* 13-20.

Cuffel, B., Heithoff, K. A., and Lawson, W. "Correlates of Patterns of Substance Abuse Among Patients with Schizophrenia." *Hospital and Community Psychiatry,* 1993, *44,* 247-251.

Cuffel, B., Shumway, M., Chouljian, T. L., and MacDonald, T. "A Longitudinal Study of Substance Use and Community Violence in Schizophrenia." *Journal of Nervous and Mental Disease,* 1994, *182,* 704-708.

Dixon, L., Dibietz, E., Myers, P., Conley, R., Medoff, D., and Lehman, A. F. "Comparison of DSM-III-R Diagnoses and a Brief Interview for Substance Use Among State Hospital Patients." *Hospital and Community Psychiatry,* 1993, *44,* 748-752.

Donovan, D. M. "Assessment of Addictive Behaviors: Implications of an Emerging Biopsychosocial Model." In D. M. Donovan and G. A. Marlatt (eds.), *Assessment of Addictive Behavior.* New York: Guilford Press, 1988, 3-48.

Donovan, D. M., Kivlahan, D. R., Walker, R. D., and Umlauf, R. "Derivation and Validation of Neuropsychological Clusters Among Male Alcoholics." *Journal of Studies on Alcohol,* 1985, *46,* 205-211.

Drake, R. E., Alterman, A. I., and Rosenberg, S. D. "Detection of Substance Use Disorders in Severely Mentally Ill Patients." *Community Mental Health Journal,* 1993, *29,* 175-192.

Drake, R. E., and Mercer-McFadden, C. "Assessment of Substance Abuse Among Persons with Severe Mental Disorders." In A. F. Lehman and L. Dixon (eds.), *Double Jeopardy: Chronic Mental Illness and Substance Abuse.* New York: Harwood Academic Press, 1995, 47-62.

Drake, R. E., Mueser, K. T., Clark, R. E., and Wallach, M. A. "The Natural History of Substance Use Disorder in Persons with Severe Mental Illness." *American Journal of Orthopsychiatry,* 1996, *66,* 42-51.

Drake, R. E., Mueser, K. T., and McHugo, G. J. "Using Clinician Rating Scales to Assess Substance Abuse Among Persons with Severe Mental Disorders." In L. I. Sederer and B. Dickey (eds.), *Outcomes Assessment in Clinical Practice.* Baltimore: Williams and Wilkins, 1996, 113-116.

Drake, R. E., and Noordsy, D. L. "Case Management for People with Coexisting Severe Mental Disorder and Substance Use Disorder." *Psychiatric Annals,* 1994, *24,* 27-31.

Drake, R. E., Osher, F. C., Noordsy, D. L., Hurlbut, S. C., Teague, G. B., and Beaudett, M. S. "Diagnosis of Alcohol Use Disorders in Schizophrenia." *Schizophrenia Bulletin,* 1990, *16,* 57-67.

Drake, R. E., Osher, F. C., and Wallach, M. A. "Alcohol Use and Abuse in Schizophrenia: A Prospective Community Study." *Journal of Nervous and Mental Disease,* 1989, *177,* 408-414.

Drake, R. E., and Wallach, M. A. "Moderate Drinking Among People with Severe Mental Illness." *Hospital and Community Psychiatry,* 1993, *44,* 780-782.

Drake, R. E., Yovetich, N. A., Bebout, R. R., Harris, M., and McHugo, G. J. "Integrated Treatment for Dually Diagnosed, Homeless Adults." Unpublished manuscript, 1996.

Galletly, C. A., Field, C. D., and Prior, M. "Urine Drug Screening of Patients Admitted to a State Psychiatric Hospital." *Hospital and Community Psychiatry,* 1993, *44,* 587-589.

Gold, M. S., and Dackis, C. A. "Role of the Laboratory in Evaluation of Suspected Drug Abusers." *Journal of Clinical Psychiatry,* 1986, *47,* 17-23.

Goldfinger, S. M., Schutt, R. K., Seidman, L. M., Turner, W. M., Penk, W. E., and Tolomiczenko, G. "Alternative Measures of Substance Abuse Among Homeless Mentally Ill Persons in Cross-Section and over Time." *Journal of Nervous and Mental Disease,* in press.

Goodman, L. A., Dutton, M. A., and Harris, M. "Physical and Sexual Assault Prevalence Among Homeless Women with Serious Mental Illness." *American Journal of Orthopsychiatry,* 1995, *65,* 468-478.

Grant, B. F. "Prevalence of the Proposed DSM-IV Alcohol Use Disorders: United States, 1988." *British Journal of Addiction,* 1992, *87,* 309-316.

Harris, M. "Treating Sexual Abuse Trauma with Dually Diagnosed Women." *Community Mental Health Journal,* in press.

Haywood, T. W., Kravitz, H. M., Grossman, L. S., Cavanaugh, J. L., Davis, J. M., and Lewis, D. A. "Predicting the 'Revolving Door' Phenomenon Among Patients with Schizophrenic, Schizoaffective, and Affective Disorders." *American Journal of Psychiatry,* 1995, *152,* 856-861.

Jerrell, J. M., and Ridgely, M. S. "Comparative Effectiveness of Three Approaches to Serving People with Severe Mental Illness and Substance Abuse Disorders." *Journal of Nervous and Mental Disease,* 1995, *183,* 566-576.

Knudsen, P., and Vilmar, T. "Cannabis and Neuroleptic Agents in Schizophrenia." *Acta Psychiatrica Scandinavica,* 1984, *69,* 162-174.

Kofoed, L. L. "Assessment of Comorbid Substance Abuse and Other Major Psychiatric Illnesses." In K. Minkoff and R. E. Drake (eds.), *Dual Diagnosis of Major Mental Illness and Substance Disorder. New Directions for Mental Health Services,* no. 50. San Francisco: Jossey-Bass, 1991, 43-55.

Lehman, A. F., and Dixon, L. (eds.) *Double Jeopardy: Chronic Mental Illness and Substance Abuse.* New York: Harwood Academic Publishers, 1995.

Lehman, A. F., Myers, P., and Corty, E. "Assessment and Classification of Patients with Psychiatric and Substance Abuse Syndromes." *Hospital and Community Psychiatry,* 1989, *40,* 1019-1025.

Lehman, A. F., Myers, C. P., Corty, E., and Thompson, J. "Severity of Substance-Use Disorders Among Psychiatric Inpatients." *Journal of Nervous and Mental Disease,* 1994, *182,* 164-167.

Lehman, A. F., Myers, C. P., Thompson, J. W., and Corty, E. "Implications of Mental and Substance Use Disorders: A Comparison of Single and Dual Diagnosis Patients." *Journal of Nervous and Mental Disease,* 1993, *181,* 365-370.

Lieberman, J. A., Kinon, B. J., and Loebel, A. D. "Dopaminergic Mechanisms in Idiopathic and Drug-Induced Psychoses." *Schizophrenia Bulletin,* 1990, *16,* 97-110.

McHugo, G. J., Drake, R. E., Burton, H. L, and Ackerson, T. M. "A Scale for Assessing the Stage of Substance Abuse Treatment in Persons with Severe Mental Illness." *Journal of Nervous and Mental Disease,* 1995, *183,* 762-767.

Magliozzi, J. R., Kanter, S. L., Csernansky, J. G., and Hollister, L. E. "Detection of Marijuana Use in Psychiatric Patients by Determination of Urinary Delta-9-Tetrahydrocannabino-11-oic acid." *Journal of Nervous and Mental Disease*, 1983, *171*, 246-249.

Marcus, P., and Snyder, R. "Reduction of Comorbid Substance Abuse with Clozapine." *American Journal of Psychiatry*, 1995, *142*, 959.

Minkoff, K., and Drake, R. E. (eds.). *Dual Diagnosis of Major Mental Illness and Substance Disorder.* New Directions for Mental Health Services, no. 50. San Francisco: Jossey-Bass, 1991.

Monti, P. M., Abrams, D. B., Kadden, R. M., and Cooney, N. L. *Treating Alcohol Dependence.* New York: Guilford Press, 1989.

Mueser, K. T., Nishith, P., Tracey, J. I., DeGirolamo, J., and Molinaro, M. "Expectations and Motives for Substance Use in Schizophrenia." *Schizophrenia Bulletin*, 1995, *21*, 367-378.

Mueser, K. T., Yarnold, P. R., and Bellack, A. S. "Diagnostic and Demographic Correlates of Substance Abuse in Schizophrenia and Major Affective Disorder." *Acta Psychiatrica Scandinavica*, 1992, *85*, 48-55.

Negrete, J. C., and Knapp, W. P. "The Effects of Cannabis Use on the Clinical Conditions of Schizophrenics." In L. S. Harris (ed.), *Problems of Drug Dependence.* Rockville, Md.: National Institute on Drug Abuse, 1986.

Noordsy, D. L., Drake, R. E., Biesanz, J. C., and McHugo, G. J. "Family History of Alcoholism in Schizophrenia." *Journal of Nervous and Mental Disease*, 1994, *182*, 651-655.

Noordsy, D. L., Schwab, B., Fox, L., and Drake, R. E. "The Role of Self-Help Programs in the Rehabilitation of Persons with Severe Mental Disorders and Substance Use Disorders." *Community Mental Health Journal*, 1996, *32*, 71-81.

Osher, F. C. and Kofoed, L. L. "Treatment of Patients with Both Psychiatric and Psychoactive Substance Use Disorders." *Hospital and Community Psychiatry*, 1989, *40*, 1025-1030.

Prochaska, J. O., DiClemente, C. C., and Norcross, J. C. "In Search of How People Change: Applications to Addictive Behaviors." *American Psychologist*, 1992, *47*, 1102-1114.

Regier, D. A., Farmer, M. E., Rae, D. S., Locke, B. Z., Keith, S. J., Judd, L. L, and Goodwin, F. K. "Comorbidity of Mental Disorders with Alcohol and Other Drug Abuse." *Journal of the American Medical Association*, 1990, *264*, 2511-2518.

Richard, M. L., Liskow, B. I., and Perry, P. J. "Recent Psychostimulant Use in Hospitalized Schizophrenics." *Journal of Clinical Psychiatry*, 1985, *46*, 79-83.

Ridgely, M. S., Osher, F. C., and Talbott, S. A. *Chronically Mentally Ill Young Adults with Substance Abuse Problems: Treatment and Training Issues.* Rockville, Md.: Alcohol, Drug Abuse, and Mental Health Administration, 1987.

Rosenberg, S. D., Drake, R. E., and Mueser, K. T, "New Directions for Treatment Research on Sequelae of Sexual Abuse in Persons with Severe Mental Illness." *Community Mental Health Journal*, in press.

Ryglewicz, H. "Psychoeducation for Clients and Families: A Way In, Out, and Through in Working with People with Dual Disorders." *Psychosocial Rehabilitation Journal*, 1991, *15*, 79-89.

Safer, D. J. "Substance Abuse by Young Adult Chronic Patients." *Hospital and Community Psychiatry,* 1987, *38,* 511-514.

Selzer, M. L. "The Michigan Alcoholism Screening Test: The Quest for a New Diagnostic Instrument." *American Journal of Psychiatry,* 1971, *127,* 89-94.

Shaner, A., Khaka, E., Roberts, L., Wilkins, J., Anglin, D., and Hsieh, S. "Unrecognized Cocaine Use Among Schizophrenic Patients." *American Journal of Psychiatry,* 1993, *150,* 758-762.

Skinner, H. A. "The Drug Abuse Screening Test." *Addictive Behaviors,* 1982, *7,* 363-371.

Skinner, H., Holt, S., Sheu, W. J., and Israel, Y. "Clinical Versus Laboratory Detection of Alcohol Abuse: The Alcohol Clinical Index." *British Medical Journal,* 1986, *292,* 2261-2265.

Sobell, M. B., Maisto, S. A., Sobell, L. C., Cooper, A. M., Cooper, T., and Sanders, B. "Developing a Prototype for Evaluating Alcohol Treatment Effectiveness." In L. C. Sobell, M. B. Sobell, and E. Ward (eds.), *Evaluating Alcohol and Drug Abuse Effectiveness.* New York: Pergamon, 1980, 129-150.

Spitzer, R. L, Williams, J. B. W., Gibbon, M. and First, B. B. *Structured Clinical Interview for DSM-III-R-Patient Version (SCID-P).* New York: Biometric Research Department, New York State Psychiatric Institute, 1988.

Stone, A., Greenstein, R., Gamble, G., and McLellan, A. T. "Cocaine Use in Chronic Schizophrenic Outpatients Receiving Depot Neuroleptic Medications." *Hospital and Community Psychiatry,* 1993, *44,* 176-177.

Test, M. A., Wallisch, L. S., Allness, D. J., and Ripp, K. "Substance Use in Young Adults with Schizophrenic Disorders." *Schizophrenia Bulletin,* 1989, *15,* 465-476.

Toland, A. M., and Moss, H. B. "Identification of the Alcoholic Schizophrenic: Use of Clinical Laboratory Tests and the MAST." *Journal of Studies on Alcohol,* 1989, *50,* 49-53.

Yesavage, J. A., and Zarcone, V. "History of Drug Abuse and Dangerous Behavior in Inpatient Schizophrenics." *Journal of Clinical Psychiatry,* 1983, *44,* 259-261.

ABOUT THE AUTHORS

Robert E. Drake, M.D., Ph.D., is Professor of Psychiatry and Community and Family Medicine at Dartmouth Medical School and Director of the New Hampshire-Dartmouth Psychiatric Research Center. Stanley D. Rosenberg, Ph.D., is Professor of Psychiatry and Chief Psychologist, Department of Psychiatry at Dartmouth Medical School. He is a senior researcher at the New Hampshire-Dartmouth Psychiatric Research Center. Kim T. Mueser, Ph.D., is Professor of Psychiatry and Community and Family Medicine at Dartmouth Medical School and a senior researcher at the New Hampshire-Dartmouth Psychiatric Research Center.

Copyright 1996. Jossey-Bass, Inc., Publishers. Reprinted with permission.

COCAINE USE BY SCHIZOPHRENIC OUTPATIENTS WHO RECEIVE DEPOT NEUROLEPTIC MEDICATION

Andrew M. Stone, Robert A. Greenstein,
Geraldine Gamble, and A. Thomas McLellan

Reprinted from *Hospital and Community Psychiatry*, 44(2): 176-177, 1993

With the rise in drug use in the general population, hospital emergency rooms and substance dependence treatment programs have witnessed a dramatic increase in the demand for treatment of cocaine dependence. This paper presents results of a screening for cocaine use among a group of relatively stable chronic schizophrenic patients who were receiving depot neuroleptic medication at an outpatient clinic program operated by the Veterans Affairs Medical Center in Philadelphia.

SETTING

During the past 20 years, the mental health clinic of the Philadelphia VA Medical Center has treated between 65 and 85 schizophrenic patients each year with intramuscular depot neuroleptic medication (fluphenazine or haloperidol) in an outpatient clinic program (1).

The medical center's mental health clinic is a large urban outpatient psychiatric facility with about 2,400 active patients. The vast majority (93 percent) have a chronic psychiatric disorder that began or was exacerbated during their military service. Forty-seven percent have schizophrenia, 30 percent have anxiety disorders, including post-traumatic stress disorder, and 15 percent have primary affective disorders, including bipolar disorder.

The clinic's depot neuroleptic program is managed by psychiatric nurses. Patients in the program are seen at least monthly by a clinical nurse specialist who monitors their mental status and general health. Using a standardized protocol, complete blood count and relevant biochemical profiles are obtained annually or when clinically indicated. A physician also follows each patient, periodically reviewing the patient's condition and treatment.

At the time of the study in April 1989, the clinic's depot neuroleptic program had an active census of 69 patients with diagnoses of chronic schizophrenia or schizoaffective disorder. Sixty-seven of the patients were men, and two were women. The patients had a history of noncompliance with oral medication regimens. All had a history of long-term hospitalization lasting two years or more or a history of three or more psychiatric hospitalizations. The group also included one combat veteran with chronic psychosis who had never been hospitalized.

Most patients in the depot neuroleptic program reliably kept their scheduled appointments at the clinic. Between eight and 17 patients were hospitalized each year for recurrences or exacerbation of schizophrenia. Although we were aware of significant alcohol abuse and dependence in this patient population, we were not aware of other substance use disorders.

An increase in the number of dually diagnosed patients on the medical center's inpatient psychiatric unit during the preceding year and behavioral changes among patients in the depot neuroleptic program suggested the need to test for substance use among the outpatients served by the clinic.

METHODS

Urine samples from each patient in the depot neuroleptic program were screened for evidence of substance use as part of the annual standardized protocol. Urine specimens were obtained from patients using an unmonitored clinic rest room. The specimens were analyzed using thin-layer chromatography, and positive results were confirmed by radioimmunoassay. At the time of the urine screening, a nurse-therapist (GG) interviewed each patient using a semistructured format that included questions about drug use and other issues. Patients who tested positive for cocaine use were later informed of the results and were interviewed again using the same format.

Relationships between the proportion of patients with positive drug screens and other patient variables, including self-reports of drug use, were analyzed using unpaired, two-tailed t tests.

RESULTS

Of the 69 patients tested, 15 patients (21.7 percent) had urine samples that were positive for cocaine. Evidence of cocaine use was strongly associated with certain patient factors, including gender, age, use of other substances, and psychiatric hospitalization during the year before the study. All 15 patients who tested positive for cocaine use were men. Their mean age was 35.5 years, compared with 46.3 years for the patients who tested negative ($t=3.709$, $df=67$, $p<.001$). No other demographic characteristics, including ethnic group, were significantly associated with cocaine use.

Using a rating of alcohol problems based on self-reports of quantities consumed and a global rating by the treating clinician, we found that five of the 15 patients who used cocaine had a problem with alcohol, compared with ten of the 54 patients who did not use cocaine; this difference was not significant. Eight of 15 patients who tested positive for cocaine use reported that they used marijuana, compared with four of 54 patients who did not use cocaine (t=-5.425, df=65, p<.001). No patients acknowledged cocaine use before being informed about the results of the drug screen. After the results were discussed, eight of the 15 patients with positive test results admitted to using cocaine.

To measure the effect of cocaine use on clinical course, we counted the number of patients who had a psychiatric hospitalization during the preceding year. Five of the 15 patients (33.3 percent) who used cocaine had been hospitalized in the previous year, compared with nine of the 54 patients (17 percent) who did not use cocaine. Although this difference was not statistically significant in our small sample, the 2-to-1 ratio of percentages suggests a trend that could be significant in a larger sample.

DISCUSSION

Dual diagnosis of substance use disorders and major psychiatric illness has recently begun to receive long-deserved attention (2). Studies of both substance dependence in patients with primary psychiatric diagnoses and psychiatric illness in patients in treatment for substance dependence have been reported (3,4). A significant incidence of substance dependence has been found among psychiatric inpatients (5). Substance dependence in psychiatric patients correlates with increased readmission rates (6), particularly among patients who use psychostimulants (7). Outpatient treatment of schizophrenic patients with substance dependence has been described (8). However, we could find no reports of the incidence of cocaine use in a population of schizophrenic outpatients.

Cocaine (especially crack cocaine) is cheap and quite prevalent in many communities, particularly in large urban centers. Some patients reported that their cocaine use was actually an effort to conform to societal norms in their community and to reduce the stigma of their diagnosis in the view of their peers who are not mentally ill. However, self-reports cannot be accepted as a full explanation or description of patients' patterns of substance use. The diagnosis of substance use disorder must be actively sought by use of biochemical screens, direct interview, and observation for otherwise unexplained changes in patients' condition, so that this vulnerable group can receive appropriate treatment.

Based on the data in our study, younger schizophrenic patients may have a higher incidence of substance use, although no age group appears totally exempt from risk. Several factors in the study design, including use of a single random urine sample, unmonitored collection of samples, and exclusion of marginal or noncompliant patients from the depot neuroleptic program because of inability to keep appointments, could result in underreporting of substance use. In addition, thin-layer chromatography, the method used to analyze the samples, has a low sensitivity and is associated with high rates of false negatives. It is likely that the actual incidence of substance use in the sample we studied was higher than reported here.

All the patients tested in this study were known to be compliant with a neuroleptic regimen that could be expected to produce significant dopamine blockade. Neuroleptics are known to interfere with physical sensations of cocaine cravings and internal stimulus control of behavior (9). In a study of recently detoxified chronic cocaine abusers, postsynaptic dopamine receptors were found to be depleted (10). Thus any hypothesis proposing a relationship between dopamine blockade and cocaine use or effect must consider that the patients we studied used cocaine while also taking neuroleptics, potent antagonists of dopamine. Further study of the subjective experience of both cocaine craving and cocaine effects in the presence of dopamine blockade are needed for a more complete understanding of these mechanisms. Other factors that should be explored include the specificity of dopamine receptors and the extent of dopamine blockade produced by neuroleptics.

Our findings suggest that patients with chronic psychiatric illness are at risk for substance abuse and dependence. Plans for comprehensive treatment of this population must include measures to prevent, detect, and treat these disorders.

REFERENCES

1. Selander JM, Miller WC: Prolixin group: can nursing intervention groups lower recidivism? *Journal of Psychosocial Nursing and Mental Health Services* 23(11):16-20, 1985
2. Drake RE, Wallach MA: Substance abuse among the chronic mentally ill. *Hospital and Community Psychiatry* 40:1041-1046, 1989
3. Dixon L, Haas G, Weiden PJ, et al: Drug abuse in schizophrenic patients. *American Journal of Psychiatry* 148:224-230, 1991
4. Kleber HD: The use of psychotropic drugs in the treatment of compulsive opiate abusers: the rationale for their use. *Advances in Alcohol and Substance Abuse* 5(1-2):103-119, 1985-86
5. Miller F, Tanenbaum JH, Goodwin C, et al: Cocaine and polysubstance abuse in psychiatric inpatients. *Hospital and Community Psychiatry* 41:1251-1253, 1990
6. Craig TJ, Lin SP, El Defrawi MH, et al: Clinical correlates of readmission in a schizophrenic cohort. *Psychiatric Quarterly* 57:5-10, 1985
7. Richard ML, Liskow BI, Perry PJ: Recent psychostimulant use in hospitalized schizophrenics. *Journal of Clinical Psychiatry* 46(3):79-83, 1985
8. Hellerstein DJ, Meehan B: Outpatient group therapy for schizophrenic substance abusers. *American Journal of Psychiatry* 144:1337-1339, 1987

9. Colpaert FC, Niemegeers JE, Jansen PAJ: Neuroleptic interference with cocaine CHE: internal stimulus control of behavior and psychosis. *Psychopharmacology* 58:347-367, 1987
10. Volkow ND, Fowler JS, Wolf AP, et al: Effects of chronic cocaine abuse on postsynaptic dopamine receptors. *American Journal of Psychiatry* 147:719-724, 1990

ABOUT THE AUTHORS

Andrew M. Stone, M.D., Robert A. Greenstein, M.D., Geraldine Gamble, M.S.N., R.N.C.S., and A. Thomas McLellan, Ph.D., are affiliated with the Philadelphia Veterans Affairs Medical Center.

ACKNOWLEDGMENTS

The authors thank Arthur Alterman, Ph.D., for help in developing the study.

Copyright 1993. The American Psychiatric Association. Reprinted by permission.

Concurrent Validity of Clinicians' Ratings of Substance Abuse Among Psychiatric Outpatients

Kate B. Carey, Karen M. Cocco, and Jeffrey S. Simons

Reprinted from *Psychiatric Services* 47:842-847, 1996

Objective. Given the prevalence of substance abuse among persons with psychiatric disorders, substance use assessment should be an integral component of mental health evaluations. This study examined the validity of a set of two 5-point rating scales developed for use by mental health clinicians in rating individual clients' levels of alcohol and other drug use.

Methods. A sample of 116 psychiatric outpatients who were participating in a study of psychosocial functioning and substance use was assessed by researchers using an extensive battery of instruments that included the Addiction Severity Index and the Timeline Follow-Back interview. Each client's primary therapist completed the 5-point rating scales to indicate the client's levels of alcohol and drug use.

Results. Clients were grouped according to their ratings on the 5-point scales. Significant differences between the groups were found on self-reported patterns of current alcohol and drug use and substance use history.

Conclusions. Outpatient therapists provided ratings of clients' alcohol and drug use that corresponded well with substance use data obtained from an extensive research battery. The study results support use of clinician rating scales as a screening tool for identifying problematic alcohol and other drug use among psychiatric outpatients.

The high prevalence of substance abuse problems among persons with psychiatric disorders calls for more effective alcohol and drug use assessment in psychiatric settings. Epidemiological data indicate that 29 percent of persons with mental disorders in the general population also have substance use disorders (1). This population figure is exceeded by prevalence estimates of substance abuse in mental health treatment settings, which range from one-third to one-half of all patients (2-6).

These findings suggest that substance use assessment should be a critical component of an overall psychiatric evaluation. However, the accuracy of self-reported substance use or abuse in this population has been questioned due to findings that substance use is underreported in mental health contexts (6-8). In acute care settings, psychosis and behavioral disorganization may interfere with accurate reporting (9,10). Even among stable outpatients, a battery of standardized instruments identified only 75 percent of patients with schizophrenia who also had alcohol use disorders (11). These findings underscore the need to validate assessment instruments specifically for use with patients treated in psychiatric settings (12).

Guidelines for substance use assessment in mental health settings typically recommend using data from multiple sources, including patients' self-reports from periods of relative psychiatric stability, and incorporating longitudinal assessment over an extended time (13-15). An assessment strategy consistent with these recommendations is to solicit information on substance use patterns from experienced professionals who have observed the patient over time.

A set of two 5-point scales based on the work of Drake and others (16) has been developed to help clinicians integrate their observations with information from other sources to rate the level of substance use by severely ill psychiatric patients in the community. The two scales—one for rating alcohol use and the other for rating use of all other drugs combined—are anchored with descriptions that correspond to DSM-III-R criteria for substance abuse and dependence. The five points on each scale reflect the following degrees of substance use: 1, none; 2, mild use but no problems; 3, moderate use with some resulting problems; 4, use associated with severe problems; and 5, use associated with extremely severe problems, probably resulting in hospitalization. Table 1 shows the descriptions corresponding to each degree of substance use.

Clinicians' ratings are based on information obtained over a period of six to 12 months from direct observation of behavior, patients' self-reports, and a variety of collateral sources, including family members, group home or day center staff, and other community contacts. In studies using the scales, ratings covering a six-month period showed good interrater reliability, with kappas of .80 for ratings of patients' alcohol use and .95 for ratings of use of street drugs (16).

Evidence for validity of the clinician rating scales is promising. Predictable relationships have been found between clinicians' ratings of alcohol and drug use and clients' demographic and psychosocial characteristics. For example, among psychiatric outpatients, younger age, male gender, and financial and housing problems were correlated with clinicians' ratings (3,16).

Table 1. Scale for clinicians' rating of clients' use of alcohol or drugs and descriptions corresponding to ratings[1]

Rating	Description
1, none	Client has not used alcohol or drugs during this time interval.
2, mild	Client has used alcohol or drugs during this time interval, but there is no evidence of persistent or recurrent social, occupational, psychological, or physical problems related to use and no evidence of recurrent dangerous use.
3, moderate	Client has used alcohol or drugs during this time interval, and there is evidence of persistent or recurrent social, occupational, psychological, or physical problems related to use or evidence of recurrent dangerous use. Problems have persisted for at least one month. For example, recurrent alcohol or drug use leads to disruptive behavior and housing problems.
4, severe	Meets criteria for moderate use, plus at least three of the following: greater amounts or intervals of use than intended, much of time spent obtaining or using alcohol or drugs, frequent intoxication or withdrawal interferes with other activities, important activities given up because of alcohol or drug use, continued use despite knowledge of alcohol- or drug-related problems, marked tolerance, characteristic withdrawal symptoms, and alcohol or drugs used to relieve or avoid withdrawal symptoms. For example, binges and preoccupation with drinking or using drugs have caused client to drop out of job training and non-alcohol-related or non-drug-related activities.
5, extremely severe	Meets criteria for severe use, plus related problems are so severe that they make noninstitutional living difficult. For example, constant drinking or use of drugs leads to disruptive behavior and inability to pay rent so that client is frequently reported to police and seeking hospitalization.

[1]Separate versions of the scale are used for alcohol use ratings and drug use.

Enhanced levels of psychiatric symptoms have also been associated with substance use among mentally ill persons (17). Higher ratings have been associated with medication noncompliance, hostile behaviors, and disorganized speech (3,16). In addition, in a sample of outpatients with schizophrenia, 68 percent of heavy alcohol users, who were rated as having at least moderate use of alcohol, were rehospitalized over a one-year follow-up interval, compared with only 27 percent of those rated as not using alcohol (16).

This assessment approach has been validated in limited clinical use with other measures of substance use. Drake and associates (11) found excellent sensitivity (95 percent) and specificity (100 percent) for ratings of alcohol use for the previous 12 months among outpatients with schizophrenia, compared with diagnoses of alcohol abuse or dependence made by consensus of a clinical team. Notably, the clinician rating scale was the most accurate single instrument used in their study, which also included self-report questionnaires and a diagnostic interview.

The study reported here provides additional support for the validity of the rating scales for alcohol and drug use, as completed by mental health professionals in an outpatient setting. This investigation differs from previous analyses of the validity of the rating scales because the therapists who provided the ratings for this study received no special training in case identification, the rating scales for both alcohol and drug use were evaluated, and the scales were validated using an extensive, structured assessment of substance-related behaviors that focused on patterns of use rather than diagnoses. Study participants were outpatients at a public psychiatric facility who volunteered for the study; they were not selected on the basis of suspicion of substance abuse.

METHODS

Participants

Study participants were 83 men and 33 women attending outpatient clinics at a state psychiatric facility in upstate New York. Their mean age was 39.1±8.8 years, with a range from 23 to 62 years. All participants volunteered for a study of psychosocial adjustment and substance use and received modest compensation for their participation (the equivalent of $10 in food coupons or movie tickets). Participants were recruited between December 1991 and March 1995 through posters and pamphlets placed in clinic waiting rooms, announcements made in community meetings by research staff, or referrals by therapists. Table 2 shows demographic and diagnostic characteristics of the sample.

Table 2. Demographic and clinical characteristics of 116 psychiatric outpatients who volunteered for a study of psychosocial adjustment and substance use

Characteristic	Value
Gender	
Male	71.6%
Female	28.4%
Race	
White	81.7%
African American	13.0%
Native American	2.6%
Other	2.6%
Marital status	
Married	5.3%
Divorced or separated	36.9%
Never married	55.8%
Living arrangements	
Own home or apartment alone	33.3%
Own home or apartment with others	30.6%
Boarding home	33.3%
Public shelter or other setting	2.7%
Mean$\pm$SD age (years)	39.1$\pm$8.8
Mean$\pm$SD years of education	12.4$\pm$2.7
Mean$\pm$SD N hospitalizations	8.6$\pm$9.7
Primary psychiatric diagnosis	
Schizophrenia	55.2%
Bipolar disorder	19.8%
Schizoaffective disorder	11.5%
Other[1]	12.4%

[1]Includes major depression, dysthymia, psychotic disorder not otherwise specified

Procedure

All participants provided written informed consent after receiving a thorough description of study procedures from a research assistant. Participants were assessed by a trained research assistant in individual sessions that took place in private offices or conference rooms at the treatment sites or in a research office at the state psychiatric facility. Before each session, a breath analysis (using Alcosensor III, by Intoximeters, Inc.) was done; in rare cases when the reading indicated a blood alcohol level greater than 0, the session was rescheduled and the blood alcohol level screening was repeated before the next session.

Baseline assessment included several structured interviews to elicit information on alcohol and other drug use patterns, psychosocial functioning, and diagnostic status. Using the Timeline Follow-Back procedure (18), the research assistant provided visual and verbal prompts to help participants recall drinking behavior and amounts of alcohol consumed each day over the previous six months. Each day was assigned a code characterizing the study participant's drinking behavior as abstinent, light drinking (one to three standard drinks), moderate drinking (four to six standard drinks), or heavy drinking (seven or more standard drinks). Standard drinks were defined as 12 ounces of beer, four ounces of wine, or one ounce of hard liquor. In addition, the maximum number of standard drinks consumed on a single day during the previous six months was recorded. Sobell and Sobell (18) have summarized extensive evidence supporting the reliability and validity of the Timeline Follow-Back procedure.

The Addiction Severity Index (ASI), a structured interview used as a treatment planning and outcome assessment tool (19), was administered to obtain additional information on both alcohol and drug use. The drug and alcohol section of the ASI evaluates history of substance use and treatment and frequency of use in the last month as well as the range of substances used and their route of administration. These sections were supplemented with several additional questions related to age at first use and number of days since last drink or drug use. Sound psychometric properties have been reported for the ASI in a variety of substance abuse treatment samples (20-22); preliminary evidence supports its reliability among persons with both substance-related disorders and major psychiatric disorders (23).

The Structured Clinical Interview for DSM-III-R (SCID) (24) was used to obtain diagnostic information. Interrater reliability for the primary diagnosis, calculated using results from a subset of 14 interviews by two doctoral-level clinical psychologists, was excellent (kappa=1). Finally, the Symptom Check List–90–Revised (SCL-90-R) (25) was used to obtain information about current symptoms. The Global Symptom Index (GSI) from the SCL-90-R was used as an index of subjective psychological distress.

The instruments were administered to participants in varied orders; however, the ASI interview usually preceded the others. At the baseline assessment, the participant identified his or her outpatient therapist, who was typically a social worker, community mental health nurse, or psychologist. The therapists serve a coordinating role in providing services, meet with outpatients once every week or two weeks, and are responsible for maintaining progress notes and updating treatment plans in patients' charts.

The therapists completed the two versions of the clinician rating scales—one on the study participant's use of alcohol during the past six months and the other on the participant's use of all other illicit drugs during the same time period. Therapists returned the forms by mail to the research team. To determine interrater reliability of the rating scales, the two research staff members responsible for the baseline data collection reached consensus ratings on a subset of 25 cases. The kappa of 1 for the rating scale on drug use indicated perfect agreement between ratings by the research team and by the therapists. However, agreement on ratings of alcohol use was low (kappa=.36). Inspection of the ratings indicated that all discrepancies were accounted for by differences in ratings of 1 (no use) or 2 (mild use, no problems). In these cases, the research team assigned a 2 instead of a 1 based on knowledge of a single drink that was revealed during the extensive assessment of alcohol and drug use. No interrater discrepancies emerged for ratings that indicated heavier drinking.

RESULTS

Complete rating scale data were available for 99 study participants. Participants were grouped according to their ratings on the two clinician rating scales. Table 3 shows frequency counts for each of the rating categories.

Table 3. Frequency of clinicians' ratings of alcohol and drug use among 99 psychiatric outpatients assessed using 5-point clinician rating scales[1]

Ratings of alcohol use	Ratings of drug use				
	None	Mild	Moderate	Severe	All ratings
None	55	4	0	0	59
Mild	17	5	1	0	23
Moderate	8	0	6	1	15
Severe	2	0	0	0	2
All ratings	82	9	7	1	99

[1]Alcohol and drug use were rated on a scale from 1 to 5 on which 1 indicated none; 2, mild use; 3, moderate use; 4, severe use; and 5, extremely severe use. No study participants received a rating of 5, extremely severe use.

Although many participants received the same rating on the alcohol scale and the drug scale, a full third of the sample had different ratings on the two scales.

None of the participants in this study received a rating of 5, indicating extremely severe alcohol or drug use. Because only two study participants were rated as having severe alcohol use and only one participant as having severe drug use, the main analyses included only the participants whose substance use had been rated 1, none; 2, mild; or 3, moderate.

Alcohol use

One-way analyses of variance indicated significant differences between the three groups on all but one of the variables from the Timeline Follow-Back interview. Due to the unequal cell sizes, least-square means were used for between-group comparisons. As Table 4 shows, there were significant differences between participants whose alcohol use was rated 1, none, and those whose use was rated 3, moderate, on the number of abstinent days, light-drinking days, and heavy-drinking days and on the maximum amount of alcohol consumed on any one day in the last six months. In addition, participants whose use was rated 2, mild, and those whose use was rated 3 differed on the number of abstinent days and heavy-drinking days and on the maximum daily quantity. No significant differences between groups 1 and 2 emerged.

A similar pattern of results was found for group comparisons on items from the ASI. Comparisons of the least-squares means between groups 1 and 3 indicated significant differences on the number of days in the past 30 during which drinking occurred, during which the participant was intoxicated, and during which the participant experienced alcohol-related problems and on the amount of money spent on alcohol and the number of days since the participant's last drink. Groups 2 and 3 significantly differed from each other on all variables except money spent on alcohol and number of days since the last drink. No significant group differences emerged between groups 1 and 2 on any of the variables except number of days since the last drink.

Drug use

Several items from the ASI alcohol and drug use section were used in the analyses of differences between groups in drug use. As Table 5 shows, one-way analyses of variance indicated significant group differences on all ASI variables and significant differences between group 3 and groups 1 and 2 on all but one variable. Groups 2 and 3 did not differ on the number of days since last use of drugs or in age at first drug use. No significant differences were found between groups 1 and 2 except on the number of days since last drug use.

Table 4. Mean scores on measures in a comprehensive assessment of alcohol use among three groups of psychiatric outpatients whose level of alcohol use was rated by clinicians

Measure	Level of alcohol use[1]			F	df	p<
	Group 1, none (N=59)	Group 2, mild (N=23)	Group 3, moderate (N=15)			
Timeline Follow-Back						
N days abstinent in the last 180 days	178[a]	164[b]	117[ab]	22.62	2, 88	.001
N light-drinking days in the last 180 days	.72[a]	8	23[a]	5.19	2, 88	.01
N moderate-drinking days in the last 180 days	.72	1.73	5.25	2.27	2, 88	ns
N heavy-drinking days in the last 180 days	.73[a]	6[b]	35[ab]	11.11	2, 88	.001
Maximum daily quantity (N standard drinks)	2.7[a]	3.4[b]	10.9[ab]	6.88	2, 88	.01
Addiction Severity Index						
N drinking days in the last 30 days	0[a]	2[b]	5[ab]	12.35	2, 92	.001
N days intoxicated in the last 30 days	.26[a]	.27[b]	5[ab]	12.68	2, 92	.001
Amount of money spent on alcohol in last 30 days	$2.25[a]	$6.40	$11.07[a]	3.03	2, 92	.05
N days experiencing alcohol problems in the last 30 days	0[a]	0[b]	5[ab]	10.03	2, 92	.001
N days since last drink	539[ab]	159[b]	100[a]	14.43	2, 89	.001
Age at first drink (years)	16.4	16.4	14.5	.83	2, 89	ns
N previous treatment episodes for alcohol problems	.94	1.23	1.46	.36	2, 91	ns
Global Assessment of Functioning score[2]	45.5	47.6	43.5	.45	2, 87	ns
Global Symptom Index score[3]	.99	.73	1.3	2.04	2, 84	ns

[1] Means with the same superscripts differ from one another (least-square means test, p<.05).
[2] Lower scores indicate poorer functioning.
[3] Higher scores indicate more severe symptoms.

Table 5. Mean scores on measures in a comprehensive assessment of drug use among three groups of psychiatric outpatients whose level of drug use was rated by clinicians

Measure	Group 1, none (N=82)	Group 2, mild (N=9)	Group 3, moderate (N=7)	F	df	p<
Addiction Severity Index						
Amount of money spent on drugs in last 30 days	$1.08[a]	$.63[b]	$76.00[ab]	33.26	2, 93	.001
N days using more than one substance in last 30 days	.21[a]	.12[b]	3.43[ab]	12.57	2, 93	.001
N days used cannabis in the last 30 days	1.89[a]	.38[b]	4.72[ab]	14.53	2, 93	.001
N days used cocaine in last 30 days	.01[a]	0[b]	4.14[ab]	10.87	2, 93	.001
N days experiencing drug problems in last 30 days	.12[a]	.25[b]	8.29[ab]	29.57	2, 93	.001
N types of drugs used in the last 30 days	.15[a]	.22[b]	1.43[ab]	25.12	2, 97	.001
N days since last drug use	713[ab]	281[b]	10[a]	13.50	2, 79	.001
Age at first drug use (years)	21.1[a]	16.5	12.3[a]	3.87	2, 77	.05
N previous episodes of treatment for drug problems	.48[a]	.12[b]	2.43[ab]	5.14	2, 92	.01
Global Assessment of Functioning score[2]	46	40.4	44.2	.67	2, 88	ns
Global Symptom Index score[3]	.95	1.27	.99	.59	2, 85	ns

[1] Means with the same superscripts differ from one another (least-square means test, p<.05).
[2] Lower scores indicate poorer functioning.
[3] Higher scores indicate more severe symptoms.

DISCUSSION AND CONCLUSIONS

Overall, our findings support the utility of clinicians' ratings of substance use among severely mentally ill clients in the community. The interrater reliability estimate for ratings of drug use in this study compares favorably with estimates found in earlier studies using the ratings.

This finding is especially notable because the two sets of raters in this study—the primary therapists and the research team—used different methods of assessment and varying sources of information to arrive at their ratings. The therapists were instructed to base their judgments on their knowledge of patients over the last six months, which usually included behavioral observations and collateral reports. On the other hand, the members of the research team who made the consensus ratings relied on the aggregate of the assessment data, including structured interviews, paper-and-pencil questionnaires, behavioral observation during the assessments, and chart data.

Use of the different databases accounted for discrepancies reflected in the low kappas for the ratings of alcohol use. All discrepancies were accounted for by the research team's knowledge of rare, and perhaps atypical, instances of drinking reported by study participants during the comprehensive assessment of drinking behavior. The consistency between the ratings by the clinicians and the researchers suggests that ratings by clinicians based on their general knowledge of their patients are, with few exceptions, consistent with ratings based on an extensive testing battery. Although the clinicians' ratings on the 5-point scale cannot yield detailed findings on clients' patterns of substance use and substance use history, they represent an economical and practical approach to global assessment of substance use.

Earlier evidence for the concurrent validity of the clinician rating scales was derived from expected relationships between ratings of substance use and study participants' demographic and psychosocial variables (3,16). However, in these studies, clinicians' ratings of substance use were validated using clinicians' ratings of the psychosocial functioning of clients—for example, the extent of their financial problems or problems with housing.

In contrast, in the study reported here, the evidence for concurrent validity came from instruments that relied on study participants' self-reports and on ratings by the research team. In addition, the instruments addressed alcohol and drug use patterns and history of use specifically rather than a broader range of psychosocial variables. The fact that variables such as the number of days since last use, the amount of money spent on drugs, and the number of heavy drinking days correspond to the clinicians' ratings lends direct support to the accuracy of the ratings.

The data support clinicians' ability to make a distinction between the presence and absence of problems related to their clients' use of alcohol and other drugs. This finding suggests that the clinician rating scales may be used effectively to identify substance abuse problems among psychiatric outpatients. Although the rating scales would not be appropriate for initial assessment of a new patient, they could be used as a brief screening instrument with the majority of psychiatric patients who have some ongoing contact with mental health professionals. Such a screen could determine the need for further, in-depth assessment or monitoring.

We found few differences between the group who received ratings of 1, no use, and the group who received ratings of 2, mild use, perhaps because ratings of 1 and 2 do not reflect reliable differences. This interpretation is supported by the finding that study participants who received a rating of 1 from clinicians did report some, although minimal, alcohol and drug use in the comprehensive assessment (see Tables 4 and 5). Furthermore, discrepancies emerged between the clinicians' ratings and the researchers' ratings only in the distinction between no use and mild use of alcohol. Some therapists may be more likely than others to probe for this information in the absence of observable problems.

The lack of group differences on several variables is also noteworthy. The study results suggest that psychiatric outpatients with problematic drug use are more likely to have received specialized treatment for drug abuse, compared with nonusers; however, outpatients with alcohol problems are no more likely than nondrinkers to have received treatment for alcohol abuse. Although the means for age at first drink are ordered in expected patterns, with more problems associated with earlier onset, the groups were not significantly different on that variable. Because of the relatively small size of group 3, the analysis may not have had the statistical power needed to detect differences that may have existed.

Finally, the groups differentiated by the clinicians' ratings did not differ on the two indexes of general psychosocial functioning in the comprehensive assessment battery—the GAF as rated by the SCID interviewer, or the GSI. These findings are somewhat unexpected. The literature suggests that psychiatric patients with substance abuse or dependence experience more psychiatric symptoms (6,17) and greater psychosocial dysfunction (3,26) than those without these problems. However, the effect of substance use on functioning is difficult to determine without knowing participants' baseline, or abstinent, level of functioning. If, for example, substance users were less symptomatic or higher functioning when abstinent, as suggested by other researchers (5,27), then a substantial symptom exacerbation associated with substance use may not be apparent on cross-sectional comparison.

One limitation of the present study was the restricted range of ratings included in clinician rating scales. The study participants received ratings up to 4 on a 5-point scale, and, due to the infrequency of ratings of 4, we used only three groups in the analyses. The limited range of ratings is likely a result of our sample selection procedures. To obtain data on the wide range of alcohol and drug use variables reported here, we studied outpatients who volunteered to participate in an extensive clinical research battery. Outpatients who may have been rated as having severe or extremely severe problems were unlikely to make a commitment to such a study. Because of this sampling bias, we cannot address distinctions between groups 3, 4, and 5, which would have allowed validation of the full 5-point range of the clinician rating scales. This bias also restricts our ability to replicate previous findings on impairments in psychosocial functioning often observed among heavy substance abusers. Existing evidence supports the use of the clinician rating scales in screening for problematic alcohol or other drug use. However, if the scales are to be used as program evaluation tools or treatment outcome measures, additional efforts will be needed to evaluate their sensitivity to change within individuals.

REFERENCES

1. Regier DA, Farmer ME, Rae DS, et al: Comorbidity of mental disorders with alcohol and other drug abuse. *Journal of the American Medical Association* 264:2511-2518, 1990
2. Caton CL, Gralnick A, Bender S, et al: Young chronic patients and substance abuse. *Hospital and Community Psychiatry* 40:1037-1040, 1989
3. Drake RE, Wallach MA: Substance abuse among the chronic mentally ill. *Hospital and Community Psychiatry* 40:1041-1046, 1989
4. Kanwischer RW Hundley J: Screening for substance abuse in hospitalized psychiatric patients. *Hospital and Community Psychiatry* 41:795-797, 1990
5. Mueser KT Yarnold PR, Levinson DF et al: Prevalence of substance abuse in schizophrenia: demographic and clinical correlates. *Schizophrenia Bulletin* 16:31-56, 1990
6. Safer DJ: Substance abuse by young adult chronic patients. *Hospital and Community Psychiatry* 38:511-514, 1987
7. Shaner A, Khalsa ME, Roberts L, et al: Unrecognized cocaine use among schizophrenic patients. *American Journal of Psychiatry* 150:758-762, 1993
8. Test MA, Wallisch LS, Allness DJ, et al: Substance use in young adults with schizophrenic disorders. *Schizophrenia Bulletin* 15:465-476, 1989
9. Ananth J, Vandewater S, Kamal M, et al: Missed diagnosis of substance abuse in psychiatric patients. *Hospital and Community Psychiatry* 40:297-299, 1989
10. Barbee JG, Clark PD, Crapanzano MS, et al: Alcohol and substance abuse among schizophrenic patients presenting to an emergency psychiatric service. *Journal of Nervous and Mental Disease* 177:400-407, 1989
11. Drake RE, Osher FC, Noordsy DL, et al: Diagnosis of alcohol use disorders in schizophrenia. *Schizophrenia Bulletin* 16:57-67, 1990
12. Teitelbaum LM, Carey KB: Alcohol assessment in psychiatric patients. *Clinical Psychology: Science and Practice*, in press
13. Carey KB: Challenges in assessing substance use patterns in persons with comorbid mental and addictive disorders, in *Treatment of Drug-Dependent Individuals With Comorbid Mental Disorders*. Edited by Onken LS. Washington, DC, US Government Printing Office, in press
14. Drake RE, Alterman AI, Rosenberg SR: Detection of substance use disorders in severely mentally ill patients. *Community Mental Health Journal* 29:175-192, 1993
15. Skinner HA: Assessing alcohol use by patients in treatment, in *Research Advances in Alcohol and Drug Problems*, Vol 8. Edited by Smart RG, Cappell HD, Glaser FB, et al: New York, Plenum, 1984

16. Drake RE, Osher FC, Wallach MA: Alcohol use and abuse in schizophrenia: a prospective community study. *Journal of Nervous and Mental Disease* 177:408-414, 1989

17. Carey MP, Carey KB, Meisler AW: Psychiatric symptoms in mentally ill chemical abusers. *Journal of Nervous and Mental Disease* 179:136-138, 1991

18. Sobell LC, Sobell MB: Timeline Follow-Back: a technique for assessing self-reported alcohol consumption, in *Measuring Alcohol Consumption: Psychosocial and Biochemical Methods*. Edited by Litten RZ, Allen JP. Totawa, NJ, Humana, 1992

19. McLellan AT, Kushner H, Metzger D, et al: The fifth edition of the Addiction Severity Index. *Journal of Substance Abuse Treatment* 9:199-213, 1992

20. Hendricks VM, Kaplan CD, Limbeek JV, et al: The Addiction Severity Index: reliability and validity in a Dutch addict population. *Journal of Substance Abuse Treatment* 6:133-141, 1989

21. Kosten TR, Rounsaville BJ, Kleber HD: Concurrent validity of the Addiction Severity Index. *Journal of Nervous and Mental Disease* 171:606-610, 1983

22. McLellan AT, Luborsky L, O'Brien CP, et al: An improved evaluation instrument for substance abuse patients: the Addiction Severity Index. *Journal of Nervous and Mental Disease* 168:26-33, 1980

23. Hodgins DC, El-Guebaly N: More data on the Addiction Severity Index: reliability and validity with the mentally ill substance abuser. *Journal of Nervous and Mental Disease* 180:197-201, 1992

24. Spitzer RL, Williams JB, Gibbon M, et al: *Structured Clinical Interview for DSM-III-R, Patient Version (SCID-P)*. New York, New York State Psychiatric Institute, Biometrics Research, 1990

25. Derogatis LR: *SCL-90-R: Administration, Scoring, and Procedures Manual, II*. Baltimore, Clinical Psychometric Research, 1983

26. Lehman AF, Myers CP, Thompson JW, et al: Implications of mental and substance use disorders: a comparison of single and dual diagnosis patients. *Journal of Nervous and Mental Disease* 181:365-370, 1993

27. Dixon L, Haas G, Weiden PJ, et al: Drug abuse in schizophrenic patients: clinical correlates and reasons for use. *American Journal of Psychiatry* 148:224-230, 1991

ABOUT THE AUTHORS

Kate B. Carey, Ph.D., Karen M. Cocco, Ph.D., and Jeffrey S. Simons, B.A., are affiliated with the Department of Psychology, Syracuse University, Syracuse, NY.

ACKNOWLEDGMENTS

Parts of this paper were presented at the annual convention of the American Psychological Association held August 11-15, 1995, in New York City. This research was supported by grant DA07635 from the National Institute on Drug Abuse to Dr. Carey.

Copyright 1996. The American Psychiatric Association. Reprinted by permission.

HETEROGENEITY OF PERSON AND PLACE: ASSESSING CO-OCCURRING ADDICTIVE AND MENTAL DISORDERS

Anthony F. Lehman

Reprinted from *American Journal of Orthopsychiatry*, 66(1):32-41, 1996

Provision of appropriate treatment for clients with co-occurring addictive and mental disorders is hampered by difficulties in diagnosing this diverse population and in identifying and delivering necessary services via agencies that typically focus on only a portion of these clients' problems. This paper considers common pitfalls in assessment across settings and suggests approaches to identifying and meeting the needs of clients with multiple problems.

Rational and effective treatment for people with co-occurring addictive and mental disorders (COAMD) begins with accurate detection of the problems that need to be addressed. Identification of COAMD remains a challenge in most service settings despite considerable progress made in recent years in clarifying effective diagnostic methods (Drake & Mercer-McFadden, 1995; American Psychiatric Association, 1994). This article aims to assist practitioners across a wide variety of service settings in detecting cases of co-occurring disorders and in dealing with them appropriately and efficiently. First, clinically relevant groups of clients with COAMD are identified. Next, the settings in which these different groups are likely to present and the services they are likely or unlikely to be offered are discussed. Finally, common pitfalls in identifying these individuals across settings are noted and some simple methods are outlined for detecting and assessing COAMD and associated problems.

HETEROGENEITY OF THE POPULATION

There are several dimensions of heterogeneity in dual diagnosis (Lehman, Myers, & Corty, 1989; Rounsaville, Weissman, Kleber, & Wilber, 1982). These include: 1) the presence and nature of the substance use disorder, including type of drugs used, severity of substance abuse, and current status of the abuse problem; 2) presence and nature of other Axis I *DSM* disorders, their severity, duration, and current status; 3) presence and nature of any Axis II personality disorders; 4) the presence, nature, and severity of medical problems directly related to substance abuse, such as hepatitis or HIV infection; and 5) disability and social problems—such as poverty, unemployment, homelessness, legal entanglements, and family problems—directly related either to the substance abuse or to the presence of mental disorders. Although each individual will present with a unique combination of these problems, it is useful to consider major subgroupings of clients because this often dictates where they present for help and what help they are offered. It is also essential to keep in mind that, although we frequently refer to clients with "dual diagnoses," a more accurate description would be multiple diagnoses and multiple problems.

A brief review of terminology, in particular the *DSM-IV* classification of substance-related disorders (American Psychiatric Association [APA], 1994), may be helpful. Substance-related disorders (SRDs) refer broadly to "disorders related to the taking of a drug of abuse, to the side effects of medication, and to toxin exposure" (APA, p.175). The present article deals only with SRDs involving drugs of abuse. SRDs are further divided into substance use disorders (SUDs), including abuse and dependence, and substance-induced disorders (SIDs).

The *DSM-IV* defines substance abuse as a "maladaptive pattern of substance use leading to clinically significant impairment or distress," as manifested by recurrent use resulting in a failure to fulfill major role obligations, recurrent use in situations in which it is physically hazardous, recurrent use despite persistent or recurrent social or interpersonal problems related to substance use, and/or recurrent substance-related legal problems (APA, 1994, pp. 182-183). Substance dependence may include any of these symptoms of abuse, but also involves physical tolerance, withdrawal, or compulsive drug-taking. The SIDs include acute intoxication and withdrawal syndromes as well as syndromes that meet criteria for another Axis I disorder (such as psychosis, depression, or dementia), but that clearly are directly induced by a drug of abuse. Finally, for purposes of discussion here, Axis I syndromes that are not SIDs or that are not due to some other known organic factor are referred to as "independent mental disorders" (IMDs).

Substance use disorders with substance-induced disorders

As is well known, the use of psychoactive substances can lead to a variety of substance-induced mental syndromes. Among the most common patterns are the mood disorders, such as depression and anxiety, associated with chronic alcohol and sedative use and withdrawal from stimulants (Alterman, 1985; Rounsaville et al., 1991). Less common are acute and subchronic psychotic syndromes, such as delusional disorders induced by stimulants and hallucinogens (Satel & Edell, 1991; Turner & Tsuang, 1990). The critical feature of this group is that their "dual diagnosis" can be attributed primarily to the symptoms induced by their substance use. In a sense they are not dually diagnosed, in that their psychiatric syndrome is a manifestation of their substance use, but they are often perceived as dually diagnosed in service settings because of the complication of their substance use by prominent secondary psychiatric symptoms (Lehman, Myers, Dixon, & Johnson, 1994). Identifying members of this subgroup has important clinical implications since a cessation of their substance would likely resolve their psychiatric symptoms. Usually, the nature and severity of the associated mental syndrome are driven by the nature and severity of the substance abuse. Different substances will produce different psychiatric side effects, and more severe use, or use of multiple substances, will likely lead to more severe secondary psychopathology.

Substance use disorders with an independent mental disorder

Individuals with primary Axis I mental disorders are known to abuse substances at a higher rate than those in the general population (Regier et al., 1990). The major dimension of concern for this group is the nature and severity of the Axis I mental disorder, which can range from transient adjustment disorders and minor mood disorders, to more serious but time-limited mental disorders (such as a major depressive episode), to persistent and serious mental disorders (such as schizophrenia, bipolar disorders, and chronic anxiety disorders). For this group, treatment of the SUD alone will not resolve the psychiatric problem. Often, the Axis I psychiatric disorder overshadows the SUD, and the presence of the two disorders complicates their mutual diagnosis and treatment. For example, chronic use of stimulants may make the accurate diagnosis of a mood disorder difficult due to the confusion of mood symptoms induced by stimulant intoxication and withdrawal, with mood symptoms due to an underlying IMD. This differentiation generally can be made only after a period of abstinence. It has been shown that the presence of a substance use disorder substantially detracts from the diagnostic reliability of other Axis I disorders (Corty, Lehman, & Myers, 1993).

Also, a substance-use problem can easily be overlooked in someone with a major mental illness. Withdrawal or intoxication symptoms, such as increased paranoia, depression, or anxiety, can easily be attributed to the major mental illness known to be present and the possible complication of substance use never considered. Appropriate treatment for these clients consists of integrated interventions for both problems; failure to address both problems may render treatment for either ineffective. Fortunately, effective treatments exist for most Axis I disorders, so detection can lead to substantial reduction in symptoms.

Substance use disorders with Axis II personality disorders

Axis II personality disorders, especially antisocial personality disorder, commonly co-occur with substance use disorder (Lehman, Myers, Thompson, & Corty, 1993; Mirin & Weiss, 1991). *DSM-IV* defines three major clusters of Axis II personality disorders: Cluster A, consisting of paranoid, schizoid, and schizotypal disorders; Cluster B, consisting of antisocial, borderline, histrionic, and narcissistic disorders; and Cluster C, consisting of avoidant, dependent, and obsessive-compulsive disorders. Substance abuse is most common among those in the Cluster B group, who tend to be impulsive, emotional, and erratic in behavior. For Cluster B borderline personality disorder, substance use is specifically mentioned as an example of impulsive self-damaging behavior.

The type of personality disorder present may have important implications for treatment. The major problem posed by the presence of a personality disorder is that, by definition, the client will have interpersonal difficulties that are relatively intractable and that both contribute to continued drug use and interfere with engagement in treatment. Appropriate formulation of the nature of the personality disorder will permit adaptation of the treatment to account for the client's personality difficulties. The clinician may thus anticipate problems in the treatment process (e.g., the need to set limits and adjust expectations) and provide additional treatments designed to alleviate problems associated with the personality disorder (e.g., interpersonal skills training to reduce social inhibitions that motivate substance use). Failure to do this can lead to treatment burnout for clinicians who may feel that the client "doesn't want help."

It must also be kept in mind that substance use may lead to behavior that is misdiagnosed as an Axis II disorder. For example, illegal acts related to drug-seeking may be misattributed to antisocial personality. Noting that substance-abuse treatment outcomes are poorer among clients with antisocial personality disorders, Gerstley and colleagues (1990) cautioned that at least two subgroups may exist, those with "true" or idiopathic psychopathic personalities and those with psychopathic behavior related to substance use, so-called "symptomatic psychopaths." For those in the latter group, effective substance-abuse treatment may also substantially reduce antisocial behavior.

COAMD with associated major medical problems

SUDs can lead to major medical problems. The most prominent example currently is HIV infection, which dramatically alters the clinical prognosis; over time, the treatment focus becomes increasingly governed by progression of the HIV. An initial barrier to treatment can be patient reluctance to accept HIV testing. Besides fear of the diagnosis, patients may be reluctant to undergo testing because of concerns about stigma, job and housing discrimination, and loss of health insurance.

The client's knowledge of the HIV infection may affect motivation for treatment of co-occurring disorders; in turn these co-occurring disorders may interact with treatment for HIV. For example, a COAMD client's reaction to the diagnosis of HIV can be dramatically affected by the presence of an impulsive Axis II disorder (e.g., borderline personality disorder), leading to acting out (suicide attempts, unsafe sex) and HIV treatment noncompliance.

HIV infection has been found to be more common among substance abusers with an antisocial personality disorder than among those without such a diagnosis (Brooner, Greenfield, Schmidt, & Bigelow, 1993). The presence of a severe Axis I disorder, such as schizophrenia or bipolar disorder, can impair the patient's capacity to understand and comply with treatment for HIV. This is especially troubling given the relatively high rate of HIV seroprevalence among seriously mentally ill persons admitted to psychiatric hospitals (Cournos et al., 1991).

Conversely, HIV infection may complicate somatic treatments for Axis I psychiatric disorders, and can further cloud the diagnostic picture when HIV involves the central nervous system. Certain psychotropic agents used in the treatment of major mental disorders, e.g., clozapine for schizophrenia or carbamezapine for bipolar disorder, cause blood dyscrasias that may be particularly troublesome in the HIV client. Other major medical problems related to substance abuse that may impinge upon treatment for the substance abuse and psychiatric disorders include pancreatitis, liver disease, heart disease, tuberculosis and other infectious diseases, anemia, organic brain disorders, and stroke.

COAMD with associated major social problems

SUDs, IMDs, and Axis II disorders all can lead to major social difficulties. Among the most common examples are legal entanglements associated with substance-use activities and other antisocial behavior, homelessness associated with substance abuse or major mental illnesses, and unemployment due to substance use or psychiatric disability. These problems can become the focal point of a person's help-seeking and can pose major barriers to effective treatment. For example, incarceration can complicate access to mental health or substance-abuse services, as can homelessness. Unemployment may reduce access due to lack of health insurance.

These social problems can greatly complicate the assessment process. Proper, longitudinal assessment of COAMD in individuals who are homeless is extremely difficult. Incarceration may be a major barrier to assessment in penal settings that lack integrated mental health and substance-abuse treatment services (Abrams & Teplin, 1991). Finally, poverty itself can pose major obstacles to proper assessment due to lack of access to care.

HETEROGENEITY OF PLACE

What help is sought? What is offered?

The different COAMD groups described above may seek help in quite different ways, and they may be offered quite different assistance depending on where they contact the service system (Lehman, Myers, Dixon, & Johnson, 1994). The central challenge here is timely and accurate assessment so that the most appropriate array of treatments and services can be offered. Four types of treatment settings where COAMD clients may present will be considered: mental health treatment facilities, substance-abuse treatment facilities, general health-care facilities, and non-health-care service agencies and institutions.

Two general problems exist in matching client service needs with service settings. The first involves the way in which clients or their referral agents define the primary problem and search for help. Second is the fact that agencies are best at detecting the problems for which they are primarily designed to respond. These two factors are pitfalls to appropriate care regardless of the service setting.

Mental health treatment facilities. There are two primary COAMD groups that opt to seek care at, or are brought for care to, mental health facilities: those with co-occurring SUDs and severe and persistent IMDs (such as schizophrenia, major depression, or mania) and those who experience severe SIDs, such as suicidal substance-induced depression or acute substance-induced psychosis (Lehman, Myers, Dixon, & Johnson, 1994). For individuals in these groups, the initial contact is often through an emergency-room visit or an acute hospitalization. The other group that may present initially to a mental health facility includes individuals with SUDs and milder co-occurring independent Axis I disorders, such as dysthymia, anxiety disorders, or an acute adjustment disorder. These clients usually make contact via a regular outpatient route.

For all of those presenting to a mental health facility, the most common assessment problems are failure to assess and treat adequately the substance use disorder and related medical problems. The focus tends to be on the non-substance Axis I diagnosis. Studies have consistently shown the problem of underdiagnosis and undertreatment of substance use disorders in mental health treatment settings (Haugland, Siegel, Alexander, & Galanter, 1991; Ananth et al., 1989). Failure to address the SUD interferes with treatment of the Axis I psychiatric disorder (noncompliance, drug-medications interactions). Conversely, treatment may be initiated for a presumed Axis I disorder that does not exist, e.g., maintenance antipsychotic treatment for presumed schizophrenia when the problem is a substance-induced psychosis, or treatment for major depression when the problem is a substance-induced mood disorder.

Substance-abuse treatment facilities. The corollary problems exist in substance-abuse treatment settings, which do quite well at assessing the substance-abuse problem, but may overlook or downplay a significant Axis I mental disorder. Substance-abuse programs may tend to view all psychiatric problems as consequences of substance abuse or as rationalizations for continued substance use. Further complicating matters is the ideological conflict that sometimes exists in the treatment of psychiatric problems within substance-abuse treatment settings where prescribed medications are viewed negatively, essentially as another "chemical crutch." Hence a client with depression or psychosis may not receive needed pharmacotherapy. Clients with such persistent Axis I problems may drop out of substance-abuse treatment because the symptoms of the mental illness interfere with the client's capacity to comply with substance-abuse treatment and to abstain from substance use. Fortunately, substance-abuse programs have become more sensitive to the value of medications for psychiatric disorders.

General health-care facilities. A large proportion of people with mental health and substance-abuse problems present for help in general health-care settings, especially primary-care offices and clinics and emergency rooms. These settings commonly present two major impediments to adequacy of treatment for dually diagnosed clients. First, many general health providers fail to assess adequately the possibility of either a mental illness or a substance use disorder. Hence the client may be treated for a presenting somatic complaint (e.g., insomnia or pain) when in fact these symptoms are manifestations of an undetected psychiatric illness (e.g., depression) or substance-use problem (e.g., opiate addiction). Besides misdiagnosis, which may lead to failure to treat the psychiatric or substance-use problem, the treatment that is prescribed may add to the client's problem. For example, prescription of a sedative may worsen depression or lead to further addiction.

Another pattern of care for COAMD in general medical settings is that of the client who presents for care of a serious medical problem arising directly from substance abuse, such as infectious diseases due to intravenous drug use. For these clients, the ongoing mental illness and substance abuse may pose major barriers to adequate care of the medical problem. In general, morbidity due to a variety of medical problems is higher among persons with severe mental illnesses (Black, Warrack, & Winokur, 1985), presumably because of their difficulties in relating to health-care providers, in identifying their medical needs, in complying with medical care, and in maintaining proper general health habits. When a serious medical problem arises, these patterns can be life-threatening. Similarly, ongoing substance abuse can dramatically interfere with clients' compliance with medical treatment, complicate the effectiveness of medical treatments, and alienate medical staff.

Non-health-care service agencies and institutions. COAMD clients may enter the service system via non-health-care agencies, such as departments of social services, family welfare agencies, homeless service agencies, and jails or prisons. Such agencies cannot be expected to conduct full-scale health assessments that confirm the presence of substance abuse or psychiatric disorders, but one would hope that they provide at least enough problem surveillance to refer dually diagnosed clients to mental health and substance-abuse programs.

One type of client who may be more likely to present in these settings than in health-care facilities is the COAMD client with Axis II personality disorders. These individuals may shun psychiatric or substance-abuse care or may be rejected from such care because of their interpersonal difficulties. Their Axis II problems are likely to send them to non-health-care social agencies. In a demonstration project for homeless persons in Baltimore, substantial numbers of such clients were identified by social service agencies for the homeless as "severely mentally ill," even though they had no Axis I disorder other than substance abuse (Dixon, Krauss, Kernan, Lehman, & DeForge, 1995). This reflects the degree of difficulty that these clients can pose for agencies and the hopelessness that the individuals may feel about finding any agency that can care for them. Therapeutic nihilism may abound.

COMMON PITFALLS

Assessing for substance-abuse and psychiatric disorders

Although there are potential problems in the quality and accuracy of available assessment procedures (Drake & Mercer-McFadden, 1995), the omission of *any* assessment presents the major barrier to effective intervention. In any clinical context the most effective diagnostic assessment will occur in ongoing evaluation and treatment of suspected mental health and substance-abuse problems. Hence the most important step is initial screening for the possible presence of one or both disorders (Dixon et al., 1993).

A variety of simple screening measures exists to detect substance-abuse and psychiatric problems; these include the Drug Abuse Screening Test (DAST) (Skinner, 1981), the CAGE (Mayfield, McLeod, & Hall, 1978), and the Michigan Alcohol Screening Test (MAST) (Selzer, 1971), all of which can be done as brief self-reports while the client is waiting to be seen or as part of a brief screening interview. These screening approaches for substance-use problems are especially helpful in mental health treatment agencies, general health-care settings, and other social service agencies where the person may not be presenting with a complaint of substance use. In health-care settings, selective toxicology urine screens can also be quite helpful and practical. Similarly, some simple screening measures for non-substance use psychiatric problems exist that are practical for use in non-mental-health-care agencies. These include the Brief Symptom Inventory (Derogatis & Melisaratos, 1983), and the General Health Questionnaire (Goldberg, 1972).

The recommendation is that agencies institute basic, routine screening procedures for mental or substance use disorders—whichever is not the agency's primary focus of contact with the client. When problems are identified via such screening, clients should be engaged in follow-up discussion and provided with treatment or referral, as appropriate. No screening instrument is perfect; any of these will miss some cases ("false negatives") and incorrectly identify others ("false positives"). However, a standard screening procedure will substantially reduce those missed, and false positives can be identified in the follow-up assessment.

Initial screening is essential, but definitive diagnosis of COAMD typically requires a longitudinal assessment by a clinician whom the client knows and trusts. This relationship can be critical to the patient's willingness to disclose stigmatized symptoms and behavior (for example, drug tolerance or withdrawal symptoms, risk behavior such as IV drug use, or psychotic symptoms). Such disclosure permits more accurate diagnosis, often marks initial acknowledgement that a problem exists, and enables discussion of treatment options.

Along these lines, substantial progress has occurred recently in conceptualizing and assessing the stages of addiction, recovery, and treatment. Prochaska, DiClemente, and Norcross (1992) have defined five stages of change and recovery in persons with addictions: 1) *pre-contemplation* is "the stage at which there is no intention to change behavior in the foreseeable future;" 2) *contemplation* is "the stage in which people are aware that a problem exists and are seriously thinking about overcoming it but have not yet made the commitment to take action;" 3) *preparation* combines the intention to take action within the next month with lack of success in taking action during the past year; 4) *action* "is the stage in which individuals modify their behavior, experiences, or environment in order to overcome their problems;" and 5) in *maintenance,* "people work to prevent relapse and consolidate the gains attained during action" (pp. 1103-1104). Prochaska et al. noted that the process of recovery is not linear, but typically involves relapses and recycling through these stages of change, a process that they refer to as the "spiral process of change."

Similarly, Osher and Kofoed (1989) have defined four stages of treatment in persons with COAMD: 1) *engagement* refers to the initial development of a trusting relationship between the client and the treatment provider; 2) *persuasion* defines the process through which clients learn about the role that substance use plays in their lives and develop motivation to change; 3) in *active treatment*, clients use strategies and interventions to reduce their substance use and strive for abstinence; and 4) *relapse prevention* involves ongoing strategies to prevent recurrence.

In assessing a client with COAMD, it is useful to determine the individual's present position along these recovery continua. Failure to do so may result in premature efforts to treat the substance use disorder, which in turn can lead to noncompliance and premature termination of treatment (Lehman, Herron, & Schwartz, 1993). Rollnick, Heather, Gold, & Hall (1992) have developed a brief client questionnaire to assess "readiness to change" based on the Prochaska et al. framework, and Drake, Mueser, and McHugo

(1995) have devised the Substance Abuse Treatment Scale, completed by a treating clinician or case manager, to reflect the stages of treatment defined by Osher and Kofoed (1989).

Assessing for related medical problems

Brief health questionnaires can be used as quick screens for health problems. These are of two types: reviews of specific diagnoses and symptoms, and general health status measures. The former presents clients with a list of diseases and symptoms and asks whether they have had any of them. Examples include the Sickness Impact Profile (Bergner, Bobbitt, Carter, & Gilson, 1981) and the National Health Interview Survey (1991). General health status measures inquire more generally about functional limitations due to health problems and perceived general health status, for example, the Medical Outcomes Short Form (SF-36) (Ware & Sherbourne, 1992) and the Duke Health Index (Parkerson, Broadhead, & Tse, 1990). These cover such dimensions as physical functioning, role limitations due to illness, perceived health status, vitality, and pain.

Assessing for related social problems

Because of the common co-occurrence of serious social problems in connection with COAMD, assessments should at least screen for such difficulties. Failure to detect and address such problems may defeat efforts to engage the client in treatment and contribute to noncompliance. The treatment offered may seem irrelevant or insensitive to the client ("The doctor doesn't care about my real problems, just whether I take my medication."), or the press of the social problems may overwhelm the client's capacity to participate in treatment.

It is not necessarily more difficult to screen for social problems than for psychiatric, substance use, or general health problems. Clients can be asked such simple questions as whether they have a stable place to live, whether they are having any serious problems with family or social relations, whether they have enough income for basic necessities, and whether they have any legal problems. Such problems are sometimes referred to under the rubric of "quality of life," and a variety of related assessment measures have been developed (Lehman & Burns, 1996) that can be used in health-care and social-service settings. These typically cover a range of life domains, such as living situation, social and family relations, employment, finances, and legal and safety problems, and provide a reasonable inventory of important issues in everyday life. They measure both functional status and life satisfaction. Another widely used measure in substance-abuse treatment programs is the Addiction Severity Index (McLellan, Luborsky, O'Brien, & Woody, 1980; McLellan et al., 1992), which covers similar dimensions that can be affected by substance use.

Limitations on agency capacity

Most human service workers and agencies feel an obligation to help with the problems for which clients present. However, most human service agencies lack the capacity to deal directly with all of the problems of COAMD clients. Therefore, effective diagnosis and assessment of related problems can present a dilemma. What do we do about problems that we cannot treat? This is a practical problem because many agencies are required to develop a comprehensive treatment plan to address identified problems. If they identify a problem, then they must say how they will address it. If they have no capacity to address it, administrative concerns arise. Thus, there may be an incentive to underidentify problems. This can be dealt with either by developing so-called "one-stop" agencies or by developing referral networks among "single-service" agencies. The latter is often more realistic, but poses service integration challenges.

CONCLUSION

Individuals with COAMD present in a wide variety of service settings. Although the person's most pressing current problem may determine the choice of site of initial presentation, other factors—such as the availability of services, prior experience with the service system, and local social practices for dealing with problem behaviors—can influence these decisions. Regardless of where COAMD clients present initially for care, their problems are typically multiple, including not only the COAMD, but additional psychiatric, medical, and social problems, all of which conspire against success of the service plan and favorable outcome. The most common problems in effective service planning are failure to screen adequately for the presence of COAMD and associated problems, lack of capacity to deal with multiple problems when they are identified, and lack of networking among service agencies for COAMD clients who have multiple problems. These problems can be substantially reduced by the introduction of simple, routine screening procedures for multiple problems, education of staff to the importance of such screening, and development of service capacities and interagency linkages that provide a comprehensive range of service options.

REFERENCES

Abrams, K.M., & Teplin, L.A. (1991). Co-occurring disorders among mentally ill jail detainees. *American Psychologist, 46,* 1036-1045.

Alterman, A.I. (Ed.). (1985). *Substance abuse and psychopathology.* New York: Plenum Press.

American Psychiatric Association [APA]. (1994). *Diagnostic and statistical manual of mental disorders* (4th ed.). Washington DC: Author.

Ananth, J., Vandewater, S., Kamal, M., Broksky, A., Gamal, R., & Miller, M. (1989). Missed diagnosis of substance abuse in psychiatric patients. *Hospital and Community Psychiatry, 40,* 297-299.

Bergner, M., Bobbitt, R.A., Carter, W.B., & Gilson, B.S. (1981). The Sickness Impact Profile: Development and final revision of a health status measure. *Medical Care, 8,* 787-805.

Black, D.W., Warrack, G., & Winokur, G. (1985). Excess mortality among psychiatric patients: The Iowa record-linkage study. *Journal of the American Medical Association, 253,* 58-61.

Brooner, R.K., Greenfield, L., Schmidt, C.W., & Bigelow, G.E. (1993). Antisocial personality disorder and HIV infection among intravenous drug abusers. *American Journal of Psychiatry, 150,* 53-58.

Corty, E., Lehman, A.F., & Myers, C.P. (1993). The influence of psychoactive substance use on the reliability of psychiatric diagnosis. *Journal of Consulting and Clinical Psychology, 61,* 165-170.

Cournos, F., Empfield, M., Horwath, E., McKinnon, K., Meyer, I., Schrage, H., Currie, C., & Agosin, B. (1991). HIV seroprevalence among patients admitted to two psychiatric hospitals. *American Journal of Psychiatry, 148,* 1225-1230.

Derogatis, L.R., & Melisaratos, N. (1983). The Brief Symptom Inventory: An introductory report. *Psychological Medicine, 13,* 595-605.

Dixon, L., Dibietz, E., Myers, P., Conley, R., Medoff, D., & Lehman, A. (1993). Comparison of DSM III-R diagnosis and a screen for drug and alcohol use in psychiatric state hospital inpatients. *Hospital and Community Psychiatry, 44,* 748-752.

Dixon, L.B., Krauss, N., Kernan, E., Lehman, A.F., & DeForge, B.R. (1995). Modifying the PACT model to serve homeless persons with severe mental illness. *Psychiatric Services, 46,* 684-688.

Drake, R.E., & Mercer-McFadden, C. (1995). Assessment of substance use among persons with chronic mental illnesses. In A.F. Lehman & L.B. Dixon (Eds.), *Double jeopardy: Chronic mental illness and substance abuse* (pp. 47-62). New York: Harwood Academic Press.

Drake, R.E., Mueser, K.T., & McHugo, G.J. (1995). Using clinician rating scales to assess substance abuse among persons with severe mental illness. In L.I. Sederer & B. Dickey (Eds.), *Outcome assessment in clinical practice* (pp. 113-116). Baltimore: Williams & Wilkins.

Gerstley, L.J., Alterman, A.I., McLellan, A.T., & Woody, G.E. (1990). Antisocial personality disorder in patients with substance abuse disorders: A problematic diagnosis? *American Journal of Psychiatry, 147,* 173-178.

Goldberg, D.P. (1972). *The detection of psychiatric illness by questionnaire.* London: Oxford University Press.

Haugland, G., Siegel, C., Alexander, M.J., & Galanter, M. (1991). A survey of hospitals in New York State treating psychiatric patients with chemical abuse disorders. *Hospital and Community Psychiatry, 42,* 1215-1220.

Lehman, A.F., & Burns, B.J. (1996). Severe mental illness in the community. In B. Spilker (Ed.), *Quality of life and pharmacoeconomics in clinical trials* (2nd ed., pp. 919-924). Philadelphia: Lippincott-Raven.

Lehman, A.F., & Dixon, L.B. (Eds.). (1995). *Double jeopardy: Chronic mental illness and substance use disorders.* New York: Harwood Academic Press.

Lehman, A.F., Herron, J.D., & Schwartz, R.P. (1993). Rehabilitation for young adults with severe mental illness and substance-use disorders: A clinical trial. *Journal of Nervous and Mental Disease, 181,* 88-92.

Lehman, A.F., Myers, C.P., & Corty, E. (1989). Assessment and classification of patients with psychiatric and substance abuse syndromes. *Hospital and Community Psychiatry, 40,* 1019-1025.

Lehman, A.F., Myers, P., Corty, E., & Thompson, J.T. (1994). Prevalence and patterns of "dual diagnosis" among psychiatric patients. *Comprehensive Psychiatry, 35,* 106-112.

Lehman, A.F., Myers, C.P., Dixon, L.B., & Johnson, J.L. (1994). Defining subgroups of dual diagnosis patients for service planning. *Hospital and Community Psychiatry, 45,* 556-561.

Lehman, A.F., Myers, C.P., Thompson, J.W., & Corty, E. (1993). Implications of mental and substance use disorders: A comparison of "single" and "dual" diagnosis patients. *Journal of Nervous and Mental Disease, 181,* 365-370.

Mayfield, D., McLeod, G., & Hall, P. (1978). The CAGE questionnaire: Validation of a new alcoholism screening instrument. *American Journal of Psychiatry, 131,* 1121-1123.

McLellan, A.T., Kushner, H., Metzger, D., Peters, R., Smith, I., Grissom, G., Pettinati, H., & Argeriou, M. (1992). The fifth edition of the Addiction Severity Index. *Journal of Substance Abuse Treatment, 9,* 199-213.

McLellan, A.T., Luborsky, L., O'Brien, C.P., & Woody, G.E. (1980). An improved evaluation instrument for substance abuse patients: The Addiction Severity Index. *Journal of Nervous and Mental Disease, 168,* 26-33.

Mirin, S.M., & Weiss, R.D. (1991). Substance abuse and mental illness. In R.I. Frances & S.I. Miller (Eds.), *Clinical textbook of addictive disorders* (pp. 271-298). New York: Guilford Press.

National Health Interview Survey, National Center for Health Statistics. (1991). *Health, United States, 1990* (DHHS Pub. No. PHS 91-1232). Hyattsville, MD: Dept. of Health and Human Services.

Osher, F.C., & Kofoed, L.L. (1989). Treatment of patients with psychiatric and psychoactive substance abuse disorders. *Hospital and Community Psychiatry, 40,* 1025-1030.

Parkerson, G.R., Broadhead, W.E., & Tse, C.K.J. (1990). The Duke Health Profile. *Medical Care, 28,* 1056-1072.

Prochaska, J.O., DiClemente, C.C., & Norcross, J.C. (1992). In search of how people change: Applications to addictive behaviors. *American Psychologist, 47,* 1102-1114.

Regier, D.A., Farmer, M.E., Rae, D.S., Locke, B.Z., Keith, S.J., Judd, L.L., & Goodwin, F.K. (1990). Comorbidity of mental disorders with alcohol and other drug abuse. *Journal of the American Medical Association, 264,* 2511-2518.

Rollnick, S., Heather, N., Gold, R., & Hall, W. (1992). Development of a short "readiness to change" questionnaire for use in brief, opportunistic interventions among excessive drinkers. *British Journal of Addictions, 87,* 743-754.

Rounsaville, B.J., Anton, S.F., Carroll, K., Budde, D., Prusoff, B., & Gavin, F. (1991). Psychiatric diagnoses of treatment-seeking cocaine abusers. *Archives of General Psychiatry, 48,* 43-51.

Rounsaville, B.J., Weissman, M.M., Kleber, H., & Wilber, C. (1982). Heterogeneity of psychiatric diagnosis in treated opiate addicts. *Archives of General Psychiatry, 39,* 161-166.

Satel, S.L., & Edell, W.S. (1991). Cocaine-induced paranoia and psychosis patterns. *American Journal of Psychiatry, 148,* 1708-1711.

Selzer, M.L. (1971). The Michigan Alcohol Screening Test: The quest for a new diagnostic instrument. *American Journal of Psychiatry, 127,* 89-94.

Skinner, H.A. (1981). The primary syndromes of alcohol abuse: Their measurement and correlates. *British Journal of Addictions, 76,* 63-76.

Turner, W.M., & Tsuang, M.T. (1990). Impact of substance abuse on the course and outcome of schizophrenia. *Schizophrenia Bulletin, 16,* 87-95.

Ware, J.E., & Sherbourne, C.D. (1992). The MOS 36 Item Short-Form Health Survey (SF-36). *Medical Care, 30,* 473-483.

ABOUT THE AUTHOR

Anthony F. Lehman, M.D., M.S.P.H., is at the Department of Psychiatry, University of Maryland, Baltimore.

Copyright 1996 by the American Orthopsychiatric Association, Inc. Reproduced by permission.

A SCALE FOR ASSESSING THE STAGE OF SUBSTANCE ABUSE TREATMENT IN PERSONS WITH SEVERE MENTAL ILLNESS

Gregory J. McHugo, Robert E. Drake,
Heather L. Burton, and Theimann H. Ackerson

Reprinted from *Journal of Nervous and Mental Disease* 183:762-767, 1995

Substance abuse is common among persons with severe mental illness, but few measures exist for clinicians to evaluate treatment progress. The Substance Abuse Treatment Scale (SATS) combines a motivational hierarchy with explicit substance use criteria to form an eight-stage model of the recovery process. Data are presented supporting the reliability and validity of the SATS, based on its use in a community-based sample of persons with dual disorders. The SATS can be used as either a process or an outcome measure, for individuals or for groups, and its value in making explicit the stages of substance abuse treatment is discussed.

During the past 15 years, substance abuse has been identified as a common co-occurring disorder that seriously complicates adjustment among people with severe mental disorders (Lehman and Dixon, 1995; Minkoff and Drake, 1991). Initial reviews of the problem of co-occurring severe mental disorders and substance use disorders indicated that these patients interacted with the mental health system primarily around crises, that they were served poorly within both the mental health and addiction systems, and that most experts recommended programs that integrated mental health and substance abuse interventions (Ridgely et al., 1986, 1987). In parallel with the development of integrated treatments, clinical researchers began to recognize the necessity of providing motivational interventions for substance-abusing patients who were engaged in treatment but not yet ready for an abstinence-oriented intervention. This was occurring both within the general substance abuse field (Miller and Rollnick, 1991; Stark and Kane, 1985) and within dual-disorder programs (Carey, in press; Kofoed and Keys, 1988; Noordsy and Fox, 1991; Osher and Kofoed, 1989).

Following on the premotivational-motivational distinction, clinical investigators began to conceptualize a stage-wise process of treatment (Carey, in press; Drake et al., 1993; Osher and Kofoed, 1989). For example, Osher and Kofoed (1989) argued that dual disorder patients typically passed through four stages in the process of recovery (engagement, persuasion, active treatment, and relapse prevention): a) In the initial stage, they become engaged in a relationship or treatment process. b) Once engaged, they can be persuaded that substance abuse is a problem and that they have the capacity to achieve greater life satisfaction by decreasing their use of psychoactive drugs. c) When motivated to pursue abstinence, active treatment strategies can enable them to acquire the skills and supports necessary to achieve abstinence. d) After stable abstinence is achieved, they can be helped to maintain whatever resources and behavioral changes are needed to prevent relapse. These stages parallel a general description of the internal process of recovery from substance abuse (Prochaska et al., 1992), but they emphasize overt behaviors and relationships with providers as well as psychological states. The focus on overt behaviors in relation to treatment emphasizes the clinician's perspective. It also alleviates difficulties due to lack of correspondence between attitudes and behaviors and those due to unreliability in assessing internal states.

Despite the convergence of thinking regarding the stage-wise nature of treatment and the longitudinal aspect of recovery, no scale has been available to assess or document this process. Assessing the stage of substance abuse treatment might be useful for several reasons: a) Clinicians, who are often frustrated about unmet expectations, can develop more realistic expectations regarding course and outcome, based on understanding where patients are in the recovery process. b) Knowing the patient's stage of treatment, clinicians can offer a range of treatment options known to be effective for that stage (Drake and Noordsy, 1994). c) Clinicians can monitor individual patients over time to determine whether or not each is making progress at a reasonable rate. d) Programs can monitor cohorts of patients over time to determine whether they are moving toward recovery at a realistic rate or whether they are becoming stuck at a particular point.

The purpose of this paper is to describe the development and the psychometric properties of a scale for assessing the stage of substance abuse treatment in dually disordered patients, the Substance Abuse Treatment Scale (SATS). After describing the development of the SATS, we present initial studies of its reliability and validity and then provide examples of its clinical and research use.

Development of the Substance Abuse Treatment Scale

In 1988, the New Hampshire Division of Mental Health began to implement a statewide service system for patients with co-occurring severe mental disorders and substance use disorders (Drake et al., 1990b). This program was built on the four-stage model of dual-disorder treatment described by Osher and Kofoed (1989). As part of the implementation across 10 community mental health centers and various day treatment, residential, and inpatient settings, the Psychiatric Research Center and the Division of Mental Health cosponsored a monthly seminar for dual-disorder clinicians that has continued for 5 years. Clinicians in this seminar elaborated on the four-stage model and identified eight stages in the recovery process. Researchers helped these clinicians to operationalize the eight stages with explicit criteria. The SATS ratings refer to the previous 6-month period, which provides sufficient time for observation of the client by the rater and allows less influence on the overall rating by short-term aberrations in behavior. The stages of treatment and their rating criteria are shown in Table 1.

Because clinicians found the SATS so useful in monitoring their patients' progress through treatment, our research team began to use it and soon discovered that data from a variety of perspectives could be combined reliably to assess stage of treatment. Thus, the SATS is considered both a clinical and a research instrument.

Research Context

The data presented here derive primarily from a large-scale randomized clinical trial comparing two case management strategies for treating individuals with co-occurring serious mental illness and substance use disorder. This study was conducted at seven community mental health centers (CMHCs) throughout New Hampshire and involved extensive data collection over a 3-year period from clients, case managers, families, and both mental health and non-mental health treatment and service providers.

Study participants were interviewed every 6 months to assess status within several domains, such as residential situation, alcohol and drug use, symptom severity, service utilization, and quality of life. The client's case manager completed the SATS at each 6-month assessment point and also rated alcohol and drug use with the Case Manager Rating Scale (Drake et al., 1990a). Most case managers in the New Hampshire Dual Disorders Study had been trained in the use of the SATS and Case Manager Rating Scale by our research staff, and they practiced using the scales by rating several cases that were presented as vignettes.

Table 1. Substance abuse treatment scale

Instructions: This scale is for assessing a person's stage of substance abuse treatment, not for determining diagnosis. The reporting interval is the last *six months*. If the person is in an institution, the reporting interval is the time period prior to institutionalization.

1. Pre-engagement. The person (not client) does not have contact with a case manager, mental health counselor, or substance abuse counselor.
2. Engagement. The client has had contact with an assigned case manager or counselor but does not have regular contacts. The lack of regular contact implies lack of a working alliance.
3. Early Persuasion. The client has regular contacts with a case manager or counselor but has not reduced substance use more than a month. Regular contacts imply a working alliance and a relationship in which substance abuse can be discussed.
4. Late Persuasion. The client is engaged in a relationship with a case manager or counselor, is discussing substance use or attending a group, and shows evidence of reduction in use for at least 1 month (fewer drugs, smaller quantities, or both). External controls (*e.g.*, Antabuse) may be involved in reduction.
5. Early Active Treatment. The client is engaged in treatment, is discussing substance use or attending a group, has reduced use for at least 1 month, and is working toward abstinence (or controlled use without associated problems) as a goal, even though he or she may still be abusing.
6. Late Active Treatment. The person is engaged in treatment, has acknowledged that substance abuse is a problem, and has achieved abstinence (or controlled use without associated problems), but for less than 6 months.
7. Relapse Prevention. The client is engaged in treatment, has acknowledged that substance abuse is a problem, and has achieved abstinence (or controlled use without associated problems) for at least 6 months. Occasional lapses, not days of problematic use, are allowed.
8. In Remission or Recovery. The client has had *no* problems related to substance use for over 1 year and is no longer in any type of substance abuse treatment.

For the purposes of this report, the data from the NH Dual Disorders Study participants and their case managers were used to assess the validity of the SATS. Additional data collection was required for the assessment of reliability, although for the most part, the same clients and case managers were involved.

Consensus Rating Process

A major obstacle for psychometric analysis is the determination of a reliable and valid measure of current substance use and stage of treatment. Client self-reports, collateral reports (*e.g.*, family or friends), treatment-provider reports (*e.g.*, therapist, case manager, group leader), and laboratory data (*e.g.*, urinalysis) are imperfect for a variety of reasons. A preferred method of determining client status involves bringing together information from multiple sources and multiple time points, thereby assuring that the aggregate information is more valid than that from any single source. Consequently, our research team has standardized a process whereby all relevant information from 3 years of data collection is brought to bear through a consensus process in order to determine the stage of substance abuse treatment for each client at each 6-month assessment point. These consensus SATS ratings are used in this report as the criterion measure against which to test the validity of the case managers' SATS ratings.

Statistical Methods

For the assessment of interrater and test-retest reliability of the SATS, the intraclass correlation coefficient (ICC) was chosen as the appropriate statistic, following arguments and formulas given by Bartko and Carpenter (1976). The ICC is computed as a ratio of variance components from a random effects analysis of variance. Perfect agreement by two concurrent raters (interrater) or across repeated ratings (test-retest) within subjects will produce an ICC equal to 1.0, regardless of variation between subjects. The 95% confidence interval for each ICC was computed according to formulas given by Shrout and Fleiss (1979). Standards for evaluating reliability coefficients are somewhat arbitrary, depending in part on the type of reliability in question and the purposes of the assessment. Landis and Koch (1977) have suggested that a value of Cohen's Kappa above .60 indicates substantial reliability and above .40 indicates acceptable reliability. No such standards have been proposed for the ICC, although the ICC is mathematically related to Kappa. For practical purposes in services research, reliabilities less than .60 probably indicate substantial inconsistency that reduces the researcher's power to detect true relationships between measures.

Validity was determined by examining the correlation between the SATS and other measures of substance use or measures of functional status. The Pearson product-moment correlation coefficient was used when the criterion measure was continuous, and Kendall's Tau was used when the criterion measure was ordinally scaled.

RELIABILITY

Clinician interrater reliability

Because many clients with dual disorders in New Hampshire's mental health system are served by treatment teams, several clinicians often know each client well. Therefore, two concurrent SATS ratings were obtained for seven clients at each of six CMHCs, for a total of 42 paired ratings. The ICC was .90 (CI: .82 to .94).

Clinician test-retest reliability

To assess test-retest reliability, two SATS ratings were obtained, about 1 week apart, for 72 clients in four CMHCs. The same case manager provided both ratings for each client, but the raters were not aware of the second rating task when they made their initial ratings. The ICC was .91 (CI: .86 to .94).

Researcher interrater reliability

As part of the process to develop consensus SATS ratings in the NH Dual Disorders Study (described above), two members of the research team made separate SATS ratings based on all of the longitudinal research data on each client, except the case manager's SATS ratings, which were not revealed until the final stage of the consensus process. Consequently, the SATS ratings from the two raters were used to assess interrater reliability among researchers on a subset of clients (N = 65). The ICC for the intake (baseline) ratings was .75 (CI: .62 to .84), and the ICCs at the other six assessment points (6 months through 36 months) varied from .88 (CI: .81 to .93) to .95 (CI: .92 to .97). The average ICC over the seven assessment points was .89, and the ICC over all 433 pairs of ratings was .93.

VALIDITY

Concurrent validity

Using a sample of 136 clients from the NH Dual Disorders Study, we correlated the case manager's SATS ratings at each assessment point with the researchers' consensus SATS ratings. Table 2 shows that the correlations ranged from .67 to .73, with an average correlation of .70. The correlation over all ratings was .75 (N = 857). Although high, these correlations are attenuated somewhat because case managers rated clients over the previous

Table 2. Validity of the substance abuse treatment scale: correlations between the case manager SATS ratings and criterion, related, and dissimilar measures

| | Type of Validity | | | |
| | Concurrent | Convergent | | Discriminant |
Assessment Point	Consensus SATS[a]	CMRS alcohol use[b]	Follow-up calendar alcohol & drug use[a]	GAS[a]
Intake	.72**	-.42**	-.15	-.21*
6 months	.70**	-.43**	-.24**	.0
12 months	.70**	-.58**	-.37**	.23*
18 months	.67**	-.56**	-.27**	.13
24 months	.73**	-.45**	-.31**	.20*
30 months	.68**	-.52**	-.44**	.17
36 months	.68**	-.55**	-.35**	.37**

[a]Pearson product-moment correlation (GAS = Global Assessment Scale).
[b]Kendall's Tau-b (CMRS = Case Manager Rating Scale).
*p < .05, **p < .01.

6 months, whereas the researchers rated them over a several-week period, since the treatment-related information available to researchers was based on the 2 weeks prior to the client interview. In repeating these analyses with the ICC, which assesses actual agreement rather than relative rank, the coefficients were reduced by about .02, as the overall ICC was .73 and the average ICC over the seven assessment points was .68.

Convergent and discriminant validity

Campbell and Fiske (1959) argued that the assessment of validity ought to include comparing the measure in question with other measures thought to assess either similar (convergent validity) or different (discriminant validity) constructs. By this reasoning, the SATS should be moderately correlated with measures of alcohol or drug use, but only weakly correlated with measures of function in domains that are only partially affected by substance abuse (*cf.* McLellan et al., 1981).

To assess convergent validity, several measures of substance use were compared with the case managers' SATS ratings. First, SATS ratings ($N = 135$) were correlated with case managers' ratings of their clients' alcohol use during the past 6 months using the Case Manager Rating Scale (Drake et al., 1990a). The correlation (Tau-b) of the SATS with alcohol use ratings at each assessment point ranged from -.42 to -.58 (see Table 2), with an average of -.50, and the overall correlation ($N = 859$) was -.53.

Case managers' SATS ratings were also correlated with measures of alcohol and drug use taken from the 6-month follow-back calendars obtained at each assessment point (*cf.* Sobell et al., 1980). When compared with the measure of alcohol consumption (days in past 6 months), the correlation (Pearson *r*) was significant at each assessment point except intake, ranging from -.20 (at 6 months) to -.41 (at 30 months), with an average of -.30. When the follow-back measure also included days of drug use (see Table 2), the correlations with the SATS increased slightly (except at baseline), averaging -.33.

To assess discriminant validity, the SATS was compared at each assessment point with several ratings of functional status. The case managers' SATS ratings showed a weak relationship with ratings of clients by their interviewers at each assessment point on the Global Assessment Scale (Endicott et al., 1976); three of seven were significant in the expected direction; the average correlation was .13 (see Table 2). In addition, case managers' SATS ratings were compared with global ratings of change from baseline made by the consensus raters within four domains: residential (including hospital), psychiatric symptoms, activity, and socialization. Four of the 28 correlations (Tau-b) were significant, and the range was from -.08 to .37. The relationship between the SATS ratings and the combined measure of function (over the four domains) was slightly stronger, ranging from .20 (at 6 months) to .34 (at 12 months).

MONITORING PATIENTS AND PROGRAMS

The SATS has broad utility in clinical and research applications as a measure of stage of treatment for individuals and groups in substance abuse programs. Whether conceived of as a measure of process or of outcome, the SATS can be used to monitor the status of individual clients throughout the course of their treatment. In addition, treatment options can be timed better and tailored to each client if the current stage of treatment is known. In other applications, the SATS can be used to summarize and track the progress of groups of clients in substance abuse treatment. Mean SATS ratings over time should indicate the success of clinical programs or research interventions in helping groups of clients to progress toward recovery. As an additional example, Figure 1 presents the consensus SATS ratings for 125 clients in the NH Dual Disorders Study, showing the percentage of clients within each stage of substance abuse treatment at each assessment point. This plot illustrates the progress made by this cohort over the course of 3 years in dealing with their substance abuse, as more and more of them moved from the persuasion stages into active treatment, relapse prevention, and recovery.

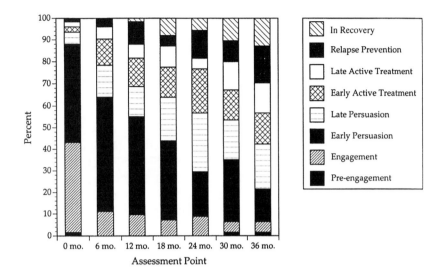

Figure 1. Consensus SATS ratings at each assessment point in the NH Dual Disorders Study (N=125).

DISCUSSION AND CONCLUSIONS

The SATS appears psychometrically sound. Reliability is high across raters and upon retesting, even though clients are moving through the stages of treatment, indicating that the classification criteria are clear and non-overlapping. The 6-month time frame for the rating and the explicit criteria for each stage concerning treatment status and substance use are two likely reasons for the high reliability of the SATS. Furthermore, case manager SATS ratings correlated highly with the criterion consensus ratings, and the degree of association with other measures of substance use and with measures of overall functional status was appropriate. Thus, with modest training and reasonable familiarity with their clients, clinicians can use the SATS consistently and meaningfully.

Some researchers have questioned whether the SATS rests on an unproven theoretical model. The underlying model was, however, derived entirely from empirical observation rather than theory: retrospective interviews with dually diagnosed clients about their process of recovery, and prospective observations across several research studies indicating that clients must first be engaged in treatment and then develop motivation for abstinence before they are ready to participate in traditional substance abuse treatments.

Questions have also been raised concerning the adaptability of the SATS to various substance abuse patterns or other domains of rehabilitation. First, the scale should be applied to the client's current pattern of substance abuse, for example, just alcohol, just cocaine, or polysubstance abuse. Furthermore, it should be possible to adapt the SATS to other rehabilitation and treatment situations that involve motivational stages. With careful attention to published studies, clinical practice, and client behavior, researchers could develop behavioral criteria for any rehabilitation process and map them onto the stages of treatment.

Another question concerns whether the stages of treatment imply a linear process. They do not, since substance abuse is recognized to be a chronic, relapsing disorder. Clients typically cycle between earlier stages, especially at the beginning of treatment, and a pattern of progress emerges only over months and years. Moreover, a client can enter treatment at any stage. The stages are meant to guide treatment planning and to monitor long-term progress, not to specify a linear pathway to recovery. Implicit in this approach to substance abuse treatment among persons with mental illness is an understanding of the chronicity of the problem and of the intermediate stages between abuse and recovery.

One problem that has arisen in using the SATS occurs when clients are relapsing and must be assessed in terms of returning to a previous stage of treatment. In this common situation, the criteria relating to time of abstinence may not make sense. In other words, a client who experiences an episode of relapse will not have a month of reduction but may well be in early active treatment, in terms of longer recent history, motivational level, and readiness for active, abstinence-oriented treatment. In this case, the client should be assessed as early active treatment rather than as persuasion stage, since appropriate treatment planning is the ultimate validity criterion for this scale as a clinical instrument.

The SATS was designed to assess progress in recovering from substance abuse in relation to treatment. What about clients who make progress outside of the treatment system? This potential conflict is mitigated by two factors. First, since these clients have severe mental illness, they typically make progress toward recovery from substance abuse in relation to some treatment process. Second, if treatment for substance abuse is broadly conceived, as continuous feedback, advice, counseling, and consequences from many sources, then progress can be construed as nearly always related to treatment.

In conclusion, the SATS provides both clinicians and researchers with a measure of progress through substance abuse treatment for persons with severe mental illness. The SATS has high reliability, and these initial analyses support its validity. The scale can be used, at the individual or group level, as a process measure to monitor treatment status or as an outcome measure to evaluate treatment program success. The conjunction of motivational level and substance use pattern at each stage of treatment accomplishes several things; it enables reliable classification, facilitates treatment planning, permits assessment of intermediate outcomes, and, perhaps most important, conveys an understanding of the interdependence between overall mental health treatment engagement and substance abuse treatment specifically in the population of individuals with dual disorders.

REFERENCES

Bartko JJ, Carpenter WT (1976) On the methods and theory of reliability. *Journal of Nervous and Mental Disease* 163:307-317.

Campbell DT, Fiske DW (1959) Convergent and discriminant validation by the multitrait-multimethod matrix. *Psychological Bulletin* 56:81-105.

Carey KB (in press) Substance use reduction in the context of outpatient psychiatric treatment: A collaborative, motivational, harm reduction approach. *Community Mental Health Journal.*

Drake RE, Bartels SJ, Teague GB, Noordsy DL, Clark RE (1993) Treatment of substance use disorders in severely mentally ill patients. *Journal of Nervous and Mental Disease* 181:606-611.

Drake RE, Noordsy DL (1994) Case management for people with coexisting severe mental disorder and substance use disorder. *Psychiatric Annals* 24:427-431.

Drake RE, Osher FC, Noordsy DL, Hurlbut SC, Teague GB, Beaudett MS (1990a) Diagnosis of alcohol use disorders in schizophrenia. *Schizophrenia Bulletin* 16:57-67.

Drake RE, Teague GB, Warren RS (1990b) New Hampshire's dual diagnosis program for people with severe mental illness and substance abuse. *Addiction and Recovery* 10:35-39.

Endicott J, Spitzer RL, Fleiss JL, Cohen J (1976) The Global Assessment Scale. *Archives of General Psychiatry* 33:766-771.

Kofoed LL, Keys A (1988) Using group therapy to persuade dual-diagnosis patients to seek substance abuse treatment. *Hospital and Community Psychiatry* 39:1209-1211.

Landis JR, Koch GG (1977) The measurement of observer agreement for categorical data models. *Biometrics* 33:159-174.

Lehman AF, Dixon L (1995) *Double jeopardy: Mental illness and substance abuse.* New York: Harwood Academic Press.

McLellan AT, Luborsky L, Woody GE, O'Brien CR, Kron R (1981) Are the "addiction-related" problems of substance abusers really related? *Journal of Nervous and Mental Disease* 169:232-239.

Miller WR, Rollnick S (1991) *Motivational interviewing.* New York: Guilford.

Minkoff K, Drake RE (Eds) (1991) *Dual diagnosis of major mental illness and substance disorder.* San Francisco: Jossey-Bass.

Noordsy DL, Fox L (1991) Group intervention techniques for people with dual disorders. *Psychosocial Rehabilitation Journal* 15:67-78.

Osher FC, Kofoed LL (1989) Treatment of patients with psychiatric and psychoactive substance abuse disorders. *Hospital and Community Psychiatry* 40:1025-1030.

Prochaska JO, DiClemente CC, Norcross JC (1992) In search of how people change: Applications to addictive behaviors. *American Psychologist* 47:1102-1114.

Ridgely MS, Goldman HH, Talbott JA (1986) *Chronic mentally ill young adults with substance abuse problems: A review of the literature and creation of a research agenda.* Baltimore: University of Maryland Mental Health Policy Studies Center.

Ridgely MS, Osher FC, Talbott JA (1987) *Chronic mentally ill young adults with substance abuse problems: Treatment and training issues.* Baltimore: University of Maryland Mental Health Policy Studies Center.

Shrout PE, Fleiss JL (1979) Intraclass correlations: Uses in assessing rater reliability. *Psychological Bulletin* 86:420-428.

Sobell MB, Maisto SA, Sobell LC, Cooper AM, Cooper T, Sanders B (1980) Developing a prototype for evaluating alcohol treatment effectiveness. In LC Sobell, MB Sobell, E Ward (Eds), *Evaluating alcohol and drug abuse treatment effectiveness.* New York: Pergamon.

Stark MJ, Kane BJ (1985) General and specific psychotherapy role induction with substance-abusing clients. *International Journal of Addictions* 20:1135-1141.

ABOUT THE AUTHORS

Gregory J. McHugo, Ph.D., and Robert E. Drake, M.D., Ph.D., are affiliated with the New Hampshire-Dartmouth Psychiatric Research Center, Department of Community and Family Medicine, Dartmouth Medical School, Hanover, NH. Heather L. Burton, M.A., is a medical student at Columbia University College of Physicians and Surgeons. Theimann H. Ackerson, M.S.W., is affiliated with the New Hampshire Department of Corrections.

ACKNOWLEDGMENTS

This work was supported by Public Health Service grants MH-46072 and MH-00839 from the National Institute of Mental Health, and grants AA-08341 and AA-08840 from the National Institutes on Alcohol Abuse and Alcoholism.

Reprinted with permission from *Journal of Nervous and Mental Disease.*

INTRODUCTION TO SECTION FOUR

The Clinical Issues section contains six articles that present an overview of what is known about the complications of severe mental illness that are related to substance abuse. Many studies have examined the relationship between substance abuse and such clinical issues as symptom severity, relapse and hospitalization, medication compliance, violence and crime, homelessness, medical problems such as infection with HIV, and overall functioning. These studies have been reviewed in detail elsewhere (Drake & Brunette, in press), and we include representative articles concerning these issues in this section.

Many researchers have tried to determine whether or not there is a clear relationship between substance abuse and symptoms of mental illness, but it has been difficult to reach a consensus on this matter. Most studies that look at a cross-sectional sample (i.e., at one point in time) have not found that substance abusers have more symptoms than nonabusers. Studies that examine the same group of persons over time provide more compelling evidence that substance abuse does cause symptom exacerbation in some persons with severe mental illness.

The relationship between substance abuse and symptoms varies with the symptoms in question and the substance of abuse. Some drugs, such as hallucinogens and amphetamines, increase positive symptoms of psychosis in laboratory settings. Prospective studies, that is, studies that follow a group of people over time, provide strong evidence that cannabis and cocaine abuse worsen positive symptoms of psychosis over time. Both prospective and correlational studies suggest that alcohol abuse is associated with worsening of depression. The article by Don Linszen and his colleagues describes a large, one-year prospective study, which showed that people with schizophrenia who were heavy users of cannabis relapsed to positive psychotic symptoms more quickly and more frequently than did mild users and nonusers of cannabis. Negative and depressive symptoms did not seem to be related to cannabis abuse.

Persons with severe mental illnesses who abuse alcohol and drugs are likely to spend more time in the hospital than nonabusers. For example, Swofford and colleagues recently showed that despite having the same levels of symptoms, substance abusers with mental illness had twice the hospitalization rate of nonusers (Swofford, Kasckow, Scheller-Gilkey, & Indrbitzin, 1996). High rates of hospitalization are not necessarily related to substance-induced clinical relapses of psychotic or depressive symptoms, since substance abusers have more difficulties with aggressive, disruptive, illegal, and suicidal behavior, all of which can precipitate hospitalization. Additionally, medication noncompliance in concert with substance abuse may lead to symptoms and behaviors that necessitate hospitalization. These factors are discussed in the remaining articles in this section.

Persons with dual disorders have more difficulties in managing finances, living independently, maintaining meaningful activities, and maintaining relationships than persons who have severe mental illnesses without substance abuse. Functioning tends to decline after episodes of substance abuse. Moreover, clients involved in treatment for their dual disorders tend to improve in overall functioning. The article by Tandy Chouljian and her colleagues shows the relationship between substance abuse and lower functional level in people with dual diagnoses.

Substance abuse is strongly related to medication noncompliance in people with severe mental illness. For example, Kashner et al. (1991) found that among people with schizophrenia, substance abusers were 13 times more likely to be medication noncompliant than nonabusers. One reason for poor medication compliance in the community may be poor adherence with treatment in general. Individuals with schizophrenia who are living in the community are less likely to receive aftercare services and more likely to miss appointments if they abuse substances than are those who do not abuse substances. This problem may be overcome by offering assertive aftercare that includes daily monitoring of medications (Osher et al., 1994). The article by Richard Owen and his colleagues provides evidence that substance abuse is strongly associated with medication noncompliance, and that those with substance abuse, medication noncompliance, and no outpatient contact form a particularly high-risk group.

Barriers to housing, treatment strategies, and ways to support homeless people with dual disorders are discussed in the article by Fred Osher and Lisa Dixon. Roughly 10-20% of homeless persons suffer from co-occurring severe mental illness and substance use disorder. People with dual disorders are more likely to become homeless or fail to achieve stable housing than those with severe mental illness alone. Drake and Wallach (1989) found that patients discharged from the state hospital with dual disorders had three times the rate of housing difficulties as those with mental illness only. Osher and Dixon argue that integrating mental health, substance abuse, and housing services improves the likelihood that homeless people with mental illnesses will attain residential stability and independent living. Moreover, attaining residential stability is associated with progress toward recovery from substance abuse.

Numerous studies have examined the relationship between substance abuse and disruptive behaviors, hostility, aggression, and actual violence. Most have found that persons with dual diagnoses have higher rates of disruptive behaviors, aggression, and violence than those without substance use disorders. For example, Swanson and colleagues studied a large number of people in the community and reported that rates of violence were much higher in persons with schizophrenia who abused any substances (30.3%) compared with those who did not (8.3%) (Swanson, Holzer, Ganju, & Jono, 1990). The article by Brian Cuffel and his colleagues presents evidence that polydrug use in particular is correlated with and predictive of violent behavior.

Substance abuse is also correlated with criminal behavior in those with severe mental illnesses (Wessely, Castle, Douglas, & Taylor, 1994), but the connection may be complex. Only a minority of criminal activities among those with severe mental illnesses is directly related to substance abuse, e.g., intoxication and possession or obtaining money to pay for substances. Rather, substance abusers become arrested and incarcerated for inappropriate and disruptive behaviors that could be induced by substance abuse in combination with other risk factors, such as psychotic symptoms, medication noncompliance, comorbid antisocial personality disorder, and homelessness.

Human immunovirus seropositivity (i.e., being HIV positive) among people with severe mental disorders is strongly related to drug abuse. Studies suggest that people with dual disorders may have a higher rate of HIV infection than those without comorbid substance abuse. Michael Carey and his colleagues summarize studies on this topic and describe implications for practice. They argue that there is a clear need for risk assessment, education, risk-reduction counseling, and antibody testing for HIV infection in those with serious mental illnesses, especially those with dual disorders.

Although substance use disorders are correlated with many clinical and social problems, these correlations should be interpreted cautiously, as correlation does not necessarily mean causation. For example, a third variable such as medication noncompliance might explain much of the relationship between substance abuse and symptoms. It is easier to believe that substance abuse causes a particular problem when many studies are consistent in their findings, and when prospective, longitudinal studies support the relationship. For now, the association between substance use and such clinical issues as symptom exacerbations, residential instability, and HIV risk should alert practitioners to the common co-occurring problems that must be monitored and addressed in comprehensive treatment.

REFERENCES

Drake, R.E., & Brunette, M.F. (in press). Complications of severe mental illness related to alcohol and other drug use disorders. In M. Galanter (Ed.), *Recent developments in alcoholism: Vol. XIV. Consequences of alcoholism*. New York: Plenum Publishing Company.

Drake, R.E., & Wallach, M.A. (1989). Substance abuse among the chronic mentally ill. *Hospital and Community Psychiatry*, 40, 1041-1046.

Kashner, T.M., Rader, L.E., Rodell, D.E., Beck, C.M., Rodell, L.R., & Muller, K. (1991). Family characteristics, substance abuse, and hospitalization patterns of patients with schizophrenia. *Hospital and Community Psychiatry, 42*, 195-197.

Osher, F.C., Drake, R.E., Noordsy, D.L., Teague, G.B., Hurlbut, S.C., Biesanz, J.C., & Beaudett, M.S. (1994). Correlates and outcomes of alcohol use disorder among rural outpatients with schizophrenia. *Journal of Clinical Psychiatry, 55*, 109-113.

Swanson, J.W., Holzer, C.E., Ganju, V.K., & Jono, R.T. (1990). Violence and psychiatric disorder in the community: Evidence from the Epidemiologic Catchment Area Survey. *Hospital and Community Psychiatry, 41*, 761-770.

Swofford, C.D., Kasckow, J.W., Scheller-Gilkey, G., & Indrbitzin, L.B. (1996). Substance use: A powerful predictor of relapse in schizophrenia. *Schizophrenia Research, 20*, 145-151.

Wesseley, S.C., Castle, D., Douglas, A.J., & Tayler, P.J. (1994). The criminal careers of incident cases of schizophrenia. *Psychological Medicine, 24*, 483-502.

CANNABIS ABUSE AND THE COURSE OF RECENT-ONSET SCHIZOPHRENIC DISORDERS

Don H. Linszen, Peter M. Dingemans, and Marie E. Lenior

Reprinted from *Archives of General Psychiatry,* 51:273-279, 1994

Objective. We sought to examine the relation between cannabis abuse and the symptomatic course of recent-onset schizophrenia and related disorders.

Design. A prospective cohort study over a year using monthly Brief Psychiatric Rating Scale assessments.

Participants. Cannabis-abusing patients (n=24) were compared with nonabusers (n=69). Eleven patients were mild and 13 were heavy cannabis-abusing patients.

Results. Significantly more and earlier psychotic relapses occurred in the cannabis-abusing group (P=.03). This association became stronger when mild and heavy cannabis abuse were distinguished (P=.002). No confounding effect of other variables, e.g., other street drugs, was found. In all but one patient, cannabis abuse preceded the onset of the first psychotic symptoms for at least 1 year.

Conclusions. Cannabis abuse and particularly heavy abuse can be considered a stressor eliciting relapse in patients with schizophrenia and related disorders and possibly a premorbid precipitant.

Studies examining the relationship between cannabis use and schizophrenic symptoms among patients with schizophrenic disorders have found the following: (1) an increase in psychotic (positive) symptoms[1-6]; (2) no difference in psychotic symptoms in comparison to non-cannabis-abusing schizophrenic populations[7,8]; and (3) a decrease in negative symptoms.[7,8] Studies are needed to continue systematic study of this relationship to understand these discrepant findings. Clarification of the relationship would have both theoretical benefits of elucidating the mechanisms of psychotic relapse and practical applications for treatment of mentally ill substance abusers. Questions such as, "Do variable amounts of cannabis consumption render different symptomatic impact on schizophrenic patients?" or "Do positive consequences such as relief of psychotic or negative symptoms occur with some level of cannabis use?" might be answered.

However, the available studies consisted of case series, in which possible relationships between cannabis abuse and psychotic symptoms were difficult to test. In a few case-control studies, psychotic symptoms were evaluated retrospectively, using hospital files.[4] Also, the observation period was only 1 week[7] and schizophrenic symptoms were evaluated once.[8]

This study seeks to make improvements over past efforts. Therefore, data were analyzed from the present prospective 1-year outpatient follow-up study to examine the relationship between reported cannabis abuse and the symptomatic course of psychotic, negative, and affective symptoms in young patients consecutively admitted to the hospital with recent-onset schizophrenia and related disorders.

Subjects and Methods

Patients were eligible for the study if they were diagnosed as having schizophrenia or a related disorder using *DSM-III-R* criteria,[9] were in need of continuous antipsychotic medication, were between 15 and 26 years of age, and were living with or in close contact with parents or other relatives. Patients with primary alcohol or drug dependence or brief drug-related psychoses who needed detoxification were excluded. All included patients participated in a 15-month treatment program. This program was composed of an inpatient phase (3 months), in which baseline data were collected. An important issue during the inpatient treatment was trying to maximize antipsychotic medication compliance. After hospital discharge, treatment was continued in a 12-month outpatient phase, composed of day hospital treatment (3 months) and community care (9 months).

The present study took place during the outpatient phase, in which patients were maintained on a regimen of optimal antipsychotic medication and received individual supportive treatment. During day treatment, patients received medication management training. Patients were seen biweekly during day hospital treatment and during the first 2 months of outpatient care. The last 7 months, individual treatment contacts took place monthly. In addition, half of the patients received an additional psychoeducative family treatment by family therapists designed to reduce family stress. Patients and their families in the latter condition were seen with the same frequency as with the individual treatment contacts.

Instruments

Parents or relatives of the patients were interviewed with the Psychiatric and Social History Schedule.[10] In this interview, data were elicited about present and past illness as well as prognostic factors and premorbid social attainment,[11] substance abuse, medication, family history of mental disorder, and other prognostic factors.

Cannabis abuse was described according to the cannabis dependence criterion of the *DSM-III-R*, defined as daily or almost daily use of cannabis.[9] Abuse was rated as present if it was reported by (1) the patient and parents or former treatment summaries as having existed prior to hospital admission *and* (2) during the 12-month outpatient treatment phase, as reported both by the patient and the treatment staff. If in any one case these criteria were not met, cannabis abuse was rated as absent. During the study, no systematic laboratory confirmation of cannabinoid derivatives in urine was made that could have verified abuse. The combined self-reports as well as reports of relatives and therapists over an extended period (with a minimum of more than 1 year) were likely to be valid, since the use of cannabis, though officially illegal, is practically not restricted in Holland. The use was and is discussed freely and it seems unlikely that nonabusers were, in fact, abusers. Within the abusing group, two subgroups were defined: mild or heavy cannabis abuse. Patients with heavy abuse smoked more than one cigarette a day before hospital admission and during the 12-month outpatient treatment period. Patients with mild abuse smoked between once a week and once a day.

Psychopathologic symptoms were assessed by an independent clinical evaluator who saw patients on a monthly basis using the Brief Psychiatric Rating Scale (BPRS).[12] The BPRS interviewer (P.M.D.) had been trained at the University of California, Los Angeles (UCLA, Department of Psychology), before and the test was recalibrated for reliability again halfway into the study. The interrater agreement between the interviewer and standardized UCLA BPRS ratings was satisfactory (K=0.79). He was blind to cannabis abuse.

The monthly collected BPRS data were used to evaluate relapses in the present study. The monthly BPRS ratings allowed us to formulate objective quantitative criteria for relapse or exacerbations of psychotic episodes. Nuechterlein et al[10] introduced a precise system for evaluating psychotic relapse. Relapse or significant exacerbation of psychotic symptoms was defined according to the following criteria.

Remission followed by relapse

The patient maintained a 3 or below on all BPRS relapse scales (hallucinations, conceptual thought disorder, formal thought disorder) during the first month of the outpatient treatment phase and a score of 6 or 7 was noted on one of these scales during the other 11 months of the outpatient treatment.

Remission followed by significant exacerbation

The patient maintained at least a 3 or below on relapse scales for at least 1 month and the patient also (1) scored 5 on a relapse scale at some point following this period, plus an increase of two points on another conceptually related scale; or she or he (2) scored 5 on a relapse scale for more than 1 month.

<u>Persisting symptoms followed by significant exacerbation</u>

The patient scored 4 or 5 on a relapse scale during the first month and (1) she or he maintained this state throughout the following period and subsequently showed an increase of two points on this scale; or (2) showed one-point increase on this scale (to a 6 or 7), accompanied by two-point increase on another conceptually related scale. In other reports on this sample,[13] data collected regularly by treating clinicians were also used to form a composite relapse criterion. However, since these clinicians contributed data to the estimate of cannabis abuse, these data could have influenced their relapse judgments. Thus, only the BPRS data were truly independent of the cannabis status of patients in the study.

Negative symptoms were operationalized with the anergy factor of the BPRS items (factor 2).[12] This factor has been found to be a parsimonious description of the negative symptom complex.[14,15] Again, a mean was calculated monthly for the anergy items for a period of 12 months; the mean was used as the negative symptom score. Affective symptoms were operationalized with the anxiety-depression factor of the BPRS items (factor 1).[12] A mean was also calculated monthly for a year for the affective items; the mean was used as the affective symptom score.

Antipsychotic medication compliance was indexed by the treating psychiatrist and the social psychiatric nurse in their regular contacts with the patient during the 12-month study period. Both interviewed the patient about compliance and compliance estimates were recorded. The social psychiatric nurse did occasional pill counts. A research assistant reviewed the compliance data for each month of the study and made ratings on a four-point scale: 1, 0% to 24% compliance: no or irregular; 2, 25% to 49%: rather irregular; 3, 50% to 74%: rather regular; and 4, 75% to 100%: regular, including depot. The recorded antipsychotic medication was rated from 1 (not prescribed) to six (more than 15 equivalents) in daily haloperidol equivalents.

Procedure

During the intake before hospital admission, the Psychiatric and Social History Schedule was assessed by a research psychologist (P.M.D.). During the inpatient phase, a research assistant and a psychiatrist (D.H.L.) verified parental Psychiatric and Social History Schedule data with psychiatric case notes, the patient's own reports, and former treatment hospital discharge summaries. Conflicting data were presented to the informants. Cannabis abuse and the use of alcohol and other psychoactive drugs during outpatient treatment were independently assessed by the treating psychiatrist and nursing personnel. From hospital admission until the end of the 12-month study period (15 months), the patients were assessed monthly with the BPRS.[12]

Data Analysis

Analyses of psychotic, negative, and affective symptoms were based on the scores of 12 monthly BPRS-E interviews during the outpatient treatment period. The data were analyzed with Statistical Package for the Social Sciences (SPSS Inc, Chicago, Ill)[16] and Biomedical Computer Programs (BMDP)[17] programs. Relapses or significant exacerbations of psychotic symptoms were analyzed by product-limit survival analyses. Survival time until the first incidence of relapse or exacerbation was analyzed with treatment condition, cannabis abuse, intensity of cannabis abuse, and duration of cannabis abuse before hospital admission as grouping variables. The effect of covariates was analyzed using proportional hazards analysis: "Cox regression" (likelihood ratio tests). Analysis of variance for repeated measures and incomplete data was carried out on the means of negative and affective symptom item scores of the BPRS.

RESULTS

Of the 97 patients consecutively admitted to the hospital, four patients dropped out before psychopathologic conditions on the BPRS could be assessed; hence, evaluations for 93 patients were available. The experimental family treatment condition did not affect the relapse rate ($P=.87$) nor did any treatment condition influence cannabis abuse ($P=.25$). The patients had a clinical hospital discharge diagnosis of schizophrenia (52 patients), schizoaffective (19 patients), schizophreniform (11 patients), and other (delusional disorder, nine patients; atypical psychosis, two patients) psychotic disorders (11 patients). Compliance with antipsychotic medication was deemed high throughout the study, as the mean ($\pm$SD) rating during day treatment was 3.8 ± 0.58 and during community care it was 3.8 ± 0.58.

According to our definition, 24 (26%) of the patients were cannabis abusers. The frequency of abuse varied from once a week to four to five cigarettes a day. The mean ($\pm$SD) age when they started cannabis abuse was 16 ± 2.2 years and the mean duration of abuse before hospital admission was 3.9 ± 2.3 years. All but one of the cannabis-abusing patients started their habit at least 1 year prior to their first psychotic symptoms (mean, 3 years; range, 0 to 7 years). Within the group of cannabis abusers, 13 (54%) heavy cannabis-abusing patients could be distinguished. The mild cannabis-abusing group consumed between one cigarette a week and one a day. Hard drug abuse was rare (two patients used cocaine and 3,4-methylenedioxymetamphetamine ["ecstasy"]; one of these patients used hard drugs sporadically in combination with heavy cannabis abuse). The characteristics of the patient group and comparisons of the nonabusing and abusing group are summarized in Table 1.

The two groups showed no statistically significant differences in variables of clinical importance: DSM-III-R diagnoses, history of illness course, sum score of positive and negative symptoms on the BPRS at the start of the study,[18] and compliance with and dosage of antipsychotic medication during treatment. Moreover, there were no differences in familial social class,[19] education, and race (data not shown). Statistically significant differences between abusers of cannabis and nonabusers were found for age at the time of hospital admission, sex, and alcohol use. No differences were found between the heavy and mild cannabis-abusing group, in particular not for compliance with medication ($P=.55$) or dosage of antipsychotic medication ($P=.47$).

In the cannabis-abusing group, 10 (42%) of 24 patients suffered relapses, whereas of the 69 patients who did not abuse cannabis, 12 patients (17%) suffered relapses or exacerbations during the 12-month study period. As compared with patients without abuse, a significant difference in time until relapse was observed ($P=.03$), indicating that cannabis abusers suffered relapses more frequently and earlier than nonabusers (Figure 1).

Eight patients (61%) in the heavy cannabis-abusing group of 13 patients suffered relapses, whereas of the 11 mild cannabis-abusing patients only two (18%) suffered relapses. With the cannabis-abusing group divided into mild and heavy abusers, an ordered effect was revealed ($P=.002$).

To test the effect of the duration of cannabis abuse prior to hospital admission, a survival analysis was conducted for three groups: no cannabis abuse, 3 years or less of cannabis abuse before hospital admission, and more than 3 years of cannabis abuse. Again an ordered effect was found ($P=.02$), revealing that with a longer period of abuse the risk of relapse increased.

The cannabis effects were tested again with age at time of hospital admission, sex, and use of alcohol as covariates. A strong trend of cannabis abuse remained, if corrected for the differences between the two groups ($P=.06$). Also, the intensity of cannabis abuse was analyzed, revealing that the effect of the intensity of cannabis abuse (no, mild, and heavy abuse) remained highly significant ($P=.01$). Finally, the effect of the duration of cannabis abuse before hospital admission was reduced when corrected for differences between abusers and nonabusers ($P=.08$). This was caused by the fact that duration of cannabis abuse was shorter for younger patients (20 years or younger) than for older patients ($P=.01$). With regard to sex and alcohol, no significant differences were found between the two groups according to duration of cannabis abuse. Likelihood tests demonstrated no significant effects of sex, age at the time of hospital admission, and alcohol use on the survival function or any interaction effect.

One may find the diagnosis of the sample too heterogeneous. Therefore, we carried out analyses in a subsample of patients with schizophrenia only (*DSM-III-R* criteria: N=52 [56%]). Post hoc analyses revealed that the relation between the intensity of cannabis abuse (no abuse, 10 of 39 patients suffering a relapse; mild abuse, one of six patients suffering a relapse; heavy abuse, five of seven patients suffering a relapse) and the time until psychotic relapse remained highly significant ($P=.01$). This effect remained when corrected for age, sex, and alcohol ($P=.01$).

Table 1. Demographic, psychiatric, and drug characteristics of all patients and of the cannabis-abusing and nonabusing groups

Variable	All Patients (N=93)	Nonabusers (N=69)	Abusers (N=24)	P Value*
Demographic				
Mean (±SD) age, yrs at admission	20.6±2.44	20.8±2.5	19.8±1.98	.04
Sex, No. (%)				
F	26 (28)	23 (33)	3 (13)	.05
M	67 (72)	46 (67)	21 (88)	
Mean (±SD) prognostic scale score (Strauss and Carpenter)[20]	61.7±11.08	62.2±11.55	60.4±9.70	.52
Psychiatric				
Mean (±SD) age, yrs at onset of schizophrenia	19.1±2.56	19.3±2.70	18.8±2.11	.38
Psychotic episodes, No. (%)				
1	52 (56)	37 (54)	15 (63)	.45
>1	41 (44)	32 (46)	9 (38)	
Schizophrenia (*DSM-III-R*), No. (%)				
No	41 (44)	30 (44)	11 (46)	.84
Yes	52 (56)	39 (57)	13 (54)	
Mean (±SD) sum score of positive and negative symptoms (BPRS)[†]	15.1±4.77	14.6±4.70	16.3±4.85	.13
Drugs				
Abuse of alcohol, No. (%)				
No	84 (91)	67 (97)	17 (74)	.00
Yes	8 (9)	2 (3)	6 (26)	
Mean compliance to antipsychotic medication, No. (%)				
0-24	3 (3)	2 (3)	1 (4)	.23
25-49	2 (2)	1 (1)	1 (4)	
50-74	13 (14)	7 (10)	6 (25)	
75-100	75 (81)	59 (86)	16 (67)	
Mean (±SD) dosage of antipsychotic medication[†]	3.6±1.2	3.5±1.2	3.8±1.0	.27

*P value for difference between nonabusers of cannabis.
[†]These Brief Psychiatric Rating Scale (BRPS) items[12] were scored from 1 (not present) to 7 (very severely); the mean item scores of the last 2 months of inpatient treatment were taken.
[‡]The mean dosage (in haloperidol [Haldol] equivalents) during inpatient and outpatient treatment was taken. Dosage was scored from 1 (no prescription) to 6 (>15 haloperidol equivalents) (3, four to six equivalents; 4, seven to nine equivalents).

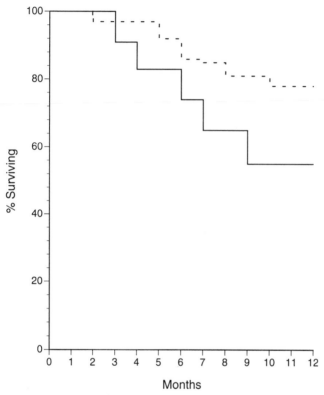

Figure 1. Survival curves of time until psychotic relapse (brief psychiatric rating scale) by no abuse (dashed line) and abuse (solid line) of cannabis.

No main effect of cannabis abuse for the course of negative symptom scores was found ($P=.286$). However, negative symptoms generally decreased over 12 months, with a significant increase at month 2 and a decrease at month 10. There was an interaction effect between cannabis and time ($P=.03$). The interaction effect became stronger when the cannabis-abusing group was divided into mild and heavy abusers ($P=.002$). A significant interaction effect was found at month 10 for mild abusers and nonabusers of cannabis. At this point, the mean negative symptom score was increasing for nonabusers while decreasing for mild abusers.

Also, no effect of cannabis abuse for the course of affective symptom scores was found ($P=.53$). However, a trend was found with the intensity of cannabis abuse ($P=.09$). In the mild cannabis-abusing group, there was a trend for less anxiety and depression than in the nonabusing and heavy cannabis-abusing group.

COMMENT

The most relevant finding of this prospective study in patients with recent-onset schizophrenia and schizophrenia-related disorders was the occurrence of significantly more and earlier psychotic relapses or exacerbations in the group of cannabis-abusing patients. When a distinction with respect to the intensity of abuse was made, it appeared that particularly heavy cannabis-abusing patients had more and earlier relapses. This finding was not confounded by exposure to alcohol and/or any other (psychoactive) drugs, nor by differences in antipsychotic medication compliance and dosage. Baseline symptom status, prognostic scale score,[20] or history of prior relapse rates were similar for cannabis abusers and nonabusers. No other demographic or clinical factors could be identified that affected this relationship. Another finding was that all cannabis-abusing patients but one started their habit at least 1 year prior to the first psychotic symptoms, suggesting that cannabis abuse can possibly be a premorbid precipitant.

These findings could have been more convincing if this study had included systematic laboratory confirmation of cannabinoid derivatives in urine. Martin et al,[21] however, found that the information on use of soft drugs given by patients is reliable. Moreover, evaluation of cannabis abuse in the present study was based on information given by various sources: the reports of the patients, parents, psychiatrist, and nursing staff. Also, the reader may not be familiar with cannabis use patterns in Amsterdam. Though not officially sanctioned, the use of cannabis products is not restricted by legislation; however, hard drugs are much more difficult to get. Levels of antipsychotic medication in the blood of the patients under study should have been measured to provide the compliance data with a solid base.

Two additional findings indicate a possible causal relation between cannabis and psychotic relapse. First, 14 of 24 cannabis-abusing patients reported an immediate increase of psychotic symptoms after cannabis abuse. Thirteen of these 14 patients were clinically in remission when they reported the increase of psychotic symptoms. Six patients noted no such increase and only one patient reported a decrease of psychotic symptoms when abusing cannabis, which is in agreement with earlier case reports.[2,3,6] Second, in all but one patient, cannabis abuse preceded the initial onset of psychotic episodes for at least 1 year. This finding is congruent with the observations of a Swedish epidemiologic study that revealed that cannabis abuse prior to illness was an independent risk factor for schizophrenia.

A biologic explanation of the demonstrated relation between psychotic symptoms of schizophrenic patients and cannabis abuse may be found in recent pharmacologic studies.[23] Delta (9)-tetrahydrocannabinol (delta-9-THC), the principal psychoactive constituent of cannabis, was found to act as a dopamine agonist in dopaminergic projections of the medial forebrain bundles.

Dopaminergic hyperactivity is generally thought to be related to the presence of psychotic symptoms of schizophrenia,[24] although other neurotransmitters may be affected as well. An increase of dopamine could undo the dopamine receptor blockade of antipsychotic medication. In our study, the intensity of abuse was correlated with an increase of psychotic relapses, suggesting that delta-9-THC acts as a dopamine agonist in the projections of the medial forebrains of the patients as well. Future studies with brain imaging techniques applied to heavy abusing and nonabusing schizophrenic patients with standard antipsychotic medication may be indicated to reveal these differences in dopamine receptor blockade or in other neurotransmission systems. Cannabis abuse may also have influenced the antipsychotic drug metabolism, lowering plasma levels of active metabolites. Thus, cannabis abusers could have been relatively undertreated, despite the finding of a lack of differences in antipsychotic dosage between heavy and mild abusers. Of course, it may not be the biologic action alone that increases the risk for relapse in these young patients. Those patients who used cannabis heavily both before and after the onset of their psychosis may represent a different population of cases from those who were nonabusers. While it is true that most of our background measures do not discriminate cannabis abusers from nonabusers, it is possible that those persons who use cannabis regularly are more vulnerable to or have less effective coping mechanisms for dealing with intercurrent life events. This same vulnerability to stress may produce a lower threshold for recurrence of the psychiatric disorder, even if these patients discontinued cannabis use.

As for cannabis abuse and negative symptoms, even though a significant interaction effect was observed between time and cannabis abuse, we consider this finding to be of limited value, since no main effect of cannabis abuse was established on the course of negative symptoms. The same consideration holds true for cannabis abuse and the course of affective symptoms. However, in the mild cannabis-abusing group, symptoms of anxiety and depression tended to be less present than in the nonabusing and heavy cannabis-abusing group. Therefore, our findings support the self-medication hypothesis only for patients with mild cannabis abuse.[25] According to this theory, schizophrenic patients successfully try to reduce their negative and affective symptoms[8,26] or side effects of antipsychotic medication[6] by using street drugs. The existence of an amotivational syndrome with an increase of negative symptoms in the cannabis-abusing group of young schizophrenic patients was not tenable, particularly not in the heavy cannabis-abusing group.

The findings of this study support the concept that cannabis abuse and particularly heavy abuse is at least a stressor for psychotic relapse and exacerbation in schizophrenia and related disorders and—possibly—a premorbid precipitant. However, the prospective nature of the study does not resolve the problem of cause and effect of cannabis abuse and psychotic relapse, because the needed nonschizophrenic cannabis-abusing controls were lacking. Nevertheless, treatment strategies have to be developed to discourage cannabis abuse by schizophrenic patients. Further studies should include cannabis abuse intervention programs, a quantitative estimation of cannabis abuse repeated in time, laboratory confirmation of cannabis abuse, and repeated assessments of dose-response effects as soon after abuse as possible in cannabis-abusing patients.[27]

REFERENCES

1. Weil AT. Adverse reactions to marijuana, classification and suggested treatment. *New England Journal of Medicine* 1970;282:997-1000.
2. Chopra GS, Smith JW. Psychotic reactions following cannabis use in East Indians. *Archives of General Psychiatry* 1974;30:24-27.
3. Treffert DA. Marijuana use in schizophrenia: a clear hazard. *American Journal of Psychiatry* 1978;135:1213-1215.
4. Negrete JC, Knapp WP, Douglas DE, Smith B. Cannabis affects the severity of schizophrenic symptoms: results of a clinical survey. *Psychological Medicine* 1986;16:515-520.
5. Cleghorn JM, Kaplan RD, Szechtman B, Szechtman H, Brown GM, Franco S. Substance abuse and schizophrenia: effect on symptoms but not on neurocognitive function. *Journal of Clinical Psychiatry* 1991;52:26-30.
6. Knudsen P, Vilmar T. Cannabis and neuroleptic agents in schizophrenia. *Acta Psychiatria Scandinavica* 1984;69:162-174.
7. Rottanburgh D, Robins AH, Ben-Arie O, Teggin A, Elk R. Cannabis-associated psychosis with hypomanic features. *Lancet* 1982;2:1364-1366.
8. Peralta V, Cuesta MJ. Influence of cannabis abuse on schizophrenic psychopathology. *Acta Psychiatria Scandinavica* 1992;85:127-130.
9. American Psychiatric Association, Committee on Nomenclature and Statistics. *Diagnostic and Statistical Manual of Mental Disorders, Revised Third Edition.* Washington, DC: American Psychiatric Association; 1987.
10. Nuechterlein KH, Snyder KS, Dawson ME, Rappe S, Gitlin M, Fogelson D. Expressed emotion, fixed dose fluphenazine decanoate maintenance and relapse in recent-onset schizophrenia. *Psychopharmacology Bulletin* 1986;22:633-639.
11. Kokes R, Strauss J, Klorman R. Measuring premorbid adjustment: the instruments and their development. *Schizophrenia Bulletin* 1977;3:186-213.
12. Overall JE, Gorham DR. The Brief Psychiatric Rating Scale. *Psychological Reports* 1962;10:799-812.
13. Linszen DH, Dingemans PMAJ, Scholte WF, et al. Behandeling, 'expressed emotion' en recent ontstane schizofrenie en verwante stoornissen. *Tijdschrift voor de Psychiatrie* 1993;9:625-640.

14. Thiemann S, Csernansky JG, Berger PA. Rating scales in research: the case of negative symptoms. *Psychiatry Research* 1987;20:47-55.
15. Czobor P, Bitter I, Volavka J. Relationship between Brief Psychiatric Rating Scale for the assessment of negative symptoms: a study of their correlation and redundancy. *Psychiatry Research* 1991;36:129-139.
16. Norusis MJ. *SPSSPC+ 4.0 Base Manual for the IBM PC/XT/AT and PS/2*. Chicago, Ill: SPSS Inc; 1990.
17. Dixon MJ, Brown MB, Engelman L, et al, eds. *BMDP Statistical Software Manual*. Berkeley: University of California Press; 1990;1-2.
18. Breier A, Schreiber JL, Dyer J, Pickar O. National Institute of Mental Health Longitudinal Study of Chronic Schizophrenia: prognosis and predictors of outcome. *Archives of General Psychiatry* 1991;48:239-246.
19. Hollingshead AB, Redlich FC. *Social Class and Mental Illness*. New York, NY: John Wiley & Sons Inc; 1968;387-397.
20. Strauss JS, Carpenter WT. Prediction of outcome in schizophrenia, III: Five-year outcome and its predictors. *Archives of General Psychiatry* 1977;34:159-163.
21. Martin GW, Wilkinson A, Kapur BM. Validation of self-reported cannabis use by urine analysis. *Addictive Behaviors* 1988;13:147-150.
22. Andreasson S, Allebeck P, Engström A, Rydberg U. Cannabis and schizophrenia: a longitudinal study of Swedish conscripts. *Lancet* 1987;2:1483-1486.
23. Gardner EL, Lowinson JH. Marijuana's interaction with brain reward systems: update 1991. *Pharmacology, Biochemistry and Behavior* 1991;40:571-580.
24. McKena PJ. Pathology, phenomenology and the dopamine hypothesis of schizophrenia. *British Journal of Psychiatry* 1987;151:288-301.
25. Schneier FR, Siris SG. A review of psychoactive substance use and abuse in schizophrenia: patterns of drug choice. *Journal of Nervous and Mental Disease* 1987;175:641-652.
26. Dixon L, Haas G, Weiden PJ, Sweeney J, Frances AJ. Drug abuse in schizophrenic patients: clinical correlates and reasons for use. *American Journal of Psychiatry*. 1991;148:224-230.
27. Thornicroft G. Cannabis and psychosis: is there epidemiological evidence for an association? *British Journal of Psychiatry* 1990;157:25-33.

ABOUT THE AUTHORS

Don H. Linszen, M.D., Ph.D., Peter M. Dingemans, Ph.D., and Marie E. Lenior, M.A., are affiliated with the Psychiatric Center of the Academic Medical Center and the Department of Psychiatry, University of Amsterdam, the Netherlands.

ACKNOWLEDGMENTS

This study was funded in part by grant 28-1241 from the "Praeventiefonds," the Hague, the Netherlands.

Jitse Verhoeff, M.D., provided continuous support of the study and Harry Büller, M.D., Ph.D., gave a critical review of the article.

Copyright 1994. American Medical Association. Reprinted with permission.

SUBSTANCE USE AMONG SCHIZOPHRENIC OUTPATIENTS: PREVALENCE, COURSE, AND RELATION TO FUNCTIONAL STATUS

Tandy L. Chouljian, Martha Shumway, Evelyn Balancio, Eleanor Valdes Dwyer, Robert Surber, and Marc Jacobs

Reprinted from *Annals of Clinical Psychiatry*, 7(1):19-24, 1995

The prevalence and course of alcohol and drug use were examined in a longitudinal, retrospective study of 100 schizophrenic outpatients. During the 18 month study period, problem substance use (abuse and dependence) was not associated with differential attrition from outpatient treatment. Thirty to forty percent of subjects were using drugs or alcohol during any evaluation period. The overall level of substance use and problem use of alcohol, marijuana, and other drugs remained stable, while problem use of cocaine and multiple substances increased over time. Problem substance use was associated with lower functional status and the detrimental effect of problem substance use appeared to increase with time. These findings underscore the need to address substance use problems in the context of outpatient schizophrenia treatment.

INTRODUCTION

Empirical evidence documents that substance use and abuse complicate the course and treatment of schizophrenic illness. Among schizophrenic persons, substance abuse has been associated with increased likelihood of symptom exacerbation (1), elevated risk of hospitalization (2-4), higher levels of disruptive and suicidal behavior (2), decreased medication compliance (3,5), reduced neuroleptic drug efficacy (6), difficulties in coping with community living (2), and limited treatment options (7,8). Additional data suggest that substance use disorders are more prevalent among persons with schizophrenia than in the general population (9) and that the prevalence rate may be increasing (10).

Although comorbid substance use in schizophrenia has received increased attention in the last decade, most published studies fail to incorporate standardized diagnostic criteria, examine substance use among nonhospitalized persons, or differentiate levels of substance use (8,11,12). Furthermore, these largely cross-sectional studies provide little information about the longitudinal course or impact of comorbid substance use.

To begin addressing these issues, we conducted a retrospective longitudinal study of 100 schizophrenic outpatients in a culturally diverse urban area to characterize the extent and nature of substance use during the 18 months following an acute illness episode. The goals were (a) to estimate the prevalence of substance use among schizophrenic outpatients and determine whether prevalence changes over time, (b) to determine whether substance use is associated with differential attrition from outpatient treatment, and (c) to examine the relationship of substance use to functional status. Based on existing research evidence, we hypothesized that 10 to 65% of patients would use drugs or alcohol during the evaluation period, that substance users would be more likely to drop out of treatment, and that patients who used substances would evidence lower levels of functioning than those who did not.

METHODS

Subjects

One hundred subjects were identified through sequential screening of clinical records of all patients seen in the outpatient schizophrenia research clinic at San Francisco General Hospital between 1985 and 1989. All were age 18 to 55 and had primary DSM-III-R diagnoses of schizophrenia, schizoaffective disorder or schizophreniform disorder [verified by the SCID (Structured Clinical Interview for DSM-III-R)] (13). All subjects entered the clinic following an acute psychotic episode after agreeing to participate in a randomized clinical trial. Some never entered the clinical trial and were treated only with standard neuroleptic medication. Those entering the clinical trial were treated with a combination of double blind fluphenazine decanoate (in one of three dosage levels) plus known strength fluphenazine as needed to control symptoms. All patients were medicated to maximum clinical response, permitting evaluation of the three dosage levels without allowing patients to relapse.

Measures

All data were collected through retrospective chart review. Baseline demographic data consisted of gender, age, ethnicity, marital status, level of educational attainment, age at first hospitalization, number of prior psychiatric admissions, and baseline ratings of severity of illness on the Clinical Global Impressions Scale (14), ranging from 1 = not at all ill to 7 = among the most severely ill patients.

Research assistants rated substance use and functional status in each 3-month interval for up to 18 months based on review of progress notes written by psychiatrists, nurses, and social workers, as well as toxicology reports indicating evidence of substance use. The comprehensive and intensive treatment provided in the research clinic yielded frequent, extensive clinical notes from a variety of different clinicians. Since the clinic provided family treatment and case management to all participants, the notes reflect reports from family members and other collateral contacts which are likely to provide a more accurate picture of client course than could be obtained through client contacts alone. Although ratings of substance use were not conducted prospectively, substance use was of general concern to both clinicians and family members and was routinely assessed during clinical contacts. These extensive clinical notes, evaluated in three-month time intervals, provide a solid basis for assessment of substance use and functioning. Toxicology results were not obtained frequently or systematically and provide only an occasional, corroborative information source.

To establish standard rating procedures, the authors attained consensus ratings on five cases which were used to train research assistants. Eleven additional randomly selected reliability cases were completed to ensure stability of rating practices.

Level of use was recorded for four classes of substances (alcohol, marijuana, cocaine and other drugs) using a 4-point rating scale reflecting DSM-III-R diagnostic criteria for substance use disorders, where 1 = no use, 2 = use, 3 = abuse, and 4 = dependence (15). Weighted kappa statistics (16) were calculated to assess interrater agreement on the four-level substance use ratings made for the four substance classes in each of the six evaluation periods. Agreement was good, with a mean kappa of .84.

Level of functioning at the end of each 3 month period was rated using the 100 point Global Assessment Scale (GAS) (17). Intraclass correlations (ICCs) were calculated to assess interrater reliability on the GAS scores using the Case 1 formula of Shrout and Fleiss (18). The mean ICC was .62, indicating adequate reliability. The somewhat restricted range of scores (encompassing approximately 50 points of the 100 point scale) may have attenuated these correlations.

RESULTS

Demographic characteristics

The sample was largely young (mean age, 27.18 ± 6.23 years), male (81%), and ethnically diverse (29% white, 37% black, 14% Asian, 5% Latino, and 15% other). Most subjects had completed high school (75%) and had never been married (84%). On average, study subjects were first hospitalized in their early twenties (mean age, 23.21 ± 4.93 years), had been psychiatrically hospitalized twice (mean number of hospitalizations 2.14 ± 2.56), and were rated as moderately ill (mean rating 4.12 ± 1.07) on the 7 point CGI severity of illness scale at clinic admission.

Prevalence of substance use over time

The overall level of substance use, aggregated across substance classes, remained stable over time. In all evaluation periods, as shown in Table 1, the majority of subjects (61 to 71%) were not using substances, between 3 and 12% were using substances, 14 to 22% were abusing substances, and 6 to 12% were substance dependent. Repeated measures analyses (SAS PROC CATMOD) (19), conducted on 59 subjects with complete data, indicated that usage levels did not vary significantly over time [$\chi^2(5) = 4.72$, ns]. A chi square test for trend, conducted on all available data, yielded a similar nonsignificant association between time and usage level [$\chi^2(15) = 9.22$, ns].

Examination of the full range of usage levels for each of the four substance classes was not feasible with the modest sample available. Therefore, we collapsed the original four levels for subsequent analyses. Abuse and dependence were combined into a single "problem use" category. No use and use were combined into a "no problem use" category because minimal, intermittent use was probably subject to underreporting and underrecording.

Problem use of some individual substances did appear to change over time. As shown in Table 2, repeated measures analyses (SAS PROC CATMOD) (19), conducted on 59 subjects with complete data, indicated that there were statistically significant increases in problem use of cocaine [$\chi^2(5) = 10.97$, $p = .05$] and problem use of multiple substances [$\chi^2(4) = 9.54$, $p = .05$]. Problem use of alcohol, marijuana and other drugs remained stable over time [largest $\chi^2(4) = 8.26$, ns]. The less powerful chi-square tests for trend, conducted on all available data, showed no association between time and problem use of any substance [largest $\chi^2(5) = 6.57$, ns].

Substance use and treatment dropout

Differential attrition could obscure longitudinal trends in substance use if key variables were associated with treatment dropout during the 18 month evaluation period. We used life table procedures (SAS PROC LIFETEST) (19) to examine the relationships of problem substance use (abuse and dependence) and functional status to time in treatment. Problem substance users were not more likely to drop out of treatment [$\chi^2(1) = .48$, ns]. Lower-functioning persons were more likely to drop out [increment $\chi^2(1) = 7.54$, $p < .01$], but there was no interaction between problem substance use and functional status [increment $\chi^2(1) = .08$, ns]. Since substance use was not associated with treatment dropout, trends in substance use and the relationship between substance use and functional status should be interpretable and generalizable.

Table 1. Overall level of substance use

	Time period					
Usage level	Mos 1-3 (n = 100)	Mos 4-6 (n = 80)	Mos 7-9 (n = 69)	Mos 10-12 (n = 67)	Mos 13-15 (n = 61)	Mos 16-18 (n = 59)
No use	64% (64)	71% (57)	64% (44)	61% (41)	66% (40)	68% (40)
Use	11% (11)	8% (6)	9% (6)	12% (8)	3% (2)	7% (4)
Abuse	19% (19)	14% (11)	22% (15)	21% (14)	20% (12)	15% (9)
Dependence	6% (6)	8% (6)	6% (4)	6% (4)	12% (7)	10% (6)

Table 2. Problem use[a] by substance class

	Time period					
Substance class	Mos 1-3	Mos 4-6	Mos 7-9	Mos 10-12	Mos 13-15	Mos 16-18
Alcohol	14% (14)	13% (10)	17% (12)	18% (12)	20% (12)	17% (10)
Marijuana	11% (11)	10% (8)	12% (8)	12% (8)	10% (6)	7% (4)
Cocaine/crack	11% (11)	6% (5)	7% (5)	13% (9)	18% (11)	14% (8)
Other drugs	2% (2)	4% (3)	6% (4)	2% (1)	5% (3)	9% (5)
Multiple substances	4% (4)	1% (1)	6% (4)	8% (5)	7% (4)	9% (5)

[a]Abuse and dependence.

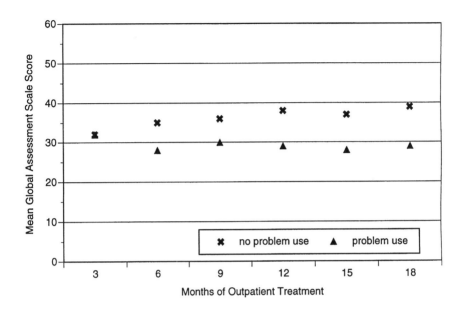

Figure 1. Level of functioning and problem substance use over time

The lack of association between problem substance use and treatment dropout does not completely eliminate concern about attrition during the study period (of 100 subjects seen in the research clinic in months 1 through 3, only 59 were still in treatment in months 16 though 18). We attempted to address this concern in subsequent analyses by using statistical procedures which made use of all available data instead of relying on analyses of subjects with complete data at all time points.

Problem substance use and functional status

The longitudinal relationship between problem substance use and functional status was examined using a mixed-model, repeated measures analysis (SAS PROC MIXED) (20), which permitted use of all available data on all subjects. As shown in Figure 1, results suggested that problem substance use was associated with lower GAS scores and that the difference between problem users and nonproblem users became more pronounced over time (problem use x time interaction, $F = 4.18$, df = 1,433, $p = .04$).

DISCUSSION

This sample of schizophrenic outpatients evidenced rates of substance use similar to those reported previously, with 30 to 40% of subjects using drugs or alcohol during each 3-month evaluation period. Despite this relatively high level of substance use, substance use was not associated with differential attrition from outpatient treatment, nor did the overall level of substance use increase over time. These results suggest that persons with comorbid substance use problems can and do participate in outpatient schizophrenia treatment and that this treatment may moderate the progression of these problems. Although these patients were participating in a research treatment program which included ongoing medication management and psychosocial family interventions that may have been more intensive than typical community outpatient treatment, the treatments were not focused on substance use problems. It is possible that specialized interventions would be more beneficial.

Despite the overall stability of substance use, there were statistically significant increases in problem use of cocaine and multiple substances. These increases may reflect the highly addictive nature of cocaine or the cumulative impact of prolonged polysubstance use. They may, however, be artifacts of subjects' reluctance to report illicit substance use in the early months of treatment in a new setting.

Although problem substance users were not more likely to drop out of treatment, they did experience lower functional status levels than did nonproblem users. Although problem and nonproblem users were functioning similarly in months 1-3, probably because all entered outpatient treatment following an acute illness episode, problem users had mean GAS scores 5 to 9 points lower than nonproblem users in all subsequent evaluation periods and the magnitude of the difference appeared to increase with time, possibly indicating that continued substance use had a cumulative, detrimental effect on functioning.

The relatively small observed differences appear clinically significant. For example, in months 16 through 18, nonproblem users had a mean GAS score of 37.7, indicating "major impairment in several areas," while problem users had a mean GAS score of 28.5, indicating "inability to function in almost all areas." While a 9-point difference on a 100 point scale may seem modest, it can represent a critical decrement in functional capacity in this low functioning patient population.

The observed association between problem substance use and low functioning could be explained by either substance use leading to decreased functioning or poor functioning leading to substance use as a remedy for psychotic symptoms, medication side effects, or general demoralization. Although prospective studies are needed to reach definitive conclusions, the time trend seen here is more consistent with the first causal hypothesis. The indication that the detrimental effects of problem substance use become more prominent with time suggests that persistent substance use has a detrimental effect on functioning. If a low functional status predisposed patients to substance use, the association would be as likely in the early evaluation periods as in the later ones.

The retrospective nature of this study limits the precision of these findings to some extent. Since ratings of substance use were based on existing chart notes, without systematic queries about substance use, it is likely that problematic use was recorded more often than nonproblematic use, regardless of the extent of use. It is also likely that clients under-reported their substance use, particularly their use of illegal substances. In addition, the available sample size was too small to permit detailed examination of the impact of the full range of substance usage levels or of specific substance classes.

Nevertheless, the results of this short term longitudinal study illustrate that substance use is a prominent, enduring factor in schizophrenic illness which is associated with reductions in functional status. These findings underscore the need for substance abuse treatment among schizophrenic outpatients. However the social and cognitive impairments which characterize schizophrenic illness often limit patients' ability to tolerate the confrontational nature of many traditional substance abuse interventions and many patients require maintenance antipsychotic medication which may be incompatible with the drug-free philosophies of many substance abuse programs.

Clearly, this patient population requires specialized programs which integrate substance abuse treatment with traditional outpatient schizophrenia treatment. Several model programs have shown promising results with approaches that emphasize nonconfrontational therapies, psychoeducation, and development of alternative social and coping skills (21-25). In our sample, substance users were no more likely than non-users to drop out of treatment, demonstrating that substance users can and do participate in and benefit from outpatient treatment. It seems likely that such patients would derive even greater benefit from treatments that specifically addressed their substance use problems as well as their schizophrenic illness.

REFERENCES

1. Galanter M, Castaneda R, Ferman J: Substance abuse among general psychiatric patients: Place of presentation, diagnosis and treatment. *American Journal of Drug & Alcohol Abuse* 1988; 142:211-235
2. Drake RE, Wallach MA: Substance abuse among the chronic mentally ill. *Hospital and Community Psychiatry* 1989; 40:1041-1046
3. Kashner TM, Rader LE, Rodell DE, Beck CM, Rodell LR, Muller K: Family characteristics, substance abuse, and hospitalization of patients with schizophrenia. *Hospital and Community Psychiatry* 1991; 42:195-197

4. Kivlahan DR, Heiman JR, Wright RC, Mundt JW, Shupe, JA: Treatment cost and rehospitalization rate in schizophrenic outpatients with a history of substance abuse. *Hospital and Community Psychiatry* 1991; 42:609-614

5. Pristach CA, Smith CM: Medication compliance and substance abuse among schizophrenic patients. *Hospital and Community Psychiatry* 1990; 41:1345-1348

6. Bowers MB, Mazure CM, Nelson JC, Jatlow PI: Psychotogenic drug use and neuroleptic response. *Schizophrenia Bulletin* 1990; 16:81-85

7. Haugland G, Siegel C, Alexander MJ, Galanter M: A survey of hospitals in New York state treating psychiatric patients with chemical abuse disorder. *Hospital and Community Psychiatry* 1991; 42:1215-1220

8. Salloum IM, Moss HB, Daley DC: Substance abuse and schizophrenia: Impediments to optimal care. *American Journal of Drug & Alcohol Abuse* 1991; 17:321-336

9. Regier DA, Farmer ME, Rae DS, Locke BZ, Keith SJ, Judd LL, Goodwin FK: Comorbidity of mental disorders with alcohol and other drug abuse. *Journal of the American Medical Association* 1990; 264:2511-2518

10. Cuffel BJ: Prevalence estimates of substance abuse in schizophrenia. *Journal of Nervous and Mental Disease* 1992; 180:589-592

11. Mueser KT, Yarnold PR, Levinson DF, Singh H, Bellack AS, Kee K, Morrison RL, Yadalam KG: Prevalence of substance abuse in schizophrenia: Demographic and clinical correlates. *Schizophrenia Bulletin* 1990; 16:31-56

12. Turner WM, Tsuang MT: Impact of substance abuse on the course and outcome of schizophrenia. *Schizophrenia Bulletin* 1990; 16:87-95

13. Spitzer RL, Williams JBW, Gibbon M, et al.: *Structured Clinical Interview for DSM-III-R - Patient Version* (SCID-P, 5/1/89). New York: Biometrics Research Department; 1989

14. Guy WM: *ECDEU Assessment Manual*. Bethesda, MD: National Institute of Mental Health, DHEW Publication No. (ADM) 76-338; 1976

15. American Psychiatric Association: *Diagnostic and Statistical Manual of Mental Disorders*, 3rd ed. rev. Washington, DC: American Psychiatric Association; 1987

16. Fleiss JL: *Statistical Methods for Rates and Proportions*. New York: Wiley; 1981

17. Endicott J, Spitzer RL: The global assessment scale: A procedure for measuring overall severity of psychiatric disturbance. *Archives of General Psychiatry* 1976; 33:766-771

18. Shrout PE, Fleiss JL: Intraclass correlations: Uses in assessing rater reliability. *Psychological Bulletin* 1979; 86:420-428

19. SAS Institute Inc.: *SAS/STAT User's Guide, Version 6*, 4th ed. Cary, NC: SAS Institute Inc.; 1989

20. SAS Institute Inc.: SAS Technical Report P-229, *SAS/STAT Software: Changes and Enhancements, Release 6.07*. Cary, NC: SAS Institute Inc.: 1992

21. Alfs DS, McClellan TA: A day hospital program for dual diagnosis patients in a VA medical center. *Hospital and Community Psychiatry* 1992; 43:241-244

22. Carey KB: Emerging treatment guidelines for mentally ill chemical abusers. *Hospital and Community Psychiatry* 1989; 40:341-349

23. Minkoff K: An integrated treatment model for dual diagnosis of psychosis and addiction. *Hospital and Community Psychiatry* 1989; 40:1031-1036

24. Drake RE, Antosca LM, Noordsy DL, Bartels SJ, Osher FC: New Hampshire's specialized services for the dually diagnosed. *New Directions for Mental Health Services* 1991; 50:57-67
25. Rosenthal RN, Hellerstein DJ, Miner CR: Integrated services for treatment of schizophrenic substance abusers: Demographics, symptoms and substance abuse patterns. *Psychiatric Quarterly* 1992; 63:3-26

ABOUT THE AUTHORS

Tandy L. Chouljian, M.S., Martha Shumway, B.A., Evelyn Balancio, M.S.W., Eleanor Valdes Dwyer, M.S.W., Robert Surber, M.S.S.W., and Marc Jacobs, M.D., are affiliated with the Department of Psychiatry, University of California and San Francisco General Hospital, San Francisco, CA.

ACKNOWLEDGMENTS

This work was supported by National Institute of Mental Health Grant MH40042 and Biomedical Research Support Grant RR05755. The authors thank Margaret Riordan, Carolee Waidelich, and Patricia McKenna for their assistance with data collection, William Hargreaves, Teh-wei Hu, and Brian Cuffel for their data analytic advice, and Patricia Arean, Cynthia Battle, David Gibson, Maria Juarez-Reyes, Jeanne Miranda, and Kathleen Schutte for their editorial comments.

Reprinted with permission from *Annals of Clinical Psychiatry*.

Medication Noncompliance and Substance Abuse Among Patients with Schizophrenia

Richard R. Owen, Ellen P. Fischer, Brenda M. Booth, and Brian J. Cuffel

Reprinted from *Psychiatric Services*, 47:853-858, 1996

Objective. The study examined the effect of medication noncompliance and substance abuse on symptoms of schizophrenia.

Methods. Short-term inpatients with a diagnosis of schizophrenia were enrolled in a longitudinal outcomes study and continued to receive standard care after discharge. At baseline and six-month follow-up, Brief Psychiatric Rating Scale (BPRS) scores and data on subjects' reported medication compliance, drug and alcohol abuse, usual living arrangements, and observed side effects were obtained. The number of outpatient contacts during the follow-up period was obtained from medical records. Relationships between the dependent variables—medication noncompliance and follow-up BPRS scores—and the independent variables were analyzed using logistic and linear regression models.

Results. Medication noncompliance was significantly associated with substance abuse. Subjects who abused substances, had no outpatient contact, and were noncompliant with medication had significantly greater symptom severity than other groups.

Conclusions. Substance abuse is strongly associated with medication noncompliance among patients with schizophrenia. The combination of substance abuse, medication noncompliance, and lack of outpatient contact appears to define a particularly high-risk group.

Compliance with a prescribed regimen of medication can be an important factor in determining the effectiveness of treatment for schizophrenia (1-3), as well as for several other medical (4,5) and psychiatric disorders (6-8). For patients with psychiatric disorders, estimates of medication compliance vary by treatment setting, with greater compliance observed among inpatients than among outpatients (9,10). The rate of medication noncompliance among outpatients with schizophrenia has been reported to be as high as 50 percent (3,11,12).

In the treatment of any medical disorder, patients' lack of compliance with a medication regimen is affected by many factors. Factors related to providers' behavior include the dose of medication prescribed and the complexity of the medication regimen. Factors related to patients' behavior include the perceived benefit from medication (13,14) and the degree of daily supervision, often assessed by whether the patient is living alone, with others, or in a controlled environment (6,12). Side effects, another important factor related to patients' behavior, are particularly significant in neuroleptic pharmacotherapy (13,15-18).

Moreover, lack of awareness of illness, which is common among patients with schizophrenia, may increase medication noncompliance (19,20). Patients may also modify medication intake to exercise control and to attempt to feel better (13). In addition, characteristic symptoms of schizophrenia, such as suspiciousness or persecutory delusions (21), grandiosity (22,23), and anxiety or depression (24), may predispose affected patients to medication noncompliance.

Comorbid substance abuse is common among patients with schizophrenia. The Epidemiologic Catchment Area study found that 47 percent of persons with schizophrenia had a lifetime diagnosis of a substance use disorder (25). The prevalence of current substance abuse among inpatients may be even higher (26,27). Individuals with a dual diagnosis of schizophrenia and substance abuse have been reported to have high rates of noncompliance with a prescribed medication regimen (28-31). In addition, both medication noncompliance (1-3) and substance abuse (28,30,32,33) have been associated with poor outcomes among patients with schizophrenia. However, little information is available about the relationship between substance abuse and medication compliance among these patients. Although each condition may independently affect symptom severity over time, it is also possible that medication noncompliance mediates the effects of substance abuse on symptom severity (34).

We used data from a longitudinal study of outcomes of routine care for patients with schizophrenia to test two specific hypotheses about relationships between patient characteristics, medication noncompliance, and substance abuse. First, we wanted to determine whether current substance abuse, unsupervised living arrangements, infrequent outpatient mental health care visits, and medication side effects are associated with medication noncompliance. Second, we assessed whether medication noncompliance is associated with greater symptom severity.

METHODS

Subjects

Subjects were recruited from among short-term inpatients on psychiatric units at either the Little Rock Veterans Affairs Medical Center or Arkansas State Hospital between February 1992 and May 1993. To be eligible, patients had to meet *DSM-III-R* criteria for schizophrenia, assessed using the Structured Clinical Interview for DSM-III-R (SCID) (35); to be between age 18 and 55; and to provide written informed consent after the study was described to them in detail.

Data collection

Subjects were interviewed at baseline during the index hospitalization and again six months later to obtain information on demographic characteristics, medication noncompliance, substance abuse, symptom severity, and medication side effects. The interviews were conducted by trained research assistants.

Demographic characteristics. In addition to questions about basic demographic characteristics, subjects were asked about their usual living arrangements during the preceding 30 days. The level of supervision associated with these arrangements was coded on a 4-point scale on which 0 indicated a controlled or supervised environment, 1 indicated living with others, 2 indicated living alone, and 3 indicated that living arrangements were unstable.

Medication noncompliance. Subjects were asked about medication compliance within the 30 days before the hospital admission during which they were recruited for the study and the 30 days before the six-month follow-up interview. Of 135 subjects who provided complete information on medication compliance and symptom severity at follow-up, 130, or 96.3 percent, reported that medication had been prescribed for them for the preceding 30-day period. These subjects were asked to rate their compliance with their oral or injectable medication regimen during that period on a 5-point scale developed by Miklowitz and colleagues (36,37). On that scale, 1 indicates never missed medication; 2, missed a couple of times, but essentially took all prescribed doses; 3, missed several times, but took at least half of prescribed doses; 4, took less than half of the prescribed doses; and 5, stopped taking medication altogether.

Informants close to the patient, including family members or health professionals, were asked to rate the subject's medication compliance on the same scale. We determined that this scale had excellent test-retest reliability among subjects with a diagnosis of schizophrenia (intraclass correlation coefficient [ICC]=.89) and adequate concordance between subject and informant responses (ICC ranged from .51 to .75).

Because the majority of subjects rated their compliance 1 or 2 on the 5-point scale, indicating that they never missed taking medication or missed only a couple of times, a dichotomous variable was created. Subjects who rated their compliance 1 or 2 were classified as compliant, and the remaining subjects were classified as noncompliant. A total of 110 subjects, or 84.6 percent, were classified as compliant, and 20 subjects, or 15.4 percent, were classified as noncompliant.

This classification is clinically relevant because minor omissions of medication would be less likely than major oversights to result in symptom exacerbation, and major omissions are more likely to be reported accurately by patients (38). Moreover, Miklowitz and associates (37) found that this method of classification resulted in the strongest association between noncompliance and relapse among patients with bipolar disorder.

Substance abuse. Substance use disorders were diagnosed at baseline using the SCID. A screen for current substance abuse during the month before the follow-up was developed from responses to questions on the CAGE questionnaire (39,40), to questions from the CAGE adapted for use in detecting drug use, and to questions about frequency of use. Subjects were classified as currently abusing substances if they responded positively to one or more CAGE questions (for alcohol or drugs) and reported substance use at least one or two days per week in the preceding 30 days. These criteria demonstrated 81 percent sensitivity and 86 percent specificity for detecting current drug abuse, and 74 percent sensitivity and 78 percent specificity for detecting alcohol abuse at baseline, compared with *DSM-III-R* diagnoses derived using the SCID.

Symptom severity. The anchored version of the 18-item Brief Psychiatric Rating Scale (BPRS) (41,42) was administered by trained lay interviewers. Interrater reliability for the BPRS total score was excellent (ICC=.97). The BPRS includes specific items that are rated on a scale from 1 to 7, with higher ratings indicating greater symptom severity. Nine of the items are based on subjects' self-report. Data for these items were listed as missing if the subject did not give a meaningful answer. For subjects who had three or fewer missing items, the missing values were imputed using the average item score for that subject.

Side effects. The presence or absence of tardive dyskinesia, parkinsonism, or akathisia was rated by the interviewer. A dichotomous variable was created to indicate the presence or absence of any observed side effect. We used the baseline observation of side effects in the analysis of the relationship between side effects and medication compliance at follow-up.

Additional information on treatment variables was obtained through review of subjects' medical records, as described below.

Outpatient treatment. We defined outpatient services to include outpatient clinic visits, case management contacts, and partial hospitalization services. One visit to or one day of any of these services was counted as one unit of outpatient service. We defined three levels of a categorical variable to represent the amount of outpatient services: 0, no outpatient services; 1, one to six units of service, representing up to one unit per month on average; and 2, greater than six units.

Depot neuroleptics. Medical record reviewers determined which subjects were prescribed depot neuroleptic medication in the two months before follow-up. These patients may represent a distinct group in terms of medication compliance (11) because their compliance with a regimen of neuroleptics is at least partly determined by compliance with appointments for injections.

Data analysis

Bivariate analysis was used to identify and exclude from multivariate analyses demographic variables that were not significantly associated with the respective dependent variable.

Factors associated with medication noncompliance. The relationship between medication noncompliance at follow-up and follow-up substance abuse, usual living arrangements, observed side effects at baseline, and outpatient contacts was analyzed using multiple logistic regression.

Factors associated with follow-up symptom severity. Multiple linear regression was used to analyze the relationship between follow-up BPRS total score and the independent variables included in the logistic regression plus self-reported medication compliance at follow-up, sex, and baseline symptom severity as indicated by the BPRS total score. Interaction terms for medication noncompliance, substance abuse, and outpatient contact were fit according to the results of descriptive analysis.

RESULTS

Subjects

We enrolled 161 subjects during an index hospitalization and were able to reinterview 147 subjects, or 91 percent, at six-month follow-up. Complete BPRS scores and complete data on compliance were available for 135 subjects. The subjects who were not included in the analysis were not significantly different from the final sample in demographic characteristics, baseline symptom severity, or proportion with a SCID-confirmed diagnosis of a substance use disorder.

Seventy-four subjects, or 55 percent, were enrolled at the state hospital, and 61, or 45 percent, were enrolled at the VA medical center. Although the state hospital subsample contained a significantly greater proportion of female subjects—16 percent, compared with 5 percent in the VA group—subjects enrolled at the two facilities were not significantly different with respect to race, age, education, baseline BPRS total score, duration of illness, or number of previous hospitalizations.

Table 1. Clinical and demographic characteristics of 135 patients with schizophrenia at baseline and six-month follow-up

Characteristic	Baseline[1]		Follow-up	
	N	%	N	%
Current substance abuse or dependence	57	42	31	23
Observed side effects present	25	19	20	15
Usual living arrangements				
Unstable	6	5	10	7
Alone	35	27	36	27
With others (family or friends)	73	55	75	56
Controlled environment	18	14	13	10
Medication compliant	69	53	110	81
Medication noncompliant	47	36	20	15
Not prescribed medication	14	11	5	4
Outpatient contacts				
None	—	—	38	29
One to six	—	—	40	30
More than six	—	—	53	41
On depot neuroleptic	—	—	42	31
Mean±SD score on the				
Brief Psychiatric Rating Scale	39.5±9.5		36.8±10.7	

[1]With the exception of side effects and BPRS total score, which were observed at the baseline interview, all baseline measures refer to the 30-day period before the index hospitalization.

Eighty-nine percent of the subjects were male. The sample mean±SD age was 38±7 years, and median illness duration was 16 years. Fifty-seven percent of the subjects were African American, and 43 percent were Caucasian.

Table 1 shows the distributions of the clinical and demographic characteristics at baseline and follow-up. Medication noncompliance was significantly more likely before the index hospitalization than at follow-up (McNemar X^2=20.5, df=1, p<.001; subjects who were not prescribed medication were excluded from this analysis).

Factors associated with medication noncompliance. Table 2 shows rates of medication noncompliance associated with the clinical and demographic variables examined in the study. Table 3 presents the results of the logistic regression analysis predicting medication noncompliance at follow-up as a function of substance abuse, outpatient contacts, usual living arrangements at follow-up, and observed side effects at baseline.

Table 2. Clinical and demographic characteristics of 20 subjects who were medication noncompliant at six-month follow-up, among 130 subjects who were prescribed medication

Characteristic	N	%
Current substance abuse (at follow-up)		
Present (N =29)	12	41
Absent (N=101)	8	8
Outpatient contacts in six months[1]		
None (N=35)	10	29
One to six (N=39)	5	13
More than six (N=54)	4	7
Observed side effects (at baseline)[1]		
Present (N=25)	1	4
Absent (N=103)	19	18
Living arrangements[1]		
Unstable (N=10)	2	20
Alone (N=33)	7	21
With others (N=73)	11	15
Controlled environment (N=13)	0	0
Sex		
Female (N=15)	0	0
Male (N=115)	20	17
Race		
African American (N=72)	13	18
Caucasian (N=58)	7	12

[1]Total N for this variable is less than 130 due to missing data.

Subjects with current substance abuse were at substantially increased risk of reporting medication noncompliance (odds ratio [OR]=8.1, p<.001). Baseline observed side effects and increased outpatient contact appeared to decrease the likelihood of medication noncompliance, with these relationships approaching statistical significance (OR=.53, p=.09, and OR=.13, p=.07, respectively). Living arrangements were not significantly associated with medication noncompliance. Because all female subjects were classified as compliant with their medication regimen, sex was not included in the logistic regression model.

Factors associated with symptom severity at follow-up. The multiple linear regression model to predict BPRS total score at follow-up explained 40 percent of the variance in symptom severity (F=4.8, df=15, 109, p<.001). The model predicted follow-up BPRS score as a function of baseline BPRS score, follow-up substance abuse, medication noncompliance, outpatient

Table 3. Logistic regression model showing characteristics associated with medication noncompliance at follow-up

Characteristic	Parameter estimate	Standard error	Odds ratio	95% CI
Substance abuse (0=no abuse,1=current abuse)	2.09	.60	8.1**	2.5—26
Observed side effects (0=none,1=any side effects)	-2.03	1.13	.13*	.01—1.2
Outpatient contacts (0=none, 1=one to six, 2=more than six)	-.63	.38	.53*	.25—1.1
Living arrangements (0=unstable, 1=alone, 2=with others, 3=controlled environment)	.19	.39	1.2	.56—2.6

*p<.10
**p<.001

contacts, living arrangements, observed side effects, and sex, and all two- and three-way interaction terms involving the variables of substance abuse, noncompliance, and outpatient contact. As expected, baseline BPRS total score was positively associated with follow-up BPRS (F=33, df=1, p<.001). Outpatient contacts (F=3.5, df=2); the three-way interaction term including noncompliance, substance abuse, and outpatient contacts (F=3.3, df=2); and the two-way term including noncompliance and outpatient contacts (F=3.4, df=2) were significantly associated with BPRS total score at follow-up (p<.05 for all associations). Observed side effects and living arrangements were not associated with symptom severity at follow-up.

Table 4 presents least-squares mean BPRS total scores at follow-up, adjusted for the effects of other variables in the model, to illustrate the nature of the three-way interaction. Noncompliant subjects who abused substances and had no outpatient contact had significantly higher BPRS scores at follow-up than other groups of subjects. The group compliant with medication had no clear variation in BPRS scores by substance abuse or outpatient contacts.

The results of both the logistic and the linear regression analyses were robust and did not substantially change when we excluded female subjects, excluded subjects who had been prescribed depot neuroleptics, or classified subjects as noncompliant if either they or their informants reported medication noncompliance.

Table 4. Mean total adjusted BPRS scores at follow-up of subjects who were compliant and noncompliant with their medication regimen, by presence of current substance abuse and outpatient contacts

Characteristic	Medication compliant		Medication noncompliant	
	Mean	SE	Mean	SE
Current substance abuse				
No outpatient contact	36.6	4.4	52.5	3.1[1]
One to six outpatient contacts	37.8	2.9	39.4	5.0
More than six outpatient contacts	36.6	4.4	—[2]	
No current substance abuse				
No outpatient contact	36.0	1.9	37.6	6.1
One to six outpatient contacts	37.8	1.8	25.8	6.2
More than six contacts	33.3	1.3	36.9	5.0

[1] Adjusted mean is greater than means in every other cell (p<.05).
[2] One observation in cell (BPRS total score=27)

DISCUSSION

The rate of medication noncompliance before the index hospitalization found among subjects in this study—about 50 percent—is consistent with previous reports of rates of noncompliance among outpatients with schizophrenia (3,11,12). Because medication noncompliance has been associated with relapse or rehospitalization of patients with schizophrenia (1-3), our finding that medication noncompliance is significantly more likely before hospitalization than at six-month follow-up is not surprising.

Factors associated with medication noncompliance

The finding that current substance abuse was strongly associated with medication noncompliance is particularly important given the prevalence of comorbid substance abuse among patients with schizophrenia (25), especially in inpatient settings (26,27). Our data are consistent with other reports that persons with schizophrenia who use drugs or alcohol regularly are less compliant with their prescribed medication regimen (28-30).

Because this analysis examined data on substance abuse and medication compliance cross-sectionally, we cannot infer causality nor specify the direction of the relationship. Individuals with comorbid schizophrenia and substance abuse have been reported to stop taking medications because they have been told not to combine their medications with substances of abuse (26). Substance intoxication may cause patients to neglect to take their medication. Substance abusers may also experience increased side effects that could contribute to medication noncompliance (43,44).

Interpreting the association between substance abuse and medication compliance is complicated by the interaction of substance abuse with the amount of outpatient contact. There may be a pattern of noncompliance with both outpatient care and the medication regimen in substance-abusing subjects. Another possible interpretation, however, is that subjects with active substance abuse may be less able to obtain outpatient care for a variety of reasons and, as a result, be less able to comply adequately with their medication regimen.

Previous reports that side effects (15-18) or level of supervision (6,12) contribute to medication noncompliance were not confirmed in this analysis. Our study design was not ideal for examining the relationship between side effects and noncompliance because of the six-month interval between observation of the two variables. Such a relationship has been demonstrated when medication noncompliance is assessed soon after the development of extrapyramidal side effects (15,16). In addition, our classification of living arrangements may not adequately reflect the actual level of supervision that subjects received.

Factors associated with symptom outcomes

In our sample, the combination of current substance abuse, medication noncompliance, and no outpatient contact was associated with significantly worse symptom severity at six-month follow-up. Our interpretation is that these "worst-case" subjects constitute a particularly high-risk group of patients with schizophrenia. Interventions to decrease medication noncompliance and substance use and to increase outpatient contact could improve patient outcomes (45,46). Integrated psychiatric and substance abuse treatment may improve treatment retention for dual diagnosis patients (45-47). Intensive case management or assertive community treatment programs may be helpful because of increased patient contact and improved compliance (34,46). Depot neuroleptics should be considered for this population to enhance medication compliance.

Several limitations of this analysis must be considered. First, reliance on self-reports of medication compliance is controversial. No single method is widely accepted for measuring medication compliance (48,49). We expect that major omissions of neuroleptic medication, which are more likely to be reported accurately by subjects (38), would be more likely to affect symptoms of schizophrenia than would minor noncompliance. Thus subjects' reports provided a reasonable basis for examining the relationship between medication noncompliance and outcomes.

Subjects may underreport both medication noncompliance and substance abuse, which would result in overestimates of their relationship. The fact that our findings were not altered if subjects were classified as noncompliant when either the subject or an informant reported noncompliance suggests that such a self-report bias does not fully explain the results.

Our study examined the short-term course of illness for patients with schizophrenia who received routine care following a hospitalization. Generalizations from our subjects to the larger population of individuals with schizophrenia should be made with caution. Although subjects from both the VA and the state facility had similar demographic and clinical characteristics, relatively few female subjects were enrolled. Therefore, this sample did not allow us to specifically examine the relationships between substance abuse, noncompliance, and outcomes for female subjects.

Further research on the relationship between medication compliance and substance abuse in determining outcomes for patients with schizophrenia should compare self-report of medication compliance and substance abuse with other methods of data collection. The nature of associations among medication compliance, outpatient contact, and substance abuse also needs to be explored further, with a focus on their temporal relationships.

CONCLUSIONS

Our data clearly support the idea that individuals with schizophrenia who abuse drugs or alcohol are at increased risk for medication noncompliance and poor symptom outcomes. Moreover, lack of outpatient contact appears to interact with substance abuse to decrease medication compliance and contribute to worse outcomes. Further research is needed to clarify these relationships and identify effective interventions. Clinicians should be vigilant in detecting comorbid substance abuse among patients with schizophrenia and in encouraging treatment compliance among dual diagnosis patients.

REFERENCES

1. Fernando MLD, Velamoor YR, Cooper AJ, et al: Some factors relating to satisfactory post-discharge community maintenance of chronic psychotic patients. *Canadian Journal of Psychiatry* 35:71-73, 1990
2. Sands RG: Correlates of success and lack of success in deinstitutionalization. *Community Mental Health Journal* 20:223-235, 1984
3. Serban G, Thomas A: Attitudes and behaviors of acute and chronic schizophrenic patients regarding ambulatory treatment. *American Journal of Psychiatry* 131:991-995, 1974

4. Cramer JA, Mattson RH: How often is medication taken as prescribed? A novel assessment technique. *JAMA* 261:3273-3277, 1989

5. Morisky DE, Malotte CK, Choi P, et al: A patient education program to improve adherence rates with antituberculosis drug regimens. *Health Education Quarterly* 17:253-267, 1990

6. Blackwell B: Treatment adherence. *British Journal of Psychiatry* 129:513-531, 1976

7. Connelly CE, Davenport YB, Nurnberger JI Jr: Adherence to treatment regimen in a lithium carbonate clinic. *Archives of General Psychiatry* 39:585-588, 1982

8. Willcox DRC, Gillan R, Hare EH: Do psychiatric out-patients take their drugs? *British Medical Journal* 2:790-792, 1965

9. Irwin DS, Weitzel WD, Morgan DW: Phenothiazine intake and staff attitudes. *American Journal of Psychiatry* 127:1631-1635, 1971

10. Hare EH, Willcox DRC: Do psychiatric in-patients take their pills? *British Journal of Psychiatry* 113:1435-1439, 1967

11. Young JL, Zonana HV, Shepler L: Medication noncompliance in schizophrenia: codification and update. *Bulletin of the American Academy of Psychiatry and the Law* 14:105-122, 1986

12. Weiden PJ, Dixon L, Frances A, et al: Neuroleptic noncompliance in schizophrenia. *Schizophrenia Research* 1:285-296, 1991

13. Diamond RJ: Enhancing medication use in schizophrenic patients. *Journal of Clinical Psychiatry* 44 (June suppl):7-14, 1983

14. Janz NK, Becker MH: The health belief model: a decade later. *Health Education Quarterly* 11:1-47, 1984

15. Van Putten T: Why do schizophrenic patients refuse to take their drugs? *Archives of General Psychiatry* 31:67-72, 1974

16. Van Putten T, May PRA, Marder SR: Response to antipsychotic medication: the doctor's and the consumer's view. *American Journal of Psychiatry* 141:16-19, 1984

17. Parkes CM, Brown GW Monck EM: The general practitioner and the schizophrenic patient. *British Medical Journal* 1:972-976, 1962

18. Herz MI, Melville C: Relapse in schizophrenia. *American Journal of Psychiatry* 137:801-805, 1980

19. Amador XE, Strauss DH, Yale SA, et al: Awareness of illness in schizophrenia. *Schizophrenia Bulletin* 17:113-132, 1991

20. McEvoy JP, Aland J, Wilson WJ, et al: Measuring chronic schizophrenic patients' attitudes toward their illness and treatment. *Hospital and Community Psychiatry* 32:856-858, 1981

21. Wilson JD, Enoch MD: Estimation of drug rejection by schizophrenic in-patients, with analysis of clinical factors. *British Journal of Psychiatry* 113:209-211, 1967

22. Bartko G, Herczeg I, Zador G: Clinical symptomatology and drug compliance in schizophrenic patients. *Acta Psychiatrica Scandinavica* 77:74-76, 1988

23. Van Putten T, Crumpton E, Yale C: Drug refusal in schizophrenia and the wish to be crazy. *Archives of General Psychiatry* 33:1443-1446, 1976

24. Pan PC, Tantam D: Clinical characteristics, health beliefs, and compliance with maintenance treatment: a comparison between regular and irregular attenders at a depot clinic. *Acta Psychiatrica Scandinavica* 79:564-570, 1989

25. Regier DA, Farmer ME, Rae DS, et al: Comorbidity of mental disorders with alcohol and other drug abuse. *JAMA* 264:2511-2518, 1990

26. Pristach CA, Smith CM: Medication compliance and substance abuse among schizophrenic patients. *Hospital and Community Psychiatry* 41:1345-1348, 1990

27. Caton CLM, Gralnick A, Bender S, et al: Young chronic patients and substance abuse. *Hospital and Community Psychiatry* 40:1037-1040, 1989

28. Drake RE, Osher FC, Wallach MA: Alcohol use and abuse in schizophrenia: a prospective community study. *Journal of Nervous and Mental Disease* 177:408-414, 1989

29. Kashner TM, Rader LE, Rodell DE, et al: Family characteristics, substance abuse, and hospitalization patterns of patients with schizophrenia. *Hospital and Community Psychiatry* 42:195-197, 1991

30. Drake RE, Wallach MA: Substance abuse among the chronic mentally ill. *Hospital and Community Psychiatry* 40:1041-1046, 1989

31. Kent S, Yellowlees P: Psychiatric and social reasons for frequent rehospitalization. *Hospital and Community Psychiatry* 45:347-350, 1994

32. Martinez-Arevalo MJ, Calcedo-Ordoniz A, Varo-Prieto JR: Cannabis consumption as a prognostic factor in schizophrenia. *British Journal of Psychiatry* 164:679-681, 1994

33. Osher FC, Drake RE, Noordsy DL, et al: Correlates and outcomes of alcohol use disorder among rural outpatients with schizophrenia. *Journal of Clinical Psychiatry* 55:109-113, 1994

34. Warner R, Taylor D, Wright J, et al: Substance use among the mentally ill: prevalence, reasons for use, and effects on illness. *American Journal of Orthopsychiatry* 64:30-39, 1994

35. Spitzer RL, Williams JBW: *User's Guide for the Structured Clinical Interview for DSM-III-R.* Washington, DC, American Psychiatric Press, 1990

36. Miklowitz DJ, Goldstein MJ, Nuechterlein KH, et al: Expressed emotion, affective style, lithium compliance, and relapse in recent onset mania. *Psychopharmacology Bulletin* 22:628-632, 1986

37. Miklowitz DJ, Goldstein MJ, Nuechterlein KH, et al: Family factors and the course of bipolar affective disorder. *Archives of General Psychiatry* 45:225-231, 1988

38. Rickels K, Briscoe E: Assessment of dosage deviation in outpatient drug research. *Journal of Clinical Pharmacology* 10:153-160, 1970

39. Ewing JA: Detecting alcoholism: the CAGE questionnaire. *JAMA* 252:1905-1907, 1984

40. Brown RI: Identification and office management of alcohol and drug disorders, in *Addictive Disorders.* Edited by Fleming MF, Barry KL. St Louis, Mosby Yearbook, 1992

41. Overall JE, Gorham DR: The Brief Psychiatric Rating Scale. *Psychological Reports* 10:799-812, 1962

42. Lukoff D, Nuechterlein KH, Ventura J: Appendix A: manual for expanded Brief Psychiatric Rating Scale (BPRS). *Schizophrenia Bulletin* 12:594-602, 1986

43. Dixon L, Weiden P, Haas C, et al: Increased tardive dyskinesia in alcohol-abusing schizophrenic patients. *Comprehensive Psychiatry* 33:121-122, 1992

44. Olivera AA, Kiefer MW, Manley NK: Tardive dyskinesia in psychiatric patients

with substance use disorders. *American Journal of Drug and Alcohol Abuse* 16(1&2):57-66, 1990

45. Hellerstein DJ, Rosenthal RN, Miner CR: A prospective study of integrated outpatient treatment for substance-abusing schizophrenic patients. *American Journal on Addictions* 4:33-42, 1995

46. Drake RE, McHugo GJ, Noordsy DL: Treatment of alcoholism among schizophrenic outpatients: 4-year outcomes. *American Journal of Psychiatry* 150:328-329, 1993

47. Kofoed L, Kania J, Walsh T, et al: Outpatient treatment of patients with substance abuse and coexisting psychiatric disorders. *American Journal of Psychiatry* 143:867-872, 1986

48. Bond WS, Hussar DA: Detection methods and strategies for improving medication compliance. *American Journal of Hospital Pharmacy* 48:1978-1988, 1991

49. Lasagna L, Hutt PB: Health care, research, and regulatory impact of noncompliance, in *Patient Compliance in Medical Practice and Clinical Trials*. Edited by Cramer JA, Spiker B. New York, Raven, 1991

ABOUT THE AUTHORS

Richard R. Owen, M.D., Ellen P. Fischer, Ph.D., and Brenda M. Booth, Ph.D., are affiliated with the Veterans Affairs Field Program for Mental Health (152/NLR) at the VA Medical Center, North Little Rock, AR, and the Centers for Mental Healthcare Research at the University of Arkansas for Medical Sciences in Little Rock. Brian J. Cuffel, Ph.D., is affiliated with the Department of Psychology at Santa Clara University in Santa Clara, CA, and the Department of Psychiatry at the University of California, San Francisco.

ACKNOWLEDGMENTS

This work was supported by grant 91-005 from the Health Services Research and Development Service of the Department of Veterans Affairs, grant MH49123 from the National Institute of Mental Health, and a Research Associate award from the VA Health Services Research and Development Service to Dr. Owen. The authors thank Doris Hutchins, M.S.W., Paula McCarther, Jackie Cano, Shalini Manjanatha, and Barbara J. Burns, Ph.D.

Parts of this paper were presented at the annual meeting of the American Psychiatric Association held May 21-26, 1994, in Philadelphia; at the Institute on Hospital and Community Psychiatry held September 30 to October 3, 1994, in San Diego; and at the National Institute of Mental Health Conference on Mental Health Services Research held September 11-12, 1995, in Washington, D.C.

Copyright 1996. The American Psychiatric Association. Reprinted by permission.

Housing for Persons with Co-Occurring Mental and Addictive Disorders

Fred C. Osher and Lisa B. Dixon

Reprinted from *Dual Diagnosis of Major Mental Illness and Substance Abuse.*
Volume 2: Recent Research and Clinical Implications. New Directions for
Mental Health Services, No. 70, R.E. Drake & K.T. Mueser (Eds.).
San Francisco: Jossey-Bass, Inc. (pp. 53-64), 1996

*Homelessness is a far too common outcome for persons with dual
diagnoses. This chapter discusses existing housing barriers and suggests
housing, treatment, and support services responsive to population need.*

Case Example

Ms. B is a thirty-five-year-old Caucasian woman with a long history of
frequent psychiatric hospitalization beginning at age seventeen. She has a
diagnosis of schizophrenia (paranoid type) and at referral met criteria for
binge-pattern alcohol dependence. Her drinking was associated with impulsive outbursts of violence, both toward herself and others. When not drinking, she was childlike and friendly although persistently paranoid about the
efforts of others to "poison her." She had been living in the streets and in the
shelter system of a large urban city for ten years prior to referral to an assertive community treatment (ACT) team that targeted homeless persons with
severe mental illnesses. After a six-month period of outreach and regular
meetings at a local diner, she seemed increasingly comfortable with several
members of the case management team and agreed to a low dose of antipsychotic medication that she took irregularly. She initially refused to discuss
her alcohol use, stating "it's none of your business." Over the six months,
she acknowledged that she drank but vehemently denied that this alcohol
use created any problems for her. At this point, she agreed to live in a transitional shelter that prohibited any substance use and provided on-site AA and
NA group meetings. The ACT team was able to convince the shelter staff to
waive their program requirement that all residents attend daily self-help
meetings for Ms. B because of her behavior in groups. The team assured the
shelter staff that alcohol abuse would be addressed in individual meetings
with Ms. B. She did not drink for almost three months while living at this
shelter. During this time, the ACT team assisted her in obtaining social security disability benefits; the team was named as the representative payee for

this income support. She was assisted in finding her own apartment and being sober enabled her to gain access to housing subsidies. Although the team ensured that Ms. B's rent and bills were paid, she would sometimes use the leftover funds to buy alcohol, which induced bizarre behavior. When her landlord threatened eviction because of a behavioral disturbance, the ACT team would intervene by coming into the apartment to provide crisis counseling. These binging episodes became less frequent. Ms. B slowly became willing to acknowledge that alcohol use was not in her best interest and agreed to try group educational meetings about alcohol. She became increasingly attached to her apartment and stated that she did not want to do anything that might lead to her becoming homeless again. The team used this information to gently persuade her to examine the likely consequences of ongoing alcohol abuse and over time her drinking episodes disappeared entirely. Ms. B's compliance with medication improved somewhat but she remains suspicious and slightly paranoid.

DUAL DIAGNOSIS AND UNSTABLE HOUSING

Access to appropriate housing is a critical component of care for persons with co-occurring mental and addictive disorders. Homelessness and housing instability can exacerbate addiction and mental illness, creating a malignant cycle of increased symptomatology, disability, and exposure to harsh living environments. Studies focusing on persons with dual diagnoses have shown that they are disproportionately at risk for housing instability and homelessness (Belcher, 1989; Drake, Osher, and Wallach, 1991). Epidemiologic studies have revealed that roughly 10 to 20 percent of homeless persons suffer from severe mental illnesses and co-occurring addictions (Tessler and Dennis, 1989; Drake, Osher, and Wallach, 1991). Furthermore, the majority of persons with co-occurring disorders never receive any mental or addictive treatment services (Kessler and others, 1994).

An aftercare study of patients of an urban state hospital revealed that over one-fourth of all patients and over one-half of patients with dual diagnoses had unstable housing and were at least temporarily homeless during the six months following discharge (Drake, Wallach, and Hoffman, 1989). Another study of discharged state hospital patients found that 36 percent of patients experienced homelessness within six months of their discharge (Belcher, 1989) and patients who used alcohol or other drugs were more likely to be in the homeless group. When homeless men with mental illness were followed from shelters to community housing, 44 percent returned to homelessness within eighteen months and co-occurring substance use disorders significantly increased the risk for homelessness (Caton and others, 1993). Drake and others (1991) found that this phenomenon is not restricted to urban locations. They studied housing instability of patients with schizophrenia in a rural area where patients had extensive family supports and low-cost housing was available. Their study found that co-occurring disorders were strongly correlated with housing instability and that the majority of patients with schizophrenia and alcohol problems experienced housing instability during a six-month period.

Thus alcohol and drug abuse by persons with severe mental illness must be considered a high-risk behavior for homelessness. In fact, a cohort of five investigators funded under the Stewart B. McKinney Homeless Assistance Act cited co-occurring substance use disorder as the major clinical factor associated with prolonged and repeated homeless episodes among homeless persons with severe mental illnesses (Center for Mental Health Services, 1994). Effective treatment of co-occurring disorders is critical to enabling an individual to escape cycles of homelessness. Conversely, effective interventions should reduce the risk of homelessness for those dually diagnosed persons currently in housing.

REASONS FOR DUAL DIAGNOSIS-HOMELESS RELATIONSHIP

Consideration of systemic, legal, and clinical perspectives facilitates understanding of why persons with dual diagnoses are at risk for housing instability and homelessness. Although research on all aspects of these issues has not been conducted, these issues merit consideration in developing residential and treatment services for dually diagnosed individuals.

Systemic issues

Systemic barriers to services for persons with dual diagnoses have been well documented. Lack of a common administrative structure for alcohol, drug, and mental health services at the federal, state, and local levels; insufficient resources; historic distrust and philosophical conflicts between providers of addiction services and mental health services; and separate funding streams for treatment of both disorders have contributed to these barriers (Ridgely, Goldman, and Willenbring, 1990). Rapidly evolving health care reform initiatives that limit access to or funding for psychiatric or substance abuse services are likely to compound these barriers by failing to recognize, or respond to, the complex service needs of dually diagnosed individuals.

As a result of administrative divisions, many residential treatment programs for persons with mental illness specifically bar patients with co-occurring substance abuse problems. If they admit them, they may evict them after an episode of use. Residential addiction programs similarly bar patients with co-occurring mental illnesses, often identified as those who use prescribed psychopharmacologic medications. Clients encountering these bureaucratic barriers may experience frustration and anger or may accept the inaccessibility of the system as further justification for continued maladaptive behavior and hopelessness. The locus of responsibility for providing housing and clinical services to homeless persons with dual diagnoses is unclear and variable in different communities. The lack of clarity about whether mental health providers, substance abuse providers, or providers of housing services are responsible for assuring access to housing perpetuates the existence of housing gaps.

Legal issues

Legal issues present obstacles to housing for persons with dual diagnoses. The Fair Housing Amendments Act of 1988 extended protection of federal fair housing legislation to persons with disabilities, including persons with mental illness. The full impact of this act in protecting against discriminatory housing practices remains to be seen (Petrila, 1995). In practice, however, persons with dual diagnoses face discriminatory treatment. Individuals with histories of drug dependence are not eligible for public housing programs unless they are receiving addiction treatment (Rubenstein, 1989) that is often in short supply with long waiting lists. Thus persons with mental illnesses may be shut out of the housing programs established for their care because of disabilities associated with drug or alcohol use. In addition, potential landlords may reject persons involved with illicit drugs because of perceived liability issues (Drake, Osher, and Wallach, 1991).

Criminal records and sometimes even contact with the criminal justice system can be a barrier to housing access. Homeless persons with dual diagnoses have been shown to have greater histories of arrest when compared to homeless persons without dual diagnoses. These arrests are frequently for misdemeanors caused by bizarre symptoms and erratic behavior, publicly displayed because of their lack of shelter (Abram and Teplin, 1991). Once they have an arrest record, it may be more difficult for persons with dual diagnoses to obtain housing of any kind.

In 1994 Congress passed legislation that limits the duration of income supports and entitlements to anyone whose disability is related to a substance use disorder to thirty-six months. Although it is too early to measure the effects of this legislation, one can hypothesize that increasing numbers of persons with addictive disorders, including those with dual diagnoses, will be unable to afford even the cheapest of accommodations. These legal issues serve as examples of how housing instability of persons with dual diagnoses can be an epiphenomenon of social policy rather than a clinical correlate.

Clinical issues

Persons with dual diagnoses have been found to have greater rates of psychiatric symptoms (Negrete, Knapp, Douglas, and Smith, 1986; Drake and Wallach, 1989), noncompliance with treatment (Osher and others, 1994), psychiatric hospitalizations and use of emergency services (Safer, 1987; Bartels and others, 1993), and violent, disruptive behavior (Safer, 1987; Abram and Teplin, 1991)—including suicide (Drake, Osher, and Wallach, 1989; Dassori, Mezzich, and Keshavan, 1990; Bartels, Drake, and McHugo, 1992)—than persons with mental illnesses only. It is not surprising, then, that individuals with this clinical profile have trouble accessing housing and are at risk for losing housing.

Families already under stress from years of coping with mental illness may be unable to tolerate the additional disruption—and perhaps danger—associated with co-occurring substance abuse, resulting in eviction from the family home (Robinson, Dixon, Stewart, Harold, and Lehman, 1993). Providers in other residential settings such as board and care homes or public housing settings may also evict persons with dual diagnoses because they are unable to tolerate their erratic behaviors, their disturbance of other tenants, or their unreliable rental payments. Frequent or prolonged hospitalizations may result in loss of housing placement, particularly in locations where affordable housing is scarce and waiting lists are common.

Another important consideration is that persons with dual diagnoses may be unable to manage income or benefits, particularly if such funds are diverted to support a drug or alcohol habit. Consequently when no money for rent and other bills is available, streets, hospitals, or prisons become the only other shelter alternatives. The use of a representative payee, which can ameliorate this problem, is currently required for persons disabled as a result of a substance use disorder receiving social security income. Unfortunately, even if the need for a representative payee is obvious, it can be extremely difficult to find persons willing to serve as payees for these dually diagnosed individuals.

CLINICAL STRATEGIES THAT FACILITATE STABLE HOUSING

In order to treat dually diagnosed persons who are homeless or who are at risk for homelessness, clinicians must have an adequate understanding of the basic principles of treating persons with dual diagnoses. The heterogeneity of the dually diagnosed population with regard to both disabilities associated with their mental and addictive disorders and to their demographic, socioeconomic, and cultural backgrounds makes it incumbent on clinicians to design individualized treatment strategies. Distinguishing between substance abuse and dependence in persons with serious mental illnesses, for example, may govern the intensity of early treatment interventions (Bartels, Drake, and Wallach, 1995). Others have suggested that tailoring interventions to the unique needs of dually diagnosed women should be considered (Alexander, 1996).

As discussed by Carey (this volume),[1] an integrated treatment program for dually diagnosed individuals organized around treatment phases—engagement, persuasion, active treatment, and relapse prevention (Osher and Kofoed, 1989)—has gained widespread acceptance. Successful programs have recognized the need to attend to both disorders, persisting through multiple crises and relapses, utilizing educational and supportive groups, and in many cases providing comprehensive case management services (Drake and Noordsy, 1994). Integrating motivational interventions matched to these stages is currently being investigated (Ziedonis and Fisher, 1994). Specific effects of these and other model interventions on housing stability remain to be studied. Clinical strategies to stabilize housing for persons with dual diagnoses will be discussed in terms of the treatment phases mentioned above.

Engagement

Housing instability and homelessness complicate the already difficult engagement phase in the treatment of individuals with co-occurring mental and addictive disorders. Assertive and prolonged outreach is essential because clients in this phase generally do not come to the program office or keep appointments. Lack of money for transportation, the daily demands of obtaining food and shelter, psychiatric symptoms, ongoing substance use, and associated organic deficits may cause clients to miss appointments. This can be a critical problem in efforts to secure limited housing resources such as Section 8 certificates (Dixon, Krauss, Myers, and Lehman, 1994). Because clients often have limited access to phones and mail, tracking clients requires tenacity as well as extensive contacts with providers in the community

Providing for basic needs such as clothes, showers, and food may be helpful in the engagement process. Provision of badly needed material resources can help to draw clients into a trusting relationship in which staff can persuade them to enter treatment for substance abuse or mental illness and help them identify other long-term goals. The promise of safe, clean housing may motivate clients to enter the treatment system (Gaffney and Dixon, 1995). A treatment team must be able to access diverse housing or shelter options on an acute basis. Because housing instability persists even after housing is obtained, provision of on-site support is usually required. The capacity for crisis intervention for persons with dual diagnoses is critical. Crises, whether they are psychiatric, medical, or housing-related, may provide important opportunities to engage clients by addressing their acute needs.

---

[1]Editors' Note: The authors refer to a chapter that appears in the book where this reading was originally published. The full reference for that chapter is Carey, K. B. (1996). Treatment of co-occurring substance abuse and major mental illness. In R.E. Drake & K.T. Mueser (Eds.), *Dual diagnosis of mental illness and substance abuse: Vol. 2. Recent research and clinical implications* (pp. 19-31). San Francisco: Jossey-Bass. See also Dr. Carey's article in the Treatment section of this volume.

Assessment of homeless individuals with dual diagnoses must begin in the engagement phase and continue longitudinally. Homeless persons with co-occurring disorders frequently avoid treatment; they may be suspicious of providers and unwilling to provide much personal information. They may also try to hide their substance use pattern for fear that disclosure may restrict their access to housing (Goldfinger and others, in press).

Persuasion

Persuasion involves reducing a patient's denial about a mental illness or substance abuse problem. Progress can be measured by a patient's acknowledgment that a problem exists and by the commitment to pursue active treatment. In addition to the persuasion strategies for dually diagnosed clients mentioned elsewhere in this volume,[2] the link between housing opportunities and abstinence should be emphasized. How substance use has influenced housing arrangements in the past should be examined and, if appropriate, how access to current housing options is limited by ongoing drug use should be pointed out. Developing a discrepancy between the housing that the client hopes to obtain or maintain and the obstacles to this goal created by their ongoing drug abuse can be a key to persuading the individual to consider abstinence.

The use of representative payeeship assumes special importance in working with dually diagnosed homeless persons in the persuasion phase. Implicit in the condition of homelessness is that the client's basic needs are not being met. Although there may be a multitude of reasons for this (for example, the absence of decent affordable housing), the only way to stop the cycle of homelessness and drug use may be for the program, family, or some other individual to assume the responsibility of managing the person's finances. Stable housing requires stable finances. If a patient relapses and requires hospitalization and detoxification or simply spends some time on the streets, there can at least be a home to which he or she can return if the rent is paid. The implementation of a representative payee system fits well with the goals of the persuasion phase; it may alienate individuals during the engagement phase and may be a necessary condition for active treatment to proceed.

---

[2]Editors' Note: The authors refer to discussions of persuasion strategies in two chapters that appear in the book where this reading was originally published. The full references for those two chapters are (1) Carey, K.B. (1996). Treatment of co-occurring substance abuse and major mental illness. In R.E. Drake & K.T. Mueser (Eds.), *Dual diagnosis of mental illness and substance abuse: Vol. 2. Recent research and clinical implications* (pp. 19-31). San Francisco: Jossey-Bass; and (2) Mueser, K.T., & Noordsy, D.L. (1996). Group treatment for dually diagnosed clients. In R.E. Drake & K.T. Mueser (Eds.), *Dual diagnosis of mental illness and substance abuse: Vol. 2. Recent research and clinical implications* (pp. 33-51). San Francisco: Jossey-Bass. The chapter by Mueser and Noordsy is reprinted in the Treatment section of this volume. See also Carey's journal article that is reprinted in the Treatment section.

Related to the use of a representative payee is the use of other strategies that patients may perceive as coercive. The frequent legal entanglements of dually diagnosed persons offer opportunities for clinicians to use the requirement for court-ordered treatment. The clinician's attitude and approach in using coercion are critical. There is clearly an obligation to honor court-ordered requirements; additionally, concrete contingencies with direct consequences for failure to meet these conditions may be an important way to persuade people to begin treatment. Coercive approaches are *not* substitutes for treatment but may be an important component of an overall treatment strategy. Future research may reveal the extent to which structure and rules are themselves therapeutic at different phases of treating persons with dual diagnoses.

Active treatment

In the active treatment phase, patients develop the skills and relationships necessary to achieve and maintain sobriety and minimize disabilities associated with their mental illness. The basic strategies useful in this phase are discussed elsewhere in this volume (Carey, Chapter Two)[1] and include individual and group therapies, education, and psychosocial rehabilitation. During this phase, the client's housing status should be reviewed and environmental or situational threats (living in a heavy drug trafficking zone, for example) to attaining abstinence should be identified.

Relapse prevention

Both addictions and mental illnesses tend to be relapsing disorders. The relapse prevention phase focuses on minimizing the extent of and damage caused by a patient relapse. The lack of social and family supports of the homeless individual with dual diagnoses may lead to increased fragility and greater vulnerability to relapse, both in terms of addiction and mental illness. Unanticipated relapses can lead to another episode of homelessness. It is thus especially important for programs and clinicians to plan contingencies if relapses occur to minimize the risk of repeated homelessness.

HOUSING STRATEGIES TO FACILITATE RECOVERY

Housing strategies for homeless or marginally-housed persons with dual diagnoses must be developed in tandem with clinical strategies. Development of housing strategies requires consideration of types of housing, associated support, organization, and funding. Newman (1992) describes two different philosophies that have been organizing principles of housing programs for severely and persistently mentally ill persons. The first, more traditional program uses a *level of care,* or *continuum* approach. The varying needs of the heterogeneous mentally ill population are addressed by offering several settings, each with different levels of service and supervision as well as restrictiveness. In this model, treatment and housing are linked. A second model has been called the *supported housing* model. In this model, the intensity of supported services varies with client need and the residential site remains the same (Ridgeway and Zipple, 1990; Harp, 1990).

Although some view these models as mutually exclusive, the authors and others believe that supported housing is simply another important part of the continuum of residential housing. The objective of housing diversity is to optimize choice, maintain community tenure, and ultimately to improve effectiveness (Fields, 1990; Kline, Harris, Bebout, and Drake, 1991). For persons with dual diagnoses, housing choice will be determined by community alternatives. This selection should be made by an assessment of the clinical needs and personal preferences of the individual. Housing selection may vary depending on what phase of treatment the person is in and what support needs exist. In addition to factors important to the housing choice of any citizen such as location, costs, and convenience, housing for dually diagnosed individuals requires the following special considerations.

Residential tolerance

A critical question for persons with dual diagnoses is whether treatment can or should be separated from housing. Residential options must include settings that will tolerate the lengthy adjustment process required to feel safe and simultaneously struggle to control two disabling disorders. Kline, Harris, Bebout, and Drake argue (1991) that "transitions necessitated by administrative factors such as arbitrary time constraints, rather than by clinical needs, should be avoided."

The arguments to separate housing from treatment can lead to practical clinical problems. So-called *wet housing,* or housing in which the use of drugs and alcohol is tolerated, may be the only housing choice acceptable to the client in the early phases of engagement and treatment. Yet some clinicians believe that allowing substance use in housing sustains or enables use and is countertherapeutic. At the same time, the achievement and maintenance of sobriety may be unlikely if not impossible, without adequate housing (Drake, Osher, and Wallach, 1991). Some patients may be motivated to stop using drugs if they are aware that their housing depends on their sobriety. Other patients will continue to use despite prohibitions, will get evicted, and will wind up on the streets in circumstances that are not conducive to pursuing sobriety. The solution to this dilemma is vexing and will require experimentation with different models and client choices.

At the present time, most housing options sponsored by mental health or substance abuse providers are *dry housing,* or housing in which alcohol and drug use is prohibited. Perhaps a housing continuum should provide for degrees of dryness, including *damp housing,* where there is an expectation of abstinence on the premises but clients are not required to agree to be abstinent off-site. At one end of the housing continuum could be shelters and other safe havens that are very tolerant of use, whereas toward the other end of the continuum there could be stronger expectations and limits. In a housing demonstration in which homeless persons were empowered to make house rules, alcohol was initially allowed on-site but later banned by the residents as they became aware of its destabilizing influence (Center for Mental Health Services, 1994).

The engagement phase might require flexible housing regulations while intensive and assertive support services are provided. High levels of structure and supervision may be unacceptable to persons during engagement. Once engagement is achieved, however, clients might tolerate a greater degree of structure and supervision during the persuasion and active treatment phases when peer interaction and clear limits may be therapeutic. Less structure and supervision consistent with supported housing models may be more appropriate during later phases of treatment such as the relapse prevention phase. The duration of on-site residential care remains a critical question for future investigations.

Safety

As mentioned above, homeless individuals are frequently victims of crime, and life on the streets is wrought with danger. Consideration of this fact is essential in planning housing for persons with mental illness who have drug addiction problems. Housing must be safe, whether it is a transitional shelter with a time-limited stay, a group home with other residents with mental illness, or an independent apartment fully integrated into the community.

Client preference

In making choices about housing, programs must balance housing availability, client preferences, and client needs. Schutt and Goldfinger (1996) have found that although most people prefer independent housing, they do not always succeed at this choice. Clients with active addiction problems may prefer independent living but may have previous experience that suggests that they need more structure and supervision. Dixon, Krauss, Myers, and Lehman (1994) have shown that it was possible to honor the housing preferences of the majority of homeless mentally ill patients treated in their program that had a limited number of Section 8 certificates.

Shelterization

Unique to the long-term homeless individual is the phenomenon of *shelterization*. This refers to a process of acculturation and adaptation that homeless persons who use shelters may experience (Gounis and Susser, 1990; Grunberg and Eagle, 1990). Although it helps homeless persons cope with their surroundings in the short term, this process may impede the process of moving out of the shelter system that becomes a social community with familiar social rules. Some formerly homeless clients may experience loneliness when they make the transition from the noisy, busy shelter system to independent housing. There is some evidence that more intensive support during transition from shelter to housing may result in increased residential stability (Center for Mental Health Services, 1994). If programs attend to these issues as well as clinical needs, housing stability should be enhanced.

Cooperative Agreements Between Providers and Housers

Given the complex and varied requirements of providing housing and clinical care as well as the historic administrative and economic separation of housing and treatment services, mental health, substance abuse, and housing providers should all agree prospectively to work together. Otherwise there is considerable danger that patients will fall between the cracks, receiving housing without mental health and addiction services or vice versa. Cooperative agreements should outline the respective roles and responsibilities of housing providers, mental health providers, and substance abuse providers. The specific details of such an agreement will need to reflect community resources. The common goal will be to maintain individuals with dual diagnoses in the community.

CONCLUSION

Hypotheses about the optimal degree of structure, supervision, and support in housing for dually diagnosed persons await future research. Evaluators of the Robert Wood Johnson Foundation HUD Demonstration Program on Chronic Mental Illness noted, "It is particularly difficult to serve active substance abusers and those with recent histories of destructive behaviors using an independent housing strategy" (Newman, 1992). Inclusiveness has been advocated (Kline and others, 1991) as a principle of program development in which the goal is to provide services to as diverse a set of people as possible.

Although models for providing housing to individuals with co-occurring disorders have not been fully explicated and evaluated, reducing the morbidity and mortality associated with homelessness for these persons is critical. Dually diagnosed persons who are homeless or at risk for homelessness have special needs and characteristics that must be considered in treatment planning. Common principles must guide approaches to this population until empirical data are available. These include the following guidelines: individualized housing and treatment planning must be derived from thorough assessments, flexibility and creativity must outweigh intolerance and categorical programs, and ongoing therapeutic relationships must be established over time.

REFERENCES

Alexander, M. J. "Women with Co-Occurring Addictive and Mental Disorders: An Emerging Profile of Vulnerability." *American Journal of Orthopsychiatry,* 1996, *66* (1), 61-70.

Abram, K. M., and Teplin, L. A. "Co-Occurring Disorders Among Mentally Ill Jail Detainees." *American Psychologist,* 1991, *46,* 1036-1045.

Bartels, S. J., Drake, R. E., and McHugo, G. J. "Alcohol Use, Depression, and Suicide in Schizophrenia." *American Journal of Psychiatry,* 1992, *149,* 394-395.

Bartels, S. J., Drake, R. E., and Wallach, M. A. "Long-Term Course of Substance Use Disorders Among Patients with Severe Mental Illness." *Psychiatric Services,* 1995, *46* (3), 248-251.

Bartels, S. J., Teague, G. B., Drake, R. E., Clark, R. E., Bush, P., and Noordsy, D. L. "Substance Use in Schizophrenia: Service Utilization and Costs." *Journal of Nervous and Mental Disease,* 1993, *181,* 227-232.

Belcher, J. R. "On Becoming Homeless: A Study of Chronically Mentally Ill Persons." *Journal of Community Psychology,* 1989, *17,* 173-185.

Caton, C. L., Wyatt, R., Felix, A., Grunberg, J., and Dominquez, B. "Follow-Up of Chronically Homeless Mentally Ill Men." *American Journal of Psychiatry,* 1993, *150* (11), 1639-1642.

Center for Mental Health Services. *Making a Difference: Interim Status Report of the McKinney Research Demonstration Program for Homeless Mentally Ill Adults.* Rockville, Md.: Center for Mental Health Services, Substance Abuse and Mental Health Services Administration, 1994.

Dassori, A. M., Mezzich, J. E., and Keshavan, M. "Suicidal Indicators in Schizophrenia." *Acta Psychiatrica Scandinavica,* 1990, *81,* 409-413.

Dixon, L., Krauss, N., Myers, P., and Lehman, A. L. "Clinical and Treatment Correlates of Access to Section 8 Certificates for Homeless Mentally Ill Persons." *Psychiatric Services,* 1994, *45,* 1196-1200.

Drake, R. E., and Noordsy, D. L. "Case Management for People with Coexisting Severe Mental Disorder and Substance Use Disorder." *Psychiatric Annals,* 1994, *24,* 427-431.

Drake, R. E., Osher, F. C., and Wallach, M. A. "Alcohol Use and Abuse in Schizophrenia: A Prospective Community Study." *Journal of Nervous and Mental Disease,* 1989, *177,* 408-414.

Drake, R. E., Osher, F. C., and Wallach, M. A. "Homelessness and Dual Diagnosis." *American Psychologist,* 1991, *46,* 1149-1158.

Drake, R. E., and Wallach, M. A. "Substance Abuse Among the Chronic Mentally Ill." *Hospital and Community Psychiatry,* 1989, *40,* 1041-1046.

Drake, R. E., Wallach, M. A., and Hoffman, J. S. "Housing Instability and Homelessness Among Aftercare Patients of an Urban State Hospital." *Hospital and Community Psychiatry,* 1989, *40,* 46-51.

Drake, R. E., Wallach, M. A., Teague, G. B., Freeman, D. H., Paskus, T. S., and Clark, T. A. "Housing Instability and Homelessness Among Rural Schizophrenic Patients." *American Journal of Psychiatry,* 1991, *148,* 330-336.

Fields, S. "The Relationship Between Residential Treatment and Supported Housing in a Community System of Services." *Psychosocial Rehabilitation Journal,* 1990, *13,* 105-113.

Gaffney, L., and Dixon, L. "Engagement of Homeless Persons in Treatment." Paper presented at the 148th annual meeting of the American Psychiatric Association, Miami, Fla., May 1995. Abstract published in *New Research Program and Abstracts,* 95-96.

Goldfinger, S. M., Schutt, R. K., Seidman, L. M., Turner, W., Penk, W. E., and Tolomiczenko, G. "Alternative Measures of Substance Abuse Among Homeless Mentally Ill Persons in the Cross-Section and Over Time." *Journal of Nervous and Mental Disease,* in press.

Gounis, K., and Susser, E. "Shelterization and Its Implications for Mental Health Services." In N. Cohen (ed.), *Psychiatry Takes to the Streets; Outreach and Crisis Intervention for the Mentally Ill.* New York: Guilford Press, 1990.

Grunberg, J., and Eagle, P. F. "Shelterization: How the Homeless Adapt to Shelter Living." *Hospital and Community Psychiatry,* 1990, *41,* 521-525.

Harp, H. "Independent Living with Support Services: The Goal and Future for Mental Health Consumers." *Psychosocial Rehabilitation Journal,* 1990, *13* (4), 85-89.

Kessler, R. C., McGonagle K. A., Zhao, S., Nelson, C. B., Hughes, M., Eshleman, S., Wittchen, H., and Kendler, K. S. "Lifetime and Twelve-Month Prevalence of DSM-III-R Psychiatric Disorders in the United States." *Archives of General Psychiatry,* 1994, *51,* 8-19.

Kline, J., Harris, M., Bebout, R. E., and Drake, R. E. "Contrasting Integrated and Linkage Models of Treatment for Homeless, Dually Diagnosed Adults." In K. Minkoff and R. E. Drake (eds.), *Dual Diagnosis of Major Mental Illness and Substance Use Disorder.* New Directions for Mental Health Services, no. 50. San Francisco: Jossey-Bass, 1991.

Negrete, J. C., Knapp, W. P., Douglas, D. E., Smith, W. B. "Cannabis Affects the Severity of Schizophrenic Symptoms: Results of a Clinical Survey." *Psychological Medicine,* 1986, *16,* 515-520.

Newman, S. E. "The Severely Mentally Ill Homeless: Housing Needs and Housing Policy." Baltimore, Md.: Johns Hopkins University Institute for Policy Studies, Occasional Paper No. 12, 1992.

Osher, F. C., and Kofoed, L. L. "Treatment of Patients with Psychiatric and Psychoactive Substance Abuse Disorders." *Hospital and Community Psychiatry,* 1989, *40,* 1025-1030.

Osher, F. C., Drake, R. E., Noordsy, D. L., Teague, G. B., Hurlbut, S. C., Biesanz, J., and Beaudett, M. S. "Correlates of Outcomes of Alcohol Use Disorder Among Rural Schizophrenic Outpatients." *Journal of Clinical Psychiatry,* 1994, *55,* 109-113.

Petrila, J. "The Supreme Court's Ruling in *Edmonds v. Oxford House:* Implications for Group Homes." *Psychiatric Services,* 1995, *46,* 1011-1012.

Ridgely, M. S., Goldman, H. H., and Willenbring, M. "Barriers to the Care of Persons with Dual Diagnoses: Organizational and Financing Issues." *Schizophrenia Bulletin,* 1990, *16,* 123-132.

Ridgeway, P., and Zipple, A. M. "The Paradigm Shift in Residential Services: From the Linear Continuum to Supported Housing Approaches. *Psychosocial Rehabilitation Journal,* 1990, *13,* 11-31.

Robinson, C. T., Dixon, L., Stewart, B., Harold, J., Lehman, A. F. *Family Connections of the Homeless Mentally Ill.* Poster session, 146th annual meeting of the American Psychiatric Association, San Francisco, Calif., 1993.

Rubinstein, L. *The Impact of the Fair Housing Amendments on Land-Use Regulations Affecting People with Disabilities.* Washington, D.C.: Mental Health Law Project, 1989.

Safer, D. "Substance Abuse by Young Adult Chronic Patients." *Hospital and Community Psychiatry,* 1987, *38,* 511-514.

Schutt, R. K., and Goldfinger, S. M. "Housing Preferences and Perceptions of Health and Functioning Among Homeless Mentally Ill Persons." *Psychiatric Services,* 1996, *47,* 381-386.

Tessler, R. C., and Dennis, D. L. *A Synthesis of NIMH-Funded Research Concerning Persons Who Are Homeless and Mentally Ill.* Rockville, Md.: National Institute of Mental Health, 1989.

Ziedonis, D. M., and Fisher, W. "Assessment and Treatment of Comorbid Substance Abuse in Individuals with Schizophrenia." *Psychiatric Annals,* 1994, *24,* 477-483.

ABOUT THE AUTHORS

Fred C. Osher, M.D., is Associate Professor of Psychiatry and Director of Community Psychiatry at the School of Medicine, University of Maryland. Lisa B. Dixon, M.D., is Associate Professor of Psychiatry and Research Psychiatrist at the Center for Mental Health Services, School of Medicine, University of Maryland.

Copyright 1996. Jossey-Bass, Inc., Publishers. Reprinted with permission.

A LONGITUDINAL STUDY OF SUBSTANCE USE AND COMMUNITY VIOLENCE IN SCHIZOPHRENIA

Brian J. Cuffel, Martha Shumway,
Tandy L. Chouljian, and Tracy MacDonald

Reprinted from *Journal of Nervous and Mental Disease*, 182:704-708, 1994

The authors report the findings of a longitudinal study testing the hypothesis that substance use leads to subsequent violence in the community. Subjects were 103 patients with a Structured Clinical Interview for DSM-III-R diagnosis of schizophrenia or schizoaffective disorder who were seen in an outpatient clinic for the treatment of schizophrenia. Data on substance use and violent behavior were collected by review of medical records. Results indicated that use of drugs and alcohol was associated with increased odds of concurrent and future violent behavior when compared with persons with schizophrenia and no substance use. Odds of violence were particularly elevated for individuals having a pattern of polysubstance use involving illicit substances.

Individuals with schizophrenia and comorbid substance use disorders are among the most costly to treat and often have extensive involvement with the criminal justice system (Bartels et al., 1993; Kivlahan et al., 1991). Cross-sectional research has identified several factors that may underlie difficulties in the outpatient management of these patients, including increased suicidality, noncompliance, negative attitudes toward treatment, hostility, housing instability, and contact with the legal system (Alterman et al., 1981; Bartels et al., 1991; Carpenter et al., 1985; Drake and Wallach, 1989; Drake et al., 1989; Pristach and Smith, 1990). Perhaps most troubling is the possibility that substance use predisposes these individuals to violent behavior in the community (Monahan, 1992; Swanson et al., 1990). Recent advances in the epidemiology of mental disorders have provided more conclusive evidence that mental illness is a risk factor for aggressive and violent behavior (Monahan, 1992; Swanson et al., 1990). Results of the NIMH's Epidemiologic Catchment Area study indicate that while 2% of the nondisordered population had exhibited violent behavior in the past year, rates for persons with schizophrenia (12.7%), alcohol abuse or dependence (24.57%), and drug abuse or dependence (34.7%) were considerably higher. These findings suggest that there is a reliable relationship between mental disorder and violence and that rates of violence are particularly elevated among persons with comorbid psychiatric and substance use diagnoses. Despite these advances, the existing literature is mostly cross-sectional and does not lend itself to more definitive statements about the causal role of substance use in precipitating violence in this population. As a result, we do not have convincing evidence that substance use leads to future violent behavior and that interventions designed to decrease substance use will lead to changes in the behaviors that are most problematic for the mental health system and society. Knowing whether substance use in persons with schizophrenia is associated with later violence is of clinical and social importance.

We present the first longitudinal data on the relationship between substance use and violence among persons with schizophrenia. In doing so, we hope to address two questions that are of importance in determining whether substance use disorders play a causal role in the occurrence of violence. First, is substance use in schizophrenia cross-sectionally related to the occurrence of violent behavior? Second, does substance use in schizophrenia predict the occurrence of future violent behavior? Our investigation is an initial examination of these questions using retrospective review of case histories of a sample of Structured Clinical Interview for DSM-III-R-diagnosed individuals with schizophrenia.

METHODS

Subjects

A total of 103 subjects were identified through sequential screening of clinical records of all patients seen in the outpatient schizophrenia research clinic at San Francisco General Hospital (San Francisco, CA) between 1985 and 1989. All were age 18 to 55 and had DSM-III-R diagnoses of schizophrenia, schizoaffective disorder, or schizophreniform disorder (verified by the Structured Clinical Interview for DSM-III-R; Spitzer et al., 1990). Because the subjects in this sample were participating in other clinical trials of pharmacological interventions, persons physically dependent on drugs or alcohol and persons with extensive legal histories were excluded from the sample. However, many substance use problems were quickly discovered once into the clinical trial protocols, as earlier research using this sample of schizophrenic patients has reported (Chouljian et al., 1993).

Subjects entered the clinic following an acute psychotic episode after agreeing to participate in a randomized clinical trial. Some never entered the clinical trial and were treated only with standard neuroleptic medication. Those entering the clinical trial were treated with a combination of double-blind fluphenazine decanoate (in one of three dosage levels) plus known strength fluphenazine as needed to control symptoms. All patients were medicated to maximum clinical response.

Procedures

All data were collected through retrospective chart review. Research assistants recorded basic demographic data as well as substance use and violent behavior in 3-month intervals for up to 18 months. Ratings were based on review of progress notes written by psychiatrists, nurses, and social workers, as well as toxicology reports indicating evidence of substance use. The present study limited itself to violent behavior and substance use occurring in months 1 to 3 and in months 3 to 6. An earlier report has presented substance use findings for the full 18-month course of the study (Chouljian et al., 1993). Because of sample attrition in months 6 and beyond, analyses examining more than the first two assessment periods were not considered informative because of a lack of statistical power.

Measures of substance use and violence

To establish standard rating procedures, the authors attained consensus ratings on five cases that were used to train research assistants. Eleven additional randomly selected reliability cases were completed to ensure stability of rating practices.

Substance use was recorded separately for alcohol, marijuana, cocaine, and other drugs (*e.g.*, amphetamines, opiates, sedatives, and hallucinogens). Weighted Kappa statistics were calculated to assess interrater agreement for each drug category (Fleiss, 1973). Agreement was good, with a mean Kappa of .84. Earlier research has suggested that the ability to examine the correlates of single substances is extremely difficult because of the rarity with which single substances are abused and the high rates of polysubstance abuse and dependence in this population (Cuffel et al., 1993). This earlier work empirically identified two groups of substance abusers among persons with schizophrenia using the Epidemiologic Catchment Area data: those who abuse only alcohol or marijuana and those who abuse multiple substances. This led us to classify subjects into two groups. The first group was defined as using only alcohol or marijuana (N = 9). The second group used some other substance, such as cocaine, amphetamines, opiates, sedatives, or hallucinogens (N = 11).

In other words, the "cleanest" demarcation of substance use patterns that could be achieved in this study separated use that was limited to alcohol and marijuana (alcohol and marijuana use) from use that was more pervasive involving other substances (polysubstance use). Because of the tendency of our sample to use alcohol and marijuana in connection with other substances, alcohol and marijuana use was frequently present in the polysubstance use group. Despite the overlap of substances across groups, our classification defines two important and prevalent patterns of substance use in schizophrenia. The rates of use, abuse, and dependence for the alcohol and marijuana use group were 10.7%, 12.6%, and 3.9%, respectively. The rates of use, abuse, and dependence for the polysubstance use group were 1.0%, 6.8%, and 3.9%, respectively.

For each drug category, research assistants recorded abstinence, use, abuse, and dependence using DSM-III-R criteria (American Psychiatric Association, 1987). For purposes of the present study, use, abuse, and dependence ratings were combined. This was done for two reasons. First, the substance abuse and dependence classifications were used too infrequently to permit use of the full four-level scale in subsequent analyses. Second, DSM-III-R criteria use problematic behaviors such as violence to discriminate substance abuse and dependence from use. As a result, we were concerned that a circularity in the definition of substance abuse and dependence would "build in" a relationship between substance use and violence, thus overstating any relationship we might observe between substance use and violence. As a result, we chose not to distinguish between use, abuse, and dependence in order to minimize the probability of finding a spurious association between violence and substance use. Use, abuse and dependence were, therefore, combined into a single substance use category; mean Kappa for this dichotomous classification was .85.

Violent behavior was rated by a separate research assistant who was blind to the purposes of the study. Because data collection relied on chart review, we limited ourselves to a checklist of behaviors that mental health providers and family members had directly observed. Because family members were highly involved in the clinical trials forming the sample for this study, knowledge of patient behavior was perhaps unusually high. Behaviors included verbal threats to harm others, nonverbal threats to harm others, throwing objects at others, physical assaults or altercations with others, brandishing a weapon, using a weapon, starting fires, and destroying objects in the environment. Interrater Kappa for the presence or absence of any violent behavior was .66.

Attrition

Of 103 patients seen in the clinic in months 1 through 3, 89 patients were still in treatment in months 3 through 6. Attrition bias, although low in the first two assessment periods, could pose a threat to meaningful interpretation of study findings. To examine potential attrition bias, we compared subjects who dropped out within the first 6 months of treatment with those who remained on all demographic, substance use, and behavioral measures. T-tests were used for continuous variables and chi-square analyses for categorical variables.

Treatment dropouts in months 3 through 6 were higher among women (30.0%) than in men (10.8%) ($\chi^2 = 4.75$, $p = .03$). However, treatment dropouts did not differ in age, race, likelihood of alcohol or marijuana use, likelihood of other drug use, or likelihood of violence.

Data analyses

Hypothesis tests were conducted using logistic regression in which the dependent variable was either violent behavior in the first 3 months of treatment or violent behavior in the second 3 months of treatment. Two dummy coded variables were entered into the model as indicators of substance use in the first 3 months of treatment. The first coded for presence or absence of alcohol or marijuana use. The second coded for presence or absence of any other substance use. Covariates to the model were age, sex, and minority status. Minority status was dummy coded into three groups: Anglo, black, and other ethnicity. Anglo subjects were the reference group.

RESULTS

Demographics and descriptive statistics

The average age of the sample was 27 years (SD = 6.9). The sample was predominantly male (81.6%) and was evenly divided among white (34.9%), African-American (33.0%), and other ethnic minority patients (32.0%). Rates of violence and substance use were relatively stable across the 6-month course of this study. In the first 3 months following admission to the clinic, 8.6% of the subjects reported use of substances that was limited to alcohol or marijuana and 10.6% of the subjects reported a pattern of polysubstance use. In months 4 through 6, alcohol use was 11.3% and polysubstance use was 5.7%. Rates of violent behavior remained stable throughout the study period. Violent behavior was reported in the charts of 18.4% of the sample in months 1 through 3 and 14.7% of the sample in months 4 through 6.

Is substance use cross-sectionally correlated with violent behavior?

Polysubstance use was highly associated with the occurrence of community violence in the first 3-month evaluation period, as shown in Table 1. Individuals with schizophrenia who used multiple substances had odds of violence over 12 times greater than schizophrenic individuals who did not use any substances, controlling for age, sex, and ethnic minority status. In contrast, individuals who used only alcohol or marijuana were not at higher risk for violent behavior, although the small sample size present in this study limits confidence in any negative findings. Age, sex, and race were similarly unrelated to the probability of community violence. The age, sex, and race adjusted prevalence estimates of violence for this sample were

Table 1. Logistic regression analysis predicting violence from substance use in a sample of outpatient individuals with schizophrenia

	Odds Ratios	
Predictor	Violence in months 1-3	Violence in months 4-6
Age	1.03	.91
Sex	.79	.33
Black	1.56	3.0
Other Minority	.76	2.7
Alcohol or Marijuana Use	2.35	.70
Polysubstance Use	12.56*	4.61**
Violence in months 1-3	—	1.72

*p < .01; **p < .10.

62% for individuals who used substances other than alcohol or marijuana and 11.6% for individuals who did not use such substances.

Is the use of substances predictive of future violent behavior?

Prospectively, polysubstance use was associated with more than a four-fold increase in odds of future violence, when controlling for likelihood of violence in the prior interval (see column 2, Table 1). The small sample size prevented this from reaching conventional levels of statistical significance. Again, alcohol or marijuana use did not appear to be associated with increased odds of future violence among persons with schizophrenia. Adjusting for age, sex, race, and the occurrence of violence in the first 3-month interval, the logistic model in Table 1 estimates that 31.3% of the individuals who had used substances other than alcohol or marijuana during the first 3 months of clinic treatment would go on to exhibit violent behavior in the community in the next 3 months. Only 8.1% of those not using substances were estimated to commit violent behavior in the next 3 months.[1]

---

[1]Although we included verbal and nonverbal threats of harm in our definition of violence, it appears that the present results are robust to variations in scope of behavior considered violent. When the logistic regression analysis was estimated limiting the dependent variable to physical acts of violence toward other persons, the results are comparable to those reported. In fact, the odds ratios for polysubstance use are significant at the .05 level. We do not report these results because the logistic model does not converge unless patient ethnic minority status is excluded.

DISCUSSION

The results of the present study give presumptive evidence that use of certain substances, such as stimulants, opiates, and hallucinogens, may predispose individuals with schizophrenia and polysubstance use to later episodes of violent behavior. These findings suggest that earlier reports of higher rates of hospitalization, higher treatment costs, and greater contact with the criminal justice system may be attributable in part to the fact that substance use disorders predispose individuals with schizophrenia to violent, threatening, and destructive behavior (Cuffel, 1993; Drake et al., 1993; Kivlahan et al., 1991).

Outpatient, clinical programs that seek to treat these patients must be aware of the potential for violence and disruptive behavior, particularly among those who use illicit substances. Important advances in the implementation of specialized treatment programs for the dually diagnosed have emphasized concomitant treatment of mental health and substance use problems in "hybrid" programs that integrate aspects of the mental health and the addictions treatment systems (Drake et al., 1991). One of the initial dilemmas in developing these programs was to break down the philosophical, conceptual, and organizational barriers separating treatments offered in the mental health and addictions systems (Minkoff, 1991). Our results underscore the need for dual diagnosis treatment programs to also integrate acute inpatient, residential treatment, and treatment within the criminal justice system. That is, dual diagnosis programs should provide continuity of care for patients as they move in and out of the community into inpatient detoxification programs, acute inpatient psychiatric treatment, and jail.

In addition, the literature on substance use interventions for persons with schizophrenia has focused primarily on persons who abuse alcohol (Drake et al., 1993; Hellerstein and Meehan, 1987; Kivlahan et al., 1991). Although alcohol abuse and dependence may be much more prevalent in the general population and among persons with severe mental illness, it may not be the most problematic to treat and to manage. Research examining patterns of substance abuse and dependence in this population have shown two prevalent types (Cuffel et al., 1993). The first involves abuse or dependence on alcohol and marijuana without concomitant polysubstance use. The second involves abuse or dependence on one or more illicit substances, such as cocaine and other stimulants, hallucinogens, opiates, and sedatives. In the latter group, there is also a high likelihood of alcohol or marijuana dependence (Cuffel et al., 1993). Our results suggest that these patterns of abuse and dependence may have different propensities for violence. Further research examining the unique clinical characteristics of the polysubstance-abusing patient with schizophrenia appears warranted and may have implications for the focus and intensity of substance abuse treatment for this population.

In theory, substance use disorders may contribute to violence by impairing cognitive and behavioral mechanisms of impulse control, promoting negative mood states, such as depression, paranoia, and rage, that may predispose individuals to violence, and by stimulating aggressive behaviors through their direct pharmacological effects on brain systems (Maughan, 1993; Pihl and Peterson, 1993). A recent meta-analysis of experimental literature suggests a reliable effect of alcohol on aggressive behavior in the general population (Bushman and Cooper, 1990). Less is known about the effects of other substances on violent behavior, and similar experimentation has not considered the effects of mental disorder on the alcohol—violent behavior relationship (Pihl and Peterson, 1993). The mechanisms by which substance use predisposes individuals in the general population to violent behavior are understood to be complex and involve biologically, psychologically, and socially mediated processes (Maughan, 1993; Pihl and Peterson, 1993). Understanding the mechanisms by which substance use affects violent behavior in disordered populations may yield key insights for understanding the treatment and clinical management of these individuals. The results of the present study suggest that this research may focus on the effects of illicit and polysubstance substance use.

Violent behavior may also increase the likelihood of substance use problems, as has been proposed by a number of authors (Patterson and Yoerger, 1993; Pihl and Peterson, 1993). These theories propose that deviant and disruptive behaviors such as violence produce a cascade of events within a person's community and peer group that increase the likelihood of using substances. This hypothesis was not tested in the present study and is compatible with the present results.

Some characteristics of the present study limit the generalizability of its results. First, the study sample size was small and may have prevented some otherwise meaningful relationships from approaching conventional levels of significance. Because of the small sample size, it cannot be concluded that alcohol and marijuana use are unrelated to violent behavior in the community, as found in past research on alcohol use in schizophrenia (Bartels et al., 1991). Second, the study relied entirely on medical record review in its measures of substance use and violent and threatening behavior. As a result, a reporting bias for substance use or violent behavior may have existed such that either may have been more likely to have been reported in the medical record when they co-occurred than when they occurred in isolation. Prospective research involving community surveys of larger samples of schizophrenic individuals is needed to support the results of the present study. One advantage of prospectively collected data is that it might also examine the antecedents of substance use in this population and the circumstances around which use leads to subsequent violent behavior. Finally, the sample for the present study was taken from a clinical trial for the treatment of schizophrenia that may have screened out subjects who were more severely substance dependent, noncompliant, or violent. The magnitude of the substance use—violence association in more severely dependent or violent samples cannot be estimated from the present study.

Despite limitations in generalizability, the 12-fold increase in risk for violence associated with substance use observed in this sample is alarming and requires replication in other samples with more rigorous assessment of substance use and violence. Despite methodological limitations, the results of the present study are consistent with the existence of a causal link between substance use and subsequent violence. Future research might explore events leading to substance use in persons with schizophrenia and the cascade of events that lead to episodes of violence and other forms of disruptive behavior following use of substances. The emerging research investigating specialized substance abuse treatment programs may be particularly relevant in this regard. The results of the present study suggest that interventions that decrease substance use may decrease the likelihood of future violence, particularly among persons who abuse illicit substances. However, observing changes in levels of violence following interventions designed to decrease substance use is needed to support this hypothesis.

In addition, the results of the present study corroborate the clinical observation that use of substances portends outpatient management problems and a costly course of mental health treatment. Further research examining the role that violent, threatening, and destructive behavior plays in mediating the relationship between substance use and mental health system costs would have important implications for the development of clinical programs and focusing mental health system resources on the most problematic and costly of these patients.

REFERENCES

Alterman AI, Erdlen FR, Murphy E (1981) Alcohol abuse in the psychiatric hospital population. *Addictive Behaviors* 6:69-73.

American Psychiatric Association (1987) *Diagnostic and statistical manual of mental disorders* (3rd ed, rev). Washington, DC: Author.

Bartels SJ, Drake RE, Wallach MA, Freeman DH (1991) Characteristic hostility in schizophrenic outpatients. *Schizophrenia Bulletin* 17:163-171.

Bartels SJ, Teague GB, Drake RE, Clark RE (1993) Substance abuse in schizophrenia: Service utilization and costs. *Journal of Nervous and Mental Disease* 181:227-232.

Bushman BJ, Cooper HM (1990) Effects of alcohol on human aggression: An integrative research review. *Psychological Bulletin* 107:341-354.

Carpenter MD, Mulligan JC, Bader IA, Meinzer AE (1985) Multiple admissions to an urban psychiatric center. A comparative study. *Hospital and Community Psychiatry* 36(12):1305-1308.

Chouljian TL, Shumway M, Balancio E, Dwyer EV, Surber R, Jacobs M (1993) Substance use among schizophrenic outpatients: Prevalence, course, and relation to functional status. Unpublished manuscript.

Cuffel BJ (1994) Violent and destructive behavior among the severely mentally ill in rural areas: Evidence from Arkansas' community mental health system. *Community Mental Health Journal* 30:495-504.

Cuffel BJ, Heithoff KA, Lawson W (1993) Correlates of patterns of substance abuse among patients with schizophrenia. *Hospital and Community Psychiatry* 44:247-251.

Drake RE, McHugo GJ, Noordsy DL (1993) Treatment of alcoholism among schizophrenic outpatients: Four-year outcomes. *American Journal of Psychiatry* 150:328-329.

Drake RE, McLaughlin P, Pepper B, Minkoff K (1991) Dual diagnosis of mental illness and substance disorder: An overview. In K Minkoff, RE Drake (Eds), *Dual diagnosis of mental illness and substance disorder* (pp. 3-12). San Francisco: Jossey-Bass.

Drake RE, Osher FC, Wallach MA (1989) Alcohol use and abuse in schizophrenia. A prospective community study. *Journal of Nervous and Mental Disease* 177(7):408-414.

Drake RE, Wallach MA (1989) Substance abuse among the chronic mentally ill. *Hospital and Community Psychiatry* 40(10):1041-1046.

Fleiss JL (1973) *Statistical methods for rates and proportions.* New York: John Wiley & Sons.

Hellerstein DJ, Meehan CSW (1987) Outpatient group therapy for schizophrenic substance abusers. *American Journal of Psychiatry* 144:1337-1339.

Kivlahan DR, Heiman JR, Wright RC, Mundt JW, Shupe JA (1991) Treatment cost and rehospitalization rate in schizophrenic outpatients with a history of substance abuse. *Hospital and Community Psychiatry* 42(6):609-614.

Maughan B (1993) Childhood precursors of aggressive offending in personality-disordered adults. In S Hodgins (Ed), *Mental disorder and crime* (pp. 119-139). Newbury Park, CA: Sage.

Minkoff K (1991) Program components of a comprehensive integrated care system for serious mentally ill patients with substance disorders. In K Minkoff, RE Drake (Eds), *Dual diagnosis of major mental illness and substance disorder* (pp. 13-27). San Francisco: Jossey-Bass.

Monahan J (1992) Mental disorder and violent behavior: Perceptions and evidence. *American Psychologist* 47:511-521.

Patterson GR, Yoerger K (1993) Developmental models for delinquent behavior. In S Hodgins (Ed), *Mental disorder and crime* (pp. 140-172). Newbury Park, CA: Sage.

Pihl RO, Peterson JB (1993) Alcohol/drug use and aggressive behavior. In S Hodgins (Ed), *Mental disorder and crime* (pp. 263-283). Newbury Park, CA: Sage.

Pristach CA, Smith CM (1990) Medication compliance and substance abuse among schizophrenic patients. *Hospital and Community Psychiatry* 41(12):1345-1348.

Spitzer RL, Williams JBW, Gibbon M, First MB (1990) *SCID user's guide for the Structured Clinical Interview for DSM-III-R.* Washington, DC: American Psychiatric Press.

Swanson JW, Holzer III CE, Ganju VK, Jono RT (1990) Violence and psychiatric disorder in the community: Evidence from the epidemiologic catchment area surveys. *Hospital and Community Psychiatry* 41:761-769.

About the Authors

Brian Cuffel, Ph.D., and Martha Shumway, B.S., are affiliated with the Department of Psychiatry, University of California, San Francisco. Brian Cuffel, Ph.D., Tandy Chouljian, M.A., and Tracy MacDonald, B.A., are affiliated with the Institute for Mental Health Services Research, Berkeley, CA.

Acknowledgments

This research was supported by the NIMH Center for Research on the Organization and Financing of Care for the Severely Mentally Ill in Berkeley, California (P50-MH4369).

Reprinted with permission from *Journal of Nervous and Mental Disease*.

PREVALENCE OF INFECTION WITH HIV AMONG THE SERIOUSLY MENTALLY ILL: REVIEW OF RESEARCH AND IMPLICATIONS FOR PRACTICE

Michael P. Carey, Lance S. Weinhardt, and Kate B. Carey

Reprinted from *Professional Psychology: Research and Practice*, 26(3):262-268, 1995

The authors review the research literature for estimates of the prevalence of HIV infection among the seriously mentally ill. Data from nine studies suggest that 4%-23% of the seriously mentally ill have been infected with the virus that causes AIDS. Men have been infected at a higher rate than have women, but this gender difference is less pronounced than that found in the general population. Because most of these blinded seroprevalence studies have been conducted in New York City, the representativeness of these results remains unknown. Nonetheless, the findings call attention to the need for enhanced HIV-related services for the seriously mentally ill. The authors provide screening and counseling guidelines for practitioners who work with seriously mentally ill clients.

AIDS represents the fastest growing, most serious threat to public health in the world (Mann, 1992). In the relatively brief interval from 1981 to June 1994, AIDS had been diagnosed in 401,749 Americans; 243,423 of these people have already died (Centers for Disease Control and Prevention, 1994a). Because the incubation period between infection with HIV and the emergence of an AIDS-defining condition can be quite lengthy, AIDS cases reflect HIV transmission patterns that occurred approximately 10 years earlier.

To provide more timely information about the HIV epidemic, public health officials monitor HIV seropositivity among accessible population groups. For example, since 1987 in New York State, the Department of Health has tested more than 2.5 million anonymous blood samples for HIV antibodies (New York State Department of Health [NYSDoH], 1994). One group from which anonymous blood samples are routinely tested are newborn infants. During the 1987-1993 interval, 0.63% of the 1,736,247 infants born in New York State tested positive; among infants born in New York City, 1.17% tested positive (NYSDoH, 1994). Such data can be used to inform policy decisions, health care planning, and research.

Many mental health professionals have expressed concern that life circumstances and psychiatric symptoms may increase the risk for HIV infection among the seriously mentally ill (e.g., Cournos et al., 1994; Kelly et al., 1992; McDermott, Sautter, Winstead, & Quirk, 1994). This concern, coupled with the obvious value of HIV prevalence data, has encouraged several investigators to attempt to provide estimates of HIV infection among the seriously mentally ill. To provide such estimates, most investigators have collected discarded blood samples obtained during routine admissions procedures (e.g., see procedures described by Cournos et al., 1991). All identifying information is removed from the samples, which are then forwarded to an independent laboratory for HIV antibody testing. This "blinded" procedure serves to protect the anonymity of the patients and decreases the inevitable bias that can occur with alternative (i.e., volunteer) sampling procedures.

In this article, we summarize the extant data on the prevalence of HIV infection among persons diagnosed with a serious mental disorder. Our primary goal is to apprise mental health professionals of the available evidence and its limitations. We also provide screening and counseling guidelines for practitioners who work with seriously mentally ill clients. In addition, we identify sources for additional information and for ongoing professional education.

REVIEW OF THE RESEARCH

We searched the epidemiological, medical, nursing, psychiatric, and psychological literature to obtain estimates of the seroprevalence of HIV infection among the seriously mentally ill. Our search began with computerized searches of the medical (MEDLINE) and psychological (PsycLIT) databases. After collecting obviously relevant articles, we next studied each reference cited in those articles to identify additional relevant studies. This process was repeated for each new reference located until all cited references were included or eliminated as not providing new information.

Table 1 (page 254) summarizes the nine reports that provided information on seroprevalence in the seriously mentally ill. Although not all of these studies were designed specifically to assess seroprevalence, all provided useful data. Notably, these investigations evaluated seroprevalence in persons involved in inpatient or outpatient psychiatric treatment; no information is available on nontreated individuals with a serious mental disorder.

We offer the following observations about the studies summarized in Table 1. First, and most important, is the observation that prevalence of HIV infection has ranged from 4%-23% in samples of the seriously mentally ill. Collapsing across all studies (see Table 2, page 257) yielded an overall seroprevalence rate of 8% (i.e., 189 infected persons out of 2,345 tested). This rate of infection exceeds the rate found in the U.S. general population, which is estimated to be 800,000-1,200,000 out of 260 million, or 0.3%-0.5% (Steele, 1994).

Because nearly all of the studies with the seriously mentally ill have been done in New York City, a known epicenter for HIV and AIDS, comparison of these rates with those estimated for the U.S. general population may be misleading. A more informative approach would be to compare the rate among the seriously mentally ill with that of the New York City general population. However, to our knowledge, no representative estimates of HIV seropositivity for the general New York City population are available (cf. NYSDoH, 1994).

A second observation from these studies is that men with a serious mental disorder have been infected at a higher rate (i.e., 8%) than have women (5%; see Table 2). Although the rate of HIV infection in the general population is greater for men than for women (at least 1 in 100 adult men and 1 in 600 adult women in the United States are HIV positive; Centers for Disease Control and Prevention, 1990), the gender difference in infection rates is smaller among the seriously mentally ill. This finding, which should be considered tentative given the limited database, is consistent with the second wave of the epidemic in which women are the demographic group with the faster growing infection rate (cf. Kelly, Murphy, Sikkema, & Kalichman, 1993).

Third, except for gender, it is premature to make inferences regarding the association between HIV serostatus and numerous demographic (e.g., age, education, income, racial or ethnic status) and psychiatric history characteristics (e.g., primary diagnosis, medication compliance, other comorbid conditions). These associations have not been consistently studied or reported in sufficient detail to allow meta-analysis or confident inferences at this time.

Fourth, data obtained from sites specializing in acute care, chronic care, and homeless populations suggest that the homeless may be at the greatest risk for infection. This observation is clearly tentative, as it is based on a small sample of studies; however, the association between homelessness and HIV risk should be studied further (cf. Toro & Wall, 1991). It is noteworthy that patients institutionalized in long-term care facilities are also at risk, contrary to traditional beliefs that such patients are sexually inactive.

Fifth, several investigators have reported that seriously mentally ill adults with a history of injection drug use, as well as men who have sex with other men, are at elevated risk for HIV infection in comparison with those without such a history. These associations are consistent with national data that indicate that these two exposure categories account for the largest number of AIDS cases (Centers for Disease Control and Prevention, 1994a).

Sixth, positive serological status continues to be underdetected among persons receiving psychiatric services. Cournos et al. (1991) reported that 15 of 25 (60%) patients identified as HIV positive by anonymous testing had not been reported to hospital infection control committees. At another site, 10 of 25 (40%) patients later identified as HIV positive through anonymous

Table 1. Studies examining HIV Seroprevalence Among the Seriously Mentally III

Study	Participants	Source of participants	Dates of data collection	Methods	Results (percentage HIV infected)	Correlates
1. Cournos et al. (1991)	N = 451 (237 men, 214 women). Age: 18-59. Race: 172 Af. Am., 163 Caucasian, 115 Hispanic. Diagnoses: Schizophrenia, 206; schizoaffective disorder, 39; affective disorder, 114; other psychotic disorders, 53; other diagnoses, 42.	Two public psychiatric hospitals in Queens, New York City. One acute care, one acute and chronic care.	December, 1989-July, 1990.	ELISA with Western Blot confirmation was used with discarded blood samples drawn during routine admission procedures. Anonymous testing.	5.5% (25/451); 5.1% (12/237) of men; 6.1% (13/214) of women.	Race: Af. Am. > Caucasian. Behavior: history of homosexual activity among men or women or IDU.
2. Empfield et al. (1993)	N = 203 (146 men, 57 women). Age: 18-59. Race: 93 Af. Am., 20 Hispanic, 90 Caucasian and Asian. Diagnoses: Schizophrenia, 103; schizoaffective disorder, 90; affective disorder, 7; other psychotic disorders, 9.	Homeless patients admitted to New York City state hospital for extended care.	December, 1989-May, 1991.	ELISA with Western Blot confirmation was used with discarded blood samples drawn for routine purposes. Anonymous testing.	6.4% (13/203); 6.8% (10/146) of men; 5.3% (3/57) of women.	Age: under 40 > over 40. Behavior: IDU.

Study	Participants	Source of participants	Dates of data collection	Methods	Results (percentage HIV infected)	Correlates
3. Lee et al. (1992)	*N* = 135 *Age:* NR. *Race:* NR. *Diagnoses:* Psychotic, affective, substance abuse disorders and miscellaneous diagnoses.	Consecutive admissions to New York City hospital inpatient psychiatric service.	February 1, 1989-June 30, 1989.	ELISA with Western Blot confirmation was used with discarded blood samples drawn for routine purposes. Anonymous testing.	16.3% (22/135); 16.7% of men (number of men NR); 16.0% of women (number of women NR).	*Age:* Patients 18-45 > older patients. *Diagnosis:* Psychotic disorder patients represented a lower seroprevalence than other patients.
4. Meyer et al. (1993)	*N* = 199 (131 men, 68 women). *Age:* 18-59. *Race:* NR. *Diagnoses:* Schizophrenia, 140; schizoaffective disorder, 12; mood disorders, 17; organic disorders, 8; other diagnoses, 22.	Long stay (>1 year) patients at Creedmoor Psychiatric Center, New York City (state hospital).	April 9, 1990-July 31, 1990.	ELISA with Western Blot confirmation was used with discarded blood samples drawn for annual routine testing. Anonymous testing.	4% (8/199); 3.8% (5/131) of men; 4.4% (3/68) of women.	*Behavior:* IDU since 1978.
5. Sacks, Dermatis, Looser-Ott, & Perry (1992) (see also Sacks, Dermatis, Looser-Ott, Burton, & Perry [1992])	*N* = 350 (154 men, 196 women). *Age:* 18-55. *Race:* NR. *Diagnoses:* Organic mental disorder, 24; bipolar disorder, 74; depressive disorders, 101; schizophrenia, 87.	Admissions to a voluntary psychiatric hospital (Payne Whitney Clinic) in Manhattan, New York City.	November 1, 1989-May 31, 1990.	ELISA with Western Blot confirmation was used with discarded blood samples drawn for routine admissions testing. Anonymous testing.	7.1% (25/350); 12.3% (19/154) of men; 3.1% (6/196) of women.	*Gender:* men >women. *Diagnosis:* Patients with organic mental disorders more likely to be HIV positive than those with schizophrenia, bipolar disorder, or depressive disorder. *Behavior:* Male-male sex.

Study	Participants	Source of participants	Dates of data collection	Methods	Results (percentage HIV infected)	Correlates
6. Silberstein et al. (1994)	$N = 118$ (103 men, 15 women). *Age:* 19-69. *Race:* 60 Af. Am., 34 Caucasian/other, 21 Hispanic. *Diagnoses:* Schizophrenia/other psychotic disorder, 44; non-Axis I, 31; bipolar, 19; depression, 16; other, 7.	Sequential dual-diagnosis (substance abusing) admissions to psychiatric ward of general hospital.	January, 1991-April, 1991.	ELISA with Western Blot confirmation was used with blood samples given voluntarily for study. Pretest and posttest HIV counseling provided.	22.9% (27/118); 24% (24/102) of men; 20% (3/15) of women.	*Race:* Af. Am. > Caucasian/other. *Behavior:* IDU, male-male sex, prostitution, receptive anal intercourse, IDU sex partner. *Diagnosis:* Depression.
7. Susser et al. (1993)	$N = 62$ men. *Age:* 18+. *Race:* 48 Af. Am., 11 Hispanic, 3 Caucasian/other. *Diagnoses:* Schizophrenia, 42; other diagnoses, 20.	Discharges from homeless shelter psychiatric program.	Data collected over a 2-year period before August 1992.	ELISA with Western Blot confirmation. Voluntary testing available for all patients in program.	19.4% (12/62); NR by gender.	*Behavior:* IDU, male-male sex.
8. Volavka et al. (1992)	$N = 476$ (343 men, 133 women). *Age:* NR *Race:* 270 Af. Am. 107 Hispanic, 99 Caucasian.	New admissions to state psychiatric hospital in New York City for long-term treatment.	February 15, 1990-February 15, 1991.	ELISA with Western Blot confirmation. Voluntary testing. Patients not informed of results.	7.4% (26/352); NR by gender.	Results of Risk Behavior Questionnaire (high risk group—higher seroprevalence)
9. Zamperetti et al. (1990)	$N = 475$ *Age:* NR *Race:* NR *Diagnoses:* NR	Psychiatric ward patients.	Data collected over a period of two years (pre-1990).	NR	6.5% (31/475); NR by gender.	Suicide attempts among HIV positive patients.

Note. Af. Am.= African American; NR = not reported; ELISA = Enzyme Linked Immunosorbency Assay; IDU = Intravenous Drug Use.

Table 2. HIV seroprevalence among the seriously mentally ill by gender

Study	Total			Men			Women		
	N	n HIV+	% HIV+	N	n HIV+	% HIV+	N	n HIV+	% HIV+
Cournos et al. (1991)	451	25	5.5	237	12	5.1	214	13	6.1
Empfield et al. (1993)	203	13	6.4	146	10	6.8	57	3	5.3
Lee et al.(1992)	135	22	16.3	NR	NR	16.7	NR	NR	16.0
Meyer et al. (1993)	199	8	4.0	131	5	3.8	68	3	4.4
Sacks, Dermatis, Looser-Ott, & Perry (1992)	350	25	7.1	154	19	12.3	196	6	3.1
Silberstein et al. (1994)	118	27	22.9	102	24	24	15	3	20.0
Susser et al. (1993)	62	12	19.4	62	12	19.4	—	—	—
Volavka et al. (1992)	352	26	7.4	NR	NR	NR	NR	NR	NR
Zamperetti et al. (1990)	475	31	6.5	NR	NR	NR	NR	NR	NR
Total	2,345	189	8.1	832	82	9.9	550	28	5.1

Note. Dashes indicate data not applicable. *n* HIV+ = number infected with HIV; NR = not reported.

testing had not been identified on admission (Sacks, Dermatis, Looser-Ott, Burton, & Perry, 1992). Most (88%) of these HIV positive patients had risk factors recorded in their charts, suggesting that risk factor assessment should be performed routinely. In one sample of psychiatric inpatients, 39 of 77 (51%) with identifiable risk factors documented on admission left the hospital with their serological status still unknown (Sacks, Dermatis, Looser-Ott, Burton, & Perry, 1992).

Finally, nearly all of the studies cited in Tables 1 and 2 have been published in psychiatric, rather than psychological, journals. Given that many psychologists are actively involved in the care of the seriously mentally ill (cf. American Psychological Association, 1993), the relative absence of epidemiological information in the psychological literature is troublesome.

We offer three caveats about the findings of our review. First, as can be seen in Table 1, most data were obtained during 1991 or earlier. Given the rapidly changing nature of the HIV epidemic (Koziol & Henderson, 1992), estimates from these articles should not be interpreted as reflective of current prevalence data.

Second, two studies reported findings resulting from voluntary testing, whereas six remaining studies used anonymous testing of discarded blood samples. (The methods of the remaining study were not provided.) The effect that voluntary testing has on the obtained seroprevalence rate is unknown. One might speculate that it would increase the prevalence because such testing might attract higher risk patients; alternatively, higher risk patients might be inclined to avoid such testing to protect their privacy, thus reducing the prevalence estimate.

Third, nearly all of the studies have been conducted in New York City. It is widely known that New York City is an epicenter for HIV infection, with significantly enhanced seroprevalence rates relative to other areas. Thus, it is likely that rates that appear in Tables 1 and 2 reflect overestimates of HIV infection in nonepicenter environments. Additional research conducted in settings outside of New York City, including other large metropolitan areas, middle-sized cities, and rural environments, is urgently needed to determine the representativeness of data obtained in New York City.

Such limitations notwithstanding, these data highlight the need for increased vigilance on the part of mental health professionals who work with the seriously mentally ill. Regardless of the setting, individuals who have a serious and persistent mental disorder appear to be at significant risk for HIV infection. If the epidemic is to be controlled, mental health professionals must equip themselves with the information and resources they need to assess risk status and behaviors and to provide effective and potentially lifesaving advice to their clients.

IMPLICATIONS FOR PRACTICE

We suggest that professional psychologists provide three HIV-related services to their clients as a routine part of care, namely, risk assessment, education and counseling, and referral for other services (e.g., HIV testing or treatment, if indicated).

Risk assessment

Risk assessment should be conducted with all clients by all therapists. Such assessment serves to guide individualized education and prevention counseling; risk assessment will also help a therapist to determine when testing is advised.

Risk assessment requires only a basic knowledge of HIV and AIDS. Professional psychologists need to know that (a) HIV is transmitted when the blood, semen, or vaginal fluids of an infected person enter the body of another person; (b) transmission occurs most often during unprotected sexual intercourse (vaginal and anal), or during needle sharing among injection drug users; (c) sexual abstinence or mutually monogamous sex with an uninfected partner and not sharing drug use equipment provide the best protection against HIV infection; (d) use of a male or female condom and cleaning drug use equipment both reduce significantly the likelihood of HIV transmission; and (e) antibody testing is available at most public health care facilities for those clients who wish to know their serostatus. Although additional HIV-related knowledge will provide therapists with greater confidence and allow them to answer a wider array of questions, it is not necessary to be an expert to conduct basic risk assessment and screening. It is necessary, however, to communicate to clients that such assessment constitutes a routine part of mental health care. This disclosure will help to assuage client fears of prejudice or being singled out as someone at risk.

Screening should be done in a private interview setting as a routine part of a comprehensive assessment. A sensitive introduction should also include assurances of continued confidentiality. Questions, such as those presented in Table 3, are usually sufficient and can be integrated into routine psychosocial history taking. Depending on the clients' responses to these questions and their knowledge of HIV transmission and prevention, mental health care providers can determine whether further education or counseling is necessary and whether the client might profit from antibody testing.

Education and risk reduction counseling

Education and risk reduction counseling will require more sophistication on the part of a therapist. If a client is misinformed about the basics of HIV and AIDS or has simple questions about transmission and prevention of HIV infection, most therapists will be able to help immediately. If a client

Table 3. Risk assessment interview prompts

Prompt	Follow-up
1. Have you had sexual intercourse with men, women, or both in the past 10 years?	Number of partners, genders, specific sexual practices, use of protection.
2. Have you had a male sexual partner who has had sex with other men in the past 10 years?	Number of such partners, specific practices, use of protection.
3. Have you ever shared or borrowed a needle to inject yourself with a drug, or think that someone you had sex with did this?	Number of partners, disinfecting of needles between users.
4. Have you ever had a sexual partner whom you knew, or you later learned, was HIV infected or had AIDS?	Frequency of intercourse and/or needle sharing.
5. Did you receive a blood transfusion or treatment for a blood clotting problem between 1977 and 1985?	Previously tested for HIV?
6. Did a sexual or needle partner receive blood transfusion or treatment for a blood clotting problem between 1977 and 1985?	Previously tested for HIV?
7. Are you at all concerned that you might have picked up the virus?	Explore. This leaves the door open for people who may not have felt comfortable responding to questions 1-6.

has been involved in risky sexual or drug use practices, he or she should be advised promptly and specifically about which behaviors enhance risk and what preventive action can be taken to reduce risk for infection. A client who is at risk should also be encouraged to participate in intensive HIV-prevention programs (involving, e.g., training in condom use and assertiveness to avoid pressures to engage in unsafe practices) if these are available.

Provision of intensive education or prevention programs will require that the therapist be well-informed. The American Psychological Association will be providing training to therapists across the country through Project HOPE (Moses, 1992). For those therapists who wish to provide more detailed education regarding HIV and AIDS, we recommend Kalichman's (1995) guide. Practical and empirically based risk reduction strategies are contained in Kelly's (1995) manual. Therapists can also call on resource persons to provide additional education or counseling; such resource persons can be found by calling local, state, and national hotlines.

Excellent resources are available for the HIV-conscious mental health practitioner working with the seriously mentally ill. Several national information sources exist: (a) National AIDS Hotline at 800-342-7514; (b) National AIDS Hotline TTY/TDD Service (Confidential toll-free information for deaf or hearing impaired people) at 800-243-7889; (c) National AIDS Information Clearinghouse at 800-458-5231. National AIDS computer news groups exist that allow subscribers to automatically receive recent publications, post general requests for information from other readers, and discuss current HIV-relevant biomedical, legal, sociological, and psychological issues. Subscription to sci.med.aids, one such national news group, may be achieved by sending an e-mail request to: listserv@puigmal.cesca.es with the text SUBSCRIBE AIDS firstname lastname.

Locally, chapters of the American Red Cross offer HIV and AIDS resource materials and educational programs of various lengths that cover basics of viral transmission, disease progression, epidemiology, testing, and prevention. Local health departments may also be able to assist in staff training and education.

Antibody testing for HIV infection

For clients with a history of risky practices, antibody testing may be recommended. Early detection of HIV infection can help clients to obtain referrals to receive prophylactic medical care as well as other preventive, psychological, and social services. Knowledge of serostatus may also enhance motivation for safer sexual practices to avoid partner infection. Such a recommendation is complex, however, because legal, ethical, and political issues involved with HIV-antibody testing (e.g., informed consent, privacy, discrimination, and duty to protect) must be considered. As Haimowitz (1989) indicates,

> since no statute has been enacted requiring or prohibiting the HIV test in psychiatric hospitals or settings, testing remains a medical decision that should be guided by clinical judgment of the patient's best interests and by the legal principle of informed consent. (p. 732)

Therapists should consider encouraging clients to seek testing if they have had unprotected anal or vaginal intercourse with a partner whose HIV serostatus is positive or unknown, or if they have shared needles. Clients who express anxiety despite apparent low risk may also be advised to consider testing. Clients who have been abstinent or who strongly believe themselves to have been in a mutually monogamous sexual relationship with an HIV-negative partner and who have never shared an injection drug needle can be reassured and counseled to maintain low risk.

Mental health care providers can obtain information about the process of HIV-antibody testing from numerous sources, including local American Red Cross chapters and city and state Department of Health offices. These organizations can provide specific information regarding sites, types of tests offered, and fees. Two types of voluntary testing are available, and clients considering testing should be aware of the distinctions. If an individual undergoes confidential testing, the results are recorded in his or her medical files and may be disclosed to those with legal access to records. For anonymous testing, alternatively, a code number is given when blood is drawn, and the code must be presented by the client to obtain the results. In no way is the client's name associated with test results. Many states offer anonymous or confidential tests without charge.

Depending on the client's level of functioning, therapists should consider assisting with scheduling of the test and coordinating counseling efforts with the testing site. With the prospect of testing, clients may experience anxiety and increased psychiatric symptoms. Intensive therapist support, as well as increased attention to suicidal ideation (Zamperetti et al., 1990), may be necessary for some clients. Although sites that provide HIV testing are required to provide pre- and posttest counseling (cf. Centers for Disease Control and Prevention, 1994b), therapists should plan to supplement such counseling in light of the unique needs of the seriously mentally ill. If a client is infected with HIV, additional therapy that addresses HIV and AIDS-related issues will be warranted. Although this topic is beyond the scope of this article, we recommend Winiarski's (1991) guide, which discusses critical issues of AIDS-related therapy and neuropsychological effects.

By writing this article, we hope to achieve three aims: (a) to raise the awareness of practitioners who work with seriously mentally ill clients of the potential for elevated rates of HIV infection; (b) to encourage greater attention to the topic of HIV and AIDS in the seriously mentally ill in psychological training and journals; and (c) to equip practitioners with basic information regarding assessment of HIV risk status and related HIV and AIDS counseling.

REFERENCES

American Psychological Association. (1993). *Serving the seriously mentally ill: Public-academic linkages in services, research, and training.* Washington, DC: Author.

Centers for Disease Control and Prevention. (1990). HIV prevalence estimates and AIDS case projections: Results. *Morbidity and Mortality Weekly Report, 39,* 27-31.

Centers for Disease Control and Prevention. (1994a, June). *HIV/AIDS Surveillance Report (Mid-Year Edition), 6(1),* 1-27.

Centers for Disease Control and Prevention. (1994b). *HIV Counseling, Testing and Referral: Standards and Guidelines.* Atlanta: Author.

Cournos, F., Empfield, M., Horwath, E., McKinnon, K., Meyer, I., Schrage, H., Currie, C., & Agosin, B. (1991). HIV seroprevalence among patients admitted to two psychiatric hospitals. *American Journal of Psychiatry, 148,* 1225-1229.

Cournos, F., Guido, J. R., Coomaraswamy, S., Meyer-Bahlburg, H., Sugden, R., & Horwath, E. (1994). Sexual activity and risk for HIV infection among patients with schizophrenia. *American Journal of Psychiatry, 151,* 228-232.

Empfield, M., Cournos, F., Meyer, I., McKinnon, K., Horwath, E., Silver, M., Schrage, H., & Herman, R. (1993). HIV seroprevalence among homeless patients admitted to a psychiatric inpatient unit. *American Journal of Psychiatry, 150,* 47-52.

Haimowitz, S. (1989). HIV and the mentally ill: An approach to the legal issues. *Hospital and Community Psychiatry, 40,* 732-736.

Kalichman, S. C. (1995). *Understanding AIDS: A mental health practitioner's guide to the epidemic.* Washington, DC: American Psychological Association.

Kelly, J. A. (1995). *Preventing HIV infection: Practical guidelines for the helping professions.* New York: Guilford Press.

Kelly, J. A., Murphy, D. A., Bahr, G. R., Brasfield, T. L., Davis, D. R., Hauth, A. C., Morgan, M. G., Stevenson, L. Y., & Eilers, M. K. (1992). AIDS/HIV risk behavior among the chronic mentally ill. *American Journal of Psychiatry, 149,* 886-889.

Kelly, J. A., Murphy, D. A., Sikkema, K. J., & Kalichman, S. C. (1993). Psychological interventions to prevent HIV infection are urgently needed: New priorities for behavioral research in the second decade of AIDS. *American Psychologist, 48,* 1023-1034.

Koziol, D. E., & Henderson, D. K. (1992). Evolving epidemiology of HIV infection among adults. *Annals of Allergy, 68,* 375-385.

Lee, H. K., Travin, S., & Bluestone, H. (1992). HIV-1 in inpatients. *Hospital and Community Psychiatry, 43,* 181-182.

Mann, J. M. (1992). AIDS—the second decade: A global perspective. *Journal of Infectious Diseases, 165,* 245-250.

McDermott, B. E., Sautter, F. J., Winstead, D. K., & Quirk, T. (1994). Diagnosis, health beliefs, and risk of HIV infection in psychiatric patients. *Hospital and Community Psychiatry, 45,* 580-585.

Meyer, I., McKinnon, K., Cournos, F., Empfield, M., Bavli, S., Engel, D., & Weinstock, A. (1993). HIV seroprevalence among long-stay patients in a state psychiatric hospital. *Hospital and Community Psychiatry, 44,* 282-284.

Moses, S. (1992, June). Curriculum is developed to teach AIDS trainers. *APA Monitor,* p. 30.

New York State Department of Health. (1994). *AIDS in New York State, 1993.* Albany, NY: Author.

Sacks, M., Dermatis, H., Looser-Ott, S., Burton, W., & Perry, S. (1992). Undetected HIV infection among acutely ill psychiatric inpatients. *American Journal of Psychiatry, 149,* 544-545.

Sacks, M., Dermatis, H., Looser-Ott, S., & Perry, S. (1992). Seroprevalence of HIV and risk factors for AIDS in psychiatric inpatients. *Hospital and Community Psychiatry, 43,* 181-182.

Silberstein, C., Galanter M., Marmor, M., Lifshultz, H., Krasinski, K., & Franco, H. (1994). HIV-1 among inner city dually diagnosed inpatients. *American Journal of Drug and Alcohol Abuse, 20,* 101-113.

Steele, F. R. (1994). A moving target: CDC still trying to estimate HIV prevalence. *Journal of NIH Research, 6(6),* 25-26.

Susser, E., Valencia, E., & Conover, S. (1993). Prevalence of HIV infection among psychiatric patients in a New York City men's shelter. *American Journal of Public Health, 83,* 568-570.

Toro, P. A., & Wall, D. D. (1991). Research on homeless persons: Diagnostic comparisons and practice implications. *Professional Psychology: Research and Practice, 22,* 479-488.

Volavka, J., Convit, A., O'Donnell, J., Douyon, R., Evangelista, C., & Czobor, P. (1992). Assessment of risk behaviors for HIV infection among psychiatric inpatients. *Hospital and Community Psychiatry, 43,* 482-485.

Winiarski, M. G. (1991). *AIDS-related psychotherapy,* Elmsford, NY: Pergamon Press.

Zamperetti, M., Goldwurm, G. F., Abbate, E., Gris, T., Muratori, S., & Vigo, B. (1990). *Attempted suicide and HIV infections: Epidemiological aspects in a psychiatric ward.* Abstracts, VI International Conference on AIDS, 3, 182.

ABOUT THE AUTHORS

Michael P. Carey, Ph.D., is Professor of Psychology at Syracuse University. Lance S. Weinhart, Ph.D., is a graduate student in the Clinical Psychology Program at Syracuse University. Kate B. Carey, Ph.D., is Associate Professor of Psychology at Syracuse University.

ACKNOWLEDGMENTS

Preparation of this review was supported in part by a Scientist Development Award from the National Institute of Mental Health (MH01101) and a FIRST Award from the National Institute on Drug Abuse (DA07635) We thank Jeffrey A. Kelly for his generous assistance and guidance.

Copyright 1995 by the American Psychological Association. Reprinted with permission.

INTRODUCTION TO SECTION FIVE

The Treatment section contains seven articles that inform clinicians about the critical ingredients of effective interventions for persons with dual disorders. Over the past 10 years there has been a dramatic shift in the philosophy of treatment for dual disorders, and this change has begun to permeate all aspects of service provision, among both mental health and substance abuse providers. Traditionally, treatment for clients with dual diagnoses was provided by clinicians with different backgrounds and training experiences, working at separate agencies, often with access to different levels of funding. In *parallel treatment*, substance abuse and mental health services were provided simultaneously to clients by different clinicians who had little or no contact with one another. In *sequential treatment*, intervention for one type of problem was provided prior to treatment for the other. Numerous problems were associated with the traditional treatment approaches, such as treatment strategies that were incompatible with care of the other disorder, lack of communication and coordination, and difficulty accessing certain services. Comprehensive reviews of the effectiveness of these traditional treatment approaches for clients with dual diagnoses indicated dismal results (Ridgely, Goldman, & Willenbring, 1990; included in Special Issues section), paving the way for more effective interventions based on the integration of mental health and substance abuse treatment services. Several recent research studies indicate that integrated treatment approaches are effective (Mueser, Drake, & Bond, in press).

The articles in this section cover a range of topics concerning the treatment of persons with a dual disorder. The first three articles provide overviews of comprehensive approaches or programs for individuals with dual diagnoses. The next three address special topics: group treatment, self-help groups, and pharmacological treatment. The final article addresses system issues, challenging the traditional separation between mental health and substance abuse treatment services.

The article by Kenneth Minkoff was one of the first to articulate the need to integrate mental health and substance abuse services into a single program for persons with a dual diagnosis. Minkoff shows the similarities between the major mental disorders and the substance use disorders, pointing out their chronic and presumably biological nature. He also suggests similarities between the biopsychosocial and rehabilitation model of psychiatric illness and the 12-step disease and recovery model of Alcoholics Anonymous for addictive disorders. The program that Minkoff describes is an excellent example of the "new breed" of integrated treatment programs that began to develop in the mid-1980s.

In the second article, Robert Drake and his colleagues provide an overview of the essential components of comprehensive treatment for clients with dual diagnoses. The major focus is on describing nine fundamental elements of integrated treatment, rather than the various clinical methods that can be employed to achieve these ends. For example, *stagewise treatment* is an important part of any intervention program. It is based on the observation that clients with dual diagnoses who receive treatment and recover from substance use disorders typically progress through a series of motivational stages (Osher & Kofoed, 1989). In order to ensure optimal effectiveness of treatments, interventions should be geared to the client's current stage. For example, the goal of the engagement stage is to establish a relationship with the client, and hence attempts to persuade the client that substance abuse is a problem (persuasion stage) or to cut down on substance use (active treatment stage) are likely to prove ineffective.

Kate Carey next provides a model for the treatment of clients with dual diagnoses. The model is compatible with the principles of treatment espoused by Drake and colleagues, but the emphasis and organization differ. Carey's model identifies four themes from the psychological treatment literature, which she proposes are crucial in working with people who have dual diagnoses: variable intensity in accordance with clients' needs, stages of change, motivational interventions, and harm reduction. The concept of *harm reduction* as a primary goal of dual-diagnosis treatment represents a significant departure from traditional approaches to substance abuse in the United States, in which abstinence has been emphasized to the exclusion of reduction. The themes identified by Carey are employed in a model involving five steps that are consistent with the stages of treatment outlined by Osher and Kofoed (1989).

The fourth article, by Kim Mueser and Douglas Noordsy, describes group treatments for persons with a dual diagnosis. Group treatment is one of the most common forms of intervention, and Mueser and Noordsy describe four basic models: 12-step, educational-supportive, social skills training, and stagewise. The authors identify the common themes and unique characteristics of the different models, with special emphasis on stagewise groups. They also review the meager research literature on the effectiveness of group treatment.

The fifth article, by Douglas Noordsy and his colleagues, describes how self-help groups can assist people with dual diagnoses in making progress toward recovery. Self-help groups such as Alcoholics Anonymous play an important role in the recovery of persons with a primary substance use disorder, but are infrequently used by clients with dual diagnoses. This article describes some of the characteristics of those clients with dual diagnoses who are most likely to benefit from self-help groups, and the article identifies common obstacles to engaging these clients in self-help groups. The widespread availability of self-help groups in the community indicates that such groups could be an important resource for clients with dual diagnoses. The authors offer several suggestions to help clinicians link clients with self-help groups.

The sixth article in this section, from the Center for Substance Abuse Treatment, addresses the critical issue of psychopharmacological management of persons with dual diagnoses. The article does not differentiate between severe mental illnesses and other mental illnesses, but nonetheless it provides useful descriptions of the different types of psychotropic medication that are used generally in treating psychiatric illnesses. Some psychiatrists are reluctant to prescribe medications to clients with an active substance use disorder. This article makes it clear that pharmacological treatment is critical for the care of mental disorders (including severe disorders such as schizophrenia, bipolar disorder, and psychotic depression), even in clients who are continuing to abuse substances. It points out that the failure to medicate such clients substantially increases their chances of clinical deterioration, as well as subsequent risk of injury to themselves or others.

In the concluding article, Fred Osher envisions a future in which the traditional separation between mental health and substance abuse services is abandoned in favor of an integrated system that is responsive to all of the needs of its clients. He points out that the evidence has accumulated attesting to the effectiveness of integrated treatment, and that the failure to learn from these recent advances may be akin to "Nero fiddling while Rome burns." Osher provides a direction for the field, and his encouragement is a refreshing reminder that improvements in the lives of consumers with dual diagnoses are possible only if professional people are guided by a vision of integrated care that transcends the traditional divisions between mental health and substance abuse services.

REFERENCES

Mueser, K.T., Drake, R.E., & Bond, G.R. (in press). Recent advances in psychiatric rehabilitation for patients with severe mental illness. *Harvard Review of Psychiatry.*

Osher, F.C., & Kofoed, L.L. (1989). Treatment of patients with psychiatric and psychoactive substance abuse disorders. *Hospital and Community Psychiatry,* 40, 1025-1030.

Ridgely, M.S., Goldman, H.H., & Willenbring, M. (1990). Barriers to the care of persons with dual diagnoses: Organizational and financing issues. *Schizophrenia Bulletin,* 16, 123-132.

AN INTEGRATED TREATMENT MODEL FOR DUAL DIAGNOSIS OF PSYCHOSIS AND ADDICTION

Kenneth Minkoff

Reprinted from *Hospital and Community Psychiatry*, 40(10):1031-1036, 1989

A model that integrates the treatment of patients with a dual diagnosis of psychosis and addiction has been developed on a general hospital psychiatric unit. The model emphasizes the parallels between the standard biopsychosocial illness-and-rehabilitation model for treatment of serious psychiatric disorders and the 12-step disease-and-recovery model of Alcoholics Anonymous for treatment of addiction. Dual-diagnosis patients are viewed as having two primary, chronic, biologic mental illnesses, each requiring specific treatment to stabilize acute symptoms and engage the patient in a recovery process. An integrated treatment program is described, as are the steps taken to alleviate psychiatric clinicians' concerns about patient involvement in AA and addiction clinicians' discomfort with patients' use of medication.

For the past ten years or more, reports of the widespread problem of patients who have dual diagnoses of mental illness and addiction have been increasing in the literature (1-9). Despite the powerful impact of this population on the service delivery system, advances in treatment and training have been surprisingly slow (8-10). In a recent comprehensive review of treatment and training nationwide, Ridgely and associates (11) comment that the development of treatment for substance abuse in chronic mentally ill young adults is "in its infancy, characterized more by trial and error than by implementation of established treatment protocols."

One possible contributor to the problem of developing established treatment protocols for dual-diagnosis patients is the conflict that frequently arises when addiction treatment programs and mental health treatment programs try to collaborate. According to Ridgely and associates (11), "the fields of mental health and substance abuse have different foci, different philosophies, and a history of contentious behavior toward one another." As a solution, they have proposed the development of "hybrid" programs in which mental health and substance abuse treatment can be effectively integrated. One challenge that such programs face is to develop an integrated treatment philosophy that incorporates both mental health and substance abuse treatment in a unified conceptual and programmatic framework, thereby permitting clinicians from both areas to collaborate effectively.

This paper describes a model for an integrated treatment philosophy as developed in one type of hybrid program—a general hospital psychiatric unit that treats both addiction patients and general psychiatric patients. The application of the model to the treatment of dual-diagnosis patients in this setting is also discussed. In this paper, "dual diagnosis" refers only to patients who have both a primary psychotic mental disorder (major psychosis)—such as schizophrenia, schizoaffective disorder, or major affective disorder (bipolar or unipolar) with psychotic features—and a substance abuse or substance dependence disorder, as defined by *DSM-III-R* (12). Treatment of patients with substance abuse disorders who have concomitant anxiety disorder, personality disorder, dysthymic disorder, or nonpsychotic depression is not discussed.

THE TREATMENT SETTING

The model was developed at the Caulfield Center, a 21-bed voluntary psychiatric unit in a nonprofit, community general hospital located in a working-class suburb of Boston. Until 1984 the unit functioned primarily as an Alcoholics Anonymous—oriented addiction treatment program and, although licensed as a psychiatric unit, had only a vestigial psychiatric program.

In 1984 the hospital board of trustees decided to change the focus of the psychiatric service to be more consistent with its psychiatric license. A new chief of psychiatry (KM) was hired to expand and strengthen the unit's psychiatric program, while retaining the well-regarded addiction program, which was based on the 12-step program of Alcoholics Anonymous (AA). For the new psychiatric program to coexist with the addiction program on one unit, the Caulfield Center needed to develop an integrated treatment philosophy—a common language in which the 12-step addiction philosophy and standard mental health philosophy could be seen not as inherently contentious but as mutually validated and unified. The integrated model was the result.

THE INTEGRATED MODEL

The integrated model is based on AA's 12-step disease-and-recovery model for treatment of addiction (the addiction model) (13-15) and the standard biopsychosocial illness-and-rehabilitation model for treatment of serious psychiatric disorders (the psychiatric model) (16,17). Under the integrated illness-and-recovery model, both addiction and major psychosis can be viewed as chronic, biologic mental illnesses that can be treated through simultaneous application of parallel concepts from both the addiction and psychiatric models.

The development of the integrated model was based on several assumptions. The addiction model and the psychiatric model were considered equally valid when applied separately to patients with a diagnosis of addiction or major psychosis alone. Although the AA model and the psychiatric model are not the only valid models, both have been used widely and applied with reasonable success to a very broad range of patients (17,18). In addition, the necessity of developing an integrated framework was assumed to justify emphasizing the parallels between the two models, although that approach may have tended to minimize their differences. It was assumed that the contrasts could be considered clinical differences in the application of a unified model to individual patients with different diseases.

PARALLEL CONCEPTS OF ILLNESS

Clearly, the disease concept in the addiction model and the illness concept in the psychiatric model have numerous parallels. In each model the illness or disease is an incurable, biologic mental disorder, most commonly characterized by a chronic course with multiple relapses and exacerbations. Even though symptoms may remit for long periods, the potential for relapse is generally always present.

In each model the illness has a complex multifactorial etiology, in which a hereditary or congenital biologic predisposition interacts with psychosocial stressors to result in the emergence of symptoms (16,19,20). Both models emphasize that once the illness is established, the presence of an underlying biologic process requires treatment to stabilize the acute symptoms and engage the patient in a rehabilitation or recovery process rather than to undo the etiology to obtain a cure.

Profound denial is a prominent characteristic of the illness in each model, and overcoming denial is the first major task of treatment. Moreover, the impact of the illness on patients and families produces characteristic feelings of shame, guilt, stigma, and despair, and these feelings must also be addressed in the treatment process.

Both psychosis and addiction are characterized by loss of control of particular aspects of thinking and behavior. In both the psychiatric and the addiction models this loss of control is related to the underlying biologic process of the disease. For example, in schizophrenia and affective psychosis, alterations in brain structure or chemistry result in the emergence of psychotic symptoms that cannot be suppressed by will power alone.

Similarly, the disease concept of addiction postulates that heavy substance use progressively affects the biologically predisposed brain to create structural or chemical changes, causing increasingly persistent and irresistible conscious and unconscious cravings for substances and decreasing the ability to regulate substance use through will power alone (19-21). The pathognomonic lack of control in either illness becomes evident when the patient cannot regulate his thinking or behavior in the face of clear harmful consequences, such as incarceration, loss of job, or loss of residence.

Thus, in each model, the patient is powerless (15) over the primary disease—powerless over the reality of having the illness and powerless to cure it, powerless to consistently control the symptoms of the disease and powerless to consistently prevent harmful consequences of those symptoms. In neither model, however, is powerlessness equated with hopelessness. The patient can always regain control by accepting the powerlessness, accepting the illness, and asking for help by actively participating in treatment (13-15,22).

However, unlike the self-medication hypothesis of addiction (23), the integrated model states that the disease of addiction is primary and becomes independent of whatever symptom relief was originally sought through substance use. In fact, this model predicts that addictive substance use will not be controlled even when symptom relief is no longer forthcoming. The integrated model further states that the primary disease of addiction requires specific addiction treatment and cannot be treated solely by finding alternate means of relieving "underlying" symptoms (14).

Similarly, unlike psychodynamic hypotheses of psychotic illness, the integrated model implies that schizophrenia and affective psychoses are primary and eventually become independent of whatever psychodynamic or family stresses may have originally contributed to their onset. The primary mental illness therefore requires specific psychiatric treatment, such as medication, and cannot be treated solely by attempting to resolve underlying psychodynamic issues through psychotherapy (16).

Thus addiction and major psychoses are specific examples of primary, chronic, biologic mental illnesses. They have numerous parallels despite differences in symptoms and treatment.

APPLICATION TO DUAL-DIAGNOSIS PATIENTS

Patients with a dual diagnosis of major psychosis and substance dependence have two primary, chronic, biologic mental illnesses that require concomitant and equally intensive and specific treatment. Although each primary disease can be ameliorated to some extent by treatment of the other disease alone, this approach does not eliminate the need for specific treatment of both diseases simultaneously.

Applying the integrated model at the Caulfield Center required training clinicians to carefully distinguish between secondary symptoms and primary disease as part of the assessment process. For example, many patients with drug or alcohol addiction may develop secondary affective or psychotic symptoms during persistent intoxication or withdrawal. However, once the patient is abstinent, secondary psychoses or affective syndromes resolve; such patients are diagnosed as having primary addiction with a secondary organic psychosis. Although these patients may temporarily require medication therapy, their treatment focuses primarily on addiction alone. Patients with coexistent primary psychoses, however, will not improve with abstinence alone and will require ongoing, specific, parallel treatment for primary mental illness.

Similarly, some patients with mental illness may use substances in a controlled manner for a wide variety of reasons—recreation, socialization, anxiety reduction, and symptom relief. For most such patients, even controlled use of mind-altering substances may be harmful or potentially harmful because of the documented deleterious effect of even minimal substance use on the course of mental illness (4,5,24). Such patients therefore can be diagnosed as having a primary mental illness and a secondary substance abuse disorder, according to *DSM-III-R*. These patients receive substance abuse treatment in the context of a comprehensive approach to recovery from mental illness, through education about the need for making better choices about substance use because of the deleterious effects of substance use on recovery. Abstinence is recommended, but engagement in psychiatric treatment, not addiction treatment, is emphasized.

In some patients with primary mental illness, substance abuse has progressed, or will progress, to the point of loss of control in the face of clear harmful consequences. These patients will meet *DSM-III-R* criteria for substance dependence, and, according to the integrated model, will then have two primary diseases and will require specific, parallel, abstinence-oriented treatment for the additional primary disease of addiction. (Most studies indicate that the prevalence of substance abuse in mentally ill patients is 60 to 85 percent [1,4,6,7], and the prevalence of substance dependence is only 15 to 35 percent [3,7].)

Obviously, assessment is frequently complicated by the fact that the line of demarcation between abuse and dependence is not always clear. However, as training in the parallel disease model has progressed, clinicians from both sides have gradually developed a common language for evaluating dual-diagnosis patients. For patients who present difficulties in assessment, philosophic battles about which diagnosis should be primary have shifted to clinical discussions about how to evaluate the available clinical data to make a specific diagnosis and treatment plan for each individual to work toward recovery.

Parallel Concepts of Recovery

Both the addiction model and the psychiatric model have concepts of recovery or rehabilitation that describe a process of continued growth despite the presence of a chronic, incurable mental illness. Both models emphasize that the process of recovery requires focusing not merely on stabilizing the more prominent—and incurable—biologic aspects of illness, but also on treating the person who has the illness and engaging that person in active participation in the treatment and rehabilitation process (13,16,25).

The program of recovery for addiction has been well described in 12-step programs of recovery such as AA. The steps emphasize the importance of overcoming denial and accepting one's powerlessness to control substance use on one's own; admitting the need to ask for help from others to gain the power to maintain sobriety; maintaining sobriety through continued participation in treatment over many years; and, once sobriety is attained, being willing to use the treatment program actively and honestly to learn new skills for coping with life without substances (13-15).

In recent years, an analogous recovery process has been described for people with chronic mental illnesses. Long-term (30-year) follow-up studies of seriously mentally ill patients in Vermont have indicated surprising levels of clinical improvement and remission (26).

In some studies, factors that appear to help mentally ill patients in the recovery process (22,26) have been similar to factors that contribute to recovery from addiction: acceptance of the illness, compliance with treatment, using help to learn new coping skills, and willingness to actively collaborate in treatment (22). In addition, both the psychiatric and the addiction models describe a parallel process of recovery, with phases of acute stabilization, engagement, prolonged stabilization (maintenance), and rehabilitation. Discussions of the phases follow.

Acute stabilization

The acute stabilization phase of the integrated model may last from three days to three months. In the acute stabilization phase of mental illness, acute psychotic symptoms are stabilized with medication, usually in an inpatient setting. Treatment may be involuntary, generally lasts between two weeks and three months, and should include assessment for the effects of substance abuse and for the presence of addiction.

In the acute stabilization phase of addiction treatment, detoxification from substances takes place, usually with medication and in an inpatient setting. Treatment may be involuntary, generally lasts from three days to two weeks, and should include assessment for concomitant psychiatric disorders.

Engagement

Once the patient is stabilized, the process of engagement in treatment begins. Engagement involves establishing a beginning treatment relationship, educating the patient about the illness, teaching the patient how to maintain stabilization through compliance with treatment, and overcoming denial and other resistances to making a commitment to an ongoing treatment program.

For both illnesses, engaging the patient in ongoing treatment is crucial for recovery to proceed. Unfortunately, addiction patients may experience repeated cycles of detoxification and relapse—and mentally ill patients may have prolonged cycles of "revolving-door" admissions and persistent medication noncompliance—before acknowledging the need to engage in continuous treatment. Both illness models emphasize that a combination of empathic, long-term relationship building and a judicious use of leverage and confrontation by family and other caretakers or by the legal system are necessary for engagement to succeed (16,27).

Prolonged stabilization

In both the addiction and the psychiatric models, the phase of prolonged stabilization lasts approximately one year. Prolonged stabilization of addiction involves maintaining complete abstinence through intensive participation (not less than four to as many as seven times per week in a self-help program of recovery such as AA or Narcotics Anonymous [NA]. Prolonged stabilization of mental illness involves attaining maximum possible symptom control (not necessarily symptom removal) through ongoing medication compliance.

In the integrated model, medication and AA attendance are parallel treatments for parallel diseases. For either illness, establishing prolonged stabilization may also require one to 12 months of a combination of inpatient treatment, day treatment, or residential rehabilitation in addition to participation in an outpatient support system to overcome denial, promote acceptance of the illness, and reinforce continued compliance. Family education and participation in ongoing support programs such as Al-Anon and the Alliance for the Mentally Ill may also be necessary components of ongoing treatment.

The phase of prolonged stabilization establishes a period of "convalescence" (27) during which a patient can regroup from the chaotic disruption of the illness and prepare for future progress. Maintaining stability must be the major focus; in both addiction and psychiatric treatment, patients are advised that trying to make major life changes during early recovery may risk decompensation (13,27).

Rehabilitation

The rehabilitation phase can last from one to 30 years. In both the psychiatric and the addiction models, prolonged stabilization alone does not constitute recovery; stability merely begins the recovery phase by creating the possibility of growth and change (13, 22). Once stabilized, patients who continue active participation in a treatment program (and many do not) can begin to address the feelings of shame, guilt, despair, and helplessness that are engendered by the illness, to learn new skills for coping with daily living, and to participate in a process of social and vocational rehabilitation.

For both illnesses, rehabilitation is regarded as a slow, incremental, "one-day-at-a-time" process with frequent, and sometimes prolonged, plateaus. This process of rehabilitation or recovery is always ongoing, never completed (hence, "a recovering alcoholic"). Ideally, as the rehabilitation-recovery process progresses over many years, patients can achieve not only better levels of functioning but also a greater sense of mastery over their disease and, ultimately, greater peace of mind through acceptance of their limitations regardless of the extent of their disability (14,22). Thus, in this model, even though people recovering from mental illness are more likely to remain symptomatic and disabled than people recovering from addiction, the outcome of recovery for both illnesses is essentially the same.

The integrated model allows major psychosis and addiction to be viewed as parallel illnesses with parallel processes of recovery. Under this model, therefore, dual-diagnosis patients can be given a cohesive message about their condition: "You have two primary mental illnesses. There is a different treatment and recovery program for each illness, but the process of treatment and recovery is the same."

PRINCIPLES FOR TREATMENT OF DUAL-DIAGNOSIS PATIENTS

The integrated model can be applied to developing specific principles and programs for concomitant treatment of dual-diagnosis patients.

Parallel treatment programs

In the Caulfield Center, using the integrated model has permitted us to construct parallel, yet integrated addiction and psychiatric programs in the same inpatient unit. Each program treats patients with and without a dual diagnosis. Consequently, dual-diagnosis patients in the addiction program can receive the same specific treatment for their addiction as patients with addiction only, and dual-diagnosis patients in the psychiatric program can receive the same specific treatment for psychotic illness as patients with psychosis only.

Patients participate in one of four different treatment schedules, depending on individual needs: full addiction, full psychiatric, mixed addiction (full addiction plus two days of psychiatric treatment per week), and mixed psychiatric (full psychiatric plus two days of addiction treatment per week). Each schedule provides approximately four to six hours of treatment each day, including daily one-and-a-half-hour didactic sessions. (Treatment program schedules are available from the author on request.) The average length of stay is approximately three weeks; maximum stay is 60 days.

Selection of treatment program for dual-diagnosis patients

At the Caulfield Center, there is no one correct treatment program for dual-diagnosis patients. Treatment interventions vary according to severity of substance diagnosis (abuse versus addiction) and phase of recovery.

Patients with a dual diagnosis of psychosis and addiction require parallel treatment for both illnesses, and medication compliance, abstinence, and AA participation are required simultaneously. On our unit, such parallel treatment is provided in the mixed addiction program.

However, patients who abuse substances but are not addicted receive treatment for substance abuse solely through an educational program to encourage abstinence in the context of a comprehensive approach to recovery from mental illness. On our unit, such treatment is provided in the mixed psychiatric program. AA participation is voluntary.

In addition, patients with a dual diagnosis of psychosis and addiction may require different programs at different times during a single admission, depending on the phase of recovery. For example, a patient who is admitted for detoxification and acute stabilization of psychosis may start in the full psychiatric program while the psychosis clears with medication. As the patient's thinking clears, the need for substance education can be addressed, and the patient may begin mixed psychiatric treatment. Once the psychosis is stabilized, the patient can be confronted about the need for addiction treatment and, if willing, may enter the mixed addiction or full addiction program.

Finally, patients with a dual diagnosis of psychosis and addiction may cycle through multiple admissions for stabilization of psychosis or for detoxification before making a commitment to engage in either ongoing psychiatric or ongoing addiction treatment. As Ridgely and associates (11) have observed, each cycle of interrupted treatment represents an opportunity for clinicians to focus on the next step in the engagement process and build on previous gains. Thus, although there are parallel treatments and phases of recovery for each illness, progress usually occurs one step at a time in one illness at a time. A patient may stabilize psychosis during one admission but refuse addiction treatment, then return to deal with the addiction in a subsequent admission months or years later.

Consequently, simultaneous treatment often means maintaining the stabilization of one illness while focusing intensely on engaging the patient in a program to stabilize the other. Regardless of whether psychosis or addiction is stabilized first, both illnesses must be stabilized over time for significant progress to occur in recovery.

Issues in implementation of parallel treatment

Concerns by mental health clinicians about the use of 12-step programs to treat addiction in dual-diagnosis patients are well documented (7,11) and include concerns about religious concepts (the "higher power"), discouragement of medication compliance, and overstimulation in meetings leading to patient disorganization. However, successful attainment of abstinence is associated with AA attendance for alcoholics in general (28), and some researchers continue to advocate the use of these programs for dual-diagnosis patients (10).

Similarly, addiction clinicians tend to feel uncomfortable about any use of medication, and they may have difficulty distinguishing between psychotropic medication and psychoactive substances (13).

At the Caulfield Center, resolution of these concerns involved the following steps:

- Consistent validation of each treatment methodology as a specific treatment for each disease.
- Documentation in AA literature that prescribed medication is acceptable (13) and that patients with ancillary physical or psychiatric disorders are welcome: "The only requirement for membership is a desire to stop drinking" (15).
- Demonstration to addiction clinicians that antipsychotic medication is necessary to enable dual-diagnosis patients to benefit from or even participate in addiction treatment.
- Emphasis in medication practice on using medication to treat only specific primary psychotic illnesses in dual-diagnosis patients and not to relieve nonspecific symptoms of depression and anxiety. Benzodiazepines are specifically avoided, except during detoxification.
- Education of mental health clinicians that the idea of a "higher power" is not necessarily a religious concept but instead a reflection of the patient's need to accept help from a "power greater than himself" (15). For the dual-diagnosis patient, this concept can mean accepting the power of medication and the prescribing physician in treating psychosis or the power of attending AA for treating addiction.
- Acknowledgment that although dual-diagnosis group meetings may be desirable for these patients (11), they are not sufficiently available to permit daily attendance. Therefore, patients who learn to use AA on a regular basis (four to seven meetings per week) have a better chance of maintaining sobriety (10).
- Demonstration to both mental health and addiction clinicians that with special preparation (11) dual-diagnosis patients can participate in and benefit from AA and NA.

Special preparation at the Caulfield Center includes individualized education on how to behave in meetings, patient participation in a weekly dual-diagnosis group, selection of meetings that are most suitable for dual-diagnosis patients by staff who are themselves recovering from addiction, integration of dual-diagnosis patients with nonpsychotic addicts for both meetings and groups so that they do not stand out, and consideration of resistance to AA participation as a manifestation of denial of addiction rather than as inherent in a chronic psychosis. For example, psychotic patients who say they are too paranoid to attend AA often admit they are not too paranoid to enter far more dangerous settings to obtain alcohol or drugs.

As training in the implementation of this integrated treatment approach has proceeded, and as clinicians have observed medicated, dual-diagnosis patients becoming sober through AA involvement, philosophic disagreements about the merits of AA and medication have shifted to individualized clinical discussions about the best technique for integrating AA and medication for each dual-diagnosis patient. Increasingly, clinicians from both areas have adopted the belief that in dual-diagnosis patients, once the primary psychosis is stabilized with medication, the addiction can be treated much like addiction in any other patient.

CONCLUSIONS

This paper has described a model for integrating treatment of patients with a dual diagnosis of addiction and psychosis in a general hospital psychiatric unit. The model uses parallel concepts of disease and recovery for psychosis and addiction. However, despite the model's potential value for treating dual-diagnosis patients, there are limits to its generalizability.

First, the model was developed in a short-term acute care setting in which there was a clear administrative mandate to develop a hybrid program; generalizability to other settings may be limited. Second, this model was developed in a setting in which a psychiatric program was incorporated into an addiction unit; the integrated model may not work as well in the reverse situation. Third, the model was developed in an urban area with a great variety, proximity, and flexibility of 12-step programs; other areas may not provide similar availability of adaptable addiction treatment resources.

Finally, the integrated model emphasizes similarities and parallels between treatment for addiction and treatment for psychiatric illness. The assumption that most, if not all, philosophic differences between psychiatric and addiction treatment can be resolved through the use of this approach remains to be tested in other settings with controlled research.

REFERENCES

1. Pepper B, Kirshner MC, Ryglewicz H: The young adult chronic patient: overview of a population. *Hospital and Community Psychiatry* 32:463-469, 1981
2. Schwartz SR, Goldfinger SM: The new chronic patient: clinical characteristics of an emerging subgroup. *Hospital and Community Psychiatry* 32:470-474, 1981
3. Alterman AI: Substance abuse in psychiatric patients, in Substance Abuse and Psychopathology. Edited by Alterman AI. New York: Plenum, 1985
4. Safer D: Substance abuse by young adult chronic patients. *Hospital and Community Psychiatry* 38:511-514, 1987
5. McCarrick AK, Manderscheid RW, Bettolucci DE: Correlates of acting-out behaviors among young adult chronic patients. *Hospital and Community Psychiatry* 36:848-853, 1985

6. Ridgely MS, Goldman HH, Talbott JA: *Chronic Mentally Ill Young Adults With Substance Abuse Problems: A Review of Relevant Literature and Creation of a Research Agenda*. Baltimore, Mental Health Policy Studies Center, University of Maryland, 1986

7. Galanter M, Castaneda R, Ferman J: Substance abuse among general psychiatric patients: place of presentation, diagnosis, and treatment. *American Journal of Drug and Alcohol Abuse* 14:211-235, 1988

8. Bachrach LL: The context of care for the chronic mental patient with substance abuse. *Psychiatric Quarterly* 58:3-14, 1986-87

9. Barry H III: Psychiatric illness of alcoholics, in *Substance Abuse and Psychiatric Illness*. Edited by Gottheil E, McLellan AT, Druley KA. New York, Pergamon, 1980

10. Kofoed L, Kania J, Walsh T, et al: Outpatient treatment of patients with substance abuse and coexisting psychiatric disorders. *American Journal of Psychiatry* 143:867-872, 1986

11. Ridgely MS, Osher FC, Talbott JA: *Chronic Mentally Ill Young Adults With Substance Abuse Problems: Treatment and Training Issues*. Baltimore, Mental Health Policy Studies Center, University of Maryland, 1987

12. *Diagnostic and Statistical Manual of Mental Disorders*, 3rd ed, rev. Washington, DC, American Psychiatric Association, 1987

13. *Living Sober*. New York, Alcoholics Anonymous World Services, 1975

14. *Alcoholics Anonymous*, 3rd ed. New York, Alcoholics Anonymous World Services, 1976

15. *Twelve Steps and Twelve Traditions*. New York, Alcoholics Anonymous World Services, 1952

16. Lamb HR: *Treating the Long-Term Mentally Ill*. San Francisco, Jossey-Bass, 1982

17. Strauss JS, Boker W, Brenner HD (eds): *Psychosocial Treatment of Schizophrenia*. Toronto, Hans Huber, 1987

18. Holden C: Is alcoholism treatment effective? *Science* 236:20-22, 1987

19. Donovan JM: An etiologic model of alcoholism. *American Journal of Psychiatry* 143:1-11,1986

20. Nace EP: Recent advances in alcohol and drug treatment. Presented at the 40th Institute on Hospital and Community Psychiatry, New Orleans, Oct 22-27, 1988

21. Gawin FH, Kleger HD, Bych R, et al: Desipramine facilitation of initial cocaine abstinence. *Archives of General Psychiatry* 46:117-121, 1989

22. Strauss JS, Harding CM, Hafez H, et al: The role of the patient in recovery from psychosis, in *Psychosocial Treatment of Schizophrenia*. Edited by Strauss JS, Boker W, Brenner HD. Toronto, Hans Huber, 1987

23. Khantzian EJ: The self-medication hypothesis of addictive disorders: focus on heroin and cocaine dependence. *American Journal of Psychiatry* 142:1259-1264, 1985

24. Drake RE, Osher FC, Wallach MA: Alcohol use and abuse in schizophrenia: a prospective community study. *Journal of Nervous and Mental Disease* 177:408-414, 1989

25. Minkoff K: Beyond deinstitutionalization: a new ideology for the postinstitutional era. *Hospital and Community Psychiatry* 38:945-950, 1987

26. Harding CM, Brooks GW, Ashikaga T, et al: The Vermont longitudinal study of persons with severe mental illness, II: long-term outcome of subjects who retrospectively met DSM-III criteria for schizophrenia. *American Journal of Psychiatry* 144:727-735, 1987
27. Greenfeld D: The Psychotic Patient. New Haven, Conn, Yale University Press, 1987
28. Hoffman H, Noem AA: Criteria for the differentiation of success and failure in alcoholism treatment outcome. *Psychological Reports* 39:887-893, 1976

ABOUT THE AUTHOR

Kenneth Minkoff, M.D., is Chief of Psychiatry at Choate-Symmes Health Services, Woburn, MA.

ACKNOWLEDGMENTS

This paper was part of a special section in *Hospital and Community Psychiatry* on patients with dual diagnoses of mental illness and substance abuse.

Copyright 1989. The American Psychiatric Association. Reprinted by permission.

TREATMENT OF SUBSTANCE ABUSE IN SEVERELY MENTALLY ILL PATIENTS

Robert E. Drake, Stephen J. Bartels, Gregory B. Teague,
Douglas L. Noordsy, and Robin E. Clark

Reprinted from *Journal of Nervous and Mental Disease*, 181:606-611, 1993

Substance abuse is the most common comorbid complication of severe mental illness. Current clinical research converges on several emerging principles of treatment that address the scope, pace, intensity, and structure of dual-diagnosis programs. They include a) assertive outreach to facilitate engagement and participation in substance abuse treatment, b) close monitoring to provide structure and social reinforcement, c) integrating substance abuse and mental health interventions in the same program, d) comprehensive, broad-based services to address other problems of adjustment, e) safe and protective living environments, f) flexibility of clinicians and programs, g) stage-wise treatment to ensure the appropriate timing of interventions, h) a longitudinal perspective that is congruent with the chronicity of dual disorders, and i) optimism.

Substance use disorders are increasingly recognized as frequent comorbid conditions that adversely affect the adjustment of persons with severe mental illnesses (Minkoff and Drake, 1991). Approximately 50% of persons with severe mental disorders develop alcohol or other drug use disorders at some point in their lives, and the rate of dual diagnosis is even higher among those who are in clinical settings (Regier et al., 1990). Substance abuse among severely mentally ill patients is associated with a variety of problems, such as symptomatic worsening, disruptive behavior, homelessness, and institutionalization (Alterman et al., 1980; Bartels et al., 1993; Carey et al., 1991; Drake et al., 1989, 1991c).

The rapidly developing literature on dual-diagnosis treatment reflects substantial progress since the original Alcohol, Drug Abuse, and Mental Health Administration reviews of treatment, training, and policy issues in the mid-1980s (Ridgely et al., 1986, 1987). Randomized clinical trials currently underway (National Institute on Alcohol Abuse and Alcoholism, 1991; National Institute of Mental Health, 1989) will add significantly to knowledge in this area. Nevertheless, current findings from a variety of clinical demonstrations and clinical research studies merit discussion at this time because many state and local mental health authorities are actively developing and implementing dual-diagnosis programs for severely mentally ill persons.

The aim of this paper is, therefore, to identify and clarify emerging treatment principles from current clinical research related to the treatment of substance use disorder among severely mentally ill patients. To develop these principles, we have surveyed the published clinical research, reviewed the 13 demonstration projects on young adults with serious mental illness and substance abuse problems funded by the NIMH between 1987 and 1990 (Mercer-McFadden and Drake, in press; Teague et al., 1990b), and drawn extensively from our work in progress at the New Hampshire-Dartmouth Psychiatric Research Center.

PRINCIPLES OF TREATMENT

We will review nine principles: assertiveness, close monitoring, integration, comprehensiveness, stable living environment, flexibility and specialization, stages of treatment, longitudinal perspective, and optimism. These principles denote structural elements that underlie successful programs rather than specific clinical procedures or guidelines. Our review begins with the cross-sectional scope and intensity of services and moves to their longitudinal pace and pattern.

Assertiveness

Successful programs incorporate active interventions, such as outreach in the community and assurance of practical assistance with basic needs, as a precondition for effective, continuous engagement in treatment. Furthermore, they assertively address substance abuse as a central problem that destabilizes severe mental illness and interferes with rehabilitation.

People with dual disorders tend to be noncompliant with treatment (Drake and Wallach, 1989; Pristach and Smith, 1990; Safer, 1987). They do not fit well into either the mental health system or the substance abuse system; they often appear unmotivated for treatment; and they are difficult to engage in outpatient treatment or rehabilitation programs (Ridgely et al., 1990).

Treatment, therefore, needs to be assertive and flexible, with an emphasis on outreach and practical assistance. Assertive interventions include meeting patients where they live, work, and pass time; providing medication management, skills training, and general assistance in the community; and working with family members, landlords, employers, and others who may be able to provide support. In addition, assertiveness often entails close monitoring, such as using payeeships, guardianships, or legal sanctions as inducements to engage in treatment (discussed below).

One common approach to assertive treatment involves interdisciplinary teams, often called continuous treatment teams, that take full responsibility for a small but discrete group of patients, with an explicit focus on engagement and stabilization (Test, 1990; Torrey, 1986). For example, continuous treatment teams in New Hampshire's community mental health centers combine assertive case management, mental health treatment, and substance abuse treatment (Drake et al., 1990b, 1991a)—an approach that has been successful in engaging dually diagnosed patients in long-term treatment (Drake et al., 1993b).

Once dually diagnosed patients are involved with a continuous treatment team, assertive approaches can also be used to connect them with substance abuse treatments. For example, among 240 dually diagnosed patients in one study, those randomly assigned to continuous treatment teams, which have low caseloads and provide extensive outreach, rather than standard case management services were six times as likely to attend dual-diagnosis treatment groups (Teague et al., 1990a).

Close monitoring

Close monitoring refers to intensive supervision, which is sometimes provided with the patient's consent and at other times on an involuntary basis. Various forms of intensive supervision are often necessary to initiate and sustain early treatment. For people who are not psychiatrically disabled, close monitoring improves outcomes for the treatment of alcoholism (Moos et al., 1990), cocaine addiction (Higgins et al., 1991), and narcotics dependence (Vaillant, 1966). Close monitoring may be even more important for patients whose lives are ravaged by two chronic illnesses with the resultant instability, lack of insight, poor judgment, self-destructiveness, and demoralization.

Disability often renders dually diagnosed persons dependent on several systems—mental health, welfare, legal, housing, and family—that can provide a range of options for close monitoring. For example, when public entitlements are being used for alcohol and other drugs, legal procedures such as payeeships and protective guardianships can help dually diagnosed persons to manage their funds. For patients who have engaged in crimes or dangerous behaviors, substance abuse treatment can sometimes be included in the conditions of probation, parole, outpatient commitment, or conditional discharge from the hospital. Pharmacological treatments, such as antipsychotic drugs and disulfiram, and urine drug tests can also be mandated and supervised by staff (Nikkel and Coiner, 1991; Osher and Kofoed, 1989). In addition, mental health systems often have available a continuum of supervised living situations (Bebout and Harris, 1992) and day treatment settings (Carey, 1989a), in which close monitoring can be provided as needed.

Clinicians' experiences across a range of programs indicate that these methods of close monitoring, ranging from voluntary to involuntary, are key components of dual-diagnosis treatment (Mercer-McFadden and Drake, in press). Patients themselves often report ambivalence regarding involuntary interventions—they fear losing independence but recognize that some external controls may be necessary and helpful. As they recover from substance abuse, patients typically need less intensive supervision and steadily move toward genuine independence.

Integration

Combining mental health and substance abuse interventions in a concurrent and coordinated fashion is referred to as integrated treatment (Minkoff and Drake, 1991). For historical reasons, the mental health and substance abuse systems are quite separate. Extruding patients from each system because of the other disorder remains common (Ridgely et al., 1990). For example, active alcohol abuse frequently results in exclusion from psychiatric treatment centers, while active psychosis prevents admission to alcohol treatment units. Treating only one disorder or treating the two disorders sequentially also generally fails because the overlooked disorder frequently undermines treatment of the targeted disorder. For example, patients who are actively drinking and using drugs show poor compliance with prescribed antipsychotic medications (Drake et al., 1989; Pristach and Smith, 1990).

Concurrent, parallel treatments in the two systems—another common approach to dual diagnosis—often results in fragmented, contradictory, and inadequate care. Parallel treatment is problematic for several reasons: It places on the patient the burden of integrating two systems with disparate philosophies, treatments, and clinicians; it allows each system to continue to provide a standard form of treatment and to resist specific modifications for special populations; and it maximizes the potential for miscommunications, contradictory recommendations, and noncompliance (Galanter et al., 1988; Kline et al., 1991; Ridgely et al., 1990; Wallen and Weiner, 1989). Too often, the patient in parallel treatment becomes lost between the two treatment systems.

Integrated treatment programs, in which the same clinicians provide mental health and substance abuse treatments in the same setting, have been demonstrably effective, at least in open clinical trials. Kofoed and colleagues (1986) treated 32 dually diagnosed patients in a group setting and found that those who remained in treatment for 1 year (34%) had a reduced rate of hospitalization. Hellerstein and Meehan (1987) found that 10 substance-abusing schizophrenic patients who participated in a weekly outpatient dual-diagnosis group reduced their days in the hospital during 1 year of treatment. Ries and Ellingson (1989) found that 12 of 17 dually diagnosed patients (70.6%) who attended drug and alcohol discussion groups while in the hospital were abstinent 1 month after discharge. Bond and colleagues (1991) found that 19 young adults with major mental illness and substance use disorder who were treated in a dual diagnosis group for 18 months reduced their use of marijuana, though not of alcohol and other drugs. Drake et al. (1993b) found that 11 of 18 schizophrenic patients with alcohol use disorders (61%) achieved stable remission from alcoholism during 4 years in an integrated treatment program that included assertive case management and substance abuse treatment groups. Lehman and colleagues (1993) found that 29 dually diagnosed patients assigned to an experimental group intervention showed no improvements in substance abuse but had fewer days in the hospital during 1-year follow-up than a control group. Most of these studies are limited by small samples, brief follow-ups, lack of controls, and insufficient data on the natural history of substance abuse in this population. Nevertheless, these are the best clinical studies currently available.

Substance abuse treatment can be integrated into most community mental health programs as a core component at a relatively low cost (Bartels and Drake, 1991). The substance abuse treatment can be provided on an individual basis by clinical case managers or continuous treatment teams and in groups by the same staff. The expense of initiating such a program involves little more than educating and supporting the clinical staff while they develop skills for treating dual disorders.

Comprehensiveness

Comprehensive treatment programs address not just the specific manifestations of a disorder, but a wide range of skills, activities, relationships, and supports. Substance abuse treatment for non-dually diagnosed persons is most effective when it is broad based and comprehensive (McLellan et al., 1992; Miller, 1990). Living context, relationships, and vocational and interpersonal skills are critically related to engagement in treatment (Higgins et al., 1991) and to long-term recovery (Moos et al., 1990). Persons with problems related to substance abuse typically need structure, such as new relationships and activities, in their lives. Long-term follow-up studies indicate that recovery typically occurs during intervals of increased structure rather than during episodes of intensive treatment (Vaillant, 1983).

The need for broad-based, comprehensive treatment is even more evident in people who have co-occurring severe mental illness, because they tend to be deficient in the skills, relationships, supports, and living contexts that are associated with stable recovery from substance abuse (Mercer-McFadden and Drake, in press). Mental health programs organized according to the community support system model (Stroul, 1989) have an advantage over other programs that would need to create extensive new services or link their services with outside agencies in a parallel treatment model. In a dual-diagnosis program, each of the service components may need to be modified in correspondence with the complexities of dual diagnosis. For example, family psychoeducation includes information on not only mental illness, but also substance abuse and dual diagnosis (Ryglewicz, 1991).

Stable living situation

Dually diagnosed persons need to have access to a range of housing options that provide safety, freedom from alcohol and drugs, support, and companionship. Living situation critically affects recovery from alcoholism for nonpsychiatrically impaired persons as well; the posttreatment environment predicts outcomes more strongly than the treatment environment across a range of inpatient and residential alcohol treatment programs (Moos et al., 1990). Persons with severe mental illness, especially in urban areas, tend to reside in drug-infested neighborhoods and settings for the homeless (Belcher, 1989; Drake et al., 1989, 1991b). The toxicity of the living environment, including the ubiquity of drugs, may explain why dually diagnosed individuals in urban areas are often attracted to the hospital as a living environment (Drake and Wallach, 1992). Clinicians who work with homeless dually diagnosed persons observe that active treatment and recovery are difficult, if not impossible, without access to decent housing (Drake et al., 1991b).

A significant proportion of these patients do well while in hospitals or residential treatment settings, but have difficulty transferring gains or skills for maintaining abstinence to the community. For example, Bartels and Thomas (1991) found that 17 of 46 patients (37%) admitted to a dual-diagnosis residential program had no difficulty maintaining abstinence for 3 months, but all relapsed soon after discharge to their usual community living situation. Conversely, dually diagnosed patients who achieved and maintained stable recovery in several studies typically resided in supportive housing situations in the community (Bartels et al., 1993; Mercer-McFadden and Drake, in press). For example, in a Washington, DC study of 168 homeless, dually diagnosed patients, the vast majority of those who are achieving stable abstinence are living in structured, congregate living settings (Drake et al., 1993a).

Flexibility and specialization

Since dual-diagnosis treatment differs from traditional substance abuse and mental health treatments, successful administrators and clinicians modify previous beliefs, learn new skills, and try new approaches empirically; they become dual-diagnosis specialists (Mercer-McFadden and Drake, in press; Minkoff and Drake, 1991). Clinicians with a substance abuse treatment background alter previous approaches based on basic information about treating major mental illness. For example, confrontation and other intensive, emotionally charged interventions are often ineffective and increase the risk of dropout or relapse of psychiatric symptoms in this population; effective treatments proceed slowly and gently, with a low level of affect, a high level of structure, and attention to psychotic vulnerability (Carey, 1989b; Fariello and Scheidt, 1989). At the same time, mental health clinicians alter their approaches in accordance with basic facts about drugs of abuse and addictive behaviors. They learn to discern cognitive changes that are due to drugs rather than to mental illness, to use laboratory tests for monitoring drug use, to be aware of behaviors and interventions that are reinforcing (or enabling) substance abuse, and to help their patients develop skills for achieving and maintaining abstinence (Drake et al., 1993a).

Stages of treatment

Substance abuse can be conceptualized as a chronic, relapsing disorder that is to some extent independent of the mental illness, and that is treatable in a program oriented toward rehabilitation and recovery (Minkoff, 1989). Like the treatment of major mental illness, substance abuse treatment proceeds in stages. Osher and Kofoed (1989) conceptualized four stages—engagement, persuasion, active treatment, and relapse prevention—that refer to overlapping processes: developing a trusting relationship, or working alliance, with the patient (engagement); helping the patient to perceive the adverse consequences of substance use in his or her life and to develop motivation for recovery (persuasion); helping the patient to achieve stable recovery, whether that is controlled use or abstinence (active treatment); and helping the patient to maintain a stable recovery (relapse prevention).

A stage model of treatment serves mainly heuristic purposes, since treatment rarely proceeds in a linear pathway. Patients typically cycle back and forth between engagement and persuasion early in treatment and may also relapse from active treatment or relapse prevention stages. The stage model does, however, guide clinicians in planning and deciding what interventions are appropriate at a particular point in time. For example, since many of these patients do not perceive their substance use as problematic (Drake et al., 1990a; Test et al., 1989), insisting on abstinence when they are in the engagement stage of treatment often drives them away from treatment. Once engagement occurs, clinical work involves helping them gradually to develop awareness of the negative consequences of using alcohol and other drugs by observing and reviewing the effects of many episodes of substance use over time (Kofoed and Keys, 1988; Noordsy and Fox, 1991), often in the context of crisis intervention and stabilization (Fariello and Scheidt, 1989; Nikkel and Coiner, 1991).

The longitudinal perspective

Substance abuse is a chronic, relapsing disorder. The need for a longitudinal perspective in viewing severe mental disorders like schizophrenia (Group for the Advancement of Psychiatry, 1992) applies equally to substance abuse (Vaillant, 1983). Treatment occurs continuously over years rather than episodically or during crises. Progress can be observed and measured after years rather than weeks or months. For example, the 11 schizophrenic patients with alcoholism who became stably abstinent in our pilot program in New Hampshire did so after an average of 2 years of treatment (Drake et al., 1993b).

Standard substance abuse treatment in the United States has been criticized for concentrating service resources at the beginning phase of treatment in a brief but intensive and expensive model, such as the 28-day inpatient treatment model, with minimal follow-up care (Holder et al., 1991). Most controlled studies do not show that intensive inpatient treatment for alcoholism is superior to outpatient treatment (Holder et al., 1991; McLellan et al., 1992; Miller and Hester, 1986). Longitudinal research also demonstrates that recovery from alcoholism (Vaillant, 1983) or narcotics addiction (Vaillant, 1966) usually occurs over years.

Experience with dually diagnosed patients also supports the need for a long-term perspective. Stable recovery from substance abuse does not typically occur in the first year of treatment, perhaps because most patients are in the persuasion stage and are not yet ready for active treatment (Lehman et al., 1993). The majority of these patients are unable to benefit from intensive residential substance abuse treatment. For example, we found that nearly two thirds of the 46 dually diagnosed patients admitted to an intensive, 90-day, residential treatment program left prematurely (Bartels and Thomas, 1991). Of the 11 schizophrenic patients with alcoholism who became stably abstinent in another study, none did so in conjunction with an inpatient substance abuse admission, while all recovered gradually in the context of outpatient dual-diagnosis treatment (Drake et al., 1993b).

Optimism

Patients, families, and treatment providers need to have hope for recovery. Demoralization among patients and their families occurs almost inevitably as part of adjusting to a chronic illness (Frank, 1974; Smyer and Birkel, 1991). People with dual disorders are particularly likely to become discouraged and hopeless about the future—a state often misconstrued and labeled as poor motivation. Defining motivation as a fixed attribute can result in blaming the patient for treatment failure, whereas conceptualizing motivation as a psychological state emphasizes that motivation can be influenced by various psychological and behavioral strategies (Miller, 1985).

Treatment of chronic illness inevitably addresses demoralization (Frank, 1974). As patients begin to trust their caregivers and to experience some improvement, their attitudes typically change. They develop some hope for the future, greater expectations for themselves, and more wishes and demands for treatment. They, therefore, appear to be more motivated. Families go through parallel stages in adjusting to their relatives' chronic illnesses (Tessler et al., 1987). Clinicians also tend to be pessimistic about treating dual disorders.

Observations of successful dual-diagnosis treatment programs indicate that patients, families, and caregivers achieve and maintain a hopeful attitude toward recovery (Mercer-McFadden and Drake, in press). For example, rather than extruding or rejecting patients who appear to be unmotivated, clinicians recognize that motivation appears naturally during the persuasion stage of treatment. Several mechanisms can serve to enhance and maintain clinicians' optimism. In New Hampshire, the dual-diagnosis teams from across the state meet monthly for peer supervision and training sessions. These meetings serve not only to increase knowledge and skills, but also to develop a secure identity for team members as dual-diagnosis specialists.

CONCLUSIONS

Despite the lack of controlled clinical trials, our review of demonstration programs and clinical research has identified several emerging principles of dual-diagnosis treatment. These elements are common to successful dual-diagnosis programs: an assertive style of engagement, techniques of close monitoring, integration of mental health and substance abuse treatments, comprehensive services, supportive living environments, flexibility and specialization of clinicians, stage-wise treatment, a long-term perspective, and optimism.

REFERENCES

Alterman AI, Erdlen FR, McLellan AT, Mann SC (1980) Problem drinking in hospitalized schizophrenic patients. *Addictive Behaviors* 5:273-276.

Bartels SJ, Drake RE (1991) Dual diagnosis: New directions and challenges. *California Journal of the Alliance for the Mentally Ill* 2:6-7.

Bartels SJ, Teague GB, Drake RE, Clark RE, Bush P, Noordsy DL (1993) Service utilization and costs associated with substance abuse among rural schizophrenic patients. *Journal of Nervous and Mental Disease* 181:227-232.

Bartels SJ, Thomas WN (1991) Lessons from a pilot residential treatment program for people with dual diagnoses of severe mental illness and substance use disorder. *Psychosocial Rehabilitation Journal* 15:19-30.

Bebout RR, Harris M (1992) In search of pumpkin shells: Residential programming for the homeless mentally ill. In HR Lamb, LL Bachrach, FI Kass (Eds), *Treating the homeless mentally ill* (pp. 159-181). Washington, DC: American Psychiatric Press.

Belcher JR (1989) On becoming homeless: A study of chronically mentally ill persons. *Journal of Community Psychology* 17:173-185.

Bond GR, McDonel EC, Miller LD, Pensec M (1991) Assertive community treatment and reference groups: An evaluation of their effectiveness for young adults with serious mental illness and substance abuse problems. *Psychosocial Rehabilitation Journal* 15:31-43.

Carey KB (1989a) Treatment of the mentally ill chemical abuser: Description of the Hutchings day treatment program. *Psychiatric Quarterly* 60:303-316.

Carey KB (1989b) Emerging treatment guidelines for mentally ill chemical abusers. *Hospital and Community Psychiatry* 40:341-342, 349.

Carey MP, Carey KB, Meisler AW (1991) Psychiatric symptoms in mentally ill chemical abusers. *Journal of Nervous and Mental Disease* 179:136-138.

Drake RE, Antosca L, Noordsy DL, Bartels SJ, Osher FC (1991a) New Hampshire's specialized services for people dually diagnosed with severe mental illness and substance use disorder. In K Minkoff, RE Drake (Eds), *Dual diagnosis of major mental illness and substance disorder* (pp. 57-67). San Francisco: Jossey-Bass.

Drake RE, Bebout RR, Quimby E, Teague GB, Harris M, Roach J (1993a) Process evaluation in the Washington, DC dual diagnosis project. *Alcoholism Treatment Quarterly* 10:113-124.

Drake RE, McHugo GJ, Noordsy DL (1993b) A pilot study of outpatient treatment of alcoholism in schizophrenia: Four-year outcomes. *American Journal of Psychiatry* 150:328-329.

Drake RE, Osher FC, Noordsy DL, Hurlbut SC, Teague GB, Beaudett MD (1990a) Diagnosis of alcohol use disorder in schizophrenia. *Schizophrenia Bulletin* 16:57-67.

Drake RE, Osher FC, Wallach MA (1989) Alcohol use and abuse in schizophrenia: A prospective community study. *Journal of Nervous and Mental Disease* 177:408-414.

Drake RE, Osher FC, Wallach MA (1991b) Homelessness and dual diagnosis. *American Psychologist* 46:1149-1158.

Drake RE, Teague GB, Warren RS (1990b) New Hampshire's dual diagnosis program for people with severe mental illness and substance use disorder. *Addiction and Recovery* 10:35-39.

Drake RE, Wallach MA (1989) Substance abuse among the chronic mentally ill. *Hospital and Community Psychiatry* 40:1041-1046.

Drake RE, Wallach MA (1992) Mental patients' attraction to the hospital: Correlates of living preference. *Community Mental Health Journal* 28:5-11.

Drake RE, Wallach MA, Teague GB, Freeman DH, Paskus TS, Clark TA (1991c) Housing instability and homelessness among rural schizophrenic patients. *American Journal of Psychiatry* 145:330-336.

Fariello D, Scheidt S (1989) Clinical case management of the dually diagnosed patient. *Hospital and Community Psychiatry* 40:1065-1067.

Frank JD (1974) *Persuasion and healing.* New York: Schocken Books.

Galanter M, Castenada R, Ferman J (1988) Substance abuse among general psychiatric patients: Place of presentation, diagnosis, and treatment. *American Journal of Drug & Alcohol Abuse* 142:211-235.

Group for the Advancement of Psychiatry (1992) *Beyond symptom suppression: Improving long-term outcomes of schizophrenia.* Washington, DC: American Psychiatric Press.

Hellerstein DJ, Meehan B (1987) Outpatient group therapy for schizophrenic substance abusers. *American Journal of Psychiatry* 144:1337-1339.

Higgins ST, Delaney DD, Budney AJ, Bickel WK, Hughes JR, Foerg F, Fenwick JW (1991) A behavioral approach to achieving initial cocaine abstinence. *American Journal of Psychiatry* 148:1218-1224.

Holder H, Longabaugh R, Miller WR, Rubonis AV (1991) The cost effectiveness of treatment for alcoholism: A first approximation. *Journal of Studies on Alcohol* 52:517-540.

Kline J, Bebout RR, Harris M, Drake RE (1991) A comprehensive treatment program for dually diagnosed homeless people in Washington, DC. In K Minkoff, RE Drake (Eds), *Dual diagnosis of major mental illness and substance disorder* (pp. 95-106). San Francisco: Jossey-Bass.

Kofoed LL, Kania J, Walsh T, Atkinson RM (1986) Outpatient treatment of patients with substance abuse and coexisting psychiatric disorders. *American Journal of Psychiatry* 143:867-872.

Kofoed LL, Keys A (1988) Using group therapy to persuade dual-diagnosis patients to seek substance abuse treatment *Hospital and Community Psychiatry* 39:1209-1211.

Lehman AF, Herron JD, Schwartz RP (1993) Rehabilitation for young adults with severe mental illness and substance use disorders: A clinical trial. *Journal of Nervous and Mental Disease* 181:86-90.

McLellan AT, Metzger D, Alterman AI, Cornish J, Urschel H (1992) How effective is substance abuse treatment—compared to what? In CP O'Brien, J Jaffe (Eds), *Advances in understanding the addictive states* (pp. 232-252). New York: Association for Research in Nervous and Mental Disease.

Mercer-McFadden C, Drake RE (in press) *A review of 13 NIMH demonstration projects for young adults with severe mental illness and substance abuse problems.* Rockville, MD: Community Support Program, Center for Mental Health Services, U.S. Department of Health and Human Services. Manuscript in preparation.

Miller WR (1985) Motivation for treatment: A review with special emphasis on alcoholism. *Psychological Bulletin* 98:84-107.

Miller WR (1990) Alcohol treatment alternatives: What works? In HB Milkman, LI Sederer (Eds), *Matching substance abuse patients and treatments* (pp. 253-264). Lexington, MA: D.C. Heath.

Miller WR, Hester RK (1986) Inpatient alcoholism treatment: Who benefits? *American Psychologist* 41:794-805.

Minkoff K (1989) An integrated treatment model for dual diagnosis of psychosis and addiction. *Hospital and Community Psychiatry* 40:1031-1036.

Minkoff K, Drake RE (Eds) (1991) *Dual diagnosis of major mental illness and substance disorder.* San Francisco: Jossey-Bass.

Moos RH, Finney JW, Cronkite RC (1990) *Alcoholism treatment: Context, process, and outcome.* New York: Oxford.

National Institute on Alcohol Abuse and Alcoholism (1991) *Synopses of cooperative agreements for research demonstration projects on alcohol and other drug abuse treatment for homeless persons.* Rockville, MD: U.S. Department of Health and Human Services.

National Institute of Mental Health (1989) *Currently funded research grants on services for persons with mental disorders that co-occur with alcohol and/or drug abuse disorders.* Rockville, MD: Division of Biometry and Applied Sciences.

Nikkel R, Coiner R (1991) Critical interventions and tasks in delivering dual diagnosis services. *Psychosocial Rehabilitation Journal* 15:57-66.

Noordsy DL, Fox L (1991) Group intervention techniques for people with dual disorders. *Psychosocial Rehabilitation Journal* 15:67-78.

Osher FC, Kofoed LL (1989) Treatment of patients with psychiatric and psychoactive substance abuse disorders. *Hospital and Community Psychiatry* 40: 1025-1030.

Pristach CA, Smith CM (1990) Medication compliance and substance abuse among schizophrenic patients. *Hospital and Community Psychiatry* 41:1345-1348.

Regier DA, Farmer ME, Rae DS, Locke BZ, Keith SJ, Judd LL, Goodwin FK (1990) Comorbidity of mental disorders with alcohol and other drug abuse: Results from the Epidemiologic Catchment Area (ECA) study. *Journal of the American Medical Association* 264:2511-2518.

Ridgely MS, Goldman HH, Talbott JA (1986) *Chronic mentally ill young adults with substance abuse problems: A review of the literature and creation of a research agenda.* Baltimore: University of Maryland Mental Health Policy Studies Center.

Ridgely MS, Goldman HR, Willenbring M (1990) Barriers to the care of persons with dual diagnoses: Organizational and financing issues. *Schizophrenia Bulletin* 16:123-132.

Ridgely MS, Osher FC, Talbott JA (1987) *Chronic mentally ill young adults with substance abuse problems: Treatment and training issues.* Baltimore: University of Maryland Mental Health Policy Studies Center.

Ries RK, Ellingson T (1989) A pilot assessment at one month of 17 dual diagnosis patients. *Hospital and Community Psychiatry* 41:1230-1233.

Ryglewicz H (1991) Psychoeducation for clients and families: A way in, out, and through in working with people with dual disorders. *Psychosocial Rehabilitation Journal* 15:79-89.

Safer DJ (1987) Substance abuse by young adult chronic patients. *Hospital and Community Psychiatry* 38:511-514.

Smyer MA, Birkel RC (1991) Research focused on intervention with families of the chronically mentally ill elderly. In E Light, B Lebowitz (Eds), *The elderly with chronic mental illness* (pp. 111-130). New York: Springer Publishing.

Stroul BA (1989) Community support systems for persons with long-term mental illness: A conceptual framework. *Psychosocial Rehabilitation Journal* 12:9-26.

Teague GB, Drake RE, McKenna P, Schwab B (1990a) *Implementation analysis of continuous treatment teams for dually diagnosed clients.* Presented at the NIMH Community Support Program conference, Washington, DC.

Teague GB, Schwab B, Drake RE (1990b) *Evaluating programs for young adults with severe mental illness and substance use disorder.* Arlington, VA: National Association of State Mental Health Program Directors.

Tessler RC, Killian LM, Gubman GC (1987) Stages in family response to mental illness: An ideal type. *Psychosocial Rehabilitation Journal* 10:3-16.

Test MA (1990) *The training in community living model: Delivering treatment and rehabilitation services through a continuous treatment team.* Madison, WI: Mental Health Research Center.

Test MA, Wallisch L, Allness DJ, Burke SS (1989) Substance use in young adults with schizophrenic disorders. *Schizophrenia Bulletin* 15:465-476.

Torrey EF (1986) Continuous treatment teams in the care of the chronic mentally ill. *Hospital and Community Psychiatry* 37:1243-1247.

Vaillant GE (1966) A twelve-year follow-up of New York narcotic addicts: IV. Some characteristics and determinants of abstinence. *American Journal of Psychiatry* 123:573-584.

Vaillant GE (1983) *The natural history of alcoholism.* Cambridge, MA: Harvard University Press.

Wallen MC, Weiner HD (1989) Impediments to effective treatment of the dually diagnosed patient. *Journal of Psychoactive Drugs* 21:161-168.

ABOUT THE AUTHORS

Robert E. Drake, M.D., Ph.D., Stephen J. Bartels, M.D., Gregory B. Teague, Ph.D., Douglas L. Noordsy, M.D., and Robin E. Clark, Ph.D., are affiliated with the New Hampshire-Dartmouth Psychiatric Research Center, Concord, NH.

ACKNOWLEDGMENTS

This study was supported by Robert Wood Johnson Foundation grant 13539, NIMH grants R18-MH-46072 and K02-MH-00839, and NIAAA grants R01-AA-08341 and U01-AA-08840.

Reprinted with permission from *Journal of Nervous and Mental Disease.*

SUBSTANCE USE REDUCTION IN THE CONTEXT OF OUTPATIENT PSYCHIATRIC TREATMENT: A COLLABORATIVE, MOTIVATIONAL, HARM REDUCTION APPROACH

Kate B. Carey

Reprinted from *Community Mental Health Journal*, 32(3):291-306, 1996

A conceptual model for reducing substance use within the context of outpatient psychiatric treatment is described. The proposed model incorporates four themes from the psychological treatment literature: treatment intensity, stages of change, motivational interventions, and harm reduction. The five steps of the model include (1) establishing a working alliance, (2) evaluating the cost-benefit ratio of continued substance use, (3) individualizing goals for change, (4) building an environment and lifestyle supportive of abstinence, and (5) anticipating and coping with crises. This model attempts to integrate clinical realities of mental health treatment with empirically-grounded strategies applicable to substance abuse problems.

Substance abuse exacts an enormous toll on physical and psychological health. Problems stemming from substance use and misuse occur in every segment of society. Negative consequences arising from use of alcohol and/or illicit drugs may be enhanced in persons who already suffer from psychological disabilities. Epidemiological data suggest that persons with mental disorders have three times the risk of alcohol or drug abuse problems than those without mental disorders (Regier et al., 1990). Among certain diagnostic groups, such as schizophrenia, prevalence of substance use disorders approaches 50% (Mueser, et al., 1990; Test, Wallisch, Allness, & Ripp, 1989). Thus, in some mental health treatment settings, comorbidity of substance abuse and mental disorders may be the rule rather than the exception (Bergman & Harris, 1985).

The presence of substance abuse adversely affects the process and outcome of mental health treatment. Persons dually diagnosed with these classes of disorders experience more frequent inpatient hospitalizations (Drake & Wallach, 1989; Safer, 1987), display more hostile behavior and suicidal tendencies (Drake & Wallach, 1989), exhibit poor response to neuroleptic treatments (Bowers, Mazure, Nelson, & Jatlow, 1990), leave the hospital against medical advice more frequently (Hall, Stickney, Gardner, Perl, & LeCann, 1979), and receive aftercare less consistently (Solomon & Davis, 1986). With regard to outpatient treatment, the dually diagnosed exhibit poor medication compliance (Drake & Wallach, 1989; Pristach & Smith, 1990), report greater symptom levels (Carey, Carey, & Meisler, 1991), miss appointments frequently (Hall, Popkin, DeVaul, & Stickney, 1977), and involve themselves minimally in structured treatment programs (Carey & Carey, 1990). Over all, dually diagnosed persons with severe mental illness spend more time not involved in treatment when compared with their non-abusing counterparts (Richardson, Craig, & Haugland, 1985).

Mental health treatment providers have increasingly recognized the need to address substance use among their clients' many treatment needs. Unfortunately, most chemical dependency treatment agencies have neither the staff nor the flexibility in programming to accept many clients with major mental disorders. By necessity, most dual diagnosis clients receive treatment exclusively in the mental health system. However, relatively few treatment models truly integrate psychiatric and substance abuse treatment (e.g., Evans & Sullivan, 1990; Osher & Kofoed, 1989; Minkoff, 1989; Minkoff & Drake, 1991; Rosenthal, Hellerstein, & Miner, 1992). Thus, given the prevalence of clients with substance use disorders in mental health treatment settings, and the generally poor results achieved by standard psychiatric treatment approaches, specific treatment guidelines are needed.

Consider for example, a very basic problem faced by mental health treatment providers when faced with a dual diagnosis client. Although abstinence from nonprescribed drugs and alcohol may be a long-term goal, abstinence is not a realistic or acceptable goal for many clients. What treatment options exist for a therapist or case manager? Withholding treatment is usually not an option for clients in crisis or for those with major Axis I disorders. Their mental illness may require medication therapy, symptom monitoring, and possibly psychosocial interventions. Implementing such a treatment plan necessitates regular contact with mental health treatment staff. What is needed is a model for addressing substance abuse behavior that is consistent with the mental health treatment process, and that offers the option for client-therapist collaboration on mutually acceptable goals.

RELEVANT THEMES

Fortunately, several themes emerge from the literature on psychosocial substance abuse treatments that are relevant to this task. These include providing treatment options of varying intensity, identifying stages of change, motivational interventions, and harm reduction approaches. Each of these themes will be discussed briefly as it relates to the treatment of substance abuse in persons with psychiatric disorders.

Treatment intensity

Recognition of the heterogeneity among abuse patterns and abusers, and the need for multivariate models to understand substance abuse problems (e.g., Blane & Leonard, 1987) has direct implications for treatment. Since alcohol problems vary in scope and severity, the intensity of treatment should be matched to the severity of the disorder (Institute of Medicine, 1990). The Institute of Medicine (1990) recommends that least restrictive treatment options be explored first (e.g., brief interventions, outpatient counseling) and more intensive approaches (e.g., structured inpatient programs) be employed only if necessary. Because many dual diagnosis clients do not experience symptoms of physical dependence and exhibit dysfunction at lower levels of substance use (Drake, Osher, & Wallach, 1989), interventions incorporated into ongoing outpatient mental health treatment are, in many cases, consistent with the Institute of Medicine's recommendations. Since neither inpatient rehabilitation programs nor structured substance abuse treatment programs are available to many of the dually diagnosed, the integration of substance abuse treatment principles into outpatient mental health treatment is also a practical approach.

Stages of change

The second relevant theme is the recognition that substance abusing individuals vary in their readiness to change their behavior. The trans-theoretical model articulated by Prochaska and DiClemente (1992) outlines five stages of change applicable to changing addictive and other problem behaviors: precontemplation, contemplation, active change, maintenance, and relapse. Importantly, different intervention strategies may be appropriate at each stage. For example, drink refusal skills training may be effective for individuals ready for active change and/or maintaining treatment gains; however, it may not be well-accepted by persons in the precontemplation stage who have not yet decided that they need to refuse drinks. Since people cycle in and out of the stages of change, interventions designed to enhance readiness to change may be necessary before people can engage in active treatment strategies.

The stages of change model fits well with a four phase model described by Osher and Kofoed (1989). They proposed that treatment of the dually diagnosed client involves engagement, persuasion, active treatment and relapse prevention. Significantly, the bulk of strategies developed for the treatment of substance use disorders focus on active treatment and relapse prevention. Relatively few interventions address concerns about engaging dual diagnosis clients in treatment, and persuading them that substance use behaviors need to be changed. However, the data documenting poor treatment attendance and compliance suggests that greater attention should be paid to processes of engagement and persuasion. Any model of dual diagnosis treatment must then incorporate awareness of stages of change and include strategies to ready clients for active change.

Motivational interventions

The third theme relevant to the task of treating the dually diagnosed is motivational interviewing (Miller & Rollnick, 1991). Motivational interviewing describes an approach to establishing a collaborative therapeutic alliance and enhancing motivation to change addictive behaviors. This approach is based on a social learning perspective (in contrast to a disease model). Motivational interviewing is designed to minimize resistance to change. Techniques are nonconfrontational, in an effort to avoid the defensiveness and psychological reactance often created by commonly used confrontational approaches. It is assumed that clients are ambivalent about changing their substance use, and must come to their own conclusion about the need to change. Toward this end, the interviewer elicits evidence for alcohol or drug problems and the client is helped to make connections between substance use and frustration of important life goals. Key to this process is enhancement of self-efficacy by focusing on past or present successes in controlling substance use.

Motivational interventions have particular utility with the dually diagnosed for several reasons. First, nonconfrontational interactions are more consistent with the way mental health treatment staff relate to their clients. Clients with schizophrenia, in particular, do not tolerate well emotionally charged interactions, and their inability to benefit from confrontational methods may explain in part their lack of comfort with and success in traditional substance abuse treatment programs. Second, motivational interventions attempt to enhance self-esteem and self-efficacy, both of which tend to be undermined by the many social and developmental disappointments experienced by persons with mental illness (Pepper, Kirshner, & Ryglewicz, 1981). Lastly, motivational interviewing can be enacted over many treatment contacts, gradually marshalling evidence over time for the impact of substance use on a person's functioning.

Harm reduction

The final theme adopted from psychological approaches to addictions treatment is that of harm reduction (e.g., Marlatt & Tapert, 1993). Underlying the harm reduction approach is the notion that substance use exists on a continuum of abstinence to problematic use or abuse. If a person successfully reduces the quantity and/or frequency of substance use, the likelihood of suffering negative consequences should also go down. Although abstinence may constitute the ideal goal, any movement in the direction of reduced use is encouraged. The harm reduction philosophy provides an alternative to traditional abstinence-oriented philosophies, and is more likely to engage persons who will not or cannot embrace abstinence as a goal. Importantly, adopting a harm reduction attitude in treatment does not reject abstinence outcomes; rather, it accepts other outcomes (often on the way to abstinence) if they represent a reduction in the risks associated with substance use.

THE PROPOSED MODEL

Against the backdrop of the treatment themes just articulated, I propose a five-step model for structuring treatment of dual diagnosis clients. This is a pragmatic model, emerging from my own experience (see Carey, 1989), and the shared experiences of many therapists who have worked diligently with substance abusing persons with severe and persistent mental illnesses. The model assumes an outpatient mental health context, broadly defined, that involves a primary therapist or case manager. The five steps include (1) establishing a working alliance, (2) evaluating the cost-benefit ratio of continued substance use, (3) individualizing goals for changes in substance use, (4) building an environment and lifestyle supportive of abstinence, and (5) anticipating and coping with crises. These steps are not comprehensive prescriptions nor do they imply an invariant temporal sequence. Rather, they provide a schema for integrating treatment planning for substance use reduction into ongoing treatment for major mental disorders, focusing attention on important therapeutic tasks. In the remainder of this article, the steps and strategies for accomplishing each will be described.

Establishing a working alliance

Building a relationship between the client and a member of the treatment team constitutes a critical first step towards changing substance use patterns. Forging a therapeutic alliance may take months or even years. Specific strategies to establish a working alliance include providing medications, and assistance in obtaining entitlements, food and recreational opportunities. During this relationship-building period, the treatment provider must communicate a sincere acceptance of the person, if not his/her substance use behavior. The goal is to establish trust, a prerequisite for the client to openly talk about substance use and the functions it serves. The time involved in building trust serves at least two purposes. First, the therapist gains credibility and reinforcement value, if the client perceives the therapist to have a sincere commitment to his/her welfare. Second, a safe environment is created for the client to express concerns and fears about changing. Such an environment helps to support the client through initial, perhaps physically and mentally painful, efforts to control substance use.

Importantly, it may be necessary to continue symptom management while a client is still using drugs and/or alcohol. Although this is not an optimal arrangement, many psychiatrists are uncomfortable withholding medications from a substance abusing client with psychotic, manic, or serious depressive symptoms. The risks of not attempting to control debilitating symptoms (even if substance use is contributing to them) must be weighed against the risks of drug interactions. Regular education about the actions of medications, their side effects, and potential interactions between prescribed and nonprescribed drugs is an important component of medication management.

The process of establishing a working treatment alliance aims to engage the client in treatment and to maintain sufficient contact for additional therapeutic work to take place (Osher & Kofoed, 1989). Clients in immotive/precontemplative stages of change may take longer than clients in contemplative or active stages. Once the client has established a connection to, and faith in, someone on the treatment staff, then it is possible to exploit naturally occurring events, or windows of opportunity, that enhance the person's readiness to change.

Evaluating costs and benefits of continued substance use

The next step involves attempts to enhance readiness to change. These activities begin when the client is willing to discuss his/her substance use and the effects it has on his/her life. Clients are likely to be in the contemplative stage and therapeutic goals include persuading the client that substance use patterns have to change (Osher & Kofoed, 1989). To do this, the stage may be set by general discussion about substances and their effects, as well as about the client's life goals. The client then evaluates pros and cons of continued substance use. Motivational interviewing techniques play an important role at this step. Preliminary activities relevant to this step include providing accurate information about the short- and long-term effects of substance use, and specifically their effects on cognitive, emotional, and behavioral symptoms experienced by the client. Although this type of education may be initiated by the therapist, the effectiveness of the message may be enhanced if the information is provided when relevant to issues raised by the client. For example, if complaints of increased anxiety appear to be temporarily related to evidence of cocaine use, the therapist may encourage speculation about the causal relations, and offer a brief discussion of cocaine-induced physical and psychological changes.

It is important to keep in mind that educational interventions alone rarely result in behavior change. In fact, one current model applied to another problem behavior, changing AIDS risk behaviors, emphasizes the concurrent needs for knowledge, motivation, and behavioral skills for successful risk reduction (Fisher & Fisher, 1992). However, knowledge can serve to set the stage, by raising awareness of consequences attributable to substance use rather than other causes (e.g., psychiatric or medical problems).

A second preliminary activity consists of identifying and discussing the client's life goals. These could be getting an apartment or a job, or staying out of the hospital for a certain length of time. It may take time for the client to be able to articulate or to feel comfortable talking about personal goals. Furthermore, the therapist may need to shape initially unrealistic goals (e.g., publishing a book) into more appropriate forms. Goal setting is central to many models of motivation, and the greatest motivational impact occurs when goals are specific (rather than vague), proximal (rather than distal), attainable, and accompanied by performance feedback (Miller, 1985). Goal-setting also provides a focus for discussions about what needs to change in order for goals to be met. For psychiatric outpatients, substance use almost always interferes with attaining desired outcomes. I have found that focusing on the goal (that requires a reduction in substance use) rather than focusing on the substance use per se is an effective strategy early in the change process.

With these preliminary activities, the therapist and client have engaged in a dialog that may serve consciousness raising functions (see Prochaska, Velicer, DiClemente, & Fava, 1988, for further discussion of matching therapeutic processes to stages of change). The costs and benefits of continued substance use can now be addressed. Inquire about the reasons why a client uses alcohol and/or drugs; encourage honest reporting of the perceived benefits by maintaining a nonjudgmental, information-seeking attitude. Often substance use serves significant functions in a person's life. Commonly sought-after effects include social facilitation, relief from unpleasant emotions, changes in cognitive states (e.g., ruminations, racing thoughts, uncomfortable self-focus), and promoting a certain self-image or feelings of control (Dixon, Haas, Weiden, Sweeney, & Frances, 1990). Principles of functional analysis as they have been applied to addictive behaviors are relevant here (Miller & Munoz, 1982). Briefly, functional analysis can help understand motivations for using substances by identifying antecedents and consequences of a particular behavior. The reasons for use and the effects of alcohol and drugs can vary for different individuals. As therapists, we must respect the functions of substance use and validate the needs underlying the desire to use. The needs can be distinguished from the methods used to achieve them. Attend also to the differences between perceived benefits and real benefits; this discrepancy can serve to illustrate the ultimate ineffectiveness of substances in achieving the very outcomes that motivate their use.

Assess also the pain and costs of substance use. Optimally, these should be elicited from the client; taking too active a role in defining costs may create psychological reactance. Reactance refers to the oppositional way a person behaves when that person feels he/she is being influenced in a certain direction (Brehm & Brehm, 1981). In this context, a person may resist acknowledging the costs of continued use if the therapist attempts to point these out. Miller and Rollnick (1991) suggest that techniques such as open-ended questions, reflective listening, and elaboration can help to elicit such information. Empathy (vs. an "I told you so" attitude) is needed in order to promote honest self-disclosure. The time devoted to trust-building pays off here. Over time, the therapist can reframe problems whenever possible (e.g., an arrest or hospitalization) to include the contributions of substance use, gradually increasing the lists of costs. Increased acknowledgment of costs related to drinking distinguishes individuals ready for active change from those in earlier stages (King & DiClemente, 1993). The therapist can then relate the benefits and costs of substance use articulated by the client back to life goals. Maintaining a focus on desired goals is a way of integrating substance use with the many other therapeutic concerns addressed in outpatient mental health treatment.

In summary, the tasks discussed in this section serve as groundwork for substance abuse treatment planning. Within an ongoing treatment relationship, clients can begin talking about substance use patterns, learning accurate information about substance effects, verbalizing realistic goals, identifying both the benefits and costs of substance use, and relating changes in substance use to achieving desired outcomes. These tasks also help to move clients in the contemplative stage of change towards active change.

Individualizing goals for change

The acceptability of moderation vs. abstinence goals in addictions treatment remains a hotly debated topic. Empirical evidence supports moderation goals for some persons; however, psychological and social stability are associated with successful moderate drinking outcomes (Rosenberg, 1993). Although outcome goals for persons with psychiatric disorders have not been studied, it is generally assumed that abstinence from non-prescribed drugs is the safest outcome for psychiatrically impaired substance abusers. Nonetheless, the harm reduction approach to intervention emphasizes the value of changes in the direction of abstinence. It may be better to work with a client on reducing substance use if that is what the client is willing and able to do. Marlatt and Tapert (1993) argue that one advantage of the harm reduction philosophy is that it engages more people in addictions treatment than an abstinence-only, "zero tolerance" philosophy. If reduced use is a realistic goal for change, it can be construed as the first step in the change process. Abstinence may continue to be the desired goal, but abstinence occurs along a continuum, starting with one day, then one week, up to a lifetime. Thus, flexibility in outcome goals constitutes a collaborative approach that may enhance the involvement of abusers in treatment.

For persons who use drugs or alcohol irregularly, initial goals may be to use less often or to use smaller amounts. For persons who have been unable to voluntarily abstain in the past, 24 hours of abstinence may constitute a reasonable initial goal. Noticeable changes in pattern, such as interruptions of using days with brief strings of sober days may represent significant progress consistent with the harm reduction objective. The effort should be recognized, and labeled a success, so that the client may feel an enhanced sense of self-efficacy and control over substance use. Feelings of personal efficacy are central to many psychological models of change (Bandura, 1986; Marlatt & Gordon, 1985).

Early in this active stage of change, the therapist can help the client anticipate some of the changes in mood, symptoms, lifestyle, and peer relations that might occur. The therapist must also be attuned to the fears and concerns expressed by the client about reducing substance use. Recovering persons often feel worse before they feel better, and the physical and emotional changes can be painful and scary. They may experience self-doubt about their abilities to succeed, and concern about losing the degree of control or predictability they may have had over their lives. Again, the therapeutic relationship plays an important role. The client has to trust that the therapist will support him/her through the difficult time and that the therapist will be available to offer tangible assistance (medical referral, hospital admission) if needed. Experience suggests that attention, empathy, and encouragement from the therapist may be the primary source of reinforcement during initial efforts to change.

In summary, it has been proposed that a therapist's willingness to individualize treatment goals may encourage more clients to modify their substance use patterns than a strict abstinence-for-life approach. Establishing meaningful but attainable goals for substance use reduction or abstinence can be considered the first step in the evolution of control over the role substances play in a person's life. First steps, however, can be intimidating and sometimes painful. A collaborative alliance between client and treatment staff can help to ensure that initial efforts are reinforced and perceived as success experiences.

Building an environment and lifestyle supportive of abstinence

Personal efforts to change substance use behaviors must be paralleled by social/environmental changes that support abstinence rather than substance use. Will power alone rarely suffices. Thus, the construction of these supports is an essential part of treatment planning. Evans and Sullivan (1990) describe an "outside-in treatment strategy" consistent with both mental health and addictions treatment models. This strategy refers to the temporal staggering of treatment priorities. Priorities early in the active treatment stage involve simple goals (e.g., staying sober, taking medications) and putting into place external structures (e.g., an AA meeting schedule, day treatment attendance) that help to maintain stability and reduce stress. Later in the process, more fundamental social, emotional, and cognitive changes are addressed.

The treatment program constitutes one such source of support and re-inforcement for abstinence. During early stages of change, as much structure as possible should be provided to the client, in the form of a day treatment program or frequent clinic appointments. Many recovering persons have said that they need to know that someone knows what they are going through and cares about the outcome of their quit efforts. In addition, skills training can facilitate recovery by enhancing adaptive functioning and providing alternative social and coping options (e.g., Nikkel, 1994). However, treatment contact should be supplemented by additional social supports.

Typically, sources of environmental support for recovery include family, work, church, and/or community groups. However, many chronically mentally ill persons are not well-integrated into these naturally occurring support systems. Consequently, they may feel that they have little to lose by continuing to abuse substances. In fact, they may not be reinforced for sobriety unless environmental and lifestyle restructuring is part of the treatment plan. For example, family members can be apprised of the treatment plan and instructed about ways in which they can provide moral support as well as tangible assistance (e.g., transportation, meals) contingent upon sobriety.

Note that building social support for abstinence may require avoidance of friends and acquaintances, if these individuals also abuse substances. One of the strongest predictors of substance use is a substance-abusing peer group (Murray & Perry, 1985); it is highly unlikely that recovery can be maintained if the client continues to associate with persons who drink or use drugs. Replacing friends and related social activities is difficult, especially for persons whose social skills are poor. Although loneliness may contribute to the onset of alcohol abuse, research shows that it is also associated with recovery (Akerlind & Hornquist, 1992). This suggests that establishing social supports and rebuilding social networks during recovery is a particularly important challenge.

Self-help groups can provide social support and structured activities. Not all persons with psychiatric disorders find self-help groups tolerable or helpful, but most should be encouraged to try at least a couple of meetings. Treatment staff may want to accompany a client to his/her first meetings, to overcome the fear of the unknown. Clients whose symptoms or behaviors get in the way of participation in community groups may want to seek out "Double Trouble" groups, which are created for persons with both mental illness and addictions problems. Note that models have been developed for modified step-work tailored to various psychiatric disorders which can supplement (or in some cases substitute for) 12-step oriented self-help groups (e.g., Evans & Sullivan, 1990).

An environment supportive of abstinence also must include the client's residence. Every attempt should be made to create a drug-free living environment. Supportive housing which does not tolerate substance use can provide needed external limits on one's own as well as others' behavior. In essence, housing often gives a client "something to lose" if substance use gets out of control.

Finally recovering persons often need help in finding activities to structure time that had previously been occupied with substance-related behaviors. Ideally, ideas regarding activities that the client finds enjoyable have emerged during previous alliance-building stages. These may include recreational activities, volunteer work, and educational or training opportunities.

In summary, recovery attempts involve a transaction between personal commitment and effort, and an environment that supports and promotes a healthier lifestyle. Neither component alone is sufficient for lasting change to take place. Persons with psychiatric disorders may need additional assistance to manage necessary lifestyle changes if they experience deficits in interpersonal relationships, or organization and planning skills.

Coping with crises

Substance use disorders and most major mental illnesses are relapsing disorders. Both treatment traditions incorporate relapse prevention concepts; in the case of coexisting disorders, relapse prevention is broadly defined to address setbacks in both. In fact, relapse in one domain can trigger relapse in the other. Acknowledging that recovery is usually a long-term process, interrupted by periodic relapses, several authors advocate a continuum of care plan for dual diagnosis clients (e.g., Carey, 1989, 1995; Drake, Teague, & Warren, 1990). Access to detoxification, psychiatric evaluation for medication adjustments, inpatient psychiatric hospitalization, or temporary housing may be periodically necessary, and coordinated management of such transitions helps to limit the scope of inevitable setbacks. Thus, treatment planning should anticipate relapses and prepare to cope with crises.

Several causes of relapse occur frequently among recovering substance abusers with psychiatric disorders (Evans & Sullivan, 1990). Three classes of determinants consist of biological, psychological, and social factors. Biological factors include withdrawal symptoms that trigger substance use to counteract discomfort; a poor response to psychiatric medications that leaves a client symptomatic; an extroverted temperament prone to sensation seeking; and extreme physiological states, captured in the acronym HALTS (i.e., hungry, angry, lonely, tired, or sick). Psychological factors include negative emotional states, positive expectations of drug effects, patterns of distorted thinking (e.g., "I can't do anything right"), and an impoverished lifestyle which provides little meaningful engagement with anything other than substance use and its rituals. Finally, social factors include lack of social support for the work involved in recovery, peer pressure to drink or use drugs, holidays or social occasions associated with substance use, and interpersonal conflict.

The functional analysis that occurred earlier in the treatment process ought to yield information about situations in which substances have been used in the past, and the needs that alcohol/drugs typically have met. Thus, it is often possible to anticipate the types of situations that are likely to precipitate relapse for individual clients. Relapse prevention, broadly defined, is a collaborative process in which the client tries to identify and cope with difficult events, and the treatment staff offers early intervention to reduce the harm if a relapse does occur. With regard to substance use, staff can reinforce continued contact with treatment after periods of use, and help to evaluate what happened and why. Thus, relapses should not be construed as failures but as opportunities to learn for the future. Similarly, early signs of psychiatric decompensation can be monitored, medications reevaluated, and sources of stress can be identified before the desire to resort to chemical management becomes overwhelming.

Coping with crises refers to the active, ongoing process of anticipating the multiple determinants of relapse, and coping with setbacks as they occur, optimally with a continuum of comprehensive care. Work with mentally ill substance abusers requires a broad definition of relapse that encompasses both psychiatric and substance abuse setbacks, because outcomes of each are mutually dependent. If relapses are framed within a collaborative learning experience, they can serve to refocus treatment efforts towards areas that prove to be high risk for a person at a given time. Expectations of a longitudinal recovery process are appropriate and adaptive for both clients and treatment staff.

CONCLUSIONS

The substance abuse treatment model just described offers several advantages over exclusively abstinence-oriented, 12-step models. First, and most importantly, it provides an alternative to not addressing substance use among psychiatric clients, or relying solely on referrals to standard alcohol/drug treatment programs in which persons with serious mental disorders rarely succeed. Second, this can be individualized for clients with varying degrees and types of psychopathology, as well as different degrees of willingness and ability to change. Third, the proposed model shifts the focus from motivation for treatment to readiness to change, from static traits to more fluid states that can be influenced by external circumstances such as motivational interventions and critical life events. Fourth, this model explicitly addresses the early stages of engagement and persuasion (Osher & Kofoed, 1989) that receive relatively little attention. Most substance abuse treatment models emphasize activities relevant to active change and relapse prevention stages. Fifth, this model takes a longitudinal perspective on the change process. This contrasts with the finite duration of many substance abuse treatment programs. For persons with limited social and psychological resources, and with destabilizing relapses due to psychiatric disorders interfering with a recovery focus, a long-term treatment model appears essential. Finally, the proposed model allows for flexibility in defining success. The harm reduction philosophy (contrasted with the zero-tolerance philosophy) provides more opportunities for success experiences and tries to avoid unrealistic goals that set clients up for failure. Furthermore, encouraging therapists to perceive incremental change may enhance their sense of accomplishment when working with very challenging clients.

In sum, a five-step model for reducing substance use within the context of outpatient psychiatric treatment has been proposed. The influence of themes from the psychological treatment literature appears throughout the model, which attempts to integrate clinical realities of mental health treatment with empirically-grounded strategies applicable to addiction problems. This type of cross-fertilization is needed to stimulate new ideas that will improve practice and research in the area of comorbid substance use and psychiatric disorders.

REFERENCES

Akerlind, I., & Hornquist, J.O. (1992). Loneliness and alcohol abuse: A review of evidence of an interplay. *Social Science and Medicine, 34,* 405-414.

Bandura, A. (1986). *Social foundations of thought and action: A social cognitive theory.* Englewood Cliffs, NJ: Prentice-Hall.

Bergman, H., & Harris, M. (1985). Substance abuse among young adult chronic patients. *Psychosocial Rehabilitation Journal, 9,* 49-54.

Blane, H.T., & Leonard, K.E. (1987). *Psychological theories of drinking and alcoholism.* New York: Guilford.

Bowers, M.B., Mazure, C.M., Nelson, C.J., & Jatlow, P.I. (1990). Psychotogenic drug abuse and neuroleptic response. *Schizophrenia Bulletin, 16,* 81-85.

Brehm, S.S., & Brehm, J.W. (1981). *Psychological reactance: A theory of freedom and control.* New York: Academic Press.

Carey, K.B. (1989). Treatment of the mentally ill chemical abuser: Description of the Hutchings day treatment program. *Psychiatric Quarterly, 60,* 303-316.

Carey, K.B. (1995). Treatment of substance abuse with schizophrenia. In A.F. Lehman & L. Dixon (Eds.) *Double jeopardy: Chronic mental illness and substance abuse.* London: Harwood.

Carey, K.B., & Carey, M.P. (1990). Enhancing the treatment attendance of mentally ill chemical abusers. *Journal of Behavior Therapy and Experimental Psychiatry, 21,* 205-209.

Carey, M.P., Carey, K.B., & Meisler, A.W. (1991). Psychiatric symptoms in mentally ill chemical abusers. *Journal of Nervous and Mental Disease, 179,* 136-138.

Dixon, L., Haas, G., Weiden, P., Sweeney,, J. & Frances, A. (1990). Acute effects of drug abuse in schizophrenic patients: Clinical observations and patients' self-reports. *Schizophrenia Bulletin, 16,* 69-79.

Drake, R.E., Osher, F.C., & Wallach, M.A. (1989). Alcohol use and abuse in schizophrenia: A prospective community study. *Journal of Nervous and Mental Disease, 177,* 408-414.

Drake, R.E., Teague, G.B., & Warren, S.R. (1990). Dual diagnosis: The New Hampshire Program. *Addiction and Recovery, June,* 35-39.

Drake, R.E., & Wallach, M.A. (1989). Substance abuse among the chronic mentally ill. *Hospital and Community Psychiatry, 40,* 1041-1046.

Evans, K., & Sullivan, J.M. (1990). *Dual diagnosis: Counseling the mentally ill substance abuser.* New York: Guilford.

Fisher, J.D., & Fisher, W.A. (1992). Changing AIDS risk behavior. *Psychological Bulletin, 111,* 455-474.

Hall, R.C.W., Popkin, M.K., DeVaul, R., & Stickney, S.K. (1977). The effect of unrecognized drug abuse on diagnosis and therapeutic outcome. *American Journal of Drug and Alcohol Abuse, 4,* 455-465.

Hall, R.C.W., Stickney, S.K., Gardner, E.R., Perl, M., & LeCann, A.F. (1979). Relationship of psychiatric illness to drug abuse. *Journal of Psychedelic Drugs, 11,* 337-342.

Institute of Medicine (1990). *Broadening the base of treatment for alcohol problems.* Washington, DC: National Academy Press.

King, T.K, & DiClemente, C.C. (1993). *A decisional balance measure for assessing and predicting drinking behavior.* Poster presented at the Annual Meeting of the Association for Advancement of Behavior Therapy, Atlanta, GA.

Marlatt, G.A., & Gordon, J.R. (1985). *Relapse prevention: Maintenance strategies in the treatment of addictive behaviors.* New York: Guilford.

Marlatt, G.A., & Tapert, S.F. (1993). Harm reduction: Reducing the risks of addictive behaviors. In J.S. Baer, G.A. Marlatt, & R.J. McMahon (Eds.). *Addictive behaviors across the lifespan: Prevention, treatment, and policy issues.* (pp. 243-273). Newbury Park, CA: Sage.

Miller, W.R. (1985). Motivation for treatment: A review with special emphasis on alcoholism. *Psychological Bulletin, 98,* 84-107.

Miller, W.R., & Munoz, R. (1982). *How to control your drinking: A practical guide to responsible drinking* (Rev. Ed.). Albuquerque, NM: University of New Mexico Press.

Miller, W.R., & Rollnick, S. (1991). *Motivational interviewing: Preparing people to change addictive behavior.* New York: Guilford.

Minkoff, K. (1989). An integrated treatment model for dual diagnosis of psychosis and addiction. *Hospital and Community Psychiatry, 40,* 1031-1036.

Minkoff, K., & Drake, R.E. (1991). *Dual diagnosis of major mental illness and substance disorders.* San Francisco: Jossey-Bass.

Mueser, K.T., Yarnold, P.R., Levinson, D.F., Singh, H., Bellack, A.S., Kee, K., Morrison, R.L., & Yadalam, K.G. (1990). Prevalence of substance abuse in schizophrenia: Demographic and clinical correlates. *Schizophrenia Bulletin, 16,* 31-56.

Murray, D.M., & Perry, C.L. (1985). The prevention of adolescent drug abuse: Implications of etiological, developmental, behavioral, and environmental models. In C.L. Jones & R.J. Battles (Eds.). *Etiology of drug abuse: Implications for treatment* (DHHS Publication No. ADM 85-1335). Washington, DC: US Government Printing Office. 235-255.

Nikkel, R.E. (1994). Areas of skill training for persons with mental illness and substance use disorders: Building skills for successful community living. *Community Mental Health Journal, 30,* 61-72.

Osher, F.C., & Kofoed, L.L. (1989). Treatment of patients with psychiatric and psychoactive substance abuse disorders. *Hospital and Community Psychiatry, 40,* 1025-1030.

Pepper, B., Kirshner, M.C., & Ryglewicz, H. (1981). The young adult chronic patient: Overview of a population. *Hospital and Community Psychiatry, 32,* 463-469.

Pristach, C.A., & Smith, C.M. (1990). Medication compliance and substance abuse among schizophrenic patients. *Hospital and Community Psychiatry, 41,* 1345-1348.

Prochaska, J.O., & DiClemente, C.C. (1992). Stages of changes in the modification of problem behaviors. In M. Hersen, R.M. Eisler, & P.M. Miller (Eds.), *Progress in behavior modification* (pp. 184-218). Newbury Park, CA: Sage.

Prochaska, J.O., Velicer, W.F., DeClemente, C.C., & Fava, J. (1988). Measuring processes of change: Application to the cessation of smoking. *Journal of Consulting and Clinical Psychology, 56,* 520-528.

Regier, D.A., Farmer, M.E., Rae, D.S., Locke, B.Z., Keith, S.J., Judd, L.L., & Goodwin, F.K. (1990). Comorbidity of mental disorders with alcohol and other drug abuse. *Journal of the American Medical Association, 264,* 2511-2518.

Richardson, M.A., Craig, T.J., & Haugland, G. (1985). Treatment patterns of young chronic schizophrenic patients in the era of deinstitutionalization. *Psychiatric Quarterly, 57,* 104-110.

Rosenberg, H. (1993). Prediction of controlled drinking by alcoholics and problem drinkers. *Psychological Bulletin, 113,* 129-139.

Rosenthal, R.N., Hellerstein, D.J., & Miner, C.R. (1992). A model of integrated services for outpatient treatment of patients with comorbid schizophrenia and addictive disorders. *American Journal of Addictions, 1,* 339-348.

Safer, D.J. (1987). Substance abuse by young adult chronic patients. *Hospital and Community Psychiatry, 38,* 511-514.

Solomon, P., & Davis, J.M. (1986). The effects of alcohol abuse among the new chronically mentally ill. *Social Work in Health Care, 11,* 65-74.

Test, M.A., Wallisch, L.S., Allness, D.J., & Ripp, K. (1989). Substance use in young adults with schizophrenic disorders. *Schizophrenia Bulletin, 15,* 465-476.

ABOUT THE AUTHOR

Kate B. Carey, Ph.D., is affiliated with the Department of Psychology, Syracuse University.

ACKNOWLEDGMENTS

This research was supported by National Institute on Drug Abuse Grant DA07635.

Reprinted with permission from *Community Mental Health Journal*.

GROUP TREATMENT FOR DUALLY DIAGNOSED CLIENTS

Kim T. Mueser and Douglas L. Noordsy

Reprinted from *Dual Diagnosis of Major Mental Illness and Substance Abuse.*
Volume 2: Recent Research and Clinical Implications. New Directions for
Mental Health Services, No. 70, R.E. Drake & K.T. Mueser (Eds.).
San Francisco: Jossey-Bass, Inc. (pp. 33-51), 1996

*Group treatment is a widely practiced intervention for persons with
dual diagnoses. This chapter reviews the rationale for group treatment
and discusses four different approaches to group intervention: twelve-
step, educational-supportive, social skills, and stagewise treatment.*

It is now widely accepted that dually diagnosed individuals require interventions that simultaneously address both mental health and substance use disorders. In addition to recognizing the need to treat both dual disorders when present, integrated treatment models have embraced the concept of stages of recovery from substance use disorder. Accordingly, treatment must motivate clients to address their substance abuse prior to attempting to reduce substance use (Miller and Rollnick, 1991; Prochaska, Velicer, DiClemente, and Fava, 1988). Drake and others (1993) have proposed four stages of treatment designed to provide maximally relevant interventions: engagement (client is not engaged in treatment), persuasion (client is engaged in treatment but is not convinced of the importance of reducing substance use), active treatment (client is attempting to reduce substance use), and relapse prevention (client has reduced or stopped substance use and is trying to prevent relapses). The stage concept provides a heuristic to clinicians by identifying the critical goals at each stage, and leads to the selection of stage-specific interventions (for example, at the persuasion stage the clinician works to establish awareness of the consequences of substance use).

A core component of integrated treatment programs is the inclusion of group-based intervention. There are three reasons for including group treatment. First, there is a strong tradition of nonprofessional self-help groups such as Alcoholics Anonymous (AA) in the primary addiction field. The group format is an ideal setting for capitalizing on the common need for support and identification shared by persons with an addiction. Second, substance abuse among psychiatric clients frequently occurs in a social context (Dixon and others, 1991; Test, Wallisch, Allness, and Ripp, 1989). Addressing substance use-related issues in a group setting makes it clear to clients that they are not alone and provides an opportunity for the sharing of experiences and coping strategies. Third, there are economical advantages to offering group therapy rather than individual therapy because less clinician time is required.

MODELS OF GROUP TREATMENT

Different approaches to group treatment can be divided into four general models: twelve-step, broad-based educational-supportive, social skills training, and stagewise. Although this categorization facilitates the discussion of different group methods, many interventions are hybrids of more than one model (for example, stagewise treatment may include elements of twelve-step, social skills training, and educational-supportive models). Furthermore, for group intervention to be effective it must be provided in the context of a comprehensive treatment program, including elements such as ongoing assessment, case management, and pharmacotherapy (Drake and others, 1993).

Twelve-step models

Twelve-step models are based on the self-help group approach popularized by AA and adapted for other substances or disorders (narcotics addiction or gambling, for instance). A number of different approaches to dual diagnosis include aspects of twelve-step programs, such as clinician-led groups that prepare clients for community AA-type meetings and consumer-led self-help meetings with a focus on individuals with dual diagnoses. The clinician-led models, described by Minkoff (1989) and Bartels and Thomas (1991), include twelve-step principles and philosophy adapted from the AA model blended with education and support for mental-illness management. Treatment is usually delivered by clinicians with some personal or professional experience with the twelve-step model working in a mental health system. Their focus is on integrating substance abuse treatment with mental health care. These groups promote supplementary attendance at AA meetings but attempt to deliver comprehensive treatment through the group to those who never attend.

We have previously described the difficulty persons with dual disorders have linking to self-help groups for substance abuse (Noordsy, Schwab, Fox, and Drake, 1996). We therefore designed a pre-AA model of group treatment for the New Hampshire study of dual diagnosis. This model is designed to facilitate the linkage of clients to self-help treatment in the community by developing an awareness of the consequences of substance use, motivation for treatment, and familiarity with the twelve-step approach. Although initial work in this model parallels the persuasion model by necessity (see section below on Stagewise Treatment), the language and milieu of the group differ. Twelve-step concepts such as denial, rationalization, working the steps, and surrender are central to the pre-AA group but not in persuasion groups. Members are also encouraged to attend self-help meetings and listen to others' stories to further their motivation to change.

The group discusses typical barriers clients experience to attending self-help groups, such as social discomfort, the emphasis on religion, and the negative stance some AA members have toward psychotropic medications, and strategies for overcoming those barriers. Members' attendance at self-help meetings and their reactions to them are regularly reviewed. Although pre-AA groups are clearly distinguished from twelve-step meetings, some rituals, such as reading aloud from twelve-step books and closing meetings by holding hands and reciting a prayer together, are practiced in group to increase members' comfort with them and to stimulate discussion. The active treatment phase of this model is attending AA or other self-help meetings with sobriety as a goal. Members in this phase are encouraged to continue attending the pre-AA group to serve as mentors to their peers.

Several authors have described twelve-step self-help groups that specialize in serving a membership with dual disorders (Bricker, 1994; Hendrickson and Schmal, 1994). These include groups initiated by community AA volunteers (Kurtz and others, 1995; Woods, 1991) and groups initiated by professionals (Caldwell and White, 1991). The former follow a standard AA format but also include discussion of "recovery" from mental illness (Kurtz and others, 1995). The latter generally follow an AA format with some modifications, such as allowing professional involvement.

Broad-based educational-supportive models

This approach posits that change in substance abuse occurs because of education about the effects of substances and social support from others experiencing similar difficulties. An explicit educational curriculum is provided, interspersed with the sharing of personal experiences and open discussion of recent substance abuse. Other than a shared focus on education and engendering social support among group members, applications of this model vary widely in terms of their eligibility requirements, duration of treatment, and specific clinical methods employed (for example, psychoeducational techniques, skills training, and problem solving).

Some approaches limit participation in the group to persons who are motivated to reduce substance abuse (Hellerstein and Meehan, 1987; Hellerstein, Rosenthal, and Miner, 1995), whereas others do not (Alfs and McLellan, 1992; Sciacca, 1987; Straussman, 1985). The approach described by Hellerstein, Rosenthal, and Miner differs from others in that groups are offered on a time-unlimited basis. Common across the different educational-supportive group treatments is avoidance of direct confrontation, maintaining an affectively benign and supportive milieu, helping clients understand how substance abuse affects their psychiatric illness, and familiarizing clients with how AA-type groups in the community work. For example, in Sciacca's (1987) group, speakers from AA and Narcotics Anonymous (NA) are invited to describe their groups to members.

In general, the educational-supportive model is the least theoretically distinct model of integrated group treatment for dually diagnosed individuals. The approach is compatible with stagewise treatments without explicitly endorsing the stage model of recovery. For example, the approaches of Alfs and McLellan (1992), Sciacca (1987), and Straussman (1985) resemble persuasion groups, whereas Hellerstein and Meehan's (1987) groups resemble active treatment groups (described below). Members are encouraged to try AA and other self-help groups, but the main purpose of educational-supportive groups is not to prepare clients for self-help groups in the community. Finally, although some skills training techniques may be used in some of these groups, they do not embrace a social-learning conceptualization of treating dual disorders.

Social skills training

Social skills training (SST) refers to a social learning approach to improving interpersonal competence through modeling, role playing, positive and corrective feedback, and homework assignments (Liberman, DeRisi, and Mueser, 1989). SST procedures have traditionally been used to teach interpersonal skills, but can also be used to teach self-care skills such as grooming and hygiene. Although SST methods are employed by other group models, the SST model differs in two respects. First, the SST model conceptualizes the needs of dually diagnosed persons in terms of skill deficits that interfere with the ability to develop a lifestyle free from substance abuse. Thus, deficits in areas such as the ability to resist offers to use substances, recreational skills, or skill in managing interpersonal conflicts are thought to contribute to substance abuse. Second, because the focus of SST is on teaching new skills or relearning old ones, an emphasis is placed on explicit modeling of skills and repeated behavioral rehearsals, guided by the principle that over-practice of skills is necessary to achieving mastery (Ericsson and Charness, 1994). In contrast, other group models are more likely to facilitate skill development by *implicit* use of modeling (for example, skills are used by leaders, but are not specifically demonstrated for participants) and talking about skills, with only occasional use of role plays and behaviorally based feedback.

In order to teach an array of specific skills to clients, SST models employ detailed, preplanned curricula and follow a specific agenda. Despite the structure of the groups, the SST approach places high value on fostering supportive relationships between group members, improving understanding about the effects of substances, and addressing the emergent needs of clients (Jerrell and Ridgely, 1995). As with other models, specific SST programs vary in their content, format, and structure. Nikkel (1994) has described a long-term SST program based on training modules developed by Liberman and others (1987), with skills taught in areas such as relationships, resisting offers to use substances, self-care, money management, sleep hygiene, leisure, and vocational and educational functioning. The group format and other formats (for example, family psychoeducation and individual therapy) are used to teach skills. Carey, Carey, and Meisler (1990) describe a skills training approach in which problem-solving skills are systematically taught to outpatients to enable them to more effectively manage stress and interpersonal situations. We have recently developed a time-limited inpatient SST group with a focus on teaching interpersonal skills, strategies for managing negative emotions, and alternative recreational activities (Mueser and others, 1995).

As with the educational-supportive group model, a key distinction between the social skills model and stagewise treatment is that the skills approach does not formally incorporate the distinction between persuasion and active treatment into the group. Similarly, skills training and other behavioral strategies are typically included in stagewise treatment (as indicated in the following section), as well as a range of other clinical methods. Consistent with the other group models, the SST model incorporates education into the curriculum and endorses the potential benefits of self-help groups such as AA (for example, Nikkel, 1994).

Stagewise treatment

Stagewise treatment refers to group interventions designed to meet the unique needs of clients at different stages of recovery from substance abuse. Over the past several years, we have developed and implemented stagewise group treatments at different community mental health centers throughout New Hampshire (Noordsy and Fox, 1991). Although four different stages of recovery have been proposed, for the purposes of group treatment, clients in the second stage (persuasion) participate in one type of group (a *persuasion group*), and clients in the last two stages (active treatment and relapse prevention) participate in a second type of group (an *active treatment group*). Clients in the engagement phase may attend some persuasion groups, but regular attendance does not typically occur until they complete this stage.

The unique feature of this approach is recognition that many individuals with dual diagnoses lack motivation for treatment, and that motivation must be developed for treatment to succeed. This approach draws on the techniques of the other three group intervention models, using them as they are relevant for individuals within groups and subdividing their use across two motivational stages. Leaders must be skilled in the techniques of the other approaches to be able to use them when needed.

Persuasion Groups. By definition, clients in the engagement and persuasion stages of recovery do not recognize that they have a substance abuse problem, and do not endorse the goal of reducing substance use. Therefore the primary goal of persuasion groups is to develop clients' awareness of how substances complicate their lives. A combination of clinical strategies is employed to assist participants in examining the consequences of their substance use, including education and motivational interviewing techniques (Miller and Rollnick, 1991), such as empathic listening and helping clients perceive the discrepancy between their personal goals and substance use. Persuasion groups can be conducted either with inpatients (Kofoed and Keys, 1988) or outpatients (Noordsy and Fox, 1991). We provide below a brief description of how these groups are conducted on an outpatient basis at several community mental health centers in New Hampshire.

The optimal format for groups is to have two leaders, one with expertise in treating mental illness and the other with expertise in addictive disorders. Groups are held weekly, often shortly after the weekend so that periods of heavy substance use are likely to be fresh in clients' minds. Some groups run for 45-60 minutes, whereas others have two 20-30 minute sessions separated by a short break. Brief sessions reduce the intensity and enable clients with limited attention spans to participate. Groups are open to all clients and weekly attendance is encouraged but not required. Because initial attendance is usually a problem, the groups serve refreshments, include activities (for example, community trips and videos), and are extremely supportive. Clients need not acknowledge a problem with substances in order to attend and those who have been using substances are allowed to attend group if they behave appropriately.

Persuasion groups are not confrontational. They assume instead that recognition of a substance abuse problem occurs over time in the context of peer group support and education. The stated goal of the group is to help members learn more about the role that alcohol and drugs play in their lives. Group leaders provide didactic material on substances and mental illness, but they spend most of their effort facilitating peer interactions and feedback about substance use. Leaders actively limit the level of affect, monitor psychotic behaviors, and maintain the group's focus on substance abuse. Members who turn up at group inebriated are allowed to participate (if they are not disruptive), and members are permitted to leave early if they choose. Those who are reluctant to participate are invited to contribute at least once or twice during each meeting. The overriding theme is to encourage participation in the group and to gently, repeatedly expose members to opportunities to explore the reinforcing and destructive effects of their substance use.

Persuasion group sessions often begin with a review of each member's use of substances over the previous week. This discussion is nonjudgmental so that members feel safe in reporting their use honestly. As a member discusses a recent period of intoxication, others help to identify antecedents, including internal emotional states, and consequences of use. All members are encouraged to contribute to this process, perhaps offering advice or relating a similar experience. Leaders field questions and provide brief information on addiction, the effects of various substances on physical and mental health, and the interactions between drugs and medications. Relevant films, short readings, or group outings are occasionally used to stimulate interest and discussion if needed, although lengthy didactic presentations are avoided. Group members often ask leaders about their own use of substances. Leaders are typically open about their use; those who are recovering from addiction may share their own experiences, and those who are not honestly relate their past experimentation, subsequent consequences if any, and current choices, facilitating discussion of distinctions between use and abuse.

Active Treatment Groups. These groups are focused, behavioral, and aimed at reducing substance use and promoting abstinence. Members working toward a common goal of abstinence actively give each other feedback and support. Unlike persuasion groups, there is an assumption of sobriety during participation in active treatment groups. Although not required, members are encouraged to try out self-help meetings as a form of active treatment work or one route to sobriety. Members often accompany each other to meetings. The group work includes review of members' experiences using self-help and focuses on developing the skills to successfully negotiate a self-help program (at times similar to pre-AA groups).

Behavioral principles of addiction treatment (Monti, Abrams, Kadden, and Cooney, 1989) guide active treatment groups. This approach is less stimulating than some others and addresses the development of skills that dually diagnosed clients often lack. Members learn social skills through role plays and group interaction and use one another for support and assistance in attending self-help meetings. They are trained in assertiveness, giving and receiving criticism, drink or drug refusal skills, making new friends, and managing thoughts about alcohol or other drug use. Clients learn to develop constructive substitutes for substance use, to manage craving, difficult emotions, or symptoms. Another common focus of these groups is on learning coping strategies. For example, clients experiencing cravings for substances may be taught the use of imagery by transforming positive images for a desired substance into negative images, such as hangovers, psychotic relapses, or fights.

Clients also learn to recognize situations that increase their risk of substance use and to use relapse prevention techniques for managing these situations (Marlatt and Gordon, 1985). For example, relaxation training and principles of sleep hygiene are used to regain control over anxiety and insomnia that may lead to the use of substances. Many members need help with concrete situations such as learning how to set limits on substance-abusing friends. The cognitive and behavioral chain of events leading up to episodes of craving or substance use are identified and strategies for preventing future episodes are developed. Members are encouraged to write down their internal or interpersonal struggles during the week so that they can work on them in the group. Leaders help them discover and label strategies for managing emotional experiences that they had been obliterating with substance use and to appreciate the gradual improvements in their mental health and stability that come with sobriety. Members often gain a greater sense of responsibility for managing both of their illnesses during this process. When relapses do occur, group members offer support and help in developing plans to minimize the severity of the relapse in order to arrest the backslide to substance abuse and dependence.

Combined Persuasion and Active Treatment Groups. In some settings where persuasion and active treatment groups have been running for several years, it may be advantageous to combine the two formats into a single group. Despite the fact that all clients participate in the same group, intervention is tailored to the specific stage of recovery for each client. We provide several clinical vignettes illustrating stagewise treatment in a combined group.

CLINICAL VIGNETTES

The following vignettes illustrate typical interactions at different stages of group development in the stagewise model.

Beginning the group

The leaders start group by asking each member to describe their use of substances or craving for them over the past week. This exercise is used to provide continuity from group to group and to develop material for the session.

LEADER: Good morning. Let's go ahead and get started. How was your week, George?

GEORGE: I'm still drinking and smoking and I just can't stop. I'm awake half the night because I can't breathe, and I cough and hack my guts out every morning. I've got to stop. It's killing me.

LEADER: You've been struggling with this for a while. Would you like to develop a plan for quitting in group today? There's a lot of experience in this room that you could put to work for you.

GEORGE: Couldn't hurt.

LEADER: Good, we'll get back to that. How was your week, Jim?

JIM: This has been a pretty intense week for me. I didn't sleep much over the weekend and I got pretty manic.

LEADER: Were you using?

JIM: I haven't had a drink in three months. Drinking didn't have anything to do with how I was feeling this weekend. I was going through some intense personal exploration and my medications got all screwed up.

LEADER: You have often mentioned smoking pot to the group.

JIM: Well, sure I was smoking, but that had nothing to do with it. I smoke less when I'm manic because I don't need it as much.

LEADER: Would it be fair to look at that some more later?

JIM: Fair enough.

LEADER: How was your week, Brian?

BRIAN: Pretty lousy. I couldn't sleep good and I had pains in my neck and back and shoulders. I hurt all over.

LEADER: Were you using?

BRIAN: No, it's been a year since I've had a drink or a drug. I didn't want to wreck that, but I sure was thinking that a beer would help kill the pain.

Developing a plan to quit

George is a fifty-two-year-old divorced male with diagnoses of schizophrenia and alcohol dependence. His psychotic illness had onset in his mid-thirties and was characterized by frequent medication discontinuation and episodes of behaviorally disruptive psychosis. He has used alcohol heavily since his teens except for five years during his marriage when his wife disallowed it. During one severe episode of drinking and psychosis, he stole a car in response to his delusions. He was convicted of auto theft and his probation required medication compliance and abstinence. Since the probation ended three years ago, he has remained medication compliant and has not had another severe psychotic episode, but he returned to daily drinking. He attended the stagewise group regularly during his probation, but now drops out for a month or two at a time. He is in group for the first time in five weeks today. He has repeatedly identified an abstinence goal and made attempts at quitting drinking, placing him in the early active treatment stage.

LEADER: George, you mentioned a lot of problems related to smoking and drinking. Would you like some help figuring out how to change?

GEORGE: Well, I'm moving to a new place so I was thinking of quitting then. Is that what you mean?

LEADER: That's excellent. Starting in a new place would help to avoid craving being triggered by the reminders of using around your old home. Would you like to pick a quit date?

GEORGE: I'm going to be way out in the boonies. I just won't bring it with me and I won't go out to see anyone anymore. Everyone I know drinks and smokes, even my girlfriend. I've had enough of her. I wish someone would just lock me up in detox for a few weeks, but they don't do that anymore. I can't do it around my friends.

BILL: I wouldn't be alone. That'll drive you to drink.

MARY: Won't you get bored? I'd be pacing the floor thinking about using the whole time.

GEORGE: No, I like to be alone. When I quit before, nine years ago, I just went out in the woods for a few weeks and quit everything, even medication.

LEADER: How did that work out?

GEORGE: Well I ended up in the hospital, but I didn't drink for two years.

JIM: You don't want to end up back in there. Besides, you'll need to go to the store sometime and there's always beer there begging you to take it home. I think you should go to AA.

LEADER: Maybe we can develop a plan using the things that worked for you before and some of these other suggestions to help you get to your goal. One thing that might help is establishing a date and time now for starting your new healthy lifestyle. You are less likely to just keep using out of habit and miss the opportunity of using your move to help you if you make a clear plan for yourself.

GEORGE: Well, I'm moving this weekend.

LEADER: Would you like to be using during the move?

GEORGE: Yeah, I'll probably be drinking some that day. I'll be all in by Saturday night.

LEADER: Would you like to stop using then?

GEORGE: Yeah, that's it. I'll stop using Saturday night at, say six o'clock.

LEADER: What other things have helped people to get sober?

JIM: I needed to have people to talk to to get through it. Sober people. That's why I went to AA.

GEORGE: The guy I'm renting from is real nice and he doesn't drink or smoke. I can hang around with him. I guess I could try AA again. I went years ago on probation but it just made me want to drink more to hear all those stories.

LEADER: It might be worth trying AA again. You might hear those stories differently now that you want to quit. Could you use any family members for support?

GEORGE: They're all drunks too for the most part except for my sister. She quit about three years ago. She goes to AA actually.

JIM: You could talk to her for support and ask her to take you to a few meetings, too.

LEADER: Would the folks in this group be willing to help George out if he needed support?

JIM: Sure, call me anytime George. We could have coffee and talk.

MARY: I'd be happy to help out, but I don't have a phone. I still live in the same place.

BRIAN: Yeah, I'll help.

LEADER: I'll make sure your case manager knows about this plan so she can work with you on it, too. You know Mary mentioned craving before. Maybe we can generate a list of things to do to get through a craving.

GEORGE: When I get craving a drink I can just taste it. It's hard to think of anything else. That's what gets me.

MARY: You could keep a list with you that tells you what to do.

LEADER: You know, Mary's right. It's hard to think when you are in the middle of a craving, but if you have a list handy you can just read it. Why don't each of us come up with a personal list of things to do to get through a craving. I'll pass around index cards and let's each write down ten things we could do to get through a craving and then we'll go around the room and share ideas....

Persuasion work

Jim is a thirty-five-year-old man with advanced degrees in philosophy who has been diagnosed with a bipolar affective disorder. He used alcohol and other drugs extensively throughout his postsecondary schooling and subsequent employment. He suffered a head injury in a car accident at age twenty-five and subsequently developed chronic bipolar symptoms with psychotic features exacerbated by severe alcoholism and marijuana abuse. Jim has attended stagewise treatment groups intermittently in the last two years. Initially he did persuasion stage work in group, recognized severe physical consequences of his alcohol use, and developed a goal of abstinence from alcohol. He developed active treatment plans in individual and group settings and used AA meetings as well. During this time his group participation became erratic, attending for several sessions after each relapse back to alcohol use and psychosis. After several state hospital admissions he reestablished an abstinence goal and has been attending group regularly for nine months. He had a brief, severe relapse to drinking three months ago and has been abstinent from alcohol since. He continues marijuana use. He is therefore doing relapse prevention work around alcohol, but still requires persuasion stage work focusing on his marijuana use.

LEADER: Jim, you mentioned that you had a rough weekend with some medication problems and mania, and you were smoking some too.

JIM: Nothing different from usual. Actually when I'm manic I smoke less; I don't need it as much. It's just that I cut back on the lithium for a little while and things got a little out of hand. I got pretty psychotic, but I just took some [chlorpromazine] and got back in control. I'm all set now.

LEADER: How much were you smoking?

JIM: Oh, you know, whenever I got the chance. Marijuana has been a really positive drug for me. I don't look at it as a drug for me any more than I would psychiatric medications. It's a tool that helps me have insights and understand life.

LEADER: Were you smoking any more than usual last week?

JIM: Well, I did get a good supply last week so you could say that I was smoking a fair amount until it ran out.

LEADER: When did it run out?

JIM: Friday night.

LEADER: When did you get psychotic?

JIM: I don't know. I guess it started Friday during the day.

LEADER: Do you like being psychotic?

JIM: It's interesting to a point but I don't like getting real paranoid. I usually quit smoking before it gets too bad.

LEADER: But you didn't this time. How come?

JIM: It was really good stuff and I had a lot of it. I guess I just didn't want to stop badly enough.

LEADER: What do you think, Brian?

BRIAN: I don't know. Sounds like he couldn't stop.

LEADER: George?

GEORGE: I know where he's coming from. It's hard to say no when it's right there under your nose.

LEADER: And you usually don't feel the consequences until it's too late. Jim, no one can decide what's right for you except yourself but it sounds like your pot use wasn't all that pleasurable this week.

JIM: Yeah, I was pretty hurting by the end.

LEADER: What did it cost you to buy?

JIM: Forty bucks.

LEADER: Was it worth it?

JIM: If you'd have asked me Thursday I would have said yes. I don't know now.

COMMON AND UNIQUE FACTORS IN GROUP MODELS

Different models of integrated group treatment share many common characteristics. All the approaches educate clients about the effects of substance use and avoid the confrontation typical of many programs for primary substance abuse. Each of the models strives to create a supportive social milieu within the group and encourages socialization between members outside of the group. All the models also recognize the role that psychiatric disorders play in increasing clients' risk to substance abuse (for example, symptoms, stigma, and lack of leisure activities) and attempt to address illness-related factors that may contribute to this vulnerability through education, skills training, and supportive techniques. Finally, all the models endorse the potential benefits of self-help organizations such as AA in aiding clients in their recovery from substance use disorders.

The models of group treatment can be distinguished primarily in their philosophy of recovery. By its very nature, only stagewise treatment explicitly identifies goals and targets interventions based on the client's stage of recovery and focuses on self-assessment of motivational development as a prerequisite to sobriety-oriented work. Twelve-step groups have a strong orientation toward recovery based on the traditional AA model and toward trying to engage clients in self-help groups available in the community. The skills training approach places a premium on the acquisition of new skills and downplays the possible role of insight in aiding recovery. Although none of these foci are unique to one model, their emphasis differs across the models. Thus the twelve-step, educational-supportive, stagewise, and social skills models are each based on somewhat different but compatible philosophies. Overall, the integrated approaches to group treatment have more in common than they are unique.

RESEARCH ON GROUP TREATMENT

Over the past decade a number of studies have examined the effectiveness of group treatment in the context of integrated programs for dually diagnosed persons. The results of these studies are summarized in Table 1. As can be seen from inspection of this table, research has been limited by the paucity of controlled studies, especially those involving random assignment to treatment groups. None of the three studies in which clients were randomly assigned to *group treatment* and *no group treatment* categories found an added effect for the group intervention (Carey, Carey, and Meisler, 1990; Hellerstein, Rosenthal, and Miner, 1995; Lehman, Herron, Schwartz, and Myers, 1993). These studies were limited, however, by the relatively brief intervention period (ranging from six weeks to one year), small sample sizes (ranging from twenty-nine to fifty-four), and nonattendance in the group condition (for example, Lehman, Herron, Schwartz, and Myers, 1993). Bond, McDonel, Miller, and Pensec's (1991) quasi-experimental study was unique in that clients who received group treatment over eighteen months improved more in substance abuse outcomes than clients who received either ACT or standard treatment. It is possible that nonrandom assignment of clients to treatment condition contributed to the differential outcome in substance abuse. Jerrell and Ridgely's (1995) study suggests that different approaches to integrated treatment produce similar results, with some advantage for the skills training model. By and large, however, the outcomes for the different integrated treatments in this study were similar. In a recently completed study, Drake and others (1996) reported that integrated substance abuse and mental health treatment, with a heavy reliance on cognitive-behavioral groups, resulted in better alcohol abuse and housing outcomes for homeless dually diagnosed persons than standard services that employed twelve-step groups. Similar to Jerrell and Ridgely's (1995) study, however, the two treatment conditions studied by Drake and others differed in a variety of respects other than the group models used, so it is difficult to ascribe differences in outcomes to the group models employed.

Although the experimental evidence supporting the added benefits of group treatment is meager, more naturalistic pre-post study designs suggest that group treatment, when provided with other elements of integrated treatment, is associated with improved outcomes compared to standard care. There is also a trend for integrated treatments that include groups to more successfully engage and retain clients in treatment, which is associated with better outcomes (Drake, McHugo, and Noordsy, 1993; Hellerstein and Meehan, 1987; Hellerstein, Rosenthal, and Miner, 1995; Kofoed and Keys, 1988; Kofoed, Kania, Walsh, and Atkinson, 1986). These findings are consistent with the positive results of the NIMH Community Support Program Demonstration Studies of Services for Young Adults with Severe Mental Illness and Substance Abuse (Mercer-McFadden and Drake, 1993), which examined the effects of integrated treatment, including group intervention, across thirteen different sites.

It appears that one obstacle to demonstrating the effects of group treatment is that integrated approaches are so powerful that it is difficult to show the added advantage of a single component of the model. At the same time, a systematic dismantling of the different components of integrated treatment models is a formidable task, both because of the sheer number of components (for example, case management, family intervention, group models, use of monitoring techniques, control over contingencies such as funds, housing, and hospitalization) and because of the variety of articulated integrated treatment models. An additional research problem is that only 50 to 75 percent of dually diagnosed clients will attend groups even minimally, and 30 to 50 percent regularly. Therefore the group must have very strong effects to exceed the "noise" of nonattenders.

Table 1. Summary of research on group treatment for dually diagnosed clients

Investigator	Number Clients	Treatment Groups	Duration of Treatment	Research Design	Outcomes
Kofoed and others (1986)	32	Educational-supportive	Up to 2 years (weekly sessions)	Pre-post	35% of clients remained in treatment for more than 3 months Clients who remained in treatment spent less time in hospital.
Hellerstein and Meehan (1987)	10	Educational-supportive	1 year (weekly sessions)	Pre-post	50% of clients remained in treatment 1 year. Clients who remained in treatment spent less time in hospital.
Kofoed and Keys (1988)	109	Stagewise (persuasion)	Inpatient-brief (2 sessions/week)	Non-experimental comparison of two wards	Clients in treatment group referred for outpatient substance abuse treatment more than clients who did not receive treatment group.
	109	No inpatient group treatment			No differences in rehospitalization over 6 months.
Carey and others (1990)	17	Social skills training (problem solving)	6 weeks (2 sessions/week)	Random assignment to group/no group treatment	At 1 month follow-up, no difference in problem-solving skills between groups.
	12	No group treatment			

Investigator	Number Clients	Treatment Groups	Duration of Treatment	Research Design	Outcomes
Bond and others (1991)	23	Educational-supportive	18 months (variable group session frequency)	Quasi-experimental	Group treatment and ACT clients remained in treatment longer.
	31	Assertive community treatment (ACT) (no group treatment)			Group treatment clients had fewer hospitalizations; ACT clients spent less time in hospital.
	43	Control (no group treatment)			Group treatment clients used less alcohol and drugs. All clients improved in quality of life.
Noordsy and Fox (1991)	18	Stagewise	3 years (weekly sessions)	Pre-post	Approximately 60% of all clients attained stable abstinence and 80% of group attenders
Alfs and McClellan (1992)	145	Educational-supportive	6-8 weeks (daily meetings in day hospital; weekly evening aftercare)	Pre-post	66% of clients completed program. 33% of clients in active treatment relapsed.
Lehman and others (1993)	29	Educational-supportive and twelve-step and intensive case management	1 year (daily sessions)	Random assignment to group/no group treatment	Clients in group treatment attended 20% of the groups. No differences or changes in symptoms, substance abuse, or life satisfaction.
	25	Control (no group treatment)			

Investigator Clients	Number Groups	Treatment Treatment	Duration of Design	Research Outcomes
Hellerstein and others (1995)				
24	Educational-supportive	8 months (2 sessions/week)	Random assignment to group/no group treatment	36% of clients remained in treatment. Clients improved in substance abuse and symptoms, but no differences between group treatment and controls.
23	Control (standard, nonintegrated, no group treatment)			
Jerrell and Ridgely (1995)				
39	Twelve-step	18 months	Quasi-experimental	Clients improved on most measures of substance abuse, symptoms, social functioning, and service utilization.
45	Case management (CM) and sporadic educational groups			Clients in SST tended to do best, followed by CM, followed by 12-step
48	Social skills training (SST)			
Drake and others (1996)				
158	Integrated treatment and cognitive-behavioral groups	18 months	Quasi-experimental	Clients in integrated treatment improved more in alcohol abuse, spent less time in hospitals, and had more stable housing. Clients in both treatments improved in symptoms and quality of life.
59	Standard treatment with 12-step groups.			

Recommendations for Future Research on Group Treatment

Significant progress has been made over the past decade in the treatment of dually diagnosed persons. Coincident with the recognition that these individuals need comprehensive interventions that simultaneously address both disorders, an understanding has developed that short-term treatments produce short-term benefits, and that long-term strategies are required for meaningful results to accrue. Group intervention has consistently been included as a vital component of integrated treatment programs, yet there are scant data to support this important role. In fact, only two controlled studies suggest added benefits of group treatment, and both included quasi-experimental, not fully randomized designs (Bond and others, 1991; Jerrell and Ridgley, 1995).

Several avenues of research may shed light on the effects of group treatment. First, there is a pressing need for more controlled research that compares the effects of integrated treatment with versus without group therapy. In order for such research to be meaningful, the treatments must be provided long-term (preferably at least eighteen months), the group model must be sufficiently specified, and a moderate proportion of the clients must attend the groups. Studies in which few clients regularly attend groups tell us little about the efficacy of group intervention (for example, Lehman, Herron, Schwartz, and Myers, 1993). It may be fruitful to identify characteristics of clients most likely to attend treatment groups so that research on the efficacy of group treatment can focus primarily on these clients, and clinicians can explore strategies for increasing attendance at groups.

Second, there is a need to examine whether specific client attributes are predictive of clinical response to group treatment in general or to specific models of group intervention. For example, it might be argued that social skills deficits will predict a better response to social skills training, an external locus of control will be related to improvements in a twelve-step approach, whereas antisocial personality characteristics predict a poor response to all group interventions. Although such correlational research is necessarily speculative, it can form the basis for hypothesis generation that can be subsequently evaluated in experimental designs.

Finally, research into group treatment may provide valuable insights into the relationship between specific dimensions of client participation in the group (for example, level of participation and specific content of verbal contributions) and their current and future clinical functioning. At present, there is little available information to aid clinicians in understanding when and for whom the group intervention is working. Research on client group behavior and patterns of substance abuse may assist clinicians in identifying clients who are ready to begin tapering their substance use, who are at increased risk for relapse, or who may be on the verge of dropping out. Such information would enable clinicians to take proactive steps to enhance outcomes.

Substantial advances have been made in treating this difficult population. The positive effects of many different interventions that have included a group treatment component bode well for the efficacy of this modality. Despite this, the benefits of group treatment remain to be empirically demonstrated. The recent specification of a number of coherent group treatment models poises the field to address this important question.

REFERENCES

Alfs. D. S., and McClellan, T. A. "A Day Hospital Program for Dual Diagnosis Patients in a VA Medical Center." *Hospital and Community Psychiatry,* 1992, *43,* 241-244.

Bartels, S. J., and Thomas, W. N. "Lessons from a Pilot Residential Treatment Program for People with Dual Disorders of Severe Mental Illness and Substance Use Disorder." *Psychosocial Rehabilitation Journal,* 1991, *15,* 19-30.

Bond, G., McDonel, E. C., Miller, L. D., and Pensec, M. "Assertive Community Treatment and Reference Groups: An Evaluation of their Effectiveness for Young Adults with Serious Mental Illness and Substance Use Problems." *Psychosocial Rehabilitation Journal,* 1991, *15,* 31-43.

Bricker, M. "The Evolution of Mutual Help Groups for Dual Recovery." *TIE-Lines,* 1994, *11,* 1-4.

Caldwell, S., and White, K. K. "Co-Creating a Self-Help Recovery Movement." *Psychosocial Rehabilitation Journal,* 1991, *15,* 91-95.

Carey, M. P., Carey, K. B., and Meisler, A. W. "'Training Mentally Ill Chemical Abusers in Social Problem Solving." *Behavior Therapy,* 1990, *21,* 511-518.

Dixon, L., Haas, G., Weiden, P., Sweeney, J., and Frances, A. "Drug Abuse in Schizophrenic Patients: Clinical Correlates and Reasons for Use." *American Journal of Psychiatry,* 1991, *148,* 224-230.

Drake, R. E., Bartels, S. J., Teague, G. B., Noordsy, D. L., and Clark, R. E. "Treatment of Substance Abuse in Severely Mentally Ill Patients." *Journal of Nervous and Mental Disease,* 1993, *181,* 606-611.

Drake, R. E., McHugo, G. J., and Noordsy, D. L. "Treatment of Alcoholism Among Schizophrenic Outpatients: Four-Year Outcomes." *American Journal of Psychiatry,* 1993, *150,* 328-329.

Drake, R. E., Yovetich, N. A., Bebout, R. R., Harris, M., and McHugo, G. J. "Integrated Treatment for Dually Diagnosed Homeless Adults." Unpublished manuscript, 1996.

Ericsson, K. A., and Charness, N. "Expert Performance: Its Structure and Acquisition." *American Psychologist,* 1994, *49,* 725-747.

Hellerstein, D. J., and Meehan, B. "Outpatient Group Therapy for Schizophrenic Substance Abusers." *American Journal of Psychiatry,* 1987, *144,* 1337-1339.

Hellerstein, D. J., Rosenthal, R. N., and Miner, C. R. "A Prospective Study of Integrated Outpatient Treatment for Substance-Abusing Schizophrenic Patients." *American Journal on Addictions,* 1995, *4,* 33-42.

Hendrickson, E., and Schmal, M. "Dual Disorder." *TIE-Lines,* 1994, *11,* 10-11.

Jerrell, J. M., and Ridgely, M. S. "Comparative Effectiveness of Three Approaches to Serving People with Severe Mental Illness and Substance Abuse Disorders." *Journal of Nervous and Mental Disease,* 1995, *183,* 566-576.

Kofoed, L. L., Kania, J., Walsh, T., and Atkinson, R. M. "Outpatient Treatment of Patients with Substance Abuse and Coexisting Psychiatric Disorders." *American Journal of Psychiatry,* 1986, *143,* 867-872.

Kofoed, L. L., and Keys, A. "Using Group Therapy to Persuade Dual-Diagnosis Patients to Seek Substance Abuse Treatment." *Hospital and Community Psychiatry,* 1988, *39,* 1209-1211.

Kurtz, L. F., Garvin, C. D., Hill, E. M., Pollio, D., McPherson, S., and Powell, T. J. "Involvement in Alcoholics Anonymous by Persons with Dual Disorders." *Alcoholism Treatment Quarterly,* 1995, *12,* 1-18.

Lehman, A. F., Herron, J. D., Schwartz, R. P., and Myers, C. P. "Rehabilitation for Adults with Severe Mental Illness and Substance Use Disorders: A Clinical Trial." *Journal of Nervous and Mental Disease,* 1993, *181,* 86-90.

Liberman, R. P., DeRisi, W. J., and Mueser, K. T. *Social Skills Training for Psychiatric Patients.* Needham Heights, Mass.: Allyn & Bacon, 1989.

Liberman, R., and Associates. *Psychiatric Rehabilitation of the Chronic Mental Patient.* Washington, D.C.: American Psychiatric Press, 1987.

Marlatt, G. A., and Gordon, J. R. *Relapse Prevention Maintenance Strategies in the Treatment of Addictive Behaviors.* New York: Guilford Press, 1985.

Mercer-McFadden, C., and Drake, R. E. *A Review of NIMH Demonstration Programs for Young Adults with Co-Occurring Severe Mental Illness and Substance Use Disorder.* Center for Community Mental Health Services, SAMSHA. Rockville, Md.: U.S. Department of Health and Human Services, 1993.

Miller, W. R., and Rollnick, S. *Motivational Interviewing: Preparing People to Change Addictive Behavior.* New York: Guilford Press, 1991.

Minkoff, K. "An Integrated Treatment Model for Dual Diagnosis of Psychosis and Addiction." *Hospital and Community Psychiatry,* 1989, *40,* 1031-1036.

Monti, P. M., Abrams, D. B., Kadden, R. M., and Cooney, N. L. *Treating Alcohol Dependence.* New York: Guilford Press, 1989.

Mueser, K. T., Fox, M., Kenison, L. B., and Geltz, B. L. *The Better Living Skills Group.* Treatment manual, 1995. Available from New Hampshire-Dartmouth Psychiatric Research, Main Building, 105 Pleasant St., Concord, NH, 03301.

Nikkel, R. E. "Areas of Skills Training for Persons with Mental Illness and Substance Use Disorders: Building Skills for Successful Living." *Community Mental Health Journal,* 1994, *30,* 61-72.

Noordsy, D. L., and Fox, L. "Group Intervention Techniques for People with Dual Disorders." *Psychosocial Rehabilitation Journal,* 1991, *15,* 67-78.

Noordsy, D. L., Schwab, B., Fox, L., and Drake, R. E. "The Role of Self-Help Programs in the Rehabilitation of Persons with Severe Mental Illness." *Community Mental Health Journal,* 1996, *32,* 71-78.

Prochaska, J. O., Velicer, W. F., DiClemente, C. C., and Fava, J. "Measuring Processes of Change: Application to the Cessation of Smoking." *Journal of Consulting and Clinical Psychology,* 1988, *56,* 520-528.

Sciacca, K. "New Initiatives on the Treatment of the Chronic Patient with Alcohol/ Substance Use Problems." *TIE-Lines,* 1987, *4,* 5-6.

Straussman, J. "Dealing with Double Disabilities: Alcohol Use in the Club." *Psychosocial Rehabilitation Journal,* 1985, *8,* 8-14.

Test, M. A., Wallisch, L., Allness, D. J., and Ripp, K. "Substance Use in Young Adults with Schizophrenic Disorders." *Schizophrenia Bulletin,* 1989, *15,* 465-476.

Woods, J. D. "Incorporating Services for Chemical Dependency Problems into Clubhouse Model Programs: A Description of Two Programs." *Psychosocial Rehabilitation Journal,* 1991, *15,* 107-112.

ABOUT THE AUTHORS

Kim T. Mueser, Ph.D., is Professor of Psychiatry and Community and Family Medicine at Dartmouth Medical School and a senior researcher at the New Hampshire-Dartmouth Psychiatric Research Center. Douglas L. Noordsy, M.D., is Medical Director of The Mental Health Center of Greater Manchester, Manchester, NH, and is Assistant Professor of Psychiatry at Dartmouth Medical School and Research Associate at the New Hampshire-Dartmouth Psychiatric Research Center.

Copyright 1996. Jossey-Bass, Inc., Publishers. Reprinted with permission.

THE ROLE OF SELF-HELP PROGRAMS IN THE REHABILITATION OF PERSONS WITH SEVERE MENTAL ILLNESS AND SUBSTANCE USE DISORDERS

Douglas L. Noordsy, Brenda Schwab,
Lindy Fox, and Robert E. Drake

Reprinted from *Community Mental Health Journal*, 32(1):71-81, 1996

Substance abuse treatment programs in the United States frequently incorporate self-help approaches, but little is known about the use of self-help groups by individuals with dual disorders. This paper brings together several current studies on the role of self-help programs in treating substance use disorders among individuals with severe mental illness. These studies indicate that only a minority of individuals with dual disorders become closely linked to self-help. Psychiatric diagnosis and possibly social skills are correlates of participation. Dually disordered consumers often experience the use of 12-step philosophy and jargon by mental health professionals as alienating and unempathic. The authors propose suggestions for incorporating self-help approaches into the comprehensive community care of individuals with dual disorders.

The high prevalence of co-occurring substance use disorders among individuals with severe mental illness is now widely recognized (Minkoff & Drake, 1991). As patients with dual disorders have poor short-term outcomes in traditional mental health programs and do not readily fit into traditional substance abuse treatment programs (Ridgely et al., 1990), models that integrate mental health and substance abuse treatments have been developed (Drake et al., 1991a, 1993a; Hellerstein and Meehan, 1987; Kofoed et al., 1986; Lehman et al., 1993; Minkoff, 1989). Linkage with Alcoholics Anonymous (AA) and other self-help groups for people with substance abuse has been included in many of these models. However, little information is available about how individuals with severe mental illness use these self-help groups.

The purpose of this paper is to report (a) findings from several studies on the use of AA and other self-help groups by patients who have coexisting severe mental illness and substance use disorder, and (b) our clinical observations regarding the use of self-help groups, based on working for several years in dual-disorder programs. The context for these studies and observations is New Hampshire's statewide service program for people with coexisting severe mental illness and substance use disorder (Drake et al., 1990b, 1991a; Noordsy and Fox, 1991).

RESEARCH STUDIES

Treatment of alcoholism among schizophrenic outpatients

Based on a pilot sample of outpatients with schizophrenia, we have previously reported the rate and correlates of alcohol use disorders (Drake et al., 1990a, 1991b; Noordsy et al., 1991; Osher et al., 1994), and the rate of recovery from alcohol use disorders over a four-year follow-up period (Drake et al., 1993b). We will present here previously unreported findings on the use of self-help in this study group.

The 18 patients with alcoholism and schizophrenia were treated continuously between 1987 and 1991 in a community mental health center-based dual-disorder program that included intensive case management, substance abuse treatment groups, and linkage with self-help groups in the community. Linkage to self-help was promoted through work on development of motivation to attend meetings, education about the content and format of meetings, transportation, and a "Double Trouble" AA meeting specifically for people with dual disorders held at the mental health center after hours. Patients were reevaluated approximately four years after their original evaluation. Alcohol use and street drug use were assessed through a combination of hospital records, mental health center records, psychiatric interviews, case manager ratings, and intensive case reviews to resolve disagreements. Use of self-help programs was assessed by case managers based on client reports, behavioral observations in the community and collateral information from families, community contacts, and other caregivers.

The 11 people who attained full remission from alcohol use disorders as defined in DSM-III-R (Remission group) were compared with the 7 people who did not (Active Abuse group). The two groups did not differ significantly at baseline in age, sex, diagnosis, marital status, or the number of months of prior hospitalization. There was a trend towards higher average MAST scores (29.3 vs. 20.6, $t(16)=-1.31$, $p=.21$) in the Active Abuse group at baseline.

Of the 18 patients, five (28%) attended self-help meetings during the four-year follow-up interval, and only one (5.6%) attended regularly (at least once a month). In contrast, 13 (72%) attended specialized dual-disorder treatment groups in the mental health center, and six (33%) attended these groups regularly (most attended nearly weekly). There was a weak trend towards patients being more likely to attend clinician-led groups than self-help groups during the interval (Fisher's exact test, $p=.150$).

The five individuals with schizophrenia who had attended self-help meetings were all diagnosed with alcohol dependence syndrome and two had co-occurring drug abuse. They had an average MAST score of 28.8. They all attended clinician-led dual-disorders treatment groups in addition to self-help meetings. Four of them were in the Active Abuse group at follow-up. Members of the Active Abuse group were more likely to use self-help during the study interval than were members of the Remission group (Fisher's exact test, $p=.047$).

An ethnographic study of dual-disorders treatment

This study reports on the ethnographic component of a randomized clinical trial of standard and intensive case management for persons with co-occurring severe mental illness and substance use disorders (Schwab, 1991). For two years, two ethnographers conducted participant observation and qualitative interviews with clients and case managers in both community and treatment settings, including self-help meetings (see Schwab, 1991; and Schwab et al., 1991 for a description of the ethnographic procedures). We will summarize findings on clinicians' efforts to promote self-help attendance, not on the use of twelve-step groups by consumers.

Several clients in this study found self-help programs helpful and were committed to participation. However, many reacted negatively to the use of twelve-step philosophy and jargon by clinicians. Consumers perceived this approach as minimizing the considerable problems they faced in living with their disabilities. One of the central precepts that seemed to contribute to misunderstandings and impasses in treatment was the attempt to challenge denial. Case managers used jargon such as "stinkin' thinkin'" to confront explanations for substance use. Clients were told, "It's your disease talking," to signify that an explanation for behavior was not coming from a client him- or herself; or the phrase, "people, places, and things," was used to refer to a person's blaming other persons or situations for his/her drug use rather than blaming the drug use for causing these problems (Schwab et al., 1991).

One consequence of using these standard responses was that case managers often missed opportunities to explore meanings from the client's perspective and, in some instances, used the concept of denial to discount the client's complaints about aspects of treatment. Clients perceived case managers' use of jargon, particularly in reference to the concept of denial, as a negation of their reasoning. Applying the concept of denial to clients' explanations and statements thus gave many clients the impression that case managers were ignoring their experience and their suffering (cf. Kleinman et al., 1992). Another consequence was that clients would admit to alcohol use and declare their intention to attend AA meetings in order to avoid discussion about their cocaine or other drug use and lack of participation in other aspects of treatment.

Resistance to self-help was seen by some case managers as noncompliance with treatment or failure to accept therapeutic goals and strategies (cf. Estroff, 1991; Kaljee & Beardsley, 1992). Use of standard phrases or statements about self-help participation became a kind of currency used between clients and case managers to negotiate treatment. In such discussions, self-help meeting attendance was treated as if it was a major goal of treatment, rather than a means to an end.

A significant limitation of this study was that the suitability of the model could not be separated from idiosyncrasies in staff characteristics. During the first year of this study, some staff with little addictions treatment training were acquiring experience and expertise on the job. Over time they became more sophisticated at integrating twelve-step approaches with other treatment strategies. The ethnographic methods had the power to distinguish one fairly clear finding despite the limitations: when attempting to promote self-help among individuals with dual diagnoses, the case manager's use of a monolithic, inflexible approach was experienced as alienating by many clients.

Our observations are consistent with other anthropological findings in a variety of clinical settings. Impasses in treatment occur when clinicians do not explore or share the explanations or meanings patients attribute to their problems (Good & Good, 1981; Katon and Kleinman, 1981; Kleinman, 1981, 1988). Research shows that consumers of psychiatric services have ideas about their illnesses and medications that affect their behavior (Estroff, 1991; Kaljee & Beardsley, 1992; Rhodes, 1984). A more meaning-centered approach (Good & Good, 1981) to the treatment of substance abuse among mental health clients would emphasize listening to clients' explanatory models of their distress, rather than trying to impose a specific model of addiction on them.

Preliminary findings from other studies

This section surveys preliminary findings of two studies that are in preparation. One is a survey of self-help use among a group of individuals with dual disorders treated by case management teams in the community (Noordsy et al., in preparation), and the other is a follow-up of attendees of a residential dual-diagnosis program to evaluate outcomes including self-help use (Bartels, 1992; Bartels & Thomas, 1991).

Preliminary evaluations of these studies show some consistent themes. First, both studies show that few individuals use self-help groups consistently over time, despite the fact that the programs were successful in getting the majority of individuals to attend self-help meetings at some point. Second, diagnosis appears to be associated with intensity of self-help use in these study groups. Regular attendance at self-help programs seems to be more common among individuals with affective disorders than among those with schizophrenic disorders. Third, better social ability appeared to be associated with use of self-help programs.

We expect that these studies will demonstrate that self-help programs can be used by some clients with dual-disorders, although they do not usually participate fully. Social impairment may be an intervening variable between diagnosis and difficulty using self-help intensively, and deserves further study.

CLINICAL OBSERVATIONS

We have frequently heard from individuals with severe mental illness about their experiences attempting to use self-help groups in the recovery process. Several recurring themes are described here.

Many individuals reported avoiding initial attendance at self-help meetings because of a fear of large crowds and the feeling that everyone would be watching them. Symptoms of mental illness, medication use, and associated side-effects made them feel different from others. Some consumers reported that other self-help members encouraged them to discontinue psychiatric medications because all they needed were meetings.

Individuals who attempted to use self-help programs reported dropping out or finding it hard to make a regular commitment for several reasons. Some stated that once at a meeting they had difficulty sitting still, but felt uncomfortable getting up and leaving. If they were able to listen, many found the stories increased their desire to use substances. They often were unable to relate to the negative side of the stories they heard, as they hadn't experienced the same losses. They usually hadn't had a spouse, job, or car to lose because of substance abuse. Other individuals had difficulty distinguishing the spiritual recovery of 12-step programs from religious themes. Talk of spiritual awakening and advice to "let go and let God" became laden with delusional significance.

Although encouraged to attend self-help in order to develop a sober peer group, many individuals had difficulty finding people whom they felt similar to there. They often reported an inability to relate to others at meetings, and intimidation by the expectations that sponsorship would have placed on them. Their negative symptoms, suspiciousness, and social deficits were often misunderstood and responded to with confrontation. Some consumers who had trouble affiliating with self-help groups in the early stages of treatment attended more regularly in the later stages when they had established an abstinence goal.

Those people with dual diagnoses who were successful in linking to community self-help groups for management of their addiction generally described them as extremely helpful. Some obtained sponsors and got a list of members' phone numbers. They pointed to the network of support, broad availability, and flexibility to speak or just listen. In some instances they were able to talk about not only drug and alcohol problems, but also problems in living and coping on a daily basis. They liked feeling that they were not alone.

The religious aspects of 12-step meetings were very appealing to some clients who had strong religious backgrounds. Some found that the "one day at a time" approach worked for them and liked the routine and structure the meetings brought to their lives. A self-help meeting in one part of town had many of the same elements as a meeting anywhere.

Some of these consumers had accompanied their peers to self-help meetings or helped start special self-help meetings for people with dual disorders. They described being able to help a fellow addict or alcoholic as a very empowering experience.

DISCUSSION

Our data and observations suggest that self-help has an important but limited role in the treatment of substance use disorders among individuals with severe mental illness. We found evidence in several settings that only a small proportion of individuals with severe mental illness attend self-help programs regularly, despite extensive efforts at linkage by their treatment providers. We also found a trend towards greater use of clinician-led dual-diagnosis groups than self-help groups in one study. This supports the view that offering multiple treatment options for substance use disorders is important to comprehensive care for individuals with dual diagnoses (Drake & Noordsy, 1994).

The finding that vigorous attempts to promote self-help as the treatment of choice frequently alienated clients suggests the importance of using client preferences to guide treatment planning. Some clients who refuse self-help group membership initially may join at later treatment stages, which suggests that client's receptiveness to self-help promotion efforts may vary over time. The finding that active abusers in the first study were more likely to attend self-help suggests that linkage could occur over time for those dually diagnosed individuals who are still struggling with substance use.

Linkage to self-help appears to be related to diagnosis and possibly to social skills, which are also related to diagnosis (Samson et al., 1988). People with affective disorders may have different service needs and preferences than people with schizophrenia, and treatment should be tailored accordingly. Social ability deserves further study as a potential predictor of likelihood to affiliate with self-help groups.

The fact that some consumers affiliated strongly with self-help groups and found them helpful in their recovery indicates that self-help approaches remain a viable treatment option for people with dual-diagnoses. As difficulty fitting-in was a problem cited by many consumers in these studies, self-help groups specific to dual disorders may have some advantage (Bricker, 1994). Double Trouble groups, for example, are self-help meetings based on AA specifically for individuals with dual disorders (Hendrickson & Schmal, 1994). Such groups were available in the mental health centers during these studies on a once weekly basis, but were not otherwise broadly available. The trend towards higher rates of affiliation with clinician-led groups than with self-help in general could reflect the greater presence of peers with dual disorders in the former groups.

Those consumers who did affiliate with self-help cited the importance of a network of support, structure, wide availability, and the option to just listen. Assuming that self-help is not optimal treatment for all consumers, there may be value in investigating the incorporation of these factors into clinician-provided treatment.

It is not clear how the intensity of self-help affiliation found here would compare to a sample without mental illness. Less intensive use of self-help may be optimal for some individuals. Individuals with serious mental illness may be self-selecting a comfortable level of involvement with self-help programs that does not include establishing a sponsor or frequent attendance.

These findings were generated under conditions of considerable support and assistance in using self-help and the simultaneous availability of extensive case management and other substance abuse treatment services. As these studies took place in the context of assertive treatment in residential and community settings in rural and small urban environments, the applicability of these findings to other treatment settings is unknown. The context of treatment initiation in these studies was also different from most substance abuse treatment settings, although typical of work with individuals with severe mental illness. Clients were identified by clinicians and research instruments as having substance abuse problems, often well before they identified such problems themselves.

CLINICAL GUIDELINES

These studies suggest that without careful attention to clients' explanatory models and tolerance for intensity of intervention we may have difficulty developing plans for treatment of substance abuse that clients can comfortably participate in. The approach we have developed provides an array of addictions treatment services, including self-help promotion, brought to the individual with mental illness in their natural environment and fit to their needs. Basic needs such as housing (Drake et al., 1991b) and vocational rehabilitation (Becker & Drake, 1994) are attended to in a fashion that supports engagement around substance use issues. Multiple addictions treatment models are tried, with their relative effectiveness guiding further application for each individual. We feel that self-help programs have their greatest potential when chosen by individuals in this context. Suggested guidelines are as follows:

1) Introduce self-help programs as one treatment option that is helpful for many people, and make other treatment options available.
2) Help clients to sample self-help by offering to accompany them to meetings. Help them overcome the social barriers by introducing them to people at the meeting and translating the meeting during and afterwards.
3) Treat the mental illness, addiction and underlying social skills deficits aggressively to increase clients' ability to function independently in self-help.
4) If the client doesn't like self-help, back off. Don't pair yourself so tightly with self-help that the client has to reject you to reject self-help. Use other treatment approaches to help the client make progress and gain trust in you. At later treatment stages gently introduce self-help options again.
5) Encourage attendance at Double Trouble or similar groups when possible to improve member-group fit. Recovering individuals with dual disorders can be helpful in facilitating the affiliation process as well.

CONCLUSIONS

We have compiled several perspectives on the role of self-help interventions from our work on the treatment of substance use disorders among individuals with severe mental illness. Collectively these suggest that a minority of consumers with dual diagnoses affiliate closely with self-help programs, that diagnosis and possibly social function are associated with successful linkage, that most achieve remission without using self-help, and that emphasizing a twelve-step model with those who don't gravitate to it can be counter-productive. Our clinical experience suggests that self-help programs are experienced as most helpful by consumers when the program philosophy is consistent with their own explanatory models and chosen voluntarily.

REFERENCES

Bartels, S.J. (1992). *Programming for mentally ill substance abusers.* Washington: Presented at the 145th American Psychiatric Association annual meeting, May 4th.

Bartels, S.J. & Thomas, W. (1991). Lessons from a residential program for people with dual diagnoses of severe mental illness and substance use disorder. *Psychosocial Rehabilitation Journal, 15,* 19-30.

Becker, D.R. & Drake, R.E. (1994). Individual placement and support: A community mental health center approach to vocational rehabilitation. *Community Mental Health Journal, 30,* 193-206.

Bricker, M. (1994). The evolution of mutual help groups for dual recovery. *Tie Lines, 11,* 1-4.

Drake, R.E., Antosca, L., Noordsy, D.L., Bartels, S.J. & Osher, F.C. (1991a). New Hampshire's specialized services for the dually diagnosed. In K. Minkoff & R.E. Drake (Eds.), *Dual Diagnosis of Major Mental Illness and Substance Disorder.* San Francisco: Jossey-Bass.

Drake, R.E., Bartels, S.J., Teague, G.B., Noordsy, D.L. & Clark, R.E. (1993a). Treatment of substance abuse in severely mentally ill patients. *Journal of Nervous and Mental Disease, 181,* 606-611.

Drake, R.E., McHugo, G.J. & Noordsy, D.L. (1993b). Treatment of alcoholism among schizophrenic outpatients: Four-year outcomes. *American Journal of Psychiatry, 150,* 328-329.

Drake, R.E. & Noordsy, D.L. (1994). Case management for people with coexisting severe mental disorder and substance use disorder. *Psychiatric Annals, 24,* 427-431.

Drake, R.E., Osher, F.C., Noordsy, D.L., Hurlbut, S.C., Teague, G.B. & Beaudett, M.S. (1990a). Diagnosis of alcohol use disorders in schizophrenia. *Schizophrenia Bulletin 16,* 57-67.

Drake, R.E., Teague, G.B. & Warren, R.S. (1990b). New Hampshire's dual diagnosis program for people with severe mental illness and substance use disorder. *Addiction and Recovery, 10,* 35-39.

Drake, R.E., Wallach, M.A., Teague, G.B., Freeman, D.H., Paskus, T.S. & Clark, T.A. (1991b). Housing instability and homelessness among rural schizophrenic outpatients. *American Journal of Psychiatry, 148,* 330-336.

Estroff, S.E. (1991). Everybody's got a little mental illness: Accounts of self among people with severe, persistent mental illness. *Medical Anthropology Quarterly, 5,* 331-369.

Good, B.J. & Delvecchio-Good, M.J. (1981). The meaning of symptoms: A cultural hermeneutics model for clinical practice. In L. Eisenberg & A. Kleinman (Eds), *The Relevance of Social Science for Medicine.* Boston: D. Reidel Publishing.

Hellerstein, D.J. & Meehan, B. (1987). Outpatient group therapy for schizophrenic substance abusers. *American Journal of Psychiatry, 144,* 1337-39.

Hendrickson, E. & Schmal, M. (1994) Dual Disorder. *Tie Lines, 11*:10-11.

Kaljee, L.M. & Beardsley, R. (1992). Psychotropic drugs and concepts of compliance in a rural mental health clinic. *Medical Anthropology Quarterly, 6,* 271-287.

Katon, W. & Kleinman, A. (1981). Doctor-patient negotiation and other social science strategies in patient care. In L. Eisenberg & A. Kleinman (Eds.), *The Relevance of Social Science for Medicine.* Boston: D. Reidel Publishing.

Kleinman, A. (1981). On illness meanings and clinical interpretation. *Culture, Medicine and Psychiatry, 5,* 373-377.

Kleinman, A. (1988). *The Illness Narratives: Suffering, Healing and the Human Condition.* New York: Basic Books.

Kleinman, A., Brodwin, P.E., Good, B.J., Good, M.J., DelVecchio (1992). Pain as human experience: An introduction. In M.J.D. Good, P.E. Good, B.J. Good, A. Kleinman (Eds.), *Pain as Human Experience: An Anthropological Perspective.* Berkeley: University of California Press.

Kofoed, L., Kania, J., Walsh, T. & Atkinson, R. (1986). Outpatient treatment of patients with substance abuse and coexisting psychiatric disorders. *American Journal of Psychiatry, 143,* 867-872.

Lehman, A.F., Herron, J.D. & Schwartz, R.P. (1993) Rehabilitation for young adults with severe mental illness and substance use disorders: A clinical trial. *Journal of Nervous and Mental Disease, 181,* 86-90.

Minkoff, K. (1989). An integrated treatment model for dual diagnosis of psychosis and addiction. *Hospital and Community Psychiatry, 40,* 1031-1036.

Minkoff, K. & Drake, R.E. (Eds.) (1991). *Dual Diagnosis of Major Mental Illness and Substance Disorder.* San Francisco: Jossey-Bass.

Noordsy, D.L., Drake, R.E., Teague, G.B., Osher, F.C., Hurlbut, S.C., Beaudett, M.S., Paskus, T.S. (1991). Subjective experiences related to alcohol use among schizophrenics. *Journal of Nervous and Mental Disease, 179,* 410-414.

Noordsy, D.L. & Fox, L. (1991). Group intervention techniques for people with dual diagnoses. *Journal of Psychosocial Rehabilitation, 15,* 67-78.

Noordsy, D.L., Kremzner, S.A., Parker J., Drake R.E. (in preparation) Self-help use among dually diagnosed individuals in treatment.

Osher, F.C., Drake, R.E., Noordsy, D.L., Teague, G.B., Hurlbut, S.C., Paskus, T.S., Beaudett, M.S. (1994) Correlates and outcomes of alcohol use disorder among rural schizophrenic outpatients. *Journal of Clinical Psychiatry, 55,* 109-113.

Rhodes, L.A. (1984). "This will clear your mind": The use of metaphors for medication in psychiatric settings. *Culture, Medicine and Psychiatry, 8,* 49-70.

Ridgely, M.S., Goldman, H.H. & Willenbring, M. (1990). Barriers to the care of persons with dual diagnoses: Organizational and financing issues. *Schizophrenia Bulletin, 16,* 123-132.

Samson, J.A., Simpson, J.C. & Tsuang, M.T. (1988). Outcome studies of schizoaffective disorders. *Schizophrenia Bulletin, 14,* 543-554.

Schwab, B. (1991). *Explanatory models in conflict: Substance abuse treatment for persons with chronic mental illness.* Chicago: Presented at the American Anthropological Association annual meeting, November 2nd.

Schwab, B., Clark, R.E. & Drake, R.E. (1991). An ethnographic note on clients as parents. *Psychosocial Rehabilitation Journal, 15,* 95-99.

ABOUT THE AUTHORS

Douglas L. Noordsy, M.D., is Medical Director of The Mental Health Center of Greater Manchester, Manchester, NH, and is Assistant Professor of Psychiatry at Dartmouth Medical School and Research Associate at New Hampshire-Dartmouth Psychiatric Research Center. Brenda Schwab, Ph.D., is a faculty member in the Department of Anthropology at Dartmouth College. Lindy Fox, M.A., is Research Associate at New Hampshire-Dartmouth Psychiatric Research Center. Robert E. Drake, M.D., Ph.D., is Director of New Hampshire-Dartmouth Psychiatric Research Center and Professor of Psychiatry and Community and Family Medicine at Dartmouth Medical School.

Reprinted with permission from *Community Mental Health Journal.*

PHARMACOLOGIC MANAGEMENT
Center for Substance Abuse Treatment

Reprinted from *Assessment and Treatment of Patients with Coexisting Mental Illness and Alcohol and Other Drug Abuse,* Treatment Improvement Protocol (TIP) Series 9. DHHS Publication No. (SMA) 94-2078. Rockville, MD: U.S. Department of Health and Human Services, Public Health Service, Substance Abuse and Mental Health Services Administration, (pp. 91-103), 1994

PHARMACOLOGIC RISK FACTORS

Addiction is not a fixed and rigid event. Like psychiatric disorders, addiction is a dynamic process, with fluctuations in severity, rate of progression, and symptom manifestation and with differences in the speed of onset. Both disorders are greatly influenced by several factors, including genetic susceptibility, environment, and pharmacologic influences. Certain people have a high risk for these disorders (genetic risk); some situations can evoke or help to sustain these disorders (environmental risk); and some drugs are more likely than others to cause psychiatric or AOD[1] use disorder problems (pharmacologic risk).

Pharmacologic effects can be therapeutic or detrimental. Medication often produces both effects. Therapeutic pharmacologic effects include the indicated purposes and desired outcomes of taking prescribed medications, such as a decrease in the frequency and severity of episodes of depression produced by antidepressants.

Detrimental pharmacologic effects include unwanted side effects, such as dry mouth or constipation resulting from antidepressant use. Side effects perceived as noxious by patients may decrease their compliance with taking the medications as directed.

Some detrimental pharmacologic effects relate to abuse and addiction potential. For example, some medications may be stimulating, sedating, or euphorigenic and may promote physical dependence and tolerance. These effects can promote the use of medication for longer periods and at higher doses than prescribed.

Thus, prescribing medication involves striking a balance between therapeutic and detrimental pharmacologic effects. For instance, therapeutic antianxiety effects of the benzodiazepines are balanced against detrimental pharmacologic effects of sedation and physical dependency. Similarly, the desired therapeutic effect of abstinence from alcohol is balanced by the possibility of damage to the liver from prescribed disulfiram (Antabuse).

---

[1]AOD = alcohol and other drug

Pharmacologic Risk Factors

A medication may have:
- Psychoactive potential (causes acute psychomotor effects)
- Reinforcement potential (decreases negative symptoms and increases positive symptoms)
- Tolerance and withdrawal potential (a higher dose is needed to gain the effect or to avoid ill effects)

Side effects of prescription medications vary greatly and include detrimental pharmacologic effects that may promote abuse or addiction. With regard to patients with dual disorders, special attention should be given to detrimental effects, in terms of 1) medication compliance, 2) abuse and addiction potential, 3) AOD use disorder relapse, and 4) psychiatric disorder relapse (Ries, 1993).

Psychoactive potential

Not all psychiatric medications are psychoactive. The term *psychoactive* describes the ability of certain medications, drugs, and other substances to cause acute psychomotor effects and a relatively rapid change in mood or thought. Changes in mood include stimulation, sedation, and euphoria. Thought changes can include a disordering of thought such as delusions, hallucinations, and illusions. Behavioral changes can include an acceleration or retardation of motor activity. All drugs of abuse are by definition psychoactive.

In contrast, certain nonpsychoactive medications such as lithium (Eskalith) can, over time, normalize the abnormal mood and behavior of patients with bipolar disorder. Because these effects take several days or weeks to occur, and do not involve acute mood alteration, it is not accurate to describe these drugs as psychoactive, euphorigenic, or mood altering. Rather, they might be described as *mood regulators*. Similarly, some drugs, such as antipsychotic medications, cause normalization of thinking processes but do not cause acute mood alteration or euphoria.

However, some antidepressant and antipsychotic medications have pharmacologic side effects such as mild sedation or mild stimulation. Indeed, the side effects of these medications can be used clinically. Physicians can use a mildly sedating antidepressant medication for patients with depression and insomnia, or a mildly stimulating antipsychotic medication for patients with psychosis and hypersomnia or lethargy (Davis and Goldman, 1992). While the side effects of these drugs include a mild effect on mood, they are not euphorigenic. Nevertheless, case reports of misuse of nonpsychoactive medications have been noted, and use should be monitored carefully in patients with dual disorders.

While psychoactive drugs are generally considered to have high risk for abuse and addiction, mood-regulating drugs are not. A few other medications exert a mild psychoactive effect without having addiction potential. For example, the older antihistamines such as doxylamine (Unisom) exert mild sedative effects, but not euphoric effects.

Reinforcement potential

Some drugs promote *reinforcement,* or the increased likelihood of repeated use. Reinforcement can occur by either the removal of negative symptoms or conditions or the amplification of positive symptoms or states. For example, self-medication that delays or prevents an unpleasant event (such as withdrawal) from occurring becomes reinforcing. Thus, using a benzodiazepine to avoid alcohol withdrawal can increase the likelihood of continued use. *Positive reinforcement* involves strengthening the possibility that a certain behavior will be repeated through reward and satisfaction, as with drug-induced euphoria or drug-induced feelings of well-being. A classic example is the pleasure derived from moderate to high doses of opiates or stimulants. Drugs that are immediately reinforcing are more likely to lead to psychiatric or AOD use problems.

Tolerance and withdrawal potential

Long-term or chronic use of certain medications can cause tolerance to the subjective and therapeutic effects and prompt dosage increases to recreate the desired effects. In addition, many drugs cause a well-defined withdrawal phenomenon after the cessation of chronic use. Patients' attempts to avoid withdrawal syndromes often lead them to additional drug use. Thus, drugs that promote tolerance and withdrawal generally have higher risks for abuse and addiction.

A Stepwise Treatment Model

As can be seen, there are pharmacologic as well as hereditary and environmental factors that influence the development of AOD use problems. All of these factors should be considered prior to prescribing medication, especially when the patient is at high risk for developing an AOD use disorder. High-risk patients include people with both psychiatric and AOD use disorders, as well as patients with a psychiatric disorder and a family history of AOD use disorders.

One aspect of this issue relates to the pharmacologic profile of certain medications that are used in the treatment of specific psychiatric disorders. For instance, many medications used to treat symptoms of depression and psychosis are not psychoactive or euphorigenic. However, many of the medications used to treat symptoms of anxiety, such as the benzodiazepines, are psychoactive, reinforcing, have potential for tolerance and withdrawal, and have an abuse potential, especially among people who are at high risk for

AOD use disorders. Other antianxiety medications, such as buspirone (BuSpar), are not psychoactive or reinforcing and have low abuse potential, even among people at high risk.

Thus, decisions about whether and when to prescribe medication to a high-risk patient should include a risk-benefit analysis that considers the risk of medication abuse, the risk of undertreating a psychiatric problem, the type and severity of the psychiatric problem, the relationship between the psychiatric disorder and the AOD use disorder for the individual patient, and the therapeutic benefits of resolving the psychiatric and AOD problems.

For example, the early and aggressive medication of high-risk patients who have severe presentations of psychotic depression, mania, and schizophrenia is often necessary to prevent further psychiatric deterioration and possible death. For these patients, rapid and aggressive medication can shorten the length of the psychiatric episodes. In contrast, prescribing benzodiazepines to high-risk patients with similarly severe anxiety involves a substantial risk of promoting or exacerbating an AOD use disorder. For these high-risk patients, the use of psychoactive medication should not be the first line of treatment.

Rather, for some high-risk patients, treatment efforts should involve a stepwise treatment model that begins with conservative approaches and progressively becomes more aggressive if the treatment goals are not met (Landry et al., 1991a). For example, the stepwise treatment model for treating high-risk patients with anxiety disorders may involve three progressive levels of treatment: 1) nonpharmacologic approaches when possible; 2) nonpsychoactive medication when nonpharmacologic approaches are insufficient; and 3) psychoactive medications when other treatment approaches provide limited or no relief (Landry et al., 1991).

Nonpharmacologic approaches

Depending upon the psychiatric disorders and personal variables, numerous nonpharmacologic approaches can help patients manage all or some aspects of their psychiatric disorders (Weiss and Billings, 1988). Examples include psychotherapy, cognitive therapy, behavioral therapy, relaxation skills, meditation, biofeedback, acupuncture, hypnotherapy, self-help groups, support groups, exercise, and education.

Nonpsychoactive pharmacotherapy

Some medications are not psychoactive and do not cause acute psychomotor effects or euphoria. Some medications do not cause psychoactive or psychomotor effects at therapeutic doses but may exert limited psychoactive effects at high doses (often not euphoria, but sometimes dysphoria).

For practical purposes, all of these medications can be described as nonpsychoactive, since the psychoactive effect is not prominent. Medications used in psychiatry that are not euphorigenic or significantly psychoactive include but are not limited to the azapirones (for example, buspirone), the amino acids, beta-blockers, antidepressants, monoamine oxidase inhibitors, antipsychotics, lithium, antihistamines, anticonvulsants, and anticholinergic medications.

Psychoactive pharmacotherapy

Some medications can cause significant and acute alterations in psychomotor, emotional, and mental activity at therapeutic doses. At higher doses, and for some patients, some of these medications can also cause euphoric reactions. Medications that are potentially psychoactive include opioids, stimulants, benzodiazepines, barbiturates, and other sedative-hypnotics.

Stepwise treatment principles

One of the emphases of stepwise treatment is to encourage nondrug treatment strategies for each emerging symptom before medications are prescribed. Nondrug treatment strategies alone are inappropriate for acute and severe symptoms of schizophrenia and mood disorders, but nondrug strategies do have their place in the treatment of virtually any psychiatric problem, and may provide partial or total relief of some symptoms related to severe psychiatric disorders. For example, relaxation therapy can minimize or eliminate somatic symptoms of anxiety that may accompany an agitated depression.

A second emphasis of stepwise treatment is to encourage the use of medications that have a low abuse potential. This conservative approach must be balanced against other therapeutic and safety considerations in acute and severe conditions, such as psychosis or mania. On the other hand, a conservative approach is not the same as undermedication of psychiatric problems. Undermedication often leads to psychiatric deterioration and may promote AOD relapse. There should be a balance between effective treatment and safety.

A third emphasis of stepwise treatment is to encourage the idea that different treatment approaches should be viewed as complementary, not competitive. For example, if psychotherapy or group therapy does not provide complete relief from a situational depression (such as prolonged grief), then antidepressants should be considered as an adjunct to the psychotherapy, but not as a substitute for psychotherapy.

A Stepwise Management Approach For Mild and Moderate Mental Disorders*

Step One: Try nonpharmacologic approaches
Step Two: Add nonpsychoactive mediations if Step One is unsuccessful
Step Three: Add psychoactive medications if Steps One and Two are unsuccessful.

* For severe conditions, such as psychotic depression, mania, and schizophrenic disorders, rapid and aggressive use of medications is needed to prevent danger to self or others and further psychiatric deterioration.

In practice, treatment providers often use a combination of drug and nondrug strategies. This practice includes medication to treat the acute manifestations of the disorder while the individual learns long-term management strategies. For example, an individual may be prescribed nonpsychoactive buspirone to reduce anxiety symptoms while learning stress reduction techniques and attending group therapy.

These guidelines are broad, general, and more applicable to chronic than to acute psychiatric problems. Also, these guidelines have limited application to very severe psychiatric problems.

SPECIFIC MEDICATIONS AND RECOVERY

Antihistamines

Several antihistamines are approved for sale as over-the-counter hypnotics, including diphenhydramine (Nytol, Benadryl), doxylamine (Unisom), and pyrilamine (Quiet World). The efficacy of these drugs is not uniform, and tolerance to the anxiolytic and hypnotic effects is rapid, limiting their utility for episodic use. Antihistamines are frequently prescribed for mild anxiety and insomnia, particularly for patients in general hospitals, patients with physical illness (Salzman, 1989), and elderly patients.

Antihistamines and Recovery. In general, the early antihistamines exert very mild anxiolytic and hypnotic effects, but lack euphoric properties and do not promote physical dependence (Meltzer, 1990). While lacking significant abuse potential themselves, antihistamines may cause problems for some patients by reinforcing the idea of self-medication of insomnia and anxiety. Taken in high doses, antihistamines may cause acute delirium, alter mood (often causing dysphoria), or cause morning-after depression. Under close medical supervision, the conservative use of antihistamines can be valuable in treating brief episodes of insomnia during an otherwise drug-free recovery process. Patients in recovery should be discouraged from purchasing and using over-the-counter antihistamines.

Antidepressants

The antidepressants include several types of medication, such as tricyclics, monoamine oxidase inhibitors (MAOIs), and other, newer, antidepressants such as trazodone (Desyrel), bupropion (Wellbutrin), sertraline (Zoloft), and fluoxetine (Prozac). Antidepressants are effective for the treatment of depression, and several are valuable for the treatment of anxiety disorders, including generalized anxiety disorder, phobias, and panic disorder.

Antidepressants and Recovery. The antidepressants are not euphorigenic, and do not cause acute mood alterations. Rather, they are mood regulators and diminish the severity and frequency of depressive episodes; they also have anti-panic capabilities unrelated to sedation.

While the general effects of most of the older tricyclic antidepressants are similar, they differ considerably with regard to side effects. For example, some antidepressants such as doxepin (Sinequan) exert a mild sedating effect, while others such as protriptyline (Vivactil) exert a mild stimulating effect. These side effects can be clinically useful. For example, clinicians might give antidepressants with slight sedating effects to depressed patients with insomnia or give those with mild stimulating effects to depressed patients who experience low energy and hypersomnia (Davis and Goldman, 1992).

Other side effects of tricyclic antidepressants are common. Anticholinergic effects such as dry mouth, blurred vision, constipation, urinary hesitancy, and toxic-confusional states are common anticholinergic effects. Adrenergic activation symptoms may include tremor, excitement, palpitation, orthostatic hypotension, and weight gain. These noxious side effects are frequently the cause of requests to switch from one medication type to another. Also, side effects often prompt discontinuation of medication, which may provoke reemergence of the psychopathology. Tricyclics unfortunately are quite toxic when combined with AODs. Therefore use of tricyclic antidepressants in early recovery should be carefully monitored.

More expensive, but much less toxic when used with AODs, are the newer serotonin reuptake inhibitors including fluoxetine, paroxitine (Paxil), and sertraline. These agents also have anticompulsive effects, and their side effects tend to be slight to moderate stimulation rather than sedation. They are much safer to use in early recovery.

Overall, the use of antidepressants is consistent with a psychoactive-drug-free philosophy, does not compromise recovery from addiction, and enhances recovery from depressive and panic disorders. However, patient information must include clear explanations of the reasons for prescribing, the expected results, and the risks of adverse effects, including overdose. The risk-benefit analysis must include the risk of lethal overdose with tricyclic antidepressants, especially for depressed patients (Reid, 1989).

β-blockers

The beta-blockers such as propranolol (Inderal) are well-recognized medications for the treatment of hypertension, cardiac arrhythmias, and angina pectoris. They also have clinical efficacy as an adjunct in the treatment of anxiety (Lader, 1988). The β-blockers may reduce or eliminate the adrenergic discharge associated with panic attacks, thus blocking the somatic components of some anxiety states, especially when somatic symptoms predominate (Trevor and Way, 1989). β-blockers diminish the tremor and restlessness related to lithium or antipsychotics in some patients.

β-Blockers and Recovery. The β-blockers are not psychoactive, euphorigenic, or mood altering. Since tolerance to the anti-panic effects of β-blockers develops rapidly, they cannot be used for extended periods of time for this purpose. Rather, they are often used prophylactically for anticipated panic-producing situations, or for episodes of anxiety that may last a few days. The β-blockers are also used to decrease acute and subacute anxiety symptoms during detoxification from sedative-hypnotics such as the benzodiazepines. Overall, the use of β-blockers is consistent with a psychoactive-drug-free philosophy, does not compromise recovery from addiction, and can be an important adjunct to anxiety management.

Benzodiazepines

While all of the benzodiazepines have anxiolytic characteristics, they differ in their effectiveness in treating generalized anxiety disorder, mixed anxiety and depression, panic attacks, phobic-avoidance behaviors, and insomnia. In general, the benzodiazepines promote sedation, central nervous system depression, and muscle relaxation, and thus are effective for anxiety reduction and, at higher doses, for short-term management of insomnia.

The Benzodiazepines and Recovery. The benzodiazepines are psychoactive, mood altering, and reinforcing. Chronic use and subsequent cessation can cause withdrawal symptoms. Studies have shown that the benzodiazepines are not uniformly euphorigenic. Also, patients with a family and personal history of AOD abuse and addiction are more likely to experience euphoria with the benzodiazepines (Ciraulo et al., 1988, 1989).

Benzodiazepines are the most commonly used agents to moderate alcohol withdrawal and prevent dangerous withdrawal conditions such as delirium tremens and seizures. They are also widely used during detoxification from sedative-hypnotics. The benzodiazepines are frequently prescribed for use alone and in combination with antipsychotics during the treatment of acute psychotic symptoms caused by mania, schizophrenia, and drugs of abuse such as cocaine. Such treatment should be limited to the acute episode for most patients with dual disorders, so that one problem (psychosis) is not replaced by another problem (physical dependence or addiction). The benzodiazepines are not usually recommended for long-term use in patients with dual disorders unless all nonpsychoactive approaches have failed. That is, if all other less potentially adverse medications have proven inadequate and the benzodiazepines are indicated, then careful dispensing, regulation of dose, and scrupulous monitoring are required.

Overall, the use of benzodiazepines after the medical management of withdrawal is not consistent with a psychoactive-drug-free philosophy and may compromise recovery from addiction (Zweben and Smith, 1989). However, they can be used in the management of acute and severe withdrawal, panic, and psychosis with special guidelines in nonroutine situations.

Buspirone

Buspirone is the most well known of a new group of drugs (the azapirones) that selectively diminish multiple symptoms of anxiety without the acute mood alteration, sedation, or associated somatic side effects seen in the sedative-hypnotic anxiolytics. Buspirone is useful for generalized anxiety disorder, chronic anxiety symptoms, anxiety with depressive features, and anxiety among elderly patients. Buspirone is generally equivalent to the benzodiazepines with regard to anxiety management (Petracca et al., 1990; Strand et al., 1990). However, it takes several weeks for the maximal therapeutic effect of buspirone to occur.

Buspirone and Recovery. Buspirone is not psychoactive, mood altering, or euphorigenic (Balster, 1990). In particular, buspirone does not cause the mood alteration, central nervous system depression, sedation, and muscle relaxation associated with the benzodiazepines. However, many people with experience taking benzodiazepines may associate these mood alterations with relief of anxiety. As a result, patients who have experience with the benzodiazepines may misinterpret the absence of these side effects as evidence that the medication is ineffective. Educating patients about the distinction between anxiety reduction and sedation and about treatment expectations can avoid these misinterpretations.

Overall, the use of buspirone is consistent with a psychoactive-drug-free philosophy, does not compromise recovery from addiction, and enhances recovery from anxiety disorders.

Clonidine

Used in the form of a patch (Catapres Transdermal Therapeutic System patches) or tablets (Catapres), clonidine is well recognized as a treatment for symptoms of hypertension, including hypertensive symptoms that occur during withdrawal from depressant drugs, especially the opioids. In addition, clonidine appears to have anxiolytic and anti-panic properties comparable to the antidepressant imipramine. Patients may become less anxious but remain symptomatic. Some patients who have anxiety-depression or panic-anxiety experience significant antianxiety effects from clonidine. The anti-panic effect is the result of clonidine's ability to decrease locus ceruleus firing and thus decrease adrenergic discharge. Thus, clonidine may be useful for short-term use in the treatment of refractory anxiety with panic (Domisse and Hayes, 1987; Uhde et al., 1989).

Clonidine and Recovery. Clonidine is not psychoactive, euphorigenic, or mood altering. Clonidine may have significant antianxiety effects when administered to patients with anxiety-depression and panic-anxiety. However, tolerance to the anti-panic effects of clonidine can develop within several weeks. Thus, clonidine may be most useful for short-term use in the treatment of refractory panic disorder.

Overall, the use of clonidine is consistent with a psychoactive-drug-free philosophy, does not compromise recovery from addiction, and may be an adjunct in the treatment of anxiety symptoms.

Neuroleptic (antipsychotic) medications

The neuroleptic medications are most effective in suppressing the positive symptoms of psychosis such as hallucinations, delusions, and incoherence. In addition, they may help reduce disturbances of arousal, affect, psychomotor activity, thought content, and social adjustment (Africa and Schwartz, 1992). These psychotic symptoms may accompany schizophrenia, brief reactive psychosis, schizophreniform disorder, mania, depression, and organic mental disorders induced by AODs and medical conditions (Ries, 1993).

Although neuroleptic medications are equally effective in suppressing psychotic symptoms, individuals may respond to one medication better than another. The chief differences among the neuroleptics relate to dosage, onset of effects, and (especially) side effects. Some side effects may be clinically useful, such as nighttime sedation with chlorpromazine (Thorazine) or avoidance of appetite stimulation with molindone (Moban) (Africa and Schwartz, 1992).

In general, low-potency neuroleptics, for example, chlorpromazine, thioridazine (Mellaril), and clozapine (Clozaril), have significant sedative and hypotensive properties. Tolerance to these properties may develop within a few weeks. Also, low-potency neuroleptics are inherently anticholinergic, so that the use of additional anticholinergic drugs to prevent extrapyramidal symptoms may be unnecessary. The high-potency neuroleptics such as fluphenazine (Prolixin) and haloperidol (Haldol) cause more extrapyramidal side effects than the low-potency medications.

Neuroleptic Drug-Induced Extrapyramidal Symptoms. The extrapyramidal system is a network of nerve pathways that links nerves in the surface of the cerebrum (the deep mass of the brain), the basal ganglia deep within the brain, and parts of the brain stem. The extrapyramidal system influences and modifies electrical impulses that are sent from the brain to the skeletal muscles.

When this system is damaged or disturbed, execution of voluntary movements and muscle tone can be disrupted, and involuntary movements, such as tremors, jerks, or writhing movements, can appear. These disturbances are called extrapyramidal syndromes, which can be caused by all of the neuroleptic medications except clozapine.

Medicating Extrapyramidal Symptoms. Extrapyramidal symptoms are unwanted, noxious, and uncomfortable. Compliance with neuroleptic medications is worsened because of the onset of these drug-induced symptoms. A class of medications called anticholinergic agents can eliminate the muscle spasms in the neck, oral, facial, cheek, and tongue regions. Several other types of medications may also be helpful, including amantadine and beta-blockers.

Anticholinergic agents can also reduce the extrapyramidal movement disorder called akathisia, which consists of purposeless movements, usually of the lower extremities, often accompanied by the experience of severe, uncomfortable restlessness. These medications include benztropine (Cogentin), biperiden (Akineton), diphenhydramine (Benadryl), trihexyphenidyl (Antitrem), and procyclidine (Kemadrin). Patient response should be monitored because some anticholinergic medications may be mildly psychoactive for some AOD patients.

Neuroleptic Medications and Recovery. Neuroleptic drugs are not euphorigenic and do not cause acute mood or psychomotor alterations. However, side effects are common. Most of the neuroleptics cause sedation as a side effect, although adaptation to the sedative (but not the antipsychotic) effects develops within days or weeks. The anticholinergic side effects of neuroleptic medications can include dry mouth, constipation, and blurred vision. The neuroleptics can also cause extrapyramidal symptoms. The adverse side effects of neuroleptic medications are a frequent cause of medication compliance problems. These adverse effects can also prompt patients to use AODs to self-medicate noxious symptoms.

Because patients with psychotic symptoms often experience significant biopsychosocial problems, the neuroleptics allow them to engage in problem-solving and recovery-oriented interpersonal activities. Overall, the use of neuroleptics is consistent with a psychoactive-drug-free philosophy, does not compromise recovery from addiction, and enhances recovery from psychotic disorders.

Lithium

Lithium is the standard and first-line treatment for manic episodes, even though 10-14 days may be required before full effect is achieved. The initial symptoms managed by lithium include increased psychomotor activity, pressured speech, and insomnia. Later, lithium diminishes the symptoms of expansive mood, grandiosity, and intrusiveness. Lithium also treats signs related to disorganization of the form of thought such as flight of ideas and loosening of association.

Lithium and Recovery. Lithium does not cause acute mood alteration, and is not psychoactive or mood altering. Rather, lithium is a mood regulator, and diminishes symptoms of acute mania. The common adverse effects of lithium include thirst, urinary frequency, tremor, and gastrointestinal distress. Lithium allows patients who may have seriously disabling symptoms to engage in problem-solving and recovery-oriented interpersonal activities. Overall, the use of lithium is consistent with a psychoactive-drug-free philosophy, does not compromise recovery from addiction, and enhances recovery from bipolar disorders.

Anticonvulsants

Anticonvulsants have a role in the management of bipolar disorders, mania, schizoaffective disorder, and alcohol and benzodiazepine withdrawal.

In addition, these medications may be prescribed for "flashbacks" related to drug use or post-traumatic stress disorder. These medications, such as carbamazepine (Tegretol) and valproic acid, are not psychoactive. The typically minor side effects of sedation and nausea may emerge as treatment is initiated. Rarely, carbamazepine causes a decrease in white blood cell count. Both medications are monitored according to blood levels. For the treatment of bipolar disorder, the anticonvulsants are most often used when lithium has failed. However, they are occasionally used by highly skilled physicians as first-line treatment. These medications are consistent with a psychoactive-drug-free philosophy, and may enhance the abilities of those who need them to participate in the recovery process.

DRUG INTERACTION CAUTIONS

There are certain risks associated with AOD use and withdrawal among patients who are also being administered medications to treat psychiatric disorders. Because of these risks, serious consideration should be given to inpatient treatment for withdrawal.

- Alcohol and barbiturates can cause increased tolerance by increasing the amount of liver enzymes responsible for their metabolism. These same liver enzymes are also responsible for metabolizing many antidepressant, anticonvulsant, and antipsychotic medications. Thus, serum levels of medications will be decreased, possibly to subtherapeutic levels. Without assessing for possible AOD use, some physicians may mistakenly increase medication doses.
- Alcohol interferes with the thermoregulatory center of the brain, as do antipsychotic drugs. Patients taking both medications may be unable to adjust their body temperature in response to extremes in the external environment.
- The interaction of stimulants in a person taking monoamine oxidase inhibitor antidepressants can lead to a life-threatening hypertensive crisis.
- Alcohol and cocaine enhance the respiratory depression effects of opioids and some neuroleptics such as the phenothiazines. This effect can increase vulnerability to overdose death.
- Marijuana has anticholinergic effects. In combination with the anticholinergic medications such as Cogentin, marijuana use can lead to an anticholinergic (atropine) psychosis.
- Patients who are vulnerable to hallucinations, such as schizophrenic patients, are at high risk for having hallucinations during the withdrawal from alcohol and other sedative-hypnotics. Antipsychotics and antidepressants lower the seizure threshold and enhance seizure potential during withdrawal from sedative-hypnotics and alcohol.

- Alcohol intoxication and withdrawal disturbs the fluid electrolyte balance in the body, which can lead to lithium toxicity.

REFERENCES

Africa, B., and Schwartz, S.R. Schizophrenic disorders. In: Goldman, H.H., ed. *Review of General Psychiatry, Third Edition.* Norwalk, Connecticut: Appleton & Lange, 1992. pp. 226-241.

Balster, R.L. Abuse potential of buspirone and related drugs. *Journal of Clinical Psychopharmacology* 10(3, Suppl.):31S-37S, 1990.

Ciraulo, D.A., Barnhill, J.G., Ciraulo, A.M., Greenblatt, D.J., and Shader, R.I. Parental alcoholism as a risk factor in benzodiazepine abuse: A pilot study. *American Journal of Psychiatry* 146:1333-1335, 1989.

Ciraulo, D.A., Barnhill, J.G., Greenblatt, D.J., Shader, R.I., Ciraulo, A.M., Tarmey, M.F., Molloy, M.A., and Foti, M.E. Abuse liability and clinical pharmacokinetics of alprazolam in alcoholic men. *Journal of Clinical Psychiatry* 49:333-337, 1988.

Davis, G.C., and Goldman, B. Somatic therapies. In: Goldman, H.H., ed. *Review of General Psychiatry, Third Edition.* Norwalk, Connecticut: Appleton & Lange, 1992. pp. 370-390.

Domisse, C.S., and Hayes, P.E. Current concepts in clinical therapeutics: anxiety disorders, Part 2. *Clinical Pharmacy* 6:196-215, 1987.

Lader, M. β-Adrenoreceptor antagonists in neuropsychiatry: an update. *Journal of Clinical Psychiatry* 49:213-223, 1988.

Landry, M.J., Smith, D.E., McDuff, D.R., and Baughman, O.L., 3rd. Anxiety and substance use disorders: the treatment of high-risk patients. *Journal of the American Board of Family Practice* 4:447-456, 1991.

Landry, M.J., Smith, D.E., and Steinberg, J.R. Anxiety, depression, and substance use disorders: diagnosis, treatment, and prescribing practices. *Journal of Psychoactive Drugs* 23(4):397-416, 1991a.

Meltzer, E.O. Performance effects of antihistamines. *Journal of Allergy and Clinical Immunology* 86(4, Part 2):613-619, 1990.

Petracca, A., Nisita, C., McNair, D., Melis, G., Guerani, G., and Cassano, G.B. Treatment of generalized anxiety disorder: preliminary clinical experience with buspirone. *Journal of Clinical Psychiatry* 51(9, Suppl.):31-39, 1990.

Reid, W.H. *The Treatment of Psychiatric Disorders.* New York: Brunner/Mazel, 1989.

Ries, R.K. The dually diagnosed patient with psychotic symptoms. *Journal of Addictive Diseases* 12(3):103-122, 1993.

Salzman, C. Treatment with antianxiety agents. In: *Treatments of Psychiatric Disorders.* Washington, D.C.: American Psychiatric Association, 1989. pp. 2036-2052.

Strand, M., Hetta, J., Rosen, A., Sorensen, S., Malmstrom, R., Fabian, C., Marits, K., Vetterskog, K., Liljestrand, A.-G., and Hegen, C. A double-blind, controlled trial in primary care patients with generalized anxiety: a comparison between buspirone and oxazepam. *Journal of Clinical Psychiatry* 51(9, Suppl.):40-45, 1990.

Trevor, A.J., and Way, W.L. Drugs used for anxiety states and sleep problems. In: Goldman, H.H., ed. *Review of General Psychiatry, Second Edition.* Norwalk, Connecticut: Appleton & Lange, 1989.

Uhde, T.W., Stein, M.B., Vittone, B.J., Siever, L.J., Boulenger, J.P., Klein, E., and Mellman, T.A. Behavioral and physiologic effects of short-term and long-term administration of clonidine in panic disorders. *Archives of General Psychiatry* 46(2):170-177, 1989.

Weiss, D.S., and Billings, J.H. Behavioral medicine techniques. In: Goldman, H.H., ed. *Review of General Psychiatry, Second Edition.* Norwalk, Connecticut: Appleton & Lange, 1989. pp. 574-579.

Zweben, J.E., and Smith, D.E. Considerations in using psychotropic medication with dual diagnosis patients in recovery. *Journal of Psychoactive Drugs* 21(2):221-226, 1989.

ABOUT THE AUTHORS

The Center for Substance Abuse Treatment (CSAT) is part of the Substance Abuse and Mental Health Services Administration in the U.S. Department of Health and Human Services.

ACKNOWLEDGMENTS

This article was originally published as a chapter in CSAT's Treatment Improvement Protocol (TIP) 9, titled *Assessment and Treatment of Patients with Coexisting Mental Illness and Alcohol and Other Drug Abuse.*[2] Richard Ries, M.D., served as the Consensus Panel Chair for this TIP. The publication was written under contract number ADM 270-91-0007 from the Center for Substance Abuse Treatment of the Substance Abuse and Mental Health Services Administration (SAMHSA). Anna Marsh, Ph.D., and Sandra Clunies, M.S., served as the Government Project Officers. Elayne Clift, M.A., Carolyn Davis, Joni Eisenberg, Mim Landry, and Janice Lynch served as contractor writers.

---

[2]The TIPs are prepared by the Quality Assurance and Evaluation Branch to facilitate the transfer of state-of-the-art protocols and guidelines for the treatment of alcohol and other drug (AOD) abuse from acknowledged clinical, research, and administrative experts to the Nation's AOD abuse treatment resources. The dissemination of a TIP is the last step in a process that begins with the recommendation of an AOD abuse problem area for consideration by a panel of experts. These include clinicians, researchers, and program managers, as well as professionals in such related fields as social services or criminal justice. The opinions expressed herein are those of the consensus panel participants and do not reflect the official position of CSAT or any other part of the U.S. Department of Health and Human Services (DHHS). No official support or endorsement of CSAT or DHHS is intended or should be inferred. The guidelines proffered in this document should not be considered as substitutes for individualized patient care and treatment decisions.

A VISION FOR THE FUTURE: TOWARD A SERVICE SYSTEM RESPONSIVE TO THOSE WITH CO-OCCURRING ADDICTIVE AND MENTAL DISORDERS

Fred C. Osher

Reprinted from *American Journal of Orthopsychiatry*, 66(1):71-76, 1996

Identified by providers, family members, administrators, and consumers as an issue creating frustration, high costs, and a profoundly negative impact on quality of life, co-occurring addictive and mental disorders cry out for creative and alternative clinical responses. With empirical research and clinical experience supporting the effectiveness of integrated approaches, the time has come to reconsider the systemic division of addictive and mental health services. A change toward integrated systems of care is likely to benefit the mental health and addiction treatment needs of all people, not just those with co-occurring disorders.

At the heart of our current difficulties in serving persons with co-occurring addictive and mental disorders (COAMD) are archaic administrative structures and policies that inadvertently confound and compartmentalize conditions which, for many individuals, are inseparable. In spite of this, some providers and communities have made advances in the last ten years to integrate care. These approaches must be replicated, evaluated, and, if found effective, generalized. Systems that resist integrative strategies remain open to criticism linking their ineffective models of care to continued morbidity and mortality amongst a large, vulnerable population with COAMD. Is this a case of Nero fiddling while Rome burns?

As this nation's health care system moves from specialty to general practice, the time has come for behavioral health to do the same. This concluding article in a special section devoted to COAMD[1] summarizes principles that can be used to guide the development of future systems of integrated care and suggests systemic strategies for developing effective and cost-efficient approaches.

---

[1]Editors' Note: The author refers to a special section of the *American Journal of Orthopsychiatry*. The special section focuses on dual diagnosis and appears in Number 1 of Volume 66, January 1996. Four of the articles originally published in this section are included as readings in this volume.

ENVISIONING AN INTEGRATED SERVICE SYSTEM

In order to plan for an ideal system of care, it is necessary to share a vision of what it would look like, what its goals and objectives would be, and what mechanisms would be used for implementation. While this system would, in part, be evaluated by its success in reducing the morbidity and mortality associated with COAMD, it must preserve the strengths of existing systems also to serve individuals with "only" a mental *or* an addictive disorder. We would be ill-advised to develop a third system of care for dually diagnosed individuals when such a high percentage of all those in current systems have, or are at risk for, co-occurring illnesses. Establishing a third service system would create new boundaries at all administrative and clinical levels, and would undoubtedly be inefficient. In terms of public policy, genuine service integration would eliminate the need for grant set-asides and mandates targeting the dually diagnosed population. A system of care that is effective for persons with COAMD, whose needs are among the most challenging and extensive, can continue to be effective for "singly diagnosed" individuals.

A truly integrated behavioral health system would promote the seamless delivery of mental and addictive services through a variety of agencies across all behavioral health fields. It would avoid structural deficits, identified as barriers to care by Talbott, Bachrach, and Ross (1986), by maintaining a broad range of services including specialized services adapted to address the needs of individuals with COAMD. Ongoing evaluations to assess whether service supply meets patient demand would be integral and the system of care would be flexible enough to shift resources according to evaluation findings. One measure of a system's integration would be the extent to which an individual with a mood, thought, or behavioral disorder could enter any service portal and be accurately assessed and matched to appropriate services.

Treatment components

Bachrach (1981) has argued that services in an ideal system are longitudinal and continuous, individualized, comprehensive, flexible, personal, accessible, and cohesive. Each of these dimensions could serve as objectives of an integrated system responsive to the needs of individuals with COAMD.

Continuity of care. The importance of a longitudinal perspective cannot be overemphasized in working with disorders notorious for relapses and chronicity. Continuity of care must be assured by stable and predictable resources with multi-year commitments to maintain program integrity and a cadre of well-trained providers. The ideal system would shift from the inpatient-outpatient separation that currently exists to a continuum of care in which client need determines appropriate setting and practitioners work across all settings. As Minkoff (1991) has suggested, an integrated dual diagnosis case-management program is an essential component in ensuring continuity of care.

There must also be a blurring of the boundaries between public and private care to assure access for everyone to the widest array of programs. Disruptions in service, which can occur when transitions between systems are required, must be avoided. Complementary programs should be created by the public and private sectors to ensure that the treatment site is not determined by ability to pay or the unique benefit limitations imposed by various managed care organizations. This elimination of a two-tiered service system could maximize resource efficiency and is consistent with current managed-care approaches in "carving out" behavioral health services.

Individualized planning. Given the heterogeneity of the population with need for mental or addictive services, individualized treatment planning is essential. Patients are heterogeneous in terms of their demographics, substances of abuse, psychiatric disorders, and range of disability. The young Caucasian man with schizophrenia who regularly uses cocaine is likely to have quite different needs than the elderly African-American woman with recurrent depressive episodes who is alcohol-dependent. Providing patients with unique needs identical interventions will invariably lead to less than optimal outcomes.

Comprehensive services. Patient diversity raises the need for comprehensive services. While a system may only be responsible for behavioral health care, its capacity to interact with housing and other supportive services clearly will affect client-level outcomes. Poverty, homelessness, and unemployment are conditions that exacerbate addiction and mental illness, creating a malignant cycle of increased symptomatology, disability, and exposure to harsh living environments. Individuals with COAMD may enter the health system through non-behavioral settings, and the utility of efficient responses to addiction and mental health problems in medical settings has been demonstrated (Fuller, 1995). In addition, management of individuals with COAMD by behavioral health providers makes improved communications with primary care providers imperative (Lee, 1995).

Some in the field have suggested that behavioral services should be but one step toward integrated, comprehensive health care systems (Mauch, 1995). In creating structures that join physical and mental health care, the discriminatory limits on benefits and services can be eliminated. As Jean Thorne, Oregon Medicaid director, stated:

> At some time in the future, we want to have a client sign up for a managed care plan: we make a payment to that plan, and the plan is responsible for providing and arranging for a full range of services and making referrals to a dermatologist or a mental health professional, whatever the need might be. (Helf, 1994, p. 7)

Flexibility. Because of the inevitable shifting sands of health care financing and societal priorities, flexibility is key. A review of mental and addiction policy changes over the last three decades can be linked to unforeseen or unanticipated sociopolitical events. The widespread experimentation with drugs in the 1960s and the AIDS epidemic of the 1980s are examples of powerful cultural phenomena that have dramatically shifted public health system priorities. Likewise, the remarkable penetration of behavioral health managed care organizations into the health-care landscape has created opportunities for developing benefit packages with varying degrees of service accessibility.

Personalized services. An ideal system must also be perceived as personal. The engagement of persons with COAMD into treatment is a challenge unique to health care. Chest pain brings people into clinical settings; however, the paralyzing effects of anxiety or affective disorders are more likely to impede care-seeking. Human relationships developed over time can engage and maintain patients in care. The recruitment and nuturance of well trained, compassionate personnel is a key systemic responsibility. To be truly effective, practitioners must shift their perspective from directing care to listening and working with the consumer to address matters of mutual concern.

Accessibility. Accessible services for a broad array of people must be assured. Barriers imposed by transportation needs, cultural and ethnic differences between providers and recipients of care, and health-care costs must be minimized. Outreach efforts and public education campaigns should be sponsored and the bulk of services should be provided within the communities where patients reside. System planners must recognize the toll that not treating COAMD can take in terms of morbidity, mortality, and cost and must value the effectiveness of current integrated approaches. By doing so, the service network will be compelled to offer accessible services.

Cohesive care. That the system of care should be cohesive is synonymous with the need for integration. Our fragmented systems of care have up to now put the burden of integration on the least capable members of society—those persons disabled by their illnesses. The designers of future systems must strive for a rational delivery system that is cohesive, understandable, and responsive to its consumers.

GETTING THERE

In 1994, the Clinton administration attempted to develop a set of sweeping changes to address cost, access, and quality issues in the United States health care system. Managed competition, a mechanism for introducing managed care principles into the health care reform process, was proposed but soundly rebuked in the ensuing national debate. Members of the mental health subgroup of the President's National Health Care Reform Task Force reported no fundamental problems with tackling behavioral health issues (encompassing both mental and addictive disorders) within the commonly defined plan benefits, structure, and spending caps. In fact, the common sense of developing integrated mental health and addictive services far outweighed existing self-imposed barriers.

History will show that the Clinton administration's effort to design a rational system of care underestimated the complexity of the task and the conflicting interests of the myriad components of the U.S. health care industry. As a result, states have taken the center stage in considering proposals to restructure health care services for the public sector, and large managed care companies are increasingly shaping the private care environment. Managed care organizations, by their very nature, are intolerant of inefficient services that characterize many of our current fragmented systems. Rather than a threat to our capacity to serve persons with COAMD, managed care represents an opportunity to redress the problems of fragmentation, accountability, comprehensiveness, continuity, and effectiveness that hamper our current approaches.

Advocates for the large number of persons with, or at risk for, co-occurring conditions must anticipate the impact of various coverage strategies. Ridgely, Goldman, and Willenbring (1990) have identified eligibility, benefit, and payment limits as potential barriers to the development of a responsible system of care for dually diagnosed individuals. Effective integrated services may either be unavailable within a certain plan or have limits affecting their utility. If mental health and addictive services are lumped within a benefit plan, and not provided in an integrated fashion, inpatient or ambulatory limits may quickly be exceeded. Finally, providing services to a person with complex bio-psycho-social needs is necessarily costly, a fact that must be appreciated and incorporated into financing strategies. Risk adjustments must be taken into account so as to demonstrate that while treating persons with COAMD is costly, not treating them will ultimately break the health-care bank (Fuller, 1995). Planners must be wary of limits on access or funding enforced through the design of capitation strategies that may underpay for the complications associated with co-occurring disorders. Recent experience with managed Medicaid in Tennessee (Gottlieb, 1995) continues to highlight the obvious: if the behavioral health system is grossly underfunded, neither good design nor good intentions will matter; outcomes will be poor.

Progressive policies within private and public sectors can produce incentives for integrated efforts. The federal program for homeless persons with serious mental illnesses is a good example of knowledge generation and policy development supporting integrative strategies (Center for Mental Health Services, 1992; Straw, Levine, & Osher, in press). The progressive language embedded within a small McKinney homeless program for persons with severe mental illnesses, the Program for Assistance in the Transition from Homelessness, can teach us much about creating incentives to care for those with COAMD. This legislation simply states that only entities that have the capacity to coordinate the provision of services to meet the needs of homeless persons with COAMD may be recipients of program funds. This legislative language did more to increase interest in integrated approaches then any other exhortation toward this objective. The federal government could include similar nondiscriminatory language in its behavioral health service and research grants, block grants, or requests for managed care proposals. There are also a number of state and local strategies for systems integration that may help to ensure that the needs of persons with COAMD are addressed. These include interagency agreements, joint program development, cross-training of providers, and the specific identification of individuals with COAMD as a priority population within all strategic planning initiatives (Ridgely & Dixon, 1995). Consumers and families must continue to demand that systems be responsive to the complex needs of these people.

At the community and program level, Minkoff (in press) has outlined a process for implementing integrated services. This starts with the development of an integrated philosophy among relevant stakeholders. After agreeing on an integrated mission, an assessment of current organizational capacity is performed and service gaps are identified. Participants then prioritize modest steps in program development and move toward creating a continuum of assessment and treatment services responsive to the needs of persons with COAMD. Ongoing psychiatric and addiction training is provided to all staff. Minkoff emphasized the importance of leadership and ongoing process and outcome evaluation to ensure continued progress toward identified goals for service integration.

CONCLUSIONS

If the integration of mental health and substance abuse systems of care cannot be accomplished, what hope is there for effective behavioral health services? Naysayers will point to the long waiting lists of singly diagnosed persons that exist and question the advisability of shifting resources. Yet the risks of losing authority and control over separate systems could be offset by the sharing of knowledge, by being a part of a system that does not turn away people in need, and by the strength that comes from unity.

Smaller integration efforts in serving persons with COAMD have produced positive outcomes (Drake, Noordsy, & Ackerson, 1995). Larger efforts would have to be evaluated to measure their effectiveness in terms of improved quality of life for those served, increased numbers of people utilizing services, and management of expenses. The mental health and addiction fields share a history of stigma and discrimination, yet they have data on effectiveness every bit as good as somatic health data (National Institute of

Mental Health, 1993). Principles of care within the two fields historically converge on respect for the individual, reaching out to engage those who cannot yet trust, and the importance of community, family, and peers to recovery.

A note of optimism

A principle espoused for the treatment of persons with COAMD, missing from the aforementioned systems principles is that of optimism (Drake, Bartels, Teague, Noordsy, & Clark 1993). Just as the "myth of incurability" led to locking up people with mental disorders within institutions in the first part of this century, so does a similar myth shroud our efforts to serve persons with COAMD. We can find hope in the collection of articles within this special section,[1] which help to transcend our frustration and despair by identifying effective responses to persons with COAMD. For organizations to move forward, demoralization must be addressed and enthusiasm for an improved way of doing things has to be maintained. Consumers, families and practitioners who maintain a hopeful attitude toward recovery are associated with effective dual diagnosis treatment programs. So too, advocates for integration of the mental health and addiction fields must be optimistic about the opportunities and potential of integrated efforts. People with mental, addictive, or both disorders deserve no less.

REFERENCES

Bachrach, L.L. (1981). Continuity of care for chronic mental patients: A conceptual analysis. *American Journal of Psychiatry, 138,* 1449-1455.

Center for Mental Health Services. (1992). *Integrating mental health and substance abuse services for homeless people with co-occurring mental and substance use disorders.* Rockville, MD: Author.

Drake, R.E., Bartels, S.J., Teague, G.B., Noordsy, D.L., & Clark, R.E. (1993). Treatment of substance abuse in severely mentally ill patients. *Journal of Nervous and Mental Disease, 181,* 606-611.

Drake, R.E., Noordsy, D.L., & Ackerson, T. (1995). Integrating mental health and substance abuse treatments. In A.F. Lehman & L. Dixon (Eds.), *Double jeopardy: Chronic mental illness and substance use disorders* (pp. 251-264). Chur, Switzerland: Harwood Academic Publishers.

Fuller, M.G. (1995). More is less: Increasing access as a strategy for managing mental health care costs. *Psychiatric Services, 46,* 1015-1017.

Gottlieb, M. (1995, October 1). The managed care cure-all shows its flaws and potential. *The New York Times,* p.1.

Helf, C. (1994). *Medicaid managed care and mental health: An overview of Section 1115 programs.* Washington, DC: Intergovernmental Health Policy Project, George Washington University.

Lee, F.C. (1995, January/February). What is the future for providers in managed care? *Journal of Practical Psychiatry and Behavioral Health,* pp. 77-82.

Mauch, D. (1995). Public-private behavioral health-care integration trends: A vision for the '90s and beyond. *Behavioral Healthcare Tomorrow, 4*(2), 78-80.

Minkoff, K. (in press). Integration of addiction and psychiatric treatment. In K. Minkoff & D. Pollack (Eds.), *Public sector managed care: A survival manual.* Chur, Switzerland: Harwood Academic Publishers.

Minkoff, K. (1991). Program components of a comprehensive integrated care system for seriously mentally ill patients with substance disorders. In K. Minkoff & R.E. Drake (Eds.), *Dual diagnosis of major mental illness and substance disorder* (pp. 13-27). San Francisco: Jossey-Bass.

National Institute of Mental Health. (1993). *Health care reform for Americans with severe mental illnesses: A report of the National Advisory Mental Health Council.* Rockville, MD: Author.

Ridgely, M.S., & Dixon, L.B. (1995). Policy and financing issues. In A.F. Lehman and L. Dixon (Eds.), *Double jeopardy: Chronic mental illness and substance use disorders* (pp. 277-295). Chur, Switzerland: Harwood Academic Publishers.

Ridgely, M.S., Goldman, H.H., & Willenbring, M. (1990). Barriers to the care of persons with dual diagnoses: Organizational and financing issues. *Schizophrenia Bulletin, 16*(1), 123-132.

Straw, R.B., Levine, I.S., & Osher, F.C. (in press). Developing effective solutions for social problems: What is the federal role? In J.W. Thompson & W.R. Breakey (Eds.), *Innovative programs for the homeless mentally ill.* Chur, Switzerland: Harwood Academic Publishers.

Talbott, J.A., Bachrach, L., & Ross, L. (1986). Noncompliance and mental health systems. *Psychiatric Annals, 16,* 596-599.

ABOUT THE AUTHOR

Fred Osher, M.D., is affiliated with the Department of Psychiatry, University of Maryland School of Medicine, Baltimore, MD.

Copyright 1996 by the American Orthopsychiatric Association, Inc. Reproduced by permission.

INTRODUCTION TO SECTION SIX

The Special Issues section contains six articles that address important and sometimes-neglected issues in discussions of dual disorders. Some issues are controversial, for example, disability benefits, coercive treatment, or the barriers to effective services. Other issues have been neglected in the literature on dual disorders, for example, the needs and concerns of specific groups such as women or families. Consequently, omission of an issue from this section does not mean that it is less important, but simply, that less has been written about it.

A literature on ethnicity and dual disorders has just begun to appear. Little is known about the epidemiology of dual disorders for minority groups, such as African Americans, persons of Hispanic descent, or Native Americans, but some data suggest that the rates of co-occurring substance abuse and severe mental illness are higher than general population rates. For example, the strong connection between dual disorders and homelessness is well established, as is the fact that members of minority groups are overrepresented among those who are homeless (Jencks, 1994). Higher rates of poverty and drug abuse among some minority groups may also place them at greater risk for dual disorders.

The importance of ethnicity when addressing dual disorders is not confined to greater risk exposure; access to culturally appropriate treatment is severely limited also. Nonetheless, dual-disorders demonstration projects have shown a variety of strategies for culturally sensitive programming (Mercer-McFadden, Drake, Brown, & Fox, 1997). Some studies suggest that matching clients with treatment providers of the same ethnic group (e.g., matching African-American clients with African-American case managers) encourages clients to remain in treatment longer and to be more satisfied with their treatment, factors that are critically important for recovery (Jerrell & Wilson, 1996).

Age is a factor in dual disorders about which surprisingly little has been written. Although many adults with dual disorders report that they began to abuse alcohol or other drugs during adolescence, we know little about the development or treatment of dual disorders in this age group (Greenbaum, Foster-Johnson, & Petrila, 1996). Children and adolescents are usually served by different types of providers, have a distinct legal status, and have developmental needs that require a treatment approach that is different from that used for adults. Similarly, aging persons with dual disorders are likely to have more physical problems than their younger counterparts and are often served by different health care providers. They too have needs that require special attention (Bartels & Liberto, 1995).

Many studies show that a greater percentage of men than women have dual disorders, and treatment interventions have not often taken into account the special characteristics and needs of women. Mary Jane Alexander reviews the literature on women with dual disorders. She outlines important differences between the experiences of women and men with dual disorders, such as greater vulnerability to physical and sexual assault, higher poverty rates, preferences for different types of treatment, and higher treatment dropout rates. Although we have much more to learn about tailoring treatment to gender-specific needs, Alexander suggests some areas on which treatment providers and researchers can focus their efforts.

Families play a significant role in providing basic support for a relative with mental illness. The article by Robin Clark on family support for persons with dual disorders summarizes findings from a number of studies about relationships between family members and their relatives with dual disorders. Persons with dual disorders often find it hard to comply with therapeutic regimens and drop out of treatment, leaving their families as the sole source of emotional and material support. Interventions that strengthen family ties and that provide social support and education about coping strategies can reduce stress on family caregivers and lower relapse rates in their relatives with dual disorders. The studies discussed in this article also point to the importance of maintaining family support by fostering a healthy interdependence between persons with dual disorders and their families, a shift from earlier approaches that emphasized independence.

Money is an important theme in this section. In many forms, it plays a critical role in treatment for persons with dual disorders. Together with the organizational structure of mental health and substance abuse treatment systems, financing influences the types of treatment available and who can access them. The article by Susan Ridgely and her colleagues illustrates how separate ways of structuring and paying for public mental health and substance abuse services, which developed for political and administrative reasons, serve as barriers to treatment for persons with dual disorders. When integrated treatment is required, as is the case for persons with severe mental illness and co-occurring substance use disorders, separate treatment systems place the burden of sorting out conflicting rules and philosophies on clients, who may be poorly equipped for the task. This article has helped policymakers realize that effective treatment requires changes in the systems that administer and pay for services as well as improvements in the specific techniques that service providers use.

Concern about the costs of treating various disorders, and about the societal costs of not treating them, are at the center of health care policy debates today. The perception that treatment costs are higher for persons with dual disorders has motivated public and private groups to devote more attention to improving assessment and treatment of dual disorders in recent years. Barbara Dickey and Hocine Azeni use data from Massachusetts' public mental health and Medicaid systems to show that public systems spend significantly more on persons with dual disorders than on others with mental illness but no substance abuse. Their study provides a strong reason for treatment providers to address the problems of dual disorders, even though in the short term, it may cost slightly more to treat substance abuse in addition to mental illness. Other studies suggest that treatment resulting in reduced use or abstinence may lower costs in the long term (e.g., Bartels et al., 1993). It is also possible that effective treatment of dual disorders reduces public costs associated with arrests, incarceration, and income support, which would offset short-term increases in mental health treatment.

How income affects substance use and whether persons with substance use problems should have full control over their finances has been hotly debated by treatment providers, policymakers, families, and consumers. At issue has been the concern that persons with substance use problems who have ready access to cash may spend it for drugs or alcohol. Some studies indicate that placing money management authority in the hands of a family member, treatment provider, or other legally designated person can reduce substance abuse (e.g., Spittle, 1991; Higgins et al., 1994). Understandably, persons with dual disorders are reluctant to yield authority over their finances to someone else. Treatment providers and public welfare agencies rely increasingly on court-appointed guardians or "representative payees" as a means of gaining control. Opponents of this approach argue that the potential benefits of such an approach do not justify such a violation of consumers' individual rights to manage their own affairs.

A controversial study published by Shaner et al. (1995) illustrates one side of the argument for making money management part of treatment for dual disorders. The study showed an increase in drug levels in the blood, psychiatric symptoms, and admissions to psychiatric hospitals among veterans with schizophrenia and cocaine abuse disorders in the days immediately following receipt of their monthly disability payments. The authors argued that the disability payments contributed to substance abuse and therefore should be controlled or possibly eliminated. Sally Satel's companion article to this study, which we include in this section, is a further elaboration of these points. Partially in response to this study, Rosenheck and Frisman (1996) published their study, again with a population of veterans, showing that those who received public benefits were no more likely than others to have substance abuse disorders. The implication of the two studies is that the amount of money received at a particular time may be a more important factor in substance abuse than whether the payment comes from public or private sources. Currently, there is little agreement about the contribution of public support to sustaining substance abuse, or about the circumstances under which coercive measures are ethical and therapeutic, such as making access to money contingent on getting treatment.

Coercion is strong medicine that can have negative as well as positive outcomes. Ronald Diamond's article examines in a more general way the advantages and disadvantages of using various types of coercion in treatment. Viewing these measures on a continuum from weak to strong impact, Diamond provides a framework that clinicians, family members, persons with dual disorders, and others can use to evaluate the possible consequences of coercive treatment. The article explores questions of how to tell when coercion may be helpful and justified, and when it may be destructive to the relationship between treatment providers and persons with dual disorders. It concludes with a discussion of how the need for coercive measures can be reduced.

The readings in this section leave many questions unanswered, but they offer food for thought for anyone concerned about dual disorders. We encourage readers to use these discussions as a starting point for further learning and to monitor future developments in each of these areas.

REFERENCES

Bartels, S.J., & Liberto, J. (1995). Dual diagnosis in the elderly. In A.F. Lehman & L.B. Dixon (Eds.), *Double jeopardy: Chronic mental illness and substance use disorders* (pp. 139-157). Chur, Switzerland: Harwood Academic Publishers.

Bartels, S.J., Teague, G.B., Drake, R.E., Clark, R.E., Bush, P., & Noordsy, D.L. (1993). Substance abuse and schizophrenia: Service utilization and costs. *Journal of Nervous and Mental Disease*, 181, 227-232.

Greenbaum, P.E., Foster-Johnson, L., & Petrila, A. (1996). Co-occurring addictive and mental disorders among adolescents: Prevalence research and future directions. *American Journal of Orthopsychiatry*, 66, 52-60.

Higgins, S.T, Budney, A.J., Bickel, W.K., Foerg, F.E., Donham, R., & Badger, G.J. (1994). Incentives improve outcome in outpatient behavioral treatment of cocaine dependence. *Archives of General Psychiatry*, 37, 568-576.

Jencks, C. (1994). *The homeless.* Cambridge: Harvard University Press.

Jerrell, J.M, & Wilson, J.L. (1996). The utility of dual diagnosis services for consumers from nonwhite ethnic groups. *Psychiatric Services*, 47, 1256-1258.

Mercer-McFadden, C., Drake, R.E., Brown, N.B., & Fox, R.S. (1997). The Community Support Program demonstrations of services for young adults with severe mental illness and substance use disorders. *Psychiatric Rehabilitation Journal*, 20, 13-24.

Rosenheck, R., & Frisman, L. (1996). Do public support payments encourage substance abuse? *Health Affairs*, 15, 192-200.

Shaner, A., Eckman, T.A., Roberts, L.J., Wilkins, J.N., Tucker, D., Tsuang, J.W., & Mintz, J. (1995). Disability income, cocaine use, and repeated hospitalization among schizophrenic cocaine abusers: A government-sponsored revolving door? *New England Journal of Medicine*, 333, 777-783.

Spittle, B. (1991). The effect of financial management on alcohol-related hospitalization. *American Journal of Psychiatry*, 148, 221-223.

Women with Co-Occurring Addictive and Mental Disorders: An Emerging Profile of Vulnerability

Mary Jane Alexander

Reprinted from *American Journal of Orthopsychiatry*, 66(1):61-70, 1996

The heterogeneity of those with co-occurring addictive and mental disorders has only recently begun to be recognized, and treatment strategies for different segments of this population are still being developed. This article reviews the literature on alcohol and drug problems in women, and on women with severe mental illness who are at high risk for substance abuse—as well as other forms of abuse and deprivation—due to poverty and victimization. As public health and mental health agendas are threatened by budget cuts, it is critical that initial gains in acknowledging and addressing their needs not be lost or abandoned.

When alcohol and drug co-morbidities were first identified among individuals with diagnoses of severe mental illness (schizophrenia and major affective disorders), those with co-occurring addictive and mental disorders (COAMD) were profiled as young, male, interpersonally demanding and treatment-resistant (Bachrach, 1987; Pepper, Kirshner, & Ryglewicz, 1981; Sheets, Prevost, & Reiman, 1982). This perspective reflects the prevalence rates reported in the Epidemiological Catchment Area (ECA) community-based studies, in which men are twice as likely as women to meet criteria for alcohol disorders, and four times as likely to meet criteria for substance use disorders (Regier et al., 1990). Many studies in psychiatric settings continue to identify significantly more men than women as having COAMD (Alexander, Craig, MacDonald, & Haugland, 1994; Cuffel, Heithoff & Lawson, 1993; Eisen, Grob, & Dill, 1989; Kanwische & Hundley, 1990; Kay, Kalathara & Meinze, 1989; Schmidt, 1992; Zisook et al., 1992). Others find no significant differences in the proportions of men and women with COAMD (Dixon, Haas, Weiden, Sweeney, & Frances, 1991; Kivlahan, Heiman, Wright, Mundt, & Shupe, 1991), and some identify from half to three quarters of women in their samples as having COAMD (Caton, Gralnick, Bender, & Simon, 1989; Ananth et al., 1989). Only recently has attention been drawn to COAMD among women, primarily because of the high-risk behavior and circumstances associated with women's drug and alcohol use (Fullilove & Fullilove, 1994); the poverty, residential instability and social isolation associated with severe mental illness (Cohen, 1993); and the poverty and exposure to physical and sexual violence associated with being female (Browne, 1993). These factors make it likely that combined disabilities will increase women's risk for adverse health and social outcomes. Yet, gender-specific analyses or discussion in studies of COAMD have been sparse.

This article will review findings on the effects of alcohol or substance use alone on women's health and social outcomes, examine the developing literature describing COAMD among women who have been victims of violence or are homeless or both, and survey the treatment literature that addresses access to gender-appropriate interventions for alcohol and drug use in these health and social contexts. Special attention will be given to the identification of COAMD and victimization, which is important in formulating treatments for women with COAMD.

WOMEN AND SUBSTANCE USE

A literature describing women's alcohol use has developed in the past decade (Gomberg, 1991), but treatment models as well as research regarding treatment outcome have historically been based on men's addictions (Nunes-Dinis, 1993; Weisner & Schmidt, 1992). This may be due to the greater numbers of men than women with alcohol and drug problems (Warner, Kessler, Hughes, Anthony, & Nelson, 1995), particularly in cohorts born before World War II, or to male substance use and its consequences being more visible and more frequently antisocial. Still, alcohol and substance use among women present significant individual and societal problems, especially since gender differences in the rates of problem drinking and in substance use are decreasing among younger adults (Gomberg, 1991; Warner, Kessler, Hughes, Anthony, & Nelson, 1995; Wilsnack & Wilsnack, 1991).

The physical consequences of both alcohol and substance use are serious for women. Alcohol is the third leading cause of death among women aged 35-55 years, and women who drink heavily are at higher risk than their male counterparts for rapid development of liver disease and for death due to cirrhosis (Van Thiel & Gavalier, 1988). Women experience the adverse effects of drinking—liver, cardiovascular, and gastrointestinal disease—more quickly, and at lower drinking rates, than do men, a phenomenon known as "telescoping" (Ashley et al., 1977). Reproductive consequences of alcohol and other drug use include an increased risk for amenorrhea, spontaneous second trimester abortions (Mello, 1988), breast cancer (Longnecker, Berlin, Orza, & Chalners, 1988) and sexually transmitted diseases (STDs) including HIV infection (Center for Substance Abuse Treatment 1994a;

Silberstein, Galanter, Marmor, Lifsjutz, & Krasinski 1994). Alcohol use, while less sensational than drug use, is much more prevalent than other substances in general (Regier et al., 1990), and more prevalent among individuals with severe mental illness in particular (Drake, Osher, Noordsy, Hurlbut, Teague, & Beaudett, 1990).

Life-styles associated with substance use among women exacerbate the reproductive and health consequences. Crack use, which in some cities during the 1980s reached epidemic levels, has been accompanied by the exchange of sex for drugs as well as by more traditional prostitution (Fullilove & Fullilove, 1994). While roughly half of women with AIDS inject drugs themselves, an additional 21% are sexual partners of intravenous (IV) drug users, and some studies suggest that women who use crack cocaine may be at equal or greater risk for HIV than are IV drug users (Center for Substance Abuse Treatment, 1994a; Inciardi, Lockwood, & Pottieger, 1991). Although data on the incidence of STDs are not available for women with alcohol or substance abuse problems, there were dramatic increases during the 1980s in prevalence rates of STDs, which have been linked to crack use (Inciardi et al., 1991). The health consequences of untreated STDs (e.g., pelvic inflammatory disease, infertility, ectopic pregnancy) are heightened in women who, because they tend to be relatively asymptomatic, do not seek treatment for long periods following infection (Center for Substance Abuse Treatment, 1994a).

VIOLENCE AND VICTIMIZATION

Women experience striking levels of physical and sexual violence (Browne, 1993). In U.S. community-based samples, from 20%-30% of women report that they were sexually victimized as children (Finkelhor, Hotaling, Lewis, & Smith, 1990); by legal definition, 14%-25% of adult women in the U.S. have been raped (Koss, 1993). Women who abuse alcohol or have drug problems are more likely than other women, and more likely than men, to have been exposed to sexual, physical, or emotional abuse as children (Miller, Downs, Gondoli, & Keil, 1987; Wallen, 1992; Wilsnack, 1984).

Social perceptions of women who drink increase their risk of being sexually victimized. Both men and women viewers of identical videotaped situations judged women who ordered an alcoholic drink as more sexually available than men, especially if a male paid for the drink, and more available than women who ordered a soft drink (George, Gournic, & McAfee, 1988). Indeed, outside of the laboratory, women who drink or use drugs are likely to be victimized, and to initiate conflict as well.

Wilsnack (1984) reviewed studies in which 41%-74% of women in treatment for alcohol or drug treatment reported being childhood or adult victims of sexual abuse. The increased risk for major depression among alcoholic women in the ECA studies—four times the rate for alcoholic men

(Helzer & Pryzbeck, 1988)—may reflect the long-term effects of violence and sexual victimization, which may be manifest as depression (Russo, 1990). In a sample of women in treatment for drinking, 38% reported that they had been victims of violent crime, compared to 18% of controls, and 16% reported having been raped, compared to none of the controls (Miller, Downs, & Gondoli, 1989). These women also reported partner-initiated violence ranging from verbal abuse to serious assaults (Miller, Downs, Gondoli, & Keil, 1987). Among heavy drinkers, women report more instances than men of starting fights with their spouses or with unrelated others (Clark & Midanik, 1982; Robbins, 1989), and, regardless of their spouse's alcohol problems, women in treatment for alcoholism reported more moderate and extreme levels of violent conflict with their spouses than did women in a random household sample (Miller et al., 1989).

The evidence is growing that women with severe mental illness are more likely to have experienced childhood physical and sexual abuse than are women in community samples (Jacobson, 1989; Jacobson & Richardson, 1987; Muenzenmaier, Meyer, Struening & Ferber, 1993), and that women with COAMD are more likely to have experienced childhood physical and sexual abuse than severely mentally ill women without substance use problems. Among a random sample of women inpatients hospitalized for more than one year in state facilities, the 46% who reported having been victims of incest were younger and had had more sexual delusions, depressive symptoms, substance abuse, and major medical problems (Brown & Anderson, 1991). Among 947 consecutive admissions to an Air Force psychiatric unit, women had experienced more childhood sexual abuse than men; among those with physical abuse histories, more women met criteria for current, prior, and lifetime drug abuse (Craine, Henson, Colliver, & MacLean, 1988). Despite the growing awareness of early sexual trauma among women with severe mental illness, only 10%-20% of severely mentally ill women whose abuse histories were identified reported that these traumas were adequately addressed in treatment (Craine, Henson, Colliver, & MacLean, 1988; Muenzenmaier, Meyer, Struening, & Ferber, 1993).

Among homeless women with a diagnosis of schizophrenia, higher rates of alcohol and drug abuse, antisocial personality disorder, and less adequate family support were found than among women with schizophrenia who had never been homeless (Caton et al., 1995). Except for inadequate family support, these risk factors were similar to those found in men by the same investigators (Caton et al., 1994). Women's addiction co-morbidities were more important than any factors related to their schizophrenia, and the investigators suggest that this is the critical component in women's loss of family support and subsequent homelessness. Addiction may also play a role in placing homeless mentally ill women in dangerous situations. In a sample of recently rehoused homeless mentally ill women, in which almost half reported co-occurring substance use disorders, 42%-64% reported adult physical abuse, and 21%-38% reported adult sexual assault (Goodman, Dutton, & Harris, 1995).

ACCESSING TREATMENT

Despite the serious health and mental health consequences of substance use, women are underrepresented in alcohol and drug treatment services. Lower proportions of women than men enter drug and alcohol treatment (Weisner & Schmidt, 1992), and higher proportions drop out (Reed, 1987), even relative to their lower prevalence of alcohol and drug abuse. Furthermore, Weisner and Schmidt (1992) have reported greater symptom severity among women problem drinkers when they do access services. Women problem drinkers identified across drug, alcohol, mental health, and medical treatment sectors were more likely than were male problem drinkers to report that they use mental health treatment and primary care treatment services. Women may use the treatment sectors they do because they attribute the problems associated with excessive drinking to health or mental health problems, whereas men may use alcohol and substance-use treatment services because they see the problems associated with excessive drinking as explicitly alcohol-related (Thom, 1986). If this observation is valid, then the traditional design of alcohol and drug treatment programs that focus on the behavior associated with addiction may be seen as exacerbating the gender differences in treatment selection. This traditional focus may be effective for the men in such programs; however, the historical lack of training in addiction treatment in the mental health and primary care sectors (Galanter et al., 1989) raises the question of whether alcohol or drug problems are effectively addressed in the settings that women with COAMD most frequently use. It may be that co-occurring disorders among women are more likely to be missed or, when they are identified, remain peripheral in their treatment in mental health and primary care settings (Moore et al., 1989).

Furthermore, women's "style of deviance" is typified by solitary drinking (Kagle, 1987), abuse of prescription drugs (Anthony, Warner, & Kessler, 1994; Cooperstock & Parnell, 1982), depression (Helzer & Pryzbeck, 1988), and victimization (Miller, Downs, Gondoli, & Keil, 1987) rather than antisocial behavior (Hesselbrock, Meyer, & Keener, 1985). This style, together with the social norms that severely stigmatize women who drink or use drugs (Blume 1990; Gomberg, 1991), contributes to the under-identification of COAMD in women. It has been proposed that internalization of these norms contributes to women's denial and to health professionals' missing cues to women's drinking (Moore et al., 1989). Women's need for alcohol or drug treatment, then, is frequently extreme before it is recognized; women who are in treatment for drinking have more severe symptoms than men in treatment

(Weisner & Schmidt, 1992). These findings may extend to women with severe mental illness, as is suggested by the anecdotal comments of clinicians to the effect that women with COAMD have more severe symptoms of addiction than do their male counterparts.

Assessment

Recognition by mental health professionals that criteria for COAMD need to be developed that are specific to the life circumstances of individuals with severe mental illness (Drake, Alterman, & Rosenberg, 1993; Lehman, 1996) has been a major advance. The difficulties in identifying women with alcohol or substance use problems alone suggest that we need to evaluate current methods of assessing these problems among women with severe mental illness. For instance, both survey and ethnographic approaches have been used to identify a set of novel indicators of women's alcohol problems that do not appear in standard clinical or survey instruments (Ames, Schmidt, & Klee, 1995; Klee, Schmidt, & Ames, 1991; Schmidt, Klee, & Ames, 1990). They include lethargy, fatigue, frequent illness, and neglect or deterioration of physical appearance. A similar investigation of relevant indicators perceived by women with COAMD, and by the clinicians who treat them, would broaden the basis for identification and highlight those indicators that lack specificity. The high prevalence of physical and sexual victimization among women with COAMD and the known sequelae of abuse and trauma make it important that women's experience of trauma be included in assessment and treatment decisions (Friedman & Schnurr, 1995).

Treatment

As discussed elsewhere in this special section[1] (Drake, Mueser, Clark, & Wallach, 1996; Osher & Drake, 1996) over the last decade integrated, comprehensive approaches have evolved in the mental health sector that represent the state of the art in the treatment of COAMD. As these innovative models are disseminated into the treatment culture, gender-specific findings about sexuality, relationship, victimization, depression, and empowerment will be necessary if assessment of and services for COAMD are to address women's needs effectively. (Similarly, age, ethnicity, and culture represent other aspects of the diverse population with COAMD that must also be incorporated into evolving models of treatment.)

Program components that are important for women in both the addiction and psychiatric literature include adequate and early identification of associated problems, and a treatment philosophy based on competency-building and empowerment in safe, accessible, community-based treatment

---

[1]Editors' Note: The author refers to a special section of the *American Journal of Orthopsychiatry*. The special section focuses on dual diagnosis and appears in Number 1 of Volume 66, January 1996. Four of the articles originally published in this section are included as readings in this volume.

(Abbott, 1994; Burman, 1994; Center for Substance Abuse Treatment, 1994a; Finkelstein, 1993; Hagan, Finnegan, & Nelson-Zlupko, 1994; Harris, 1994; Reed, 1987; Wilke, 1994). For those with COAMD, programs should be multidisciplinary, comprehensive, and coordinated to address the full range of their needs as they progress toward and remain in recovery.

Needs of women with COAMD include physical health care, a recognition of their adult sexuality, preventive education regarding pregnancy and STDs, and help in dealing with role loss, including their roles as parents. In New York State in 1991, 16% of children in foster care (or more than 10,000 children) and 21% of children receiving preventive services (another 8,600 children) had at least one parent with severe mental illness (Blanche, Nicholson, & Purcell, 1994). Skills are needed for even noncustodial parents to cope adequately with the complexities of their relationships to their children and to their caretakers within and outside of the foster care system.

The close associations among COAMD, victimization, and homelessness mean that both residential needs and victimization must be addressed in treating women with COAMD. Provision of safe space for women with abuse histories may range from physical privacy to accommodating unusual sleeping times and places in a supported residence. Because women with COAMD are at risk for violence from a partner, they need to develop "safe plans" that includes strategies for resolving abuse. They should also be aware of shelters for battered women that accept dually diagnosed women, and they should know how to obtain and use restraining orders and hot-lines (Hagan, Finnegan, & Nelson-Zlupko, 1994). In addition, women with COAMD need to understand what abuse is, and how abuse affects their psychiatric symptoms, their addictive behavior, and their living circumstances (Harris, 1994).

If supported housing is not available, at least case management must be provided to women with COAMD to coordinate services and help identify risk of relapse, or actual relapse. Relapse among women with COAMD includes "engagement in any unsafe behavior including alcohol or other drug use, self harm, [and] noncompliance with medications" (Center for Substance Abuse Treatment, 1994b). Further, it is important that treatment staff and clients recognize that recovery is a life-long process, and that relapse may be a stimulus to review the program's effectiveness for this client (Center for Substance Abuse Treatment, 1994a; Drake et al., 1996). Elements of relapse prevention that are important for dually diagnosed women include learning to identify and develop resources to deal with stress, learning to structure leisure time to maintain abstinence, and using individual and group work to address issues of destructive relationships that compromise recovery (Center for Substance Abuse Treatment, 1994b).

Many of these services should be available in women-only groups that function in both therapeutic and supportive modes. Women with histories of sexual abuse who attend single-gender groups are more likely to attend and complete treatment programs than are similar women in mixed groups (Copeland & Hall, 1992). Women themselves cite single-gender groups as the most useful component of addiction treatment (Reed, 1987). Women-only groups have been described as more empowering for their participants because of gender differences in communication. Women use more uncertain language, are more likely to be interrupted, and use less total talking time when men are present in a group (Argyle, Lalljee, & Cook, 1968; Swacker, 1975). They are also more likely to be intimidated by the higher frequency of hostile words used by men (Gilley & Collier, 1970). Thus, single-gender groups can provide a forum for more frank discussion of sexual and physical issues than may be possible in mixed groups.

The stigma and disability associated with severe mental illness foster deeply ingrained feelings of powerlessness and lack of control in both women and men, which continue to be reflected when there is a co-occurring disorder. While traditional 12-Step programs may provide a supportive setting in which to admit to this lack of control, peer-directed self-help groups for individuals with COAMD are beginning to emerge. These groups, which are based on shared decision-making and peer support, extend the concept of recovery to psychiatric diagnoses as well as addiction problems, provide participants with strong common bonds, and have led to positive outcomes (S. Carpinello, personal communication, March 1995).

Although, in general, women with COAMD who enter treatment are more likely than men to be poor, to be poorly educated, and to have fewer job skills, women with schizophrenia actually have higher levels of psychosocial and vocational skills than their male counterparts (Cook, 1994). Furthermore, schizophrenic women have better premorbid social and heterosexual functioning, are more likely to be married and occupationally competent, are older on average at onset, have fewer negative symptoms, are more compliant with and responsive to neuroleptic and psychiatric interventions, and are more likely to recover with fewer relapses (Bardenstein & McGlashan, 1990; Goldstein, 1988). These strengths should lead us to expect a reasonably good treatment outcome for women with COAMD if their substance use and associated problems are identified and addressed in treatment.

CONCLUSIONS

Significant gains have been made since the absence of research in women's health care was first identified as a barrier to effective treatment of women with COAMD (Bachrach, 1984). In 1987, the National Institute of Mental Health developed a research agenda on women's health; more women are leaders in health and mental health, and are setting treatment and research priorities (Blanche & Feiden-Warsh, 1994). Women diagnosed with severe mental illness speak with increased candor about their experiences, prompted by the attention and respect that consumer voices have gained. Information and innovative treatment models are emerging from both the mental health and the addiction treatment sectors that raise the next level of questions.

We need to know more about the rates of COAMD among women with severe mental illness, their profiles of substance use, and their service use patterns. For instance, do prescribed psychoactive medications present problems for severely mentally ill women with both experience of and access to them, as they do for women in general? Will the current rise in heroin use exacerbate the already alarming increase in HIV infection among women? Although crack cocaine use has diminished among the general population, will its use continue or spread among severely mentally ill women?

We need to know more about the social networks of dually diagnosed women: To what degree do they support recovery or promote relapse? Does the woman with a severe psychiatric diagnosis experience violence and victimization differently from the woman with a less serious psychiatric disability? How do early and ongoing experiences of violence and abuse affect the course of treatment for both severe psychiatric disorders and co-occurring addictive disorders?

With respect to services, we must ask to what degree existing models adequately address the broad range of service needs of dually diagnosed women: To what degree, and how, do these models achieve linkage with community-based supports? To what extent are they willing to accept responsibility for women with severe psychiatric diagnoses? And what treatment components are effective in promoting recovery for dually diagnosed women?

However, these questions may be rendered moot by present political circumstances. The research and practice that have been developed to delineate and address domestic violence, sexual abuse, and addiction—particularly as they affect women at our extreme economic margins—are likely to be undermined by current and impending budget cuts (Bassuk 1995; Davis, 1995). It would be tragic indeed, for the individuals most directly involved as well as for the society as a whole, if our emerging knowledge about women with co-occurring addictive and mental disorders is never to have the opportunity to shape future practice.

REFERENCES

Abbott, A.A. (1994). A feminist approach to substance abuse treatment and service delivery. *Social Work in Health Care, 19*, 67-83.

Alexander, M.J., Craig, T.J., MacDonald, J., & Haugland, G. (1994). Dual diagnosis in a state psychiatric facility: Risk factors, correlates and phenomenology of use. *American Journal on Addictions, 3*, 314-324.

Ames, G., Schmidt, C., & Klee, L., (1995). New measures of women's drinking problems. Unpublished manuscript.

Ananth, J., Vanderwater, S., Kamal, M., Brodsky, A., Gamal, R., & Miller, M. (1989). Missed diagnosis of substance abuse in psychiatric patients. *Hospital and Community Psychiatry, 40*, 297-299.

Anthony, J.C., Warner, L.A., & Kessler, R.C. (1994). Comparative epidemiology of dependence on tobacco, alcohol, controlled substances, and inhalants: Basic findings from the National Comorbidity Survey. *Experimental and Clinical Psychopharmacology, 2*, 244-268.

Argyle, M., Lalljee, M., & Cook, M. (1968). The effects of visibility on interaction in a dyad. *Human Relations, 21*, 3-17.

Ashley, M.J., Olin, J.S., leRiche, W.H., Kornaczewski, A., Schmidt, W., Jur, D., & Rankin, J.G. (1977). Morbidity in alcoholics: Evidence for accelerated development of physical disease in women. *Archives of Internal Medicine, 137*, 883-887.

Bachrach, L.L. (1984). Deinstitutionalization and women: Assessing the consequences of public policy. *American Psychologist, 39*, 1171-1177.

Bachrach, L.L. (1987). The chronic mental patient with substance abuse problems. *New Directions for Mental Health Services, 35*, 29-41.

Bardenstein, K.K., & McGlashan, T.H. (1990). Gender differences in affective, schizoaffective and schizophrenic disorders: A review. *Schizophrenia Research, 3*, 159-172.

Bassuk, E.L. (1995). Legislating away reality. *American Journal of Orthopsychiatry, 65*, 460-461.

Blanche, A.K., & Feiden-Warsh, C. (1994). Women's mental health services: The need for women in mental health leadership. *Journal of Mental Health Administration, 21*, 332-337.

Blanche, A.K., Nicholson, J., & Purcell, J. (1994). Patients with severe mental illness and their children: The need for human services integration. *Journal of Mental Health Administration, 21*, 388-396.

Blume, S.B. (1990). Alcohol and drug problems in women: Old attitudes, new knowledge. In H.B. Milkman & L.I. Sederer (Eds.), *Treatment choices for alcoholism and substance abuse* (pp. 183-200). Lexington, MA: Lexington Books.

Brown, G.R., & Anderson, B. (1991). Psychiatric comorbidity in adult inpatients with childhood histories of sexual and physical abuse. *American Journal of Psychiatry, 148*, 55-61.

Browne, A. (1993). Violence against women by male partners: Prevalence, outcomes and policy implications. *American Psychologist, 48*, 1077-1087.

Burman, S. (1994). The disease concept of alcoholism: Its impact on women's treatment. *Journal of Substance Abuse Treatment, 11*, 121-126.

Caton, C.L.M., Gralnick, A., Bender, S., & Simon, R. (1989). Young chronic patients and substance abuse. *Hospital and Community Psychiatry, 40*, 1037-1040.

Caton, C.L.M., Shrout, P.E., Dominguez, B., Eagle, P.F., Opler, L.A., & Cournos, F. (1995). Risk factors for homelessness among women with schizophrenia. *American Journal of Public Health, 85*, 1153-1156.

Caton, C.L.M., Shrout, P.E., Eagle, P.F., Opler, L.A., Felix, A., & Dominguez, B. (1994). Risk factors for homelessness among schizophrenic men: A case control study. *American Journal of Public Health, 84,* 265-270.

Center for Substance Abuse Treatment (1994a). *Practical approaches in the treatment of women who abuse alcohol and other drugs.* Rockville, MD: SAMSHA.

Center for Substance Abuse Treatment (1994b). *Assessment and treatment of patients with coexisting mental illness and alcohol and other drug abuse.* Rockville, MD: SAMSHA.

Clark, W.B., & Midanik, L. (1982). Alcohol use and alcohol problems among U.S. adults: Results of the 1979 national survey. In *National Institute of Alcohol Abuse and Alcoholism, Alcoholism Consumption and Related Problems,* Alcohol and Health Monograph No.1 (DHHS Publication No. ADM 82-1190). Washington, DC: U.S. Government Printing Office.

Cohen, C.I. (1993). Poverty and the course of schizophrenia: Implications for research and policy. *Hospital and Community Psychiatry, 44,* 951-958.

Cook, J. (1994). Independent community living among women with severe mental illness: A comparison with outcomes among men. *Journal of Mental Health Administration, 21,* 361-373.

Cooperstock, R., & Parnell, P. (1982). Research on psychotropic drug use: A review of findings and methods. *Social Science in Medicine, 16,* 1179-1196.

Copeland, J., & Hall, W. (1992). A comparison of predictors of treatment drop out of women seeking drug and alcohol treatment in a specialist women's and two traditional mixed-sex treatment services. *British Journal of Addiction. 87,* 1293-1302.

Craine, L.S., Henson, C.E., Colliver, J.A., & MacLean, D.G. (1988). Prevalence of a history of sexual abuse among female psychiatric patients in a state hospital system. *Hospital and Community Psychiatry. 39,* 300-304.

Cuffel, B.J., Heithoff, K.A., & Lawson, W. (1993). Correlates of patterns of substance abuse among patients with schizophrenia. *Hospital and Community Psychiatry, 44,* 247-251.

Davis, K. (1995). The federal budget and women's health. *American Journal of Public Health, 85,* 1051-1052.

Dixon, L., Haas, G., Weiden, P.J., Sweeney, J., & Frances, A.J. (1991). Drug abuse in schizophrenic patients: Clinical correlates and reasons for use. *American Journal of Psychiatry, 148,* 224-230.

Drake, R.E., Alterman, A.I., & Rosenberg, S.R. (1993). Detection of substance use disorders in severely mentally ill patients. *Community Mental Health Journal, 29,* 175-192.

Drake, R.E., Mueser, K.T., Clark, R.E., & Wallach, M.A. (1996). The course, treatment, and outcome of substance disorder in persons with severe mental illness. *American Journal of Orthopsychiatry, 66,* 42-51.

Drake, R.E., Osher, F.C., Noordsy, D.L., Hurlbut, S.C., Teague, G.B., & Beaudett, M.S. (1990). Diagnosis of alcohol use disorders in schizophrenia. *Schizophrenia Bulletin, 16,* 57-67.

Eisen, S.V., Grob, M.C., & Dill, D.L. (1989). Substance abuse in an inpatient psychiatric population. *McLean Hospital Journal, 14,* 1-22.

Finkelhor, D., Hotaling, G.T., Lewis, I.A., & Smith, C. (1990). Sexual abuse in a national survey of adult men and women: Prevalence characteristics and risk factors. *Child Abuse and Neglect, 14,* 19-20.

Finkelstein, N. (1993). Treatment programming for alcohol and drug-dependent pregnant women. *International Journal of the Addictions, 28,* 1275-1309.

Friedman, M.J., & Schnurr, P.P. (1995). The relationship between trauma, post-traumatic stress disorder and physical health. In M.J. Friedman, D.S. Charney & A.Y. Deutsch (Eds.), *Neurobiological and clinical consequences of stress: From normal adaptation to PTSD* (pp. 507-523). Philadelphia: Lippincott-Raven Publishers.

Fullilove, M.T., & Fullilove, R.E. (1994). Post-traumatic stress disorder in women recovering from substance abuse. In S. Friedman (Ed.), *Anxiety disorders in African Americans* (pp. 89-101). New York: Springer.

Galanter, M., Kaufman, E., Taintor, Z., Robinowitz, C.B., Meyer, R., & Halikas, J. (1989). The current status of psychiatric education in alcoholism and drug abuse. *American Journal of Psychiatry, 146,* 35-39.

George, W.H., Gournic, S.J., & McAfee, M.P. (1988). Perceptions of post-drinking female sexuality: Effects of gender, beverage choice and drink payment. *Journal of Applied Social Psychology, 81,* 1295-1317.

Gilley, H.M., & Collier, S.S. (1970). Sex differences in the use of hostile verbs. *Journal of Psychology, 76,* 33-37.

Goldstein, J.M. (1988). Gender differences in the course of schizophrenia. *American Journal of Psychiatry, 145,* 684-689.

Gomberg, E.S.L. (1991). Women and alcohol: Psychosocial aspects. In D.J. Pittman & H.R. White (Eds.), *Society, culture and drinking patterns reexamined* (pp. 263-284). New Brunswick, NJ: Rutgers Center of Alcohol Studies.

Goodman, L.A., Dutton, M.A., & Harris, M. (1995). Episodically homeless women with severe mental illness: Prevalence of physical and sexual assault. *American Journal of Orthopsychiatry, 65,* 468-478.

Hagan, T.A., Finnegan, L.P., & Nelson-Zlupko, L. (1994). Impediments to comprehensive treatment models for substance dependent women: Treatment and research questions. *Journal of Psychoactive Drugs, 26,* 163-171.

Harris, M. (1994). Modifications in service delivery and clinical treatment for women diagnosed with severe mental illness who are also the survivors of sexual abuse trauma. *Journal of Mental Health Administration, 21,* 397-406.

Helzer, J.E., & Pryzbeck, T.R. (1988). The co-occurrence of alcoholism with other psychiatric disorders in the general population and its impact on treatment. *Journal of Studies on Alcohol, 49,* 219-224.

Hesselbrock, M.N., Meyer, R.E., & Keener, J.J. (1985). Psychopathology in hospitalized alcoholics. *Archives of General Psychiatry, 42,* 1050-1055.

Inciardi, J., Lockwood, D., & Pottieger, A. (1991). Crack dependent women and sexuality: Implications for STD's acquisition and transmission. *Addiction and Recovery, 4,* 25-28.

Jacobson, A. (1989). Physical and sexual assault histories among psychiatric outpatients. *American Journal of Psychiatry, 146,* 755-758.

Jacobson, A., & Richardson, B. (1987). Assault experiences of 100 psychiatric inpatients: Evidence of the need for routine inquiry. *American Journal of Psychiatry, 144,* 908-913.

Kagle, J.D. (1987). Women who drink: Changing images, changing realities. *Journal of Social Work Education, 23,* 21-28.

Kanwische, R.W., & Hundley, J. (1990). Screening for substance abuse in hospitalized psychiatric patients. *Hospital and Community Psychiatry, 41,* 795-797.

Kay, S.R., Kalathara, M., & Meinze, A.E. (1989). Diagnostic and behavioral characteristics of psychiatric patients who abuse substances. *Hospital and Community Psychiatry, 40,* 1062-1064.

Kivlahan, D.R., Heiman, J.R., Wright, R.C., Mundt, J.W., & Shupe, J.A. (1991). Treatment cost and rehospitalization rate in schizophrenic outpatients with a history of substance abuse. *Hospital and Community Psychiatry, 42,* 609-614.

Klee, L., Schmidt, C., & Ames, G. (1991). Indicators of women's alcohol problems: What women themselves report. *International Journal of the Addictions, 26,* 879-895.

Koss, M.P. (1993). Rape: Scope, impact, interventions and public policy responses. *American Psychologist, 48,* 1062-1069.

Lehman, A. (1996). Heterogeneity of person and place: Assessing co-occurring addictive and mental disorders. *American Journal of Orthopsychiatry, 66,* 32-41.

Longnecker, M.P., Berlin, J.A., Orza, M.J., & Chalners, T.C. (1988). A meta-analysis of alcohol consumption in relation to risk of breast cancer. *Journal of the American Medical Association, 260,* 652-656.

Mello, N.K. (1988). Effects of alcohol abuse on reproductive function in women. In M. Galanter (Ed.), *Recent developments in alcoholism, Vol. 6* (pp. 291-304). New York: Plenum Press.

Miller, B.A., Downs, W.R., & Gondoli, D.M. (1989). Spousal violence among alcoholic women as compared to a random household sample of women. *Journal of Studies on Alcohol, 50,* 533-540.

Miller, B.A., Downs, W.R., Gondoli, D.M., & Keil, A. (1987). The role of childhood sexual abuse in the development of alcoholism in women. *Violence and Victims, 2,* 157-172.

Moore, R.D., Bone, L.R., Geller, G., Mamon, J.A., Stokes, E.J., & Levine, D.M. (1989). Prevalence, detection and treatment of alcoholism in hospitalized patients. *Journal of the American Medical Association, 261,* 403-408.

Muenzenmaier, K., Meyer, I., Struening, E., & Ferber, J. (1993). Childhood abuse and neglect among women outpatients with chronic mental illness. *Hospital and Community Psychiatry, 44,* 666-670.

Nunes-Dinis, M. (1993). Drugs and alcohol misuse: Treatment outcomes and services for women. In R.P. Barth, J. Pietrzak, & M. Ramler (Eds.), *Families living with drugs and HIV* (pp. 144-176). New York: Guilford Press.

Osher, F.C., & Drake, R.E. (1996). Reversing a history of unmet needs: Approaches to care for persons with co-occurring addictive and mental disorders. *American Journal of Orthopsychiatry, 66,* 4-11.

Pepper, B., Kirshner, M.C., & Ryglewicz, H. (1981). The young adult chronic patient: Overview of a population. *Hospital and Community Psychiatry 32,* 463-469.

Reed, B.G. (1987). Developing women-sensitive drug dependence treatment services: Why so difficult? *Journal of Psychoactive Drugs, 19,* 151-164.

Regier, D.A., Farmer, M.E., Rae, D.S., Locke, B.Z., Keith, S.J., Judd, L.L., & Goodwin, F.K. (1990). Comorbidity of mental disorders with alcohol and other drug abuse: Results from the Epidemiologic Catchment Area (ECA) study. *Journal of the American Medical Association, 264,* 2511-2518.

Robbins, C. (1989). Sex differences in psychosocial consequences of alcohol and drug abuse. *Journal of Health and Social Behavior, 30,* 117-130.

Russo, N.F. (1990). Overview: Forging research priorities for women's mental health. *American Psychologist, 45,* 368-373.

Schmidt, C., Klee, L., & Ames, G. (1990). Review and analysis of literature on indicators of women's drinking problems. *British Journal of Addiction, 85,* 179-192.

Schmidt, L.A. (1992). Profile of problem drinkers in public mental health services. *Hospital and Community Psychiatry, 43,* 245-250.

Sheets, J.L., Prevost, J.A., & Reiman, J. (1982). Young adult chronic patients: Three hypothesized subgroups. *Hospital and Community Psychiatry, 33,* 197-203.

Silberstein, C., Galanter, M., Marmor, M., Lifsjutz, H., & Krasinski, K. (1994). HIV-1 among inner city dually-diagnosed inpatients. *American Journal of Drug and Alcohol Abuse, 20,* 101-113.

Swacker, M. (1975). The sex of the speaker as a sociolinguistic variable. In B. Thorne & N. Henley (Eds.), *Language and sex: Difference and dominance* (pp. 76-83). Rowley, MA: Newbury House.

Thom, B. (1986). Sex differences in help-seeking for alcohol problems—1: The barriers to help-seeking. *British Journal of Addiction, 81,* 777-788.

Van Thiel, D.H., & Gavalier, J.S. (1988). Ethanol metabolism and hepatic toxicity: Does sex make a difference? In M. Galanter (Ed.), *Recent developments in alcoholism, Vol. 6* (pp. 291-304). New York: Plenum Press.

Wallen, J. (1992). A comparison of male and female clients in substance abuse treatment. *Journal of Substance Abuse Treatment, 9,* 243-248.

Warner, L.Y., Kessler, R.A., Hughes, M., Anthony, J., & Nelson, C.B. (1995). Prevalence and correlates of drug use and dependence in the United States: Results from the National Comorbidity Survey. *Archives of General Psychiatry, 52,* 219-229.

Weisner, C., & Schmidt, L. (1992). Gender disparities in treatment for alcohol problems. *Journal of the American Medical Association, 268,* 1872-1876.

Wilke, D. (1994). Women and alcoholism: How a male-as-norm bias affects research, assessment, and treatment. *Health and Social Work, 19,* 29-35.

Wilsnack, S.C. (1984). Drinking, sexuality and sexual dysfunction in women. In S.C. Wilsnack and L.J. Beckman (Eds.), *Alcohol problems in women* (pp. 189-227), New York: Guilford Press.

Wilsnack, S.C., & Wilsnack, R. (1991). Epidemiology of women's drinking. *Journal of Substance Abuse, 3,* 133-157.

Zisook, S., Heaton, R., Moranville, J., Kuck, J., Jernigan, T., & Braff, D. (1992). Post substance abuse and clinical course of schizophrenia. *American Journal of Psychiatry, 149,* 552-553.

ABOUT THE AUTHOR

Mary Jane Alexander, Ph.D., is affiliated with the Statistical Sciences and Epidemiology Division, Nathan S. Kline Institute for Psychiatric Research, Orangeburg, NY.

Copyright 1996 by the American Orthopsychiatric Association, Inc. Reproduced by permission.

FAMILY SUPPORT FOR PERSONS WITH DUAL DISORDERS

Robin E. Clark

Reprinted from *Dual Diagnosis of Major Mental Illness and Substance Abuse,
Volume 2: Recent Research and Clinical Implications.* New Directions for
Mental Health Services, No. 70, R.E. Drake & K.T. Mueser (Eds.).
San Francisco: Jossey-Bass, Inc. (pp. 65-78), 1996

*Families are critically important sources of housing, financial support,
and direct care for persons with dual disorders.*

Michael was twenty years old when he was diagnosed with schizophrenia. His family had noticed that he was spending more time alone in his
room and that he increasingly voiced thoughts that they found bizarre or
frightening. Still, they were surprised when his boss called one day to say
that he had begun shouting at co-workers, accusing them of trying to poison
him. After three months in a private hospital, a psychiatrist confirmed
Michael's diagnosis and prescribed antipsychotic medication. Insurance covered only a portion of the medical bills, so his family took out a second
mortgage on their home to pay the additional hospital charges.

In the ensuing years, Michael was rehospitalized a number of times. A
local mental health center arranged for him to live in a group home, but he
had difficulty complying with the rules and eventually left to live in a rented
room downtown. Complaining that it made him feel like "a crash-test
dummy" and that he really did not need it, he went for long periods without
taking his medication. Michael, who had been a moderate drinker in high
school, began getting into minor scrapes with the police when he drank.
Sometimes he disappeared for long periods of time. Eventually his family
received a call from a distant hospital, police department, or shelter asking
them to come take him home.

Relations with his family, which had been tense since his teens, have
become even more strained since Michael, now thirty-eight, began to suspect that his parents are conspiring with the FBI to implant "thought ampli-
fiers" in his brain. Fearful of a widening conspiracy, Michael tells his case
manager that his family hates him and that he rarely sees them. In spite of
their difficulties, Michael's mother continues to call him and often takes him
out for lunch and on shopping trips during which she buys him clothes or
furnishings for his room. Michael periodically runs out of money toward the
end of the month and his parents give him money for food or help him pay

his rent. When he gets in trouble with the police or is hospitalized away from home, it is almost always his father who comes to post bail or to take him home.

Michael's father is now in his mid-seventies and is becoming increasingly immobile from arthritis and heart disease. His mother, who spends most of her time looking after Michael and his father, feels isolated and worries about what will happen when she and her husband are no longer able to give Michael the help he needs. Michael worries, too.

BENEFITS AND BURDENS OF FAMILY SUPPORT

Like Michael, most persons with severe mental illness and substance disorders rely heavily on others to assist them with the basics of daily living. Families are the primary source of much of this help. Recent research suggests that they play a central role in the survival and well-being of their relatives with dual disorders, supplying large amounts of direct care and financial support (Carpentier and others, 1992; Clark and Drake, 1994; Franks, 1990; Tausig, Fisher, and Tessler, 1992). Still, we know relatively little about how families cope with these added demands, how treatment affects clients and families, and how family support—or the lack of it—influences a person's recovery from mental illness and substance disorders. As a consequence of our lack of understanding, treatment providers often underestimate the importance of families in the lives of their clients with dual disorders.

Persons with severe mental illness who also abuse alcohol or other drugs have difficulty managing tasks of daily living and have higher rates of unemployment than do persons with mental illness alone (Drake and Wallach, 1989; Kay, Kalathara, and Meinzer, 1989). Because of these problems they often depend on families or friends for assistance in securing the basic necessities of life. Although families make many other important contributions to their relatives, the basic assistance they give is, for many persons with dual disorders, a primary means of survival and the foundation on which formal treatment and rehabilitative services are built. Without first satisfying these primary needs, persons with dual disorders are unlikely to participate in or respond fully to treatment interventions.

Having a relative with dual disorders clearly places significant additional demands on families. A study of New Hampshire parents with adult children revealed that when a son or daughter had a dual disorder they spent over twice as much time giving direct care and contributed significantly more financial support than when their children were free of chronic illnesses (Clark, 1994). Parents of persons with dual disorders spent a good deal more time providing general care, for example, cooking and cleaning. They also spent more time giving rides, intervening in crises, and creating structured leisure activities for their relatives. A comparable amount of service provided by formal caregivers—case managers or home health aides, for example—would have cost almost $14,000 per year in 1992 dollars. Economic support given by parents in the dual disorder group totaled almost 16 percent of their annual income, whereas comparison families contributed an amount equal to about 6 percent of their annual income.

Family support may also have different long-term results for recipients. Financial assistance for adult children without dual disorders tends to be for purposes that could be considered investments, such as college tuition or a downpayment on a car or house. Economic support for persons with dual disorders is most often for basic necessities like food, clothing, or shelter. For persons without dual disorders, family assistance may provide a boost to economic status or earning potential. For those with dual disorders, family assistance has the far more immediate consequence of ensuring adequate nutrition and a place to stay. Losing this support could have serious consequences.

Homelessness is a potential result of lost family support. Although being homeless is stressful in itself, it also increases the risk that one will acquire AIDS, or be assaulted, robbed, or incarcerated (Fisher and Breakey, 1991; Torres, Mani, Altholz, and Brickner, 1990). Evidence for a connection between lack of family support and homelessness comes from separate studies of men and women with schizophrenia in the New York area conducted by Caton and others (1994, 1995). Matching one hundred men with schizophrenia currently living in a homeless shelter with one hundred who were similar in other characteristics but who had never been homeless, Caton and her colleagues found that a lack of adequate current family support was more strongly associated with homelessness than any of the other variables they considered. Positive psychiatric symptoms, drug abuse, antisocial personality, and treatment engagement were also important in explaining differences between the two groups, but less so than current family assistance in the form of money, shelter, food, clothing, advice, and companionship. A second study of homeless women produced very similar results: inadequate current family support was again the factor most strongly associated with homelessness (Caton and others, 1995).

In a separate study Tessler and others (1992) found that persons with mental illness who had been homeless during the previous year were more dissatisfied with and had less faith in their families than those who had not been homeless. Families of the homeless group reported less involvement, gave less care, and had more negative attitudes toward them than families of the never-homeless group. When combined with other patient characteristics such as gender, deficits in daily living, work, and incarceration history, however, family variables were not significantly associated with previous homelessness.

Although family support may benefit persons with dual disorders it can also be a burden to families. Intuitively it seems likely that substance abuse would add to the burden that families of persons with severe mental illness feel, but current research does not allow us to confirm or refute this supposition or to say how much more burden substance abuse might add.

Typically family burden is seen as a combination of objective (how much families do) and subjective (how they feel about what they do) factors (Hoenig and Hamilton, 1966; Thompson and Doll, 1982). Family caregivers may perform certain types of tasks frequently, such as preparing meals, but may not feel especially burdened by them. Other tasks, like restraining an intoxicated or angry relative, occur less often but are experienced as more burdensome.

Tessler and Gamache (1994) have further refined tasks assisted by families according to whether they are related to care (routine support) or control (behavioral problems). Care items mentioned frequently include providing transportation, time and money management, and preparing meals. Control items include attention seeking, night disturbances, embarrassing behavior, substance abuse, and a range of other troublesome behaviors (Tessler and Gamache, 1994). Some studies indicate that family members experience the care tasks as more burdensome; this finding may be influenced, however, by specific characteristics of the groups studied or by the relative infrequency of control tasks (Maurin and Boyd, 1990). Logically one would expect that persons with dual disorders would require more family efforts to control behaviors than persons with mental illness alone. It is less clear how dual disorders might affect the amount of general supportive care required.

FACTORS THAT INFLUENCE FAMILY SUPPORT

The sheer burden of caring for a relative with multiple problems might seem enough to discourage families, but the New York study of homeless men did not find differences in the level of burden reported by families of homeless and domiciled men (Caton and others, 1994). The two groups did score differently on an index of family disorganization. Men in the homeless group were over four times more likely to come from families that were inconsistent in nurturing, had unstable housing, inadequate income, and relied on public assistance. Parents of men in this group were more likely to have a history of criminal involvement, mental illness, and substance abuse. Family history does not appear to be strongly associated with homelessness among women with schizophrenia (Caton and others, 1995).

It is not entirely clear from this study why traditional patterns of family support break down. Low family support could be the result rather than the cause of homelessness, but the combination of differences between the two groups in reported family histories of disorganization and similarities in levels of current family burden suggests that the seeds of lower support are sown before the men become homeless. Families beset by extreme poverty, illness, and a range of other problems are likely to have fewer resources to give to their relatives than do others. It is important to note that not all of the study subjects came from impoverished, disorganized families, and that current behaviors like psychiatric symptoms and substance abuse are also associated with homelessness.

Although poor family support and substance abuse are both associated with homelessness, this does not necessarily mean that families of persons with dual disorders are unwilling or unable to help. Most give substantial amounts of economic and direct care support to their relatives despite active substance use. As substance abuse becomes more severe, the amount of economic support that families give decreases, but the amount of direct care appears to be unaffected (Clark and Drake, 1994).

When it comes to living together, drug and alcohol use seem to exert a more complex influence on family decisions. In an unpublished statewide survey of over 2,000 people receiving publicly funded treatment for severe mental illness in New Hampshire, clients who used alcohol were significantly less likely to live with their families. This could be interpreted as evidence that families are less willing to house a substance-abusing relative. However, there are other explanations for the finding. For example, people who do not live with their families may have less supervision and are therefore more likely to abuse drugs or alcohol; substance abusers initially may be more socially competent and therefore may be more likely to form relationships outside the home; different living situations may reflect different levels of psychiatric impairment that may be related in turn to substance abuse.

Another study of persons enrolled in specialized treatment for dual disorders suggests that parents are more willing than other relatives to house someone who is actively abusing substances (Clark and Drake, 1994). Persons who abuse drugs or alcohol more severely are less likely to live with relatives in general. When they do live with family, they are more likely to live with parents than with siblings or other relatives. This somewhat confusing picture may be explained by thinking of parents as service or housing providers of last resort.

Substance abuse decreases the range of available living options. The New Hampshire study indicates that substance abuse is associated with more stress and less appropriate housing wherever the person lives. This is generally consistent with other data that show that persons with dual disorders tend to live in less desirable housing (Uehara, 1994). When their adult children with dual disorders leave or are asked to leave their present accommodations, parents may, with some reluctance, be their only housing option. In one survey of family caregivers for persons with schizophrenia, over two-thirds of whom were parents, practical concerns like "being able to keep an eye on the patient's drinking" were the benefits of living together that caregivers cited most frequently (Winefield and Harvey, 1994). Filial relationships seem to be a critical buffer against homelessness for persons with dual disorders.

Housing a relative with dual disorders is not purely a burden; relatives with mental illness often contribute positively to their families, both financially and otherwise (Greenberg, Greenley, and Benedict, 1994). Still, living together is not without its risks. Increased contact is associated with more family stress, particularly for spouses and parents (Anderson and Lynch, 1984; Winefield and Harvey, 1994). Living together increases the risk that parents or spouses will be assaulted (Gondolf, Mulvey, and Lidz, 1990; Straznickas, McNiel, and Binder, 1993). Substance abuse seems to increase further the likelihood that the relative with mental illness will threaten or attack a family member (Monahan, 1992; Swan and Lavitt, 1988). Families who house a relative with a dual disorder are thus particularly in need of support.

Cohabitation may also be difficult for the person with a dual disorder. About one-fourth of persons with severe mental illness say they prefer to live with their families (Massey and Wu, 1993). It is not clear if substance abuse alters these preferences. In most cases persons with mental illness and their families agree on the decision to live together, but substance abuse may reduce consensus. Disagreement about the desirability of living together leads to conflict and dissatisfaction. Stressful family atmospheres are associated with increased relapse rates (Kashner and others, 1991; Kavanagh, 1992), and persons with dual disorders report more dissatisfaction with family relations and a greater desire for family treatment than do persons with mental illness alone (Dixon, McNary, and Lehman, 1995). Moreover, evidence linking parental substance abuse to current substance abuse by adult offspring means that in some cases the family environment may not be conducive to controlling substance abuse (Gershon and others, 1988; Noordsy, Drake, Biesanz, and McHugo, 1994).

Even though increased contact, behavioral problems, and greater demands for direct care add to family burden, there is no clear relationship between these stressors and a family's decision to terminate support for a relative with dual disorders. Evidence from studies of family caregivers for elderly relatives who are frail or have Alzheimer's disease suggests that the decision is influenced by a combination of the ill relative's behavior, the family's financial resources, and their attitudes toward caregiving. One study found that family caregivers were more likely to place their relatives with Alzheimer's disease in a nursing home when they felt frustrated or trapped by the caregiving role (Aneshensel, Pearlin, and Schuler, 1993). Other factors such as more severe functional impairment, caregiver stress, and having enough money to pay for out-of-home care were also associated, albeit more weakly, with the decision to place.

Help and emotional support from other family members almost certainly make the difficult aspects of caregiving more bearable. Single caregivers report more stress than married ones (Carpentier and others, 1992). Family cohesiveness and support appear to be particularly important in reducing the frustration that family caregivers feel (Greenberg, Seltzer, and Greenley, 1993). The extent to which burden can be reduced or to which family ties can be maintained by formal services is still unknown.

Many families continue providing direct and financial support in the face of great demands and stress. Why some families continue and others distance themselves from their relatives with dual disorders is a puzzle whose answer has important implications for relatives, treatment providers, and families. Preserving family support has obvious benefits for persons with dual disorders and probably for their families as well. Knowing what factors lead to family estrangement would enable more appropriately focused interventions to prevent family breakup.

TREATMENT AND FAMILY RELATIONSHIPS

Because there are few longitudinal studies of family support, we know almost nothing about how treatment of persons with dual disorders affects family support or what roles families play in recovery. Evidence from the mental health literature provides some clues. For example, it seems logical to conclude that treatment that reduces hospitalization will increase family contact and will thereby lead to greater family burden (see, for example, Goldman, 1982), but there is little recent documentation to support this notion. Most studies find no relationship between amount of hospitalization and measures of objective or subjective family burden (Maurin and Boyd, 1990). One study reported that families of persons who received intensive community services and less hospital care than customary actually preferred the community intervention (Reynolds and Hoult, 1984).

There appears to be little difference in the impact of various client-focused treatments on families, but interventions that target families (primarily families of persons with schizophrenia) have specifically shown significant changes in patterns of family interaction and in patient relapse rates (Bellack and Mueser, 1993).

Two studies illustrate these findings. Falloon and others (1982) compared in-home family therapy to individual treatment for a small group of patients with schizophrenia who were receiving psychotropic medication. Over a nine-month period, patients in the family therapy group had significantly fewer relapses and lower levels of psychiatric symptoms than those who participated only in individual treatment. In a larger study, Hogarty and others (1986) compared the effects of a family-focused intervention to those of individual treatment for patients with schizophrenia who came from high *expressed emotion* households. Expressed emotion covers a range of strong negative affects in family interactions, particularly criticism and emotional overinvolvement. After one year of treatment, patients whose families participated in a psychoeducational intervention designed to "lower the emotional climate of the home while maintaining reasonable expectations for patient performance" had significantly fewer relapses than persons whose families did not participate. No patients relapsed in families who successfully changed from high to low expressed emotion status. Although neither of the studies discussed above focused specifically on persons with dual disorders, the high levels of dissatisfaction with family relations among persons with dual disorders suggest that family-focused interventions may prove beneficial for them as well.

Interventions that attempt to improve family interactions have sometimes been criticized for focusing only on the family's response to the identified relative's behavior rather than on the behavior of both parties (Kanter, Lamb, and Loeper, 1987). Evidence suggests that the combination of difficult behaviors presented by the person with mental illness and his or her family's reactions contribute to the phenomenon known as expressed emotion (Kavanagh, 1992). Approaches that blame either party for relationship difficulties are likely to be less effective than those that view expressed emotion as an interactive phenomenon. Although recent theories posit a more complex interaction between persons with mental illness and their families (Maurin and Boyd, 1990; Mueser and Glynn, 1990), it is not clear that those ideas have been widely incorporated into treatment practice.

We do not know whether there is any association between the criticism and emotional overinvolvement that characterize high expressed emotion situations and the amounts of direct caregiving and economic assistance that families provide. This is an area in which further research may help. For now we should be careful not to confuse the amount of objective family support with the emotional content of family interactions. We cannot assume that emotional overinvolvement means that the family is giving too much direct support or that families who are giving a great deal of support are doing so inappropriately.

A limitation of virtually all treatment studies that include measures of family burden is that they tend to be relatively brief, often lasting for a year or less. Recent work by Tessler and Gamache (1994) suggests that continuity of service rather than the type or intensity of treatment a person receives may be a critical factor in reducing the burden that person's family experiences. In their analysis of data from three sites in Ohio, Tessler and Gamache found a significant relationship between the continuity of a relative's treatment and aspects of family burden for families with whom the client lived. They defined continuity as having a case manager or other formal caregiver who "helped them plan and obtain the services they needed" at each of three points over a two-year period. Continuity did not have the same benefits for families who lived separately from study participants. Consistent with other studies, being a parent and sharing a residence were associated with higher levels of family burden.

Family services specifically designed for persons with dual disorders, a relatively new phenomenon, are often incorporated into integrated treatment programs (Fox, Fox, and Drake, 1992; Sciacca, 1991). Most take a group psychoeducational approach that provides information about the effects of substance use for persons with mental illness and discusses strategies for behavior management (Clark and Drake, 1992). Typical psychoeducational groups are shorter in duration than the groups for families of persons with schizophrenia mentioned earlier; information on substance abuse can easily be incorporated into long-term family groups, however (Ryglewicz, 1991).

As yet there is little information about the effectiveness of family interventions specifically targeted for relatives of persons with dual disorders. Additional research could help determine the effectiveness of these approaches for persons with psychiatric diagnoses other than schizophrenia. Existing research and clinical opinion suggest that a "one size fits all" approach may not be appropriate for family services (Pfeiffer and Mostek, 1991). Not only may different psychiatric diagnoses present different problems, but family members may experience them differently depending on their relationship to the person with a dual disorder. Spouses, who often drop out of family groups composed primarily of parents, are more likely to remain engaged in a group of their peers (Mannion, Mueser, and Solomon, 1994). Evidence also shows that siblings have views of their brothers and sisters with mental illness that are substantially different from those of their parents (Horwitz, Tessler, Fisher, and Gamache, 1992). Services must be tailored to fit differing needs of family members.

One area of potential conflict between persons with dual disorders and their families is money management. Persons with dual disorders may have a particularly difficult time managing their funds (Drake and Wallach, 1989). Families often become involved as informal money managers or more formally as payees for government programs like supplemental security income or social security disability insurance. Although money management is a frequent subject of disagreement within families, it can be an effective way of reducing substance abuse and relapse rates (Spittle, 1991). Whether or not families are the most appropriate money managers is currently debated, but the fact is that many family members find themselves in that role. Given its potential importance, this issue should be addressed explicitly in psychoeducational interventions for families.

Although research shows that substance abuse has negative consequences for families as well as for persons with dual disorders, families often do not make the connection between substance abuse and these difficulties. In one survey of preferences for additional education, families whose relatives had schizophrenia ranked information on drug and alcohol abuse last on a list of forty-five topics; families whose relatives had a major affective disorder ranked the topic slightly higher at thirty-second out of forty-five (Mueser and others, 1992). Other studies show that families often do not see incidents of drug or alcohol abuse as particularly disturbing (Gubman, Tessler, and Willis, 1987; Hatfield, 1978). In contrast, families usually do report behaviors that are associated with substance abuse—such as temper tantrums, violence, or symptom exacerbations—as disturbing or stressful. Thus families' apparent lack of interest in substance abuse problems could stem from their attribution of behavioral problems to the mental disorder rather than to substance abuse.

Just as persons with dual disorders go through progressive phases of treatment readiness, from engagement to persuasion to active treatment (Drake and others, 1993), families may also need to be convinced that the formal treatment system has something helpful to offer them. Many families feel frustrated or disappointed about their relationships with the providers who serve their relatives and may be wary of offers to help (Hanson and Rapp, 1992). An unknown percentage of families have little or no contact with their relatives and therefore may be particularly difficult to engage (Wasow, 1994). A cooperative approach to working with families, one that recognizes and appreciates their knowledge and skills, is needed to establish a trusting, working relationship with families. This does not mean that treatment providers should wait for families to make the first move. An assertive but respectful approach to establishing a relationship with families is likely to be most effective.

CLINICAL IMPLICATIONS OF FAMILY SUPPORT

The goals of provider-family relationships are multifaceted. Providers may be able to reduce some of the stress or burden on families by providing timely crisis response and training in management of substance abuse and other behavioral problems. As emphasized in earlier schizophrenia studies, support and education for families can benefit clients by reducing relapse rates and perhaps improving symptoms. Providers can also learn a great deal from families that will help them anticipate crises and generally improve treatment effectiveness. Better provider-family relationships are likely to benefit all parties.

Maintaining family ties is a critically important goal of treatment and rehabilitation that has largely been ignored. Recent research documents the potential life-saving benefits of the basic support that families give. Although the strains that dual disorders place on family relations can cause providers, families, or their relatives with dual disorders to conclude that a respite is needed, the value of maintaining strong family ties should not be discounted.

Informal discussions with treatment providers suggest that they are often unaware of the substantial amounts of direct care and economic support that families give their clients. The reasons for this are not clear. Perhaps their clients prefer to keep such matters private, or perhaps providers do not ask about family support. In either case, the result is that providers may not fully appreciate the vital role that families play in the lives of their clients. Studies indicate that although the amount of family support varies widely, the percentage of families who give direct or financial support is impressive (Clark, 1994; Franks, 1990). Current clinical assessment techniques focus on problems in family relations but are not adequate for documenting family support. Providers may need to make a special effort to understand the extent to which a family gives concrete support to a client. This often means talking directly with the family about the kinds of support they extend in a typical month (see Clark, 1994 or Clark and Drake, 1994 for examples of support categories).

Although the intensity of conflict may lead providers and family members to conclude that a temporary separation is necessary, the potential negative impact of emotional conflict should be weighed against possible loss of family support that can be caused by separation. Indeed, preservation and enhancement of family support systems should be considered an important measure of treatment effectiveness.

CONCLUSION

Despite the stresses imposed by severe mental illness and substance abuse, families play a critical role in the lives of most persons with dual disorders. That role is broader than the one traditionally afforded them by treatment providers. Family concerns include not only their effect on clinical outcomes and the inevitable difficulties they encounter in caring for a relative with a severe, chronic illness, but also the effects of the direct support they give in the form of time, money, and in-kind gifts.

Although community mental health and psychosocial rehabilitation programs place a high premium on helping persons with severe mental illness to live independently, independence cannot be achieved at the expense of informal social support from family and friends. Improved functioning may reduce reliance on these systems, but evidence from surveys of the general population shows that mutual support among family members throughout the lifespan is overwhelmingly the norm rather than the exception (MacDonald, 1989; Marks, 1993). Perhaps a more fitting goal than independence, one that reflects more accurately the experience of most people, is *effective interdependence.* Such a goal suggests that optimal functioning, or, to use a term from psychosocial rehabilitation, recovery, is not something a person achieves independently but rather in the context of a supportive system. Research suggests that this system is particularly important for the survival of persons with dual disorders. This view has yet to be fully integrated into current treatment interventions for persons with dual disorders. Incorporating services that strengthen family relationships is a challenge that clinicians and policy makers must learn to meet.

REFERENCES

Anderson, E. A., and Lynch, M. M. "A Family Impact Analysis: The Deinstitutionalization of the Mentally Ill." *Family Relations,* 1984, *33,* 41-46.

Aneshensel, C. S., Pearlin, L. I., and Schuler, R. H. "Stress, Role Captivity, and the Cessation of Caregiving." *Journal of Health and Social Behavior,* 1993, *34,* 54-70.

Bellack, A. S., and Mueser, K. T. "Psychosocial Treatment for Schizophrenia." *Schizophrenia Bulletin,* 1993, *19,* 317-336.

Carpentier, N., Lesage, A., Goulet, J., Lalonde, P., and Renaud, M. "Burden of Care of Families Not Living with Young Schizophrenic Relatives." *Hospital and Community Psychiatry,* 1992, *43* (1), 38-43.

Caton, C.L.M., Shrout, P. E., Dominguez, B., Eagle, P. F., Opler, L. A., and Cournos, F. "Risk Factors for Homelessness Among Women with Schizophrenia." *American Journal of Public Health,* 1995, *85* (8), 1153-1156.

Caton, C.L.M., Shrout, P. E., Eagle, P. F., Opler, L. A., Felix, A., and Dominguez, B. "Risk Factors for Homelessness Among Schizophrenic Men: A Case-Control Study." *American Journal of Public Health,* 1994, *84* (2), 265-270.

Clark, R. E. "Family Costs Associated with Severe Mental Illness and Substance Use." *Hospital and Community Psychiatry,* 1994, *45* (8), 808-813.

Clark, R. E., and Drake, R. E. "Substance Abuse and Mental Illness: What Families Need to Know." *Innovations and Research,* 1992, *1* (4), 3-8.

Clark, R. E., and Drake, R. E. "Expenditures of Time and Money by Families of People with Severe Mental Illness and Substance Use Disorders." *Community Mental Health Journal,* 1994, *30* (2), 145-163.

Dixon, L., McNary, S., and Lehman, A. "Substance Abuse and Family Relationships of Persons with Severe Mental Illness." *American Journal of Psychiatry,* 1995, *152* (3), 456-458.

Drake, R. E., Bartels, S. J., Teague, G. B., Noordsy, D. L., and Clark, R. E. "Treatment of Substance Abuse in Severely Mentally Ill Patients." *Journal of Nervous and Mental Disease,* 1993, *181* (10), 606-610.

Drake, R. E., and Wallach, M. A. "Substance Abuse Among the Chronic Mentally Ill." *Hospital and Community Psychiatry,* 1989, *40* (10), 1041-1046.

Falloon, I.R.H., Boyd, J. L., McGill, C. W., Razani, J., Moss, H. B., and Gilderman, A. M. "Family Management in the Prevention of Exacerbations of Schizophrenia: A Controlled Study." *New England Journal of Medicine,* 1982, *306* (24), 1437-1440.

Fisher, P. J., and Breakey, W. R. "The Epidemiology of Alcohol, Drug, and Mental Disorders Among Homeless Persons." *American Psychologist,* 1991, *46* (11), 1115-1128.

Fox, T., Fox, L., and Drake, R. E. "Developing a Statewide Service System for People with Co-Occurring Mental Illness and Substance Use Disorders." *Innovations and Research,* 1992, *1* (4), 9-14.

Franks, D. D. "Economic Contribution of Families Caring for Persons with Severe and Persistent Mental Illness." *Administration and Policy in Mental Health,* 1990, *18* (1), 9-18.

Gershon, E. S., Delisi, L. E., Hamovit, J., Nurnberger, J. I., Maxwell, M. E., Schreiber, J., Dauphinais, D., Dingman, C. W., and Guroff, J. J. "A Controlled Family Study of Chronic Psychoses: Schizophrenia and Schizoaffective Disorder." *Archives of General Psychiatry,* 1988, *45,* 328-336.

Goldman, H. H. "Mental Illness and Family Burden: A Public Health Perspective." *Hospital and Community Psychiatry,* 1982, *33* (7), 557-560.

Gondolf, E. W., Mulvey, E. P., and Lidz, G. W. "Characteristics of Perpetrators of Family and Nonfamily Assaults." *Hospital and Community Psychiatry,* 1990, *41* (2), 191-193.

Greenberg, J. S., Greenley, J. R., and Benedict, P. "Contributions of Persons with Serious Mental Illness to Their Families." *Hospital and Community Psychiatry,* 1994, *45* (5), 475-480.

Greenberg, J. S., Seltzer, M. M., and Greenley, J. R. "Aging Parents of Adults with Disabilities: The Gratifications and Frustrations of Later-Life Caregiving." *Gerontologist,* 1993, *33* (4), 542-550.

Gubman, G. D., Tessler, R. C., and Willis, G. "Living with the Mentally Ill: Factors Affecting Household Complaints." *Schizophrenia Bulletin,* 1987, *13* (4), 727-736.

Hanson, J. G., and Rapp, C. A. "Families' Perceptions of Community Mental Health Programs for Their Relatives with a Severe Mental Illness." *Community Mental Health Journal,* 1992, *28* (3), 181-197.

Hatfield, A. B. "Psychological Costs of Schizophrenia to the Family." *Social Work,* 1978, *23,* 355-359.

Hoenig, J., and Hamilton, M. W. "The Schizophrenic Patient in the Community and His Effect on the Household." *International Journal of Social Psychiatry,* 1966, *12* (3), 165-176.

Hogarty, G. E., Anderson, C. M., Reiss, D. J., Kornblith, S. J., Greenwald, D. P., Javna, C. D., and Madonia, M. J. "Family Psychoeducation, Social Skills Training, and Maintenance Chemotherapy in the Aftercare Treatment of Schizophrenia." *Archives of General Psychiatry,* 1986, *43,* 633-642.

Horwitz, A., Tessler, R., Fisher, G., and Gamache, G. "The Role of Adult Siblings in Providing Social Support to the Seriously Mentally Ill." *Journal of Marriage and the Family,* 1992, *54,* 233-241.

Kanter, J., Lamb, H. R., and Loeper, C. "Expressed Emotion in Families: A Critical Review." *Hospital and Community Psychiatry,* 1987, *38* (4), 374-380.

Kashner, T. M., Rader, L. E., Rodell, D. E., Beck, C. M., Rodell, L. R., and Muller, K. "Family Characteristics, Substance Abuse, and Hospitalization Patterns of Patients with Schizophrenia." *Hospital and Community Psychiatry,* 1991, *42* (2), 195-197.

Kavanagh, D. J. "Recent Developments in Expressed Emotion and Schizophrenia." *British Journal of Psychiatry,* 1992, *160,* 601-620.

Kay, S. R., Kalathara, M., and Meinzer, A. E. "Diagnostic and Behavioral Characteristics of Psychiatric Patients Who Abuse Substances." *Hospital and Community Psychiatry,* 1989, *40* (10), 1061-1064.

MacDonald, M. M. *Family Background, the Life Cycle, and Inter-Household Transfers.* National Survey of Families and Households working paper no. 13. Madison, Wis., Center for Demography and Ecology, University of Wisconsin, Madison, 1989.

Mannion, E., Mueser, K., and Solomon, P. "Designing Psychoeducational Services for Spouses of Persons with Serious Mental Illness." *Community Mental Health Journal,* 1994, *30* (2), 177-190.

Marks, N. F. *Caregiving Across the Life-Span: A New National Profile.* National Survey of Families and Households working paper no. 55. Madison, Wis., Center for Demography and Ecology, University of Wisconsin, Madison, 1993.

Massey, O. T., and Wu, L. "Service Delivery and Community Housing: Perspectives of Consumers, Family Members, and Case Managers." *Innovations and Research,* 1993, *2* (3), 9-15.

Maurin, J. T., and Boyd, C. B. "Burden of Mental Illness on the Family: A Critical Review." *Archives of Psychiatric Nursing,* 1990, *4* (2), 99-107.

Monahan, J. "Mental Disorder and Violent Behavior: Perceptions and Evidence." *American Psychologist,* 1992, *47* (4), 511-521.

Mueser, K. T., and Glynn, S. M. "Behavioral Family Therapy for Schizophrenia." In M. Hersen, R. M. Eisler, and P. M. Miller (eds.), *Progress in Behavior Modification.* Vol. 16. Newbury Park, Calif.: Sage, 1990.

Mueser, K. T., Bellack, A. S., Wade, J. H., Sayers, S. L., and Rosenthal, C. K. "An Assessment of the Educational Needs of Chronic Psychiatric Patients and Their Relatives." *British Journal of Psychiatry,* 1992, *160,* 674-680.

Noordsy, D. L, Drake, R. E., Biesanz, J. C., and McHugo, G. J. "Family History of Alcoholism in Schizophrenia." *Journal of Nervous and Mental Disease,* 1994, *182* (11), 651-655.

Pfeiffer, E. J., and Mostek, M. "Services for Families of People with Mental Illness." *Hospital and Community Psychiatry,* 1991, *42* (3), 262-264.

Reynolds, I., and Hoult, J. E. "The Relatives of the Mentally Ill: A Comparative Trial of Community-Oriented and Hospital-Oriented Psychiatric Care." *Journal of Nervous and Mental Disease,* 1984, *172* (8), 480-489.

Ryglewicz, H. "Psychoeducation for Clients and Families: A Way In, Out, and Through in Working with People with Dual Disorders." *Psychosocial Rehabilitation Journal,* 1991, *15* (2), 79-89.

Sciacca, K. "An Integrated Treatment Approach for Severely Mentally Ill Individuals with Substance Disorders." In K. Minkoff and R. Drake (eds.), *Dual Diagnosis of Major Mental Illness and Substance Disorder.* New Directions for Mental Health Services, no. 50. San Francisco: Jossey-Bass, 1991.

Spittle, B. "The Effect of Financial Management on Alcohol-Related Hospitalization." *American Journal of Psychiatry,* 1991, *148* (2), 221-223.

Straznickas, K. A., McNiel, D. E., and Binder, R. L. "Violence Toward Family Caregivers by Mentally Ill Relatives." *Hospital and Community Psychiatry,* 1993, *44* (4), 385-387.

Swan, R. W., and Lavitt, M. "Patterns of Adjustment to Violence in Families of the Mentally Ill." *Journal of Interpersonal Violence,* 1988, *3* (1), 42-54.

Tausig, M., Fisher, G. A., and Tessler, R. C. "Informal Systems of Care for the Chronically Mentally Ill." *Community Mental Health Journal,* 1992, *28* (5), 413-425.

Tessler, R., and Gamache, G. "Continuity of Care, Residence, and Family Burden in Ohio." *Milbank Quarterly,* 1994, *72* (1), 149-169.

Tessler, R. C., Gamache, G. M., Rossi, P. H., Lehman, A. F., and Goldman, H. H. "The Kindred Bonds of Mentally Ill Homeless Persons." *New England Journal of Public Policy,* 1992. *8* (1), 265-280.

Thompson, E. H., Jr., and Doll, W. "The Burden of Families Coping with the Mentally Ill: An Invisible Crisis." *Family Relations,* 1982, *31,* 379-388.

Torres, R. A., Mani, S., Altholz, J., and Brickner, P. W. "Human Immunodeficiency Virus Infection Among Homeless Men in a New York City Shelter." *Archives of Internal Medicine,* 1990, *150* (10), 2030-2036.

Uehara, E. S. "Race, Gender, and Housing Inequality: An Exploration of the Correlates of Low-Quality Housing Among Clients Diagnosed with Severe and Persistent Mental Illness." *Journal of Health and Social Behavior,* 1994, *35,* 309-321.

Wasow, M. "A Missing Group in Family Research: Parents Not in Contact with Their Mentally Ill Children." *Hospital and Community Psychiatry,* 1994, *45* (7), 720-721.

Winefield, H. R., and Harvey, E. J. "Needs of Family Caregivers in Chronic Schizophrenia." *Schizophrenia Bulletin,* 1994, *20* (3), 557-566.

ABOUT THE AUTHOR

Robin E. Clark, Ph.D., is Associate Professor of Community and Family Medicine and Psychiatry at the Dartmouth Medical School, Research Associate at the New Hampshire-Dartmouth Psychiatric Research Center, and Director of the Cost-Effectiveness Laboratory at Dartmouth Medical School.

Copyright 1996. Jossey-Bass, Inc., Publishers. Reprinted with permission.

BARRIERS TO THE CARE OF PERSONS WITH DUAL DIAGNOSES: ORGANIZATIONAL AND FINANCING ISSUES

M. Susan Ridgely, Howard H. Goldman, and Mark Willenbring

Reprinted from *Schizophrenia Bulletin*, 16(1):123-132, 1990

Among the frustrations of managing the dual disorders of chronic mental illness and alcohol and drug abuse is the fact that knowing what to do (by way of special programming) is insufficient to address the problem. The system problems are at least as intractable as the chronic illnesses themselves. Organizing and financing care of patients with comorbities is complicated. At issue are the ways in which we administer mental health and alcohol and drug treatment as well as finance that care. Separate administrative divisions and funding pools, while appropriate for political expediency, visibility, and administrative efficiency, have compounded the problems inherent in serving persons with multiple disabilities. Arbitrary service divisions and categorical boundaries at the State level prevent local governments and programs from organizing joint projects or creatively managing patients across service boundaries. When patients cannot adapt to the way services are organized, we risk reinforcing their overutilization of inpatient and emergency services, which are ineffective mechanisms for delivering the care these patients need. This article reviews the barriers in organization and financing of care (categoric and third party financing, including the special problem of diagnosis-related groups limitations) and proposes strategies to enhance the delivery of appropriate treatment.

The National Institute of Mental Health (NIMH) Epidemiologic Catchment Area (ECA) study, which investigated the prevalence of mental, alcohol, and drug abuse disorders among the general population, found the co-occurrence of these disorders is quite frequent (Boyd et al. 1984). Recent reviews of the mental health and the alcohol and drug abuse literature (Ridgely et al. 1986; Galanter et al. 1988) indicate that the problem of multiple illnesses or disabilities is the rule rather than the exception among individuals seeking mental health and alcohol and drug treatment in the public sector.

In addition, the clinical and social consequences of co-occurrence have been the focus of much attention. Within the mental health literature, the combination of alcohol and drug abuse and chronic mental illness has been found to exacerbate psychiatric illness (Janowsky and Davis 1976; Knudsen and Vilmar 1984; Negrete et al. 1986), result in costly rehospitalization and other treatment (Bassuk 1980; Safer 1987; Drake et al. 1989), and often increase the chance of acting-out and suicidal behavior (Caton 1981; Richardson et al. 1985). Within the alcohol and drug abuse literature, the co-occurrence of psychiatric symptomatology with alcohol and drug abuse is associated with poor prognosis, regardless of treatment modality (Alterman et al. 1982; McLellan et al. 1983). Mental health interventions that do not attend to alcohol and drug abuse problems produce poor outcomes for individuals with dual diagnoses[1] (Cohen and Klein 1974; Hall et al. 1975; Safer 1987).

Patterns of service utilization are of particular concern. Commentators have noted that chronic mentally ill young adults have become regulars of the general hospital emergency and psychiatric emergency units (Bassuk 1980; Egri and Caton 1982; Goldfinger et al. 1984). Richardson et al. (1985), reporting on a retrospective longitudinal treatment utilization study of 56 young schizophrenic patients, characterized their treatment utilization as "heavy, discontinuous, and episodic with these patterns intensified for patients with histories of drug abuse" (p. 104). They also reported significantly more inpatient admissions, admissions of shorter duration, and more nontreatment periods for the drug-abusing study group. Less than 10 percent of the drug-abusing sample received any care from a drug abuse facility. These findings were consistent with studies by other investigators in the late 1970's (Cohen and Klein 1974; Hall et al. 1977). In addition to the reticence of patients to seek care and remain in treatment, it is clear that persons with dual disorders are often refused admission or discharged prematurely from care facilities in both sectors (Galanter et al. 1988).

Current approaches to treating persons with dual diagnoses emphasize the necessity of providing intensive and specific treatments for both illnesses concomitantly, combining the resources of mental health and alcohol and

---

[1]The authors are aware that the term *dual diagnosis* is not acceptable to some, although we choose to use it as a shorthand descriptor for the co-occurrence of chronic mental illness and alcohol or other drug abuse. *Chronic mental illness* refers to several mental disorders, including, primarily, schizophrenia, but also personality disorders and major affective disorders. Regardless of diagnosis, mental illness is considered chronic if it is sufficiently severe and enduring to cause lasting disability and recurrent contact with the mental health system. *Alcohol or other drug abuse* refers to the use of drugs and/or alcohol singly or in combination, resulting in a *DSM-III-R* (American Psychiatric Association 1987) diagnosis of substance abuse or substance dependence. Co-occurrence, co-morbidity, and dual diagnosis are used interchangeably. It is also recognized that the broad category of "dually diagnosed" patients includes a diagnostically and functionally heterogeneous group of individuals with a variety of clinical needs.

drug abuse services (Ridgely et al. 1987; Lehman et al. 1989; Minkoff 1989; Osher and Kofoed 1989). However, producing *hybrid* services requires breaking out of the conventional categorical boundaries now separating the two service systems. This act of organizational innovation and coordination has rarely been initiated, despite the far-reaching consequences of not doing so. Beyond the cost of inappropriate service utilization and the mutual frustration it engenders in caregivers and patients are the tragic and costly deterioration, lost productivity, and lost lives it ultimately produces. Individuals with dual diagnoses are a challenging clientele, under the best of organizational arrangements, but now they are suffering from the excess burden of trying to deal with service systems designed for *single disabilities* and as yet unable to accommodate their particular needs (Ridgely et al. 1986). Bachrach (1987) refers to this problem as an externally imposed disability, but one amenable to intervention.

HISTORICAL PERSPECTIVE ON THE ORGANIZATION AND FINANCING OF MENTAL HEALTH, ALCOHOL, AND DRUG SERVICES

By the 20th century, public treatment of persons with mental disorders was the domain of the States. Early treatment of mental disorder amounted mostly to custodial care within State asylums. Later reforms brought a shift of mentally ill patients out of asylums and into a variety of specialized private and public mental health facilities. Public hospitals cared for the most disturbed and disadvantaged patients. The advent of health insurance in the 1930's (and public insurance, Medicaid, and Medicare in the 1960's) spurred a new private industry in mental health services, especially inpatient services (for which there were more comprehensive benefits). One of the reasons for the limitations of insurance benefits was the large well-developed system of public services already in place. Insurers had little incentive to cover illnesses already financed by government. With the advent of third-party payment, payers (and regulators) were concerned with the appropriateness, effectiveness, and cost of care (Ridgely and Goldman 1989).

The Federal Government had a principal role in financing the development of community-based inpatient and outpatient services in the 1960's and 1970's (through the establishment of the Community Mental Health Center and Community Support Program grant-funding mechanisms at NIMH). With consolidation of the various grant mechanisms into block grants under the Omnibus Reconciliation Act (OBRA) of 1981, the States resumed their role as principal player in determining the character of mental health services (La Jolla Management Corporation 1988).

Alcohol and drug treatment developed in a distinct, though parallel way, from the development of psychiatric care. In 1935, Alcoholics Anonymous (AA) was founded by two recovering individuals as a means to help each other become sober through mutual support. Proponents of AA were clearly frustrated that many physicians (and, especially, psychiatrists) subscribed to the view that alcoholism was due to an underlying personality disorder (Vaillant 1980). Many of the public felt that alcohol and other drug abuse reflected moral weakness rather than medical illness. Modern treatment approaches, such as the "Minnesota model," began to be developed in the 1950's and 1960's (Laundergan 1982). In the 1950's the American Medical Association and the World Health Organization recognized alcoholism as a disease amenable to medical treatment, and the courts began challenging the criminality of public drunkenness. Passage of decriminalization laws in the early 1970's served to redirect the responsibility for "inebriety" from the criminal justice to the health sector (Finn 1985) where a continuum of coordinated treatment (and rehabilitation) services was to be available. Before the passage of decriminalization legislation in 34 States in the last 20 years, custodial care was also provided for many public inebriates—in jails. Even with decriminalization, in many places detoxification continues to be the principal service available to the indigent.

Early services relied on lay counselors—many of whom were recovering individuals. However the development of an alcohol and drug treatment industry[2] included a push to bring alcohol and drug treatment into the medical field for legitimacy and access to third-party payment. It led to the development of services in a variety of settings; in general hospitals, detoxification centers, freestanding treatment centers, and private hospitals. Typically, coverage for alcohol and drug treatment was limited in health insurance, however, because of the continued belief that alcohol and drug abuse is a self-inflicted disorder. (Limitations in coverage for alcohol, drug, and mental disorders are discussed in more detail below.) Legitimization brought to the field licensing rules, training requirements and accountability which had not characterized AA and lay treatment services, and which were not necessarily welcomed by the industry. Alcohol and drug treatment is an evolving field; while many programs still treat all entrants in essentially the same way, it is increasingly recognized that different treatment may be required for different people with different problems (Zinberg and Bean 1981).

Notwithstanding the move by the treatment industry toward increasing professionalization, many in the alcohol and drug field continue to distrust medicine—in particular, psychiatry—and consider the use of any mind-altering substance to be unacceptable. At the extremes, alcohol and drug abuse counselors may believe that mental illness is simply a symptom or manifestation of alcohol or drug abuse. Alternatively, mental health workers

---

[2]This treatment industry is to be differentiated from AA, even though AA principles may be part of treatment and staff may themselves be recovering individuals. The alcohol and drug treatment industry is similar to other medical business concerns, with lobbyists and official spokespersons, in contradiction of the traditions of AA (e.g., no one individual can speak for the organization).

may believe that alcohol and drug abuse is merely self-medication for an underlying mental disorder. While these extremes do not represent the fields at large, such conflicts are often played out in the day-to-day management of patients with dual diagnoses. Even within the alcohol and drug field, there is no clear consensus about the optimal treatment for patients with dual diagnoses.

The Federal Government exerted its influence through legislation creating grant-funding mechanisms to expand service capacity and developing national institutes on Alcohol Abuse and Alcoholism (PL 91-616) and Drug Abuse (PL 92-255). State agencies carried the prime responsibility for providing public alcohol and drug abuse services and for funding private services. The National Institute on Alcohol Abuse and Alcoholism (NIAAA) and the National Institute on Drug Abuse (NIDA) funded no service projects from 1981 to 1988, when NIAAA resumed using its demonstration authority with appropriations from the Stewart B. McKinney Act to provide treatment services for homeless persons. Currently the Federal Government also asserts its influence on the availability of alcohol, drug, and mental health services across the States through the benefit structure of Medicare and Medicaid.

ORGANIZATIONAL AND CATEGORICAL FUNDING BARRIERS: THE PUBLIC SYSTEMS OF CARE

The lack of a common administrative structure for alcohol, drug, and mental health services in most States cannot be overemphasized as an impediment in developing systems of care for individuals with comorbid conditions. Before there was a focus on the need for concurrent treatment of patients with dual diagnoses, highlighting the need for collaboration across service system boundaries, the chasm between alcohol/drug and mental health systems in many States and communities was widely acknowledged. The organizational discontinuities are manifested in some areas in the lack of one *authority* to which both systems are responsible and in the reality that separate authorities may mean different structures and the lack of contiguous service or planning areas across the State.

According to the National Association of State Mental Health Program Directors (personal communication, October 1989), in 22 of the 55 States and territories, the State Mental Health Authority (SMHA) administers the State's alcohol and drug programs. In at least 12 additional States, the SMHA and the Alcohol and Drug Abuse Authority are separate but relate to the same State administrative department (usually the State's Health or Human Services Department). That means that *in the remaining 21 States/territories, the SMHA and the Alcohol and Drug Authority are entirely separate administrative structures and report to separate State supraordinate departments.* And, according to data from the National Drug and Alcoholism Treatment Utilization Survey (personal communication, October 1989), in at least eight States/territories, Alcohol Authorities and Drug Authorities are distinct entities.

Further complicating the landscape, in some States/territories, *separate levels of government* are in charge. For example, in the case of New York, the city has a Mental Health, Mental Retardation and Alcoholism agency that is responsible for oversight of programs in these three fields. Drug abuse treatment, however, is purely a State responsibility. In Iowa, Polk County (Des Moines) is responsible for administering hospital and community mental health programs, but the State's Alcohol and Drug Authority funds community alcohol and drug treatment in Polk County by direct contract with individual agencies. The county's mental health authority has no administrative or planning oversight. Interestingly, the SMHA provides the only State-funded, hospital-based care for alcohol and drug abuse—within the State mental hospitals.

The fact that there are three separate institutes that make up the Federal Alcohol, Drug Abuse, and Mental Health Administration (NIMH, NIAAA, and NIDA) both reflects and exacerbates the problem at the State level. Even though there is a Federal Alcohol, Drug Abuse and Mental Health block grant, monies are distributed to State categorical agencies and no significant comingling of such funds has been noted.

These service divisions are not an accident of history but, rather, reflect purposeful attempts to create structures to improve administrative efficiency and visibility for various illness/disability groups. To ensure that categorical monies were spent for appropriate target populations, service systems set up eligibility requirements, usually focused on diagnosis. Utilization review and licensing standards were mechanisms used to ensure that *eligible* individuals were served with categorical monies. When categorical funding became especially tight, competition for scarce resources reinforced the necessity to screen out ineligible, though often needy, individuals. When individuals with multiple needs approached service systems, the initial view was toward determining the *primary diagnosis* as a way of determining eligibility. This might result in one of two poor outcomes: identifying persons as needing what one is equipped to provide (without reference to other needs) or identifying persons as needing what someone else provides, as a way of denying access to services. Both are forms of *institutional denial.* An associated problem results from the fact that individuals requesting services are likely to be assigned to programs according to their immediate, presenting problem. Because both chronic mental illness and alcohol and drug abuse are chronic disorders characterized by acute exacerbations, attention to immediate symptoms may not result in good long-term placement.

Concerns about scarce resources result in requests for collaboration being seen as attempts to encroach on one another's territory. Though remarking on phenomena in other parts of the psychiatric system, Goldberg and Fogel (1989) have noted that "paranoia tends to develop when institutions approach each other with issues involving loss of control" (p.1060). If it is not agreed that there are mutual patients across the service systems, there is the suspicion that "they want our money to treat their clients." Added to this suspicion is the history of mistrust and philosophical differences across the service systems. As characterized in a recent policy report in New York State,

> The Commission was aware that this problem has existed for decades, that it has been exacerbated by ingrained patterns of behavior of separate service delivery systems... and that these patterns of behavior are themselves reflective of the absence of a clear clinical consensus on appropriate treatment strategies. [Sundrum 1986, p. iii]

Philosophical conflicts, different training and credentialing of caregivers (especially the differential focus on professional credentials in the mental health field), and lack of respect for one another's competency have exacerbated the barriers between the service systems. Stereotyped attitudes are fueled by a lack of information about the respective fields, as well as a general lack of questioning of preconceptions about effective treatment approaches (Harrison et al. 1985). The problem might be addressable were it not for the complication of the multiplicity of views within each field about the nature of the disorders and philosophies of intervention.

Regardless of the origins or reasons for the perpetuation of existing administrative boundaries, for direct providers of service who wish to serve persons with dual diagnoses, the result is devastating. In most States, providers are licensed and funded exclusively either as mental health or alcohol and drug treatment facilities. They respond to differing administrative structures with specific rules regarding suitable buildings, staffing, and, to a lesser extent, programming. In most cases funding is granted to them to provide specific units of service, allowing them little to no ability to comingle funds (or even provide mental health and alcohol/drug services in the same location). Were it possible to draw down funding from separate funding pools, programs would still be faced with potentially conflicting rules and regulations, and would be subject to audit and other controls of more than one State administrative authority. All of these factors aid and abet institutional denial. There are negative incentives for the identification of individuals with dual diagnoses and certainly no positive incentives for stretching a program beyond its institutional bounds to address individual needs.

BARRIERS "OUTSIDE" OF THE PUBLIC SYSTEMS: THE PRIVATE SECTOR AND THIRD-PARTY FUNDING

The proliferation of facility types providing mental health and alcohol and drug services (mentioned above) was largely the result of the introduction of public and private insurance and the fields' response to these new payer sources. Of note is that mental health and alcohol and drug abuse treatment coverage was mandated in a number of States.

Before the issues in third-party payment are addressed, it is important to note the increasing importance of the private sector facility in psychiatric care. Because of restrictions on payment to freestanding psychiatric facilities (e.g., Medicaid prohibitions on paying for care to beneficiaries in such "Institutions for Mental Disease"), general hospitals have become increasingly important providers of acute psychiatric care. Similarly, general hospitals (and private, freestanding psychiatric hospitals) have been major players in the provision of alcohol and drug treatment. In general hospitals, alcohol and drug treatment programs are often profitable ventures and help to subsidize other hospital services. Although these endeavors may increase the overall availability of treatment beds, they may also systematically exclude public, indigent patients. Even when there are designated "indigent beds," these programs generally demand "motivation" and involvement of the family as prerequisites to admission, allowing them to enroll the less difficult patients (who cost less to treat). Apart from its effect on access to care, the proliferation of multiple providers has created a patchwork of providers who can act as "free agents" in a system, resulting in lack of systemwide coordination. Similarly, a patchwork of payers operates to fund various aspects of needed treatment and support in local communities.

PROBLEMS IN THIRD-PARTY FUNDING: ELIGIBILITY LIMITS

For some individuals, having a history of mental illness *or* alcohol or drug abuse may prevent them from being eligible for coverage by a third-party payer. Some private insurance companies impose strict underwriting rules on preexisting conditions, blocking individuals with a history of illness from joining the risk pool of insured individuals. Although this is an understandable risk protection mechanism for the third-party payer, it poses serious problems in access to health care for an individual disabled by mental illness and/or alcohol and drug abuse disorders.

For individuals with general medical conditions who are denied private insurance through underwriting, it is expected that the most disabled among them will be served in the public sector. It is assumed that they will qualify for disability benefits, making them eligible for public health care benefits, as well. For example, they may qualify for disability benefits from the Veterans' Administration (VA) or the Social Security Administration (SSA). Thereby, the disabled veteran gains access to the VA health care system, and the SSA disabled individual gains access to Medicare (after 2 years, if eligible for Social Security Disability Insurance [SSDI] payments) or Medicaid (in 34 States, if eligible for Supplemental Security Income [SSI]). This mechanism, however, is more complicated and less certain for the individual who is disabled by mental illness, alcoholism, or other drug abuse—or some combinations of such problems.

In recent years individuals disabled by mental illness have encountered difficulty in claiming their entitlements from the SSA (Goldman and Gattozzi 1988). Although these problems have been rectified for individuals with schizophrenia and other mental disorders, access to the disability programs of the VA and SSA may be severely limited for individuals who are disabled by alcohol and drug abuse disorders. Both the VA and the SSA have special restrictions on benefits for such individuals. In recent years, moreover, there has been a tendency to expect full recovery from alcohol and drug dependence among SSI recipients, which is seldom, if ever, achieved. Recipients may be denied benefits for failing to continue in treatment, even though the only treatment available may be inappropriate to their needs. Claimants with dual diagnoses, however, may be able to qualify for benefits under the criteria for schizophrenia or some other nonalcohol- and drug-related disorder. Special restrictions impose significant limitations in access to both income support and health care benefits.

PROBLEMS IN THIRD-PARTY FUNDING: BENEFIT LIMITS

Once individuals have qualified for coverage by a third-party payer, they then must be able to gain access to covered services. A new barrier is encountered for individuals with dual diagnoses, who may find that services designed to serve them are not covered or are covered with limits, restricting their utility. Many insurance programs do not provide services for the treatment of alcohol and drug abuse. Almost all policies provide separate limits for mental illness and related treatments. This is true for both private and public sector payers. Until recently, benefits have favored inpatient programs in hospitals, rather than residential and nonresidential alternatives to the hospital. Cost-containment efforts, however, have begun to encourage the alternatives. Programs developed in inpatient settings may now be confronted with efforts to restrict hospital stays, denying patients access to special programs. For older benefit packages, newer programs developed in ambulatory settings may not be covered. Basically, an emerging treatment technology is trapped in a period of transition from strict limits of one type (on benefits) to limits of another type (on costs). As a result, access to coverage may be limited in insurance programs.

PROBLEMS IN THIRD-PARTY FUNDING: PAYMENT LIMITS

Cost-containment policies have brought with them new payment strategies, including the use of various prospective payment mechanisms (Scherl et al. 1988). Any prospective system that pays for care at a prearranged rate for a category of service will tend to underpay for complicated cases. That is true, unless the distinguishing characteristics of those complicated patients are reflected in some adjustment to the payment system (such as a casemix measure like diagnosis-related groups [DRGs]). If no distinctions are made for different types of patients, as in health maintenance organizations (HMOs), then there are limited financial incentives to provide costly care to patients with special needs, such as patients with comorbidities. The tendency is for special needs patients (especially the chronically ill) to be underserved in such settings.

When the DRGs were introduced for use in Medicare, the categories for alcohol and drug abuse made no distinctions for different types of treatment needs. Although DRGs have limited explanatory power for resource use (or length of stay) for alcohol, drug abuse, and mental illness categories (Jencks et al. 1987), they were improved for alcohol and drug abuse. Modifications adjusted, first, for patients' need for rehabilitation services, and, second, for the presence of comorbid conditions, such as mental illness.

In all cases, if there is to be an incentive to provide care for patients with dual diagnoses, payment systems must recognize the increased costs associated with their care. A specific issue raised by some providers is that DRGs force short hospital stays when longer initial lengths of stay might be appropriate for diagnosis and assessment of complicated cases, due to the length of time required to detoxify patients from some specific psychoactive substances. Saving on the initial admission may be lost in repeated readmission.

In addition, rates of reimbursement for specialized programs must be high enough to provide the incentive to deliver quality services. Only then will intensive, specific treatment for comorbidities be available.

STRATEGIES TO ENHANCE SERVICE DELIVERY TO INDIVIDUALS WITH DUAL DIAGNOSES

While there is some evidence of a developing treatment technology for these comorbid conditions (Harrison et al. 1985; Ridgely et al. 1987; Lehman et al. 1989; Minkoff 1989; Osher and Kofoed 1989), there is by no means a consensus in the field; and the inertia of the systems of care threatens the implementation of newly developed treatment interventions. As we have asserted above, instead of being based on individual need, treatment may be provided according to historical system structure, treatment philosophy, training of staff, or other factors not related to the costs or benefits of the various alternatives. Changing the status quo may mean altering the behavior of administrators, payers, providers, and individual clinicians. Unfortunately, therefore, the potential solutions are rarely simple or short term. We will address them below, from the simpler to the more complex, starting with organizational barriers.

PERMEATING ORGANIZATIONAL BARRIERS

At the highest levels of administration (as well as at the local level), it is possible to permeate the barriers through the use of cooperative agreements and jointly funded programs. Although cynics will assert that cooperative agreements "aren't worth the paper they are written on," those inclined to make changes in the administration of systems of care have made use of such arrangements. (The most important ingredient for success may be the will of the parties and the power of signatories to institute the agreed upon initiatives.) For instance, in New Jersey, one of the first States to engage in a statewide effort to address the special needs of individuals with dual diagnoses, the Division of Mental Health and Hospitals (within the New Jersey Department of Human Services) and the Divisions of Alcoholism and Narcotic & Drug Abuse Control (in the New Jersey Department of Health) have established joint working agreements for data collection, planning, and program development. One of the "outputs" has been the development of "service oriented guidelines" that are being utilized statewide by county authorities and treatment providers (alcohol, drug, and mental health) in the development of appropriate services for individuals with dual diagnoses (Bonnie Schorske, New Jersey Division of Mental Health and Hospitals, personal communication March 1986). In addition to cooperative agreements, joint funding of local programs has been used as a mechanism for developing specialized programs to treat patients with dual diagnoses. In Los Angeles County, the county's Alcohol, Drug, and Mental Health authorities jointly funded a 26-bed residential program called the River Community. While this endeavor has not been without its problems (early clashes over philosophy and later problems with oversight by all three authorities), it provides an example of joint funding with lessons for future endeavors. Observers have concluded that while three funding streams can be used, one authority should be designated for day-to-day administration, oversight, and evaluation of any joint programs. The consultation of the other two authorities will be important to maintaining a quality hybridized program.

The State of Virginia represents a case study in the importance of "top-level interaction and collaboration" along with the use of financial incentives to alter the status quo of program development in the community (Thacker and Tremaine 1989). The State Office of Substance Abuse Services and the Office of Mental Health Services designed a request for proposal (RFP) for mental health funds (which had been earmarked for day support and psychosocial rehabilitation) to focus on the needs of persons with dual diagnoses. The response was a significant number of proposals for treating comorbidity and the development of 18 new community-based dual-diagnosis programs within a single funding cycle.

Briefly, among the approaches to overcoming organizational barriers in local communities are the following: comprehensive local planning, the development of comprehensive assessment and referral programs, and the development of managed care programs. Most observers would agree that regardless of what level of government is empowered to administer or finance mental health and alcohol and drug abuse treatment, comprehensive planning (involving the alcohol, drug, and mental health authorities) must be done at the local level. Local planning does not necessarily mean local control. It does imply, however, that there is local agreement (with the participation of State authorities) on what services should be provided within the overall system of care and by whom.

Local planning does not address the fact that there are many "doors" into which individuals can enter the system and that their needs are often defined by which door they have entered. Comprehensive evaluation can be an expensive undertaking but is necessary to match individuals to appropriate treatment opportunities. The development of a communitywide assessment and triage program may be an appropriate endeavor, provided the program is staffed with the appropriate expertise and has access to the referral networks across the two (or three) systems of care. There is potential for cost savings as well; triage allows for the substitution of less expensive outpatient alternatives. Interagency tracking mechanisms can enhance the total system's ability to prevent people from "falling through the cracks."

While not an organizational strategy, per se, the development of educational programs at the local level is important to mention. Educational programs (that impart information but also build skill and competency) should be undertaken for agency personnel. Training programs should focus on the uniqueness and special needs of patients with dual diagnoses, preparing clinicians to address the practical issues faced by caregivers in either system.

Managed care has been proposed as a solution to the discontinuities of care, especially for high-risk, high-cost patients. Balancing access and cost containment are two goals of such a system. High-risk patients are identified for more intensive management (often employing case managers). Instead of relying on patient demand or willingness of the provider, a managed care program determines the appropriateness of a particular intervention (for that patient at that time), only allowing access to the most appropriate, efficient service. Managed care programs would, for example, offer alternative programming to decrease the repetitive use of psychiatric hospitalization and residential treatment for alcohol and drug abuse—expensive services without clear evidence of superiority to less expensive outpatient alternatives. Substitution is only possible in those communities where such quality alternatives exist.

ALTERING FISCAL INCENTIVES

Approaches to addressing the financing problems were imbedded in the earlier discussion (e.g., expansion of benefits, removing barriers to access). Two additional approaches deserve mention: performance contracting and capitation financing.

Performance contracting for service is a third-party payment mechanism that might be used to provide specialized services to persons with dual diagnoses. A Mental Health or Alcohol or Drug Authority or agency might agree to contract with a specialized provider of services, instead of developing a program of its own. Or an agency might require that a certain proportion of the services provided by a contractor will be devoted to patients with dual diagnoses. In either case, the rate of payment is a concern. Contracts should specify the expected quantity of service and the specific target population. Without such specification and without adequate reimbursement, the incentive for a contract provider is to treat only lower cost (or less impaired) clients or to underserve most clients.

Capitation is a method of payment in which the provider is at financial risk to provide an unspecified amount of service to a predetermined population for a fixed amount per time period. The idea of capitated financing is often raised in connection with managed care. Such a mechanism provides a fiscal incentive to reduce cost. What is not yet clear from current experimentation, is whether it is possible to construct risk-adjusted capitation rates for vulnerable populations (such as mentally ill persons) based on factors such as age, disability, and poverty (Lehman 1986; Ridgely and Goldman 1989). It is more complicated for patients with dual diagnoses because of the higher costs associated with their care. None of the current capitation experiments have been targeted to systems of care for persons with dual diagnoses. The lack of clear experience with the development of such rates makes capitation a strategy fraught with difficulties.

CONCLUSION

As Talbott et al. (1986) have noted, systems can fail in one of two ways: because of *structural deficits* (the lack of an appropriate range of alternative services) or because of *process failures* (in which the system fails to provide continuity of care). Both structural deficits and process failures are evident in the mental health and alcohol and drug abuse treatment systems in many communities.

As has been noted, these problems are not accidents of history but represent negative (prejudice and turf protection) and positive (attention to target populations, administrative efficiency) aspects of the way we have organized and financed services. Altering the status quo will take the concerted effort of all stakeholders. It is hoped that as consensus develops around appropriate treatment interventions for individuals with dual diagnoses, agreement about appropriate organizational and financing changes will also evolve.

REFERENCES

Alterman, A.I.; Erdlen, D.L.; and Murphy, E. Effects of illicit drug use in an inpatient psychiatric population. *Addictive Disorders,* 7:231-242, 1982.

American Psychiatric Association. *DSM-III-R: Diagnostic and Statistical Manual of Mental Disorders.* 3rd ed., revised. Washington, DC: The Association, 1987.

Bachrach, L.L. The context of care for the chronic mental patient with substance abuse. *Psychiatric Quarterly,* 58:3-14, 1987.

Bassuk, E.L. The impact of deinstitutionalization on the general psychiatric emergency ward. *Hospital and Community Psychiatry,* 31:623-627, 1980.

Boyd, J.H.; Burke, J.D.; Gruenberg, E.; Holzer, C.E. III; Rae, D.S.; George, L.K.; Karns,M.; Stoltzman, R.; McEvoy, L.; and Nestadt, G. Exclusion criteria of DSM-III: A study of co-occurrence of hierarchy-free syndromes. *Archives of General Psychiatry,* 41:983-989, 1984.

Caton, C. The new chronic patient and the system of community care. *Hospital and Community Psychiatry,* 32:475-488, 1981.

Cohen, M., and Klein, D. Post-hospital adjustment of psychiatrically-hospitalized drug users. *Archives of General Psychiatry,* 31:221-227, 1974.

Drake, R.E.; Osher, F.C.; and Wallach, M.A. Alcohol use and abuse in schizophrenia: A prospective community study. *Journal of Nervous and Mental Disease,* 177:408-414, 1989.

Egri, G., and Caton, C.L. Serving the young adult chronic patient in the 1980s: Challenge to the general hospital. In: Pepper, B., and Ryglewicz, H., eds. *New Directions for Mental Health Services: The Young Adult Chronic Patient.* Vol. 14. San Francisco: Jossey-Bass, Inc., 1982. pp. 25-31.

Finn, P. Decriminalization of public drunkenness: Response of the health care system. *Journal of Studies on Alcohol,* 46:7-22, 1985.

Galanter, M.; Castaneda, R.; and Ferman, J. Substance abuse among general psychiatric patients: Place of presentation, diagnosis and treatment. *American Journal of Drug and Alcohol Abuse,* 14:211-235, 1988.

Goldberg, R.J., and Fogel, B.S. Integration of general hospital psychiatric services with freestanding psychiatric hospitals. *Hospital and Community Psychiatry,* 40:1057-1061, 1989.

Goldfinger, S.M.; Hopkin, J.T.; and Surber, R.W. Treatment resisters or system resisters: Toward a better service system for acute care recidivists. In: Pepper, B., and Ryglewicz, H., eds. *New Directions for Mental Health Services: Advances in Treating the Young Adult Chronic Patient.* Vol. 21. San Francisco: Jossey-Bass, Inc., 1984. pp. 17-27.

Goldman, H.H., and Gattozzi, A.A. Balance of powers: Social security and the mentally disabled, 1980-1985. *Milbank Quarterly,* 66:531-551, 1988.

Hall, R.C.; Poplin, M.K.; DeVaul, R.; and Stickney, S.K. The effect of unrecognized drug abuse on diagnosis and therapeutic outcome. *American Journal of Drug and Alcohol Abuse*, 4:455-465, 1977.

Harrison, P.A.; Martin, J.A.; Tuason, V.B.; and Hoffman, N.G. Conjoint treatment of dual disorders. Chapter 13. In: Alterman, A.I., ed. *Substance Abuse and Psychopathology*. New York: Plenum Publishing Co., 1985. pp. 367-390.

Janowsky, D., and Davis, J. Methylphenidate, dextroamphetamine and levamfetamine: Effects on schizophrenic symptoms. *Archives of General Psychiatry*, 33:304-308, 1976.

Jencks, S.F.; Horgan, C.; Goldman, H.H.; and Taube, C.A., eds. Bringing excluded psychiatric facilities under the Medicare prospective payment system: A review of research evidence and policy options. *Medical Care*, 25(Suppl.):Sl-S5l, 1987.

Knudsen, P., and Vilmar, T. Cannabis and neuroleptic agents in schizophrenia. *Acta Psychiatrica Scandinavica*, 69:162-174, 1984.

La Jolla Management Corporation. *Quality of Care and Outcome Measures for Alcohol, Drug Abuse and Mental Health Care*. Columbia, MD: The Corporation, November 11, 1988.

Laundergan, J.C. *Easy Does It! Alcoholism, Treatment Outcomes, Hazelden, and the Minnesota Model*. Center City, MN: Hazelden Publications, 1982.

Lehman, A.F. Capitation payment and mental health care: A review of opportunities and risks. *Hospital and Community Psychiatry*, 38:31-38, 1986.

Lehman, A.F.; Myers, C.P.; and Corty, E. Assessment and classification of patients with psychiatric and substance abuse syndromes. *Hospital and Community Psychiatry*, 40:1019-1025, 1989.

McLellan, A.; Luborsky, L.; Woody, G.E.; O'Brien, C.P.; and Druley, K.A. Predicting response to alcohol and drug abuse treatments: Role of psychiatric severity. *Archives of General Psychiatry*, 40:620-625, 1983.

Minkoff, K. Development of an integrated model for treatment of dual diagnosis of psychosis and addiction. *Hospital and Community Psychiatry*, 40:1031-1036, 1989.

Negrete, J.C.; Knapp, W.P.; Douglas, D.E.; and Smith, W.B. Cannabis affects the severity of schizophrenic symptoms: Results of a clinical survey. *Psychological Medicine*, 16:515-520, 1986.

Osher, F.C., and Kofoed, L.L. Treatment of patients with both psychiatric and psychoactive substance use disorders. *Hospital and Community Psychiatry*, 40:1025-1030, 1989.

Richardson, M.A.; Craig, T.J.; and Haughland, G. Treatment patterns of young chronic schizophrenic patients in the era of deinstitutionalization. *Psychiatric Quarterly*, 57:243-249, 1985.

Ridgely, M.S., and Goldman, H.H. Mental health insurance. Chapter 14. In: Rochefort, D.A., ed. *Handbook on Mental Health Policy in the United States*. Westport, CT: Greenwood Press, 1989.

Ridgely, M.S.; Goldman, H.H.; and Talbott, J.A. *Chronic Mentally Ill Young Adults With Substance Abuse Problems: A Review of the Literature and Creation of a Research Agenda*. Baltimore, MD: Mental Health Policy Studies, University of Maryland School of Medicine, 1986.

Ridgely, M.S.; Osher, F.C.; and Talbott, J.A. *Chronic Mentally Ill Young Adults With Substance Abuse Problems: Treatment and Training Issues.* Baltimore, MD: Mental Health Policy Studies, University of Maryland School of Medicine, 1987.

Safer, D.J. Substance abuse by young adult chronic patients. *Hospital and Community Psychiatry,* 38:511-514, 1987.

Scherl, D.J.; English, J.T.; and Sharfstein, S.S., eds. *Prospective Payment and Psychiatric Care.* Washington, DC: American Psychiatric Association, 1988.

Sundrum, C.J. *The Multiple Dilemmas of the Multiply Disabled.* Albany, NY: Commission on Quality of Care for the Mentally Disabled, 1986.

Talbott, J.A.; Bachrach, L.L.; and Ross, L. Non-compliance and mental health systems. *Psychiatric Annals,* 16:596-599, 1986.

Thacker, W., and Tremaine, L. Systems issues in serving the mentally ill substance abuser: Virginia's experience. *Hospital and Community Psychiatry,* 40:1046-1049, 1989.

Vaillant, G.E. Natural history of male psychological health: VIII: Antecedents of alcoholism and orality. *American Journal of Psychiatry,* 137:181-186, 1980.

Zinberg, N.E., and Bean, M.H. *Dynamic Approaches to the Understanding and Treatment of Alcoholism.* New York: The Free Press, 1981.

ABOUT THE AUTHORS

M. Susan Ridgely, M.S.W., J.D., is Associate Professor in the Department of Mental Health Law and Policy, Louis de la Parte Florida Mental Health Institute, University of South Florida. Howard H. Goldman, M.D., Ph.D., is Professor of Psychiatry and Director of the Mental Health Policy Studies Program, University of Maryland School of Medicine, Baltimore, MD. Mark Willenbring, M.D., is Associate Professor of Psychiatry at the University of Minnesota and is Assistant Chief of Psychiatry at the Veterans Administration Medical Center, Minneapolis.

Reprinted with permission from *Schizophrenia Bulletin.*

PERSONS WITH DUAL DIAGNOSES OF SUBSTANCE ABUSE AND MAJOR MENTAL ILLNESS: THEIR EXCESS COSTS OF PSYCHIATRIC CARE

Barbara Dickey and Hocine Azeni

Reprinted from *American Journal of Public Health*, 86:973-977, 1996

Objectives. This study examined the costs of psychiatric treatment for seriously mentally ill people with comorbid substance abuse as compared with mentally ill people not abusing substances.

Methods. Three different sources of data were used to construct client-level files to compare the patterns of care and expenditures of 16,395 psychiatrically disabled Medicaid beneficiaries with and without substance abuse: Massachusetts Medicaid paid claims; Department of Mental Health state hospital inpatient record files; and community support service client tracking files.

Results. Psychiatrically disabled substance abusers had psychiatric treatment costs that were almost 60% higher than those of nonabusers. Most of the cost difference was the result of more acute psychiatric inpatient treatment.

Conclusions. Although the public health and financial costs of high rates of comorbidity are obvious, the solutions to these problems are not. Numerous bureaucratic and social obstacles must be overcome before programs for those with dual diagnoses can be tested for clinical effectiveness.

INTRODUCTION

Use of alcohol and street drugs has been widely reported to have adverse consequences for those with serious mental illness, with important implications for treatment of such individuals.[1] Although increasing attention is being given to methods of engaging these patients in special programs that address both psychiatric and substance abuse disorders, virtually no studies have documented the increased costs associated with care provided to those with dual diagnoses. The purpose of this study was to examine the patterns and costs of psychiatric treatment for 16,395 psychiatrically disabled Medicaid beneficiaries in Massachusetts with major mental illness, some of whom have comorbid substance abuse, and to compare these patterns and costs with those of psychiatrically disabled beneficiaries not having problems of substance abuse.

BACKGROUND

The use of alcohol and street drugs is more common among individuals with serious psychiatric disorders than in the general population.[2,3] The results from the Epidemiologic Catchment Area study showed that very high levels of comorbid substance abuse occur among those with schizophrenia (47%) and bipolar disorders (56%).[4] Substance abuse is also associated with an unwillingness to seek psychiatric treatment, with homelessness, and with increases in psychiatric hospitalization.[5-7] Studies of violent behavior in mentally ill people have also found substance abuse to be a significant predictor, along with lack of medication compliance.[8,9] In addition to the problems known to occur when comorbid substance abuse is identified, another set of problems arises when substance abuse is present but undiagnosed. One of the most worrisome is inappropriate treatment,[10] such as increased doses of psychotropic medication in response to apparent treatment failure due actually to covert substance abuse.

Recent studies have shown that homeless mentally ill adults[11] who have co-occurring substance abuse diagnoses account for at least 20% of the homeless population. Other studies have found a strong correlation between mental illness, substance abuse, chronic homelessness, and housing instability. One example is a study conducted by Drake et al.,[11] who reported that the patterns of care for homeless mentally ill adults include much higher rates of admission and more bed-days among those who abuse substances as compared with those who do not. Perhaps the strongest evidence to date concerning the problems associated with mental illness and comorbid substance abuse has been summarized in an interim report on five McKinney Research Demonstration Programs for homeless mentally ill adults.[12] According to this report, participants in the programs "appeared to be unable to find or keep housing primarily because they abuse alcohol or other drugs, not because they have mental illnesses."[12(pii)]

Evidence is mounting to confirm adverse effects on mentally ill people who use even moderate amounts of alcohol. Drake and Wallach[1] found that about 25% of a group of severely mentally ill clients, assessed as moderate drinkers, had an alcohol use disorder when followed up 4 to 7 years later. The authors concluded that moderate drinking among those with major mental illness carries the risk of eventual substance abuse. This finding is not surprising, according to the authors, given the overlay of damaging effects of substance abuse on the brain dysfunction characteristic of major mental illness.

Previous cost studies have focused on the medical care cost offset predicted to occur when substance abuse is treated. An example is a study conducted by Holder and Blose,[13] who used insurance claim data to assess changes over an 8-year period, comparing the mean monthly cost of all medical care before and after treatment for alcohol abuse. They concluded that there is an offset effect: treatment reduced mean monthly medical costs (including treatment for alcohol abuse) more than 20% during the 4-year follow-up period. In a smaller comprehensive study of the costs of substance abuse in a sample of 75 adults with schizophrenia, Bartels et al.[14] found that current abusers were far more likely to use institutional care and that, overall, they had much higher treatment costs than the comparison groups. Other studies have demonstrated that the social costs associated with substance use among mentally ill people are substantial.[15,16]

METHODS

Design

This cross-sectional study investigated the patterns and costs of treatment for 100% of adult psychiatrically disabled Medicaid beneficiaries in the Commonwealth of Massachusetts during fiscal year 1992. The study was based on administrative data (i.e., the paid claims for these individuals). Comparisons were made between three groups: those who had been treated for a comorbid substance abuse disorder, those who showed evidence of a disorder but had not been treated, and those with no evidence of substance abuse.

Study population

The study included 16,395 treated adult Medicaid beneficiaries in Massachusetts (18 to 64 years of age) who were psychiatrically disabled and had been treated for a major mental illness (an *International Classification of Diseases*, 9th edition, [ICD-9] diagnosis of schizophrenia, major affective disorder, or other psychoses) in fiscal year 1992. The mean age of the study population was 41 years (SD = 12); 88% were White, and 43% were male. About 36% of this population submitted a claim for treatment reimbursement with substance abuse as a primary or secondary diagnosis. The sociodemographic characteristics of the clients are summarized in Table 1. Those with substance abuse, in comparison with those not so identified, were more likely to be male, to be younger, and to have a diagnosis of major affective disorder.

The treated substance abuse group (n = 1,493) was defined as individuals with evidence of a claim for substance abuse treatment during the year (in addition to treatment for major mental illness). The untreated substance abuse group (n = 4,393) was defined as individuals who had at least one claim with a secondary diagnosis of substance abuse but no claim for substance abuse treatment. All others (n = 10,509) were assumed not to

Table 1. Sociodemographic characteristics of 16,395 mentally ill Medicaid beneficiaries in Massachusetts, by substance abuse status

	Treated for Substance Abuse (n = 1,493)	Not Treated for Substance Abuse (n = 4,393)	No Substance Abuse (n = 10,509)
Mean age, yrs	37	40	42
Male, %	49	37	44
Diagnosis, %			
Schizophrenia	31	35	50
Major affective disorder	61	57	43
Other psychosis	8	7	7

have a substance abuse problem. This method of grouping individuals resulted in a conservative estimate[10] of those with substance abuse because some beneficiaries may actually have had substance abuse problems that were not documented on the claim form.

Data

Three different sources of data were combined into client-level files and used to compare the patterns of care and expenditures of these beneficiaries: Massachusetts Division of Medical Assistance paid claims (Medicaid) for medical as well as mental health treatments, Department of Mental Health state hospital inpatient record files, and community support service client tracking files. These sources provided all of the information necessary to account for the treatment, support, and residential care delivered to these clients, except for self-help substance abuse treatment, which was not included. Client-level longitudinal files were created by clustering all psychiatric care (claims involving a primary psychiatric diagnosis or a psychiatric revenue/procedure code, state hospital admissions, residential treatment, and case management) by type and site of treatment. Substance abuse treatment and medical care were organized similarly and added to each file by type and site of care. Each database is described subsequently.

Medicaid paid claims. We used a two-part algorithm to identify all Medicaid claimants of psychiatric and substance abuse treatment and to extract all of their claims from the Medicaid claims database. First, we selected persons with at least one paid claim that included an ICD-9 diagnosis between 295.00 and 299.90. We then used these individuals' Medicaid identification numbers to extract all of their paid claims submitted during the study period, including claims for treatment of medical disorders. Inpatient episodes were organized to capture room and board, ancillaries, and professional fees associated with each admission. Using the Medicaid membership files, we added variables for date of birth, sex, race, aid category, and residence zip code for each person in the study. Expenditures reported were the paid claims for treatment.

Client inpatient and community support service files. In Massachusetts, the Department of Mental Health maintains computerized files of all client admissions to and discharges from the department's inpatient beds. The client tracking system provides data on client-specific case management hours and department residential placements. These data are reported monthly to the department by case managers. Using unique identification numbers, we merged these data with the Medicaid claims database. Descriptions of the methods used to calculate per unit costs of Department of Mental Health community support services have been reported elsewhere.[17]

Data reliability. We carried out a pilot study to test the reliability of the Department of Mental Health client data on residential care, case management, and community support services. Residential and community support client tracking data were consistent with vendor records, but case management data were difficult to assess. The latter may underestimate time spent, according to a senior Department of Mental Health administrator who reviewed the data; however, there is no way to cross check this information because case managers fill out the client tracking reports using their own records. The cost of case management, however, was not underestimated here because we used the department's line-item budget (for each region) to calculate the cost (the total number of hours reported for the year for the region was the denominator in fixing the price per unit). The possible consequence of underreporting the time spent was to make the per unit price high, but the fewer hours of management reported resulted in an accurate estimate of the mean cost of providing case management to a client over 1 year.

Measurement of patterns of care and expenditures

Patterns of care. We quantified two different patterns of psychiatric care: (1) the probability of treatment in a general hospital psychiatric inpatient unit or a state hospital, psychiatric residential treatment, or medical treatment and (2) the amount of psychiatric hospital treatment annually (in days). We report these patterns of care for each of the three groups of interest: those with treated comorbid substance abuse, those with substance abuse as an untreated comorbidity, and those with no evidence of substance abuse.

Expenditures. The expenditure data are organized so that psychiatric and substance abuse inpatient, outpatient, and total expenditures are reported separately. We grouped facility-based 24-hour substance abuse treatment with inpatient care rather than outpatient treatment even though, strictly speaking, it is not inpatient treatment. We clustered all inpatient expenses together so that room and board, ancillaries, and attending physician or professional fees were included. Finally, the analyses are summarized in tables that display total costs (i.e., the sum of Department of Mental Health and Medicaid per patient expenditures) and costs broken down by Medicaid costs and costs to the Department of Mental Health.

Outpatient expenditures were defined to include any paid claim in one of three categories of outpatient treatment: a visit to any hospital outpatient department, health clinic, or mental health clinic; a visit to a physician's office; or the use of any one of a set of specialized mental health services, such as psychological testing or day treatment.

Analyses

Because the data we report were derived from a population rather than a sample, we did not carry out any inferential statistical tests of differences between groups. Instead, we report mean expenditures based on the total number of adults in each group, including both those who did and those who did not use the service reported. The purpose of providing means calculated in terms of the total number of claimants in the group is to allow comparison between groups, taking the total number of claimants in each group into account. Claimant means are similar to rates that are population based. We also report age- and sex-adjusted mean expenditures, by diagnostic category, because of the differences in the distribution of sociodemographic and diagnostic characteristics across the three groups. We used multiple regression analyses to arrive at age- and sex-adjusted figures.

RESULTS

Patterns of care

Individuals we categorized as having a substance abuse problem (those with a primary or a secondary diagnosis of substance abuse on a claim during fiscal year 1992), in comparison with those not having a substance abuse problem, were four times more likely to be admitted to a hospital for acute inpatient treatment and spent more time hospitalized over the course of a year; however, they were only half as likely to receive residential care. The patterns of care summarized in Table 2 are consistent with what we know about the behavior of substance abusers: they are more likely to be hospitalized, and, after discharge, they are seldom welcomed into residential treatment programs. If placed, they are more likely to lose their placement by violating substance use policies. The substance abusers also had a slightly higher probability of using any medical care.

Table 2. Characteristics of health services use among mentally ill medicaid beneficiaries, by substance abuse status

Characteristic	Treated for Substance Abuse (n = 1,493)	Not Treated for Substance Abuse (n = 4,393)	No Substance Abuse (n = 10,509)
Psychiatric admission to general hospital, %	45	36	10
State hospital admission, %	15	11	9
Mean annual bed-days in general and state hospitals	22	19	11
Medical expenditures, %	97	96	86
Residential placement, %	5	6	9

Costs of care

Comparisons of costs of treatment in fiscal year 1992 across the three treatment groups show that large differences occurred between those with no known abuse, whose annual mean treatment costs were $13,930, and those with either treated ($22,917 annually) or untreated ($20,049) substance abuse. The largest differences were in general hospital inpatient treatment, with both the proportion of those treated and the number of days hospitalized the greatest within the treated group. Overall, the substance abuse treatment expenditures were a fraction of the psychiatric treatment expenditures. Only a handful in the treated group were admitted to substance abuse treatment facilities, and virtually all received outpatient treatment ($868 annually). There were small differences in the costs and patterns of treatment between those treated and those not treated for substance abuse.

Treatment for medical problems was nearly universal among those with comorbid substance abuse but somewhat lower among those without (see Table 3), and the mean annual costs were high relative to medical costs in the general US population ($2,752 per capita in 1992[18]). These high costs are not surprising because substance abusers have been shown to have high rates of medical treatment,[16] and rates of chronic medical disorders are known to be higher among those with serious mental disorders.[1] We found that individuals without evidence of substance abuse had medical costs that were about $1,200 lower than those of substance abusers.

When age and sex adjustments were made to the expenditure data, the differences in total annual psychiatric treatment costs increased between those with and those without substance abuse. As can be seen in Table 4, which summarizes these differences by diagnostic category, there was an increase in total expenditures by about a factor of two when abusers were compared with nonabusers.

Table 3. Comparison of health services expenditures among mentally ill Medicaid beneficiaries, by substance abuse status

Type of Service	Treated for Substance Abuse (n = 1,493)		Not Treated for Substance Abuse (n = 4,393)		No Substance Abuse (n = 10,509)	
	Users, %	Mean per Claimant, $	Users, %	Mean per Claimant, $	Users, %	Mean per Claimant, $
Department of Mental Health						
State hospital	15	3,934	11	3,605	9	4,049
Residential	5	674	6	941	9	1,362
Case management	16	66	17	66	22	85
Emergency visits	9	27	9	22	7	12
Medicaid						
Hospital/facility based						
Psychiatric	45	8,369	36	6,513	10	1,590
Substance abuse	7	540	…	…	…	…
Outpatient						
Psychiatric	97	1,486	99	1,974	99	1,141
Substance abuse	98	868	…	…	…	…
Total psychiatric services costs	…	14,529	…	13,099	…	8,227
Total other medical services costs	97	6,952	96	6,927	86	5,691
Total costs	…	22,917	…	20,049	…	13,930

Table 4. Age- and sex-adjusted mean annual psychiatric treatment expenditures among mentally ill medicaid beneficiaries, by substance abuse status

Diagnosis	Treated for Substance Abuse (n = 1,493), $	Not Treated for Substance Abuse (n = 4,393), $	No Substance Abuse (n = 10,509), $
Schizophrenia	23,169	19,568	12,350
Major affective disorder	10,049	9,836	4,686
Other psychosis	6,722	5,440	3,455

When age and sex adjustments were made to the expenditure data, the differences in total annual psychiatric treatment costs increased between those with and those without substance abuse. As can be seen in Table 4, which summarizes these differences by diagnostic category, there was an increase in total expenditures by about a factor of two when abusers were compared with nonabusers.

DISCUSSION

To summarize our findings briefly, we found that the costs of psychiatric treatment were substantially higher for those who had a comorbid substance abuse diagnosis. The expenditures reported reflect care delivered in a fee-for-service environment before the advent of managed care. Combining administrative paid claims and Department of Mental Health inpatient files had the advantage of capturing relatively complete treatment information about a very large population. However, in this study, we have probably underestimated the number of substance abusers, considering the higher levels of comorbidity reported in other studies. Low rates of detection are a more likely explanation for this than selective coding to take advantage of reimbursement rates (outpatient payment rates are equivalent). We strongly suspect that not all clients who abuse substances are given that diagnosis on a paid claim, and thus they may be included in the non-substance abuse group inappropriately. As a result, our comparisons would be conservative because differences would have increased rather than decreased, if substance abuse had been more precisely identified.

The relatively low expenditures on substance abuse treatment may reflect the reluctance of patients to enter or maintain treatment regimens but are unlikely to reflect differences in diagnostic coding for the purposes of increasing revenues. They might also be explained by the fact that claims data do not record participation in self-help groups, which are a widely used form of support. Many of those in the untreated group may actually participate in such groups. It is also possible that the untreated group included some individuals admitted to a psychiatric inpatient unit for detoxification, although the paid claim records a psychiatric diagnosis first and the substance abuse diagnosis second. This might have occurred if substance abuse led to an acute exacerbation of psychiatric symptoms.

The differences we found may be the result of unmeasured clinical differences in the groups. Our data do not provide enough clinical information to allow adjustments for differences in health status that may account for differences in psychiatric hospital bed-days. Those we identified as non-substance abusers had higher state hospital (nonacute) inpatient and community support (e.g., residential, case management) service costs, suggesting that these individuals are more disabled (we know they are more likely to have schizophrenia) and thus require more institutional and residential treatment. Also, these facilities prohibit the use of alcohol and street drugs, making abuse less likely. Thus, long state hospital stays and greater regulation of abstinence in residential facilities reduce the probability of acute admissions to general hospital psychiatric units.

A cross-sectional study does not permit the long-term follow-up of treated clients to estimate the cost offset of substance abuse treatment. If treated clients were followed over time, one would hope to see reductions in both substance abuse and psychiatric expenditures. These data show no cost offset at all, but treated patients may be the heaviest abusers and the most difficult to treat psychiatrically. Furthermore, successful treatment of dual-diagnosis patients is, unfortunately, the exception rather than the rule. Being treated and no longer abusing are not synonymous. A host of problems, from access to appropriate care to lack of follow-up, discourage even the most determined individuals from seeking treatment.

The message these data convey is that substance abuse is a major public health problem, both economically and socially. Increased detection may help, but detection is only the first step. Recommending "improved" treatment programs is simplistic, given the complex relation between mental illness and substance abuse. Nevertheless, it is an urgent challenge to those who treat seriously mentally ill people to find mechanisms to bridge the gaps that exist between the experts in substance abuse and the experts in mental illness. In many states, different agencies are responsible for treatment programs for each disorder, with few resources to develop and test specialized treatment for those with dual diagnoses. Yet these data suggest that money currently spent on psychiatric treatment could be put to better use in treatment programs that emphasize treatment of both disorders. Beginning with substance abuse detection and treatment training programs for all levels of professional and paraprofessional staff and continuing through the establishment of dual-diagnosis residential programs and long-term support services, state agencies must consider large-scale changes in how they deliver services. A specialized program for dual-diagnosis clients in New Hampshire designed to promote abstinence has reported high rates of remission: 61% of those enrolled in a pilot program had a mean length of remission of

26.5 months. These rates were achieved by including active case manager outreach efforts, medication and psychosocial services, housing support, and other services designed to support abstinence.[19] Other states are testing different mechanisms for coordinating services, such as centralized intake and referral, case management, colocating treatment programs, and interagency network models.[20]

Such programs should improve the treatment of dual-diagnosis patients elsewhere, but the problems of treating this group will not be easily overcome. Individuals who are substance abusers tend to congregate in large cities, where drugs are relatively easy to obtain but housing and mental health services may be relatively less accessible. Mental health professionals derive little satisfaction from working with these very difficult patients, and self-help groups often exclude them because of their reliance on psychotropic medication. These patients rarely seek treatment on their own and, even if admitted to a detoxification facility, may not follow up with rehabilitation.

Although these data are specific to the adult Medicaid population in Massachusetts, it is likely that analyses of other statewide insurance databases, either public or private, would yield similar findings. As concerns about the costs of mental health care increase, the lesson from these data is that substance abuse among those with major mental illness is very costly. What is less certain is that treatment of substance abuse will reduce the annual costs of psychiatric care. It is hoped that longitudinal studies of seriously mentally ill people who are also substance abusers will conclude that treatment designed to end that abuse is cost-effective in the longer term.

REFERENCES

1. Drake RE, Wallach MA. Moderate drinking among people with severe mental illness. *Hospital and Community Psychiatry.* 1993;44:780-782.
2. Drake RE, Osher FC, Noordsy DL, Hurlbut SC,Teague GB, Beaudett MS. Diagnosis of alcohol use disorders in schizophrenia. *Schizophrenia Bulletin.* 1990;16:57-66.
3. Weisner C, Schmidt L. Alcohol and drug problems among diverse health and social service populations. *American Journal of Public Health.* 1993;83:824-829.
4. Regier DA, Farmer ME, Rae DS, et al. Comorbidity of mental disorders with alcohol and other drug abuse. *Journal of the American Medical Association.* 1990;264:2511-2518.
5. Drake RE, Wallach MA. Substance abuse among the chronically mentally ill. *Hospital and Community Psychiatry.* 1989;40:1041-1045.
6. Belcher JR. On becoming homeless: a study of chronically mentally ill persons. *Journal of Community Psychology.* 1989;17:173-185.
7. Koegel P, Burnam MA. *The Epidemiology of Alcohol Abuse and Dependence Among Homeless Individuals: Findings from the Inner-City of Los Angeles.* Los Angeles, Calif: University of California, Department of Psychiatry; 1987.
8. Torrey EF. Violent behavior by individuals with serious mental illness. *Hospital and Community Psychiatry.* 1994;45:653-662.

9. Mulvey EP. Assessing the evidence of a link between mental illness and violence. *Hospital and Community Psychiatry.* 1994;45:663-671.

10. Ananth J, Vanderwater S, Kamal M, Brodsky A, Gamal R, Miller M. Missed diagnosis of substance abuse in psychiatric patients. *Hospital & Community Psychiatry.* 1989;40:297-299.

11. Drake RE, Osher FC, Wallach MA. Homelessness and dual diagnosis. *American Psychologist.* 1991;46:1149-1158.

12. Center for Mental Health Services, Substance Abuse and Mental Health Services Administration. *Making a Difference: Interim Status Report of the McKinney Research Demonstration Program for Homeless Mentally Ill Adults.* Rockville, Md: US Dept of Health and Human Services; 1994.

13. Holder HD, Blose JO. The reduction of health care costs associated with alcohol treatment: a 14-year longitudinal study. *Journal of Studies on Alcohol.* 1992;53:293-302.

14. Bartels SJ, Teague GB, Drake RE, Clark RE, Bush PW, Noordsy DL. Substance abuse in schizophrenia: service utilization and costs. *Journal of Nervous and Mental Disease.* 1993;181:227-232.

15. Franks DD. *The High Cost of Caring: Economic Contribution of Families to the Care of the Mentally Ill.* Waltham, Mass: Brandeis University; 1987. Dissertation.

16. Rice DP, Kelman S, Miller LS, Dunmeyer S. *Economic Costs of Alcohol, Drug Abuse, and Mental Illness.* San Francisco, Calif: US Dept of Health and Human Services; 1985.

17. Dickey B, Fisher W, Siegel C, Altaffer F, Azeni H. The cost and outcomes of community-based care for the seriously mentally ill. Unpublished manuscript.

18. Levit KR, Cowan CA, Lazenby HC, et al. National health spending trends, 1960-1993. *Health Affairs.* 1994;13(5):14-31.

19. Drake RE, McHugo GJ, Noordsy DL. Treatment of alcoholism among schizophrenic outpatients: 4-year outcomes. *American Journal of Psychiatry.* 1993;150:328-329.

20. Baker F. *Coordination of Alcohol, Drug Abuse and Mental Health Services.* Washington, DC: Center for Substance Abuse Treatment; 1991. DHHS publication ADM 91-1742.

ABOUT THE AUTHORS

Barbara Dickey, Ph.D., and Hocine Azeni, M.A., are affiliated with Harvard Medical School, Boston, MA.

ACKNOWLEDGMENTS

This work has been supported by the Massachusetts Department of Mental Health, the Department of Medical Assistance, and National Institute of Mental Health grant RO-1 MH46522. We acknowledge the editorial assistance of Lydia Ratcliff.

Copyright 1996. American Public Health Association. Reprinted with permission.

WHEN DISABILITY BENEFITS MAKE PATIENTS SICKER

Sally L. Satel

Reprinted from *The New England Journal of Medicine*, 333(12):794-796, 1995

Schizophrenia and addiction are two disorders that are difficult to treat, but when combined—resulting in a compound condition, or "dual diagnosis"—each disorder usually complicates the other. Drugs and alcohol may exacerbate hallucinations and delusions, and the cognitive and social deficits of schizophrenia can make people especially vulnerable to substance abuse and less able to benefit from standard treatment of addiction.[1,2]

Treating patients with dual diagnoses is challenging enough, but it becomes even more daunting when patients use their disability checks to buy drugs and alcohol. In this issue of the *Journal,* Shaner and colleagues* describe a cohort of cocaine-dependent schizophrenic veterans who spent some or all of their monthly disability income—in most cases, their sole source of support—on cocaine, aggravating their symptoms.[3]

For 15 weeks, the authors collected data on 105 patients attending a dual-diagnosis clinic at an urban department of Veterans Affairs (VA) medical center. Sharp rises in cocaine use, symptom severity, and rates of psychiatric hospitalization were observed during the first week of each month, coincident with the arrival of government checks (median amount, $645) from the VA or the Social Security Administration (SSA).

The SSA directs a means-tested welfare program for the disabled, called Supplemental Security Income (SSI), which has recently come under congressional and public scrutiny.[4] A number of federal investigations have specifically examined the problem of addicted benefit recipients who spend their disability payments on drugs.[5,6] These investigations relied on anecdotal evidence since documentation of the phenomenon was unavailable at the time.

The study by Shaner et al. now offers systematic data on the misuse of disability payments and the destructive effects of this misuse on the health of the recipients. The study also underscores the relation between welfare policy and health and suggests a process of social iatrogenesis: the inadvertent exacerbation of disease by an economic policy intended to promote well-being.

---

*Shaner, A., Eckman, T.A., Roberts, L.J., Wilkins, J.N., Tucker, D., Tsuang, J.W., & Mintz, J. (1995). Disability income, cocaine use, and repeated hospitalization among schizophrenic cocaine abusers: A government-sponsored revolving door? *New England Journal of Medicine*, 333, 777-783.

Although the authors caution against overgeneralizing from their results, my own clinical experiences and those of my colleagues have persuaded me that mentally ill recipients of disability payments who abuse drugs are likely to subsidize their addictions with public funds. Like other substance abusers, those with psychiatric disorders experience the physical dependence on cocaine and psychological reward from its use, which can be so powerful that use persists despite the harrowing consequences, including the worsening of psychosis. To avert these adverse effects of disability benefits on persons with dual diagnoses, psychiatric intervention may appropriately involve the interception of benefit payments.

The SSA may be able to provide payees who will manage the funds on behalf of the patients, but many clinicians do not know about this possibility. Even those who are aware of the provision may become entangled in red tape when they attempt to use it. Some clinicians address the problem of misuse of SSI benefits by requesting that patients sign over their monthly checks to the treatment program in which they are enrolled. The SSA then considers the program the "representative payee" and thus responsible for paying the patients' rent and other basic expenses and for making the remaining funds available to them.

Even small amounts of cash, however, can be abused. A large dual-diagnosis clinic in Washington has devised a creative approach to that problem. The clinic, as payee, manages the bank accounts of patients who receive SSI payments and allows the patients to "earn back" discretionary funds when they participate in treatment and demonstrate an ability to manage cash responsibly (Ries R: personal communication). The patients' behavior is monitored by case managers, who evaluate drug use, mental status, and compliance with a plan of care that combines psychiatric treatment and rehabilitation with services for substance abuse.

Small programs cannot always afford to assume the payee role. Size, however, is not the only reason programs may reject this role; they may be dissuaded by the prospect of "collection visits" from drug dealers to whom patients owe money. Sometimes the addicted beneficiaries themselves refuse to let the treatment program manage their funds and may even refuse treatment altogether in order to retain control over their funds.

A clinician who observes and documents flagrant misuse of benefit payments can, despite the patient's wishes to the contrary, file a formal request with the SSA to halt direct payments to the patient and forward them to a representative payee. If the program cannot or will not assume the role of payee, the clinician is faced with the difficult task of finding another willing and responsible payee, usually a family member or friend not involved with drugs. Even if a payee is found, however, he or she may lack the training or temperament for dealing with eccentric or threatening patients, not to mention their drug suppliers.

If these attempts fail, the psychiatrist can request that the local probate court appoint a conservator of estate. Conservatorship can be a useful arrangement for incompetent patients—it is most commonly invoked in cases of dementia, mental retardation, or severe mental illness—but its use is limited. Probate judges are reluctant to appoint a conservator for a patient with a dual diagnosis unless the patient's financial incompetence can be traced directly to his or her mental illness. A judge who views the patient's purchase of drugs as simply a bad decision may deny the application for conservatorship.

The application may also be denied if the patient is only mildly impaired when abstinent, even though he or she becomes violent and delusional, requiring hospitalization, when using drugs. This type of patient is exemplified by the now-infamous Larry Hogue.[7] A Vietnam-era veteran, Mr. Hogue was relatively calm when free of cocaine but became dangerous and psychotic when he smoked crack. He terrorized an Upper West Side neighborhood in New York City, where he lived on the streets despite receiving tax-free disability benefits of $3,000 per month.

What can be done to promote the representative-payee arrangement through the SSA and the VA? First, these agencies need to recognize that such an arrangement is essential for good care. A payee arrangement, optimally paired with treatment, serves three functions: curbing access to illicit drugs and alcohol, which exacerbate the primary psychiatric condition; ensuring that rent and other essential bills are paid; and reducing institutional facilitation of substance abuse. The risk of such abuse can be assessed by the clinicians who determine patients' eligibility for disability benefits or by those who treat the recipients of such benefits when they seek care.

Second, the agencies that provide disability benefits should be more aggressive in acting on the risk of misuse of benefits. Congress is considering revising the SSI program so that persons with dual diagnoses who are new recipients of SSI benefits are automatically assigned representative payees and administrative case managers to coordinate treatment and disbursement of benefits. Under such an arrangement, the treatment program would automatically serve as the representative payee. If treatment is not available, one of the not-for-profit community agencies with which the SSA contracts for related services could assume the payee role. For a patient with a dual diagnosis who is already receiving benefits, SSA should, at the request of the treating psychiatrist, arrange for involuntary monitoring by a not-for-profit community agency that will provide a representative payee.

Third, when patients with dual diagnoses receive VA benefits, the VA treatment program itself should act as the payee—a role the VA currently prohibits. As a self-contained and coordinated system of treatment, rehabilitation, and financial support, the VA is a rich laboratory for the development of incentive programs. On the basis of the contingency model described above, the VA would pay rent and other bills directly and allow the patient to earn back funds by complying with treatment plans, including vocational training. Funds not earned back would be held in trust for the patient, who would regain access to them only when he or she proved capable of using discretionary moneys responsibly. Ultimately, the money could be disbursed directly to the patient on the clinician's recommendation. Supervision of funds is especially important for VA beneficiaries, because their monthly benefits can be much higher than those of SSI recipients. An added advantage of the contingency scheme is that, for addicted VA beneficiaries not now in treatment, it creates an incentive to enroll in treatment programs.

Those who treat persons with dual diagnoses have long recognized that teaching patients how to manage money—and managing it for them when necessary—should be a routine feature of rehabilitation.[8,9] Unfortunately, the burden of addressing the misuse of benefits rests on the clinician's shoulders. Only if the agencies that disburse the benefits, such as the SSA and the VA, become active partners in this effort can the unintended adverse consequences of disability policy be averted.

REFERENCES

1. Osher FC, Kofoed LL. Treatment of patients with psychiatric and psychoactive substance abuse disorders. *Hospital and Community Psychiatry* 1989;40:1025-30.
2. Minkoff K, Drake RE, eds. *Dual diagnosis of major mental illness and substance disorder.* San Francisco: Jossey-Bass, 1991.
3. Shaner A, Eckman TA, Roberts LJ, et al. Disability income, cocaine use, and repeated hospitalization among schizophrenic cocaine abusers—a government-sponsored revolving door? *New England Journal of Medicine* 1995;333:777-83.
4. MacDonald H. Welfare's next Vietnam. *City Journal of the Manhattan Institute* 1995;5(1):23-38.
5. Tax dollars aiding and abetting addiction: Social Security Disability and SSI cash benefits to addicts and alcoholics. Investigative staff report of Senator William S. Cohen. Washington, D.C.: February 7, 1994.
6. Social Security: major changes needed for disability benefits for addicts. Washington, D.C.: General Accounting Office. May 1994. (GAO-HEHS-94-128.)
7. Dugger CW. Threat only when on crack: homeless man foils system. *New York Times.* Sept. 3, 1992:A1.
8. Drake RE, Bartels SJ, Teague GB, Noordsy DL, Clark RE. Treatment of substance abuse in severely mentally ill patients. *Journal of Nervous and Mental Disease* 1993;181:606-11.
9. Center for Substance Abuse Treatment. *Assessment and treatment of patients with coexisting mental illness and alcohol and other drug abuse.* Treatment improvement protocol (TIP) series 9. Rockville, Md.: Department of Health and Human Services, 1994. (DHHS publication no. (SMA)94-2078.)

ABOUT THE AUTHOR

Sally L. Satel, M.D., is affiliated with Yale University School of Medicine, New Haven, CT, and the University of Pennsylvania, Philadelphia, PA.

Copyright 1995. Massachusetts Medical Society. All rights reserved. Reprinted with permission.

COERCION AND TENACIOUS TREATMENT IN THE COMMUNITY: APPLICATIONS TO THE REAL WORLD

Ronald J. Diamond

Reprinted from *Coercion and Aggressive Community Treatment: A New Frontier in Mental Health Law*, D. L. Dennis and J. Monahan (Eds.). New York: Plenum Press (pp. 51-72), 1996

Coercion in community-based programs has become an increasing concern (Parrish, 1992). Much of this concern has coincided with the development of assertive (or aggressive) community treatment programs. Prior to active community outreach teams, attempts to coerce the behavior of clients living in the community were limited by practical realities. Clients in traditional mental health systems always had the option of just not showing up. It is true that clients could be threatened with rehospitalization under court order, but enforcing such orders required cooperation from police, who typically had little interest in searching for a mentally ill client who had not committed any crime (Cesnik & Puls, 1977).

The development of Program for Assertive Community Treatment (PACT), assertive community treatment (ACT) teams, and a variety of similar mobile, continuous treatment programs has made it possible to coerce a wide range of behaviors in the community (Test & Stein, 1972). The staff on these ACT teams can visit clients who miss appointments or, if needed, go to a client's apartment on a daily basis to ensure that medication is being taken. Staff often have regular communication with landlords, families, and employers. The ACT teams can apply to the Social Security Administration to get a financial payee assigned to control the client's Supplemental Security Income (SSI) money, or apply for a guardianship to control other aspects of the client's life. The involvement of the treatment team in all aspects of the client's life and with all elements of the client's support system is responsible both for the effectiveness of these teams and for their potential coerciveness.

These mobile treatment teams are, in essence, a new technology that raises many ethical issues not previously perceived as a problem in the community (Diamond & Wikler, 1985; Curtis & Hodge, 1995). What should be the appropriate goals of community-based treatment for persons with serious and persistent mental illness? Is stability enough, or is something more than stability needed to help our clients make life worth living? Whose goals should be considered—how much say should clients have in setting goals for their own life? How much say should the client's family, or the rest of society, have in setting goals? What kind of role relationships do we want to be in with our clients? These issues concerning the appropriate place of paternalism are closely connected to decisions on the appropriate use of coercion in community settings.

It is easy to argue in the abstract that we should always place our clients' goals first. Unfortunately, when working with real people, these issues become very confused. For a client with a history of many relapses and rehospitalizations, the family's demands for maintained supervision or no medication reduction often seem legitimate—even when the client strongly disagrees. Alan Rosen, a well-known Australian community psychiatrist, outlines the differences between working on the high ground and working in the swamp. On the high ground, questions are carefully asked so that research can provide clear answers. Ethical principles are well defined. Decisions are clear and pristine. Everything is easy because you can see into the distance. Down in the swamp, everything is dirty and mucky. Lines do not stay straight, questions are complex, and research gives ambiguous answers. Unfortunately, almost everyone lives in the swamp, and the swamp is where all of the important questions are to be found. One can believe that it is important to support the consumer/client's own goals, important to be a client advocate, and important to avoid being an agent of social control. When working with real people in the real world, however, it is frequently hard to be clear how to make decisions based on these values. Clinicians are often confronted with the need to make decisions in the face of competing goals and concerns.

This chapter will discuss (1) paternalism as the basis of coercion in most clinical situations, (2) coercion and the range of coercive interventions available in the community, (3) court-ordered treatment as the most extreme end of the continuum of coercive interventions, and (4) how the need for coercion can be decreased.

PATERNALISM IN ASSERTIVE COMMUNITY TREATMENT PROGRAMS

Paternalism has been a part of assertive community treatment from its very beginning. In the original PACT research project that began more than 20 years ago in Madison, Wisconsin, staff from a nearby state hospital provided community-based treatment for clients who would otherwise have been committed to that same state hospital (Stein & Test, 1980). Paternalism was to a large extent accepted with little question. All the clients would have been coerced had they been hospitalized, and whatever the community-based team did was considered less coercive than the alternative.

In the early stages of PACT, consumer empowerment was not a serious consideration (Chamberlin, Rogers, & Sneed, 1989). Although the original model attempted to build on the client's strengths, it was designed to "do" for the client what the client could not do for himself or herself. Staff were assumed to know what the client "needed." Even the goal of getting clients paid employment was a staff-driven value that was at times at odds with the client's own preferences (Russert & Frey, 1991). Current assertive treatment programs continue to be influenced by traditions that arose from this early history. Paternalism continues to be reinforced by mandates from the community to "control" the behavior of otherwise disruptive clients or at the least to decrease need for psychiatric hospitalization by keeping these clients stable in the community.

Twenty years ago, paternalism was not a significant concern and was rarely discussed if a program was successful in keeping clients out of the hospital, if it improved clients' quality of life as the staff understood it, or if staff were "doing good things." Our current concern about the limits and justification of paternalism is based on a deeper examination of values and an attempt to inject a sense of humility into what we are doing as clinicians (Kalinowski, 1992; Freund, 1993; Everett & Nelson, 1992). It is an acknowledgment that what we think is best for a client may not give us the entire answer to what we should be doing. There is recognition that paternalism, even well intentioned, can interfere with the client's own sense of personal effectiveness and rehabilitation.

This is not to argue that paternalism can be entirely dismissed. Many ACT teams are willing or even targeted to work with clients who may initially not want any services, yet have dramatically demonstrated through multiple hospitalizations or arrests that they cannot maintain themselves in the community without help. It is not unusual for an ACT team to continue to visit a client and attempt to establish a relationship despite initial protests from the potential client to "stay away." The relationship thus often starts off from a paternalistic premise of involving a client in treatment for their own good. To stop the "revolving door" of repeated psychiatric hospitalizations, staff may initially feel the need to make sure that rent is paid from the client's SSI check or that food money is budgeted to last throughout the month.

Despite the paternalism inherent in these programs, many community-based programs have been working to redefine the basic relationship between staff and client from one that is paternalistic to one that is more collaborative. Assertive community treatment is changing to tenacious community treatment. This is not just a question of semantics, but an attempt to refocus on the nature of the relationship between staff and client and increasing interest in making treatment programs and staff behavior more client-centered. Staff may need to continue to establish and maintain a relationship over a client's objection, but as much as possible treatment focuses on the client's own goals and involves the consumer in all aspects of treatment planning. These "new-generation" ACT teams are typically more willing to take risks to support client decisions and to demonstrate more concern over issues such as autonomy. Increasingly, staff in ACT teams struggle between being "too paternalistic" and abandoning clients to live with the consequences of their own decisions when their lives have been devastated by an illness that at times makes it extremely difficult for them to make appropriate decisions.

COERCION IN THE COMMUNITY

There are a number of different justifications for coercion (Wertheimer, 1993). Police commonly use maintenance of safety and public order as legitimate justifications for coercion. Treatment programs, on the other hand, typically use paternalism to justify coercion. Mental health staff have a clear obligation to do what they can to prevent violence toward others, but their primary concern is to do what they feel is best for their client.

Coercion is much more than just court-ordered treatment. A National Institute of Mental Health (NIMH) roundtable that included consumers, families, and mental health professionals considered coercion to be "a wide range of actions taken without consent of the individual involved" (Blanch & Parrish, 1993). Coercion exists on a continuum—from friendly persuasion to interpersonal pressure to control of resources to use of force (Lucksted & Coursey, 1995). Mental health commitment and other court-ordered treatment is thus just the extreme end of the spectrum of pressures or restrictions that makes up coercion. Coercion based on a court order is relatively rare, while coercion of the type included in the NIMH roundtable definition is extremely common.

In Madison, Wisconsin, only a minority of people that the police bring into the emergency services unit of the mental health center end up being hospitalized under a commitment order. Most of the people either go back to their own home, go to a crisis home, are given shelter in a nearby hotel, stay temporarily with family or friends, or agree to a "voluntary" hospitalization. All the outpatient options include follow-up mental health services. Considerable persuasion or coercion may have been applied to some of these clients, either under the threat of an emergency commitment or through other kinds of pressures such as use of resources (see Chapter 1).[1]

For example, the client may be allowed to go back to his apartment rather than being hospitalized if he agrees to start taking medication, or allows his family to be contacted, or agrees to a follow-up visit the next day. A client who does not want to return home may be allowed access to a resource such as a crisis home if she takes medication, or the crisis team may pay

---

[1] Editors' Note: The author refers to a chapter that appears in the book where this reading was originally published. The full reference for that chapter is Monahan, J., Hoge, S.K., Lidz, C.W., Eisenberg, M.M., Bennett, N.S., Gardner, W.P., Mulvey, E.P., & Roth, L.H. (1996). Coercion to inpatient treatment: Initial results and implications for assertive treatment in the community. In D.L. Dennis & J. Monahan (Eds.), *Coercion and aggressive community treatment: A new frontier in mental health law* (pp. 13-28). New York: Plenum Press.

for a motel room if the client agrees to let the treatment team temporarily control how he spends his next SSI check.

Controlling a client's behavior by controlling resources is commonly used in community-based treatment programs. When clients are told that they can leave the hospital only if they agree to live in a group home, the coercion is fairly blatant. The coercion is more subtle if a client is told that he can live anywhere he wants, but the only available place for him to live is a group home. Often, what is meant is that there is no other "appropriate" place for the person to live and that the only place that staff feel is an appropriate discharge residence is the group home.

The situation becomes more complicated when the treatment staff support the client's own choice of where to live, but because of low income and lack of housing subsidies the only affordable option is a bed in a group home. A lack of resources may be unfortunate but is not necessarily coercion— many of us lack the resources to live where we want and do what we want. The issue in many cases, however, is more than just a limitation of resources. Policy decisions that make beds available in group homes rather than making subsidies available to support people in their own apartments reflect decisions about where and in what kind of settings people with a mental illness should live. Group homes are funded because that is where people "should" live; that is where they will "do best." Use of resources in this way is clearly paternalistic and can be considered coercive in that resources are allocated so as to force people to live in particular places.

Housing for persons with psychiatric disabilities often comes with special rules (Segal & Aviram, 1978). Group homes and other congregate living arrangements often specify that residents must be out of the house during the afternoon or that they are not allowed to entertain overnight guests even if they have a room of their own. Often, a client living in housing controlled by the mental health system does not even have a key to his or her own home, and mental health staff regularly enter the client's home and bedroom without permission. Even when clients do have their own apartments, housing is often contingent on continuing in a particular treatment program or continuing to take medication. Clients can be evicted from housing with little due process protection for reasons that would never lead to eviction for someone without a mental illness. This can all be considered coercion— control of a person's behavior without the person's consent.

The other resource, besides housing, that is commonly used to coerce behavior is money. A significant number of the clients in the community support programs in Dane County, Wisconsin, where I work have been assigned a financial payee who controls their SSI or Social Security Disability Insurance (SSDI) income. If a client is on either SSI or SSDI and has repeatedly had serious crises related to poor financial decisions, staff can apply to the Social Security Administration to have a financial payee assigned who then controls the person's entitlement money (Brotman & Muller, 1990) (see also Chapter 7).[2] It is to be hoped that a number of noncoercive steps will have been taken first, including voluntary assistance with budgeting and other kinds of collaborative problem solving, but both client and staff know that a financial payee is an option that can be imposed with little due process protection.

This kind of coercion can be extremely effective in helping to stabilize someone in the community. The use of a payee can ensure that rent and utilities are paid. At times, money can be used to provide the client a degree of structure in the community. For example, the payee can forward money to the treatment program that staff will use to go grocery shopping with the client or arrange for vouchers that the client can use at specific restaurants or a laundromat. Obtaining spending money can be made to some degree dependent on participating in other parts of treatment. A client can be required to come in daily to pick up spending money, and can then be pressured by staff to take prescribed medication. Legally, the client can demand the money and refuse the medication, but the pressure to take the required medication in this kind of situation can be enormous.

Control, if it is needed in a community setting, can be kept very focused. While money from SSI or SSDI is controlled with some frequency, money from other sources is rarely controlled. Legally, ethically, and clinically, SSI or SSDI money is commonly treated as different from earned income. Legally, it is extremely easy to have a financial payee assigned to control SSI money, but extremely difficult to have a guardian assigned to control other money. Ethically, staff makes distinctions between money from SSI and money that is "really the client's money." SSI or SSDI can be considered an entitlement given to the recipient to be used however he or she wants. Alternatively, one can consider SSI or SSDI to be provided as part of an implicit social contract to provide for basic necessities of living. Staff who feel that SSI or SSDI is part of this implicit contract will feel more comfortable in taking control of the money to make sure it is used as intended. The same staff that is involved in controlling a client's SSI money may also help the client find a job with the clear understanding that the client can keep and control all money received from work. Clinically, money from SSI or SSDI is also somewhat different from money earned by the client. SSI or SSDI money continues to come, even if it is used to buy drugs or alcohol that increases the client's behavioral difficulty. Money earned by work can also be used to

---

[2] Editors' Note: The author refers to a chapter that appears in the book where this reading was originally published. The full reference for that chapter is Cogswell, S.H. (1996). Entitlements, payees, and coercion. In D.L. Dennis & J. Monahan (Eds.), *Coercion and aggressive community treatment: A new frontier in mental health law* (pp. 115-125). New York: Plenum Press.

buy drugs or alcohol, but this kind of problem rapidly takes care of itself without any need for staff intervention. If a client is too "stoned" or intoxicated to go to work, he will earn less money and subsequently have less money to buy drugs. Clients either learn to control their drug and alcohol use or lose their jobs and stop having money available to buy the drugs and alcohol anyway.

While control of housing and control of money are the most common and obvious forms of coercion in the community, other kinds of control are also possible. An important part of the effectiveness of modern community support programs lies in their ability to coordinate all parts of the client's treatment and support system. This process may include communication with other treaters, friends, family, landlords, employers, family physician, or minister. This communication, even when done with the client's permission, allows enormous pressure to be applied for the client to take medication, stay in treatment, live in a particular place, or "follow the plan" in any number of ways. This pressure can be almost as coercive as the hospital in controlling behavior, but with fewer safeguards.

Staff often justify a given intrusion into a client's life by asking themselves whether the proposed restriction on the client is likely to prevent more severe restrictions in the future. For example, if taking control of money will keep the person out of the hospital and in the community where he has more choices, taking control of money may be justified. Similarly, forcing a client to take medication may be justified if doing so will allow the client to have more control over many other spheres of his life. Staff may justify limiting a client's autonomy in a particular way if they feel this will increase the client's autonomy in other ways or in the future. This paternalism must be balanced by clients' own views on how to maximize their autonomy and their desire to stay in control of their own lives. There is also the problem of agreeing about the severity of a restriction (Hoffman & Foust, 1977; Gardner et al., 1993; Byalin, 1993). For example, some clients may feel that forced medication is more restrictive than prolonged hospitalization.

COURT-ORDERED TREATMENT—THE EXTREME
END OF THE CONTINUUM

Court-ordered treatment, be it hospital- or community-based commitment, is the most extreme use of coercion and thus attracts the most attention. In most jurisdictions, the finding of dangerousness either to self or others is required whether the commitment is to a hospital or to the community. Mental health commitment and other court-ordered treatments are commonly used even in treatment systems that are trying to be more client-centered and less coercive. In Dane County, there has been a continuing decrease in mental health commitments over the past ten years.[3] There is surprisingly little data about the frequency of court-ordered coercion in different jurisdictions.

In Wisconsin, mental health commitment is to a county human services board rather than to a hospital. This procedure means that a client might initially require a brief hospitalization, but may continue on a commitment order in the community for several months. While there are problems and limitations with any commitment, either to a hospital or in the community, extending commitment into the community may help get some clients out of the "revolving door" (Appelbaum, 1986; Hiday & Scheid-Cook, 1991; Schwartz, Vingiano, & Bezirganian, 1988; Tavolaro, 1992). Community commitment, within the context of a good community-based treatment system, can allow a period of community stability to develop so that the client can make more appropriate decisions, as the following two case illustrations demonstrate.

> Susan was a 28-year-old woman with a history of many psychiatric hospitalizations. She responded well to medication in the hospital, but always discontinued it immediately upon discharge. She would then rapidly become very disorganized and paranoid, raving at people on the street, threatening her parents, and stopping up her toilet to keep out the voices. When she initially began working with one of the tenacious treatment teams, she was on a mental health commitment that extended for several months after hospital discharge. She initially threatened to discontinue medication and drop out of treatment the day her commitment expired. By the time that date arrived, however, she had an apartment that she liked, a volunteer job that she felt good about, and friends with whom she got together weekly to play cards, and had reestablished a relationship with her parents. As the date for the expiration of her commitment passed, she stopped talking about dropping out of treatment, and staff elected to just avoid talking about the change in her legal status.

The ability to force medication can, at times, make it safer to use less medication. Marge was a 58-year-old woman who would do well for long periods of time, then discontinue her medication and continue to do well for a year or more, but would then inevitably become more reclusive, stop her very active social life, drop out of her many volunteer jobs, stop eating, and

---

[3]In 1993, there were 128 involuntary hospitalizations in Dane County, Wisconsin (360,000 population). This number included 12 involuntary hospitalizations from the jail and 11 patients who came into a psychiatric hospital voluntarily but were not allowed to leave because they were felt to be dangerous. Of the involuntary hospitalizations, 33 led to a mental health commitment, 52 led to a settlement agreement, and 8 were converted to a guardianship. With the other 35 patients, the commitment was either dropped by consent of both parties or discontinued by the hearing examiner.

eventually be rehospitalized after her condition became medically dangerous. Normally, she was willing to continue taking medication, but in the past had been unwilling to restart medication once this process of decompensation had begun. She was initially placed on a limited guardianship during one of these dysfunctional periods, but it became very evident that she was fully competent when she was functioning at her baseline. She elected to stay on the guardianship because it made it much safer for her to go off the medication, knowing that it might be a year or more before she would really need it, but that it could then be restarted before she had completely decompensated.

Just as there can be positive effects from coercion, coercion can also lead to significant problems (Durham & LaFond, 1985). Commitment laws are typically introduced with the explanation that they will be used only for those few individuals who absolutely need to be coerced for the good of themselves or the community. The data suggest that if commitment laws are available they will be used (Durham, 1985; Hasbe & McRae, 1987). There are a great number of people who are potentially dangerous, and it is difficult if not impossible to predict who in this large group will actually engage in dangerous behavior. There would be legal liability as well as a sense of personal responsibility if a mental health commitment might stop a person from engaging in dangerous behavior and a commitment were not sought. As a result of mental health workers' desire to avoid "false negatives," many people end up with a mental health commitment under a dangerousness standard who would not actually have done anything dangerous if they had not been committed.

In addition to the problem of overuse, five observations can be made about the operation of court-ordered treatment.

1. Coercion will not lead to more effective treatment if the treatment system itself is inadequate. In many parts of the United States, there is pressure to change the law to make it easier to commit someone with a mental illness. It is often argued that easier commitment, and particularly easier community-based commitment, will improve the treatment and outcome for persons who are now dropping out of treatment (Mulvey, Geller, & Roth, 1987). Changing the commitment laws is often seen as a way to keep clients in treatment after they leave the hospital. It is very unclear, however, how coercion will help increase a client's connection with treatment in the community if there is no effective community-based follow-up (Zusman, 1985).

The problem of people with serious mental illness refusing treatment is due more often to failures in the treatment system than to failures in commitment laws (Stein, Diamond, & Factor, 1990; Diamond & Factor, 1994). In most treatment systems, there is little response to clients who fail to follow through. There may be a letter or phone call, but rarely will staff try to find the client in the community or try to establish a treatment program that seriously considers what the client wants for his or her own life. When effective community-based treatment teams are available, the effectiveness of community-based coercion increases, but the need for such coercion is less. This is not to say that community commitment laws are completely ineffective, but they are unlikely to be a panacea when the treatment system is the problem.

2. What can be coerced in the community is extremely limited. Most often, attempts are made to coerce medication. In order to force someone to take medication, courts must be willing to order it, clinicians must be comfortable working with a coerced client, and police must be willing to implement the treatment plan. With few exceptions, medication can be forced only by threatening the client with further hospitalization. The only medications that can be truly forced in the community are long-acting injections, and even then the police must be willing to find the client, bring him to the mental health center or hospital, and hold him down for the injection if necessary (Geller, 1987).

3. There are major interpersonal costs in coercion—in moving from a collaborative to a controlling relationship. The need for court-ordered treatment is indicative of a failure of the relationship between the client and the treatment staff, at least for that moment in time. It indicates a major discrepancy between what the client feels he or she needs and what clinical staff feel is needed. It can have a major influence on the treatment relationship, an influence that can last for years after the actual event (Blanch & Parrish, 1993). Much of what we try to do in mental health requires a collaborative relationship—a sense that the clinician and the client are working together toward a commonly defined goal.

If the treatment goal is stability, a controlling relationship through the use of a commitment order may be effective. Increasingly, we are concerned with more than stability. Issues of working with the client to increase his or her quality of life require the development of personal goals, hope, a sense of growth and accomplishment, and a sense of personal autonomy. Control of our own life is important for most of us, and persons with mental illness are no exception. Stability is an important component of quality of life, but not the only component. There is an inherent conflict between encouraging the client to take control of his or her life and instituting a coercive relationship that constantly reinforces the sense that the client really has little control.

4. Coercion is often a short-term solution to a long-term problem. Coercion is typically used as part of a response once a crisis has developed. Once police have brought a client into an emergency room in handcuffs, there are often few options available other than an emergency detention. Too often, the client is much too upset to consider other options, the staff in the

emergency room is too busy with too many other clients to have the time to develop a noncoercive option, and too often no other options are really available other than hospitalizing the client or letting him or her return to the street. The frequent use of emergency commitment and other coercion is often the result of a crisis-oriented system of care, rather than one based on providing ongoing supports and treatment.

Most episodes involving coercion involve clients with a chronic illness. These clients require an ongoing rather than an episodic approach to treatment. The current treatment system in most of the United States (and indeed most of the world) provides enormous resources to hospitalize mentally ill individuals who are in crisis. When a client is brought in by police, emergency staff are mobilized to respond, hospitalization at many hundreds of dollars a day is made available, and tremendous pressure is brought to stabilize a client's behavior rapidly. This approach often means doing whatever is necessary to get the client to take medication as soon as possible.

Most serious mental illness is persistent. The problem is not just to manage the crisis over the next few days or weeks, but to help the client manage his or her illness over the next few years. The issue is not whether the medication-responsive client is taking medication a week later, but whether the client is taking medication a year later. Coercion tends to be a relatively short-term solution to this long-term problem. Hospitalizing a client under a commitment order and forcibly starting medication may in a particular situation help that person stabilize and agree to continue taking the medication after discharge. In many other situations, however, the process of committing a client to a hospital and forcing medication may make it less likely that the client will be willing to stay connected with the treatment system or continue to take medication after discharge from the hospital. A commitment may get the client back on medication rapidly, but a more collaborative approach in the community over weeks or months may increase the likelihood that the client will use medication appropriately over the long haul (Diamond, 1983).

5. Coercion is often used only because other options are not available. The corollary to this is that coercion could often be avoided if other resources were available. In the emergency room of many hospitals, the only options available for persons in psychiatric crisis are hospitalization or release with little follow-up. Where clients can be offered a range of options, both the frequency of use of coercion and the degree of coercion can be decreased. For example, a client coming into the crisis service in Madison, Wisconsin, can be offered follow-up the next day, overnight accommodations in a nearby hotel, the short-term use of a crisis home (a bedroom in a private home rented by the crisis team), or a variety of other options. Often, a plan can be worked out that feels acceptable to all parties with little sense of coercion. At other times, some degree of coercion is present. A client may agree to stay

overnight at a hotel and come back to see the crisis team in the morning rather than go back to his apartment, where he has been arguing with his roommate. The degree of coercion in such cases is less than what would have been imposed if fewer alternatives were available.

The development of these less coercive options takes considerably more staff time than just committing someone to a hospital and requires that alternative resources be available. It may take some hours to establish a relationship with an angry client, bring in the client's family or friends, call around to see what alternatives are available, and work with the client to come up with a collaborative solution. Many clinical situations that initially seem as though commitment will be inevitable can end with a less coercive solution if the staff have the time, resources, training, and attitude to look for alternatives (Factor & Diamond, in press).

A Natural Experiment on the Effect of Court-Ordered Coercion in the Community

A recent Wisconsin Supreme Court decision led to a natural experiment that allowed data to be collected on the effects of changing from a coercive to a noncoercive approach to treatment. Wisconsin statutes allow several ways of legally coercing treatment in the community. Mental health commitment is not to a hospital, but to the county mental health board. While the first few days or weeks of this commitment may be in a hospital, it is not unusual for a client to be discharged from the hospital and continued under commitment in the community for several additional months.

Alternatively, clients who are adjudicated to be incompetent can have a guardianship assigned. A limited guardianship can be assigned for purposes of making medication-related decisions for persons who are adjudicated as incompetent only in this one area. As of October 1992, 129 people were on guardianships for mental illness in Dane County, of whom 87 were on limited guardianship for medications. Most of the individuals on limited guardianships had schizophrenia and were living in the community in their own apartments or homes. In October 1992, the Wisconsin Supreme Court ruled that limited guardianships could not be used to coerce the use of psychotropic medications. (The law governing limited guardianships has since been rewritten, and guardians can again coerce the use of medication by court order.) Ten months after the court ruling, follow-up data were collected on clients who had previously been on a limited guardianship.

Of the total group of 87 who had been on limited guardianship, 16 clients were reported to have had difficulty following the termination of coerced medication. When initially questioned, staff felt that most of the problems incurred by these clients could have been avoided if the coercive force of the guardianship had still been in place. Often, clients went through transient difficulties before restarting their medication voluntarily. For example, staff would say things like, "John went off medication and got really crazy for a while before he finally decided to take medication voluntarily, and now he's doing fine. He didn't lose his job." Or, "Susan stopped coming in and we had to go after her—it was hard to work with her for a while. Thank God she stabilized and she didn't have to go back to the hospital." It seemed, in retrospect, that many of the problems identified by staff were part of the conversion process from a more coercive to a more collaborative treatment relationship. Few of these difficult periods led to longer-term problems.

On reassessment, it appeared that 6 of these clients, approximately 7% of the entire group of people on limited guardianships, had more significant relapses, either hospitalization or other major life disruptions, that seemed connected to medication noncompliance that was in turn related to the change in guardianship. This natural experiment can simultaneously be used to justify the need for coercion and to justify that coercion is probably unnecessary for the vast majority of clients to whom it is applied. Over the 10-month follow-up, most clients had few problems after coercion was discontinued. It also appears, however, that a small but significant number of clients who had been doing well with coercion got into difficulty once it was discontinued.

There are significant limitations to this "experiment." The survey may have missed some clients who got into difficulty, the outcomes were anecdotal, and the follow-up was only 10 months. It is unclear to what extent all the clients in this group really knew their rights and knew that they could now refuse medication. It is also important to remember that these clients were in a comprehensive community-based system of care and had a significant, ongoing relationship with staff. This study was about what happened when coercion was discontinued, not what would happen if coercion had not initially been used. The initial period of coercion may have been important in initially stabilizing the person in the community, even if it was no longer needed to maintain that stability. It is also clear that terminating a court order does not stop a whole range of persuasion and pressure that staff use to encourage clients to take prescribed medication.

DECREASING THE NEED FOR COERCION

Given the problems inherent in coercion, it would seem important to do everything possible to decrease the need for court-ordered treatment. Many states are discussing changes that would make it easier to commit people, under the assumption that doing so will get more people with serious illness into the treatment system earlier. Much of the pressure to change the commitment laws seems to come from areas where the current mental health treatment system is inadequate. As already discussed, commitment laws and other kinds of coercion will not work if the treatment system is not both effective and available. If treatment designed to meet the real needs of persons with mental illness is available, many previously "treatment-refusing" individuals will accept help. There are at least five ways that a treatment system can minimize the need for coercion (Blanch & Parrish, 1993).

1. Develop a continuous range of service options. Too often, we offer a person in crisis one kind of treatment and consider him or her a "treatment refuser" if he or she rejects that one option. We call clients "treatment-resistant" if they refuse hospitalization or refuse to take prescribed medication. Many of us would refuse hospitalization on a locked ward of a state hospital, no matter how much distress we are in. Many clients will instead accept hospitalization on an open, unlocked hospital unit, especially if it is physically nice and staff seem friendly. Other clients who refuse a hospitalization will gladly accept a place to stay for a few days during a crisis, especially if it is decent and comes with supportive people. People who initially refuse medication might be willing to talk to someone or have a cup of coffee with a staff person, and in doing so perhaps establish enough of a trusting relationship to eventually accept medication. The more different options and approaches that we can offer, the more likely will a person in crisis, even if psychotic, paranoid, and afraid, be willing to accept one of them.

2. Be clear about the goals of coercion. It is important to be clear about the goals of any clinical intervention, but particularly an intervention that involves coercion. Too often, mental health workers commit a client in reaction to a problem or crisis, without thinking through how the commitment will help. A decision to commit a person to a hospital is merely a decision about where the person will live. It is important to also be clear about what treatment interventions are necessary and whether there are any alternative interventions that might be effective in meeting the same goals (Diamond, 1979). It is also important to consider from the beginning how long the commitment is likely to continue and what will happen after that. The following case illustrates a number of these issues:

At a recent case conference, staff discussed whether a petition should be filed to initiate the process for forcing Sam to stay in treatment and stay on his medication. Sam was an angry, often threatening man who firmly believed that a large amount of money had been stolen from him by the police. Staff from a mobile community program had begun to establish a relationship with him over the past several months, but he had recently stopped taking his prescribed antipsychotic medication.

On further discussion, staff agreed that there was little evidence that the medication had helped very much, and Sam's behavior had not changed since he stopped taking it. He was generally threatening toward the world, but did not make any specific threats toward any specific person. If anything, when staff tried to pressure Sam to take medication, he became more angry and threatening. It became apparent to staff during the ensuing discussion that medication was not effective enough to justify coercion and that there was little else that coercion would accomplish. He was not so acutely dangerous as to require social control, and there was a large risk that being coercive would interfere with his slowly developing relationship with staff.

3. Ensure that persons with psychiatric disability have a chance for a decent quality of life. Hope is important for all of us. It is especially important that people with serious mental illness can have a realistic hope that their life will get better. People with a biologically caused illness can fight to stay in control or can give up. For example, one of my clients used to spend several months every year in a psychotic state on a locked psychiatric unit. She now has her own apartment and a job and is fighting to regain custody of her child. She still hears voices that tell her to "do things," but as she now says, she "has to stay in control"—she now has too much to lose to let herself get that crazy and out of control. She still needs to go to the hospital, but it is typically for a few days or a few weeks and is voluntary. She still takes medication, but she has become skilled in telling staff when she needs more and when she can get by with less. Other clients find that they are much more able to control their behavior when they have something worth keeping—an apartment, a job, friends, or other elements that make their life worth living.

4. Develop treatment systems that support respectful relationships developed over time. Most treatment systems are designed to respond to a crisis, but are not designed to support people in ways to avoid a crisis. Resources are available to hospitalize someone who comes into an emergency room saying that the voices are telling him to kill himself. Too often, it is not possible to spend that same money to prevent the next crisis by hiring staff to drop by the same person's apartment to see that he is OK, to help him find decent housing, or to make sure that he knows how to use the bus system. Most important, treatment systems have traditionally not encouraged the development of long-term, trusting, and respectful relationships (Kanter, 1989). If the focus of most interactions with staff is to pressure a client to take a medication that he does not like, he is likely to feel unheard and distrustful. If staff are willing to take time to develop a relationship and to start that relationship with the client's own goals—be it a better apartment, a better job, a ride to the grocery store, or just someone to talk to—the client is more likely to listen to the staff person's suggestions about medication and everything else. We listen best to people who listen best to us. This kind of listening, especially with people with serious mental illness who find it difficult to connect with people, takes time. After staff and client know each other over years, a different kind of relationship develops than one that starts in a busy emergency room.

5. Be aware of the values of the treatment system and of how decisions about paternalism or coercion support or interfere with these values. I have

already mentioned that coercion is often a short-term solution to a long-term problem. The issue is not how to get the person to take his or her medication now or for the next week; the issue is how to help this person have a better quality of life over the next few years. If we feel that medication is an important part of this improved quality of life, the issue becomes how we can develop the kind of collaborative relationship that will encourage the client to see medication similarly to the way we see it. In this process, we will need to understand the world more from the client's point of view. Paternalism and coercion may be necessary, but it is important to be aware of how they promote or interfere with long-term goals. An important part of these goals is attention to the relationship between staff and client and support for the client's sense of control over his or her own life.

CONCLUSION

Coercion in the community refers to much more than court-ordered treatment. The hallmark of an assertive community treatment (ACT) team is their involvement in all parts of a client's life. ACT teams often control important resources—example being access to housing or help getting a job—and communicate with many of the people who are important to the client—from family members to landlords. This comprehensive engagement in the client's life allows these programs to be effective, but also gives them the ability to exert sufficient pressure to be coercive. Coercion is not necessarily bad. In specific situations, coercion, either through a court order or implemented through a less formal mechanism, may be necessary to help clients maintain both their stability and their quality of life. At the same time, there are major ethical and clinical problems with coercion and the paternalism that underlies it.

Historically, mental health staff have assumed that they know what is best for their clients. This kind of paternalism, by its very nature, limits clients' autonomy and implicitly encourages them to settle for stability rather than growth. It now appears that many clients will achieve a higher quality of life if helped to achieve their own goals, rather than being forced to follow paths laid down by a therapist or case manager. There has been growing interest in taking seriously the ideas that in most cases clients know best what they need and that the job of the mental health system is to help clients achieve goals that they themselves have set.

To take this view is not to discard all paternalism. Many of the clients initially referred to ACT teams would refuse all services if the team were not tenacious in continuing to engage until a relationship was established. Other clients may need some limits on their autonomy, be it persuasion to take medication or control over their SSI money, or even more severe restrictions on autonomy would be likely to ensue. Increasingly, however, the assumptions that underlie traditional assertive community treatment have been called into question. Historically, ACT teams made decisions for their clients and slowly gave back control once staff felt it safe to do so. "New-generation" assertive community treatment programs start with the value that it is the client's life and that the client should be in control of his or her own life. The core issue in relationship with the client is collaboration rather than control, and the goals are those of the client rather than those of the staff.

Assertive community treatment will inevitably continue to have some elements of paternalism. Coercion, broadly defined, will continue to be a part of at least some of the therapeutic interventions. Assertive community treatment is neither needed nor best for everyone. Other treatment models are available that seem effective for some clients, without the inherently paternalistic overlay. Some clients, however, will have both a better and a more stable life when given the special supports available only through an ACT team. Some of these clients will need a team that is willing to be tenacious in maintaining a relationship even over the client's objection. At times, the team will need to provide help that the client may not want and may even need to enforce a structure that the client objects to. ACT teams will continue to struggle with the problems raised by paternalism and coercion. These issues will always be more difficult for teams that "go to the client," rather than working with clients willing to come in to treatment. At the same time, many ACT teams now find that they can function effectively while being much less paternalistic and less coercive than in the original model of assertive community treatment. A clear articulation of the underlying ethical and clinical principles of these "new teams" does not yet exist. The underlying ideology of the new teams is likely to develop out of the cauldron of actual clinical work. It is clear that assertive community treatment is no longer a single entity, but rather is an admixture of different ways of working with clients, different degrees of tenaciousness, different uses of coercion, and different approaches to the problem of paternalism.

References

Appelbaum, P.S. (1986). Outpatient commitment: The problems and the promise. *American Journal of Psychiatry, 143,* 1270-1272.

Blanch, A. K., & Parrish, J. (1993). Reports of three roundtable discussions on involuntary interventions. *Psychiatric Rehabilitation and Community Support Monograph, 1,* 1-42.

Brotman, A. W., & Muller, J. J. (1990). The therapist as representative payee. *Hospital and Community Psychiatry, 41,* 167-171.

Byalin, K. (1993). In defense of "restrictiveness": A critical concept in consumer-oriented treatment planning. *Journal of Psychosocial Rehabilitation, 16,* 93-100.

Cesnik, B., and Puls, M. (1977). Law enforcement and crisis intervention services: A critical relationship. *Suicide and Life-Threatening Behavior, 7,* 211-215.

Chamberlin, J., Rogers, J. A., & Sneed, C. S. (1989). Consumers, families and community support systems. *Psychosocial Rehabilitation Journal, 12,* 93-106.

Curtis, L. C., & Hodge, M. (1995). Old standards, new dilemmas: Ethics and boundaries in community support services. *Psychosocial Rehabilitation Journal* (in press).

Diamond, R. J. (1979). The role of the hospital in treating chronically disabled. In L. Stein (Ed.), *New Directions in Mental Health Services* (pp. 45-55). San Francisco: Jossey-Bass.

Diamond, R. J. (1983). Enhancing medication use in schizophrenic patients. *Journal of Clinical Psychiatry, 44,* 7.

Diamond, R. J., & Factor, R. M. (1994). Treatment resistant patients or a treatment-resistant system? *Hospital and Community Psychiatry, 45,* 197.

Diamond, R. J., & Wikler, D. I. (1985). Ethical problems in the community treatment of the chronically mentally ill. In L. I. Stein & M. A. Test (Eds.), *The training in community living model—A decade of experience* (pp. 85-93). San Francisco: Jossey-Bass, *New Directions in Mental Health Services.*

Durham, M. L. (1985). Implications of need-for-treatment laws: A study of Washington State's involuntary treatment act. *Hospital and Community Psychiatry, 36,* 975-977.

Durham, M. L., & LaFond, J. Q. (1985). The empirical consequences and policy implications for broadening the statutory criteria for civil commitment. *Yale Law and Policy Review, 3,* 395-446.

Everett, B., & Nelson, A. (1992). We're not cases and you're not managers: An account of a client-professional partnership developed in response to the "borderline" diagnosis. *Journal of Psychosocial Rehabilitation, 15,* 77-86.

Factor, R. M., & Diamond, R. J. (in press). Emergency psychiatry and crisis resolution. In J. V. Vaccaro & G. H. Clark (Eds.), *Community psychiatry, a practitioner's manual.* Washington, DC: American Psychiatric Press.

Freund, P. D. (1993). Professional role(s) in the empowerment process: "Working with" mental health consumers. *Journal of Psychosocial Rehabilitation, 16,* 65-73.

Gardner, W., Hoge, S. K., Bennett, N., Roth, L. H., Lidz, C. W., Monahan, J., & Mulvey, E. P. (1993). Two scales for measuring patients' perceptions for coercion during mental hospital admission. *Behavioral Sciences and the Law, 11,* 307-321.

Geller, J. L. (1987). The quandaries of enforced community treatment and unenforceable outpatient commitment statutes. *Journal of Psychiatry and the Law, 17,* 288-302.

Greeman, M., & McClellan, T. A. (1985). The impact of a more stringent commitment code in Minnesota. *Hospital and Community Psychiatry, 36,* 990-992.

Hasbe, T., & McRae, J. (1987). A ten-year study of civil commitments in Washington State. *Hospital and Community Psychiatry, 38,* 983-987.

Hiday, V. A., & Scheid-Cook, T. (1991). Outpatient commitment for "revolving door" patients: Compliance and treatment. *Journal of Nervous and Mental Disease, 179,* 83-88.

Hoffman, P., & Foust, L. (1977). Least restrictive treatment of the mentally ill: A doctrine in search of its senses. *San Diego Law Review, 14,* 1100-1154.

Kalinowski, C. (1992). Beyond compliance: An approach to client-directed prescribing of psychotropic medication. Unpublished manuscript.

Kanter, J. (1989). Clinical case management: Definition, principles, components.

Hospital and Community Psychiatry, 40, 361-368.

Lucksted, A., & Coursey, R. D. (1995). Consumer perceptions of pressure and force in psychiatric treatments. *Psychiatric Services, 46,* 146-152.

Marx, A. J., Test, M. A., & Stein, L. 1. (1973). Extro-hospital management of severe mental illness. *Archives of General Psychiatry, 29,* 505-511.

Morse, S.J. (1982). A preference for liberty: The case against involuntary commitment of the mentally disordered. *California Law Review, 70,* 54-106.

Mulvey, E. P., Geller, J. L., & Roth, L. H. (1987). The promise and peril of involuntary outpatient commitment. *American Psychologist,* 571-584.

Parrish, J. (Ed.). (1992). Proceedings of roundtable discussion on the use of involuntary interventions: Multiple perspectives. Report of a meeting held in Washington, DC, October 1-2, 1992.

Russert, M. G., & Frey, J. L. (1991). The PACT vocational model: A step into the future. *Psychosocial Rehabilitation Journal, 14,* 7-18.

Schwartz, H. I., Vingiano, W., & Bezirganian, C. (1988). Autonomy and the right to refuse treatment: Patients' attitudes after involuntary medication. *Hospital and Community Psychiatry, 39,* 1049-1054.

Segal, S. P., & Aviram, U. (1978). *The mentally ill in community-based sheltered care.* New York: John Wiley.

Stein, L. I., Diamond, R. J., & Factor, R. M. (1990). A system approach to the care of persons with schizophrenia. In M. I. Herz, S. J. Keith, & J. P. Docherty (Eds.), *Handbook of schizophrenia,* Vol. 4, *Psychosocial treatment of schizophrenia.* Amsterdam: Elsevier.

Stein, L. I., & Test, M. A. (1980). An alternative to mental hospital treatment. I. Conceptual model, treatment program and clinical evaluation. *Archives of General Psychiatry, 37,* 392-397.

Tavolaro, K. B. (1992). Preventive outpatient civil commitment and the right to refuse treatment: Can pragmatic realities and constitutional requirements be reconciled? *Medical Law, 11,* 249-267.

Test, M. A., & Stein, L. I. (1972). Practical guidelines for the community treatment of markedly impaired patients. *Community Mental Health Journal, 12,* 72.

Wertheimer, A. (1993). A philosophic examination of coercion for mental health issues. *Behavioral Sciences and the Law, 11,* 239-258.

Zusman, J. (1985). APA's model commitment law and the need for better mental health services. *Hospital and Community Psychiatry, 36,* 978-980.

ABOUT THE AUTHOR

Ronald J. Diamond, M.D., is affiliated with the Department of Psychiatry, University of Wisconsin Hospital, Madison, WI.

Reprinted with permission obtained from Plenum Press.

CONCLUSION

Although tremendous advances have occurred in just a decade, many aspects of the problem of dual diagnosis remain poorly understood. Personal observations and research have begun to illuminate the effects of the problem—and the barriers to its resolution—from the perspectives of individuals, families, and communities. The causes of increased substance use disorders among people with severe mental illnesses continue to elude simple explanation. Assessment and treatment planning for substance abuse among people with severe mental illnesses have improved greatly, due in large part to better instruments and the concept of stage-wise treatment. With increased clinical wisdom and controlled research about dual diagnosis, the difficult issues that arise in clinical practice—e.g., medication compliance —are better delineated though still intractable. The treatment philosophy for dual diagnosis has shifted dramatically over the last 10 years, and guidelines and manuals for new treatments are now available; yet the effectiveness of even the most promising treatments remains to be fully proven. Special issues complicate the resolution of the dual diagnosis problem; some special issues—e.g., coercive treatment—are often discussed because they are so controversial, and others—e.g., the special needs of women and minorities —are too infrequently discussed despite their obvious importance.

All of the 33 articles in this volume were originally published during the years since 1984. Yet the articles spanning the brief period between 1984 and today represent the earliest reports as well as the latest reviews. Although the field is still new, a sizable literature now covers the many intriguing and important questions that pertain to dual diagnosis. Space did not permit us to address all of these questions in this volume. For additional information, we suggest that readers consult two recent books and a special journal section.

The publishers of one book graciously permitted us to reprint four chapters in this volume. We refer readers to the entire book:

• Drake, R.E., & Mueser, K.T. (Eds). *Dual Diagnosis of Major Mental Illness and Substance Abuse. Volume 2: Recent Research and Clinical Implications.* New Directions for Mental Health Services, No. 70. San Francisco, CA: Jossey-Bass, Inc., 1996.

We also recommend a second recently published book:

• Lehman, A., & Dixon, L. (Eds.). *Double Jeopardy: Mental Illness and Substance Abuse.* Chur, Switzerland: Harwood Academic Publishers, 1995.

The publishers of the American Journal of Orthopsychiatry kindly permitted us to reprint four articles from a Special Section in the journal. We refer readers to the entire Special Section in:

• *American Journal of Orthopsychiatry*, 66(1):4-76, 1996.

Finally, we will be happy to provide a list of publications available from our Center concerning the assessment and treatment of people with dual diagnoses. Write, call, or check our home page:

- New Hampshire-Dartmouth Psychiatric Research Center, Main Building, 105 Pleasant Street, Concord, NH 03301.

    Phone: (603) 271-5747

    Home page: www.dartmouth.edu/dms/psychrc

–The Editors

SEP 2002

Middlesex County College

3 9320 00091861 2

RC 564.68 .R42 1998

Readings in dual diagnosis

WITHDRAV

Middlesex County College
Library
2600 Woodbridge Avenue
Edison, NJ 08818